PRAISE FOR

Rachel Abramowitz's

IS THAT A GUN IN YOUR POCKET?

"Brightly written . . . There are plenty of juicy tidbits in Rachel Abramowitz's *Is That a Gun in Your Pocket?* . . . Instead of writing a catalog of the slights women have suffered at the hands of chauvinistic males, Abramowitz wisely chose a more complicated task: assembling what she calls a 'history of consciousness' of the town's most powerful women that probes the often contradictory impulses underlying female ambition. . . . Her access to name talent is extraordinary. . . . She writes a great profile, so these sections are often hard to put down. . . . Her descriptions of even the most well-known people are original and dead-on. . . . When Abramowitz [puts] her formidable descriptive powers to good use, the results are both fascinating and moving."

—LOS ANGELES TIMES

"This is the movie behind the movie, the story of what women in Hollywood did for power, and what power did to them. Tough-minded, detailed, generous, and fascinating, *Is That a Gun in Your Pocket?* exposes the working conditions in America's dream factory, a reality more cautionary than anything it puts on film."

—Gloria Steinem

"An entertaining, dishy read about women in film. I devoured it."

—Erica Jong

"A knockout. Based on extensive interviews with women of power in Hollywood, this book makes clear how much women had to pay to win the right to make movies and how worthwhile that fight has been. Mesmerizing, un-put-downable."

—Elaine Showalter

"Forget what your mother told you. Here's everything you need to know about what a woman runs into, not only in Hollywood, but just about everywhere else on earth, including a hair salon. This is an invaluable book for many reasons. It's funny, well-written, impeccably researched, a great read, but also an important and original history. How many readable histories of the female experience do we have anyway? This is one that counts."

—Jeanine Basinger

"A mesmerizing account . . . Celebrity may sell in Hollywood, but one of the strengths of Abramowitz's exposé is that she gives us the stories of the women behind the scenes as well. . . . The beauty of the book lies in its encyclopedic ability to address almost every notable woman in Hollywood over the last thirty years. Abramowitz's strength as a writer lies in her ability to let her subjects speak candidly and openly about their experiences and passions; the resulting collection celebrates Hollywood's irrepressible ability to entertain while plumbing the dark reaches of its soul."

—KIRKUS REVIEWS

"A wise and funny examination of women in power in Hollywood."

—MIRABELLA

RACHEL ABRAMOWITZ has covered Hollywood
for the last decade, with her work appearing in
such publications as THE NEWS YORK TIMES
MAGAZINE, NEW YORK, PREMIERE, VOGUE, and
ELLE. She is now a writer for the LOS ANGELES
TIMES. She graduated from Yale and lives in
Venice, California, with her husband and son.

IS THAT A
GUN IN YOUR
POCKET?

RANDOM HOUSE TRADE PAPERBACKS   NEW YORK

IS THAT A GUN IN YOUR POCKET?

THE TRUTH ABOUT FEMALE
POWER IN HOLLYWOOD

RACHEL ABRAMOWITZ

RANDOM HOUSE TRADE PAPERBACKS and colophon are trademarks
of Random House, Inc.

This work was originally published in hardcover
by Random House in 2000.

Library of Congress Cataloging-in-Publication
data is available.

ISBN 0-375-75869-0

Random House website address: www.atrandom.com

Printed in the United States of America on acid-free paper

2 4 6 8 9 7 5 3

FIRST TRADE PAPERBACK EDITION

Book design by Barbara M. Bachman

For Morton, Sheppie, and Josh

CONTENTS

INTRODUCTION

The day of Dawn Steel's funeral was one of those bright, wintry days when the smog recedes and the palm trees with their jagged fronds stand like paper cutouts against a cloudless blue sky. It was December 23, 1997, and the studio lots were bare. The phones had ceased to ring. Practically the only members of the Hollywood elite left in town were the eighty who gathered that clear morning at Mount Sinai Cemetery, an unnaturally lush green cliff overlooking the candy-colored buildings of the Disney lot. They had come to bury the diminutive former studio chieftain, a colorful and determinedly outrageous figure, famed for her name, which sounded like a moniker in a trashy novel, her vituperative mouth, which popped off swearwords like fireworks, and her thick, lustrous tresses, to which celebrity hairdressers routinely paid homage.

The mourners included the billionaire David Geffen, who used to commiserate with Steel about their respective issues with anger; and former beau Richard Dreyfuss, whom she had once bullied out of a depressive funk. There was the director Joel Schumacher, who had made the New Age thriller *Flatliners*, one of the few hits to emerge from her tenure as president of Columbia Pictures; and Ray Stark, the wily, Machiavellian power broker producer who had helped place her in that job. Close to eighty, Stark looked old and withered, while the producer Dan Melnick, the onetime Hollywood smoothie who had deciphered the town's mores for Steel, looked shattered.

When Steel arrived in L.A. in 1978, she was a thirty-one-year-old college dropout who wanted nothing more than to be accepted by the men who ran Hollywood. That Dawn Steel would have been overjoyed by the appearance of so many members of the boys' club at her funeral. It was a narcissist's fantasy, the ultimate validation that she had mattered in a town where significance was as fleeting as your last hit movie.

Dawn Steel and Chuck Roven at the seventeenth annual
American Film Institute Life Achievement Awards,
Beverly Hills, California, March 9, 1989.

That Dawn Steel, however, would have been shocked by the women, the female industry titans arrayed in dark business suits who lined up to carry her casket. In those days, if she thought of women at all, it was usually as competitors. For years Steel had felt competitive with Sherry Lansing, the first woman to be named president of a studio. She had feuded with Lynda Obst over *Flashdance* and had ignored Lucy Fisher until the two became the highest-ranking women in the business to bear children. Amy Pascal had been her protégée, her kid sister who had grown up and become a studio president in her own right, an inversion of roles that had created its own stresses. Indeed, many of the women present at the funeral had warred at one time or another with Steel, who tended to treat relationships like a high-contact sport, with head-on confrontations representing the only sign of authenticity and true intimacy.

Her ten-year-old daughter, Rebecca, was the first to speak. She was poised, blunt, and uncannily Dawn-like.

"My mother could do anything," she told the well-heeled crowd. "She was the first woman ever to run a studio. She wrote a book. She even found time to have me. That's because my mother thought she could do anything." She paused. "I want to tell you a story about my mother. She couldn't figure out how to work anything. She was never able to turn on the TV. She couldn't make the phone work. She could never make the VCR work. You can imagine what life was like at our house. Every other minute, she would be yelling, 'Rebecca, the TV's broken. Chuck, the phone's broken. Rebecca, the VCR's broken.' You see, those things had to be broken because my mother could do anything. If she didn't know how to work it, it had to be broken."

Steel's death had not been unexpected. When the news had filtered out over a year earlier that Dawn Steel had developed a brain tumor, the town had roiled with shock. For those who liked her, it was unthinkable that someone so vital should be so cruelly smote. For those who didn't— and there were many—it was divine retribution caused undoubtedly by the ubiquitous cell phone, and roundly deserved for a lifetime of temper tantrums, of heaping humiliation on a legion of secretaries, assistants, maître d's, generally anyone less powerful than she, and certainly anyone who didn't meet her exacting standards.

There was a tendency to look upon Steel's life and death as a Hollywood fable. In her heyday she had represented for many of her peers the shadow self, the female Fury, the woman unsexed. She was someone who aped the testosterone-fueled antics of the town's men—yelling, screaming, controlling, demanding fealty and obeisance from all who came into her purview. She was the ultimate ball buster. Now the angry woman—the woman who had it all—was being punished. What was essentially a freak occurrence was being cast as a moral comeuppance.

It was a neat narrative but a flawed one, and certainly not an explanation for cancer or for Dawn Steel, a charismatic figure who often turned to aggressiveness out of fear. Ironically, if she had been a man, her death would have been not the stuff of myth but just another one of life's tragedies.

Women and power—perhaps no other confluence of subjects has launched as many myths, or stirred as much gossip.

When I began reporting this book, almost every woman I met came with a kind of urban legend attached, usually a pejorative back story that purported to be the secret key to her identity or success. Most of the stories were about sex, or sexual attractiveness. The *Fatal Attraction* producer Sherry Lansing, more than a few people assured me, had slept her way to the top. Penny Marshall hadn't gotten over the fact that she wasn't as pretty as the starlets who stocked Hollywood. Steel, of course, had simply become a man. A number of Hollywood players confessed to me that they had had long conversations with their therapists over whether they "were turning into Dawn Steel."

It was 1992, and I had been asked by Susan Lyne, then the editor in chief of *Premiere* magazine, to write an article about women in the movie business. The rise of the women's movement had coincided with the death of the studio system, and the baby boomers (and a handful of those a bit older) had systematically infiltrated the entertainment industry. While there was a plethora of material devoted to the representation of women in films, not much had been written about the women trying to make films.

Nineteen ninety-two was an odd lull for women in Hollywood. It was a time when women were prevalent enough in the motion picture business that no one was alone in her foxhole, yet expectations seemed curiously diminished.

No one had followed in the wake of Steel, who had been pushed out of her job when Sony bought Columbia in 1989. "Women as studio chiefs. It's a novelty act that only happens once," quipped the agent Elaine Goldsmith. There was no female Rupert Murdoch, and not one of the seven major studios boasted a female studio chief. Many of the women who were considered for that job or even president of production had pointedly taken their names out of the running. They ostensibly weren't interested in that kind of power, or that kind of headache. "Women really don't care about the hierarchy. They don't feel the thrill that a man feels when they are top dog," posited the producer Lindsay Doran. "When I was asked to run a studio, I felt really thrilled. It was really flattering, and it lasted about twenty seconds before [I realized] the power was of no interest to me. The money was of no interest to me, not if it meant selling my life down the river," she said adamantly at the time (although later she became president of United Artists). On the talent side, the ranks were even thinner. Only Penny Marshall, the former sitcom star, was considered an A-list director.

The women of Hollywood were a curiously diffident lot, at once fiercely political about the issues of the day—the aftermath of Anita Hill, the emerging candidacy of Bill Clinton—and curiously much less politicized or vocal about their fates as working women in an industry dominated not just by men but by the likes and dislikes of the young male consumer, and by a certain saber-rattling ethos of masculinity, in which women were relentlessly sexualized, their gender constantly accessed and reaccessed as a key component of their professional abilities. It was a business where the leading women's professional society, Women in Film, was determinedly apolitical and generally dismissed by the haves in the business as an organization for the have-nots. While antidiscrimination lawsuits had forced change in the newspaper and television industries, they had failed utterly to transform the studios or the talent agencies.

The writer-director Nora Ephron has often commented that what has helped her most in her journey through Hollywood has been "denial." Willful blinders, the ability to keep one's focus amid the daily setbacks and dramas, combined with perpetual politicking, kept women relatively mute about their plight. There was, and is, a fierce desire to assimilate.

Yet how these women thought of themselves had impact far beyond the shores of Malibu. For better or worse, movies constitute much of the national dialogue on gender, and the Hollywood women were intimately involved in the processes that bore fruit such as *Fatal Attraction*, *Thelma & Louise*, *Pretty Baby*, *Flashdance*, and *A League of Their Own*. Sometimes their visions emerged intact. More often, they were bastard children—

whittled, refined, plundered by more powerful entities, their shape often determined by commercial imperatives. But these films are still the Hollywood women's legacy, one that has brought as much approbation as applause.

The challenge in writing about women in Hollywood was to puncture the mythology and to circumvent the silence. Lyne suggested that I simply try to assemble the women's stories, in their own voices, an oral history, free from cant and posturing and vague, politically correct pronouncements on the meaning of gender. I was twenty-six, and it was a young woman's dream assignment, carte blanche to call up all the most powerful women in town and ask them simply how they got to where they were, and how they felt about it. My goal was to elicit the kinds of intimacies women discuss with one another, usually when men aren't around. I wanted the messy, unpredictable truth, and I wanted to hear it in their voices.

Fortunately, public reticence did not equate to private quietude. Almost every one had a story to tell—of job interviews that began with "Take off your clothes" and of bosses who started each morning with a call announcing, "I'm holding my big, veiny dick in my hand." Or about male agents who asked their female assistants to track down phone numbers of cute girls they had spotted in cars driving along Wilshire Boulevard. Discussing sexism, indeed sexual harassment, in Hollywood was a little like discussing the fact that the sea was blue. It was just a fact of nature, keenly noted but largely accepted as the cost of doing business.

But I quickly found that there was another story, one full of unresolved, contradictory impulses, of feints and dodges, of id-driven behavior. It was the story of a group of unusual, gutsy women who'd arrived in Hollywood at a time when women were largely employed as either secretaries or actresses. Some came as helpmates of great men—successful directors like Peter Bogdanovich and Bob Rafelson and George Lucas—or helpmates to great women like Barbra Streisand and Jane Fonda. Others found positions as development girls—later called D-girls—a new title for script readers, the only opening traditionally afforded women, the so-called literate sex. For some, their novelty was emancipating.

"One of the great things about being an early woman was that there was nobody there to tell you what to do. You did what you thought you wanted to do. And that was so appealing, to be able to develop freely," says Paramount's chairman, Sherry Lansing, who arrived in Hollywood in 1966 to try her hand as an actress before segueing into development work. For others, their own ambition was the novelty, an inchoate, desperate yearning, born of the winds of the women's movement and of guilt bred by the expectations of their postwar childhoods. They wavered between self-righteousness and self-loathing.

They came at a time when Hollywood itself was undergoing a dramatic transformation. By the early seventies the studio system was in sorry shape. Movie attendance had plunged from an all-time high of 78.2 million a week in 1946 to 15.8 million a week in 1971. For a brief period the spotlight focused on a group of renegade male directors, men like Rafelson, Scorsese, Friedkin, and Coppola—whose output was often brilliant but devoted to plumbing the male psyche, and whose personal lives often seemed to thrive on rampant womanizing. Slowly, however, the studios were taken over by larger conglomerates determined to bureaucratize the unruly feudal system. By 1977, *Jaws* and *Star Wars* had ushered in the era of the blockbuster, when every movie had to gross a hundred million dollars to be deemed a success. The movie industry became obsessed with the teenage boy—the primary audience for such fare—at a high cost to other kinds of entertainment.

Over the next seven years I interviewed more than 150 women about their lives in Hollywood, many repeatedly. I cross-referenced their stories with one another and with those of another 150 men and women whose lives they had touched. Of the movie business, William Goldman once famously said, "Nobody knows anything." Its axiom might be "All business is deeply personal." Tales of work often bled into tales of life, because Hollywood was more than just a place to work: It was a mind-set, a secular religion, a deeply inbred community whose denizens increasingly married one another. It was a fishbowl existence where friendships rose and fell according to business dealings, where marriages prospered and crashed on the shoals of mutual ambition, where grosses determined social standing. Outrageous behavior—particularly by men—was tolerated, even celebrated. Many of the women in this book rose less through systematic strategy than through force of personality coupled with strategic alliances, crashing over the barriers with a blend of brass balls and charm, insouciance, and the proverbial ability to "eat a lot of shit and keep going." Usually their status was consecrated with hits—commercial ones, the only kind that really count in Hollywood.

I quickly abandoned the idea of writing an oral history, perhaps an impossible dream in the capital of spin and narcissism. I've tried, however, to give primary importance to these women's interpretations of events. I wanted to know how *they* felt. For this is not only a history of facts but a history of consciousness, of these women's—elite, well-educated, deeply psychotherapized—changing consciousness. What has emerged is a study of how these women played in a man's world, the conscious and unconscious strategies each fomented to deal with the impact of her sex. It is an examination of the pleasure and the cost of power.

As Dawn Steel lay dying, almost every power broker in Hollywood trekked to her Coldwater Canyon mansion to pay their respects. Hillary Clinton stopped at Johnny Rockets to fulfill her special request for junk food. Even President Clinton called. "The operator on the line said, 'Please hold for the president.' And then put her on hold," says Steel's husband, Chuck Roven, who'd answered the phone. "Well, Dawn never liked being put on hold. So it didn't really matter who called. After sixty seconds she hung up the phone. So about a minute later a rather frustrated operator gets on the phone and says, 'Dawn Steel, please.' And I said, 'Dawn, he's probably running calls, why don't you give him a chance to get on the phone?' She grabs the phone and says to the operator, 'Tell him to hurry up, I've got a tumor here.' So, he gets on the phone and they have a very lovely chat, and she says, 'Why are you wasting your time calling me? Get off the phone. You've got a country to go run.' "

IS THAT A
GUN IN YOUR
POCKET?

1.

ROUGH BEGINNINGS

THE GUILTIEST PERSON ALIVE

Sherry Lansing is holding court at her corner table on the patio of the Paramount commissary, the dingiest and noisiest of all the studio cafeterias. While the Warners and Sony corporate dining rooms are oases of good taste and expensive china, here at Paramount the decor is haute Howard Johnson's and the food is indistinct. Unfazed by its lack of charm, Lansing eats here religiously, to announce her presence and availability, to justify having made them change the menus to include low-fat items, one of her first decrees when she became chairman of the studio.

She sits in the farthest recess of the patio, under an umbrella. She has a view of the entire room, yet she is not on display, except when she winds her way through the restaurant, stopping to greet people—mainly the top-level employees, the top producers. It is strange to hear her effusive salutations tossed off in the brash, nasal squawk of her Chicago accent, and to see the men greet her with a belabored nonchalance that doesn't quite mask their obsequiousness.

Lansing carries herself like an old-fashioned movie star, her authority worn with casual grace, accessible but intimately aloof. She stands five feet, ten inches tall, with a Rubenesque figure that is unfamiliar in the land of the deeply aerobicized. Her uniform is an array of almost identically cut, feminine suits, largely in colors like taupe, celadon, and buttercup (and occasional black), usually worn with a piece of arresting jewelry. She is fifty-one years old, with frizzy dark hair cut below the ear, large, deep-set, blue eyes, and a girlish sensuousness that has begun to fray, though Lansing does not seem to mind. In her youth her beauty preceded her wherever she went. Now her power does. She seems comfortable with herself in a way that most people in Hollywood don't. In a few months she'll sign a new five-year contract that will net her $20 million. Paramount insiders call her the Queen.

Lansing has often cloaked her shrewdness and intelligence under a Teflon veneer of girlish warmth, a tactic that helped her navigate the Hollywood of the seventies and irritated her peers in the Hollywood of the eighties; they groused that she was fake. In the nineties Lansing resides in that rarefied Hollywood where people won't say much about her. She purposely hasn't made any enemies. She stays friendly with old boyfriends. She is not the kind of person who elicits hate. Her detractors are merely the disappointed and the frustrated. The trades bemoan Hamlet-like indecisiveness at Paramount; the agents complain about her propensity for proffering only the good news, making them uncertain about when the other shoe will drop. "She's the velvet glove," says her friend and former boyfriend, the onetime *M*A*S*H* TV star Wayne Rogers. "If this were a Communist dictatorship, she would be excellent at that, not because she's a totalitarian but because she's able to appear to be on both sides, yet she's not on both sides. She has a position, but not everybody is necessarily going to know exactly what that position is."

Few can resist the allure of Lansing's deliberate niceness, at least the first couple of times out. Her style is effusive and unslick. She frequently hugs hello, sometimes crushing people against her bosom—an embrace both seductive and maternal. Everyone is "hon" or "honey." Her huge blue eyes peer out at you. She too wants to be liked, to appear virtuous.

It is late September, and she is full of positive, if improbable, public pronouncements. She has just returned from the 1995 Venice Film Festival, where the thriller *Jade*, by her husband, William Friedkin, made its debut to a "five-minute standing ovation," she says brightly, a tacit rebuttal to the groundswell of bad advance word. "Let's knock on wood," she adds, and raps her hand across the table, though the gesture certainly doesn't dissipate the tension that surrounds Lansing and *Jade*. She has long dealt with the charge of nepotism, and her public response is unapologetic: There's nothing wrong in hiring sons or daughters, husbands and wives. She does not mention that she herself has labored over the marketing campaign, or that she has rearranged the entire Paramount release schedule in order to take *Jade* to Venice, where an old boyfriend, Count Giovanni Volpi, presides over the festival. In a few weeks, *Jade*, which cost close to $40 million, will flop spectacularly, its total U.S. gross not even reaching $10 million.

Reams of explicit sexual footage were shot but never made it into the U.S. version of this psychosexual, violent phantasmagoria by Joe Eszterhas about a married psychiatrist who doubles as a high-class call girl—Jade. On the surface, there are many similarities to the kinds of movies that made Lansing famous—slick sex and dubious women—though Lansing prefers movies with moral conundrums, especially ones that push audience buttons. *Fatal Attraction, Indecent Proposal,* and even *The Accused* all touch on issues of sexual guilt, but Lansing protests this interpretation, taking it personally. Her face becomes infinitesimally more rigid. She is not sexually uptight. She prefers to see her movies as parables of ethical responsibility. "You are responsible for your actions," she says, as she has said many times before.

Plain old guilt, she understands. "I used to be the guiltiest person alive." She laughs. "When I worked for David Stern, he wanted to create a character based on me. Every time she came into the room, she'd say, 'I'm sorry.'"

Lansing learned charm from her mother. Throughout Chicago's South Side, Margot Lansing was famed for her tall, athletic beauty, her red hair, a dust of freckles across her nose. In her family Margot was known for being able "to talk to anyone and convince them of something," recalls Lansing's sister, Judy Lansing Kovler. "If she was unhappy with something at a store, she would manage somehow to get her way, or if the policeman would stop her for a ticket, she always could talk herself out of it. My mother had an ability to present her case in a way that people would understand." It was a potent survival skill. Margot had been born in Mainz, Germany, the beloved younger daughter of a prosperous Jewish businessman. Because of Hitler, the seventeen-year-old fled to America, arriving on her uncle Max's doorstep in Chicago: no baggage, no money, no English. Her sister Lora was already there, and her parents escaped soon after, though they had to abandon all their money and assets. The rest of the family died in Hitler's concentration camps, but Margot never spoke about it. Her father went on to work in his brother's clothing shop, Hyman's, in Chicago's working-class Jewish corridor. Margot sold dresses and quickly became assimilated into America, her harsh Germanic accent soon completely replaced by the flattened vowels of the Midwest.

At twenty-one she married David Duehl, a decade her senior, a romantic, blond aesthete who listened to opera every day, playing Verdi and Mozart at full volume. The Duehl family moved into a spacious apartment, then to a house in the city, Duehl supporting them with the income from a number of apartment buildings he owned. Lansing's memories of her father are largely romantic. She was the "apple of his eye." Every Sunday he'd take eight-year-old Sherry to the Museum of Science and Industry. "We'd go to Coal Mine, see the Chick Patch," recalls Lansing. "There was a thing called the nickelodeon, and you could see silent movies. We'd laugh at Charlie Chaplin. We'd laugh at Harold Lloyd. I think that's why I went into the movie business, because I loved sitting with him and listening to him."

Duehl was already plagued by arterial sclerosis and frequent bouts of angina. When Margot was only twenty-six, the doctor informed her that her husband wouldn't live another ten years. "I remember coming home from school, and he was sitting on somebody's lawn and he couldn't make it around the block because he had gotten short of breath. I felt embarrassed because my father couldn't make it around the block, and ashamed that I felt that way," says Lansing. Later, her parents moved her father's bed into the living room because he couldn't easily navigate the stairs. He was mostly confined to his bed.

When Lansing was nine, Duehl died suddenly of a heart attack. He was forty-two. The night before his death had been one of the hottest in the hot Chicago summer. Her father had tried to escape the heat by sleeping on the porch next to Sherry's bedroom. She had heard him coughing. "Oh be quiet!" she remembers calling out to him. "Why are you up?"

The next morning she awoke to a house full of people—relatives, friends—but her mother wouldn't tell her what had happened. She went to ride her bike, and as she circled back to the house, she could hear people whispering, "Why is Sherry so happy?" Her mother finally told her that her father was really sick in the hospital and "wasn't coming home at all." Lansing began to cry hysterically. One of her female relatives barked at her sternly. "Behave yourself, Sherry," she told the young child. "If you're not a good girl, the same thing will happen to your mother."

Margot refused to allow Sherry, or her baby sister, Judy, to attend the funeral. For years Lansing wasn't quite convinced that her father was dead. Sometimes she thought her father had left them for another family because she had been bad. Whenever they took the freeway around Lake Michigan, she'd stare out the window and look for him. She feared that her angry words had killed him, a secret she kept to herself until the eve of her first marriage, at twenty, when she confessed her guilt to her fiancé. After her father's death she clung more tightly to Judy, six years her junior, adopting her almost as a "baby doll." They shared a room for years. A line was drawn down the middle. Sherry kept her side immaculate.

At age thirty-two, Margot had to figure out how to support them all. "I remember people were coming over to sit shivah, and I was with my mother," Lansing says. "I remember seeing her downstairs in the basement, where my dad had an office, and there were these huge books. Ledgers with all the accounts for the different apartment buildings, and it had the rents of the apartments. I remember seeing her cry, and there was this man who ran my dad's business coming over to tell her that he would take it over for her and that she didn't need to worry. And I remember hearing her say, 'I'm going to learn how to do this and you're not going to take it over for me.' I think that was the first role model I had. 'Teach me. I can do it.' She learned how to do the books, and then we'd go and collect the rent. I would go with her.

"She used this expression, 'Pull up your socks. Pick yourself up and get on with your life.' " Sometimes Lansing could hear her mother crying in the basement, but whenever she walked in, Margot pretended nothing was wrong. "She'd go, 'Oh, I didn't know you were here. What are you here for?' "

As a young girl Lansing told everyone she was going to be a big movie star; they all laughed. She would stage plays in their living room, with Judy as her sidekick, and invite all the neighbors. She and Bonnie Driver were the only two kids at Parkside public school without two parents. Lansing desperately wanted her mother to remarry, to make them normal. Every time her mother would go out on a date, Sherry would ask, "How about him?" Margot's men friends often plied her with candy; eventually, though, they simply disappeared. "And none of them said good-bye," recalls Lansing. "That was a really strong thing to me, that Lester Grand never said good-bye, or Mr. Aaron. Because my father didn't say good-bye because he died, and how come they just disappeared? And I was so hurt because I thought they liked me."

Lansing couldn't get rid of the feeling that something bad lurked around the corner. As a child she believed that life came in four-year cycles, a good year followed by an okay year, a less okay year, then a bad year. When she had a number of good years in a row, she wondered if the cycles had grown longer. Margot was always telling her, "If you sing before breakfast, you'll cry before dinner," or "Never say anyone is pretty because there'll be a scar on her face later."

When Lansing was twelve, Margot married the widower Norton Lansing. Margot wanted to erase her shattered past and live in her happy present. She couldn't understand why Sherry wanted to attend the Yom Kippur mourner's service for her father. Her father—Norton—was alive. Now, said Margot, they were a perfect family, and Margot quit working and devoted herself to her family's care with 1950s zeal.

Norton Lansing was the antithesis of David Duehl, an aggressive and vital businessman, the number-two man at the company that produced BarcaLoungers, totems of middle-class, middlebrow comfort. As the company zoomed to immense profitability, he never exalted in his success or its attendant perks. He didn't want a big office. He'd keep his cubicle near the salesmen. From the first day his Cadillac rolled up to their house, Lansing both resented and feared him. She found him "very cold, very demanding, very critical," as well as strict and intensely opinionated. But she angled for his approval.

While he was withholding with the children, Norton doted on Margot, openly affectionate, greeting her with a big kiss every evening, after which they would retreat to drink martinis alone, the children pointedly told to stay out. For Lansing, it was a vivid introduction to the world of complicated adult emotions. "We would all have dinner, and then we would sit and watch television, and I can remember him groping her. We all remembered his hand going down." Lansing laughs. "I saw he wasn't cold with her."

Norton brought two children to the newly merged family: Andrea, five years Sherry's senior, and Richard, one year her junior. In the beginning there was friction between Margot and Andrea, who treated her stepmother with wariness and cool reserve. Richard and Sherry were wildly competitive, fighting over almost everything, with Sherry usually tattling when Richard went to the dog races or otherwise stepped out of line.

"One of the rivalries I had with my brother was that he wanted to be a basketball player," recalls Lansing. "So they set up a basketball thing, and he practiced. I was a huge tomboy, but only as a little kid. I was really good at sports. Well, I liked to beat him. My dad, whose approval I wanted, would go, 'Jesus. You should be out in the street.' [Eventually] my mother and stepfather said, 'You're not supposed to beat the boys. You should calm down with those things.' "

Her freshman year in high school, Lansing quit sports and began to worry about finding a boyfriend. "I was so skinny and awkward and so tall and my mother was embarrassed that I was that tall. She would go to the doctor and ask, 'Oh my God, what can you do?' "

The doctor made Lansing drink a milk shake every night, but that hardly made her less tall.

"I remember asking people to dances and them saying no. I was crying and this girlfriend of mine's brother said, 'Just you wait. You're not filled out yet. Someday those boys are going to be so sorry that they didn't go with you.' "

Still, Lansing always managed to have boyfriends. "Sometime around my junior year in high school, I must have started to develop, because I remember this guy who was the most popular guy in the college asked me out, and that was like a movie star asked me out. I was so nervous I didn't talk the entire night. I must have looked okay, otherwise I think he wouldn't have been asking me out again. That was the first time I thought I mustn't be ugly, because up until then I thought I was ugly. My mother was really beautiful, so I was never in my mind like my mother. She was truly gorgeous." (But at the age of sixteen Lansing began to earn extra money modeling and playing "the young bride" in department store bridal shows.)

Lansing's relationship with her mother was volatile. On the one hand, she believed her mother loved her more than all the other children; on the other, she found her intensely critical and controlling, the kind of woman who never, ever complimented her and who relentlessly criticized her appearance. "I used to tell my mother when I was nine years old that I hated her and I wished she were dead. I screamed like a lunatic," recalls Lansing. "And my mother never got upset. I used to say to my mother, 'I hate you so much that if you don't let me do what I want, I'm going to jump out the window.' And she used to open the window." When Margot tried to bar her from dating a non-Jew, Sherry simply announced that it was better to let her date the man in question, otherwise she'd just spend the night at a friend's and do as she wished.

Margot couldn't understand why Sherry wasted so much time studying. She wanted her daughter to attend a fancy girls' school, but agreed to let her go to the school of her choice as long as it was private.

Lansing chose the Lab School of the University of Chicago, a progressive, academically rigorous school that was racially and ethnically integrated. "There were geniuses in this school, and I was like below the average. I did better than everybody else because I studied," says Lansing. "I wanted to be attractive. I wanted to be popular. I was popular because I think I worked hard on my personality. I never felt like I was in the cool group. I was always one of the straightest girls in the world. I became a cheerleader through sheer will, I'm telling you. I just kept practicing and wanting to be a cheerleader more than anything."

A WOMAN'S LESSON THAT SHOULD NOT BE LEARNED

Polly Platt arrived in Nuremberg, Germany, in 1945, not long after the Allies had decimated that city with bombs. "Everywhere we went was rubble. And those awful Germans! Even at six years old I fantasized about killing them with a gun," recalls Platt. The boat from America had taken two weeks to cross the Atlantic, and when it docked the German children leapt into the icy water for the trinkets the soldiers tossed into the sea. They chased after her mother, scooping up her trail of cigarette butts. There were no stores, no restaurants, no food; the electricity ran from six in the morning to six at night. The German kids would roam the city in gangs.

Her father, Army colonel John (Jack) Platt, was serving on a military tribunal at the war-crime trials. Platt missed her life in America. She missed ice cream and chewing gum. She felt guilty that she hadn't suffered like these people her father told her about: the Jews. She heard how the Germans had killed them, but what she couldn't understand, no matter how he explained it, was why: "I have this memory of going to a museum that had wax figures dressed in SS uniforms with whips," recalls Platt. "They were whipping little girls in striped dresses, the concentration camp uniform. The whips had little wire barbs on them."

Platt knew there had been a time before the mass killing, the bombed-out buildings, the decay: "I always wanted to restore everything artistically to the way it was before. I started fantasizing that I had these incredible powers, that I could rebuild all the broken buildings. I had this idea that there used to be perfection."

A year later she contracted polio and was taken to an American-run hospital in Munich, several hundred miles away. She lived in the children's ward for three months. The male nurses gave her shots, three times during the day, three times at night. Sulfa shots, because they didn't have antibiotics. In the morning her backside was often covered with bruises. Once she woke up with a realization: "No matter how frightened I am, no matter what I do, I always get the shots in the end. So why didn't I just roll over and let them do it? It was like an amazing discovery. The nurses started treating me better. The doctors started treating me better. My life got better because I gave in," says Platt.

"This is a woman's lesson that should not be learned," she adds ruefully. "I think it's what made me give in with things like Peter [Bogdanovich, her second husband] leaving, or when the real sad stuff would come in my life, I think I would roll over and take the shots. But artistically it was never an option."

It's late on a Friday night—the night L.A. waits for the verdict in the second Rodney King trial—and Polly Platt is lingering in her art deco office at the Gracie company, one of the largest independent production companies on the Columbia lot. She can't bring herself to go home, and, as doyenne of Gracie's film division, she always has something to do, whether it be production design, script analysis, budget breakdowns, studio politicking, or simply delineating the fascinating but baroque intricacies of the mind of the director James L. Brooks, Gracie's Sun King, creative eminence, and Platt's boss. "I understand Jim, which is a thrill in itself. I know Jim better than I know myself," says Platt.

Platt is a small woman with a pageboy haircut, and although she claims (with a smirk) to be forty-nine, she remains at once childlike and sexual. She seems to have two wardrobes—the monochromatic, vaguely depressed, power business look, and artsy, youthful peasant dresses, often in rich, vibrant colors. Today she's in a white Mexican peasant dress with a magenta velour jacket. She's wearing rubber bands around her calves to keep up her suede elf boots.

Her office—like many offices in Hollywood—is a testament to her life in the business. One wall features the stars she has known—a curly-haired Platt with a curly-haired Streisand on *A Star Is Born*; the directors she has known and loved—Orson (Welles), John (Ford), and her ex-husband Peter (Bogdanovich); Ryan O'Neal, his arm around Platt, who's wearing an Ali MacGraw *Love Story* do ("I was stoned out of my mind. Peter had just left me for Cybill [Shepherd], and I was just so happy to have a movie star's arm around me"). Another wall displays posters and slates from some of her movies—*Pretty Baby, Broadcast News, Terms of Endearment.* Another wall is a shrine to her family— mostly pictures of her two daughters, though smack in the center is a picture of Bogdanovich nestling the newborn Antonia. There are no pictures of her late third husband, the production manager Tony Wade, although she still wears his engagement ring.

Platt seems to quiver with unexpressed emotions. Everything about her is primal and visceral—she has big loves and big hates, and she doesn't bother to censor much. She often seems in a state of suppressed fight or flight. Brooks, her collaborator and friend of more than a decade, describes her as "amazingly tough and totally vulnerable at precisely the same moment—so that she can either kill you or burst into tears."

Right now she's ebullient, charged up by her recent discovery of two young filmmakers from Texas. She curls up in a chair and asks her assistant Kelly, who also happens to be her stepdaughter, for a bottle of wine, which is promptly delivered, with heavy pauses and sidelong looks. Platt, who began drinking again during dailies on *I'll Do Anything*, will quit again in another week. She whips out the Texans' tape for *Bottle Rocket*, the first ten minutes of a proposed feature about three mutton-headed, middle-class guys who start an addled life of crime. *Bottle Rocket* makes her giddy, and its discovery has pulled her out of the postpartum slump she's been wallowing in ever since they stopped principal photography on *I'll Do Anything* several weeks ago.

Later her twenty-five-year-old daughter, Antonia, wanders in. Platt got her a job as an assistant to the editor of *I'll Do Anything*. In torn purple jeans and a purple velvet vest, Antonia looks like a sultry street-urchin version of Bogdanovich. The intensity of Platt's maternal scrutiny seems to make her daughter squirm. Platt plugs in *Bottle Rocket* again and watches Antonia watch the movie. It takes on a bit of the feeling of a test. Antonia comments on good editing shots. When one of the characters begins yelling, "Fuck you! Fuck you! Fuck you!" at his partners, both Antonia and Polly giggle. "That's just like my old friends," says Antonia. When her daughter leaves, Platt sighs. "If I were young, I'd give up everything—boyfriend, home—and go to Texas and beg these guys, please, please, please let me work on [your] movie.

"I can't," she says, slugging back more red wine. "I'm old now. I can't go back to that."

Buoyed by the wine, she decides to call Bogdanovich. They've been trading calls for the last couple of days. When he picks up, all her expansiveness disappears. She seems to contract into an almost fetal position. Her voice becomes tight, careful. The conversation has a ritualistic quality—all the habits of intimacy but no longer the trust. She thanks him for flowers he sent her, coddling him with all the good buzz she's heard about his latest venture, *The Thing Called Love.* Bogdanovich directed *Targets, What's Up Doc?, Paper Moon,* and, most famously, *The Last Picture Show,* with Platt as his production designer, truth teller, creative consigliere. But he hasn't had a real hit since she stopped working on his movies twenty years ago.

She tells him about *Bottle Rocket.* "It's in Texas and there's no Larry McMurtry, but it has a bit of the feel of *The Last Picture Show.* . . . I'm Bert Schneider now," she says too gaily.

She asks him to consent to an interview about her, much like the plethora of times she has sat down to talk about him. He refuses.

"I've been talking all these fucking years about you!" she erupts.

She hangs up. Bogdanovich has agreed to an interview.

"Success makes Peter nicer," she says with an edge, and works on finishing off the bottle of wine.

Polly Platt used to think that if it weren't for the movie business, she might have ended up like her mother—in a mental hospital, alongside other women with unusual talents and no place to put them. She was the first woman to be allowed to join the art directors' guild. A score of films succeeded because of her creative input and vision. Along the way she raised four kids, buried two husbands, and watched Bogdanovich, the love of her life, betray her and then self-destruct in horrifying Grand Guignol fashion. Many thought she had the talent to be the first great woman director, but Platt is of a certain generation and temperament. Instead she invested her energy and brilliance into making men brilliant.

She wound up in other people's fictions. Her friend Larry McMurtry dedicated *Somebody's Darling* to her and Bogdanovich. The book focuses on the brilliant Jill Peel, who becomes one of Hollywood's first woman directors. McMurtry denies that Peel is modeled on Platt, though he admits he has borrowed from Platt and her daughter Antonia: "I wouldn't say they had nothing at all to do with *Terms of Endearment*," says the novelist, referring to the central bond between Aurora and Emma. "Polly is passionate about a number of things sequentially. She might be passionate about Antonia's relationship to [her younger sister], and five minutes later she's passionate about a cut of a movie, and five minutes later she's passionate about a script."

Platt is famed for her compulsive and often corrosive honesty, a quality that makes some people in a town of group-thinkers think she's eccentric or even insane. "I don't like for people to tell me that I'm nuts. It's degrading. You need a little self-confidence to have these opinions or to believe in yourself or what's in your heart."

Jim Brooks, however, borrowed that precise quality for one of the characters in *I'll Do Anything*: "There's a mood she has that's sort of reckless, that's sort of great," he says. "Polly has a gear that most other people don't have. The I-don't-care-what-the-fuck-happens—that gear."

The director rhapsodizes about Platt's long history of working with great filmmakers and consequently truly knowing what constitutes great filmmaking. For almost a decade she served as his artistic integrity police. Emotionally similar in makeup, they worked in a way that's not logical to outsiders and spoke in an often indecipherable lingo of nuances and looks. "She fills a huge void—a visualization that he's not able to do," says Penney Finkelman-Cox, who co-produced *Broadcast News* and *I'll Do Anything* with the pair. "Jim knows what he likes and doesn't like, but he doesn't know how to get there. There's just this sense of destiny. Polly can make him express his inspiration and aspirations, and can put that into concrete visuals, when he's only able to express them in dreamlike terms."

"When you watch someone else's movie with Polly, she's just so open, and she talks back to the screen, and she does that when you're alone in a screening room," says Brooks. "And it's just because of total sublimation of self to what it is that makes a movie. When you say somebody's about the work, people just never know quite what that means. And it means your ego automatically takes a backseat to whatever is right. You are genuinely humble."

For Platt, that humility has led to a twenty-year battle simply to grant her ambition and talent its due. There is a constant inner war between pride and self-loathing. "You know," she says, "I'm a woman who always thinks I'm wrong."

Platt has intimate experience with people who haven't come through for her. While Sherry Lansing was smothered in intense and demanding mother love, Platt suffered from parental, in particular maternal, neglect.

In the long months in the Munich hospital, her parents almost never came to visit her, or so she remembers. Years later, when she went into therapy to try to work out her relationship with her daughters, her psychiatrist asked her why her mother hadn't come.

"Because we didn't have a car. There were no buses. There were no trains."

"Why didn't she *come?*"

And, says Platt, "I finally understood: If it were my children, I would have gotten there."

Platt's mother, Vivian Marr, hadn't been prepared for life in a war zone. She had been a twenty-nine-year-old investment counselor at Loomis Sayles when she met Platt's father at a ball in Boston. Jack Platt, Sr., was almost fifty, a tall, dashing Army captain with an M.I.T. degree. He was descended from a prominent Wasp family. "Puritanical, original sin sort of people," says Polly's older brother Jack, though the Platt family genealogy is filled with artists: the famous architect Charles Platt, and Jack's own mother, who traveled from Buffalo to Egypt, writing and painting pictures. Polly never liked the Platts' Episcopalian high-mindedness, or their snobby ways. She hated how they looked down on her mother, who had come from a lower-class Irish Catholic background but nonetheless managed to attend Smith (although she graduated from Simmons). "I think my mother was sexy and hot, and I think my dad was cold, and he needed her," says Platt. "I think she's the blood."

Vivian gave up her career because she thought her husband "was going to become an important and powerful Army officer and that she was going to enjoy it," says Platt. Her mother was bitterly disappointed by her father's lack of ambition. Like that of Sherry Lansing's father, Jack Platt's health was delicate, because of serious asthma. Both Platt's parents drank heavily, and Vivian suffered a nervous breakdown when her husband left for Germany before her. Spending the summer at her parents' in Newburyport, Massachusetts, Vivian drove off a bridge with five-year-old Polly in the backseat, but fortunately the car landed in the shallow salt flats. Vivacious and gay when healthy, Vivian was dogged by mental illness for the rest of her life, and from the time Platt was fifteen her mother was in and out of state mental hospitals, where she underwent shock therapy.

In her youth Platt judged her mother harshly. Her behavior was erratic, at times scary. "I hated her for being the way she was. I thought she was weak." Platt wondered if she was failing Vivian in some way, but that was not her biggest worry, because her older brother was so clearly her mother's favorite. "I was the older brother," recalls Jack. "I had parents who wanted to have a son. I had it all. With Polly, it was just 'Go play with dolls.' " Early on Polly showed signs of being artistic and intensely observant, but "our parents really didn't encourage her. They thought she was just fucking around," says her brother. In turn, Polly felt alienated from her parents. Says Jack, "When I was fifteen and she was twelve, she said, 'Fuck the parents. It's you and me against them.' "

Later, when Platt came home from college, she'd eat dinner with her half-deaf father and brother. They studiously ignored Vivian, who was lying in bed upstairs, wailing Polly's father's name over and over again.

"And my father is saying to us, 'Did you hear something?' " recalls Platt. " 'No. Turn up the radio a little bit.' It is funny, but I was the only one who was able to joke about it. I'm the one who got my brother laughing.

"I believe that my mother was not insane at all," she says in retrospect, voicing an idea she seems only to half-believe. "I believe that she was not manic-depressive. I believe that she was grieving in some way. No one understood that perhaps she should have left my father, gone in her own direction. I realize now that I was driven by an idea that perhaps my mother had not fulfilled her own promise, her own gifts, her own talents."

The tenuousness of the Platt family's situation was accentuated by the fact that they were largely itinerant, moving mostly around Germany and France. Platt attended some twenty schools before her parents scraped together the money to send her to Milton Academy, a tony prep school outside Boston. She was used to solitude, to living inside her imagination. Movies had taught her most of what she knew about America. "The one thing that always struck me is that people in the movies never looked like they did in real life. It offended me, even though I loved the movies and couldn't stop going. I always thought if I had a chance to make movies, I'd make people more like they really look like, so when they wake up in the morning, they don't have lipstick on." At Milton she was rejected by the other girls, who had known one another for years, but she finally found a home in the drama department. "I found a world where my differentness was not—you know, I had compatriots," recalls Platt.

"She was the first hippie I ever met," says her brother. Platt tried a year at Skidmore, a school for genteel young ladies, but scandalized the community by going barefoot all year round and dating a townie. She transferred to Carnegie Tech (later Carnegie-Mellon), well known for its theater department. The first time she tried sex, she ended up pregnant. She dropped out, gave birth to a girl, and gave her up for adoption. She willed away any regret, although she has wondered about the child ever since. Concurrently, she met Philip Klein. He was sensitive and depressed, and dreamed of being a poet. He introduced her to Norman Mailer and Tennessee Williams. "He was a lost soul," says Jack. "There's a tradition in the Platt family for bringing home the wounded, finding people who were a little bit broken and giving them first aid."

At twenty Platt married Klein. She quit school, and they moved to L.A. for a couple of months. Platt found a job doing piecework in a factory. Finally, they moved to Arizona to start a regional theater company.

Less than five months later, on his twenty-first birthday, a car in which Klein was riding skidded off the road; the young poet was thrown from the vehicle. He landed on the ground, apparently unscathed except for a bruise on his forehead. He died moments later. Platt took his ashes up in an airplane, and scattered them over the mountains north of Tucson because, as her brother explains, "She didn't think he'd want to be in the ground."

I WANTED A GOLD STAR, SO I DIDN'T CRY

"I keep going, 'Fuck Freud. Fuck Freud,' " says Paula Weinstein. "It's ironic to me after years of analysis, five days a week on the couch working out being the daughter of a single parent and how not to have that happen to me. Here it's happened.

"I would have never had a child on my own. Never," says the unusually youthful forty-eight-year-old. Over the last twenty years Weinstein has been an agent, president of production at a studio, and most recently a producer at Warner Bros., long considered the Rolls-Royce of the studio system. She is now a single mother to one-year-old Hannah Mark Rosenberg. Her husband and producing partner, Mark Rosenberg, died suddenly in 1994 from a heart attack.

His office is still down the hall in the suite they shared on the lot. Weinstein hasn't been able to bring herself to move his belongings, so she has stayed in her office, where a photo of the great singer Paul Robeson, a friend of her mother, watches over her. Weinstein is newly slender, with well-toned arms, long brown hair, and eyes like velvet bullets. She is wearing a short skirt, sleeveless brown top, and heels. Since Rosenberg's death she has started smoking.

Weinstein often can't keep pace with the thoughts tumbling from her head. Her sentences fracture. She is animated and intense. She focuses in, with an ability to synchronize her thoughts and motions in perfect insta-intimacy. It can be jarring to realize when a meeting is over that this was just business and not a friendship.

As a child Weinstein trained herself to become seductive in the purest sense; she learned how to charm her mother's friends with jokes and smiles and little songs. As an adult she used this fluency to help her rise in Hollywood, although when she was beautiful enough to attract unwanted lascivious attention, she tempered her charisma with self-righteousness, able to turn any conversation into a high-minded political discussion, any task into a moral crusade. She swaddled herself in defiance. Weinstein was one of a number of student radicals who flocked to Hollywood when the antiwar movement was over—happy to find a place where, the prevalent joke went, "they'd never have to grow up."

Weinstein too grew up in the shadow of her mother, Hannah Weinstein, a fiery left-wing political activist best known by her sobriquet, "Red Hannah." For the first few years of Paula's life, the family's activities had to be shrouded in secrecy, because it was the fifties.

"I grew up being told, Don't answer the front door," recalls Weinstein. "If you come to the front door and someone hands you a piece of paper, don't take it, because it was a subpoena." She learned that "you don't talk about certain things unless you know who's in the room. My mother made sure that her secretaries were people who could be trusted on a political level, as well as good at their jobs."

A former journalist for the *Herald Tribune* and P.R. person, Hannah Weinstein became in 1944 (the year before Paula's birth) the director of the newly formed Independent Voter's Committee of the Arts and Sciences for Roosevelt, an eclectic group whose members ranged from Albert Einstein and John Dewey to Orson Welles and Bette Davis. After Roosevelt died and the war ended, her group merged with the Hollywood Democratic Committee to become HICCASP, and grew increasingly dominated by its hard-core Communist members. A number of prominent liberals—Ronald Reagan, Olivia de Havilland, Joan Fontaine—bailed out, but Weinstein, whose daughter Lisa says she was "a Marxist and socialist but not a Communist," remained, airily telling the papers, "If [our] program is like the Communist line, that is purely coincidental."

Weinstein's politics made her a target of the House Un-American Activities Committee. Through friends she learned that she had been named before the committee. Before she could be subpoenaed she left for Paris, taking her three little girls and their striking African-American-Cherokee nanny, Hattie Stevenson.

Paula was the youngest, and she always believed that her birth marked the beginning of the end between her parents. She never knew her father well. Pete Weinstein met Hannah when they were both writing speeches for Mayor Fiorello La Guardia in the basement of Gracie Mansion. Charming and debonair, he later ran his own advertising boutique but was intimidated by his wife's far greater success and ambitions. He hadn't wanted children, or at least not so many of them. Paula was four when her father told her that he was no longer going to be living with them. Afterward Hannah's friend Harlow Shapley, an astronomer, told them if they didn't cry they'd get a gold star. "I was the youngest, and I wanted a gold star, so I didn't cry," recalls Weinstein.

Hannah refused alimony and child support. "I think for my mother to do what she did, there was absolutely no self-pity," says Weinstein. "It wasn't that she was looking to be this Herculean character. It's just that if she was seen as fragile, I think she was probably terrified that she would be, so she just didn't do it." Those were the days when people didn't flaunt their neuroses. "You don't talk about all that stuff. You just will it away by activity."

Paris was still reeling from the trauma of the war, and the Weinsteins set themselves up in an apartment building with other blacklisted Americans. Hannah threw her kids into French schools, and, after meeting such blacklisted directors as Jules Dassin and John Berry, she produced a short film, *Fait divers à Paris*, a tale about the French resistance directed by Berry, with Yves Montand in the starring role.

In an attempt to reconcile with her husband, Hannah brought the children back to America to live with their father, but the effort was doomed from the start. Hannah had tasted creative freedom, and she wasn't about to forfeit it. She bounced back and forth between the continents for more than a year before selling a TV series, *Colonel March of Scotland Yard,* starring Boris Karloff, to a fledgling commercial TV station in England. She took the girls to England, where she produced a number of successful series, which she ultimately sold in both England and America: *Robin Hood, Four Just Men, The Buccaneers.* She employed blacklisted writers, both to support their cause and because they were incredibly cheap. She bought a small TV studio in Walton-on-Thames in Surrey and a nearby mansion, where she built Robin Hood's castle and stabled Robin Hood's horses.

"I never knew any other way than to assume that everything was possible and to go after it," says Weinstein of her childhood. "My mother—as was true of her best friend, Lillian Hellman, and the other women who were her friends—never talked in feminist terms. I think they were quite male-identified, and barreled through without a sense of sisterhood."

Paula's two older sisters, Lisa and Dina, went off to boarding school, and Paula had Hannah all to herself. Hannah's life was big and important; Paula's was small and adjunctive. "My memory is very much of me in my mother's world, not my mother in my world," recalls Weinstein. Most of their time together was spent at Hannah's job: finding new locations, visiting sets, Paula sitting at Hannah's feet as she edited the TV shows, wandering around the studio waiting for Hannah. She used to sit with Hannah as she took her bath before she went out for the evening. On weekends their country mansion (all twenty-two bedrooms) would overflow with her mother's friends, mostly expatriates, the political, the artistic, and the famous, married men with their girlfriends, surrogate uncles like Paul Robeson and Dashiell Hammett.

"I really grew up thinking that I could win anybody over. It was from a childhood of being incredibly verbally seductive," recalls Weinstein. There was stiff competition to be the cleverest, the wittiest, the fastest lip in London. "I was the entertainer in the family. I think the only way I ever got any attention was that I would come in and dance and do skits for everybody, and stand on the piano, and sing and imitate Marilyn Monroe."

At ten Weinstein wanted to be a psychiatrist, because at school she listened to all the other kids' problems. She was sometimes jealous of her friends, who had dads and moms who stayed at home, serving their children cookies when they came home from school. Sometimes she spent the night with older chums who lay across the bottoms of their parents' beds. "I always felt like an intruder because I had no comfort level with that kind of intimacy between men and women. I just hadn't experienced it."

Listening to Hannah's early-morning postmortems with her girl-friends, Paula learned that love meant passion and drama: "Unfulfilled love affairs and men you couldn't conquer. The men you did were bor-ing. I think that's why I didn't get married until I was thirty-eight." As a teenager Weinstein felt like a klutz in the boy-girl department, and, besides, she'd rather talk politics.

When Paula was eleven, Hannah was "swept off her feet" by John Fisher, a sophisticated, chiseled-featured scion of a real estate family. Imposing and forceful, he was the kind of man who could make the tough-talking studio chief feel like she was being taken care of. Nor was he put off by her three children. He wanted the finest of the fine and loved handmade suits and Piaget watches. If you told him you liked his watch, he'd take it off his wrist and give it to you.

Although she had always yearned for her mother to find a mate, Paula (and her sisters) didn't like Fisher, nor did they trust him. They resented his taking their mother from them. Paula later heard that he wrangled a divorce from his first wife by telling her he was dying of can-cer and had found a rich woman to take care of him.

Hannah entrusted the business details to Fisher and concentrated all her energies on the creative side of programming. "He was impossi-ble, and he had huge dreams," recalls Weinstein. He had worked out a pay-TV station system and was building state-of-the-art soundstages at the studio. Unfortunately, there was not enough production to support the outlay, and the studio's fortunes plummeted. Fisher disappeared for four days, leaving a string of eleven suicide notes and "a trail through England of blood in hotel rooms," says Weinstein. Weinstein's mother was plastered all over the newspapers, and the press staked out the house. "We finally found him in Edinburgh." He was alive.

Recalls Weinstein, "I didn't like this man. I didn't trust him. I hadn't for years. And now we were all living under the same roof with somebody who I held responsible for the fact that my mother spent four days sitting in a room not speaking. To see my mother in that kind of pain was unbearable to me because she was the most in-charge person in the world. And then to see her forgive him, because I understood very little about men and women and what the dynamic was. It was just unfathomable to me that we all had to pretend everything was fine." Her mother would not allow the suicide attempts to be mentioned. Her stepfather was just suffering from bronchial pneumonia. "I think the thing that hurt her the most was that we saw her really vulnerable."

Because she wanted to make sure that all the investors got their money back, Hannah put the studio into receivership. The family returned to New York and for a while lived well. On November 17, 1963, Fisher checked himself into the Waldorf-Astoria and washed down a bunch of pills with Scotch. He was rushed to Bellevue. As the news of the Kennedy assassination five days later created bedlam in the hospital, John Fisher died, surrounded by the members of the Weinstein family. Hannah contacted the bank in Switzerland to get more money. The bank wrote back that her accounts, and all her children's trust funds, had been cleared out.

IT'S LIKE I DON'T EXIST

Philip Klein's death left Polly Platt bereft and rudderless. For several months she attached herself to a Chiricahua Apache, named Mark, she had met in a coffee shop in the middle of the night. She went with him as he traveled through the Southwest selling Indian pots and jewelry from the back of a rusty red truck. He taught her how to paint the earthenware with an ocotillo flower and showed her the kind of sexual satisfaction she hadn't experienced with her husband. She confessed about the baby she had abandoned in New York.

One morning while she was cleaning out the truck, she found her father's Colt .45 wrapped in rags on the floor.

"You stole my gun," she yelled at him.

"You should have watched out for it. You deserve to lose it," her lover yelled back.

A few months later Platt packed up her convertible and drove back to New York. By the time she arrived, the top to her convertible was broken and snow filled her car.

She was rail thin, her hair bleached blond. She was shy, introverted, broken. She slept on the floor of a friend's office. Jules Fisher, a friend from Carnegie who later became a famous lighting designer, helped her find her first job designing sets Off Broadway. Later she found work in summer stock, where she met a young theatrical wunderkind named Peter Bogdanovich.

Bogdanovich was a man in whom she could lose her soul. He dazzled. At fifteen he had acted professionally with Stella Adler; at nineteen he directed a Clifford Odets play on Broadway; by the time he turned twenty-one the Museum of Modern Art had asked him to write a monograph on Orson Welles. He ran a Forgotten Film series at the New Yorker Theater and claimed to have seen some 3,999 films, the names of which he kept on file cards. He was arrogant and effusive in his love of cinema, chatting endlessly about Hawks and Ford and other directors Platt had barely heard of.

To Platt, Bogdanovich seemed to be "a young man who could take care of himself. I don't have to take care of him."

But technically he still lived with his parents. His father, Borislav, was an eccentric Serbian painter who refused to let anyone, including his wife, touch his hair, which grew straight up on his head. In his studio he wore a straw bowler with the top cut off so the air could get to his head. Borislav had met his wife Herma when as a penniless thirty-year-old artist he was hired to teach her piano. She was only thirteen. She later supported the family by making gold-leaf frames. Platt romanticized them as wonderfully eccentric émigrés, although a current of distrust coursed through the house. Years before, Herma had accidentally killed Peter's older brother when she spilled a caldron of boiling soup on the infant.

"There was a lot of unhappiness in their marriage, but I didn't see it at all. I saw it as perfect," recalls Platt, who adopted them as much as they would allow. Borislav encouraged her dream of becoming a painter, frequently taking her to the Metropolitan Museum of Art.

Bogdanovich would spend the night with Platt in the office, and when they woke in the morning he would call his mother and ask if he had received any messages. Platt clothed herself in her lover's enthusiasms, namely film. They spent their days in movie theaters, often trotting down to Forty-second Street to see five movies a day, fifty cents apiece. Platt would hold a big hat pin in her hand in case any perverts tried to put a hand on her leg. "I learned a great deal about what woke people up in that theater," says Platt. "What they laughed at. What they made fun of. We used to say if a film of ours could make it through an afternoon audience at Forty-second Street, then we had a success." Eventually, the pair moved into an apartment three blocks from his parents'. They quickly installed a film projector and screened Buster Keaton, early Henry Hathaway, Allan Dwan, and Tod Browning films for their coterie of film-fanatic friends, such as the *New York Times* critic Gene Archer, Andrew Sarris, and Robert Benton.

"You couldn't tell who influenced whom more," recalls Benton, who became a film director; he tagged them Mr. and Mrs. America. They were linked in a symbiotic relationship, able to complete each other's sentences in a running dialogue of erudite film babble.

"I used to say I brought him life, he brought me film," recalls Platt, summarizing how many perceived their relationship. She brought worldly experience, as well as an ability to navigate reality, to the brilliant but sheltered artist. In 1962 they got married at City Hall, with only the aspiring actor George Morfogen in attendance.

After Platt charmed the editor Harold Hayes at a party, Bogdanovich began writing for *Esquire.* They went together to interview his heroes: Orson Welles, Fritz Lang, John Ford, Sam Fuller, Josef von Sternberg. Platt says she asked the occasional question. Bogdanovich says she never opened her mouth. Polly transcribed most of the tapes. Influenced by French critics, Bogdanovich popularized the idea that directors are actually auteurs of their work.

In 1963 Bogdanovich decided to direct *Once in a Lifetime,* by Kaufman and Hart, Off Broadway. The couple raised $30,000 from Wall Street bankers and their wives. The play opened—and closed—on Platt's birthday, after withering reviews. Soon after, they bought a 1951 convertible for $150 and, along with Platt's one-eyed dog, Puppy, set out for L.A., determined to make it in the movie business.

Platt swore she wouldn't have children until Bogdanovich directed his first movie. She quickly secured a job designing costumes for the B-movie king Roger Corman, whose company was emerging as the nurturing ground for such young talent as Jack Nicholson, Peter Fonda, and Martin Scorsese. She supplemented their meager income by shoplifting the most expensive food items from the local grocery. (Years later she sent them a check for several thousand dollars to make restitution.) By 1967 her newly widowed father had moved in with them, adding his pension to their income, although his presence seemed to irritate Bogdanovich.

Bogdanovich continued to write homages to his idols, and the young couple charmed artists like John Ford and Orson Welles with their youth and encyclopedic knowledge of their icons' oeuvres. One night Howard Hawks took the pair out for dinner at the Flying Tiger on Ventura Boulevard. Hawks brought along Sherry Lansing, a starlet with whom he was infatuated: "We're eating and I'm just thinking, How great we don't have to buy dinner because I get to save five dollars," says Platt. "All I remember is Sherry saying, 'I have to go to the bathroom.' She gets up, stands up, and she was gorgeous. And I was not. And Peter and Howard watched her. She walked this way to the bathroom, and I remember having Howard on my right and Peter on my left, and their eyes were following her." Hawks leaned across Platt to reach Bogdanovich, and said, " 'Peter, now that is the kind of girl that you should be with.' I remember sitting there and thinking, It's like I don't exist."

IT'S NOT WHO I AM

Platt's ego-crushing encounter with Sherry Lansing was a familiar scenario, one that most women who ventured into the jungles of Hollywood had experienced. Here the apotheoses of male fantasies were not simple screen illusions but flesh and blood. They walked. They talked. They were trophies to be won, by husbands and fathers.

Sherry Lansing had arrived in Hollywood desperate to become one of those women: a movie star.

She had convinced her husband, Michael Brownstein, to do his medical internship at Cedars of Lebanon in L.A. so she could try her hand at acting. They had met when she was only sixteen, he, a nineteen-year-old student at the University of Chicago. To Lansing, Brownstein seemed like a rebellious maverick; he never studied but got straight A's. He plowed his savings into a motorcycle, and later took flying lessons. He was handsome, strong, silent, and Jewish. In the summer he drove the night shift on the local bus line. "She used to ride the bus with me so we could be together," he recalls. Lansing attended Northwestern to be nearby while he finished med school, and when she was twenty they decided to marry. She was a virgin. Lansing insisted that Brownstein get Norton's approval, but her stepfather refused to give it, mostly because they had no viable means of support. Lansing persuaded him, and eventually Norton agreed to help them financially until she finished her B.S. in liberal arts.

"We went to a lot of movies while we were in Chicago, and then

[Sherry] wanted to talk about them all the time, and I remember I wasn't always so good at that," recalls Brownstein. Nonetheless, he was the only person who didn't laugh when she told him she wanted to be in the movies.

Lansing and Brownstein had settled into a modest apartment off Franklin Boulevard, near the hospital where he worked. Caught up in the idealistic fervor of the late sixties, Lansing taught substitute math and English in the dilapidated schools of East L.A., which were still reeling from the recent Watts riots. She was often the only white face in the school yard, stepping carefully, as she says, "not to impart your middle-class values on another culture." Physical threats were common. One Thanksgiving she tried to break up a fight and was wrestled to the ground, a wastepaper basket thrown at her head. She went to find the principal, but he was AWOL, the result of a Molotov cocktail having landed in his office.

"I said, 'This isn't it,' " says Lansing. "You've got a good [brain] here, you should do something. After three years you start to lose it."

While her mornings were spent enduring grit, her afternoons were spent pursuing fantasies. After school Lansing and a girlfriend would change their clothes at a nearby gas station, put on makeup, and go looking for an agent. Johnny Grant once spotted the pretty schoolteacher making her way across the Universal lot and decided to interview her for his TV show, which featured conversations with everyday people. "She talked about how much she loved substitute teaching," he recalls. "The next day, she showed up again. She hung out by the crafts food table and talked to the crew, the makeup people. She'd schmooze anyone she wanted to." He used to joke, "She was my standby guest just in case someone didn't show up."

Lansing's statuesque figure and wide-eyed beauty did not go unnoticed, and she quickly found modeling work, eventually earning close to $80,000 a year. She did all the brunette TV spots for Alberto Culver hair products. (Farrah Fawcett played her blond counterpart.) The job consisted of tossing her long, dark hair on cue, before sitting down next to an attractive man (Tom Selleck, on occasion) and laughing. She was one of the *Laugh-In* girls, and appeared as a background model on *Playboy After Dark*, Hugh Hefner's variety show. She landed a few guest spots on TV's *The Good Guys*, played a sexpot Jack Lemmon tries to pick up at a party in *The April Fools*, and another sexpot George Segal contemplates seducing in *Loving*.

Her big break came when Howard Hawks spotted her in a TV ad for Max Factor makeup. Patrician and white-haired, he was the legendary director of *Bringing Up Baby* (1938), *His Girl Friday* (1940), and *Red River* (1948). Many film critics have written about the "Hawksian woman," an intelligent, opinionated woman who enters an all-male enclave and holds her own. Yet personally the director was "a secretive rogue, a stealthy dandy, and a ruinous womanizer," as the film historian David Thomson put it. Openly anti-Semitic and racist, Hawks had doomed his three marriages with his implicit misogyny.

He fancied himself a great Pygmalion. His first creation had been Lauren Bacall, whom his second wife, Nancy Gross, a.k.a. Slim Hawks, had spotted on the cover of *Harper's Bazaar.* For her screen debut in *To Have and Have Not*, Hawks fashioned Bacall in the sultry, confident image of his wife. Slim Keith (her later married name) wrote in her memoirs that many of her own lines found their way into Bacall's mouth, including the famous "You know how to whistle, don't you? . . . You just put your lips together and blow."

Lansing described her audition in an interview at the time that perfectly captured her pliability. "I wore makeup and my best clothes and, of course, a fresh hairdo. He said, 'Come back when you don't look so pretty,' " she gushed. The ingenue scrubbed the makeup off her face, donned blue jeans, and, when she returned, the director suggested a ritual he had promoted to countless others: Go out in the hills every morning and scream at the top of your lungs. "I live near Griffith Park, so every morning I was out there at six A.M. screaming," she recalled. "You can't imagine how many people come running out of the woods at that hour."

Hawks was the first of many paternal figures in the fatherless daughter's life. "She has been able to use men to her advantage," says her sister, Judy Lansing Kovler. "Be attractive to them and make them feel attractive so they are willing to help out. Many of them adopted her."

After several months of the director's tutelage, including a number of auditions, Lansing was cast in Hawks's last film and fifth outing with John Wayne, *Rio Lobo.* In the studio press release Hawks claimed to have written the part of Amelita for Lansing. She was going to play one of the only blue-eyed Mexicans in history, but at least she would get to be more than eye candy.

Hawks delighted in his creation. He squired Lansing to movies and restaurants. She basked in his attention but claimed she was immune from the whirlpool of the casting couch. People gossiped that she was having an affair with the director, an idea she found inconceivable. "He was eighty years old! I was so pathetically naive. When I did *Rio Lobo*, I had slept with one man, my husband. *Stupid* is really maybe a better word than *naive*."

Hawks courted Lansing through her ambition, yet she began to secretly resent his ministrations, his desire to shape and mold her.

"All of Hawks's being with me was always about how 'You could be a great movie star, if you learned how to talk with a low voice. You shouldn't have a Chicago accent. You should not use your hands,' " she recalls. "He was creating me in the image of Lauren Bacall. He was changing my voice, making me dress a certain way. Nobody said, 'Come into the room, a nice Jewish girl from Chicago, sit down and read the scene.' Everybody said, 'Come into the room with your tits up to here, and be sexy, and talk in a different voice, and have long hair,' and it's as alien from me as anything I could be."

The movie turned out to be one of the nadirs of her life. She hated acting. She hated not being herself. She suffered phantom pains; her legs felt like jelly. Her psychiatrist later explained to her, "Your body tells you when you're full of shit." She spent most of her time talking to Jennifer O'Neill, who played the ingenue, and then going home to her hotel in Tucson and crying. Everyone kept telling her how lucky she was.

"I was miserable on that set. I remember someone giving me a Valium and thinking, I am going to end up like Neely in *Valley of the Dolls*."

Perhaps she also recognized that she wasn't a very good actress. Lansing hated not being the best. Stiff and phony, she never lost the quality of a little girl playing make-believe.

She quit acting when *Rio Lobo* was over. "I can't do it. I'm just not comfortable. It's not who I am," she told Hawks.

The director was enraged. He hung up on her and never talked to her again.

Years later, when she became president of Fox, Lansing called him in an attempt to make amends.

"You know, Howard, it didn't turn out so bad, did it?" she said.

"You could have been a great actress!" he shouted, then slammed down the phone.

"Quitting acting was the beginning of my life," says Lansing, who by this time had also ended her marriage. She'd always say in retrospect that Brownstein should have been her first affair, not her first marriage.

Although she had been the one to finally instigate the divorce, Lansing was nonetheless shattered by the end of this fantasy of a white-picket-fence life, by her failure at the one thing she was raised to do. "I was ashamed," she says. "There had never been a divorce in my family. We were raised to be good little people. My mother didn't like to look at anything negative; she was so ashamed by it. She just didn't tell anybody.

"My grandmother died thinking Michael and I were still married. 'Why doesn't he come visit me in the hospital?' she'd ask. My mother would tell her, 'He'll get around to it.'"

Lansing hated her mother's deception and fought with her bitterly. Yet she recognized that "it's what made her survive [the Holocaust]; the inability to say, 'Look this isn't good,' but accept it." Indeed, her daughter absorbed Margot's strategy of willful denial all too well.

Lansing fought against taking on her mother's humiliation as her own, although she was awash in feelings that "nobody would like me. The divorce was like a Scarlet A." While her mother had tried to talk her into making another go at her marriage, her stepfather flew to L.A. on the pretext of a business trip. Lansing was shocked and gratified when he arrived on her doorstep. He huddled with Lansing in her tiny apartment, giving her all the support he could. From that time onward they were bonded.

He did, however, refuse to lend her the money to get professional help. So Lansing secured herself several part-time jobs and went into psychoanalysis. "It's the best gift I ever gave myself. I don't think I would be who I am today if I hadn't gone through it.

"It frees you of your mother. Because when you're raised with a really terrific mother but a strong mother, you want to flee." Love can be suffocating and controlling. Says Lansing, "I was criticized a lot as a kid. I swear, when my mother died, as sad as I was, there's also something that happens that's freeing, and it allowed me to choose what *I* want. Years of analysis teaches you to choose what you want, not what everybody thinks you should want."

When she was sixteen Lansing had gone to the beach with a group of girlfriends. Each girl took a turn writing in the sand her fantasies about what she wanted to be when she turned twenty-one. Each girl wrote that she wanted to be married. Lansing wrote that she wanted to work.

Peter Bogdanovich and Polly Platt on the set of
PAPER MOON, Hayes, Kansas, 1972.

UNMARRIED WOMEN

YOU CAN ONLY FEEL
FOR PEOPLE ON CELLULOID

Polly Platt's entrée with Roger Corman soon led to Peter Bogdanovich's break into the movie business. The low-budget king hired Bogdanovich to rewrite and direct the second unit on a motorcycle flick called *The Wild Angels*, telling him that "he could bring his wife too." Corman then bought a screenplay from the pair called *The Criminals*, based on an incident Platt found in a history book on World War II about a town in Poland that released all the prisoners in the jail so they could fight the invading Nazis. Corman ultimately offered Bogdanovich a chance to direct a picture of his own, with the proviso that he use part of an old horror film, *The Terror*, and two days of work from Boris Karloff, whom Corman had overpaid for a movie. Taking a note from Charles Whitman, the Texas Tower killer, as well as their heroes Alfred Hitchcock and Fritz Lang, the couple blended the tale of a drive-in movie sniper with a subplot in which Karloff, an aging motion picture star, keeps saying, "I'm a dinosaur and these horror pictures are not frightening anymore." They had gotten in the habit of showing their work to their idols, and the director Sam Fuller helped devise this film's clever finale, in which Karloff confronts the killer. Platt named their creation *Targets*.

Years later Platt would still be embarrassed about the film, but she had been happy in their filmmaking cocoon, playing the realist to her husband's optimist, the editor to his writer. Bogdanovich would type the first draft, then Platt would read it and add her thoughts. "I always thought we were failing, and he always thought we were succeeding.

And it was somewhere in between," says Platt, who served as an un-credited one-person production designer, producer, and general facto-tum for the movie, which cost $130,000 and featured snippets of a young Jack Nicholson, who had appeared in *The Terror*. They cut the film on a Moviola in their kitchen. Platt never worried about credit: "It's not about 'Gee, Peter took it from me.' He didn't. I didn't want it. Peter wanted to be a famous movie director. He wanted to be a household name. That was *his* dream."

Bogdanovich was soon on his way after *Targets* premiered in August 1968 to generous reviews and a healthy box office. Platt had finally permitted herself to become pregnant, giving birth to a daughter in November. She named her Antonia, after Peter's dead older brother. Borislav Bogdanovich came to the hospital and thanked her profusely. "He was the only person who made me feel proud," recalls Platt. "Peter had wanted a boy." The arrival of Antonia and, two years later, an-other daughter, Alexandra (nicknamed Sashy), frayed her relationship with her husband. Before, Platt had been maniacally devoted to Bog-danovich's desires. Every day they would sleep late, then Platt would clean the house; they would work together in the afternoon and go to movies at night. Now her children came first. When they were awake she was unable to focus on anything but them. Indeed, Bogdanovich refused to drive her to the hospital when she was giving birth to their second child because he was too exhausted from a location scout.

Upon the recommendation of their friend Henry Jaglom, the couple landed a meeting with the hip producer Bert Schneider, then high off the success of *Easy Rider*. Schneider asked them what projects they wanted to do; Platt piped up about a book they loved, *The Last Picture Show*. In truth, only she had read it. Sal Mineo had given the Larry McMurtry book to her in 1962, when the couple had been in Monu-ment Valley interviewing John Ford. Bogdanovich had liked the title. He thought the book was about old movies. Schneider asked for a copy of the book, and Bogdanovich retorted—in what Platt thought was high arrogance—"Buy it at a bookstore." Three days later Schneider called and wanted to make the film.

Bogdanovich finally perused the book. "He came to me and he was so angry," recalls Platt. " 'This is not about old movies at all. This is about this small town in Texas! I don't know anything about this.' "

Platt reassured him. "Yes, you do. Yes, you do."

The Last Picture Show delves into the anomie of coming-of-age in the 1950s in a small town in Texas, where sexual infidelity is almost a last-gasp cry against loneliness and boredom. Bogdanovich wrote the script with McMurtry, who tried unsuccessfully to convince the young director not to be so faithful to his book. Platt edited their work, trimming the excess and proposing script solutions to hold down the budget. When it was ready, the couple showed the script to Orson Welles, then on the skids but always Bogdanovich's mentor.

Welles was repulsed, in particular by a scene they never filmed in which the boys try to have sex with a heifer. "It's just a dirty picture about bestiality," the living legend railed. "If it's a success, the actress will get all the credit. If it's a failure, you'll get all the blame, and it's sure to be a failure." Platt began to cry, fearful that Bogdanovich would abandon the project.

Without turning his head in her direction, Welles pointed at the whimpering wife, saying, "What's the matter with her?" On the car ride home Platt tried to soothe Bogdanovich's ego and morale, reminding him that neither of his idols, John Ford and Howard Hawks, would ever make the same picture. Just because Orson hates the picture doesn't mean it's not right for you, she pleaded.

Although she was several months pregnant, Platt and Bogdanovich began scouring Texas for a location that had everything they needed—including a lake and a high school. They finally convinced McMurtry to take them to his hometown of Archer City, which turned out to be the most depressing town Platt had ever seen, replete with dusty, dilapidated buildings, big tumbleweeds blowing across an empty street, and mesquite trees that threatened to take over the countryside.

The couple decided it was perfect, and Platt went around taking color pictures of the town. When they returned to L.A., they put the pictures across the wall of their studio office. The bright blue sky and red buildings looked nowhere near as desolate as they had in real life. Platt thought about painting all the buildings gray, but Welles came by, took one look at the pictures, and peremptorily declared, "Of course, you're going to make it in black and white." He bullied Bogdanovich into it, although conventional wisdom mandated that black-and-white movies didn't make money.

The two cast the movie together. Although Bogdanovich later insisted that it was he and he alone who spotted Cybill Shepherd on the cover of *Glamour* magazine, Platt recalls them standing together in line at the supermarket when they noticed the impertinent blonde, a dead ringer for the teenage heart wrecker Jacy. Soon after her discovery, Bogdanovich and Platt deposited their toddler and their newborn baby with his parents in Phoenix and headed to Texas to begin shooting.

The Last Picture Show has often been hailed as one of the best movies of the seventies. A delectably bratty teenage vamp, Shepherd, tortures a hapless Jeff Bridges. Timothy Bottoms finds and ruthlessly severs an emotional bond to the much older Cloris Leachman, yet the movie "has a decency of feeling, with people relating to one another, sometimes on a very simple level, and becoming miserable when they can't relate," wrote Pauline Kael when she reviewed it for *The New Yorker* in 1971; Kael championed the stark black-and-white photography, which, she said, creates the sensation that "we seem to be looking at a map of life as it was," adding, however, "The film badly needs this stylization, because, of course, its shallow overview of town life is dangerously close to TV."

It was Platt who designed the spare, dust-covered sets and costumes. Recalls Jeff Bridges, "You might have a gas station—like the Texaco station. I remember her taking out the *e* and *x*, so you'd just see T   aco. It was very subtle, but something about the design—you felt like it had happened. Before we'd shoot a scene, you'd feel the evocation of time due to the particular design."

"She had as much to do with the direction as Pete did," said the grizzled character actor Ben Johnson, who played Sam the Lion. "She directed a lot of the picture herself, through Pete, of course."

"Peter and Polly were kind of partners," says Bridges. "He'd use her as a sounding board for ideas, and she gave him ideas when she felt like it."

"I think sometimes she pulled me back to reality," says Bogdanovich. "Sometimes you get carried away on a movie, you go out on a tangent. She could bring you back to where we were going."

Platt's role was a source of unspoken tension between her and her husband. Since they were trying to save money, she styled the principals' hair and applied their makeup. In particular, she made the young Shepherd into Bogdanovich's teenage fantasy. One morning while Platt was preparing Shepherd, the ingenue gaily said to her, " 'Oh, people are saying you direct it because he sits with you and you draw something on his script. You tell him what the shots will be,' " recalls Platt. "And it just wasn't true. We used to sit, and I would draw the set, and we would talk about the angles. We would have a discussion about what the scene was about, and we always used to believe that there was only one place for the camera. And we would discuss where that would be. And by and large Peter would make the decision."

Nonetheless, Shepherd's casually pointed remarks provoked a bad premonition. "I knew this was fatal," says Platt. She could see her husband's interest in Shepherd. She told herself that it was just his way of getting Shepherd to do the famous nude scene, which was scheduled for the end of the shoot. One night, on the eve of Thanksgiving, Bogdanovich didn't come home. Platt learned he had been with Shepherd.

A few hours later, Bogdanovich's mother called to say that Borislav had suffered a stroke and slipped into a coma. Several days later he died. Platt always believed that if Borislav had lived, Bogdanovich would have returned to her. His father would have made him realize that the affair with Shepherd was just sex but Platt was family. After the funeral Polly moved out of their hotel room.

"It's like a bad script," she railed at her husband one day as she drove them from Archer City to Wichita Falls. "We had read about all those directors who used to do those kinds of things, and we used to say how stupid it was. It was like a movie. It wasn't like life."

"I feel old," her twenty-nine-year-old husband answered. "I've never had a cover girl before."

Enraged, Platt drove the car off the road into a freshly plowed field. "I'll kill us both," she screamed, accelerating to seventy miles an hour. "We were going up and down and up and down, and the hood of the car came up," recalls Platt. "We came to a humiliating stop in the middle of this field. The dust started to drift away, and we both started to laugh. It was just ridiculous."

Publicly she put on a game face, popping up in interview after interview, a curiously winsome figure defending her remorseless spouse, who was just doing what directors are fated to do—fall in love with their leading ladies. Privately, some people wondered about her masochism.

Propped up by McMurtry and others, Platt tried to make Bogdanovich choose: "It's either Cybill or me," she told him one night. "He looked at me [angrily]. 'All right. All right. I'll take you,' and then he went to sleep." Lying next to him in their hotel room, Platt began to think, "He hates me. That's not the price at which I want to keep him. I want you to pick me because you love me more than you love her. She was nothing I thought compared to me."

Later Bogdanovich tried to force his wife to return to L.A. and leave him in peace. She balked at his attempt to erase her. " 'You wouldn't be making this movie if it weren't for me!' " she yelled at him. " 'I found the book. I'm not going home.' Go home to what? Go home to my empty house with my newborn child and my two-and-a-half-year-old baby? Go home to think about him fucking Cybill every night?"

Defiance emboldened Platt, giving shape to her own desires. "That's my movie as much as it was his," she says. "I don't take anything away from Peter, but I give as much to myself. I sustained him on that movie, and I knew it was going to be a very good picture. When I met Peter, I only wanted to be a great artist. More than anything else. I always wanted to be a great artist. There was no way he was going to take that away from me. No way."

When they returned to L.A., Bogdanovich moved back into their house in the Valley to make another go at their marriage. He kept telling Platt, "I love you. You're the mother of my children." She was not reassured, terrified that she would wind up as an eternally cheated-upon director's wife. She knew other directors' wives. Of such women, Platt says, "I saw how they just spent their lives redecorating their houses. Eventually their husbands all left them for younger women. I was afraid that I'd become an embittered old woman. I'd be jealous of everybody he met, and I didn't want to live like that. And so I rolled over and took the shot."

One rainy night at two in the morning, Platt was home alone with the children. Bogdanovich was supposedly cutting the picture, but Platt was sure he was out seeing Shepherd. The flu had stricken Antonia, and the toddler was vomiting and screaming. Platt called the pediatrician, who prescribed an enema. "I realized I would have to wake the baby up, put them both in the car, and drive to the Valley to get the medication. There was no one to stay home with the children. I just remember that I'd rather be alone than live with this rage that Peter's not here." She went and got the medicine, and when Antonia finally stopped throwing up, she called her husband and said, "Come home now and get your clothes and get out of the house." Bogdanovich returned to Van Nuys and packed his things.

"He stood in the doorway, and he turned and said to me, 'Just remember, you did this to us,' " recalls Platt. "You see, Peter justified his behavior by trying to find fault with me, and he had a very good partner in that. I would always agree with him that it was my fault."

Platt rearranged the furniture, something that Bogdanovich would never have permitted her to do. She dragged the TV into the bedroom and watched movies in bed. Bogdanovich hadn't liked her to wear makeup, so she went out and bought false eyelashes. She relished her newfound freedom for about two weeks, until it began to sink in that she was truly alone, with two young children to raise. She became frightened, a fear that grew exponentially after the 6.5 earthquake of 1971 devastated their house. All five thousand of their books tumbled onto the floor, along with most of their kitchenware and other possessions. Platt and the children had to be evacuated.

She kept expecting Bogdanovich to show up, to make sure that his family was okay. He never came. "He said he didn't even know there had been an earthquake. He was in his ivory tower with Cybill, probably fucking," says Platt. "It's almost impossible to hate Peter because of that. You realized he never really knew what he should do. Because he only learned things from movies. I said after we separated, 'You can only feel for people on celluloid. You have no concept what it's like in real life to feel any grief.' He just didn't understand what was the matter with me when he left. Once I said, 'Picture it in a movie, Peter, and maybe you'll get it.' "

NOBODY EVER MENTIONED MY NAME

"There was just chaos after Peter left," says Platt. "There was no meaning to my life. None." Emotionally numb, she had difficulty bonding with her second daughter.

She sought solace from the paternal figures in her life. John Ford invited her to his house and greeted her from his bed, "covered with a sheet, with chewing-tobacco stains on his pajamas. 'Oh God, come on in. I heard what happened,' he said. 'Yeah. Well I think it's an occupational hazard of the job,' I said to him. And he said, 'I never did it.' He was sitting there, and he's got this sheet over his body, and he was shaking the sheets, the ashes from his cigar. I knew he was naked underneath. He said, 'I'll tell you what, I'll move in with you.' He was the only one who said the one thing that I needed to hear. Even though it was ridiculous and I laughed."

Professionally, she was perceived by those who didn't know her as a wife simply clinging to her husband's artistry and prominence. Roger Corman tried to help, offering her a chance to direct, but she was too scared. "I think Orson Welles saved my life. He said, 'Come work for me. I need you,' " remembers Platt. She took the two girls and moved to Arizona to work with Welles on *The Other Side of the Wind*. Welles made her laugh by pointing out the cliché her life had become: "It's such a bad script. You just love that [Cybill's] worthless. There's nothing that would bother you more [than] if she were as smart as you."

Platt stayed with Bogdanovich's mother, who lived in Phoenix, but, she recalls, "Orson got so mad at me that I was leaving and going home to my children. He kept saying, 'They don't need a mother! Leave them alone. You have to work.' " Platt finally relented. She moved into Welles's house with the rest of the crew and sent the children home to L.A. with the housekeeper, setting in motion a dynamic that would haunt her for the rest of her life.

"I didn't want them around," she admits. "They were an impediment. But I kept going back to them. Antonia told me years later that our housekeeper would make her come to the table and say, 'You have to finish everything on your plate.' And she would sit there and say, 'Mommy, please come home . . . Mommy, please come home . . . Mommy, please come home'—and [I] never came."

Bogdanovich refused to be the primary caretaker, although he was generous with child support and came to visit the children often, putting them to bed in Van Nuys on a regular basis. He brought Platt flowers and sent her letters proclaiming his love.

He gaily relayed to his ex-wife that everyone in Hollywood was calling him a genius. *The Last Picture Show* hadn't been released, but a print was circulating among the private Bel Air screening rooms, where everyone marveled at its Walker Evans–like starkness, and its frankness about sex. He signed with the rising agent Sue Mengers and was soon inundated with studio offers and scripts, which he sent on to Platt to solicit her advice.

Platt talked him out of doing the action thriller *The Getaway*, saying that it was too similar in tone to *Targets* and she was afraid he'd get pigeonholed as an action director. She urged him to do a comedy. He then sent her a script called *A Glimpse of the Tiger*, which had belonged to Elliott Gould, who was separated but not divorced from Barbra Streisand.

During the first week of shooting, Gould, also the producer of the movie, suffered an emotional meltdown. According to various accounts, Gould either smacked the director Anthony Harvey (*The Lion in Winter*) and his costar Kim Darby or simply threatened to. He did, however, fire Darby, and word soon filtered back to the studio that Gould was either strung out on drugs or having a psychotic breakdown. (Gould later insisted that his behavior wasn't caused by drugs.)

Gould's producing partner frantically called Streisand, hoping she could soothe her ex-husband. She talked to him for a half hour, which seemed to work, although he would inevitably go back to acting up. By the third day the studio had to hire armed guards to protect—and mostly calm—Kim Darby, who was petrified of Gould.

By the end of the week Warners had shut down the production and sued Gould for its production costs.

Warner executive John Calley and Streisand's agent Sue Mengers hatched a plan to rewrite the film for Streisand. "Sue called me and said there was an amazing film that I think you should see and I've arranged for you to see it. It was *The Last Picture Show*," recalls Calley. "We went to Columbia. Bert Schneider let us see it. [Sue] said she'd shown it to Barbra and Barbra was excited. She thought she could put something together with Peter and Barbra." Bogdanovich hated the script but told Warners that he'd love to work with Streisand, whom he saw as the perfect heroine for a 1930s style screwball comedy like Howard Hawks's *Bringing Up Baby*. He balked at hiring the proposed costar, Ryan O'Neal, but relented after Mengers screened *Love Story* for him.

It was noted throughout town that Streisand had signed her contract without script approval. Mengers had negotiated for her a stunning 10 percent interest in the picture, as well as such perks as getting her house painted inside and out, and being allowed to take any of the furniture used in the picture. Calley had a part in the star's agreeableness. They were having an affair.

Bogdanovich hired his friends Robert Benton and David Newman (*Bonnie and Clyde*) for the rewrite, which they spent months working on, but when he sent the script to Platt, she hated it. "It was a crazy guy with a woman who was constantly trying to get him to behave himself," recalls Platt, who told her former husband that he couldn't make "Barbra be this yenta woman." She urged him to switch the parts, to give Streisand "the quirky, eccentric weirdo behavior" and make O'Neal "the lightweight, this simple stupid guy. Peter said to me, 'That is a great idea. If it works, it'll be my idea.' We were joking." While Calley liked the idea, he still thought the script was "ghastly." By this time he had broken up with Streisand, who was pissed off at him; she complained to friends that he'd only dated her to get her to do the movie. Calley hired Buck Henry, who had written Streisand's *The Owl and the Pussycat*, for another rewrite.

In the midst of the turmoil, Bogdanovich called Platt to say that Streisand wanted him to hire the production and costume designer from *The Last Picture Show* for *What's Up, Doc?* (as *A Glimpse of the Tiger* was retitled). Platt was thrilled, although, during their interview, she shocked Streisand by announcing that she was Bogdanovich's ex-wife. "I think she had designs on Peter." Platt laughs. "I said, 'Go ahead. I don't care.' "

Platt went location scouting in Chicago and decided that Streisand's kooky character needed a more idiosyncratic locale. Her father had always told her that San Francisco was the most beautiful city in the world, and she convinced Bogdanovich to switch. Scouring the city, she filled Buck Henry with wondrous descriptions of San Francisco—the bicycles, the ferry, the escalator at the Hilton, all of which he incorporated into the script. She laid out the entire chase scene without Bogdanovich's input.

Bogdanovich flew up to see her handiwork. They spent an almost magical day together, and at the end they retreated to their adjoining hotel rooms. Says Platt, "We embraced and we just never let go." They spent the night together. Shepherd had gone to New York on a modeling assignment, and Bogdanovich invited Platt to attend the L.A. premiere of *The Last Picture Show* with him. The next day he bought her an outfit in Ghirardelli Square, and that night he took her to a party at the home of his agent, Sue Mengers, the most famous hostess in L.A. "There were stars everywhere—Jack Nicholson, Warren Beatty, Marlon Brando, Paul Newman and his wife, who was knitting," Platt remembers. "Sue Mengers had this kind of a miniature Versailles house, and it had kind of a balcony on one side, and all the people who were smoking dope were going up on the balcony, and I remember the Newmans left because they were offended because people were smoking marijuana, and I was up there somehow. There were probably many, many more people in that room who were famous, but I didn't know who they were at that time. I remember there was a very famous guy who was the head of CBS and they called him the Snake. He had these really mean blue eyes." It was James Aubrey. "I remember I called him the Ana-conda. Peter laughed.

"That was the night that Sue Mengers asked me to stay late because she just didn't want to be alone. Barbra [Streisand] called, and there was this really weird conversation with Sue Mengers, who was rubbing away at her kitchen with a toothbrush and a paper towel and the phone had the longest cord I've ever seen, because she was able to walk all over the house and talk and clean. She was saying to Barbra, 'No, Buck Henry has done a wonderful job. I think it's a funny script. I think you should do it.' The whole movie was threatening to fall apart," recalls Platt, although she realized this only in retrospect, as she watched Mengers reassure her skittish client over everything from the script to the fact that the young director really did like her.

Despite Streisand's qualms, shooting began in August 1971. Prid-ing himself as a disciple of the director Ernst Lubitsch, Bogdanovich liked to act out every part and ask the actor to copy. While O'Neal sub-mitted cheerfully to his ministrations, Streisand balked. "Are you giving me line readings?" she'd yell.

Streisand had grown to hate the whole project, her mood worsened by the fact that she had begun dating O'Neal, but already the romance was souring. She could often be heard grousing at her costar, "We're in a piece of shit. I mean, we're really in trouble. I know what's funny, and *this* isn't funny." When she saw the finished picture, she was appalled. "I remember we walked out of the screening room, and Marty Erlich-man, her manager, who has been with her forever, said to me, 'Are you happy now? You have ruined her career,' " says Mengers. "And I just re-member Barbra and me kind of exchanging looks like oy, not about him, but about the picture." The Streisand contingent begged Calley not to release the picture. When he offered to buy back her 10 percent for $2 million, she happily agreed.

Nonetheless, she and Platt grew fond of each other, as Platt helped shape a sexier image for the star, sun-kissed and Californian, with blond hair swinging down her back. Streisand's interest buoyed Platt's spirits. The two drove to the beach with their kids, with Streisand singing in the car and the actress's young son begging her to stop. The star invited Platt to parties at her home, including one at which the young production designer met Milos Forman and a young Woody Allen. The next day she received a call from Sue Mengers, who told her that Allen had wanted to ask her out but was too shy. "Imagine, you could be Polly Allen," Mengers gaily told her. Platt refused, not interested in the man who'd made *Bananas*.

The movie itself turned out to be light as a cream puff, filled with restaged gags from Buster Keaton and Laurel and Hardy. Streisand, who stuck to her own rhythms and persona, fared better than O'Neal, who seemed to be imitating Cary Grant. The picture earned a smash $35 million at the box office. Platt's modern design was hailed as a witty commentary on the excesses of the sixties.

Platt and Bogdanovich's professional relationship remained the same as it had always been. She helped him visualize the scene, often sitting with him on the way to the set and drawing the floor plans and assisting him in figuring out where the camera should go. Despite their affair, he remained with Cybill Shepherd. For almost two decades Platt would prattle on nearly compulsively about her ex-husband, a wound that never seemed to heal. She began to drink heavily, which had a deleterious effect on her daughters, who bounced back and forth between their mother in San Francisco and their housekeeper in L.A.

"It's really an anesthetic. My drinking seems to be associated with suicidal tendencies," Platt says many years later. "I've never ever thought of killing myself, except once, while trying to go to work and getting my two kids to put on their shoes and go to school. I was dragging Antonia down the stairs by her arm: Boomp . . . booomp . . . booomp, and I thought, I can't believe you're doing this to your own daughter! You're dragging her down the stairs, you're screaming at her, you deserve to die if you can't treat your children better."

In retrospect she sees that the responsibility of motherhood saved her life: "I think if I hadn't had the children I would have drunk myself to death. But I was furious that I couldn't fall apart."

Platt found further solace—for her ego, at least—in the arms of O'Neal, whom she called "my Cybill Shepherd." She was happy to be seen with a boyish blond movie star, although the affair was never serious. When O'Neal went to Houston to shoot *The Thief Who Came to Dinner*, helmed by the director Bud Yorkin, Platt swallowed her fears of working away from Bogdanovich and went along as the production designer. She was still "pretty angry at that time," recalls Frank Marshall, who went with her to work on the movie. Her manner could be high-handed and presumptuous, even "brutal," says Marshall, adding, "Bud Yorkin is a pretty laid-back guy. People on the set didn't know who to go to, her or Yorkin." (Says Yorkin, "You can't be insecure and work with Polly.")

She had just been made the first woman in the Society of Motion Picture and Television Art Directors, after a fracas broke out because she was getting jobs without a union card. Finally, a man she never met, Tambi Larsen, the designer of *Hud*, stood up in a meeting and announced, "It's embarrassing that a person like that is excluded from our guild. She's what a production designer should be. I nominate Polly Platt." She was passed unanimously.

Although she was proud and pleased that her union membership allowed her to work for better wages, Platt was jealous of the acclaim and opportunities heaped on her ex-husband. She watched Bogdanovich and Shepherd at the Academy Awards from her hotel room in Texas, forgotten by both the world and her ex-husband, who was now doing with his pretty, blond girlfriend everything Platt and he had always dreamed of doing. They lived in an elegant apartment on Sunset Boulevard. They jetted off to Switzerland to meet Charlie Chaplin and attended soirees with the president, not caring that the president happened to be Richard M. Nixon. And now Bogdanovich was attending the Oscars. Platt felt abandoned and forgotten.

Ben Johnson finally went to the podium to accept his Best Supporting Actor award for his portrayal of *Picture Show*'s Sam the Lion. He looked up at the camera and announced, "I want to thank Peter Bogdanovich and his lovely wife, Polly."

Platt burst into tears. "It never occurred to me that I would be so left out. People just made a hero out of him, and nobody ever mentioned my name."

EVERYONE THINKS I'M CARRYING THE TORCH FOR YOU

Platt worked one last time with Bogdanovich, on *Paper Moon*. She had urged her former husband to take on Joe David Brown's novel *Addie Pray*, about a father-daughter con team who crisscross the Midwest during the Depression, tricking grieving families into buying Bibles, and had even recommended the daughter of her former beau Ryan O'Neal, Tatum, to play the lead. Bogdanovich later begged Platt to work on the picture with them. She refused. "I don't want to be humiliated. I can't work with you again. Everyone thinks I'm carrying the torch for you," she told him. Platt remembers that O'Neal, who was slated to play the father, "got on his hands and knees and crawled over to me and said, 'Please, I'm begging you. I figure Peter without you is only a five. With you he's a ten.' Peter was right there. 'Please do this picture.' I said, 'I'll do it if I don't have to look at Cybill coming on the set.' Ryan looked at Peter, and Peter said okay."

Creatively, they continued to work well, although their personal relationship deteriorated even more. "On *Paper Moon* she didn't care about her personal state when she was working with him," says the film's cinematographer, Laszlo Kovacs. "She only cared about the movie, and to help make the best movie she could. In those days, I knew her closely. She was very unhappy, very miserable. She never showed it. Never let anybody into it, or be affected by it. It was heroic."

Toward the end of the shoot, Platt began an affair with Tony Wade, one of the property masters who worked for her. He and his brother had been recommended to her by Ellen Burstyn, who had worked with them on *The King of Marvin Gardens.* When she interviewed him for the job, she says, "it never occurred to me that I would have a romance. He said later he thought I was hopelessly in love with Peter and all broken down emotionally. He felt sorry for me as usual. He was incredibly competent. He knew more about motion pictures in a technical way than anybody I had ever met in my life.

"I just developed the biggest crush on him. I used to follow him around. I used to ask his brother and him if I could have dinner with them. I pursued him. He was the first person who made me forget everything."

Tony Wade was huge, handsome, taciturn, and tough—they called him Big Tony, to differentiate him from her daughter Antonia, or little Tony. He was the exact opposite of Bogdanovich. He was the kind of guy who was called in to organize productions that went financially amok.

"He was like a sheriff with a gun in his pocket," recalls Platt's longtime friend Peggy Sarno. "It was very passionate. He made her feel like a woman again."

"I thought it would be only on the picture. We were doing what everybody does," says Platt. Not incidentally, her affair enraged Bogdanovich, who talked of getting back together, though he couldn't quite manage to dump Shepherd.

"She's very tough," recalls Frank Marshall, the film's associate producer. "Sometimes I think too tough. You can't take all this. Finally, on *Paper Moon*, she couldn't go on. It hurt too much."

At least Platt had begun to attract some notice as a designer, although sometimes her aggressive opinions got her in trouble. Mike Nichols fired her from *The Fortune* after she argued with him over the script and the proposed architecture of the set. She worked a bit on Robert Altman's *Thieves Like Us*. "He liked me because he couldn't seduce me," Platt once noted. "He tried in every way. He said he had affairs with all the women he worked with." Indeed, she later turned down the opportunity to work on *Nashville* because she couldn't stand how Altman treated his wife.

Bogdanovich and Platt never worked together again. Bogdanovich's muse became Shepherd, whom he put in film after film—all of them flops—until the studio refused to let him cast her in *Nickelodeon*. Bogdanovich started his long free fall from glory. "People began to think that I was even more important in Peter's success than I was," says Platt. "And so my reputation grew in inverse proportion to his failure, rather tragic actually. I was not happy about it. People would say to me, 'Oh, you directed his movies, and look at how it's been since you separated.' It's not true. I didn't direct his movies. I didn't. I was not happy with it, but it was beneficial to me in a horrible, nauseating sort of way."

Woody Allen and Sue Mengers at Regine's,
New York City, 1976.

SUE MENGERS
IS HATCHED

THE LITTLE PISHER

"The reason women haven't really achieved power in our industry is they're scared shitless," fumes Sue Mengers. It has been twenty years since Mengers ruled Hollywood as the outrageous, mouthy, impudent, muumuu-swaddled agent to the stars. She hardly looks as though she's aged. There's the little button nose, the apple cheeks, and the sharp eyes that peer out with the judgmental glare of an old yenta. Her long blond hair looks as if it has been brushed a thousand times and is held back from her face by a curiously dainty headband. She is wearing a caftan still, and dragging on her cigarette with vigor, her breath punctuating her throaty pronouncement.

She is more swaggering than bilious, her lack of politeness emphasizing her candor. "Power is still alien to women. They don't feel that it is proper. Men get on top in sex, and we are still scared of turning them off," she says vehemently, perfectly aware how this sounds.

Mengers doesn't understand why any woman in the late nineties would complain about Hollywood; these broads had it easy. In her mind, the true arrival of women into the highest circles of Hollywood is demonstrated by the fact that "there are now as many mediocre women working in our industry as there are men. But I don't believe any woman could have been as dumb or egomaniacal as Mario Kassar, Victor Kaufman, and Mickey Shulhoff. You could have the most *mediocre* women in those jobs, and they wouldn't be as stupid in having to prove their *masculinity*, in making the kind of gaffes and shit those guys did. And it infuriates me."

Mengers is sitting in the parlor of her well-appointed Beverly Hills home, a Holocaust refugee turned all-American Horatio Algerette surrounded by a veritable stage set of French-inspired gentility. The sofas are plush. Tapestries hang on the walls, cigarettes sit in silver dishes. A maid serves tea in delicate china cups. These are the only rewards left from her days as agent to Gene Hackman, Burt Reynolds, Candice Bergen, Ali MacGraw, and her onetime soul sister, Barbra Streisand.

"When I met Sue, she was like something out of a Rona Jaffe novel in the seventies," recalls the former agent Joan Hyler. "There was brilliant vulgarity about her. I would go to see her at her hotel room at the Pierre. She would be sitting there in her Christian Dior panty hose with no bra on, talking to Sidney Lumet, who she was representing. She would throw me in a cab with her, and she would say things like, 'There's another five dollars in it for you if you get me to the set in five minutes.' As opposed to talking to the cabbie: 'Gee, would you take me to . . . ?' There was always a sense of urgency about her.

"I had never seen any woman in my entire life *presume* like that," says Hyler. "I grew up watching all those Joan Crawford movies, where women were always somehow punished for presuming . . . what a man presumes. Like 'I can do it. I'm the best.' She was the first completely autonomous woman. Remember the myth of Athena, where Athena came out of Zeus's head full-grown? That was Sue. She just birthed herself. And she was at the right place at the right time."

"I was a little pisher, a little nothing making $135 a week as a secretary for the William Morris Agency in New York," Sue Mengers told Mike Wallace during a famous 1975 *60 Minutes* interview. She was one of the only agents—if not the first agent—to merit such fancy media attention, and in the segment she appears uncharacteristically ladylike and well tempered, eating lunch with Bob Evans poolside, looking positively thrilled to be in the limelight. In her low, pebbly voice she speaks like a character from a novel: "Well, I looked around and I admired the Morris offices and their executives, and I thought, Gee, what they do isn't that hard, you know. And I like the way they live, and I like those expense accounts, and I like the cars. And I used to stay late at the office, just like *All About Eve*, and I suddenly thought: That beats typing."

Mengers would ultimately have a movie to describe every phase of her life, and although the titles changed, the theme remained constant: a lonely outsider desperate to *belong*. She frequently described her childhood as *Stella Dallas*, the 1937 Barbara Stanwyck movie in which the lower-class mother ultimately sacrifices her daughter to a glamorous life of wealth.

Of course, Stella Dallas hadn't been a Jew escaping from the Holocaust. Mengers had arrived in America in 1939, an eight-year-old refugee from Hitler's Germany. Neither of her parents spoke English, and while her father had been a prosperous playboy in Europe, now both he and his wife were forced to take menial jobs in Utica, New York, where they settled. Mengers's father eventually became a traveling salesman not unlike Willy Loman. When she was thirteen, he killed himself. Mengers responded by dissociating herself, floating above her own life in an attempt to escape the guilt and the shame. "He didn't leave a note and wasn't sick—it doesn't give you the best self-image." She developed a voracious hunger to better herself.

She and her mother moved to the Jewish enclave of Washington Heights in New York City, where her mother supported them by becoming a bookkeeper. When Mengers finally became rich, she used to luxuriate in breakfast in bed, served by a Portuguese maid, because, as she explains, "It all had to do with a working mother and being left very much alone. When I was a little girl and I'd wake up, I'd be alone in the house. On the kitchen table would be a glass of milk and a muffin. For me, breakfast in bed was the symbol."

She escaped her lonely life through Saturdays at the movies, admiring Greer Garson, reveling in the sophistication of Lauren Bacall. Her mother indulged her only daughter's fantasies, scrimping so that Sue could take elocution lessons to erase her accent. She fantasized briefly about being an actress. "I looked around and saw everyone was more talented, more beautiful," says Mengers. "There goes that dream."

She used to claim she entered the movie business at the tender age of seventeen, when she answered an MCA ad for "receptionist, theatrical agency." In truth she was closer to twenty-five. It was 1955, and MCA dominated the talent trade. A secretive juggernaut where the agents sported a mandatory uniform of baggy black suits and Sulka shirts, MCA was nicknamed "the Octopus" for its habit of involving itself in every aspect of its clients' fiduciary lives, from the rental of their cars to their movie deals. The agency represented Jack Benny, George Burns and Gracie Allen, Marlon Brando, and Montgomery Clift. The few women agents were casting agents who found young talent. When a talent blossomed, he graduated to the big male agents in California.

Mengers did not last long in this buttoned-down world, sliding quickly to Baum & Newborn, a freelance theatrical agency where the style was, as one journalist has described it, "pastrami at the desk, and yelling, 'I can book 'em for two weeks at the Music Center.' "

Martin Baum at least acknowledged the cute young spark plug, teaching her, as she says, "total aggression." He also fired her repeatedly, sometimes simply for being out sick, other times for careless mistakes.

Mengers eventually moved to William Morris, the conservative industry stalwart, a powerhouse in the emerging TV business, agents to Steve McQueen and the Rat Pack. Unfortunately, she was still a secretary, although men who would eventually be her peers—Irwin Winkler, Barry Diller, Jerry Weintraub—toiled in the mail room, the long-established training ground for agents. Mengers lived in a cockroach-infested walk-up on Fifty-seventh Street between Broadway and West End Avenue.

Although Broadway had already begun its long decline, victim of television, movies, and spiraling real-estate values, Morris had a vibrant theater department, with clients like Edward Albee, *How to Succeed in Business*'s Abe Burrows, *The Music Man*'s Meredith Willson, and a very young Neil Simon. Mengers spent her time trolling Broadway, begging for tickets from press agents and trying to make herself indispensable to her bosses.

"When I was a secretary, I would stay after work to read the scripts so that I would know what my boss was talking about to the clients," she says. "And I remember once being at my desk at, like, nine o'clock and Arthur Penn calling. And he said, 'My God, I didn't think anyone would be there. Listen, Clarice Blackburn just fell out of *The Miracle Worker*'—whatever play he was doing—and he said, 'I've got to get a replacement right away and it's late, and I don't know who to call.' And I got out that casting book, and we, for an hour, went through the casting book. And I remember feeling so proud. What else would I be doing? Having dinner with some guy who would grope me later? I didn't care about dating."

The closer she got to the stars, the more unhappy she became about the glass pressed up against her nose. Mengers was once asked to deliver a script to Tyrone Power. She took the bus to his apartment on Madison and Seventy-second, the whole time fantasizing that he would come to the door, invite her to supper, and fall madly in love with her. "Of course, the minute I got there the doorman said, 'I'll take care of that, thanks,' " recalls Mengers. "I remember that feeling of total, total frustration, that I couldn't even get in to hand him the script. That terrible feeling of being left out all the time."

Unfortunately, her newfound ambition only increased her unhappiness. One weekend she went away to Atlantic City with her mother, and as they walked the boardwalk she suddenly began to cry. "It was all the frustration of wanting to be included in a world that I didn't know how to get included in," she explained later. Her mother suggested she go to one of those "head doctors: 'We have a cousin who's a psychologist—she's a relative so she won't think you're crazy.' " Mengers went and found relief. "Analysis helped me hold on till I could make it."

In her need for attention, she sometimes resorted to outrageousness. A former Morris agent told *New York* magazine about seeing Mengers in the reception area. The Marquis Chimps, who appeared at Radio City Music Hall, were sitting there with their trainer, waiting to see their agent. "Sue appeared, spotted the apes, lifted her skirt, and said, 'Monkey, want to ———?' "

In 1963 she finally quit Morris. A former Baum & Newborn colleague, Tom Korman, was starting his own agency, with backing from his father. He could pay her only $150 a week, barely more than she made as a secretary, but at least she'd be an agent. "Personally, I think he couldn't get a guy," recalls Mengers. "I'm sure he asked some of the other young agents around him; for whatever reason they didn't want to take the shot of opening an agency with the guarantee of only a year or two to make it. The father wasn't going to subsidize this forever.

"I never thought in 1960 that there was a chance for a woman to have the career that I even had three years later. Women didn't—unless you were Clare Boothe Luce—who thought in terms of a career? We didn't."

Her first day as an agent, she was determined to act like an agent. She asked her secretary to bring her coffee. Then she went down to the set of *Barefoot in the Park* and tried to sign Jane Fonda. "Now I had my credentials. *I was an agent,*" recalls Mengers at the top of her lungs. "Jane Fonda didn't know me from a hole in the wall. I knew no fear. I thought this would be great. Jane Fonda should want to sign with me. To my shock, she didn't want to sign with some unknown. I kept after her for years." Not deterred by that unsuccessful foray, Mengers went and bought a mink coat from a wholesaler who let her pay it off at twenty-five dollars a week. "That to me was the symbol."

Unlike the handful of women agents whom the industry indulged because of their literary pretensions or good taste, Mengers never even pretended to know about art or acting skill. She recognized heat and power, and consequently, she says, was only "interested in stars. I'd never discovered talent. I have no idea if someone's talented. Until I really see their work. If someone walks into an office, no matter how good looking, I can't spot it," she says. "I saw Dustin Hoffman Off Broadway—totally unimpressed. Al Pacino—signed when I was at CMA with Stephanie Phillips. She believed in him. I said, 'Are you crazy? This guy's never going to make it. He's never going to be in movies.' And she believed in him and forced me to kind of help. I never could spot it early on. But that's all right. I think stars need as much help."

Mengers took a leaf from her brief stint at MCA. Her goal was total indispensability, particularly in the early days, when she could offer more emotional support than financial savvy. She knew which buttons needed to be pushed and had answers for questions without answers.

Her first big score was Julie Harris, then Broadway's reigning star and, fortunately for Mengers, agentless. She called Harris cold, convinced her to meet, then cajoled and wheedled, a zaftig blonde determined to carry out Harris's every bidding: "There must be something you want to do that you can't get automatically." Harris admitted that she wanted to do an episode of *Bonanza*. Mengers didn't understand her agenda but dutifully looked up the name of the *Bonanza* producer in *Variety* and called him, saying that she represented Harris. "The guy said, 'Is this a joke?' He was so excited to have Julie Harris, he wanted to write an episode for her."

Mengers then laid siege to Tony Perkins for six months. He hadn't made a movie on American soil in the seven years since *Psycho*, but he was still a full-fledged star. Perkins wanted a part in René Clément's *Is Paris Burning?* Again, Mengers looked up the producer in *Variety;* it was the legendary Ray Stark. Again, she cold-called, and called, and called. Stark finally got on the phone, only to inform her the picture was entirely cast. A week later Perkins announced that he was leaving for Paris to do the movie; his L.A. agents had arranged it.

"Well, now here I'm this little pisher who means nothing to Ray Stark, so I write him a letter," says Mengers. "How unprofessional your behavior was. You were once an agent, and how could you treat another agent with such lack of sensitivity. And to Ray Stark's credit—this was an important man then, as he is now—instead of throwing this letter in the basket, he called up the agent in L.A. and said, 'Listen, I made a mistake. This girl did call me from New York. I just forgot. And she's entitled to the commission. And if you don't feel that you want to share it with her, I will pay her.' So, we got our five percent commission. And I love Ray Stark, but that was something that was a helping hand to someone that could have no meaning in his life. And on occasion I found that men were very kind to me. David Merrick, who was lousy to everyone, was lovely to me. Otto Preminger, who was like an animal, was lovely to me."

Mengers freely used every feminine wile at her disposal. She was ballsy, but always obsessed with the trappings of femininity—determined to wear the perfect outfit, the right earrings. "I was *charming.* I was *adorable,*" she insists. "I was cute. I didn't put on an act—'I'm one of you guys.' I loved what I was doing and they could see that." In her mind she was cute enough to get a seat at the table, but she didn't invite relentless sexualization—or seduction. Years later she insists that she was never harassed: "I believe it's in the way you conduct yourself. I sent off vibes of work. I never thought about them that way. They knew I was smart. They valued that more than the fact 'Here's another broad I can go to bed with.' "

Mengers assiduously curried favor with the industry's most important players by plying them with unsolicited casting advice that had no direct benefit for her. "You don't call a David Merrick when you're an unknown agent, selling him people that might be in the fourth part, unless you are going to be interesting. I would give him three ideas. When he was doing *Hello, Dolly!* we didn't represent anyone that was right for the leads, but I would call him up with what I call three ideas for the road companies. You ought to get Ginger Rogers. He took my call because I always gave him good ideas that weren't my clients, so that when the moment came that I needed something, there was a payoff."

"I remember her saying to me, 'If I could be reincarnated, I would come back as Marilyn Monroe,' " Tom Korman has quipped. "Sue's fantasy was always to be a movie star. And in a way she did become one."

Within two years Mengers was on the rise. When she was still a secretary at Morris, she had cultivated the novelist and screenwriter Gore Vidal after he caught her red-handed listening at the keyhole to his agent's office. Now she was desperate to meet Vidal's friends Paul Newman and Joanne Woodward, Hollywood's royal couple. Vidal and his companion, Howard Austen, arranged for a special dinner at the most prominent table at Sardi's, then one of New York's most glittering watering holes.

"How could I sign them? I couldn't talk to them about movies. So I would say, 'You know, Paul, you ought to have Tennessee Williams write a play for you and Joanne.' Every time I was with them, I was like this little dynamo telling them they should be doing theater. They, in turn, would go back and call their agent, Freddie Fields, and say, 'You know, we had dinner with this little agent and she's right—we ought to call Arthur Miller and Tennessee and see if they can't write a play for us.' Well, this was not something Freddie Fields or David Begelman enjoyed hearing. So, gradually, to get me out of the way, to get me to stop nudging their most important client [CMA, Creative Management Associates] hired me. What did it cost them? A couple of hundred bucks a week? They didn't pay me more than what I was making, but I knew they were the big time.

"I tried to get Tom [Korman] to come. He wouldn't. He still had that dream, that he could make this independent agency in New York work. I knew it couldn't."

Mengers felt guilty about leaving Korman. But, she says, "I knew I was limited there. I didn't have enough movie stars."

Unlike MCA's Lew Wasserman, who was motivated by power, Fields and Begelman were entranced by money. They weren't interested in clients who made less than $100,000 a year. CMA was a boutique agency for stars like Robert Redford, Steve McQueen, and Paul Newman. Fields was Mr. Hollywood himself, dressed in black safari suits, shirt open to his waist, holding court behind his six-foot-long marble desk in an office strewn with Oriental rugs and hanging plants. Begelman had the pretensions of an Ivy League gentleman and had convinced most people that he had attended Yale Law School, although in truth his only time spent in New Haven was a six-month stint in the Army. Their client Judy Garland had once tagged the pair Leopold and Loeb, after the infamous 1920s teenage killers; Fields and Begelman encouraged ruthlessness among their troops, who freely stole one another's clients and jobs.

Sue Mengers was made the head of the CMA theater department at a time when the agency "didn't want Paul Newman and Joanne Woodward or their big stars to do theater," says Mengers. There was more money to be made in TV and movies. "So my job, predominantly, was not to get them jobs. I'd come up with these plays, and Freddie and David made it clear that this was not their goal."

Every morning she donned psychic armor. "I felt like I was going into battle. Battle to get clients. Battle to hold clients. Battle to make sure my clients got enough money. Battle to make sure that the buyers liked it. I didn't make friends with any of the male agents. I wasn't interested. I always had a contempt, which was wrong. I mean, I really thought I was a genius." Others were undoubtedly afraid of her. Her bons mots gave her a reputation for profanity. While she insists she never actually used swearwords, her swaggering might have given off that impression. Unlike some women of that era, she says, "I never failed to tell men when they made a mistake. I was contemptuous sometimes in the way I may have talked. You know, 'Oh come on, don't be an idiot.' Well, to a man to hear that from a blond, overweight girl—they don't like to be wrong to a woman." Some recalled Mengers's in-your-face tactics with horror. The record producer Ben Bagley told Tony Perkins's biographer Charles Winecoff of meeting Mengers: "Tony said, 'Sue is coming and I want you to be here, because you've never met anyone as crude as this.' Well, she was the crudest person I'd ever met, and I didn't think that was possible. He delighted shocking me with her. She took her shoes off after we ate, and her feet smelled to high heaven, and she dangled them in his face. I was on the same couch and got up to move because the odor was so repellent." The New York CMA office hated her, except perhaps for Stephanie—Stevie—Phillips, agent to Liza Minnelli and Robert Redford. After an initial period of coolness, they became friends. Says Mengers, "It was because we were so different. She was very much a lady, soft-spoken and demure."

Several years after Mengers had begun there, CMA merged with another agency, General Artists Corporation. "So, they didn't know what to do with me because I didn't want to be melded into another theater department." They offered to move her to London or L.A. She had never been to the West Coast, so she chose London. "And the London office, which consisted of maybe ten agents, said, 'If she comes over here, we're quitting. En masse,' " says Mengers.

"Agents in England do not go after each other's clients. They have to die, and then someone might pick up the load. Well, in America, of course we do. Someone signs with an agent, and the next day they get three calls starting in on them. And the English agents were absolutely

appalled at the thought of my coming over. So the L.A. office unenthu-
siastically [took me], because it was either that or I'd leave the company,
and they smelled I was good."

Unleashed in L.A., Mengers transmogrified into even more of a caricature, a ribald comic-strip blonde who pulled up to Burt Lancaster on
Sunset Boulevard, rolled down her window, and yelled, "Who represents you?" "IFA," he responded. "Not for long," she yelped, as she drove
away. Lancaster resisted, although Ryan O'Neal didn't when she
strolled up to him at a party and blurted out, "When are you going to
get rid of your dumb asshole of an agent?" While her candor alienated
some, it also won her admirers in a town built on illusions. She was
unique, a fact that garnered her even more attention. She became famous for aggressiveness in the face of reason, trying to persuade the
producers of *Cabaret* to hire her personal client Anthony Newley after
they'd already chosen CMA's Joel Grey, or laying siege to Paramount
production chief Bob Evans and pressing him repeatedly to hire her
client Ryan O'Neal to play the lead in *The Godfather*.

In those days, Hollywood credited Freddie Fields for her success,
which he took upon himself: "Even Dr. Frankenstein put life into his
monster, didn't he?" Fields told *Ms.* before backtracking. "I don't mean
to imply that it could be done with anyone. . . . All I gave her was the
opportunity and the direction to allow her to become something of a
unique creature. We just kind of invented a character for her to play,
which she was able to play almost naturally at a time when the industry needed some flamboyance."

In the beginning, when Mengers would pull off a big deal, Fields
would tell her to go out and buy herself a new dress. She'd giggle—
"Thank you, Uncle Freddie"—until one day when she mentioned her
salary to a business manager and saw him pale.

She immediately marched into Fields's office and railed, "I'm not a
little girl. I'm a man doing a man's job, and I want to be paid like a
man." She was forced to use that metaphor because, as she said at the
time, "a grown-up woman means shit to them."

When Warners' John Calley dangled a studio job in front of her,
Fields went ballistic at Calley for trying to steal his manpower. Despite
their friendliness, Mengers and Stevie Phillips watched each other's
salaries like hawks. If one got a raise, Fields would quickly hear from the
other.

Mengers's business strategy was highly idiosyncratic and personalized, and fit in well with the calculated informality of the day. She liked to sit at her desk, feet slung up, smoking a cigarette, which she occasionally had her secretary lace with pot. She hardly bothered to go to the morning staff meetings, preferring to issue phone calls from the comfort of her bed. She was blunt, often amusing, occasionally crass. When a friend wrote that she was pregnant, Mengers cabled back, "You swore he wouldn't touch you." When a young woman was trying to decide between being an agent and being a manager, she quipped, "Agents are the Puerto Ricans of the business, but managers are the niggers."

Mengers combined ruthless psychologizing with breathless romanticism. Alternately bullying and coddling, she deftly played her clients' pressure points. Yet, despite the cynical exterior, Mengers believed with an immigrant's gusto in the system, in the vaunted studio heads, and in the stars, the chosen bearers of a nation's soul, charmed luminaries with charmed lives. Her faith in them bordered on messianic. "I thought being an agent was close to being Mother Teresa," she quips. "There is no question. They are more interesting," she insists years later. "Their minds are different. And also, it is very heady—fame by association. To walk into Studio 54 with Ryan O'Neal and Farrah Fawcett at the height of their fame. You like it. It rubs off on you. They're treated really nice. You hang out with talent, you feel not that any of the talent has rubbed off on you but the acceptance. Gee, I must be interesting if I can hang out with these talented people."

Her most charmed client, of course, was Barbra Streisand. In her heyday, Mengers couldn't conceive that any of her clients would ever leave her—particularly not Barbra, who was practically family. Barbra was her touchstone, the woman she might have liked to have been if she had been born with talent.

Like Mengers, Streisand was a funny-looking, fatherless, Jewish girl from New York, who deemed herself pretty and triumphed through chutzpah. They had met when Mengers was a secretary at Morris and the teenage Streisand was trying to get work singing in clubs in New York. Says Mengers, "Her manager arranged somehow to have my boss, who was the biggest snob in the world, meet with this unknown. And I went into the waiting room to bring her in. It wasn't love at first sight. She was really weird-looking. It was during her realistic 'Second-hand Rose' period. You have no idea, the beautiful woman that she is now. We made fun of her after she left, and then I saw her in her first Off Broadway revue and remember thinking, What kind of drive does a girl this unattractive have that enables her to get up and sing? I was not knocked out. We joke about this now. I mean, she never found it *that* funny."

In 1962, the nineteen-year-old Streisand created a minor sensation in her Broadway debut, *I Can Get It for You Wholesale,* with a comic spinster song entitled "Miss Marmelstein." Other agents were soon pushing one another out of the way to get in to see the rising starlet at the dingy Bon Soir, in New York's Greenwich Village, or the uptown Blue Angel. But not Mengers, although her path and Streisand's had began to cross frequently because Mengers had started representing Streisand's eventual husband, Elliott Gould. "Elliot would say, 'Come on,' and I'd be with them, but we didn't become close friends, because by this time she was taking off. Who had time to see her?" says Mengers. "But I was in love with her after *Funny Girl.* The out-of-town tryouts in New Haven." It was Streisand's first undeniable hit.

Their friendship blossomed in 1968, when both wound up single women in L.A. Streisand had split from Elliott Gould, who was overwhelmed by his wife's success and mired in a serious gambling problem. She bounced from affair to affair, from Omar Sharif to Pierre Trudeau to a fling with Warren Beatty. In between men she went out with Mengers. "We were two single women, and she was invited everywhere, and she would schlep me along," recalls Mengers. "It was a wonderful introduction for me to the industry. I can remember the New Year's Eve of 1968 or '69. We were at some New Year's Eve party together, and we locked ourselves in the bathroom so we wouldn't have to kiss all the strange people that were there. We just stayed in the bathroom till like twelve-thirty."

Mengers spent an hour in the morning and an hour at night talking to Streisand. She constantly stroked and validated the diva, soothing her woes and hearing her ideas; she was thrilled beyond belief that someone with that much talent would listen to career advice from *her,* a little pisher from the Bronx, even though the star was still officially represented by Mengers's boss, Freddie Fields.

"She didn't agree with you all the time, but she never got offended by hearing an opinion. She never got angry, hurt, or insulted," Mengers would claim, and she had little hesitation about telling the rising superstar what she thought was good for her or arguing with her like an overprotective Jewish mother. "More and more things were discussed with me because she knew I'd give her the honest reaction. Meanwhile, my boss might be thinking more in terms of commissions." When fear swept the entertainment community after the 1969 Charles Manson murders, Mengers and a distraught Streisand drove out to Steve McQueen's house in Malibu, where the action star armed himself with guns and barricaded them all inside. Mengers reassured Streisand, "Don't worry, honey, stars aren't being murdered, only featured players."

Mengers worked on making herself invaluable to Streisand, ultimately reading every potential script herself, although there was a squadron of readers to comb through the stacks of submissions. Getting Streisand to commit to a movie was "the hardest part because Barbra is not ambitious," insists Mengers. "Once she made it, it was like going crazy to get her to go to work. She's a woman of many interests, and she was offered everything for a white woman between the ages of eighteen and thirty-five." By 1970, Streisand, who had been oblivious to much of the cultural rebellion ushered in by such movies as *Easy Rider* and her estranged husband's *Bob & Carol & Ted & Alice,* became determined to update her stodgy, overproduced image, perpetuated by fare such as *Hello, Dolly!* and *On a Clear Day You Can See Forever.* Mengers introduced Streisand to her friend David Geffen, and ultimately Streisand recorded "Stoney End," a song written by Geffen's client Laura Nyro. (She went along screaming, doubting the song's appeal until it zoomed to number six on the charts, her bestselling single since "People" six years before.)

Mengers's 1971 *What's Up, Doc?* package, featuring her clients Bogdanovich, O'Neal, and Streisand, made her career, proving that she could assemble pictures like the big boys. Nonetheless, Streisand used to tell people, "Freddie is my agent, Sue is my friend." Mengers preferred to see this less as sexism than as insecurity. "Like everyone else, people want to feel like they're loved for themselves," says Mengers. "It's hard for Barbra. Everyone wanted something from her." Indeed, while Mengers focused on putting together the creative elements of a film, Fields would often follow up and negotiate the business aspects of the deal.

Mengers further cemented her status by becoming the town's most visible hostess. Since the days of the Warners, the Selznicks, and the Mayers, parties in Hollywood had been prime venues for displays of wealth and power. Freddie Fields himself had been an extravagant host, although his fetes were largely organized by his wife, the actress Polly

Bergen, or his secretary, Toni Howard. When Mengers arrived in L.A. both Fields and Begelman urged her to entertain, and CMA paid for most of it. Again, her initial calling card was Streisand. "It was very easy to get people to come to your party if you said Barbra Streisand will be there, and that was it. People came," says Mengers. "They didn't know who the fuck I was. Although I had the title of being with an agency, I wasn't someone."

Soon her house was permanently stocked with celebrities, as Mengers and her salon became in essence the embodiment of the mink coat, the breakfast in bed, the symbol of acceptance at the upper echelons of American society. Indeed, her first house was a rented one-bedroom owned by the designer Tony Duquette and decorated with set models. It was so small that it could accommodate only an exclusive thirty, and Mengers planned the parties with military precision, keeping meticulous lists of every guest who had ever been there. The mix was often eccentric, yet perfectly choreographed, with the right amount of drugs, talent, power, and available starlets. Julie Christie supped alongside Princess Margaret. "Albert Schweitzer would be playing Ping-Pong with Mick Jagger," John Calley remembers. Ultimately, Mengers bought Zsa Zsa Gabor's old estate on Bel-Air Road.

Mengers never forgot that the subtext was casting, getting her clients jobs. Ann-Margret met Mike Nichols and walked away with a part in *Carnal Knowledge.* Burt Reynolds landed *Starting Over* after dining next to the director Alan Pakula chez Mengers. Sometimes Mengers would look around the room, proud of her social accomplishments. But in later years, she would look back in bitterness at all the extras she had to provide just to become a player.

"Our house became like a restaurant," she said. "I was chasing after Rita Hayworth, just to meet her, and I was already in my thirties, folks! But the celebrities hadn't come because they wanted to see me; they wanted to see each other. I was never the star at my own parties. I was the catalyst to bring creative people together. I was the concierge. No one said, 'Let's listen to Sue's bons mots.' I was tolerated. A man in this business would not have to put on a party. Someone with another power base would not have to entertain."

But at her peak Mengers studiously, willfully ignored the impact of gender. "I never thought of myself as being like the guys, or being a woman. I was just good at what I did, and I was treated well. I didn't realize till after I retired that they weren't crazy about me. That the closeness was a professional closeness because they respected me and I could be helpful, but they were never really comfortable with me."

Dating was never a high priority. Work was her narcotic, her raison d'être. In her Tillie the Toiler days, Mengers says, she "never thought any man would marry me. I never even thought about it"; she preferred a night working the theater with her colleagues to dining with some unknown schmo. Later, when she moved to L.A., she was stunningly cognizant of where she stood on the food chain of available women. "It's six o'clock. I'm working in my little cubicle. It was 1969. Jimmy Caan, who was gorgeous at the time, came rushing in," she recalls. "And he said, 'You've got to help me out, I know this is last minute. I'm so embarrassed, but Sammy [Davis, Jr.] is opening at the Cocoanut Grove.' I'm thinking, What will I wear? Oh God, can I get my hair done? He said, 'You've got to see if Candice Bergen will go with me!' No, Jimmy Caan was not going to walk in with me." As her stature in the community grew, Mengers began to view sex as the men did—a perk of power. She liked getting set up, having affairs, particularly with well-known catches. "I was Polly Promiscuous," she bragged to journalists.

In 1970 she finally met her husband, the Belgian writer-director Jean-Claude Tramont, a romance she likens to that of Petruchio and Kate in Shakespeare's *Taming of the Shrew*. She almost forwent the dinner at the socialite Anne Ford's house where she met the handsome, erudite Tramont. She had been invited by Ford's daughter Charlotte. Mengers wanted a rich date, but none of the proposed candidates met her standards. Charlotte Ford pleaded with Mengers to come so as not to insult her mother. Because her friends Bob Evans and Ali MacGraw were also going, Mengers relented but didn't bother dressing up. Dinah Shore brought Tramont with her. He had flown in from France to shoot a UNICEF special with Shore and Marlon Brando. Mengers could tell that he was smitten with her, and, although there were only eight people at the dinner, she barely deigned to talk to him. Ten days later he called and had to remind Mengers's secretary who he was. He came over for a drink and never left. Mengers hadn't realized how lonely she was until he moved in. In 1973 they were married. Streisand was her maid of honor, and Streisand's date stood up for Tramont.

Mengers's marriage shocked the town, mostly because Tramont was movie-star handsome and relatively poor, while she was neither. After an early sojourn working in TV in New York in the 1950s, he had changed his name from Schwarz to his father's stage name, Tramont.

Her women detractors were especially peeved, while everyone gossiped about Tramont's ulterior motives. "When Ryan O'Neal said to Barbra, 'Oh God, Sue's going to be hurt. He's going to use her and he's going to dump her,' Barbra said, 'Why would that be? We love her. Why is it so surprising he'd love her?' " recalls Mengers fondly. She reveled in her husband's wit, and his ability to defuse her, to "say the one thing that would stop me from taking myself too seriously." He disdained the Sue-in-high-warrior mode: "When he would hear me on the phone at home, he used to tell me how it turned him off. I was talking like a guy. 'No, goddamnit, I'm not going to lower the price. No!' He found it so unattractive."

At first their professional accomplishments were comparable. Tramont's script *Ash Wednesday* was made into a movie with Elizabeth Taylor. But tensions grew when Tramont's career stalled and Mengers's zoomed upward in 1974. Until then she might have been CMA's most outrageous, attention-getting agent, but she wasn't the agency's most powerful player, as long as her boss Freddie Fields remained enthroned. After his former partner Richard Shephard and David Begelman left the agency to take studio jobs, Fields remained alone, at the pinnacle of CMA. He represented Newman, Redford, and McQueen, had negotiated development deals for certain directors that gave him automatic authority to green-light movies if any of five actors (four of whom he represented) agreed to star. Yet he had grown to loathe the hand-holding that was the bread and butter of an agent's existence. On December 30, 1974, he sold his agency to Marvin Josephson and his TV powerhouse, International Famous Agency, creating the behemoth known as International Creative Management.

About a month before the formal announcement of the merger, Mengers flew to New York to have dinner with Paramount's chairman, Barry Diller. She was guarding her back against any possible encroachment by Josephson, who, unlike Freddie Fields, issued dress codes and refused to put the majority of his agents under contract. She spread the rumor that she was restless. The press reported she might take her close friend Robert Evans's job at Paramount, or a similar position under her former mentor Begelman. It was a classic gambit to up your price while highlighting your potential unavailability, and it worked, landing Mengers a contract worth $200,000—more than some studio heads got—with an expense account worth $40,000.

Fields left the agency the next year. Mengers recounts, "[Barbra and I] had to confront that moment where it would become official: Barbra, I am now your agent. She said, 'You're my friend.' I said, 'I know, I know, but now we've got to make it official.' Because before it was always, 'Freddie is my agent, Sue is my friend.' She really didn't want to make that distinction, but finally she did."

Mengers received a $50,000 raise eight months later, after William Morris made a run at her. By this time the top agents Guy McElwaine and Mike Medavoy had also quit the agency business, leaving Mengers with most of ICM's stars and directors—Faye Dunaway, Bob Fosse, Gene Hackman, Jack Nicholson, Mike Nichols—clientele worth $1.5 million in commissions alone. Each came to her with a specialized mythology. Winging to New York on the Gulf + Western plane for the premiere of Streisand's *On a Clear Day You Can See Forever*, Mengers, sporting a brown T-shirt and pants, met Ali MacGraw, then married to Paramount's production chief, Bob Evans, and the star of the year's blockbuster, *Love Story*. She would become Mengers's WASP princess. "More than anyone else, Sue believed in the myth of Ali MacGraw as movie star," MacGraw told the *Los Angeles Times*. "And she believed in the myth of Bob-and-Ali. And when it was over, she took it very hard. So when people say Sue can be negative, I say, It's not negativity. It's disenchantment. Because Sue Mengers is all about enchantment."

Mengers would later say she never had time to have children because her clients were her children. It was a decision she later regretted, but her stars were all greedy for her attention, her love and care. And when they hated her, they hated their mother.

Jeannie Berlin and Elaine May at Sardi's, 1973.

4.

WOMEN CREATE

POWER IS A DIRTY WORD WHEN IT'S LINKED TO A FEMALE

"Women have been silent about their recent mistreatment in films because women are programmed to be silent—it isn't nice for a woman to scream," screamed the screenwriter Eleanor Perry on a fall evening in 1974 to a crowd of three hundred women jammed into the Donnell Library Center auditorium in Manhattan. "Women have real hang-ups about power; *power* is a dirty word when it's linked to a female," she railed. It seemed incongruous that such inflammatory words would pour forth from this elegant, older Babe Paley doppelgänger, but she was, after all, the writer of not only *David and Lisa* but also the early feminist film *Diary of a Mad Housewife*. In the years since her breakup from the director Frank Perry, her husband and former work partner, Eleanor Perry had become further radicalized by a consciousness-raising group run by Susan Brownmiller. At the 1972 Cannes Film Festival, Perry led a group of women protesters who sprayed red paint over posters for Federico Fellini's *Roma*, which featured a woman with three breasts. They also picketed screenings of the film, waving placards inscribed, WOMEN ARE PEOPLE, NOT DIRTY JOKES.

At the 1974 convocation, Perry and her copanelists (among them the feminist film critic Molly Haskell and the actress Joan Hackett) formalized their complaints, amassing evidence to prove their point: a slide show documenting the day's leading women playing prostitutes, and the latest employment statistics of women in the film business. In the Producers Guild, there were 3,060 men and 8 women. In the Directors Guild, 2,343 men and 23 women; the Writers Guild, 2,882 men and 148 women.

Perry was one of the loudest voices in a growing chorus of public protests against Hollywood's discriminatory practices toward women. In 1975 the National Organization for Women filed stockholder suits against Columbia and Paramount. Both companies rejected the call to place women on their boards of directors and to explicitly—according to NOW standards—improve the image of women in their movies. Columbia ultimately agreed to release its employment figures for the last three years, which showed that the proportion of women in management positions increased from 8 to 12 percent from 1973 to 1975. Paramount refused to cooperate at all (although NOW used the studio's equal opportunity forms to show that only 6.1 percent of Paramount executives were women).

In 1974 the American Film Institute started the Directing Workshop for Women with a $35,000 grant from the Rockefeller Foundation. Each of the fifteen participants received $350 and the use of primitive equipment to make two videotapes. The program was attacked for being elitist, a sophisticated résumé service for the rich, because, during its first three years of existence, almost every participant was either already established in her field or famous; they included the lyricist Marilyn Bergman, the producer Julia Phillips, and the actresses Anne Bancroft, Ellen Burstyn, Dyan Cannon, Marsha Mason, Cicely Tyson, and Joanne Woodward. "Famous actresses, writers are uncertain about a new field. They need a nonthreatening environment," responded the program director, Jan Haag.

The flurry of protests came largely from women who were on the margins of Hollywood. What became the largest and most long-lasting women's group, Women in Film, adopted a pointedly nonradical agenda; they wanted not to change the system but simply to find a place for women within it. The few women who had actually made strides behind the camera distanced themselves from any taint of feminism.

"They're discriminated against because they're not that good! Just get out and do it. *I* did it," Sue Mengers told *Ms.* magazine in 1975.

"I'm not against the Movement," she backtracked. "Women who want to contribute to the impotency of men, let them go right ahead. But they're hurting our work progress. By beating their chests and shouting, 'We are equal,' they're convincing the men that we're a hysterical bunch of shrews."

Nashville's screenwriter, Joan Tewkesbury, equivocated. "People think I am a feminist. I'm not a feminist. I'm for folks."

Those who did not explicitly criticize the women's movement distanced themselves from the idea that their gender in any way influenced their abilities. Carole Eastman, the screenwriter of *Five Easy Pieces*, told *Time* magazine in 1972, "There is nothing in writing that's feminine." Elaine May, who had just directed the hit *The Heartbreak Kid*, added, "I don't know if it's important if you're a man, woman, or chair. I found no sexism in getting the first job." May happened to be the only woman to direct a studio movie between 1966 and 1979.

I'M THE DIRECTOR, AND ONLY THE DIRECTOR SAYS, "CUT"

At this moment Elaine May is standing in the middle of Front Street arguing with her producer Mike Hausman. She seems gaunt and nervous in her brown shirt and tattered blue jeans, chain smoking and gesticulating with bony hands. She looks like anything but an established show biz celebrity. Shoulders hunched, head ducked, eyes staring soulfully, she resembles a teenager who has just been caught smoking on the stairs by the junior high principal. She is the meekest person on the set, and her voice is almost inaudible, but Hausman can be heard a block away.

"I can't promise to deliver that," he is screeching. "I just can't!"

May fidgets a bit. "You don't like the idea," she mumbles.

"The idea is great!" Hausman moans. "I just don't think I can deliver it, that's all."

All May wants to do is move the scene from South Street to Front Street, around the corner. . . . The crew had spent several days on South Street putting up false storefronts and arranging lights. . . . This change will require the crew to move the lights and create a few more phony stores . . . and to repave a stretch of Front Street. Oh, and if it isn't too much trouble, May would like all this done tonight, so a few takes of the scene can be shot before the sun comes up.

—Dan Rottenberg, *Chicago Tribune*

And so it went night after sweltering night from May to August 1973, according to one dispatch issued by the reporter Dan Rottenberg from the moviemaking front of the Elaine May film *Mikey and Nicky*. A bitter send-up of the Huck-and-Tom myth of male friendship, the film recounts a night in the life of two friends: Nicky (John Cassavetes), a member of a Philadelphia crime syndicate who has stolen from his boss, cheated on his wife, sadistically set up his girlfriend, and repeatedly humiliated his best friend; and Mikey (Peter Falk), the aforementioned best friend, who works for the same boss and who has now set Nicky up to be whacked. It is the grittiest of May's films, both literally and figuratively, although her first two efforts, *A New Leaf* (1971) and *The Heartbreak Kid* (1972), also turned on betrayal, namely how badly men can betray women. At the time she was roundly criticized for creating intensely unflattering portraits of womanhood—a kind of self-loathing, some thought—but the films also satirize romantic love, how foolish it is for women to expect to be fulfilled by a man, particularly the feckless heroes of these films.

From the beginning the May worldview of distrust extended to Hollywood. Despite her otherworldly, fey persona, May was fiercely protective of her vision. In her infrequent interviews she often cited a remark by her former partner Mike Nichols, "You have your work and your career. And the two are diametrically opposed."

Still, unlike most other women trying to break into the motion picture business, Elaine May never had anyone question whether she was genuinely talented. She was one-half of the most celebrated comedic duo of her age, Nichols and May. They even played JFK's legendary forty-fifth birthday bash, right before Marilyn Monroe sang her breathy version of "Happy Birthday." In 1961 *The New Yorker* rapturously described May's repertoire of characters in her Broadway skit show *An Evening with Mike Nichols and Elaine May:* "She is a short, buxom young woman, as uncompromisingly brunette as Nichols is blond, with an enormous amount of crazy hair and crazy energy. She can arrange her features and tune her voice in so many different ways that it is impossible to say what she really looks or sounds like."

Nichols and May used the Stanislavsky method of acting to create comedy sketches that aptly deflated the fatuous pieties of the Eisenhower fifties. All their routines started as improvisations, with each actor devising a part, and gradually grew into set pieces without a word being put on paper. Their dialogue often consisted of clichés lobbed upon clichés to create a fugue of absurd domestic melodramas.

In one of their most famous sketches, a mother has telephoned her son for weeks because he has not called her. It climaxes with Nichols moaning, "I feel awful," to which May responds, "Arthur, if I could only believe that I'd be the happiest mother in the world." In a radio skit version of *Oedipus Rex*, Oedipus complains to Jocasta, "Look, sweetheart, you're my mother." There was bite in their determined unraveling of the middle-class psyche; more than a little, they trafficked in human shame, in Jewish neuroses.

"It's a good thing Mike Nichols and Elaine May are partners. How could either of them find anyone else he'd distrust so much?" wrote the *New York Times* critic Walter Kerr.

"The secret we share is that neither of us really likes people very much—they have no reality for us," May explained. "The reason we're not very funny in a group is because we have this kind of communication, and people are always telling us they feel left out. It's something we can't seem to do anything about."

May's roots in theater stretched back to her toddler years, when she appeared in the stage shows written by, directed by, and starring her father, Jack Berlin, who ran a traveling Yiddish theater group. She claimed in an early studio bio that she frequently played a boy named Benny; she also appeared with the paterfamilias on a radio show called *Baby Noodnik*, in which she played a kind of Yiddish Baby Snooks. By the age of ten she had attended some fifty schools throughout the United States and Mexico, some for only weeks. ("I kept learning that Mesopotamia was the first city. I also frequently learned the multiplication tables up to five," she quipped.) Then her father died, and she and her mother moved first to Chicago, where her uncle lived, and later to Los Angeles. By fourteen she'd quit formal schooling for good, and by sixteen she'd married Marvin May, described in one magazine article in May-inspired prose as a man "whose chief occupation in life was building models of ships and airplanes." By eighteen, she had given birth to one daughter, Jeannie, but the marriage broke up. She led a nomadic existence, studying acting with Maria Ouspenskaya, a member of the Moscow Art Theater who taught the Method guru Lee Strasberg, performing in various theater troupes, hitchhiking across America. She hated L.A.: "I feel in opposition to almost everything anyway, but it comes to its height in Los Angeles."

Hearing that the University of Chicago would accept her without a high school diploma, May hitchhiked there with only seven dollars in her pocket and began unofficially auditing classes. She left Jeannie to be raised by her mother.

May struck up a relationship with Nichols while waiting for a train in the Illinois Central terminal. Nichols, a refugee from the Nazis who was now a Chicago undergrad, was on his way home from his job as a college disc jockey when he sat down next to May and said in a German accent, "May I sit down?" to which she responded, "If you weesh," and the pair started riffing as if they were foreign agents. He went home with her that night, and she made him the only thing she knew how to cook, a hamburger with cream cheese and ketchup. There was an aborted stab at romance, but quickly they evolved into friends, both bearing campus reputations for their incisive, occasionally vicious wit. May also happened to be a heartbreaker and notoriously fickle; she'd go on to a lifetime of apprehensive relations with men, caused—one husband theorized—by the untimely death of her beloved father.

Nichols and May became members of a campus improvisation group called the Compass. In 1957 they moved to New York, where they auditioned for Jack Rollins, then Woody Allen's manager, who booked them into nightclubs like the Blue Angel, and ultimately on the TV show *Omnibus*, which started their career. By 1960 they were earning $500,000 a year from their wildly successful stage show, their TV appearances, and advertising jingles they improvised for products such as Jax beer. Nichols treated money as his droit du seigneur; he moved to a penthouse overlooking Central Park and began dating great beauties like Suzy Parker. May's response to all that money was alternately giddy and skeptical. She'd barely worn heels before or had her hair done, let alone hired a decorator or been coiffed by celebrity hairdresser Mr. Kenneth. She explained at the time that "once you have money, you never have to use it—you just write checks or hand over your Diners Club card. I honestly don't know what we make now. I still get hazy when anything gets over one thousand dollars." She did, however, move her mother and now ten-year-old daughter to New York; they lived in a sprawling, book-and-paper-strewn West Side apartment where the living room was dominated by a Ping-Pong table and a portable organ. She was in psychoanalysis five days a week.

Nichols and May disbanded their act in 1961, mostly at May's instigation. She had grown bored with the routine. "I told Mike there was no way we could top ourselves," explained May, who privately believed that Kennedy's election had so changed the tone of the country that the number of bland fifties targets was shrinking.

She also wanted to focus on her writing. She had an enormous cache of unfinished plays and scenarios and devoted herself to constant revision, so marking them up with a thick black pencil that no one besides herself could decipher her notes. The first effort to be seen in public was a one-act, "Not Enough Rope," which opened Off Broadway on a bill with two other works by new playwrights. It played as an extended Nichols-and-May skit about a young girl who asks her new male neighbor if she can borrow some rope—with the intention of hanging herself—but bungles the job when all he can provide is some twine. The play flopped.

Her next play, *A Matter of Position,* concerns a young market researcher who worries obsessively that people don't like him. It was headed for Broadway, and May asked Nichols, on whom the protagonist was loosely based, to star. The debacle of that effort (which closed after seventeen performances in Philadelphia) fractured their relationship, particularly after the producers made cuts against May's wishes. "I was onstage, she was in the audience watching me, judging me. As soon as we weren't in balance . . . equals on the stage . . . we flew apart," commented Nichols, while May fumed, "I usually believe that anything can be fixed—even terminal cancer if they try. But somewhere in Philadelphia, I realized I had absolutely nothing to say about the making of my play. They didn't even want me to be in the theater. Cuts and revisions were made until they changed the material and emasculated the play." The same week the play folded May broke up with her second husband, the lyricist Sheldon Harnick. The marriage had lasted two months. More professional setbacks followed. She wrote a two-hundred-page script of Evelyn Waugh's novella *The Loved One,* but director Tony Richardson replaced her with Terry Southern and Christopher Isherwood.

May pitched a network series that ran forty-five minutes. "They said it can't be forty-five minutes. It's either a half hour or an hour," recalls John Calley, who was to produce the series. "She said, 'But that's irrational. The BBC isn't a half hour or an hour. It should be what it should be.' So she ended up in this meeting with the head of station relations and all these major guys from the network, all of whom ended the meeting apologizing for network policies." May refused to back down, and the series went down the drain. Plans for a one-act musical about a family of thieves disintegrated.

In 1963 May married a psychiatrist, *her* psychiatrist. "Why don't you just say I'm married to a doctor?" she suggested to one interviewer. Not only would that please her mother, she said, but "a psychiatrist is like a priest [and not supposed to marry his patients]. If you mention him, it will take three of his patients four years longer to get well." With her new husband, his three daughters, and the now teenage Jeannie, May moved into an enormous brownstone near the Hudson River, where periodically she descended into the basement to write. Of it she has said, "I arranged a place there. I would usually take two weeks to make sure that all the pencils were sharpened, that the pens had the right kind of points, that I had the perfect amount of three-hole notebook paper, good erasers, plenty of hot water, apples, and coffee. Then, rather than sitting down to write, I would rearrange the furniture for days. Then I would make long lists of instructions like 'Don't bother Mother under the penalty of death for anything.' Then I would find anything else to do, I would start to write, and immediately I would hear the kids yelling and I would run upstairs—spared."

In 1967 May starred in her first motion picture, Carl Reiner's *Enter Laughing.* When it was announced, Nichols, who had gone on to a celebrated directing career with such films as *Carnal Knowledge, The Graduate,* and *Who's Afraid of Virginia Woolf?,* commented, "Elaine is going to suffer in Hollywood. She must have complete control of a given situation. Out there she will be at the mercy of many people." Yet her first experience was a pleasant one. May played a bombshell actress in a second-rate acting company. "Elaine didn't know a damn thing about making movies at first," Reiner has said. "But she was deathly serious about learning. She stood around the set and soaked up everything. I had a little trouble getting through to her at first, because she talks in a funny kind of shorthand. You're walking down a path with her, and all of a sudden she takes a right turn."

Her next film, *Luv,* a farce about a trio of New York intellectuals (which Nichols had directed on stage), didn't proceed so swimmingly. Shortly after production began, May became distressed that she and her costar Peter Falk hadn't performed a scene properly; she asked to have it reshot and even offered to pay for it herself. Both the producer and the director refused, and soon a steady parade of production folk were streaming in and out of May's trailer trying to convince her that the scene had gone well. May refused to be mollified. "We all go down the drain together," she retorted. "This is a great way to get a comedy—fill everyone with an enormous sense of rage." The scene was ultimately redone, and both her costar Jack Lemmon and the director, Clive Donner, praised May effusively in the resulting press. "I think Elaine is touched with genius, like Judy Holliday," said Lemmon. "She approaches a scene like a director and a writer, not like an actor, and she can go so deep so fast on a scene, and her mind works at such great speed that it's difficult for her to work with other actors."

"When I started directing, some people said to me the first day, 'Where shall we put the camera?' And I didn't know what the camera looked like. I thought it was one of the lights," May announced in a rare public appearance as herself. "And then they took me aside and explained to me quietly what it was. Then they said to me again, 'Where shall we put the camera?' There was a hush. There was a seventy-man crew, which had been babbling incessantly. I have no idea how they heard. And everybody stopped in a row. It was like that movie scene when all the heads turn. And there was a long silence. And then somebody took me aside and said, 'You make the crew'—the crew is spoken of as something sacred, and for reasons which I don't know they are paid enormous amounts of money, and they're all sort of nice guys—'You make the crew nervous,' they said. And I had been in a terrible movie in which I had watched this director who was so panic-stricken that they had to take him out of the bathroom before a take. Literally. And I decided then that I wouldn't do that, and that if I just wasn't too cowardly to say, 'Well, I don't know,' then I'd be all right. The first movie, they thought I was insane. The second movie, after the first movie made money, they thought I had my way. 'She has her special way.' "

May was not being entirely facetious. In terms of filmmaking, she had little visual sense, less organizational and logistical ability. "She doesn't understand certain confines that the rest of us accept," says her friend Anthea Sylbert, who designed the costumes for May's movies *A New Leaf* and *The Heartbreak Kid.* "She would ultimately say, 'I don't know,' " Sylbert says, adopting May's breathy, girlish intonations. "It's the ultimate confidence. It's in all those people who know everything all the time. Walter [Matthau, star of *A New Leaf*] would say to her, 'What do you want?' 'I want you to be brilliant, Walter.' She really is an amazing mind. It's not always the most practical behavior that goes along with the amazing mind."

May's reputation as a classy genius ensured that the red carpet rolled out in front of her and helped convince Paramount to pour $1.8 million into her directorial debut, *A New Leaf.* Based on a short story she had optioned, it was the tale of a bankrupt Wasp playboy who marries a naive, otherworldly heiress, a would-be botanist, with the intention of killing her for her fortune. May was intrigued by the idea of a man who gets away with murder—he kills several people—and is redeemed by love. Despite having enlisted Matthau to star, she had been rejected by a number of studios. Learning of her problems, Arthur Penn, the director of her Broadway show, hooked her up with the producer Hillard Elkins, who brought the project back to Paramount.

"We were in a pitch with Robert Evans [head of production], Frank Yablans [head of distribution], Charles Bluhdorn [chairman of Gulf + Western], and Elaine and myself. We made the pitch. It wasn't received with overwhelming enthusiasm. I pitched very hard on the fact that having a woman director would be of consequence," says Elkins. Indeed, despite the rise of the women's movement, no woman had directed a studio movie since Ida Lupino's last film, *The Trouble with Angels,* in 1966. "The pitch seemed to work with Bluhdorn. The other two guys turned their heads from left to right; his went up and down and the deal was done."

Bluhdorn was also entranced with the financial parameters the producers (whose number grew to include Howard Koch, Sr., the former head of production at the studio) laid out. Indeed, May would take only $50,000 for acting and writing as a sweetener for being allowed to direct. Matthau would take only $250,000, and the producers $50,000 apiece; they would hope to clean up in profit participation. May had a clause inserted that if Paramount fired her as director, they would have to pay her a $200,000 penalty.

"When the camera rolled the first shot, and she says, 'cut,' we thought, God, it went great. We thought we'd press the button and go on to the next one, and she said, 'No I want to do it again,' " recalls Koch, who had a reputation for being able to corral difficult productions. "I said, 'Wow. What the hell.' After the next take, it was the same thing. 'Do it again.' The first day, we did the scene five times. We thought, Tomorrow, we'll start again, but it went on and on and on."

Besides writing, the only thing May really knew about constructing a film was performance, and she focused her energies on that, obsessively so, searching ad infinitum for the perfect rendition of a scene. After fifteen days of shooting, *A New Leaf* had fallen twelve days behind schedule. For a two-minute episode in which Matthau—incongruously cast as a haute WASP—tries to finagle money out of his uncle (James Coco), who is chomping greedily and hilariously on a turkey leg, she shot endless amounts of film. "She couldn't make up her mind. She kept changing it and changing it," says Koch. " 'Do this again.' She kept complaining she wanted it to be better. We had to go with her. She's our star, our director. What are we going to do?" Koch inadvertently made May's director's anxiety worse by hooking up a closed-circuit TV so she could watch the scenes in which she was performing. She was hardly ever satisfied with her own takes and insisted on redoing them, again and again.

"Elaine does [all those takes] because she's looking for something other than that which is presented," says Anthea Sylbert. "She's not very fond of having an actor doing the scene exactly the same over and over again. I've seen her fire an actor because each of these takes was exactly the same as the one before."

May was at once vulnerable and distrustful, and alternately attracted and repelled the kind of practical help she needed to get through her first picture. "She operates very emotionally. She only operates on trust," recalls Richard Sylbert, who designed her second film. "If she trusts you, she is the most wonderful person to work with. If she is suspicious, if she doesn't trust you on some bizarre level, you've got a problem. It's a form of paranoia."

"I think she unnerves people by her whole persona," he adds. "She scares the shit out of the executives. They're like, 'What's going to happen? Are we going to get this picture finished?' "

As the budget ballooned, diminishing drastically the possibility that the film might turn a profit, Koch went to Paramount to have May removed. Instead of paying the $200,000 penalty, the studio decided to bench Koch and send in the executive Stanley Jaffe to try to instill responsibility—and confidence—in the director. "They kept saying this movie would be funnier than *The Odd Couple* and I didn't need to work so hard," May once cracked. "I told Charles Bluhdorn, the head of Paramount, 'I'm not as good a writer as Neil Simon. It's not as good a script, so I have to work harder.' 'You are as good a writer,' he said. 'No I'm not,' I said. 'I'm not as funny.' 'Don't say that,' he said. 'You're funnier.' "

Still the film went forty days over schedule on what was originally a forty-two-day shoot, and the cost doubled to over $4 million. While most directors spend ten weeks editing their films, May spent almost ten months. Whenever Paramount asked to see a rough assemblage, May refused, avowing that she wasn't ready.

Finally Bob Evans, the head of production, took the film away from her and recut it with the aid of Koch and Jaffe. The studio promptly excised the murders, so instead of a story about a man who gets away with murder it became the watered-down, ostensibly more audience-friendly story of a man who merely contemplates the act.

May was so enraged that she tried to take her name off the film, to little avail. Upping the ante, she sued Paramount to try to bar *A New Leaf* from opening.

"We went to court and said to the judge, 'We think the picture is perfect,' " recalls Koch. "The judge said, 'Let me look at it.' The lights went down, and the judge sat there and he screamed and laughed and screamed and laughed, and the lights go up and he says, 'It's the funniest picture in years. You guys win.' "

The film opened the next day at Radio City Music Hall, to good reviews and good business. But the kudos didn't make May feel better about the whole experience. "Elaine was upset about the picture being recut and felt she was badly treated and wanted to take some action," says Elkins. "I said to her, 'What are your damages? The picture's a hit. Everybody's going to want you.' She wasn't happy with that. She wanted the picture to be exactly how she'd written it."

May later told an audience, "I went way over budget and I went over schedule and became a very hot director as a result. I think it has only to do with going over schedule, that had I come in on time, no one would have wanted me. I think it's a very funny country now. Anything that will make money, no matter what it is, they will put on. If Hitler were alive today, as somebody said, I guarantee you, $20 million at the box office."

May's uncertain directorial hand steadied noticeably in her next effort, her best film, *The Heartbreak Kid*. It was based on a Neil Simon script, in which a Jewish go-getter, Lenny (Charles Grodin), abandons his bride on their honeymoon to chase after a shiksa ideal, Kelly, personified by none other than Cybill Shepherd, a vacuous, WASPy midwestern heiress. The film is a fun-house mirror of *The Graduate*, the most celebrated film of her former partner, Mike Nichols, in which an uncertain, unconscious youth trades the wrong woman for the putatively right woman as a rite of passage to adulthood. *The Graduate* ends on a note of triumphant sentimentality; for Dustin Hoffman's Benjamin, finding Katharine Ross means finding himself, with buoyant Simon and Garfunkel tunes as backdrop. For Lenny, finding Kelly means losing himself. May lampoons the striver's capacity for self-delusion.

If the premise of the film was classic Neil Simon, the malice was all May's. Critics decried the portrayal of the jilted Jewess, Lila, as one of the most gratuitously nasty images of woman on film, an overweight caricature of sensuality, empty-headed, with a nauseating bray, overbearing presumptuousness, and slovenly table manners. This time, instead of playing the unsuspecting woman herself, May cast her daughter, Jeannie Berlin, perhaps the first mother in film history to do so. She then magnificently turned viewer expectation, as the audience's sympathy shifts from Lenny to Lila when he announces the marriage is kaput in the middle of a garish seafood palace. Lila clasps her rejecting husband, trying to stop herself from keeling over; Lenny won't even let her go throw up as he spins out his warped vision of WASP glory.

Casting Berlin had sparked a battle with Neil Simon, who didn't know she was May's daughter and proclaimed that she was too ugly for the part. Simon and the producer Edgar Scherick had hired May to direct the privately financed film, and Simon usually took a strong hand in the films made from his work. He wanted Diane Keaton to play Lila.

Simon didn't hate just Jeannie Berlin, he also hated the woman originally cast to play Kelly. Curiously enough, May initially had chosen a dark-haired, olive-skinned actress to embody the shiksa goddess. "I kept saying, 'But, Elaine, this role is about being blond,' and she kept saying, 'But you'll fix it,' " says Anthea Sylbert, who tried to dye the woman's hair blond, but, "by the first time we had the first reading, her hair was the color of a bright orange carrot. Neil Simon wasn't pleased." To keep her daughter, May traded away the carrottop shiksa. "All the while I'd been saying to her, 'Cybill Shepherd,' and she said, 'But I saw her on *The Tonight Show* and I'm not sure I like her,' " says Sylbert. "I said to her, 'The girl in the script—we don't like her either,' and we cast Cybill."

"Once we cast Cybill, Neil was happy," says Scherick. Simon had also insisted that May print at least one take where the scene was played exactly as written; then she was free to improvise as much as she chose. Curiously enough, the pressure from Simon, abetted by the support of Scherick, created May's most disciplined work and working environment. "I suspect part of the reason *Heartbreak Kid* went more smoothly is that it was somebody else's script. It divorces you slightly. You can look at the material a little more objectively than your own material," says Anthea Sylbert.

Although May had abandoned her daughter in a sense to seek her own creative satisfaction, she now took special pleasure in sharing her world with Jeannie. "She had a wonderful time with the whole idea that it was Jeannie," says Dick Sylbert. "She and Jeannie loved the idea of working on these acting problems." From an early age Jeannie had shared acting with her mother. "She was always hard on me," Berlin, who was nominated for an Oscar for *The Heartbreak Kid,* once explained. "She'd never say 'That's good' when it wasn't. She had enormous patience. If anybody is trying to learn something—really trying—that's all she needs. She reacts. And when she reacted, I was so excited. She taught me about substituting. I was about eleven. I remember singing this song to her, 'I'm Gonna Leave Old Texas Now, Ain't Got No Use for the Long-Horned Cow.' I was singing this song because I wanted to be a singer, and I had just left all my friends in California [and moved to live with my mother in New York], so my mother said to me, 'Sing the song again, and when you come to the word *Texas,* think of California, and all your friends and everything you left behind.' I sang the song again and I started to cry while I sang."

For Paramount, the first inkling that May's new film *Mikey and Nicky* might be an extraordinary production came when Gulf + Western's chairman, Charles Bluhdorn, called a board meeting and discovered that Frank Yablans, president of Paramount, was off in Philadelphia at rehearsals. Bluhdorn was furious, particularly when he found out that May had cast his studio chief in the film as a gangster. Within days Yablans was replaced—as an actor.

To Paramount stalwarts, it seemed incredible that a mere two years after the *New Leaf* fracas, Paramount—in the person of Yablans—had approved a $1.8 million budget for *Mikey and Nicky.* A forthright, funny, diminutive cabbie's son, who had no qualms telling a woman in that era, "Nice tits today, honey," Yablans was enchanted with May but had tried to protect the studio by instituting a contract that stipulated that any cost overruns would come out of May's fee. The minute the budget ran 15 percent over, Paramount had the right to take over the film, which had to be delivered on June 1, 1974, a little over a year later. In return for these concessions, May would have final cut, as well as the right to deal directly, and only, with Yablans, bypassing her *New Leaf* nemesis, Bob Evans.

While Walter Matthau, Neil Simon, and Edgar Scherick had in a sense contained May's desire to improvise and experiment, now there was no such framework. The production quickly veered offtrack. "No one was keeping the other two sane," says Anthea Sylbert of May and her costars, Falk and Cassavetes. "Together it didn't increase by three, it increased exponentially, a geometric progression. We shot it all at night, even the interiors, because she thought Peter and John would act different at night than they would during the day. I cannot explain it."

The movie was largely in the style of a Cassavetes movie, or a kind of endless Nichols-and-May routine. May didn't like to block out the actors' movements too far in advance and often kept three cameras running at once (sometimes for hours), as Falk and Cassavetes chatted both in and out of character.

On one notorious occasion, Cassavetes had left the set and Falk had wandered off down the street to talk with a friend. And still the camera rolled. After several minutes of filming a scene with no actors, a new camera operator (May had recently fired the cinematographer) called, "Cut!"

Incensed, May, who'd been sitting quietly behind the cameraman, jumped up and wanted to know why the camera had been shut off: "You don't say, 'Cut.' I say, 'Cut.' I'm the director, and only the director says, 'Cut.' "

"I know," responded the operator, but "the actors left. They walked away!"

"Yes . . . but they might come back," fumed May, furious that the director's prerogative to start and end filming was being chipped away.

On another occasion she grew enraged when the operator yelled "Cut"—because he had run out of film.

"There's a big technical side to the visual stuff, which she could never master. She can't light a cigarette without burning her hand. She works on impulses, intuitions. It's easy to do on a typewriter, but impossible to do when you have other people standing around," says Paul Sylbert (Richard's brother, and Anthea's ex-husband), who designed *Mikey and Nicky*. "She's very insecure as a director, and she's vamping it, but she's the kind of person you do everything you can to help her. She's vulnerable, and it's exposed. Look at her comedy—it's all about weird kinds of vulnerability."

By the time May had finished, after 120 days of shooting, twice the industry average, she had over two hundred hours of film.

May holed up in a set of eight suites at the Sunset Marquis Hotel in West Hollywood to try to assemble her film. She had to employ a full-time librarian just to catalog the footage, and eventually her editing crew grew to about a dozen people, working in double shifts, six days a week, often until two or three in the morning, as May seemed to thrive in the dark hours. "In all honesty I think Elaine was the brightest person I ever worked with," says the editor Sheldon Kahn, who was hired for a four-week stint but wound up staying eighteen months. "We would try it many different ways. It might take two weeks or two days to cut a scene which normally would take four or five hours. We'd cut it sixteen or seventeen ways. Elaine has a photographic memory. If we cut a scene thirteen ways, she'd go, 'The third way was the best.' She'd then recall it frame by frame." Kahn used to start every morning with a joke for May, a joke usually mangled in the telling. " 'That's not the way you should say it,' she'd say, and she'd go on to tell you all the different variations of that particular joke."

May seemed to enjoy the minutiae of editing (in its way, a visual analogue to improvisation), although at times her habits became erratic. Some nights she would return to the editing bays after the editors had gone home, with Cassavetes in tow, and systematically undo everything the editors had done that day, then disappear for forty-eight hours. Cassavetes, Falk, and the writer Peter Feibleman were among the chosen few allowed to visit. At some point during postproduction, Jeannie Berlin also moved into the Sunset Marquis. May herself rarely ventured out, save to troll from her suite to the cutting room, her figure wraithlike, her face occasionally painted with intense masklike makeup. She had forbidden the maids from entering her private bedroom for ten months, and when she left the remaining production staff found rotting banana peels and apple cores strewn in her bed, the charred remains of TV dinners in the oven, blackout curtains across all the windows. She'd written notes to herself in lipstick across all the mirrors. May seemed to live primarily on pills and health food. At one point she even commanded an underling to bring her only pink food. "If you put any salt in the food," May told one waitress, "I will die right here."

Increasingly, she seemed to spend her time consumed with scheming and fatally immobilized by suspicion. She displayed her anxiety in almost Freudian terms. "I learned to judge when to approach her and when to maintain my distance based on what she was smoking," recalls the film critic and historian Todd McCarthy, who served as her assistant through much of the postproduction on the film. "In normal circumstances, she would chain-smoke cigarettes. When things were getting a little bizarre, then she would smoke these Schimmelpennincks, which are Dutch cigarillos. In extreme moments, she would smoke big Orson Welles–size cigars."

She had reason to be nervous. May missed her ironclad delivery date by almost a year, and the budget of *Mikey and Nicky* climbed to almost $4.3 million. Eventually, her protector, Frank Yablans, was replaced by Barry Diller as the chief of Paramount. While the young Diller would undoubtedly have had trepidations about reining in the only female director working in Hollywood, he did want to get a progress report on Paramount's investment.

May, who had it written in her contract that she did not have to set foot on the Paramount lot, plotted about how to get the upper hand. She ultimately rented a tiny Ford Pinto, with a sloped roof, specifically for the meeting. Producer Michael Hausman later told the staff that he and May had forced Diller to cram himself into the car's minuscule backseat, whereupon they drove him to a greasy dive in downtown L.A. to ask for more time to edit the film. Finally, all the parties agreed that May would hand her picture over on September 15, 1975. Ten days later she told the studio she needed another $180,000 to finish.

Finally, the studio balked. Paramount refused to provide any more money and demanded that May transfer the film to an editing room on the lot, where, under her guidance, the studio technicians could finish the job much more cheaply and efficiently.

Intensely wary after her experience on *A New Leaf*, May assumed that this was merely Paramount's attempt to wrest the film away from her. She sold *Mikey and Nicky* out from under them. The price was $90,000. The buyer was Alyce Films, which turned out to be a front for Peter Falk and a number of other May allies.

Paramount promptly sued her for breach of contract, and May countersued, nonchalantly accusing the studio of breach of contract and of tampering with projects merely because they were launched under the aegis of a prior regime. A New York judge ruled that the director couldn't sell Paramount's film and that Paramount was fully in its rights to demand possession. New York sheriffs were dispatched to find the film, which they did—except for two reels. The studio believed that the missing reels were stored in the garage of a psychiatrist—a friend of May's husband—who lived in Connecticut, but the sheriffs didn't have any authority beyond New York State.

May's friend Warren Beatty, whom she had known since 1964, tried to intercede on her behalf. He phoned Diller and suggested that the studio just kick in the $180,000 and be done with it. But Diller was incensed by what he saw as a blatant attempt at blackmail. He said May could finish her film, keeping the final cut, but she had to work on the Paramount lot, and, most important, she had to return the two reels. "She is a brilliant woman and a wonderful woman," fumed Diller, within hearing of a reporter, "but she can go to jail or the madhouse for ten years before I submit to blackmail!" Paramount began contempt proceedings against May.

Several months passed, and Paramount racked up close to $5 million in legal fees, until finally the studio vice chairman, David Picker, finessed a rapprochement, and Diller and May spoke on the phone. Diller assured May that if she just returned the film, "Things will go right for you. But I won't be blackmailed, and I won't put anything in writing. You have to trust me."

Around fifteen minutes later May called Diller and asked sweetly if he was in his office to receive the reels. Moments later the missing film appeared in a box outside his suite. Ironically, for all the time she had spent improvising on the set, the final film hewed very closely to the original script.

The studio nonetheless dumped *Mikey and Nicky*, booking it into theaters for a few days to satisfy contractual obligations. The reviews ranged from dismissive to admiring. Those who liked it championed May's ability to plunge her camera into the utter nastiness of the human heart.

A decade later a new, shorter version officially approved by May was released. Not long after the Museum of Modern Art honored the film as a part of a directors' series. May made one of the few public nonperforming appearances of her life.

"I was sued," she explained to the audience, "and the movie studio gave it back to me with the word 'Here.' I think I was sued because they so hated the movie. The guy leaving the studio [Frank Yablans] told the guy coming in [Barry Diller] that it was a comedy for summer."

The *Mikey and Nicky* debacle torpedoed her career: May didn't direct again for almost a dozen years. "It was sort of difficult for me to get directing jobs because I seemed sort of crazy. They accused me of taking the negative. But then I wrote *Heaven Can Wait*, and everything was all right," she commented. "Hollywood doesn't care what you did as long as you're making money for them."

"I really do believe that she set back the cause of women directors in Hollywood by ten years," says Todd McCarthy. "Those isolated moments when she could really put all else out of her mind and concentrate on the work, she was great. But every negative notion that any male executive might want to have about how difficult it might be to work with a woman director was confirmed by her: 'She was irresponsible. She didn't know what she was doing. She couldn't be controlled.' . . . All those things that people with conventional minds wanted to believe— she confirmed them in spades."

Jodie Foster and her mother, Brandy, at the American Society
of Big Brothers dinner, Beverly Hills Hotel, 1977.

5.

A DIFFERENT KIND
OF CHILD

"Wanna get high on Ripple?" eleven-year-old Audrey asks her new friend Tommy as they trudge along the dusty streets of Tucson. Audrey is played by the young Jodie Foster, her hair short and shaggy, her gait assertive, her clothes disheveled and utilitarian; Audrey could easily pass as a boy, and it is purely her spirit of subversive nonchalance that endears her to Tommy and the audience as she instructs him in the joys of being a latchkey kid—shoplifting guitar strings, swilling down cheap booze, getting tossed into jail.

Audrey's carefully cultivated androgyny and solitary self-reliance provide a counterpoint to the besieged traditional femininity of the middle-class Alice Hyatt, the title character of 1974's groundbreaking *Alice Doesn't Live Here Anymore,* one of the first high-profile studio movies to deal explicitly with the concerns of the growing women's movement. Widowed in the first ten minutes of the film, the plucky Alice is forced to care for herself and her angry young son, and to deal with her long-postponed dreams of becoming a singer as she matures into a grown woman and travels from relationship to relationship, from oafish husband to psycho boyfriend and ultimately into the arms of her handsome prince, a sensitive yet manly rancher.

The film had been put together by Ellen Burstyn, although when studio executive John Calley asked her explicitly if she wanted producer credit, she demurred. At the time of the film's release, both the star,

Burstyn, and the director, Martin Scorsese, were careful to publicly dis-
avow any intent at feminist propaganda. Yet the National Organization
for Women emblazoned "Alice Doesn't" on their banners for a one-day
work boycott. Others—especially critics—thought the movie didn't go
far enough. Pauline Kael, who enjoyed the film's "funny malice and
breakneck vitality," described *Alice* as a modern-day *Doll's House*, mangled by Hollywood. "Alice gets a double helping of pie-in-the-sky; she
gets a warm-and-sexy good provider, and she can pursue her idiot
dream of becoming an Alice Faye."

Neither Kael nor anyone else at the time realized they were watching
the birth of another new kind of heroine, one who would grow up on
cineplexes across America to personify the woman who is not a commodity, who does not have to forgo intelligence for sex appeal. Jodie Foster was a child, both on-screen and off, of America's proliferating divorce
rate. She often played bad girls without families, orphans wise beyond
their years, ultimately maturing into a singular, self-reliant Diana—often
running on rage and forced to avenge herself and those weaker.

Foster landed in the film after Burstyn's son spotted her as Becky
Thatcher in Walt Disney's 1973 version of *Tom Sawyer.* Foster's mother
had loved Scorsese's first film, *Mean Streets,* and taken eleven-year-old
Jodie to see it four times. On the set Foster amused Scorsese mightily
with her impression of Robert De Niro, a pint-sized would-be tough guy
mouthing off.

"She was already so masculine, and even had sort of like a boy's
haircut. [Indeed, Foster shocked Scorsese by arriving on the set having
peremptorily chopped off her hair.] But it was really hard to tell that she
was a girl," recalls the film's costume designer, Toby Rafelson. "Which
might have been one of the things that Marty liked. She was bright and
sweet and quiet, and she seemed to be kind of tough. She was also very
beautiful. She had a really exquisite face." Rafelson spent a lot of time
with Foster going over Audrey's wardrobe, much of which was culled
from Foster's own clothes. Foster's mother, Brandy, hovered constantly,
vociferously announcing her presence. "You could never get her away
from you for a moment when you were working with Jodie in those
days," says Rafelson. "She was just there. She was dominating everything. She was making choices. She was bossing Jodie around. It was
weird. You kind of never knew what the reality was. You never knew
where the father was, or who—how it had happened. You know, the

only thing that existed was that woman, and the person she was living through, which was her daughter."

"Jodie was never a traditional-looking girl. And I think that has a lot to do with her success," Foster's mother said in an interview in *American Film* in 1988. "It was just at the beginning of women's liberation, and she kind of personified that in a child. She had a strength and uncoquettishness. Maybe it comes from being raised without a father to say, 'Turn around and show Daddy how pretty you look.' "

The grown-up Foster is touchy about talking about her mother, in part because Brandy's role in her success has been mythologized—as a superhuman mother-daughter bond that lasted until Foster was long out of college; as something freakish, a tie that permanently infantilizes Foster. She is both protective of Brandy, whom she has financially supported since she was a child, and wary of her controlling, intrusive nature, her opinionated personality, from which Foster often fled by retreating into a book.

"I was that vicarious outlet," says the actress-producer-director, looking back. "Everybody has some kind of psychological collaboration thing. She chose all the movies that I made from the time when I was four years old. So of course they're about issues she was working out in her life. Why would she be more interested in *Alice Doesn't Live Here Anymore* and *Taxi Driver* than she was in any four other movies with little girls at that time—*Nickelodeon, Bad News Bears,* and whatever?

"She wanted me to take it seriously. She didn't want me to be sloughed off. She wanted people when they said my name to think that I was somebody of significance," says Foster.

Jodie Foster came of age when the American home was losing its status as an impregnable sanctuary. She was a veritable poster child for the dysfunctional family, which was an apt reflection for the problems besetting Brandy Foster, who had an absentee ex-husband about whom she was openly bitter. She was struggling to raise four kids all on her own. Indeed, Jodie, officially named Alicia Christian Foster, was born November 19, 1962, five years after her closest sibling was born and months after her mother, Brandy, wound up in divorce court. Her father, Lucius Foster III, was a former Air Force colonel turned real estate broker, a dreamer from a wealthy family who already had three kids he ignored from a previous marriage. In 1954 he met pretty Brandy, née

Evelyn Almond, at a fencing club and married her during a whirlwind trip to Tijuana. Before her marriage, she had worked for a film publicist. After their rancorous split, Brandy often found herself at Lucius's real estate office begging for child support. Brandy and the children were forced to move out of their airy, expensive Hollywood Hills home. Brandy received six hundred dollars per month in support, which came irregularly and, then, was cut in half. She supported her brood living off "savings and selling things, and just surviving," Foster has recalled. It was a precarious existence, and Brandy despaired of ever being able to enter into the cultured, upper-middle-class existence she so desperately craved. "Let's just imagine a scenario where your parent spends hours in the corner crying," Foster explained at one point. "That is my great fear—to depend on somebody who is slipping away."

Brandy halted the Foster family's perilous economic decline by sending her children out to work. Buddy Foster, then eight, began acting regularly in commercials and TV. With the new influx of income, Brandy moved the family to Newport Beach, instituting a cycle of frequent dislocation as she fixed up their successive homes and sold them at a profit. The legend of Jodie's precocity was already beginning: talking at eight months, reading at age three, around which time she trailed Buddy into a commercial for Coppertone.

Already Foster's style was uniquely her own. Sporting a pair of ruffled panties and no shirt, the blond-haired tyke began to vamp for the casting directors, flexing her muscles in a series of prepubescent muscleman poses. When they asked her name, she promptly answered, "Alexander the Great." She aced her brother out of the part and became that famous little girl with the puppy tugging at her swimsuit and flashing her buttocks.

Her tomboy antics continued through the rest of her childhood. She hated any vestiges of traditional femininity. "I was always on a skateboard. I'd just go back and forth and back and forth for hours and hours. . . . Everyone that I know that I really like was a tomboy. I think there's two paths: you're either like my niece, now, who started wearing spandex pants and listening to cassettes. And getting into makeup and all that stuff, and then they take another dive, you know. They hit twenty-two and their life changes and they start worrying about things that they wouldn't normally worry about. Or, you just have the little girls who just totally block that whole thing.

"Which one was valuable, and which one's not valuable?" she points out. "Socially valuable experiences are male experiences or tomboy experiences or whatever, and the socially unvaluable experiences are the girl experiences. It's a terrible thing. But that's why being an actor, it's like the most enormous mixed message in the world. Because, you know, it's why men are so uncomfortable with it. Men actors. Because they think they're doing a girl's job. God forbid they should be talking about their emotions and working up to a scene. Somehow they're ashamed of that. I find male actors are often really ashamed of the girliness of what they have to do."

"She could read scripts cold at the age of five," Brandy says proudly. With two children working, money poured into the Foster household, now relocated back in L.A. Buddy starred on *Mayberry R.F.D.* while Jodie appeared on such shows as *The Courtship of Eddie's Father* and *Gunsmoke.* "From the very beginning Brandy pushed to get Jodie working full-time," Foster's first agent, Toni Kelman, once explained. "When Jodie first signed with me, Brandy called up complaining she wasn't working enough. 'I guess you just don't like my daughter,' she said accusingly. 'She's only six!' I said, somewhat astonished."

Brandy threatened to pull Buddy, then the bigger star, from the agency unless there was more work for Jodie. She had expensive tastes—for niceties like fine antiques—and whenever the money was tight, Kelman knew that Brandy would get the kids to work. This having been said, at one point Brandy also decided that the Foster children should shun commercials, because, she says, "when you allow yourself to become too familiar with people, that's when boredom sets in. And when somebody's on television every day, you feel that you have the right to be part of their life, or they be part of yours. I don't believe that. I think overexposure is the worst thing in the world for people, in any circumstances. In a marriage, in relationships, in everything." She was aggressive in securing money for Jodie, demanding $1,000 per week for a series when the going child rate was $420.

"My mother's very opinionated," recalls Foster. "She is a combination of being incredibly shy and incredibly bold-faced, in ways that I would just be mortified if I was that bold-faced." Brandy could spout off on a variety of topics. She indoctrinated her children in the horrors of the Vietnam War and racism. She was equally vociferous in grooming them to fulfill her elitist aspirations, sending them to cotillion classes, where they wore white gloves, and blaring opera on the weekends. "My mom used to like to go to all those newsstands for European publications, and they only had one newsstand, two newsstands when I was growing up in L.A. that actually had European magazines. And she couldn't buy them or afford to buy them—she wasn't going to pay forty dollars for an Italian *Vogue*. So she'd leave us in the car while she would read all the magazines on the newsstand. And it was like we pretty much would do that every day or every week. And we weren't allowed to get out of the car because it was Hollywood Boulevard."

In later years Foster would become irritated by her mother's insistence that her success was all a matter of style—the right style. As a child she went along with Brandy's tutelage, an education punctuated by ugly bits of reality. "We'd go on these little tours of L.A. So we would do beautiful homes, and my mom would say, 'You see that—that's the Cape Cod style,' or 'This is a Mediterranean, and this particular molding shouldn't be there, that's an interior mold, not an exterior mold,' or 'Why'd they put French windows in that house? Isn't that disgusting!' We'd have these visual training sessions. And the other thing, of course, was to ride up and down Hollywood Boulevard to see what movies were playing and what movies weren't, and who was lining up for what. We'd also go down Selma. 'These were the female prostitutes and these were the male prostitutes. This is where the young kids were, and these were the drug houses.' We'd lock our doors as we were going by."

Despite Brandy Foster's efforts to groom her children in taste and class, the household was often chaotic, the older children rebellious and uncontrollable. "The only way my mom told us to do things was that she would scream at us," says Foster. "She was big on screaming. She would always scream for us to come up and down the stairs. It drove me nuts. 'Get up here!' It was always very loud."

"There was a lot of hollering going on a lot of times," says Brandy. "I didn't ever hit them. I should have hit more and hollered less."

While her brother and sisters were volatile, Jodie was dutiful, docile, and obedient, a little adult in a child's body. "It was like a partnership [between the two of them]," recalls Clara Lisa Kabbaz, Foster's best friend—indeed, only friend—from her childhood. "Jodie was very nurturing. She would take care of her mother. Her mother would take care of her. [Jodie] loved to do little routine things like bringing the wood in, and washing the dishes. The whole routine of being a helpful kid. She loved it."

"She was small, very thin, and always had these very large horn-rimmed glasses, and she was always reading," adds Kabbaz. "She was really always involved in reading some very, very long, long book, and she could read for hours and hours and hours and not get tired of it."

Many in Hollywood who met the mother and daughter were struck by the mother's often outrageous opining and the daughter's dutiful silence. Foster's mother often took up all the oxygen in the room.

"Jodie strives to be completely inconspicuous at all times, and she was like that as a child too. She'd rather sit there with a stain developing on her pants or something from something she dropped than make a spectacle of herself and get up and try to clean it in the bathroom. That sort of thing.

"She was a funny girl, and she hated to be wrong," says Kabbaz. "She just hated to be wrong. She would argue something with you until you just gave up, you couldn't take it anymore. Or she would bet and she would be really upset if she lost, she would insist she was right on everything, on everything."

Ask her about her childhood—if she ever had a happy moment—and Foster becomes flummoxed, indeed stumped. It is easy to see why the dominant note of her childhood seems to have been free-floating anxiety. "I used to have a real fear of being poor again," she told the journalist Holly Millea. "Not that we were destitute. But for some reason, I took it really personally. And I had a lot of anxiety about just not being able to make a living."

Often her whole life seemed devoted to securing approval. "When I was a little kid, I'd be working and the director said, 'I would like you to put your toe on this left corner and twirl your head at a certain angle and do this.' It would never occur to me to say no. It's just like, What am I gonna say, no?" recalls the actress. "My whole point in life was to follow to the most minute detail absolutely everything they wanted me to be. And when I accomplished that, I got a lot of applause. When I was able to do that they would go, 'That was great! Boy, that was great!' so I learned that at a really young age. And I thought that I was never allowed to complain. I wasn't allowed to ever say no, and somehow that would be a bad thing if I were to say no."

As a child Foster would apologize profusely whenever she made a mistake and would get so upset when her studio car was late that she'd turn beet red with fury. She used to be terrified by the trips to court to get her work permit renewed. "They'd look at your fingernails, and if you bit your nails, chances are you were a really nervous person and that was one of the signs of somebody who may be having trouble with the business," she says. "I was literally petrified, and I'd go in and I'd be like this"—she closes her hands—"you know, 'cause I didn't want them to see that I bit my nails. I didn't want them to think I was bad or like psycho or something."

She landed her first movie, Disney's *Napoleon and Samantha,* when she was nine. On the set a lion bit her. "I insisted that we get out of this little town in Oregon because they just had one little local doctor," recalls Brandy. "They took us out of there in a private plane."

Foster spent four days in a Seattle hospital. The hospital priest came to visit her. "She had never talked to a priest before," says Brandy. "And she looked frightened. I thought she was rude because she would keep looking at the television and not looking at him or talking to him. And when he left, she started to cry. And I said, 'What's the matter, sweetheart?' She said, 'I'm going to die.' I said, 'You're not going to die. You have a couple of big tooth marks on your back—on your rear end—but you're not going to die.' She said, 'Well, why did the priest come here?' She had seen movies when the priest comes in and you're dying and they give you your last rites. So that ended up in a long conversation that night." When Foster returned to the set, the lion lunged at her again, although this time she managed to scamper out of its reach.

The New York Times singled out Foster's performance in the hit film as "saucy," and she followed it up with the disastrous roller-derby flick *Kansas City Bomber,* the well-received musical version of *Tom Sawyer* (which led to a singing performance on the Academy Awards), as well as various appearances on *The New Adventures of Perry Mason, The Partridge Family,* and other TV series. She took over Tatum O'Neal's role in the TV version of *Paper Moon,* which flopped after a single season. Foster blamed herself for the show's demise because the critics had complained that she played Addie with a harder edge. Jodie's paycheck soon became the dominant one in the household.

6.

THE ARSENAL
OF SEDUCTION

JANE WAS MY ANGEL

While Polly Platt initially conceived of herself as a wife and Sherry Lansing, a starlet, Paula Weinstein mimicked her mother and learned to march for left-wing causes. But whereas Hannah Weinstein's ideology was formed in the socialist fervor before World War II, her daughter came of age at the time of the New Left, the era when hundreds of thousands of angry baby boomers protested the Vietnam War.

Despite both a job as an assistant editor and night classes at Columbia's general studies program, Weinstein spent the vast amount of her time caught up in SDS, Students for a Democratic Society, meetings and rallies. Motored by righteous indignation, caught up in the heady embrace of her peers, she found her identity fighting the war. Unlike her female peers who felt so thwarted by the male leaders of the antiwar movement that they started the women's movement, Weinstein was confident of her ability to leapfrog any barriers of sexual discrimination. She was ambitious, outspoken, beautiful, and politically canny. "There were fights about why were the women running the mimeograph machine, and why were women licking the envelopes, but frankly I was in the leadership, I didn't have that," recalls Weinstein, who spent six months organizing the press relations for the Pentagon demonstrations. "I said, 'I'll lick envelopes but I'm going into the steering committee meeting.' It wasn't my nature to be sitting and waiting."

Paula Weinstein with Mark Rosenberg in Montana, 1990.

Weinstein was glamorous. Besides her upscale background, she knew how to shoot off her mouth with élan and create a splash wherever she went. "Dressing well and being chic just always mattered to me," she says in retrospect. "In the movement, trust me, I would figure out how to wear my T-shirts in a certain way that everybody would always say, 'God, she's so chic in her blue jeans and T-shirt.' "

Despite her mother's left-wing proclivities, politics became the arena in which "I played out the split with my mother," says Weinstein. Although Hannah Weinstein was deeply involved in the anti-McCarthy campaign and electoral politics, she hated the fact that her daughter was marching in the streets and getting busted by the cops. The pair engaged in furious arguments over political ideology. "She was scared for me," recalls Weinstein. "I never will forget her screaming at me, saying, 'You're supposed to be in the leadership, in the room organizing. You're not supposed to be on the street, getting your head bashed.' " After Paula's every arrest Hannah refused to speak to her. Paula quit asking her mother to bail her out after Hannah, instead of simply paying the fine, called "all the way to the Supreme Court to get her out," causing her would-be proletariat daughter embarrassment among her fellow protesters.

"I felt she wanted to make me into a mirror image of her," recalls Weinstein. "And I was going to do it my way. And she saw the fact that I dressed in a way she didn't like. Everything was an act of hostility. I kept saying, 'It's not about you. We're trying to stop the war in Vietnam.' "

Eventually Weinstein found herself with a boring job in the John Lindsay mayoral administration, arranging for artists to perform at street fairs. By 1973, she decided to follow her boyfriend out to L.A. She wasn't madly in love but she liked the idea of change. Weinstein tended to treat men as sources of exciting drama rather than beacons of emotional fulfillment. The prime exception was Mark Rosenberg, a burly, outspoken student activist. They'd slept together right after they met, but Weinstein found him too nice and too available, and consequently didn't speak to him for another six months (a tricky situation considering how often they worked together), until she relented and they became friends. After a few months in California, she called Rosenberg and begged him to come out, which he soon did.

Weinstein and Rosenberg and their radical friends typified the leftists with the cause manqué who poured into Hollywood from the battlefields of Columbia and Stanford, ready to take on life on the studio expense account. Unlike their forebears, they weren't self-made scrappers but tended to be well-tended progeny of the upper middle class with down-home hippie values. They preferred proletarian regularity to the glamour life—the déclassé chic Mexican restaurant Lucy's El Adobe to the Polo Lounge. They drank Perrier, did coke and grass, and worked eighteen-hour days, poring over scripts, which were seen as an increasingly important part of the equation (now that studios couldn't simply jam stars into whatever vehicle was lying around). Token nods were made to the values of their recent youth. There was a surface acceptance of women and the importance of equality; there was talk about making socially conscious films.

Weinstein quickly gravitated to one of the hubs of left-wing activity in Hollywood, the Indochinese Peace Campaign, a grassroots organization founded by Jane Fonda and Tom Hayden to drive home the antiwar message in states with the most electoral votes. Weinstein idolized Fonda, who had shattered her *Barbarella* sexpot image with her 1969 performance as the depressed dance marathon contestant in *They Shoot Horses, Don't They?* and her Oscar-winning portrayal of the coldhearted hooker Bree Daniel in *Klute*. Weinstein was entranced by Fonda's much publicized political awakening.

"It was such a big thing to have a movie star of Jane's stature come out against the war and be that much of an activist. I remember when all my friends from Columbia went to see her in *Klute*. We thought, Oh my God, not only is she great but she's one of us!" Indeed, Fonda and Donald Sutherland had even "gone to see my mother to ask how to be political activists and filmmakers at the same time."

Weinstein noted clearly all the times their paths had crossed, on the street at a Miami rally in 1972, and later during an interview for a radical student newspaper, which Weinstein had arranged during Fonda's cross-country tour with FTA (Free Theater Association or, unofficially, Fuck the Army), a satiric, antimilitary stage show. "All these radical New York Jews had gotten all this food because we were doing a two-hour interview with her for the paper. Of course, she ate not a morsel." Weinstein laughs. "I remember she got on the phone with Tom [Hayden], and it was a very big deal that she was really with Tom at that point."

Fonda didn't remember Paula Weinstein at all, but she remembered Hannah Weinstein, and hence agreed to meet the daughter, who'd been recommended by an IPC cohort for a script-reading job. They met at the

Hamburger Hamlet on Sunset Strip, and the two bonded less over movies than over politics. After a while Fonda's IFA agent, Mike Medavoy, strolled in, and Fonda announced she had found her reader. "Mike thought that I was much closer to Jane than I was, so he said, 'Oh my God this left-wing woman is going to get this left-wing woman back to work. She will find a piece of material that will get Jane working again,'" says Weinstein. Although it was extremely unusual at the time, Medavoy agreed to pay Weinstein to read out of her home. (Fortunately, she was living with a man who had a good salary.)

By then Fonda was deep into her incarnation as the revolutionary Hanoi Jane, perched atop the antiaircraft gun aimed at American planes, proclaiming that the POWs returning from Vietnam with stories of torture were "liars and hypocrites." The actress would tell journalists that she had been unofficially "graylisted" by the studios because of her politics.

"They were scared of her, there was no question about it," recalls Weinstein, who points out, however, "It wasn't as if she was putting herself up and being turned down." The actress had refused parts in *The Exorcist*, because the movie was too shallow, and *Chinatown*, because the part was too small. In truth it was Fonda who was ambivalent about Hollywood. She "wasn't part of the Hollywood scene anymore," says Weinstein. "The thing about Hollywood, if they don't see you and you don't go to the parties, then you're not part of it."

Fonda had already started her own film company—IPC Films (after the Indochinese Peace Campaign)—with the intention of making socially relevant movies whose profits she could use to bankroll her political causes. As her partner she had chosen Bruce Gilbert, her daughter Vanessa's teacher from the Blue Fairy nursery school, run by the radical-chic Berkeley collective where Hayden had lived. Fonda had more than once deposited Vanessa there while she was off making movies and protesting, and Gilbert had taken good care of her. He was a wealthy Berkeley dropout from Beverly Hills. Fonda had decided to make a movie about Vietnam. After meeting the paraplegic veteran Ron Kovic (later of *Born on the Fourth of July* fame) at a peace rally, she had hired Nancy Dowd, an old FTA member and friend from the feminist movement, to write a screenplay about the consequences of the Vietnam War from the perspective of a soldier's wife.

In those days people who knew Fonda simply sent her scripts directly. (Fonda told interviewers that Hayden would read them first.)

Others sent them to the agency. Weinstein talked to Fonda on the phone but mostly dealt with Medavoy, hanging out in his office whenever she came by the agency to photocopy her coverage. Within months he had hired her to work directly with him.

"Jane was my angel. Mike was my mentor," says Weinstein. "The first day I got there, I was put in an office on the eighth floor, and he brought Hal Ashby up. Day two, Terry Malick. He felt that he wouldn't get to read everything, so let them get friendly with their reader." After a while Weinstein demanded to sit closer to Medavoy, commandeering the room across the hall, a tiny filing cubicle with what looked like bullet holes across one wall. "Everyone said, 'You're so crazy,' but you open my door and there's Mike's door. If I'm going to learn anything, I'm a lot better going in and out of his office," recalls Weinstein.

Weinstein was resentful when she realized that all the other agents had carefully taken note that she was sitting in what had once been a closet. Few let her forget that, while she had been a star in the movement, she was now nothing in the hierarchy of Hollywood: "People who I had known before [in the movement] who were agents treated me like I would never be invited to their dinner suddenly, because I was a reader there." She still felt a twinge of shame about working at a "dopey" talent agency—she who'd listened to endless tirades from her mother about the evils of the flesh-peddling agents. She rationalized her alignment with the suits by becoming a rebel with a paycheck. She endowed her job with the aura of a personal crusade, fighting for the rights of her clients.

She used her ideological zeal as armor to repel the blatant sexism of Hollywood. At least in New York men had a thin veneer of political consciousness; in L.A. "everybody was still a girl." If she rebuked someone for a crude remark, Weinstein was told she didn't have a sense of humor. If she mentioned a script that touched on women's issues, her colleagues thought she was talking about a "dark menopausal" movie. She knew she had to tread carefully with men who offered to mentor her because "uncomfortable" situations, rife with unspoken sexual expectations, could quickly evolve. She claims she was unable to flirt, and feint, at least not consciously.

Fortunately, Weinstein had her angel in Jane Fonda, a relationship she sealed by finding the galleys for *Julia*, which happened to have been written by her mother's best friend, Lillian Hellman. Part of her memoirs (which later turned out to be heavily borrowed from someone else's life), *Julia* tells of Hellman's youthful entrancement with her friend

Julia, an ignored, outspoken daughter of wealth who ended up working in the anti-Nazi underground as World War II broke out. When the film was finally made, seven years later, it would be hailed as the first female buddy picture.

"I want to produce this," the twenty-seven-year-old Weinstein begged Hellman, who simply laughed and sold the material to Columbia on behalf of the producer Richard Roth, a protégé of the studio powerhouse, Ray Stark. Weinstein nonetheless forwarded the book to Fonda, who, contrary to expectation, turned down the obvious part of Julia (not wanting to feed her critics any ammunition) and opted instead to play the self-doubting Lillian. Still only a reader, Weinstein cold-called Roth and asked plaintively if he would be interested in having Jane Fonda in his movie. Roth was deeply amused. There was talk of pairing Fonda with Barbra Streisand, but Streisand also wanted to play Lillian and Sue Mengers talked her out of it. Fonda agreed to let Roth use her name to push the movie along.

Fonda and Weinstein were slowly becoming friends. There was no trading of intimacies or baring of souls. The two spoke almost exclusively about work and marched together at political events. "I can't say we were friends right away and then suddenly we were family," says Weinstein. "I think one of the reasons our friendship survived—neither of us had big expectations from the other to be something. If we didn't talk for three months or four months, no problem. If we talked five times in a month, what a great thing.

"Jane doesn't chitchat personally," adds Weinstein. "Jane's too busy in her life. When she needs it, she gets the emotional connection, but if she's going along . . . She's different."

Within a year of Weinstein's arrival, IFA merged with CMA to form ICM and Medavoy quit to become production chief of United Artists. Weinstein wanted to follow him, but he refused, although he helped her get promoted to full-fledged agent at ICM. Fonda also proclaimed that she would stay at the agency only if Weinstein became her agent. The star seemed to have little idea of the effect of her munificence on her reader's career. In her high feminist phase Fonda had been adamant about hiring female crew members for some of her movie projects. In Weinstein's case, however, Fonda was simply happy to have found someone she could talk to, someone who was loyal. Fonda was thinking simply about her own needs. Donald Sutherland and Terrence Malick followed Fonda's lead.

Weinstein's sudden ascension thrust her into the heady limelight, as Hollywood viewed the dark-haired, outspoken beauty as Fonda's industry doppelgänger. At business functions, "people didn't talk to me," recalls Weinstein. "They would come up and say, 'Why did you'—I said, 'I didn't say it, Jane said it.' "

The town's most lascivious players took notice. "The phone would ring and some powerful guy would call and say, 'I want to meet you,' and I began to realize that this was like the new woman in town, getting a lot of attention. It always had a kind of sexual overtone to it that made me uncomfortable, because I was extremely aware for the first time in my life of the boys' club. It didn't feel about business, it felt like there was a network of 'Hey, there is this new chick, check her out.' "

Her radical politicking was now seen by many as a sophisticated form of sexual innuendo. "I remember being at a party at Sue Mengers's house, and I met two of the hugest stars and directors in America, and I got into a fight with them about the Vietnamese. I left thinking, Okay, I'm never going to get that director or that actor to be around," recalls Weinstein. "Well, the next day they were both on the telephone wanting to ask me out.".

She realized suddenly that "what makes you different becomes exactly what makes you get attention." She saw how easy it would be to sell her integrity, to use her politics as a "tool in the chest of weapons," a chic ploy for impressing people, for seducing them under a guise of intellectual high-mindedness into helping her climb the ranks of Hollywood. She vowed, "I didn't ever want to get so seduced by Hollywood that those very things became part of my arsenal of seduction myself."

YOU CAN'T SPEAK, BUT YOU SIT IN AND YOU OBSERVE

Sherry Lansing did not quit acting without a plan in mind. After her marriage to Michael Brownstein crumbled, she had begun dating the movie producer Ray Wagner. A former television executive, he was almost a prototype for her beaus, fifteen years older with a pack of young children. He had produced just one movie, but it happened to be her favorite: *Petulia*, a poster of which hung on her wall.

A zingy update of a classic 1940s woman's movie, it is the tale of a kooky sprite (Julie Christie) married to a wealthy but weak husband (Richard Chamberlain) who's controlled by his father. She hides out from her marriage with the cynical but sympathetic divorced doctor played by George C. Scott. Unlike in the forties, no one is punished or redeemed. Instead, all are trapped in the stasis of alienation. Scott can't quite grab at this last chance at love; Petulia is encased by her own expectations and returns to her abusive husband. The Beatlemeister Richard Lester, then at the height of his fame, had agreed to direct because his wife had fallen in love with Barbara Turner's script.

Wagner had met Lansing when she landed a small part in his next film, *Loving*, another succès d'estime, about the angst of a middle-class graphic artist, portrayed by George Segal, who cheats on his lovely wife because he can't face growing up. "Although it received terrific critical acclaim, audiences, particularly women audiences, did not like the movie," recalls the writer-producer Don Devlin. The tale of a married man's philandering was familiar enough, yet "in every movie that had preceded that, the wife was made to be unattractive in some way. Here, his wife was more attractive than his young lady, and that is what made the women so angry. Because the women couldn't do anything about it. I must have heard a hundred stories over the years of couples who had terrific fights after leaving the theater." Wagner was Devlin's former boss and close friend, and had been brought in as executive producer at the behest of the studio, which wanted a more experienced hand.

As was her way, Lansing chatted everybody up on the set of *Loving*, often plying people with questions about their jobs and their professions. She knew that most people assumed she was a bimbo, but Wagner was the most receptive to her probing. When she had problems with the script, she approached him. Finally, he looked at her and asked, "Why are you doing this? Why don't you read scripts or do something like that?"

They began dating when the movie was over, and stayed together for three and a half years. Paternal, idealistic, Wagner encouraged Lansing's interest in the mechanics of filmmaking, eventually asking if she'd peruse a few scripts for him. Her notes were intelligent. He asked her if she'd read for him in her spare time and offered to pay her five dollars an hour. Lansing "would keep all her hours in a little date book. She would write down 1.3 hours for reading," says Wagner. "I thought it was quite wonderful that she was extremely honest about it, and very accurate."

He began inviting her to sit in on meetings. "You can't speak, but you sit in and you observe the producer and the director, and don't be obnoxious," recalls Lansing. After a few weeks of this, they began to solicit her opinion, and soon she "just became part of the crowd." Eventually, she was no longer acting, or teaching, but working for Wagner several days a week at his office in Beverly Hills and supplementing her income by collecting unemployment.

"People always kind of wondered, they would always ask me, 'Well, why is she there? Is she there because she's beautiful?' " recalls Wagner. "I said, 'No, she just happens to be the smartest person I know doing this kind of work.' "

Wagner applauded the fact that Lansing—at work—was a woman who liked to act as a woman. Her ambition was carefully veiled. "She wasn't threatening or competitive; her ego subordinated to the project at hand. She was exceedingly communicative with people. She wasn't trying to run roughshod over anyone, or to overpower them," says Wagner.

Lansing was thrilled, happy to be free from acting, happy to spend her days talking about scripts with Wagner, although the company didn't make any movies while she was working there. "I actually thought at the time I could spend the rest of my life doing that job. I know no one believes this when I say it, but it's the truth," she gushes.

She still worried, mostly about money. She had kept almost every dime she had ever made, yet she had a pervasive, irrational fear that she'd end up as a bag lady. "I used to dream that Michael would drive by in a Rolls-Royce and I'd be sitting on the street, and he'd be sitting with this beautiful woman next to him, and she's going, 'Oh look at that poor lady. Do you know her?' He would go, 'Oh, I sort of know her.' I was always afraid that I wouldn't be able to take care of myself. And I never wanted to get married for somebody to take care of me. I never wanted to sell out."

Acting had left Lansing with other important connections. One day when she had a guest spot on the TV show *The Good Guys*, the executive producer Leonard Stern had come to visit the set with his daughter Katie, age nine, whom he was taking to lunch. "Jay Sandor was directing, and he received Katie like royalty," recalls Stern. "We had a crisis, and I was going to have to cancel lunch with her. Jay was unable to take her, but he said, 'Maybe the tall girl talking to Katie will take her to lunch.' That was Sherry. There was a fifteen-year age difference between the two, but they had enormous rapport." With her mop of dark hair and the run in her stocking, Katie reminded Lansing of herself at that age.

"Katie came home and she said to me, 'Oh, Mom, I have a new friend, Sherry Lansing.' Now doesn't that sound like a little girl's name, Sherry Lansing?" recalls Katie's mother, Gloria Stern. "And then the phone started ringing. Every other day Sherry was calling Katie and Katie was calling Sherry. I would hear Katie leave her number on a service and I was thinking, 'Gee that's funny, this little girl has a service.'

"And then Katie said that she was going to Disneyland and I said, 'Who's driving?' And Katie said, 'Oh Sherry.' I went, This little girl is driving? The day came, and the doorbell rang, I expected this little Sherry Lansing would be there with her mom. And I opened the door, and there's this long drink of water standing there. It was in the sixties. The clothes were very short then. Sherry has long legs, and she looked at Katie. She said, 'Hi, hon.' And gave her a kiss and took her by the hand and the two of them drove off in her little bug of a car."

In time, Lansing was adopted by the whole Stern family. Leonard was a TV producer, a partner in Talent Associates, the producers of such hits as *McMillan and Wife* and *Get Smart.* His gregarious wife and her best friend, Myra Silverman, became the older sisters Lansing never had, a troika of well-bred, well-meaning, wealthy Jewish ladies. Lansing used to talk about getting married again and "living in a house with a white picket fence and [going] to the ball games on Sunday," recounts Gloria Stern with a laugh. "It was so provincial what she thought she wanted. I remember thinking that would not be her fate. I just felt that it would bore her. She was also always attracted to men who had children. Always right down the line."

Leonard Stern told Lansing if she ever wanted to give up acting to let him know. A year later she began splitting her time between his office and Wagner's. "There were no women in creative development," says Stern. "I felt there should be. Here was an attractive woman, and her attractiveness would give her an advantage. She'd be unique. She'd get entrée to meet anyone in this area of the business."

Soon Lansing was working fourteen hours a day with Stern, developing scripts. He was developing some of the first movies of the week. While Hollywood movies explored male alienation and ennui, TV had begun to focus on what was a regular part of the "woman's film"— socially relevant topics that often had to do with family. Stern's plan to use Lansing as catnip worked brilliantly. "It was open sesame," says the TV producer.

Lansing was Stern's most dutiful daughter, smart, hardworking, and eager to please. "She brings out the paternal and the maternal," says Stern, who was the one who used to joke that every time she came into the room, she'd say, "I'm sorry."

The producer also admired her ability to soothe: "She can disarm and defuse tempers and Machiavellian pursuits. Her aura of warmth tempers other people's ambitions and redresses them so she's not the target. She has a calming effect."

Says his wife, "Sherry's got a first-rate mind. It has a little-girl quality, but it's a first-rate mind."

Some mistook Lansing as Stern's daughter, others as his mistress. It was the continuation of a pattern that would dog her career. The first production she handled for Stern was a pilot starring Patty Duke. "Several of the people involved in the production were gay. We would stay very late at night and talk," says Lansing. "One day one of the gay men who was married came in and said to me, 'So and so called my wife—I guess he had an arrangement with her—and said that you and I were having an affair.' And I said, 'Oh my God.' He said, 'She wasn't upset. She knows it's not true, but I just thought I'd tell you.' "

That night, Lansing went out to dinner with Barbara Feldon, *Get Smart*'s Agent 99, and her then husband. "I was really down, and I started to cry," recalls Lansing. "Barbara said, 'What's wrong?' And I said, 'No matter what I do, everybody accuses me of sleeping with everyone.' And she said, 'How can you ever worry about something like that?' And then they named a head of a studio—'People think that the reason he's got the job is that he gets girls for this corporate guy.' And I said, 'Well, that's ridiculous. You wouldn't put someone in that job, and you're dealing with billions of dollars.' She said, 'Well, it's equally ridiculous what people are saying about you, but they're saying it, so why don't you just laugh it off and forget about it? It goes with the territory.' After that, I just laughed it off."

I REALIZED FINALLY THAT THIS ACTING THING IS NOT JUST A HOBBY

"There's an atmosphere at night that's like a seeping kind of virus. You can smell it in the air and taste it in your mouth," recalls Martin Scorsese about shooting *Taxi Driver*, in the sweltering summer of 1975 in New York City, a metropolis reeling from bankruptcy and political decay. "It reminds me of the scene in *The Ten Commandments* portraying the killing of the firstborn, where a cloud of green smoke seeps along the palace floor and touches the foot of a firstborn son, who falls dead. That's almost what it's like: a strange disease creeps along the street of the city."

It was an apt setting for Scorsese's nightmare vision of America's post-Vietnam evisceration, a gritty world of pimps and hookers, haves and have-nots, where the emotionally arrested war vet Travis Bickle (Robert De Niro) cruises the streets in his yellow cab, unable to sleep, unable to find connection or meaning. In frustration he turns to violence to express himself. Scorsese would later brag about his letters from women thanking him for making a feminist film—a picture that "takes the idea of macho and takes it to its logical insane conclusion, graphically, pornographically insane."

A series of sexual rejections fans Bickle's rage. The first, a badly received attempt to pick up the candy girl at a porn theater, garners the audience's sympathy. His second brush-off comes from his dream girl, the blond, beautiful campaign worker Betsy. Bickle's initial vision of her is idealized—the untouchable madonna who fights off his clumsy advances. She was played by Cybill Shepherd.

The counterpoint of the madonna is, of course, the whore, in this case the teenage runaway Iris, who claws at Travis's fly when he tells her to keep her shirt on. When Bickle fails to shoot the senatorial candidate to win Betsy's approval, he turns his fury on the scum manipulating Iris's life with a fusillade of bullets.

Ever since the making of *Alice Doesn't Live Here Anymore*, Scorsese had had his eye on Jodie Foster for Iris. He liked her androgynous, childlike quality. He inferred—correctly—that with Foster, Iris would not simply be a Lolita-ish vamp. Her sexuality would appear not as a coquettish come-on but rather as a cheap, pasted-on disguise, a commercial persona foisted on her by adult men. Both the director and the screenwriter, Paul Schrader, were also familiar with a recent study on subliminal incitements to rape. Researchers discovered that in group therapy sessions rapists often talked about Foster's Coppertone ad. "It had just the right mixture for these rapists of adolescent sexuality, female nudity, rear entry, animals, and violence," Schrader once explained.

Brandy Foster was appalled when she first read the script, declaring that there was no way Jodie was going to play a child whore. Jodie's agent, Toni Kelman, decided to let the situation cool off, and a little while later Brandy called back, announcing that her daughter wanted the part.

Brandy and Jodie had discussed Iris. "And she knew everything." Brandy laughs. "Twelve years old, they know everything."

"I don't remember having tremendous opinions about anything when I was young," Foster recalls of the decision to make *Taxi Driver*. "I just remember going 'Okay. All right. Whatever. That sounds like a good idea.' I really liked Scorsese. My mother was a real fan of movies. She saw Cassavetes, and was into Fassbinder. She talked to me the way she would talk to an adult: '*Taxi Driver* is a really important movie. It's a social statement. It's a movie about alienation. Is this something you feel comfortable with?' That was my whole relationship with her, going to the movies and [having] sort of film criticism classes."

Before Foster could start, however, she had to pass a four-hour interview with a UCLA psychiatrist to prove to the state that she was sane enough to play a hooker. She was apparently incensed by the state's intrusion into her business. She told the board her favorite movies were *Lenny*, *Day for Night*, and *Cinderella Liberty*. Edmund Brown, the former governor of California, then in private practice, was hired to steer her through the child welfare system.

The part required financial sacrifice by all the Fosters. "I was making a lot of money in television, and I kind of had a big career," says Foster, and "[my mother] flew me to New York and said, 'We'll put ourselves up in a hotel and we'll say, [you're] a New York actor and you'll make scale.'"

An atmosphere of violence and chaos surrounded the set, a condemned building on a bombed-out strip of Manhattan's Upper West Side guarded by police from marauding gang members and junkies. During the filming of Bickle's murder of a stickup man in a bodega, a real murder occurred around the corner, and soon real cops were mingling with the guards from the movie. To cope with the stress and the night shooting, many in the cast and crew "were all doing blow," the producer Julia Phillips, a cokehead herself at the time, once noted. Scorsese would ultimately develop a major drug problem.

To prepare Foster, Scorsese arranged for her to meet a real young prostitute—from whom the actress borrowed mannerisms and gags, including the routine of juggling the various pairs of sunglasses in the coffee shop in one of her meetings with Bickle.

"I also remember Robert De Niro being kind of directive," says Foster. He picked her up every day and took her to different diners. "He would sit there, and he would run the lines ad nauseam with me, and I would sit with him. Course I'm a child actor, so I run the lines once and I'd have memorized them. And he'd just go over and over and it was so boring, it was just like, Oh, God. Do I have to? And he wouldn't talk to me. You know, in his Methody way, he'd just kind of sit there and he'd go, 'Yeah.' I was so bored that I would talk to other people in the diners or just eat my food or look at the ceiling and think about something else. Because I knew he was going to spend twenty minutes of these pregnant pauses where he wouldn't say anything. And then we would just run the lines again and he would try improvisations and stuff. So that by the time I got to the actual shooting of the scene I knew the dialogue so well that when he went off into a surprise area, it never threw me because I could always go back to the text. But I would see the text in a new way."

Foster didn't engage in Method acting; instead, she learned how to simulate actions that would read as emotions on-screen. "It was like a concentration game. To think in three different levels. To say that I'm gonna put this out and I'm gonna think this. I'm gonna feel this and I'm gonna look like I'm doing this. I found it was fun. It was like visual puzzles for me," she recalls.

"I remember getting out of the elevator at the Essex House, that's where I was staying, and saying to my mom I had never had this experience before because it had always been just *me* up there. Somebody would just say, 'Just be more like yourself,' or 'Could you do that more natural?' That's pretty much what they would say to kids, 'Just be a little more natural.' I'd never shaped a character before. And then I realized finally that this acting thing is not just a hobby, that it's actually a real thing you could do."

The adult filmmakers were ambivalent about the sexuality they were forcing onto Foster's character. When Scorsese had to explain what he wanted in the scene where Bickle first hires Iris, he began to giggle so uncontrollably that De Niro had to take charge, explaining that the scene would end with Iris trying to unzip Bickle's fly, although they adamantly didn't want her to try that. (Indeed, her older sister Connie, who looked a little like Jodie, was hired to play her stand-in— primarily the hand that yanks the zipper.)

The disconcerting moment when Iris dances with her manipulative pimp was improvised. Harvey Keitel decided the scene should play like a seductive Barry White song, in which he croons, talks, comforts her into submission. "He was nervous, she wasn't," recalls Brandy Foster. "He had a hard time with that scene. He said, 'God, I feel like a dirty old man with a little girl.' It didn't dawn on her that there was *anything*. She wasn't uncomfortable with it, because it was playacting."

"She didn't exhibit any signs that it was uncomfortable, but anybody who watched it felt real creepy," says the producer Michael Phillips. "I still am amazed that she was able to [play the part], because she was completely presexual. She was only twelve, so she was our mascot. She didn't seem to have any problems with the part at all. She is a first-take—first- and second-take—actress.

"I would probe a little bit, well, you know, Are you going to be nervous? We're coming up to the dancing scene. Do you feel okay about that? Oh yeah, sure, you know. She was always chirpy, and happy, and 'oh fine.' And she would tell herself little things, I think to help her handle these situations that were somewhat over her head. I do remember her indicating that this was one of her methods, to pretend that something was going on that would allow her to, you know, perform the sequence without having to tap into the sexual side of it. Afterwards, she could break the mood and become a twelve-year-old instantly."

In her review Pauline Kael described *Taxi Driver* as "a raw, tabloid version of *Notes from the Underground*," although critics like Robert Moss drew-and-quartered Scorsese for "diving elatedly into the blood and mire." At Cannes the movie won the Palme d'Or to the accompaniment of loud booing.

Also at Cannes, Foster further certified her growing media reputation as a child prodigy when the foreign press had trouble understanding De Niro and Scorsese, and the thirteen-year-old, who attended the Lycée Français in Los Angeles, swung into action, speaking to the crowd of admiring reporters in flawless French.

She was nominated for an Oscar, along with De Niro, Scorsese, and the film. The FBI accompanied Scorsese, who had received a threatening letter: "If Jodie Foster wins for what you made her do, you will pay for it with your life."

Foster lost. It was an excruciating moment. Foster says, "I broke out in complete huge hives, all over my face. There I was in the audience with huge, red welts. I guess there was part of me that was really disappointed that I didn't win, but I would have never been able to show it."

I COULD HAVE MADE BILLIONS

"This is going to really make me unpopular with women's lib, but they never came on to me in a way that was abusive or that I couldn't handle. I was a single woman. Nobody ever threw me down on the couch. Nobody ever said, 'If you don't do this, you don't get promoted.' Nobody ever did what I considered sexual harassment," recalls Sherry Lansing. "But if you consider sexual harassment someone asking you out on a date or telling you, 'You look pretty,' or cracking a dirty joke around you, then I could have made billions on sexual harassment suits.

"I *liked* being a woman. I was flattered or annoyed sometimes, but mostly it was, like, I didn't even think about it. Like a speck on your jacket."

From the beginning of her career, Lansing faced a relentless sexualization of her being. On the one hand, she tried to play it down, sporting no-nonsense, nondescript pantsuits and scant makeup at the office; on the other, she perpetuated it, with her unusual warmth, a girlish flirtatiousness and obvious desire to please and to be liked—particularly by powerful men. Her beauty sparked the interest of her male colleagues, and she knew how to leverage their interest into a kind of power. Her comfort with the mechanics of sexual attraction also made it easier for her detractors to discount her intelligence and drive. "Quite honestly, I think I've been accused of sleeping with every man I've ever worked with. Every single man: married, unmarried, gay, whatever," she says.

The vast amount of the talk circled around Lansing's relationship to Dan Melnick, who took the most credit for her discovery. Melnick had been Leonard Stern's business partner in New York. The pair met when Gloria Stern placed Lansing next to the newly divorced Melnick at a dinner party. In his early forties, Melnick had the look of a frayed Humphrey Bogart, with deep, hooded eyes and a penchant for gold chains, black velour shirts, and all things cutting edge.

He had run Talent Associates' burgeoning movie wing, where he had helped resuscitate Sam Peckinpah's career, first with *Noon Wine* and then the bloody, misogynistic *Straw Dogs*. He later specialized in outré, artsy fare like *All That Jazz* and *Altered States*. He was urbane, manipulative, and shrewd in keeping blood off his feet in Hollywood's bitterest political battles; he was also, as one friend put it, "very self-centered. He takes himself enormously seriously."

Newly split from the composer Richard Rodgers's daughter, Melnick was also one of the town's biggest rakes. Gloria Stern had thought Danny and Sherry would amuse each other, though she herself was surprised—and slightly chagrined—when the dinner turned into an affair.

In truth, the romance lasted only for several months, although the personal—and later professional—bond between the two would last much longer. The shadow of the relationship—the so-called original sin that would prompt the gossip, as one well-known producer quipped, "Sherry slept her way to the middle"— would stretch for almost two decades.

From the beginning Lansing knew to keep the details of their relationship to herself, but Melnick was a braggart and proud of his intimate knowledge—and implied control—of the young beauty.

Within months Melnick took Stern to lunch at the Polo Lounge. "We had created a number of situation comedies together, and we talked in that kind of sitcom shorthand," recalls Melnick. "So I said, 'Here's the scene, Leonard. Two really good friends and former partners are meeting, because one of them wants to hire away the other's creative right hand, and so what does the other guy say?' And he said, 'Dan, forget it, you can't have Sherry.' He immediately saw where I was going, and I had to wait like seven or eight months before he was able to build his operation in such a way that he could afford to let her go."

Melnick had moved to L.A. to be head of production at MGM, then in the throes of its dismantlement under the financier Kirk Kerkorian. Kerkorian had installed James Aubrey, the legendary Gatsbyesque former head of CBS, as studio chief. Aubrey was renowned for his blunt, autocratic manner, his confidence in his own instincts, and his cynical assessment of public taste, leading him to air such shows as *The Munsters* and *The Beverly Hillbillies*. His rambunctious and feral after-hours pursuits earned him the sobriquet Jungle Jim. He was immortalized in no fewer than five novels, including Jacqueline Susann's *The Love Machine*. He even swapped womanizing tales with Jack Kennedy.

Since their arrival, Kerkorian and Aubrey had decimated the one-time crown jewel of Hollywood, firing four thousand employees and selling off the riches of the backlot in a spectacular eighteen-day fire sale, where Clark Gable's jacket from *Mutiny on the Bounty* went for a dollar. Although much of his time was spent as Aubrey's hatchet man, the urbane Melnick struggled to exert his more sophisticated taste, ushering through the pipeline Michael Crichton's fantasy western *Westworld* and the offbeat thriller *Slither.* After Aubrey was fired in 1973, he continued to churn out a handful of inexpensive pictures, including such successes as *Network* and *The Goodbye Girl.*

It was into this turmoil that Lansing entered as an executive story editor, the head D-girl in charge of the story department. She had taken a month's vacation in the Amazon before starting, and when she arrived her office had been repainted, decorated with faux antiques, and a note left in the typewriter, "What took you so long?"

"She was an incredible fresh drink of water," recalls Susan Merzbach, a reader at MGM at the time. "Remember, there hadn't been many women executives, so we actually didn't know what to expect at all." An eccentric Englishman with a monocle had been the previous head of the story department. Indeed, when Merzbach had started, she had to sign her reader's reports Guy Merzerbach so none of the executives would know that their story analyst was a woman.

Although the MGM production team consisted of only a handful of people—among them Lansing's former boyfriend Ray Wagner—they were firmly segregated from the script department, until she arrived. Melnick took Lansing seriously, listened to her and educated her, inviting her into the editing room on the movies they were making. "He just kind of handed the reins to her," recalls Merzbach.

Like most bosses, he also exploited her skills. "Melnick was one of those guys who learned early that women were great and undervalued resources," recalls one woman who worked for him. "He gave us all jobs. He wouldn't even read the script, just go into the meetings with the notes I had given him, and he would take credit for it."

Lansing opened her door to whatever the other script readers had to say, and, suddenly, "we were part of MGM," says Merzbach. "Anybody who wanted to comment on the scripts in progress and also contribute to the development was welcome to it, and it was huge. For the first time, I thought I had made the suggestion and actually saw it on the screen, and then I got excited."

From the beginning Lansing threw herself into the work, instituting lunchtime screenings for the entire department so she could improve her film education. Internally, she could be forceful in her opinions about material. "She was very focused," recalls Dick Shepherd, who ultimately replaced Melnick. "She made her feelings very clear. She doesn't beat around the bush."

Externally, her soft-focus beauty and cheerleaderlike demeanor made it hard for some people to take her seriously. Once she tried to give script notes to *Dirty Harry* director Don Siegel, but he groused, "We're not taking notes from you, young lady." At the next meeting, her boss gave him the identical notes, and the director applauded him for his insights.

Lansing's style differed sharply from that of the industry's high-profile women, like Mengers, or twenty-nine-year-old Julia Phillips, who in 1974 became the first woman to win an Academy Award for Best Picture, for producing *The Sting* with husband Michael Phillips and partner Tony Bill. Alternately flirtatious, brainy, and arrogant, Phillips had an ability to either connect viscerally or pulverize, often in tones that shocked men of the era. "It was like, 'Tell him I'll rip his cock off and shove it up his fucking ass, you motherfucker'—language that was just Satanic in its profanity," described the director John Landis.

In those days a stern word from Don Siegel could render Lansing mute for an entire meeting. "If someone is so scared to reject someone or be hated, they can be manipulated," says her previous boss, Leonard Stern. Yet inside MGM she became known for her exceptional talent for smoothing ruffled egos. "Melnick could have a temper," says Merzbach, "and a temper like that just doesn't faze her in the least. She is the most calming influence."

Indeed, Lansing liked to play the indulgent beauty to the beasts, the outsize, bossy, occasionally petulant men who were her bosses. She listened to their tirades with girlish empathy. Temper tantrums—if they weren't directed specifically at her—did not bother her. Throughout her career, much has been made of her ability to negotiate abusive tempers.

"I don't take it personally," says Lansing, who credits both her mother and her stepfather for her blitheness in the face of fury. "My mother was a screamer," she explained at one point, although at another time she said, "My stepfather was very tough. Maybe that's where I learned it. And I knew that he really, really, really loved me. But he was very tough."

From the beginning Lansing worked the town like a mayor without portfolio. She seemed to have an infinite number of friendly acquaintances. "She never had a bad word to say about anyone," says her close friend Myra Silverman. "On Saturdays we'd have lunch sometimes and walk through Beverly Hills, and [we'd run into people], and she would introduce me and say, 'This is my best friend,' meaning this other person." And then they'd meet someone else who was "her best friend," and so on and so on down the street. "She never ran in groups," adds Silverman. "She was very much a loner. We'd either have lunch alone or she'd have dinner with me and my husband."

"She kept people at a certain distance," says Gloria Stern. "She would call and say, 'Hi, hon, I'm calling you from the treadmill. Do you want to go to a movie? I'll be finished at ten after eleven and the movie starts at eleven-thirty, do you want to go?' And I said, 'Oh, well, okay, do you want to have lunch later?' 'No, I can't. I've got to be somewhere at one-thirty.' I think that's partly why she accomplishes so much, because she compartmentalizes her life."

Lansing's women friends were by and large Hollywood wives, save for the agent Martha Luttrell, her closest female friend. Luttrell was a visual double for Lansing, a beautiful former dancer with dark curly hair. She had worked for years as the assistant to director Mike Nichols and was just starting out as an agent when she went to lunch with MGM's executive story editor. They were comrades in arms, girls on the town.

One year, MGM flew a number of old-time film stars—Cary Grant, Fred Astaire, Johnny Weissmuller—to Cannes, for the opening of *That's Entertainment!*, an anthology of clips from MGM's heyday. The studio threw a huge "American Dinner Party" with steaks and apple pie. Lansing and Luttrell both went along, taking a room together at the Carlton, until Lansing's friend David Z. Goodman declared they had to stay at the fabled Hôtel du Cap, and gave them his room there. Melnick and studio owner Kerkorian took them to the premiere, and gambling. In the morning they breakfasted next to Cary Grant.

"I remember looking up at the hotel and seeing Sherry's beautiful, happy face. She was waving and waving," says Goodman.

Kris Kristofferson, Barbra Streisand, and Jon Peters on
location in Tempe, Arizona, filming A STAR IS BORN, 1976.

THE POWER OF BARBRA STREISAND

YOU'LL PAY FOR EVERY LOUSY THING RAY STARK EVER DID TO ME

When Sue Mengers called, Jon Peters put down his comb. The hairdresser turned movie mogul left a frost job midstreak, and cradled the phone to his ear. Standing in the middle of his Beverly Hills salon, he stared at his reflection in the mirror, admiring his brown-and-gold sweater and platform saddle shoes. "That's *all* you can get?" he asked Mengers, his girlfriend Barbra Streisand's agent.

That *all* happened to be unprecedented. In fact, Mengers was letting Peters know that he had won the latest in a series of jihads with the studio. Not only was Peters going to produce Streisand's $6 million musical remake of *A Star Is Born* but he was now set to direct as well.

Directing was the latest booty for the thirty-one-year-old seventh-grade dropout, and he felt well-suited for its rigors. As he bragged to the journalist Marie Brenner, "Directing is a thing I've done my whole life! It's getting people to do what I want them to do!"

Peters's would-be stint in the directing chair lasted only several months, derailed perhaps by a barrage of bad publicity including Brenner's piece, which appeared on the cover of *New Times* magazine under the headline A STAR IS SHORN.

Twenty-five years later Streisand insists that she was never, ever going to let Peters direct the film, although his hubris had a clarifying effect on her inchoate ambition.

"Do you know what gave me the confidence to direct?" Streisand asks. "He said, 'Maybe I should direct it.' He said this about himself. I said, 'Man, if this guy could think *he* could direct it, then *I* can direct it.' Why am I so reticent here? He had such chutzpah."

In truth, ever since the actress auditioned for her first Broadway show, *I Can Get It for You Wholesale*, in 1961, she'd wanted to direct—at least her own part. During her tryout for the supporting role of Miss Marmelstein, the trod-upon secretary, the nineteen-year-old Streisand informed the director, Arthur Laurents, and the choreographer, Herbert Ross, that she wanted to perform the number while sitting down. Partly she was nervous, but she also envisioned herself doing comic shtick while rolling around the stage in an old-fashioned desk chair.

"I got the part, and then they proceeded to try to direct the number in a whole other way. Walking around the stage in some way. It just felt totally awkward. It didn't feel truthful. I didn't know what the hell, why I was moving where," says Streisand. "They complained about me. That I was undisciplined, that I couldn't do it the same twice, and I just said, 'Why can't I do it in my chair?' It just seemed to be so organic. I can roll around on my wheels and talk to the audience and complain as a secretary would."

Streisand continued to press her case, indeed hammer away at it until Laurents and Ross relented in exasperation. "The night before we opened in Philadelphia, they said, 'Do it in your goddamn chair.' So we did it in the chair, and it stopped the show. The next day in front of the whole cast Arthur Laurents bawled me out. But my poster in the chair went up outside the theater, and my salary was doubled from two hundred dollars a week to four hundred dollars a week. So the chair was right. . . . for me. What I'm saying is that it has always been a problem for me to do what I felt was right. In other words, people got upset by it. By the way, I think Arthur is a great screenwriter and did a fabulous job in 1972 creating *The Way We Were* for me."

In the years that followed, Streisand's opinionated nature, and habit of intense questioning, alternately impressed and rankled her collaborators. During the filming of her first movie, *Funny Girl*, the twenty-five-year-old actress would watch dailies and pick out what takes she would use if she were directing the picture. She not only did her own hair and makeup but offered unsolicited acting tips to some of the other actors and made script suggestions to the sixty-five-year-old William Wyler, the Oscar-winning director of *Ben-Hur*. "I loved Willy. I came to him every morning with many versions of each scene because I had played *Funny Girl* a thousand times in Philadelphia, in Boston, in New York and London. . . . I even talked about [writer Isobel Lennart's] first movie script, which was written when I was eleven years old, called 'My Man,' and I had these scenes broken down into folders, and I'd say, 'This is what she wrote then, and this is an interesting concept here or this is a great line here.' And he would pick and choose from what I would bring him to maybe add into the script," says Streisand. "Willy Wyler was fantastic to work with because he had a very distinct opinion and he recognized the truth when he saw it." At the end of the shoot, Wyler presented Streisand with a director's megaphone and some advice: "You should be a director."

A Star Is Born arrived just as Streisand was finishing *Funny Lady*, the last of five pictures she had in her extended contract with her mentor, the Hollywood godfather Ray Stark. The actress would later look back on the film as the beginning of her rocky middle period, an era in which she lacked the confidence to direct in her own right yet wanted more and more overt control over her material. Her solution was to produce, and to hire weak directors who, she said, "would collaborate with me, people I could have input with." It was probably the worst of all possible fixes, a strategy practically guaranteed to incite power struggles and inflict maximum pain on all involved.

A Star Is Born was a film inextricably entwined with the fate of Streisand's latest, heady romance. When Peters bragged to Brenner, "The world is waiting to see Barbra and my story," Hollywood chuckled at his hubris, but woe to those who ignored his sentiment.

The latest incarnation of this oft-told tale had begun almost two years before as the brainchild of the husband-and-wife novelists and screenwriters John Gregory Dunne and Joan Didion. One July afternoon in 1973, they were driving to the airport when Dunne uttered the fateful inspiration: "James Taylor and Carly Simon in a rock-and-roll version of *A Star Is Born*."

Dunne's idea presciently captured the anxiety of the age, in which the women's movement was blossoming. The premise was simple. A fading, self-destructive male star fosters the career of a young starlet and falls in love with her. Her stardom eventually eclipses his, and the failure of his career drives him to suicide. Adela Rogers St. Johns had written the initial story for 1932's *What Price Hollywood?*, which Dorothy Parker and her less talented husband, Alan Campbell, finessed into the 1937 version, with Janet Gaynor and Fredric March. The picture had been remade in 1954 with Judy Garland and James Mason.

The movie was immediately set up at Warner Bros., which saw huge potential in the soundtrack. John Foreman (*Serpico*) was attached as producer. Dunne and Didion wanted Warren Beatty, who passed, then Mike Nichols, who also passed. To their chagrin the script was sent to Peter Bogdanovich, who was interested in the project as a vehicle for his girlfriend Cybill Shepherd. Mark Rydell finally came on unofficially as director and submitted the project to Sue Mengers for Streisand's consideration. Uninterested in rock and roll, or a remake, Streisand passed. "I wanted Barbra to do it desperately," recalls former Warners executive John Calley. "She wouldn't do it, wouldn't do it, wouldn't do it." James Taylor and Carly Simon also turned down the project, now titled "Rainbow Road," reportedly because it too closely mirrored their own lives.

Warners eventually replaced Rydell with Jerry Schatzberg, who had worked with Dunne and Didion on *Panic in Needle Park*. The script was sent to Diana Ross and Liza Minnelli. Cher, fresh from back-to-back number-one records, and her breakup with Sonny Bono, auditioned repeatedly.

In April 1974, Peters stumbled on the script. "He didn't know this movie was made twice before," Streisand says and laughs. Belligerent, barely literate, Peters nonetheless had raw energy, a clever intuitive streak, and a certain flair for showmanship. He owned a string of splashy hair salons across L.A. He styled celebrity hair, often seducing his women clientele and entertaining male clients, like Jack Nicholson and Warren Beatty, by getting his haircutting assistants to reveal their latest sexual high jinks.

Peters had met Streisand almost a year before, when she was looking for a hairstylist for *For Pete's Sake*. He drove a red Ferrari to his interview at her Beverly Hills estate. After chastising the superstar for keeping him waiting, he gushed, "You've got a great ass."

Peters landed the job as Streisand's hair and wardrobe consultant and was flown for the shoot to Manhattan, where he resided at the Plaza Hotel. He ushered Streisand out of her muumuu phase into tight jeans, revealing tops, and a flattering short coif. The pair began a volatile affair, punctuated by intense battles and cooing reconciliations. He later promised to introduce the world to a "new, sensual Barbra."

Within a year Peters was unofficially serving as Streisand's manager and pressuring her to fire her real manager and close friend of more than fifteen years, Marty Erlichman. Streisand argued for Erlichman's loyalty. Peters pointed out that the manager had talked her into the inane *For Pete's Sake*, a huge flop that featured Streisand in the atavistic role of a woman who would do anything, including sell her body, to bolster her husband's business prospects. (Ironically, Streisand had turned down *Klute, Cabaret*, and *Alice Doesn't Live Here Anymore*, the movies that respectively won Oscars for Best Actress of 1971, '72, and '74.) Ultimately, Streisand left Erlichman to go with Peters, allowing her new boyfriend a staggering 15 percent of all her earnings. Hollywood gossiped that Peters had "an absolute iron grip on Barbra," in the words of the columnist Robin Adam Sloan.

Peters tended to act like a rabid cheerleader for whatever it was his girlfriend wanted. "He just made her believe in herself," says Polly Platt, the film's production designer and once a close friend. "I do believe that if it hadn't been for Jon, she wouldn't have directed ever. He pushed her. 'You've got to direct. You've got to direct.' Everything was about her directing."

Peters persuaded Streisand to reconsider "Rainbow Road" because, as he later explained, "She'd done *Funny Lady*, and I thought, Why should a young girl be playing an old lady? She's a young, hot, sexy woman—a little ball of fire. None of that had been conveyed on film. She should be playing things that are hot and young and contemporary." Warner Bros. began to salivate over the possibility of a Streisand musical, which they projected to earn at least $50 million.

Streisand's first requirement—she told her former boyfriend John Calley—was that Jon Peters be named producer of this $6 million project. John Foreman, the producer who had shunted the project along for more than a year, would get a consolation prize, the position of executive producer.

The studio then acquiesced to every one of Streisand's deal points. Her company, First Artists and Barwood, would produce the picture, making her an executive producer and giving her final cut. "Freddie Fields muscled us into doing that," says Calley. She would take no salary for producing or starring but would get 25 percent of the net profit. She also demanded that the studio relinquish the soundtrack and its profits to her recording company, Columbia Records. By the time the movie went into production in early 1976, Peters and Streisand had gone through fourteen screenwriters, three directors, and four musical collaborators.

Dunne and Didion were the first to go. Streisand had met the pair several years earlier at a party at Sue Mengers's. In the summer of 1974 the Dunnes visited her Malibu ranch several times for script discussions. The meetings were amiable enough, filled with wine and reefer. They brought their daughter, Quintana, to play with Streisand's son, Jason Gould: "I wasn't crazy about their playing in the cage with the pet lion cub," Dunne wrote in *Esquire,* "but I figured what the hell, this was Hollywood."

Streisand wanted more "schmaltz" and more prominence for her character, which she viewed as "being so passive in the earlier versions," she later explained. "All she did was love him and watch him come apart. But this is the seventies. I don't believe it. She shouldn't stand around and watch him disintegrate. I want her to say, 'Fight for me, goddamnit, protect yourself or *I'll* kill you.' "

Dunne and Didion began to realize that Streisand and Peters saw the movie as a reflection of their relationship. Two weeks after Streisand boarded the production, the couple tried to be released from their contract, to no avail, but after their third draft Streisand let them go with lucrative compensation, and subsequent screenwriters began to come and go: Jonathan Axelrod, Jay Presson Allen, Buck Henry, and Alvin Sargent. Streisand even toyed with the idea of switching the parts, making it even more reflective of the Barbra-Jon dynamics, with the female the great superstar, and the male the young neophyte, but abandoned that tack.

Streisand and Peters continued to float an array of silly schemes, many of which advanced Peters's career. When Kris Kristofferson initially dropped out of the movie because Streisand wouldn't allow his name to appear with hers over the title, the couple decided that Peters should star. At a meeting with then director Jerry Schatzberg, Peters attempted to sing "Don't Be Cruel," accompanied by Streisand, a fiasco of off-key warbling that led even the couple to drop that idea.

After the brief flirtation with Peters directing, the couple approached and were rebuffed by a series of A-list directors, among them Bob Fosse, Hal Ashby, Sidney Lumet, and Robert Altman. Undoubtedly, it was hard to attract major talent given the perception that whoever took the job would have to serve Streisand and Peters.

Warner Bros., meanwhile, hired Frank Pierson for a fast rewrite. At the age of fifty, the patrician Pierson was one of Hollywood's leading writers, with *Dog Day Afternoon, Cool Hand Luke,* and *Cat Ballou* to his credit. He had also directed one small, not particularly well-received movie, *The Looking Glass War.* In his view the Dunne-Didion script was tough-minded and authentic to the rock-and-roll spirit but lacked a sentimental core. He concurred with Streisand's assessment, that she had no real part to play other than to become successful, stand by, and watch Norman's self-destruction. Pierson, too, wanted to update the relationship between the sexes.

"I wanted Frank Pierson to write it and I had asked Sydney Pollack to direct it," says Streisand. "At the last minute, [Frank] kind of blackmailed me and said, 'I won't write it unless I direct it.' And I said, 'Okay, but know that I'm going to do it with you. You can have the credit as a director, but it's going to be my vision as well.' I had final cut and was also financially responsible for anything over six million dollars."

Why didn't Streisand simply direct the movie herself? According to Pierson, she didn't want to hurt Peters's feelings or ego. "I couldn't just take over as a director from Jon, could I?" she said to Pierson. "But I couldn't let Jon direct. Can you imagine Jon Peters directing?

"If this film goes down the drain, it's all over for Jon and me."

Streisand would come to see *A Star Is Born* as her feminist anthem, the tale of one woman's lonely struggle against a patriarchal society. Her ambition is validated. She's grown into her own power. "I'm for women's lib," she proclaimed at the time. Offscreen, however, the actress didn't wield her authority so confidently and often resorted to unhappy backseat driving.

She and Peters continued to look for a male costar, considering performers as diverse as Marlon Brando, Mick Jagger, and Elvis Presley, whom the pair flew to Las Vegas to seduce. They went backstage after Presley's show at the Hilton, and the King, then in his waning fat years, confessed to Streisand, "You're the only one that ever intimidated me. I came to your show and I came back to see you and you never looked me in the face. All you did was paint your nails." Presley turned them down, so Streisand agreed to put Kristofferson's name adjacent to hers, and the Rhodes scholar turned singer signed on.

Meanwhile, the relationship between Pierson and Streisand disintegrated quickly. The actress was put off by a visit to his house, which she found to be a cold construction of steel and brick. It gave her a bad premonition. For his part, Pierson thought Streisand was indecisive, unfocused, and narcissistic in the extreme. She chastised him because he liked to write alone. She preferred to go over the script word by word together, which bored the writer-director, who later discovered that Streisand "hadn't read the descriptions or the stage directions of any of the scripts." He vowed to leave the script unfinished, "to keep everything spontaneous and fast, [and] reveal little in advance to her."

His attempt to withhold as a measure of control panicked Streisand. Pierson received a call from Peters, who told him, "Your turn—the Jewish Princess wants you! She's getting panicky, and when she's like that she starts calling in her friends."

Pierson went to lunch at Streisand's town house, where he was served lobster soufflé, one of his favorite meals, as the diva well knew. Sitting against the window, the sunlight pouring through her curls, Streisand talked about how she wanted a lot of backlight, how she preferred to be shot on her left side.

"I don't feel you really want to love me," she complained. "All my directors have wanted to make me beautiful. But I feel you hold something back, there's something you don't tell me. You never talk to me." Dismayed, Pierson realized she wasn't joking. "I love you," he told her, "but I'm not the demonstrative type."

The topic turned to directors, to the actor's need for a father figure to rely on.

"But you fight like hell with Jon. You fight like hell with everyone you rely on," Pierson told her.

"I know. Jon is so strong! I never had a father. I was always in charge of myself. I came and went as I pleased. I can't stand for someone to tell me what to do. Ray Stark always used to bully me, the son of a bitch. I made him, and he made millions from me. Millions!"

"You'll pay," she joked with Pierson, "for every lousy thing Ray Stark ever did to me."

Already Streisand contemplated firing Pierson. She suggested to Polly Platt that the two of them codirect the movie.

"She meant it," recalls Platt. "It was the dumbest idea I had ever heard. It was insane, counterproductive. It would have been extremely disloyal to Frank, who hired me." Streisand confided it was her first movie as a producer, and she didn't want to be embarrassed.

Platt knew that another kind of woman would have seized the opportunity. Instead, she set about trying to save Pierson's job. She told Streisand, "Two women can't direct a movie. It's ridiculous."

The first day of shooting, Streisand sang in a nightclub in Pasadena. Pierson was energized and delighted by her singing. Afterward she rushed up to the director and flung her arms around him. "Thank you! Thank God!"

She stayed up all night in a panic. If there was one thing she felt she knew about, it was how best to present herself singing. She liked to do her songs in one take and was upset that Pierson, without her knowledge, had changed the camera angles they had agreed on beforehand. She was worried that he seemed to have no suggestions about how she should play the character. She had asked him to choose between two variations, and he had replied, "I'm neutral."

Peters declared he would fire the director.

The next day John Calley talked Peters out of this folly with a pointed reminder that firing the director would only bring on more bad press. Streisand decided to monitor the work herself, attaching a video camera to the camera rig so that she could scrutinize each scene as they progressed. Platt suggested that instead of retreating to her trailer for two hours and then criticizing everything, the star should supervise the setups as they were being done, at least saving time.

From Pierson's perspective, this began a slow descent into Barbra-inspired madness. He alternately loved and hated her. She could be entrancing, more energetic than ten people combined; her manifest talents regularly overwhelmed him. "Barbra sings to make you forget every other thing she has ever done or said. You feel excited and wonderful. She throws it away as though it were a gift not worth having," he wrote later.

Streisand viewed Pierson as alternately weak and recalcitrant. She scolded him for his passivity with actors. "You have to be hard on them," she'd tell him. "They'll walk all over you." She had been on many more sets than Pierson, and she regularly barraged him with questions, her displeasure unleashed in a torrent of Why? Why? Why? She usually won her battles.

"He was incapable of dealing. I don't think Frank was born to be a director," says Platt. "She just blew him away. You have to have an answer for Barbra."

"Frank was in an untenable situation," says another member of the production team. Kristofferson was often caught in the middle as Pierson and Streisand bickered. Unbeknownst to Pierson, the singer-songwriter and Streisand had once enjoyed a brief fling. He now drowned his fury with prodigious consumption of tequila and beer chasers. Kristofferson's habitual drunkenness worried Streisand, who watched his performance with vigilance. During shooting he resented her meddling and blew up at Pierson for not standing up to her, although in later years he came to believe that Pierson "was out to lunch from the first day. [He hadn't] listened or remembered."

Streisand began staying up until three or four in the morning, panicking that her career was on the line, that a flop would irrevocably damage if not herself (who could always sing for her supper) then Peters. The film reflected her: She even wore her own clothes. She fiercely resented Pierson's attitude that *A Star Is Born* was only a movie. Dailies turned into ritual unspoolings of Streisand's psyche, happy when she looked good and everyone gushed over her beauty, despairing and venomous when she was displeased.

On March 29, Pierson won an Oscar for writing *Dog Day Afternoon*. His elation lasted just that night. The next day he fought vociferously with Streisand, who demanded a scene in which she and Kristofferson wrestle in the mud, then another where, dressed in red plush, she tries to bake bread and gets flour all over her dress. To Pierson, the ideas were like bad clichés right out of *I Love Lucy*. He shot them both, thinking he could edit them out.

But he was wrong, at least about the mud scene. The film wrapped in April, and when Pierson showed Streisand and Peters his first cut six weeks later, the lack of applause was deafening. Streisand stayed up till five in the morning conferring with her closest advisers, the songwriters Marilyn and Alan Bergman and her longtime friend Cis Corman. The next day the team of editors moved out to the pool house at Streisand's Malibu ranch, where the actress had installed a $500,000 state-of-the-art editing facility. They spent all summer there, working fourteen hours a day, seven days a week, under the direction of Streisand, who had her Polish cook whip up fantastic meals so no one would ever have to leave the premises.

IT WAS NOT REALLY MY JOB,
BUT I LOVED HER

Peters's bullying masked a very real fear that he would make a fool of himself. He was determined to show Hollywood that he was not simply Streisand's patsy. At times his showmanship was inspired—he was the one to suggest filming all the music live, which had never been done before, and convinced the stage-shy Streisand to sing before a crowd of 55,000. He spearheaded the marketing campaign—suggesting the steamy Scavullo photograph that became the poster and marketing tie-ins that became industry standards: a novelization, the first Barbara Walters interview. At other times he was merely silly, as when he proposed hiring Evel Knievel as Kristofferson's stuntman to ride a motorcycle off the stage in the big concert sequence.

Much of the time he stood on the sidelines barking out suggestions and generally ratcheting up the tension, so much so that, during a scene at Bernard Cornfeld's house, even Streisand yelled at him to get out. Peters was fuming.

Afterward Pierson ran into Streisand hiding in the hedges. "For God's sake, take me home," she told him. She was a quivering mass as she huddled in his car, recalled the director. "He gets so furious. I don't know what to do," she said, and Pierson realized in a flash that she was physically frightened of her lover. Peters flew into another rage after Streisand did a love scene in a bubble bath with Kristofferson. He chased her around the Warners lot until she found a ride home. The neophyte producer would always deny hitting his superstar girlfriend, although not the wrestling, the clawing tussles, the flying pieces of furniture.

"Their relationship was pretty volatile and intense," Jane Jenkins, Peters's assistant, has said. "There would be bursts of conflict. She would be a needy little girl where she would need a big strong man to protect her. Then there were times when he would decimate her. I heard him scream at Barbra once in a way I would have run a hundred miles. I remember her calling back an hour later with this little-girl voice and saying, 'Is Jon there?' and I wanted to say, 'Don't talk to him!' "

One thing Sue Mengers knew with all her heart: She hated Jon Peters. Twenty years later he is still a topic that can send her blood pressure skyrocketing and make her face redden with suppressed fury.

"Jon Peters was like the bad seed," she recalls. "He was a guy who wanted to rape the business and eventually did. And I was very protective of Streisand, which was not really my job, but I loved her. She was my dear friend. At that time I felt that Peters was like a carpetbagger, these guys that come in and make quick bucks and do very little work."

Mengers simmered over the way Peters foisted himself onto Streisand's coattails. "When Jon Peters made his first big deal at Warner Bros., he was piggybacking Streisand's overall deal," she says. Peters demanded a separate deal for himself. Streisand went along with it: "Barbra, like all women, wants to believe she's totally loved. That there's no ulterior motive in her lover's life."

Peters alienated a number of Streisand's longtime friends, like the Bergmans and Cis Corman, who he thought were old-fashioned, and her business associates, who all fiercely guarded their relationship with the superstar. "We fought day and night," says Mengers. "It was a very difficult, difficult time. And I was stupid. It would have been easier to play along with him instead of the two of us second-guessing each other all the time. Because Jon didn't want Barbra to work with any other producer, he wanted to totally be known as 'If you want Streisand for a picture, I gotta be the producer.' So I felt that this restricted Barbra, because if a producer had a good piece of material, why would he have to bring in Jon Peters in order to get Streisand? It was like paying twice for something. It was sleazy because he always had to have a place in it."

In fighting with Peters, Mengers was breaking her cardinal rule of agenting: Befriend the spouse. She had always worked hard to defuse any antagonism that a wife might have about her husband spending so much time with another woman. "If I had it to do all over again, I would never have taken on Jon Peters. Because your client is invariably going to choose their mate over you. It was very stupid of me. But I loved her and I wanted to protect her, and I thought at the time that she needed a little protecting."

A Star Is Born was excoriated by critics but nonetheless turned into the biggest hit of Streisand's career, earning $90 million at the box office, $15 million personally for Streisand and Peters. As a parting shot Frank Pierson published a detailed account of the project titled "My Battles with Barbra and Jon," one of the most devastating articles ever written about Streisand. Streisand felt horribly betrayed. Pierson directed one more film, and then didn't direct again for more than a decade.

Nineteen eighty would prove to be a watershed for Sue Mengers, the year she "broke through the glass ceiling" and, she says, consequently "hurt myself. I think the glass cut me or something. I suddenly stopped being able to do it." It was around this time she truly realized how grossly underpaid she was—at least in comparison to the hefty commissions her clients brought in. For years the privilege of doing her job had been enough. "When I got married my husband started to say, 'This is a joke what you're getting paid,' " she recalls. "And I thought he was feeling competitive with my affection for Freddie [Fields, her then boss]. I said, 'Oh, you don't know. It's so wonderful, they are going to take care of me. I don't need to get any stock, because they'll take care of me.' He kept saying, 'You are going to get screwed.' Well, I only realized it when I made my last contract that I was underpaid. By that time, Freddie Fields was no longer with that agency. It had been bought by Marv Josephson. It became ICM. I didn't want to acknowledge it before because I was just having such fun. And I would be like a little girl. 'Freddie, I need a new dress for the Golden Globes.' 'All right, kid, go out and get yourself a new dress.' I didn't feel that I could go up and say, 'Freddie, I really feel I deserve another $25,000 a year.' "

Ironically enough, it was Barry Manilow, Bette Midler's former accompanist turned singing superstar, who had made Mengers take notice. Manilow wasn't an important client for her. His strength was in concert tours, but she had managed to sign him to ICM with a promise of getting him into films. "It didn't work, but I set up meetings for him and Sinatra on a movie. I'm sitting in the office one day, and one of the music agents said, 'Do you know how much commission Manilow made last year? He made $600,000 touring arenas.' " Mengers had brought that $600,000 into the agency, as well as the 10 percent of such multimillion-dollar clients as Burt Reynolds at his peak and, of course, Streisand. But she was making only a fraction of the commissions she brought in. "There are some agents that write down, 'I made a deal today. It made so much commission.' They added it up. I never did that. And I never even said, 'Hey, Barry Manilow, guys.' I just didn't think about it. So then [in] my last deal Marvin Josephson was very fair. But it is money I should have been making a long time ago."

The money had grown in importance as the proportion of fun to *tsuris* dwindled. Inevitably clients left, often for mysterious reasons—at least, mysterious to her; people chafed at her bitter streak, and the attention she drew to herself. Still, it hurt. "I think the first that shocked me was that Candice Bergen left right after *Starting Over*," says Mengers. "Candy and I are very close now, but at that time we always kind of had battled, but I remember that in *Starting Over* she wanted the Jill Clayburgh part. Being one of the most beautiful women in the world, it was hard to think of casting her as a divorcée that couldn't get a date. But that was a shock to me. She had just been nominated for the Academy Award. But I think she went over to CAA, they were the hot new guys at the time. Who knew?" Soon after, Mengers lost Burt Reynolds, and Ali MacGraw.

"It is a job that really wears you down. From 1963 to 1986, that's a long time to be in the personal service business. Do you know what that means, to be at the beck and call of talent who could be very erratic and demanding? And every morning you wake up saying, 'Is this going to be the day someone leaves?' "

The war with Peters continued unabated, although their clashes were often less about differences in taste than a struggle for influence over Streisand. Both had urged her to make *The Main Event*, a screwball tale of a female perfume mogul who goes broke and decides to manage her one remaining asset, a washed-up sexist prizefighter. Knowing that Streisand was sure to reject this piece of fluff, Mengers threw a party at her home, where the producers, Howard Rosenman and Renée Missel, could meet the actress amid the chitchat of Paul Newman and Gore Vidal. She even instructed Rosenman, a neophyte producer, on what to wear (his hippest clothes) and what to say (appeal to her intellectual, serious side). Rosenman proclaimed that the film was an American riff on Lina Wertmuller's classic *Swept Away*, about a woman who literally owns a man.

Streisand decided to use *The Main Event* to fulfill her last commitment to First Artists, the production company she had launched to great fanfare with Sidney Poitier and Paul Newman in 1969, with the intent of gaining more control over her product. As soon as Rosenman began negotiating the deal, Peters balked at paying the agreed-upon price and demanded that the producer cut his fee in half. An irate Peters ultimately caved, although Mengers informed Rosenman he'd have to stay away from the set. He would be allowed to attend the premiere, but, she warned him, "When you see Barbra and she forgets your name, smile!" Again Streisand hired a director (Howard Zieff) but wound up recutting the film herself. Again the film dismayed critics and impressed fans, but it left Streisand feeling besmirched and slightly embarrassed.

The actress wanted to make an important movie, a meaningful one, and for years had nursed her dream project, *Yentl.* Based on a story by Isaac Bashevis Singer, it is the shtetl tale of a rabbi's teenage daughter who yearns to study the forbidden Torah and masquerades as a boy so she can attend the local yeshiva. She falls for her male study partner, who convinces her to marry—and bed—his former fiancée.

Streisand had stumbled upon the material in 1968, when she was only twenty-six. When she spent her first weekend with Peters in 1973, she read him the story and acted out all the parts. Peters was impressed by her ambition but wondered if she was too old to play Yentl. By 1976 Streisand had begun to talk of directing the movie herself. Peters remained leery. He recalled an incident during the making of *The Main Event:* "We were standing there in the snow, and she said, 'I hate this movie. I'm going to do *Yentl!*' I said, 'You're not going to do it!' I had offers for her to go to Vegas to do shows for twenty million, thirty million. She turned them all down. I said, 'You're not going to ruin your life and mine. You can't play a boy! We're gonna do something else together.' . . . I was a little domineering, I guess, and I remember her looking at me and saying, 'Just because you said that, I'm going to do the movie no matter what!' "

Mengers was equally discouraging, and not at all unsympathetic to the concerns of the studio chiefs who had made millions off Streisand, the biggest female star in the world, but turned her down on this project. No woman had ever been allowed to helm a big-budget Hollywood feature, although Streisand's male counterpart Warren Beatty had successfully codirected (with Buck Henry) *Heaven Can Wait* and Clint Eastwood had helmed a number of films. Yet Mengers thought that the idea of Streisand dressed up in *payot,* the long forelocks worn by religious Jews, wasn't particularly commercial, and she knew that even those who weren't sexist weren't necessarily off the mark to wonder if Streisand—a woman who could take hours to decide what she wanted to eat—would be able to make up her mind over camera angles and costume changes. Her opposition softened, however, when Streisand decided to make *Yentl* into a musical, a much more commercially viable project.

In April 1978, Peters managed to land a producing deal at Orion, which had grown out of a burgeoning friendship between himself and Streisand and Orion head Mike Medavoy and his wife, Marcia. The deal was designed to include one Streisand picture, preferably a musical, and in 1979, it was announced that Orion would make *Yentl.*

By the spring of 1980, Mengers finally saw a way to dislodge Peters's grip on all of Streisand's film projects. That the plan suited her own goals didn't invalidate its merits, or so she told herself. Indeed, as Streisand had assiduously helped Peters secure a toehold in the entertainment business, Mengers fretted about her own husband's career. Her success—and her obsession with working—created tension between them, and she hated how cruel Hollywood could be to a man who wasn't making it in the industry, particularly one she loved so desperately. His directorial debut, *Le Point de mire,* had fared badly, although Tramont had managed to set up another film, the offbeat satire *All Night Long,* at Universal—as part of a sweetheart deal for the producers Jerry Weintraub and Leonard Goldberg. The film also happened to star one of Mengers's key clients, Gene Hackman, as George Dupler, a beleaguered family man who works at an all-night drugstore and falls in love with Cheryl Gibbons, his son's Marilyn Monroe–like girlfriend.

Mengers was getting a massage when Streisand called up one day. "I remember it as clear as day," says Mengers. "She said, 'How come you didn't show me Jean-Claude's script? Cis Corman tells me it's very good.' I said, 'Well, I didn't think that you would like it.' She said, 'I'd like to read it.' " A few days after reading the script, Streisand came over to rehearse with Hackman and Tramont. "And the two men fell in love. They wanted her desperately. And she was intrigued, but as I told you, it was impossible to get her to make up her mind," says Mengers. "The only time I saw her react quickly to a project was *The Way We Were.* And even though she was tempted by this, and the money, it took her weeks to make up her mind. Weeks," says Mengers. "And finally she said yes. Jean-Claude and I had many fights afterwards about it. He said, '[You] should have left it alone.' I said, 'What could I do? She wanted to see the script. She was curious.' " Indeed, the film started production with starlet Lisa Eichhorn playing Gibbons, but soon Tramont and, apparently, Hackman, were displeased with her. There was talk of firing the actress.

According to Streisand, she was at home, working feverishly on the script for *Yentl*, when Mengers approached her about *All Night Long*. In fact, Universal was willing to pay Streisand a stunning $4 million salary for three weeks of work in an essentially supporting role, as well as 15 percent of the gross. "It was flattering because I was offered the highest salary paid to any actor—male or female—at the time," Streisand explains. "It wasn't the money. I just needed to get out of my house, and be around people and function as an actress and have someone tell me what to do. I just needed to get away from writing *Yentl* in this tunnel. It was lonely."

As word seeped out that Streisand was replacing Eichhorn, the press filled with accounts of the starlet's divalike behavior on the set and developing tensions with both Hackman and Tramont. The film's budget zoomed from $7 to $14 million with the addition of Streisand and her entourage, and the production shut down for three weeks to allow time for the actress to prepare and the script to be readjusted. "She behaved very professionally, there were no complaints about her at all," says Mengers. "But it was getting very dicey between Jon and me. And it was very important to Jon that the industry think Streisand would never do anything that he wasn't involved in." Indeed, the antipathy between Mengers and Peters erupted into an open feud.

Streisand, however, wasn't happy with how the film was turning out or with Mengers. "I said, 'How do you represent *me?*' " recalls the actress. " 'Because you're representing your husband, who doesn't want to rewrite it, and I'm screwed.' They promised to rewrite the second act before I committed, and then they didn't."

All Night Long fared badly in the preview process, and Universal took it away from Tramont and reedited the film to feature Streisand more prominently—to little avail. The movie would turn into one of the biggest flops of her career. In November of that year, Orion put *Yentl* into turnaround because Streisand's team had presented a budget $2 million higher than the studio was willing to spend, and because Orion was further spooked by the spectacular debacle of *Heaven's Gate*. Peters hadn't been particularly fond of the Jewish spiritual kick that *Yentl* had stirred in his girlfriend; he had even tried to bully Streisand out of making the film, reducing her to tears by yelling in front of friends, "Barbra, you have one year left before you turn into an old bag!" He now pressured Streisand to do a concert tour, while Mengers, in her blunt manner, told Streisand that she couldn't imagine how the thirty-eight-year-old actress was going to play a teenage boy as well as produce and direct a musical. It was the death knell to the fabled Streisand-Mengers alliance.

"My agent David Begelman didn't want me to do *Yentl*," Streisand says. "Sue Mengers didn't want me to do it. Jon Peters said, 'You'll never make *Yentl*.' Everybody who didn't believe in me got canned. I had to leave them. I had to prove them wrong. I had to prove to myself that I could do it. I was scared, but I had to do it anyway."

At first the actress had told Mengers that she was just going to work with an attorney, but that attorney brought her to Stan Kamen, Mengers's biggest rival at William Morris. The agent was shocked, angry, stunned. She couldn't believe how "anybody could be better than I was for her." Stories circulated of how Streisand had balked at paying the commission on *All Night Long*. Swathed in a white mink and a frosty attitude, Streisand did attend a private screening of the film hosted by Tramont and Mengers, but she didn't speak to her former friend and agent.

In April 1986, Mengers quit agenting after more than two decades. The loss of Streisand had been a watershed. It was a wound that festered, an unimaginable blow to her confidence. The magic talisman was gone. The fun had vanished. Mengers grew to hate the barbs slung at Tramont, who had his own angry streak. "When you live with someone and you begin to really appreciate them, and you see them hurt— not that people set out to hurt him, it's just the nature of the machine, the machine demands success. And if you don't have success in this particular industry, you are a nonperson. And for a man as proud as my husband, it was hard. As I became more and more aware of how difficult it was for him, some of it changed for me too." Mengers's critical yenta proclivity turned into outright negativity. Clients fled, and, when her contract was up, she fled too.

8.

PRETTY BABIES

NOW I UNDERSTAND THE WORLD WARS

It's Polly Platt's greatest fear that somehow she has betrayed her talent, that she could have been, should have been her literary counterpart: Jill Peel, director. The subject makes her testy and uncomfortable, but she can't leave it alone. She used to have dreams about the dailies of her movies—all blank screens. "I was so afraid I was nobody, that I had nothing to say. I'm not afraid of that anymore. But I still would be a little scared that it might be just pure light. It's a heavy-duty thing. It is like taking all your clothes off and walking around at a cocktail party."

After a long, intermittent romance, Platt eventually moved in with Tony Wade. They lived with his two children and her two children. Between movie stints Sashy and Antonia often went to stay with their father, Peter Bogdanovich, with whom Platt was convinced they were happier. "I felt that I robbed them of everything, their house in Bel Air, their experience of growing up with someone artistic and brilliant. Peter is a great talker. Peter's eloquent. Peter is interesting. I felt dull, and I seem not to be eloquent and interesting with my children. I wasn't any fun. When they would go there, they would really have fun."

Platt was often happier when Sashy and Antonia were away with their dad. She worked. And drank with Big Tony. The summer after the miserable experience of *A Star Is Born*, she moved to a ranch she'd bought near Tucson. She imbibed her way through seventeen cases of beer and wrote *Pretty Baby*—"drunk as a lark." One of the more controversial movies of the 1970s, it told the tale of a little girl raised in a whorehouse; the film launched the acting career of Brooke Shields.

Polly Platt and Ryan O'Neal, 1972.

Platt had been writing scripts between her stints as a production designer. David Picker, head of Paramount, the husband of her friend Nessa Hyams, read a sample and introduced her to the French director Louis Malle. Arty, sophisticated, and polished, Malle, the heir to a French sugar fortune, had consistently courted the controversial and trendy. His films included a coldhearted study of infidelity, *The Lovers* (1958), a meditation on mother-son incest in *Murmur of the Heart* (1971), and an exploration of French wartime collaboration in *Lacombe, Lucien* (1974). Malle wanted to make his American debut a film about wetbacks—Mexican illegal aliens—coming across the border.

Platt was aghast. She had no interest in that topic and thought it was arrogant for Malle to begin his Hollywood career wagging his European finger at America. She asked the director what he actually knew about America, as opposed to what he thought he knew. It turned out that Malle knew a great deal about New Orleans—its jazz, its long history of bordellos—and he was particularly fascinated by prostitution.

Platt was nonplussed. She'd never even met a prostitute, she told Malle. "I wouldn't even know what to write about that. All I can think of is a really bad cliché," she kept saying.

She then remembered a location scout for *The Last Picture Show* in which she had wandered through a Mexican brothel in the daytime. She thought of her own daughter, Antonia, age nine, and how little children care about what their parents do for a living. "Whether you're a prostitute or a famous production designer, or a good writer, or a famous producer, or a famous director, they don't care. They just have their needs." She realized she could write the movie from the point of view of a child, with prostitution a parallel for "the work I did, which is something that appears to be dirty and sick and that most people don't do." An image popped into her head of what would turn into the opening sequence of the film—a child being allowed to watch the birth of a baby, then running down the hallway as the viewer realizes the child is in a whorehouse.

"Mainly what fascinated me about child prostitution is that it is as old as patriarchy," Malle later told *The New York Times*. "That tells you something about our society: The male power structure can make its fantasies come true. You don't see male whorehouses for women. The very idea is shocking. It's a very strong fantasy, and related to the fantasy of incest—and of rape."

In the spring of 1976, Platt and Malle pored over a book by E. J. Bel-locq, who had photographed prostitutes in New Orleans at the begin-ning of the century. At first Platt was delighted to be collaborating with Malle. Her French was excellent, a product of her days as an Army brat. Malle was fluent in English and open and supportive. They devised the story of a girl raised in a whorehouse who at the age of twelve is hoisted atop a silver platter to be sold to the highest bidder. An enigmatic and repressed photographer—a Bellocq stand-in—photographs the prosti-tutes of Storyville and falls disastrously in love with the child-whore.

"Louis and I communicated with lots of wine and lots of cheese and we really worked and he was brilliant," recalls Platt. "I really thought we understood each other. And then we started making the movie, and I said, 'Now I understand world wars.' "

Their rift came over the casting of Bellocq. The studio was having difficulty finding the right actor, and her old friend and studio president David Picker called Platt to ask who she envisioned. She deliberated for a moment—"Well, Nicholson."

Platt knew Jack Nicholson from the days when they all had offices at BBS, the swinging production company that had financed *The Last Picture Show* as well as Nicholson's *Easy Rider* and *Five Easy Pieces.* Picker told her to give the script to Nicholson. In a serious breach of eti-quette, she called Nicholson directly and drove the script to his house on Mulholland that very afternoon; she did not bother to tell Malle what she had done, although giving a script to a star of that magnitude usually constituted an offer.

Platt and Malle went off to cast in New Orleans, Houston, and Dal-las, where she finally got a call from Picker. Nicholson wanted to do the movie. "I went running in to Louis, and said, 'Look at this. Isn't this great?' I was fairly naive. It was the first picture I had written on my own. If it had been Peter, I never would have consulted him. I consid-ered the picture to be mine as much as Louis's.

"Louis was infuriated. He refused to even entertain the notion of Jack being in the film, and accused me of trying to take over the picture. It was like an ABC lesson in politics," says Platt. Not surprisingly, Malle insisted on doing the casting himself, and Platt was enraged that the di-rector was sacrificing—in her view—what was best for the picture to preserve his ego. "I ultimately loathed what happened. I can't forgive Louis. But the picture comes first."

Malle chose Keith Carradine for Bellocq. "A man of good looks. A man tall and thin. The way Keith eventually played it, the character was almost effete and nonsexual," says Platt. To her, Bellocq truly loved the women he photographed. "I can remember saying to Louis, 'I think Bellocq is like a director. A director who wanted to sleep with everyone—man, woman, and child. Who had a visceral interest in everything, but who abstained, either because he was unable, or because they found him repulsive in that role.' "

Platt thought Malle wrongly shifted the focus of the film from the photographer to the prostitutes: "My point was that prostitution is not just a way of life that demeans and destroys women. It also destroys men who are looking for love."

Despite her simmering fury at Malle, Platt remained fiercely committed to the picture. Picker left the studio, and the new regime—headed by Michael Eisner—contemplated canceling the project, saying it was too expensive. Platt swung into battle. "I don't know how I had the courage to do this, but I went to see Eisner and I said, 'Michael, are you telling me that when you open the big vault at the bank that has Paramount's money in it, there's no money in there? Are you telling me there's dust?' And he laughed really hard and he said, 'You deserve an answer.' And we had a go in twenty-four hours."

Bogdanovich refused to take the children while Platt went to New Orleans to shoot the movie, so they remained behind with the housekeeper, except for a few visits, when Antonia got to be Shields's stand-in. It had hurt Platt's feelings that Wade wasn't more enthusiastic about the script; nonetheless he came along as production manager.

"It was kind of a nightmarish shoot," recalls Susan Sarandon. "It was plagued by accidents, death. The parts weren't of great complexity, and Louis doesn't really talk to actors. At least he didn't when I was working with him. I kind of did all the talking to the actors." Much of the controversy swirled around twelve-year-old Shields, who was being subjected not only to her first nude scenes but to her mother's overweening ambition. The competition between Antonia and Polly, which had given birth to the movie's conflicted mother-daughter relationship, found a counterpart in the relationship between Shields and her mother, Teri. A failed actress, "the mother was relegated too soon to the background, and she had this beautiful daughter. Brooke couldn't cope with it and neither could the mother," recalls Platt.

A particularly virulent *New York* magazine article detailed Teri Shields's determined sale of her daughter to the movies and magazines. It probed whether the two nude scenes—one shot with Brooke in a body stocking, the other with only Malle and cinematographer Sven Nykvist present—were destroying young Brooke's psyche.

Platt adamantly told the magazine, "There was a lot of nonsense about the nudity being traumatic for Brooke. That was silly. She'd posed nude before. There's even a book containing nude photos of her. Some of the other girls got to her and told her she shouldn't do it. I was more worried about Brooke's family problems than about the sex scenes. Her mother is supposed to be looking after Brooke, but she's just living vicariously through her. That's the real tragedy."

When Teri Shields was arrested for drunk driving and thrown into jail, Platt made the decision to leave her there, explaining to Brooke— and *New York*—that this was the best way to deal with a woman with a drinking problem, that it was "in Teri's own interest. She has to realize what she's doing. She's a sick woman." Soon after, Teri was banned from the set for several weeks.

The movie debuted in April 1978 to mixed reviews and bitter denouncements from both the right wing and feminists who called it, in the words of one critic, "the biggest boost child pornography has ever had in the country." It was banned throughout Canada. Yet it opened the prestigious Cannes Film Festival and received applause from critics like Penelope Gilliatt, who championed its fey, lyrical quality, writing in *The New Yorker* that "this may be a film set in a brothel, but it is not more lewd than a Bonnard of a naked woman in a bath. . . . [Malle] has made a bordello picture without a single, naked sex scene in it."

Indeed, what Gilliatt celebrated was probably the movie's greatest flaw. Malle's restraint toward his subject bathed prostitution in a rosy, nonjudgmental, and profoundly lifeless glow. His Bellocq was effete. "In leaving out the shame and degradation of prostitution, Malle gives us a view that is close to the traditional fantasy of the colorful, uninhibited natives who exist as a reproach to uptight, churchgoing community," wrote Molly Haskell. "But freed from shame, they are also denied its corollary—spiritual aspiration."

After it was made, Platt couldn't bear to watch the movie. She veered between rage at Malle's artistic betrayal and the overwhelming feeling that she herself had failed the director "in ways you can't remember."

I HAD, UNBEKNOWNST TO MYSELF, A VERY COMPLICATED SEXUALITY

Taxi Driver defined Jodie Foster's idiosyncratic iconography. Many of her subsequent films elaborated on an image of her as a parentless child, adrift in a strange adult world. She almost always played sexualized children. She disconnected when the emotions got tricky and powered her way through on sheer acting technique. In later years, she referred to herself as an acting "technician."

A number of her films originated with the circle of talent that surrounded Harry Ufland, Scorsese's and De Niro's irascible, opinionated agent, who had a well-defined taste for cutting-edge art. After *Taxi Driver*, Foster had joined his high-testosterone brood, which also included a number of promising young British directors who honed their craft on advertising: Tony and Ridley Scott and Adrian Lyne, all of whom would go on to major careers. Jodie and Brandy Foster haunted Ufland's Malibu parties; Foster was his only child client, practically his only female client.

After *Taxi Driver* she was cast as a gangster's moll in Alan Parker's debut film, *Bugsy Malone*, a Capone-era romp in which all the adult parts are played by children who shoot one another with whipped cream and pies. Whereas Iris was distinguished by Foster's lack of organic sexuality, the moll Tallulah oozes and inspires lust in sharp contrast to the other actors' fresh-faced innocence. Parker told her to give him a combination of Mae West and Marilyn Monroe. Her big moment comes when she slinks and sings to a nightclub audience, although, to Foster's dismay, her singing voice was dubbed by the composer Paul Williams's girlfriend.

"She didn't quite understand the vampiness of that girl," recalls Brandy Foster. "We just kind of talked about that. I remember we were in a hotel, and I got up on a bed and showed her how to walk on a stage."

In retrospect, Foster insists the part wasn't even sexual per se: "There's Tallulah walking into a room, completely confident, throwing open a door, and laying a lip lock on [a costar]. We look at that and say it must be sexual, but in fact it's just being confident. I certainly don't look back on it as having a tremendous amount of sexuality, but then again, people are who they are.

"I think that even as a child, I had, unbeknownst to myself, completely unconsciously, a very complicated sexuality that I didn't have anything to do with, that was nothing about *me*," she says. "It's just who I am. It wasn't like 'Little Molly, she certainly flirts with those grown-ups.' It was something else."

Indeed, Foster seemed more comfortable with the tomboyish antics she enjoyed with male costars, wrestling with thirteen-year-old Scott Baio or karate-chopping John Cassisi, who played Fat Sam, when he dared to call her a dumb blonde.

All the girls on the movie were in love with the teenage heartthrob Scott Baio. "I made out with him the last two days," says Foster. "He didn't care about me. He never cared about me. It wasn't a bad crush. And then he would talk about all the other girls he made out with on the movie too. And that was okay. I was like twelve. I didn't mind."

For the first time Foster was treated like a true star on the set, given her own dressing room while the two hundred other children had to share two mass dressing stages. Foster could be snide about her peers' lack of technique, openly laughing or making snarky remarks when they forgot their lines. The British children repaid her by turning the fire hoses on her, a mortifying lesson in humility that she quickly absorbed.

Alternately charming and bizarre, *Bugsy Malone* was, ultimately, a hit.

Through Ufland, Foster also met Nicolas Gessner, a young Swiss director who cast her in the creepy *The Little Girl Who Lives Down the Lane*, about a mysteriously self-assured, androgynous barely teenager who lives in a rented home with a father no one has ever seen. She has an affair with a boy and fends off—to the death—the advances of a child molester.

"I remember when I first met her, she's sitting there on that chair, this twelve-year-old girl like Charles Bronson with this kind of—concentrated energy," recalls Gessner, who had just done a movie with Bronson. The director marveled at her naturalness, except when "she was confronted with situations which she had never lived through herself. Then she would change gear into kind of expressive blankness. If she didn't have the color, then automatically or consciously, she would choose not to convey any color, to protect herself from getting a false color. And I thought that was extremely clever self-protection. Seeing or knowing that she wasn't up to something, because she had not witnessed it, or she had not grown up enough.

"She always made a point of speaking fast. She had noticed that what made child actress[es] seem false and phony was that they were speaking slowly. Howard Hawks made actresses speak always fast, you know. And in a way, that's what Jodie also accomplished without Howard Hawks."

In a rare display of pique, the twelve-year-old Foster stalked off the set after the producer demanded she be more sexy in a scene and replaced her with a stand-in (her twenty-one-year-old sister!) when she refused. "It was the straw that broke the camel's back," she said at the time. "In the first place, this crazy producer kept saying he wanted me to pull my dress lower. I decided he was nuts. I used to tell him to shut up. Finally one day he said, 'We have to have sex and violence or the picture won't sell.' So I said, 'Well I'm not going to get into that.'

"A couple of weeks later I was told they were doing the scene and I wasn't in it. I talked to the producer and got emotional and started to cry because, well, I'm young and so I cry. And I walked off."

Despite their unconventional choices of parts, Brandy and Jodie Foster made sure that Jodie did not live on art alone. They cannily alternated her provocative films with a pair of Disney movies, *Candleshoe*, in which she again played an orphan, and *Freaky Friday*, one of the few films in which Foster actually has parents (her character learns civility by switching bodies with her mother for a day, a scenario rife with Freudian undertones).

By her early teens Foster had developed a seemingly artless rap, which she trotted out for a growing pack of breathless journalists, who depicted her as a fey, adorable oddity, a child with brains. Foster read all her press avidly and performed with aplomb, as a kind of mini-Brandy. She could be breezily arrogant. She was alternately businesslike and blasé about her Oscar chances: "I hate to sound like a businessperson, but if I did get an award, that would mean I could make more money because the awards are really a way to get your price higher," followed up by, "An Oscar is great, but it won't get me to the beach on a Sunday morning. I'd rather have a car of my own."

She was publicly dismissive about the traps of womanhood, boasting to journalists about her inexpensive clothes and appearing almost everywhere in a flat tweed cap. She said she didn't like boys and probably wouldn't have kids.

She was already cynical about the roles she could expect as a grown-up: "It seems to be women have to cry in every role, and if they cry well enough, they get an Oscar for it."

YOU'RE A FACE AND A BODY AND GESTURES, THAT'S ALL YOU ARE

Privately, Foster was not so confident about her looks, her career, or her ambitions.

When she was fourteen, Dino De Laurentiis had tracked her down at a sleepover birthday party at a friend's house. Like a number of producers, he wanted to circumvent Ufland, who was full of his own opinions. He convinced Foster to come in for an interview by herself. Much later she learned that he was casting *Blue Lagoon*, the romanticized tale of two youngsters who grow up alone on a desert island.

Once she was in his office, De Laurentiis asked her to take off her jacket and turn around. He made a crack about her figure. "It felt pretty bad, yeah," recalls Foster. "But in the grand scheme of things, it probably wasn't that bad, but maybe when you're fourteen . . .

"I realized immediately that I wasn't a kid anymore in a weird way," she says. "I knew how bad I felt, and I knew that somehow I had failed. I felt differently as an actor. I definitely felt that there was something that I was supposed to be externally, and that I was probably not going to be able to be it. The pressure of that, I think, was a little upsetting. When you're young you don't think about it. You just internalize things."

The part eventually went to Brooke Shields.

When Foster later told Ufland about the meeting with De Laurentiis, he was furious. Her mother tried to soften the blow: "I have to give her credit for saying, 'You're going to be a great actor, you're not going to be Marilyn Monroe, and who wants to be Marilyn Monroe anyway?' " recalls Foster. " 'You're not a model. You're an actress, and you should be proud of that, and someday they'll realize that you are a great dramatic actress, and you shouldn't forget that. You don't have to be somebody else's fantasy of who you are.' She's really a great talker, I have to say. If anything, she drives you crazy because she wants to talk about it all."

In later years Foster reconciled herself to what had happened: "He had every right in the world to do that. I mean, that's what an actor [is]—you're a commodity. You're a face and a body and gestures, that's all you are, and a voice. It's a really hard road, but you have to make peace with that."

But nonetheless, she developed an eating disorder. She was asked to lose weight for *Foxes*, and she kept going, weighing only eighty-nine pounds by the time she did *Carny*. She ate a lot of cottage cheese and played mind-and-body-numbing games of tennis.

For all of Brandy's self-empowerment lectures, she could send mixed messages. When Scorsese was casting *Raging Bull*, Brandy was adamant that Jodie be auditioned for the part of Jake La Motta's love interest—later played by Cathy Moriarty—although it was clear she was too young. Brandy arranged for a series of photographs to be taken that highlighted Jodie's sexual allure—photos that years later ended up in a skin magazine. Colleagues of Jodie's would hear Brandy make cracks about her weight.

At times, Foster seemed like Lewis Carroll's Alice wandering through a surreal wonderland of late-seventies pop culture. She chitchatted with Andy Warhol ("She and her mother are a team. It's like a marriage," he noted; "Jodie's the father") and appeared on *Saturday Night Live* during its heyday. "It's a horrible memory," she says. "They didn't know how to write for me. I was only fourteen years old. They'd write me like I was really young and they'd put me on somebody's knee and bounce me around and they would think that was funny and it wasn't.

"At the time, I was just so overconcerned about my appearance. I just had pimples and I was really fat and I was just so weird about what I was supposed to wear. I was drinking an Orange Julius right before I went on. I spilled it all over everything and I had to go on with my pants wet and I was completely humiliated. I don't think anyone noticed, but it left a horrible taste in my mouth. I get really anxious about something being bad. If it doesn't work, I feel horrible."

As Foster progressed into her teens, she and her mother spent increasing amounts of time in Paris because Brandy was infatuated with France, although she never learned to speak French proficiently. Foster bought them an apartment and navigated nearly all practical matters. She made a forgettable film there, and another in Italy.

Just before she went off to college, Foster made two pictures that dealt explicitly with her adolescence. Neither was a cute exploration of childish high jinks topped off by the loss of virginity, as was the case in films made by her ostensibly hotter peers, Brooke Shields and Tatum O'Neal.

IT'S LIKE LOOKING AT YOUR
HIGH SCHOOL YEARBOOK

Foxes, which debuted in 1980, was written by Gerald Ayres about his daughter and her friends. It's a gritty look at the tight bonds among a group of tough adolescent girls, largely neglected by their selfish and neurotic parents. They try drugs and dabble in essentially unfulfilling sex. Foster plays the self-sufficient ringleader, Sally Kellerman her dopey, occasionally well-meaning mother.

Foxes was the directorial debut of one of Harry Ufland's clients, Adrian Lyne, who later went on to great success with Flashdance and Fatal Attraction, although Foxes lacked what would become his trademark: jet-speed montages of twirling limbs and throbbing sexual tension, all to a disco beat. This time he worked under the aegis of the legendary British producer David Puttnam (whose previous film was Midnight Express). Lyne had promised Ufland to put more heft into the script before production started, a promise he couldn't keep. Even the young actresses perceived that the director was at times in over his head—spending sixty takes on shots "of a guy zipping his zipper," one recounts, laughing. Whenever Lyne fell behind, Puttnam simply cut pages out of the script as needed.

In a kind of search for authenticity, Lyne pressed the girls to improvise their ad-libs, which later constituted whole scenes. He also refused to let them wear makeup in most scenes and instructed Foster, who turned sixteen on the set, not to lose any more weight. "I look at myself and cringe," says Foster, who likes the movie. "I looked like a little kid, and I was all round. I had pimples on my forehead, and it's like looking at your high school yearbook or something."

"It was a very male atmosphere," recalls Kandice Stroh, who played one of the girls. "The guys said inappropriate things. The attitude was to keep the girls in their place. We were young enough to be intimidated."

Of course, Foster wasn't treated this way. In fact, several of the players believed that Lyne was overwhelmed by his Oscar-nominated charge.

By the time the film was ready for release, the studio had trepidations. The marketing department promptly changed the tag line—which had been in place since the start of production—"Sweet 16 and Never Been Kids," to "Daring to Do It," which served only to confuse the film with a concurrent release, *Little Darlings*, starring Kristy McNichol and Tatum O'Neal.

The reviews were mediocre, with critics questioning the ethics of using child actors in movies with nebulous morals. Foster spoke in defense of the movie: "These kids are really victims, not bad guys. If people see this movie and say we're lousy kids smoking grass and freaking out, they'll be missing the point. The movie's about what an obstacle course it can be to reach twenty-one in one piece."

PEOPLE DON'T GO TO SEE
PICTURES ABOUT GIRLS

The other film that Foster made before heading off to college was *Carny*, about the carnival folk who travel around small-town America. Based on more than forty hours of videotape made by the documentarian Bob Kaylor, the script arrived at Harry Ufland's via the legendary film critic Pauline Kael. Foster and another Ufland client, Harvey Keitel, both agreed to star when and if the money came through.

Years passed. The rocker Robbie Robertson was looking to get into the film business, and Ufland was looking to represent him, so the writer Thomas Baum revamped the script to be more of a rock-and-roll picture than a fake documentary. Foster remained attached.

Although Ufland had stressed, "Just treat her natural," Baum was shocked when he finally met Foster. "It was like she was sent from Venus to be president of the United States," says the writer. "I just thought she was extraordinary, and she would come to the meetings at Lorimar [from] Lycée Français, with a blue outfit, and she was just focused."

Foster was to play Donna, a teenager who runs away from home and joins the carnival. Gary Busey, hot off an Academy Award nomination for *The Buddy Holly Story*, and Robertson were to play two friends who happen also to be Foster's love interests. Before filming even started, the size of Foster's part began to look problematic to some involved.

"Before the read-through, there was a meeting with Gary and Robbie, and Gary said, 'You know, this is a good part for Jodie,' " recalls Baum. "He said, 'I'm not sure it isn't the best part in the book.' And they sort of tried to ease her out of the picture. The picture was really hers. The story's of a girl who runs away in a carnival, and ends up being a carny. The guys were fixed elements in her trip. And they were trying to kind of take it away. Robbie would say things like, 'People don't go to see pictures about girls. They go to see pictures about guys.' "

More pressure was put on Foster's part by the rapidly developing closeness between Robertson and Busey, who were sharing a mansion on location in Savannah. The pair would stay up late improvising new material, which they would then summon Baum to fix for them in the morning. "Some of it was great. Some of it sucked. Then Gary would be different on every take," recalls Baum. Busey's performance varied depending on which mind-altering substance he was ingesting at the moment. "They were improvising all the time, and Jodie is a crackerjack improviser—but still these guys were sort of bullying," adds Baum. Foster was one of the only people on the set who didn't ask Baum to rewrite the script for her. Everything was compounded by the weakness of the director, who on one notorious occasion retreated in disgust to his trailer while nine people stood around discussing what should be shot next.

"I just had never seen people like that," says Foster. "And there was an awful lot of downtime, because there was a lot of waiting for people to come out of the trailer. That was definitely one of my harder films. But, you know, I was really busy doing my SAT's, and all I really wanted was a car. I made a lot of films with a lot of weird people, and I just kind of said, Well, in two months it will be over, and I'm just not going to let it get to me. I was much more involved in playing tennis than I was in that film.

"Someday I would love to remake that movie the way it was about the things that it was about," she says in retrospect, "which was frankly about a quasi-latent homosexual relationship between these two men. The girl of course is incidental. She is symbolic in some ways and used as a prop, and then takes her revenge, because it wasn't about her, and she sort of asserts herself by saying, 'You have to look at me and admit that I'm here, and that I'm a part of this group or a part of this family. I'm not just a way for you to get back at each other.' For me movies are about relationships, and those three people were a really interesting relationship, and it got sidetracked."

As ever, the cast and crew gossiped about Foster. "People used to say, at that time, 'Jodie needs a boyfriend,' " recalls Baum.

"Everyone wanted to sleep with her, both men and women," Robertson remarked later, although in the filming of the seduction scene between their characters, Foster was nervous. "I have no idea what I'm doing," she told Robertson. "Just pretend we're dancing and I'll follow you."

During shooting Jodie lived in a house with Brandy, who spent the whole shoot doing her de rigueur hovering. "I actually was close with her mother," says Baum. "Brandy was a force of nature, and flirtatious. She was a Muslim. Brandy wore the equivalent to the Star of David— the Muslim Star of David—around her neck. And she would pass out books of the Koran. I remember sitting in the bar of the Master Host Inn, which was where the whole company stayed, and she was being real friendly and saying, 'Gee, you know, Islam is the best religion, but Jews make the best husbands, right?' But she was cute." (Brandy later gave an interview in *Interview* declaring her newfound belief in Islam and her intention to go on a pilgrimage to Mecca—particularly controversial given the ongoing hostage crisis in Iran and the anti-Arab sentiment that was rampant in the United States.)

But as the shoot progressed most of Brandy's concern focused on a young stalker. "He showed up and started writing letters to [Jodie] and then he tried to get on the set as an extra," recalls the producer Jonathan Taplin. "They had to throw him out. Her mother was freaking out about the whole thing. I mean, he was just obsessed."

Brandy Foster forwarded the letters to the police, who arrested the stalker. "It's funny, her mother was more freaked out than Jodie was," says Taplin. "At least, she didn't show it, you know. She did not demonstrate fear or whatever."

"I don't overreact. I don't get upset. I'm kind of WASPy that way," says Foster. "It's not easy for me to have emotional reactions or big fearful reactions. I tend to get very cool and collected and calm."

Dan Melnick with Sherry Lansing at a
Hollywood premiere, mid-1970s.

9.

___

D-GIRLS ON THE RISE

WAS IT MY FAULT?

"Was it my fault?" she asked again and again, tossing and turning in her hospital bed, her once-beautiful face swathed in bandages, her leg encased in plaster. Sherry Lansing was disoriented and confused when she awoke from sleep following a long operation, done without anesthesia because her mother had mistakenly believed that she was allergic to it. She peered up at the friendly faces surrounding her—Dan Melnick, Gloria Stern, and Myra Silverman. Melnick explained that she had been hit by a car going forty miles an hour as she crossed Wilshire Boulevard. All Lansing could think was maybe she had done something wrong. "Was it my fault?" she couldn't stop saying as they tried to soothe her. "Will I have scars?"

In truth, the doctors wondered if she'd ever walk again, at least without a limp. She had been with James Aubrey—the infamous Jungle Jim, the former head of CBS and MGM, thirty years her senior and one of the most reviled men in town. For seven years they had dated off and on. As a crowd of fifty hovered outside the young movie executive's hospital room, Aubrey lay down the hall, alone and barely visited, until he yanked his IV to go see Lansing. Weeks later she was released. The doctors had decided that she wasn't going to be crippled but that she would have to spend almost eighteen months in a twenty-pound cast with pins in it. Her first day out of the hospital, she went on crutches to the set of *The China Syndrome*, starring Jane Fonda and Michael Douglas. Part of her head was shaved, and she was racked with pain, as she would be for months. But she was back.

The China Syndrome, a controversial thriller about a near melt-down in a nuclear power plant, was one of Lansing's first projects as vice president of production at Columbia, where she had followed her mentor Melnick in November 1977. The studio was in total disarray because the studio president, David Begelman, the man responsible for such hits as *Shampoo* and *Tommy*, had been caught embezzling. For months the indecisive company CEO, Alan Hirschfield, had been warring with Herbert Allen and Ray Stark, respectively the studio's most powerful stockholder and producer, about what to do with Begelman. Melnick became acting president of production.

On her first day of work, Lansing vowed to keep herself out of the cross fire. She went to a script meeting on *The China Syndrome* with the director, James Bridges (for whom she once auditioned as an actress), and the producer Michael Douglas at Melnick's house. None of the film-makers was happy to see her. Douglas would later boast how his first appraisal of Lansing was frankly sexual. "Every possible chauvinistic thought went through my mind," he says, recalling that he watched Lansing light a Sherman's black cigarette. Melnick even took Douglas aside to assure him of Lansing's qualifications and to stress that he himself was only a phone call away. Bruce Gilbert, Jane Fonda's producing partner, feared that Lansing, with her much-touted ties to Melnick, was simply designated to be the studio hatchet woman. Besides, Lansing knew very little about atomic energy.

Lansing quickly assuaged Douglas's and Gilbert's concerns about her, playing less the authority figure than the supportive, intelligent buddy. "She doesn't talk about herself much, you know," says Douglas, "She would always focus her attention on you." Bridges's diaries of the film include myriad mentions of Lansing's suggestions and advice. "Her most obvious contributions were on script and story. She's a great logician. She has an ability to reduce everything to the lowest common denominator," says Douglas, who found that Lansing didn't use her sexual wiles. "Beyond that, in this egotistical world we live in, she was the mother figure, and she would neutralize a lot of male posturing that might go on."

It was also during her Columbia years that the legend began: Lansing returned every single phone call every single day. She was compulsive, even when the calls grew to as many as two hundred a day. If she couldn't reach someone on the phone, she'd send a note. She worked frantically, reading two to three scripts a night, after an evening of networking, and ten to eleven scripts on the weekend. It was also during these years that she firmly established herself as the lone female in a gaggle of powerful men. "It was mostly guys hanging out, plus Sherry," recalls Dick Shepherd, her former MGM boss, of a time in the mid-seventies when he'd regularly eat dinner with Melnick, Stanley Jaffe, and Lansing.

After her accident, Lansing moved into Myra Silverman's pool cabana because she couldn't climb stairs and Silverman could offer the full-time care she needed. Every day Aubrey had his son drive him over to visit. It would take her a half hour to walk up the driveway, and her former boyfriend hounded her about doing her exercises. "He was like, 'You're not going to have a limp. You're not going to have a limp,' " says Lansing.

"He was a very misunderstood person," insists Lansing, who pooh-poohs all the gossip of sexual escapades that circled Aubrey. (But her husband offers, "The rumor about him that I had heard was that he kept whips and chains in his desk and all kinds of bondage stuff in his office.") She romanticized Aubrey as like Howard Roark, out of Ayn Rand's *The Fountainhead.* While Lansing cared too much what people thought of her, Aubrey seemed not to care at all. "Jim was like a father. He was *God.* And any time I would, like, stray, he'd look at me and go, 'You're full of it now, you know.' [He'd] just keep you clean. He had a trait that I most admire in a person, and I don't have it enough. He was self-contained. They don't worry about anybody else's space, and they just concentrate on what they want," says Lansing.

Ironically, Lansing found the six months she spent recuperating one of the happiest times of her life. She was encircled with support and relieved that she had survived the bad thing she had always worried would happen to her. "When I was a kid I always thought there was good and bad in the world, and I would read these terrible things that happened to people. And I'd think, When is one of those terrible things going to happen to me?" recalls Lansing. "This is sick, and I don't think this way anymore, but it has taken me a long time not to think this way."

When she went back to work full-time, Melnick gave her his ground-floor office, which he had kept when he became head of production, as a refuge for himself.

The China Syndrome opened in New York on March 15, 1979, to rave reviews and big crowds. There were political dissenters who believed the scenario presented in the film was far-fetched. George Will of *Newsweek* declared, "The film falsely suggests that nuclear-power companies carelessly risk destroying their billion-dollar investments."

On March 28 an accident occurred at a nuclear power plant on Three Mile Island, near Harrisburg, Pennsylvania, that uncannily mirrored the reactor breakdown in *The China Syndrome*, turning the film into not only a cultural phenomenon but a box-office hit. Columbia later took the movie to the Cannes Film Festival. "Incredible reactions. Standing ovation," wrote James Bridges in his journal. "Front rows of balcony reserved for filmmakers. Everybody pushing to sit there. Sherry didn't care. Sat in back."

The *China Syndrome* would become a kind of template for the movies Sherry Lansing would like to make, mainstream adult fare, usually with a strong female character, that posed and resolved a moral question. Most tapped into female rage, although, as in the women's films of the 1940s, that rage was often subdued either externally or internally by the end of the picture. In *The China Syndrome* Fonda's anger results in enlightenment, increased activism, and ultimately triumph; in *Kramer vs. Kramer*, Lansing's other big success at Columbia, Joanna Kramer's anger results in self-abnegation.

Kramer vs. Kramer is the tale of the workaholic schmo Dustin Hoffman, who ignores his beautiful wife, played by Meryl Streep, and his young son. Finally she has a *Feminine Mystique* moment and walks out on the marriage to find herself, leaving Hoffman to struggle with raising his child and keeping his job. *Kramer* won Oscars for Best Picture, Best Actor, and Best Supporting Actress, as well as recriminations from women who found the whole idea misogynistic: the only screen character who explained the plight of the working woman happened to be played by a man.

Kramer vs. Kramer was the most successful of a slew of male-parenting movies that began appearing as both an expiation of the guilt Hollywood's male elite had toward their children, whom they often ignored, and a backlash against the women's movement and working women. These films showing women who were unfit for mothering included the Oscar-winning *Ordinary People*, in which an emotionally barren Mary Tyler Moore cannot cope with her surviving son in the wake of her favored son's death, *The Champ, Author! Author!*, and *Mr. Mom*.

Lansing had bid on *Kramer* when she was at MGM but had lost the rights to the young producer Stanley Jaffe, who set it up at Columbia. Melnick assigned it to her when she arrived at that studio, and her influence on the movie was at once diffuse, given the increasingly bureaucratized nature of the studio, and distinctly present. The film's director, Robert Benton, explained: "You're a writer. You know what it takes to write something, and then rewrite and rewrite. After sixteen drafts I was exhausted, ready to quit. That's when Sherry's enthusiasm and creative energy and support came in. She helped me go on to the seventeenth, eighteenth. . . ."

Lansing spent hours talking to Jaffe and Benton, in particular about fleshing out Joanna Kramer, to whom she could relate: "She had always been somebody's wife, somebody's mother. She never had her own identity, and you can see [my point of view] would come right out of analysis."

"She was the person closest to the picture," recalls Jaffe of Lansing. "She was the person who came into the cut and worked a couple of days in New York, gave us her notes, and was really diligent about her responsibilities on the picture."

Jaffe and Lansing bonded during the making of *Kramer.* He was the abrasive scion of Leo Jaffe, the onetime head of Columbia Pictures. Pugnacious and bald, as well as fiercely determined not to bow and scrape to anyone, Jaffe had produced *Goodbye Columbus* at the age of twenty-nine. At thirty, he had become the head of production at Paramount. At the time he bragged to a reporter, "If you're that age and someone like Charlie Bluhdorn hands you a half-billion-dollar corporation that is not feeling well and says, 'You be the doctor,' you bet you get a little cocky." He next headed production at his father's studio, Columbia, before becoming an independent producer. Like Lansing, he had lost a parent at the age of eight, although in Jaffe's case it was his mother. The theme of abandonment runs through many of the movies the pair worked on together, starting with *Kramer vs. Kramer.* They also share a birthday.

The two had met several years earlier at a dinner party held by the columnist Joyce Haber. "I don't know who brought me there, but Stanley was at that end of the table, and I was at this end, and [one of the guests] said, 'There is this math puzzle, I can't figure it out from *The New York Times*,' and he said it, and then everybody went 'uh.' Kirk Douglas was sitting next to me, funnily enough," recalls Lansing. "And I said, 'No, no, if you do this,' and Stanley said, 'And then you do that.' And we solved it together. We started talking, and he never asked me out. He never made a pass at me. We started talking." Jaffe says, "I like blondes. She wasn't a blonde."

"It really was instant," adds Jaffe. "I mean, if it were instant in another way we would have been in bed together that night." Unlike her relationships with Ray Wagner and Dan Melnick, Lansing's bond with Jaffe was always strictly platonic. He was less her father than her brother.

"There was a center, there was intelligence, there was obviously a beauty, and I'm not blind, I find it very attractive," recalls Jaffe. "And she was in a quasi-relationship with somebody I knew, so we got to see each other a little more."

PEOPLE WHO JUST BRUISE MORE EASILY

The woman who truly prevented *Kramer vs. Kramer* from turning into a simple woman-bashing soap opera was Meryl Streep. The blond-haired actress with the aristocratic cheekbones, off-kilter nose, and cerulean eyes played the wife who left as being so certain in her self-loathing that no one would miss her when she was gone. This veritable unknown had come in to read for a small part as a woman who has an affair with Hoffman, but she had so impressed Benton and Jaffe that they decided to forgo Kate Jackson for the part of Hoffman's wife.

This was but the latest stop on the ingenue's already charmed career. The oldest daughter of an advertising executive and a freelance illustrator, she had attended Vassar, where she became enamored of acting when she was cast as the heroine who discovers the power of her own sexuality in Strindberg's *Miss Julie*. Streep went on to Yale Drama School, where she developed an incipient ulcer because she was so disturbed by her ability to win the best parts at the expense of all the other students.

Her first movie role was as a snotty socialite in *Julia*. The casting director Juliet Taylor had spotted Streep on Broadway and had her flown to England to meet the film's director, Fred Zinnemann.

"A few weeks later he called and said that 'Vanessa Redgrave was going to do the part, but would I accept a smaller role?' " says Streep. "And I said, 'Well, you know, I'll check my book,' and took that role, and it was a great part, but it was cut." She laughs. "And the part that was left in took words that I was saying in another scene and put them in my mouth, and it was so disconcerting. It was a real introduction to what they do in movies as opposed to the control that you can have over your performance on the stage, which was new to me."

Jane Fonda was particularly enthusiastic about Streep. "She would encourage me to improvise in front of the camera," recalls Streep. "I'm sure all the British people that were shooting the movie were appalled, but I was going on and on, and I was just out of the Yale cabaret, and loved that kind of improvisation, being a real asshole. She was laughing till tears came of out her eyes. Then she would tell me, 'Now when you're standing over here, step over in the light because that's where they'll see you,' and stuff like that. But she was great to me. And when she got back to California, she told people about me. So I got other work probably because of it."

Ironically, Streep's next big part was in *The Deer Hunter*, a Vietnam epic whose God-and-country politics Fonda hated so much that she railed at its director, Michael Cimino, backstage at the 1979 Academy Awards. She was clutching her own Best Actress Oscar for *Coming Home*, her liberal Vietnam story about an Army wife's transformative love affair with a Vietnam vet.

By contrast, Streep's part as the forgotten fiancée of the soldier-gone-AWOL Christopher Walken was barely written into *The Deer Hunter* when filming started. The movie is an exploration of male comradeship among a group of steelworkers, from their hunting rituals in Pennsylvania to their descent into the hell of Vietnam. Robert De Niro had seen Streep in a Lincoln Center production of *The Cherry Orchard* and urged Cimino to hire her. De Niro also knew Streep through John Cazale, her boyfriend, who had played Fredo in *The Godfather*. Cazale was dying of stomach cancer, and De Niro had put up his salary against the insurance needed for Cazale to work in *The Deer Hunter*.

Streep played her most poignant scenes with De Niro. She seduces him, her missing husband's best friend, so neither of them will have to be alone in their pain and longing. "They admitted they didn't have any idea what the girl would say in any of these situations," recalls Streep. "And I'm, like, 'Oh, my God.' Whatever I thought—would be appropriate. On the one hand, you could think of it as negligence. On the other hand, it was great artistic freedom for me because I really could make my performance."

Streep devoted nine months to caring for Cazale until he died, after which she threw herself into a torrent of work: with Alan Alda in *The Seduction of Joe Tynan*, and then *Taming of the Shrew* with Raul Julia in Central Park, Woody Allen's wife who leaves him for a lesbian in *Manhattan*, and *Kramer*, simultaneously.

Although the movie required only two weeks of work spread out over several months, Jaffe demanded that Streep forgo all her other projects to be on call for *Kramer*'s entire shoot. It was at this point that Streep switched agents, moving up from two junior women agents who had nurtured her early career to the ICM powerhouse Sam Cohn. An impassioned Streep told Jaffe, who worried that she'd be too worn out, "I won't be able to ten years from now, but I can do it now. Don't worry, I won't be too tired."

The *Kramer* set was fraught with spoken and unspoken furies, with legendary battles between Dustin Hoffman and Robert Benton. Streep felt that Hoffman was competitive with her. Indeed, her costar stewed in anger—character-inspired fury. "We fought to the point where we were really pissed-off at each other," Hoffman has said.

As in *The Deer Hunter*, Streep found that her part as written in *Kramer* was merely a plot device. "I think Bob Benton and Dustin came to the story with a very strong understanding of where the man stood. He's the wronged party of this equation. What they didn't really know or care about was what her situation was. Not that they didn't care about it, but they didn't care about it when they were committing to the project. They thought of it later. And they didn't know what she would say to defend herself or why they thought she would even have any claim to the child. So I felt very strongly why she would have a very good claim."

Streep pressed her case when it came time to shoot the courtroom custody battle. Joanna Kramer has returned and wants to reclaim her child. Streep, Hoffman, and Benton were all dissatisfied with Joanna's speech as written, so they went into separate cubbyholes in the Astoria Studios to write their own renditions of what she should say in her defense.

It was Streep's vision that made it to the final cut. To find Joanna Kramer, she had scoured the playgrounds of the Upper East Side. "I remember the stillness of those playgrounds. In those days it wasn't just the nannies that sat there. There were a lot of mothers, very dressed up, Upper East Side matrons, sitting there just with their children playing, and it just seemed that they were incarcerated in silence. They had a stillness that just seemed suffocating. Here they are with everything they ever dreamed of, but they are alone. They're not happy and they don't know why. That's from an outsider's view because at that point I was a real downtown artist. I was dealing with a hot plate and a mattress. That all seemed stultifying to me.

"Everything confounds [Joanna Kramer]. Everything that she confronts, *everything*, even the responsibility of the day with her child alone. I think mentally she couldn't achieve it. And the reason that she left was that she felt he was safe with that capable person who can beat up the whole Upper East Side and swallow it for breakfast and I can't. . . . I always remember that at that time I read something Tennessee Williams said about his heroines as being people who just bruise more easily."

Unlike Jane Fonda, who had come to view every one of her roles in broader sociological terms, Streep bored into the inner life of her character. She redeemed Joanna Kramer by remembering that she wasn't simply a construct but a heroine in her own life. She was surprised by the nation's reaction. "I didn't think of it as a zeitgeist movie," says Streep. "I just thought of it as, 'This is my part, my contribution to it, and that was good,' and I was proud of it. But I didn't think that people would extrapolate out larger meanings of it, like people were mad and women's lib and backlash. Men didn't like her. Ball breaker." Streep laughs. "Who knows? You just make your little truth and hope that it works."

SHE WOULDN'T BE ABLE TO GET A MAN TO WORK FOR HER

Publicly, Sherry Lansing always played the happiest Pollyanna in Hollywood. In the increasing number of articles about women entering the movie business, she denied ever facing discrimination or prejudice. She posed like a starlet in a bright blue evening gown on the cover of *Town & Country* for a piece about women in the movie business. For *Life* magazine, she slipped back into modeling mode, and while the other women wore business attire, Lansing appeared with tousled wet hair, and stated that she didn't expect to see a woman studio chief during her lifetime. Afterward, a furious Paula Weinstein called her up and berated her for what she had said.

When David Begelman was forced out for good after the embezzlement scandal, Melnick became the official president of the studio, and

Lansing and Leonard Stern urged him to hire Frank Price as the new production head. They knew Price, the president of Universal's TV division, from their days in the TV business. Still, the power plays at the top of Columbia continued, and in June 1978 the board forced Alan Hirschfield out. No one quit in protest, but an exodus slowly began, with Melnick leaving six months later, followed by hordes of others.

Lansing stayed. There had been the predictable rumors about an affair between her and Frank Price. In truth, Lansing had finally fallen in love again with the actor Wayne Rogers, who had gained fame as Trapper John on the TV series *M*A*S*H*. They had met years earlier at MGM, when Rogers had come in with John Cassavetes and Peter Falk to pitch a movie; Lansing had trailed Melnick into the meeting. When Lansing was still in a cast from her accident they had breakfast at the Polo Lounge, and a romance began. Although the bond would stretch for six years, it was always a "tempestuous relationship," says Rogers. "I'm volatile, and underneath she's a very emotional lady. On the surface she's very calm, cool, and collected, but she's a lady of passion." Rogers was a dead ringer for her deceased father.

Rogers was dismissive of Lansing's belief that she had needed her mentors to get where she was: "If it hadn't been Melnick or Ray Wagner or Stanley Jaffe, it would have been Hyam Schmedlick, you know, and Mary Luca Lipschitz. It would have been somebody else. I think that the qualities and the abilities that she brought to the job were things that most of these guys did not have. She is the one who was the buffer between those people who were on the outside world and the people that they had to deal with. She is the oil on the water. She could say, 'Wayne didn't really mean that. What he really meant was something else.' She was very good at that.

"Now, to that extent, to any guy who did not have those qualities, she became a complementary asset. She was always the junior partner in the partnerships, not because of her abilities but because that's the way I think she perceived herself."

When Price replaced Melnick as president of the studio, Lansing angled to become head of production. She looked to her male psychiatrist for approval to forge ahead, for a way to break free from her parents' belief that work was no kind of life for a woman. "He really gave me the confidence to think I could run a studio," she recalls. "I would get a crisis in my career, and I was really confused, and people wanted me to do various different things. And he said to me, 'Why do you always say you're going to go with Dan Melnick and you'll be vice president? Why don't you ever think that you'll be the one that does it?' I never will forget that. I said, 'I could never do that.' And he said, 'Why does it always have to be them? And you're going to be the number-two person?' He said, 'Well maybe you should start thinking about it.' He gave me confidence." Worried about how her promotion would affect her counterpart and friend David Chasman, Lansing told Price it was okay if they left the post empty, as long as she reported directly to him. Price said she had the job. She was thrilled. She was only thirty-three years old and about to become the highest-ranking woman in the motion picture industry. But on Sunday night she took a call from Jim Aubrey. "Did you hear? You have a new boss," he said. "Johnny Veitch." Veitch was the head of physical production. Lansing, stunned, began to cry.

The next morning at seven-thirty, her doorbell rang. It was Aubrey, who barked at her, "Is that your favorite outfit?" She looked at him blankly. She was going to work. "Go put on your favorite outfit and more makeup," he told her.

"I said, 'What are you talking about?' And he said, 'Don't let them know you give a shit about this at all. Don't give them the satisfaction. And just plan to leave,' " recalls Lansing.

Later that morning, Price came into her office and told Lansing that the board had refused to give her the job, ostensibly because she wouldn't be able to get a man to work for her. He promised her a raise and told her that she'd have the job eventually, which she figured out was what management said to people they wanted to keep without promoting.

Her tenure at Columbia was fast becoming untenable; she found herself cut out of the loop, even on projects like *Kramer vs. Kramer*, on which she had been the studio's point person. "It became clear as it was going further and further in the process, the picture had really come off and was going to be a success, and they cut her out of the process," recalls Jaffe. In particular, Veitch refused to let her go to the test screening in Kansas City. "There was absolutely no reason for it except that they wanted the credit or the light to shine on them. And I thought it was a real bad thing that had been done to her. And I don't know if they would have done that to somebody else."

IT'S FUN TO WIELD POWER

"There was hellish competition amongst the women," says Paula Weinstein of her female peers who were trying to climb the Hollywood corporate ladder. "Roz Heller and Marcia Nasatir and Nessa Hyams always argued about who was the first woman vice president, but one of the three of them was. We all tended to compete with each other, and to think of ourselves on this ladder for the one woman job at the studio rather than coming together and saying, 'Now how do we forge ourselves as a group?' There was a natural enmity. In the beginning, we had our eyes on each other instead of on the jobs."

Lansing drew an uncommon share of approbation because of the inaccessibility that lay under her veneer of friendliness and her tendency to play up to powerful men. "Sherry was never a girl's girl," says Weinstein, echoing a widely held sentiment. It took the former radical some time to find her own sisterhood. When she arrived, Weinstein had gone to a lunch at Ma Maison sponsored by Women of the Motion Picture League, known by the tongue-in-cheek nickname Wompy. Weinstein's idea of a women's group was Gloria Steinem, Betty Friedan, and Kate Millett raising their consciousnesses and discussing politics in a West Side apartment. At the Wompy get-togethers, she says, "I felt like I was in a group of ladies who lunch." They were talking about jobs instead of revolutions. She went to three or four lunches and quit after one woman flashed her new engagement ring.

Weinstein's antipathy for the group was compounded by competitiveness. Later the rivalries shifted a bit. Through politics and Jane Fonda, Weinstein became friends with such women as Roz Heller at Columbia and Nessa Hyams at Warners.

Weinstein still acted as if she were a rebel for justice. After Fonda made a comeback hit with the comedy *Fun with Dick and Jane*, Weinstein went to Alan Ladd, the head of production at Fox, to renegotiate Fonda's $500,000 *Julia* deal. Ladd balked at the upped price. "I made a passionate plea, 'You can't do this!'" recalls Weinstein. "My image of myself in those days: Everything was a crusade. I never thought about it like a business. I was annoyed and I was righteous."

Weinstein's righteousness irritated some and even began to seem silly to her in light of the fact that all that good-intentioned passion was getting poured into agenting. Restlessness—a desire to be somewhere better and more fulfilling—would always plague her. She had tried moving to

William Morris, which brought a salary bump to $40,000 and the opportunity to work with the legendary Stan Kamen, but still she was bored. "I kept thinking, Oh great, I fight hard. Donald Sutherland wants to do Fellini. I beg. I do everything, and Donald is off on the Appian Way. What the hell am I doing?" recalls Weinstein of her frustration. "I wanted to be sweeping the floor in the Foley section. I wanted to be doing what they were doing."

Her close friend the music wunderkind David Geffen, who was moving to Warner Bros. as vice chairman, offered her a job as vice president of production. Although the studio was still small, with just a dozen or so executives, there were only two other women who weren't secretaries. One ran the story department, the other casting—both traditional female bailiwicks. Weinstein would later look back on her two years at Warners ruefully: "I had no notion of those corporate shenanigans, . . . just politicking and protecting your own turf, and I was unbelievably naive." As a young studio executive, Weinstein was often embroiled in what she came to see as the studio chairman Ted Ashley's systematic undermining of his production chief, Guy McElwaine; ironically, Weinstein's former superior at ICM. During staff meetings Ashley encouraged the junior staff to voice their opinions—of which Weinstein's was often bold and occasionally confrontational—then used their qualms to kill McElwaine's proposed list of films. McElwaine finally quit, and the pattern was repeated with his replacement, Martin Elfand. Then Ashley's distaste seemed to turn on his friend Geffen, whom he had lured to the studio with the promise of being able to green-light his own pictures, one of the first being *Greased Lightning*, produced by Weinstein's mother. *Greased Lightning* was a troubled production, and Weinstein tried to stay as far away as possible. The film flopped at the box office, as did Geffen's other projects, and ultimately the vice chairman heard on Rona Barrett's highly successful TV show that he was going to be relieved of his duties.

His departure was a big blow to Weinstein, whose own woes at the studio were growing more pronounced as she butted heads with the newest production chief, Robert Shapiro. "There were times when I felt that what was required—as a woman—was to consistently be the best assistant," Weinstein recalls. "To not always say what I felt, to be more politic. It's hard to do that when you're talking about a script. It's hard when you don't think something's good, or you think something's wonderful, and have a boss who doesn't or does. And you might go up against him, and he's threatened by you, or you're used by somebody. It was a bad time at the studio. I couldn't be the best assistant. I couldn't. I was worn out from it in some ways."

Fortunately, Alan Ladd, Jr., offered her a job as senior vice president. He had been impressed by her ballsiness ever since she had negotiated Fonda's deal for *Julia*, and she had socialized with him a number of times with her then boyfriend, David Field, who worked at Fox. When Field left for United Artists, Ladd approached Weinstein about a position. At the time "everybody [including Sue Mengers] said, 'Don't go. Don't go. Laddie and Jay [Kantor] and Gareth [Wigan], there is a triumvirate, you'll never get past them,' " recalls Weinstein. " 'Stay at Warner Bros.' " But she was miserable, and she begged John Calley to help her get out of her contract.

On the first day of her new job, Fox received thirty-two Academy Award nominations for such films as *Julia*, *An Unmarried Woman*, and *Star Wars*. It was a halcyon time at the studio, flush with the success of George Lucas's sci-fi rendition of the hero's journey as laid out by Joseph Campbell. Along with *Jaws*, *Star Wars* ushered in the age of the blockbuster, not only profoundly affecting the kind of movie being made but changing movie distribution (mass simultaneous release rather than platform release), what constituted a box-office success, and who went to the movies. To qualify as a hit, a film now had to gross a phenomenal $100 million. To do so, it had to be targeted to the new moviegoer number one: the teenage boy.

Star Wars would augur badly for the kinds of movies that market researchers would come to believe women prefer—ones with complicated characters engaged in relationships (although the characters did not have to be women, and the relationships did not have to be romantic). It would not be until the 1980s that the film's full impact would be felt in Hollywood.

Ironically, alongside *Star Wars* Ladd had backed a number of films about women—the star-laden *The Turning Point* and *Julia*, as well as the more adventurous *An Unmarried Woman*, *Norma Rae*, and Robert Altman's dream-inspired *3 Women*. While such pictures would have been ordinary in the Hollywood of the 1930s and '40s, they were extraordinary in the Hollywood of the late '70s, which was still pumping out odes to male bonding and male power that featured the usual array of prostitutes, neurotic housewives, and busty damsels in distress.

At Fox, Weinstein catapulted forward, as if suddenly released from her bridle. It was a delirious and exciting time in her career—the birth of her ambition. "When I first stepped off and flew and didn't crash, it was an incredibly thrilling experience, and then my appetite grew," she recalls.

"It's fun, in the best sense, to wield power. You get to say yes to things you believe in. I loved having a staff reporting to me. I enjoyed being a manager. It's extremely fun to have people pay you a lot of attention and very flattering and you're young. There is a reason that power is seductive. It's a lot, a lot of fun. A lot of fun to be able to get on planes and say, 'I'm going to Paris for three days,' to go meet this director you had never met before, and you get back, and then you get the movie made. It's delightful. And being that busy is delightful, because you have to think about a whole lot."

WE KNEW YOU WOULD NEVER SETTLE FOR US

Paula Weinstein was one of the new breed of Hollywood executives, nicknamed the baby moguls, baby boomers who had arrived in town with leftist credentials, informal, hippie manners, and a penchant for making fun of the stodgy ways of their elders. In the lexicon of young comers like Paramount's head of production, Don Simpson, or Universal's head of production, Thom Mount, the Polo Lounge had transmuted into the Polio Lounge. Cynics joked that the former student radicals had found the one business where they would never have to grow up. The new intoxicants were cocaine and work.

While stars were still important, the new buzzword in town was *script*. Studios were making fewer movies; conversely, audiences were tired of past genres and pumped up by the new ideas percolating in movies such as *Annie Hall, Saturday Night Fever,* and *Star Wars*. Scripts were also seen as the engines behind lucrative new revenue streams such as soundtracks and merchandising.

Of course, script had been the one area of production traditionally hospitable to female ambition. In the thirties, the script reader Kate Corbelay was known as the Scheherazade of MGM, amusing the barely literate studio chief Louis B. Mayer with movie ideas she gleaned from huge piles of plays and newspaper clippings.

As the primacy of the script became more and more apparent in the new post-blockbuster Hollywood, development executives (often called story editors) proliferated and became institutionalized, under the pejorative tag development girl or D-girl. Essentially D-girls read scripts, and soon every office boasted not only a secretary but a D-girl, a bright, college-educated woman who sifted the wheat from the chaff, the first skirmisher in the battle against failure, with the power to say no, but not the power to say yes, which rested with her boss.

Intelligent women who had left prominent jobs in other industries to work in Hollywood were often shocked by their loss in status. When Lynda Obst was an editor at *The New York Times Magazine,* she dined frequently with people like Sue Mengers. "I felt [Sue] was my friend, and when I came to California to work for Peter Guber and made the calls to all the people that I knew, Sue Mengers said to me, 'Honey, I don't mean to be mean, but I can get Peter Guber on the phone, what do I need you for?' " recalls Obst. "So it became obvious to me really fast that I had nothing that I brought to the table. None of my relationships. All Peter Guber had ultimately hired me for was to be the girl in the room. At this point in time you needed a girl creative executive in every mix to take the notes, to look good, to be intellectual, to make interesting literary references, and I was sort of that without any real high expectations that I would become a player."

By the late seventies every studio had a token woman v.p. of production. Socially, many ran and dated their male counterparts; in Weinstein's case that meant people like her executive peers—David Field and Mark Canton. She had a long, tempestuous affair with a married co-worker. Although some of her boyfriends were decent, Weinstein's relationships were often rife with power struggles and were always unsuccessful.

On a conscious level, she had adopted her mother's view of love as grand passion and drama with men who can't quite come through. "A love relationship was, he's impossible, he doesn't call," she recalls. "Men I loved were difficult men. They were demanding and they were neurotic and they were unavailable, and deeply unavailable if they were available. And they were men who liked to keep women off balance. Both liking and being repelled by being with a strong woman. [There were] subtle put-downs and not so subtle put-downs. 'I'll be there at eight,' but coming at nine. 'I'll call you,' not calling. Flirting with other women. That mind-fuck.

"I thought that's what [love] was, that you had to conquer those people. The truth is that women who go for men like that don't really want to have a relationship. They want to appear to have a relationship. The really deep [fear] was that *I* would have to come through.

"A number of them have said to me since, 'We knew you would never settle for us.' They saw that finally who they were would not interest me for a very long time, and they're right," stresses Weinstein. "There isn't any man I went out with who now I could envision ever having married, except for [the one I married]."

Her biggest emotional support often came from the volatile, gregarious Mark Rosenberg, who had followed Weinstein west, where she had found him a job reading scripts. He too became an agent. When she left Warners, "Mark was hired in my job at Warners," she recalls. "He made a much better deal than I had made. I remember being absolutely livid that he was getting paid twice as much as [I had been] when I left.

"When I had other boyfriends, Mark and I rarely saw each other. We saw each other much less when he was married. Our relationship was the strongest when we were both single. And when I broke up with the boyfriend I moved out here with, I moved in with Mark, and when he broke up with his first wife, he moved in with me."

In fact, Weinstein had swooped in and tried to convince him not to marry his first wife, Tracy Hotchner. "I said, 'I'll go down, I'll get you out of it and you don't have to do it,' " she recalls. She held the *chupah* at his second wedding, to another Paula look-alike, the neophyte producer Lauren Shuler. "We were each other's family."

With her well-worn outspokenness, Weinstein garnered a reputation for abrasiveness. While she regarded herself as one in a line of female warriors—more comfortable in a matriarchy than a patriarchy—not everyone agreed with this self-assessment. She was great to some women, such as her protégée Lucy Fisher or her political comrade Roz Heller, and dismissive of others, namely those with whom she competed, or those who weren't useful to her.

Likewise, her taste in material ran the gamut from typical Hollywood schlock to high-minded politically correct fare. She nursed an inane film about a loser who bowls his way to fame and fortune, as well as *Brubaker,* the tale of a reform-minded warden (an unlikely Robert Redford) who attempts to clean up a southern prison run by convict guards who have conspired with administrators to provide slave labor to nearby businesses. The film was marked by a brutal battle with its director, Bob Rafelson; Weinstein vetoed his choice of cinematographer,

Vilmos Zsigmond (*McCabe & Mrs. Miller*), because she thought Zsigmond was a difficult-to-handle perfectionist. Rafelson tried to defend his choice by discussing Zsigmond's unique abilities with depth of field, but, to his dismay, Weinstein didn't know what that cinematic term meant. Rafelson instructed her on the ins and outs of deep focus but still lost his job to Stuart Rosenberg, the director of *Cool Hand Luke*, after only a week of shooting.

Weinstein's most commercially successful ventures usually came through people she knew, most notably her long-standing friend Jane Fonda, a rebel who knew the best way to send a message was to wrap it in middlebrow, commercial paper. Together they worked on the best-selling feminist revenge fantasy *Nine to Five*, in which a trio of enterprising girl Fridays kidnap their boss and institute office reform.

I'M JUST NOT GOING TO CRY OVER BUSINESS

Fonda came to the issues of women in the workplace from a vantage point of well-intentioned privilege. The genesis, she would later tell audiences, was her own short-lived stint as a secretary at *The Paris Review*: "I was fired because I wouldn't sleep with the boss." She became involved with a secretaries' rights organization and later traveled around the country interviewing office workers, whose stories affronted her. "I couldn't believe what I heard. They told about sexual harassment, about being on the job fifteen years and seeing men they trained promoted right by them to being their superiors and about clerical workers at some of the wealthiest banks who are paid so little they are eligible for food stamps," she said. Fonda had also noticed how women were treated by the studios and her husband's own political organization. "They are often treated as nonpeople," she complained, working fifteen-hour days but getting paid for only forty hours a week and being forced to do such demeaning tasks as fill gas tanks and buy their bosses' lunch.

The screenwriter Patricia Resnick first read of Fonda's desire to make a film about secretaries in Army Archerd's column in *Variety*. At age twenty-six she had already cowritten two Robert Altman films, *A Wedding* and *Quintet*, as well as provided sketch material for both Lily Tomlin and Dolly Parton, Fonda's proposed costars. Moreover, both the writer and the star were represented by William Morris, and Resnick's play about waitresses, *Ladies in Waiting*, won her an interview with

Fonda and her partner in IPC Films, Bruce Gilbert. Resnick was charmed by Fonda's seeming lack of narcissism. "Basically [Jane] wanted to make a political statement about clerical workers, and she gave me a lot of statistics [about] clerical workers [not being] unionized," recalls the writer. "But she felt that the statement could be better made as a comedy. It would be more palatable to people." While working with Altman had been an intense collaboration, with the director at times treating Resnick as almost an amanuensis for his plethora of ideas, Fonda expected Resnick to come up with the story and characters that would bring her political ideas to the screen.

"I came back and I said, 'Okay, what if the three of you were secretaries who have this horrible boss and you decide to try to kill him?' " recalls Resnick. Fonda accepted the pitch, and the pair went to Fox to set up the movie with Paula Weinstein.

Resnick began researching—primarily by working undercover as a temp in a large insurance company. Fonda would drop by her tiny apartment for script meetings and impromptu workout advice. "It was like, I can't believe Jane Fonda is sitting in my living room and showing me pelvic-groin tilts." Resnick laughs.

Resnick devised a *Sullivan's Travels* kind of framing device, with Fonda playing a studio executive based on Weinstein. "The character wants to make this political statement about women in the workplace, about secretaries, and her boss says, 'You don't know anything about secretaries other than you fired a number of them. You're a white-collar worker.' So she takes her vacation and goes underground and works at an office and gets caught up in what's going on there."

Resnick's draft caught the fancy of the director Mike Nichols, although he was leery about having the secretaries kill the boss because his film *The Fortune*, in which Warren Beatty and Jack Nicholson plot to kill sanitary-napkin heiress Stockard Channing, had been a fiasco. Resnick rewrote the script according to Nichols's notes, but the studio was unhappy and Nichols quit the project. Fonda was keen on getting another A-list director. While she would give a neophyte writer a break, she preferred to leave the fate of her performance in establishment hands, which were in those days male hands. On her first effort as a producer, *Coming Home*, she had fired her close friend and screenwriter Nancy Dowd because Dowd had written a script that focused on the friendship between two women volunteers at a veterans' hospital. Fonda thought her Vietnam picture would be more effective as a love story and brought in the writers Waldo Salt and Robert Jones, as well as the director Hal Ashby, to render it so.

Alan Ladd was less enthusiastic about *Nine to Five* than were Weinstein and Fonda. "It was wonderful and odd and dark, and Laddie wanted to make a big mainstream movie, and he just didn't think it was funny," recalls Weinstein. The writer-director Colin Higgins was meanwhile angling for a chance at the script. Higgins had written *Harold and Maude* for Ladd, as well as written and directed the hit *Silver Streak.*

Resnick was fired. "Jane and Bruce took me out to lunch and told me what was happening. Jane actually wanted me to be on the set, mostly because it was Dolly's first movie and she thought I could be kind of helpful," recalls Resnick. "But [Higgins] wasn't really comfortable with that. He just kind of felt like there needs to be one captain of the ship and it would be divisive. I literally cried myself to sleep every night for about three months."

One night Resnick had an epiphany. She was only twenty-six and this was *business.* "I tried to make a pact with myself just never to cry over business again. I have been pretty good about it. Not entirely successful, but pretty good."

By the time the film reached the screen, the secretaries were no longer trying to kill their boss—they just fantasize about it. Fonda would later claim that the studio had insisted on this change. On-screen, Tomlin and Parton sparkle, but the superstar who put the project together looks anemic and dwarfed. Fonda was no longer a powerful executive posing as an ordinary woman—she was now a naive divorcée reentering the workforce after a long marriage, sporting a frumpy fifties hairdo, oversized glasses, and prim dress-for-success work wear, envisioning herself as one of those women defined by their husbands all their lives.

Unlike stars such as Streisand, Fonda managed to diminish her own presence in the movie. "The only trouble I ever had with her was that she would care so much about making Dolly's and Lily's parts good enough, that she didn't make a part for herself," says Weinstein. "And I would go, 'Excuse me, your character is standing in the room, don't we want to make this a little bit about her?' [And she would go] 'No, no, don't worry about me, I'll figure it out later.' "

This said, as the producer Fonda earned record fees, a million-dollar salary and 10 percent of the gross on what turned out to be a huge hit. With its catchy Dolly Parton soundtrack, *Nine to Five* earned more than

$100 million domestically, a fortune in 1980 dollars. The silly, forgettable romp was trumpeted as a women's buddy picture—the fun counterbalance to the male buddy pictures that swamped the marketplace.

Although lighthearted female buddy pictures, such as Bette Midler's *Outrageous Fortune*, would continue to do well when they appeared every couple of years, it was not until the mid-1990s that Hollywood would figure out money might be made in female bonding.

Amy Heckerling and Judge Reinhold on the set
of FAST TIMES AT RIDGEMONT HIGH, 1982.

10.

———

THE FILM SCHOOL
IMPERATIVE

"How could you after doing *Nashville* do a piece of shit movie like this?" the angry female journalist asked Joan Tewkesbury as the writer-director discussed her directorial debut, *Old Boyfriends*, at a press conference at the 1979 Cannes Film Festival. Every time a hard question had come up, the film's writer and executive producer, Paul Schrader, had kicked Tewkesbury under the table and prodded her to answer. "I looked at her and I smiled," says Tewkesbury. "She was very antagonistic about it. And she said, 'Was it because this was the only way you could direct a movie?' And I said, 'Yes. And it was great.' But that was it."

Tewkesbury hated how *Old Boyfriends* had turned out. The tale of a woman who seeks out her former flames had seemed propitious, but her fantasy of autonomy was just that—a fantasy. "I thought it was going to be like an Altman movie. I thought I would have control in this kind of loose, friendly environment. And it wasn't it." Indeed, Schrader supervised a reedit of the movie against her wishes.

By the late seventies Tewkesbury was one of a handful of women who had found a way into directing. Another was a housewife turned director, Joan Micklin Silver, whose husband, Raphael Silver, had grown so distressed by watching his wife's frustrated ambitions that he personally raised the money to finance her 1975 directorial debut, *Hester Street*, about a neglected Jewish wife at the turn of the century living in Manhattan's Lower East Side. Made for only $370,000, the movie was a critical hit at Cannes and went on to earn a staggering $5 million. Although Silver signed with Sue Mengers, Hollywood did not run to embrace her, offering her neither jobs nor financing for her next proposed film, *Between the Lines*, a kind of *Big Chill* forerunner set at an alternative newspaper. Claire Townsend at United Artists finally hired Silver to write and direct *Chilly Scenes of Winter* (1979), but the studio despised the finished product and dumped it. In 1978 Claudia Weill, a young Harvard graduate, independently made one of the first feminist-inspired films to explore the vagaries of female friendship, the rough-hewn *Girlfriends;* her follow-up, United Artists' *It's My Turn*, starred Michael Douglas, and Jill Clayburgh as a woman struggling to balance a relationship and a career. Unfortunately, the stars walked all over Weill.

None of these films was a financial success, and neither Tewkesbury nor Weill directed a film again, although they worked extensively in TV. Silver's *Chilly Scenes of Winter* had garnered some good reviews, but it took the director almost ten years to land another go picture, *Crossing Delancey*, which came primarily upon the recommendation of Steven Spielberg, the husband of her proposed star, Amy Irving.

"The fact that the door had opened a crack for women didn't mean dick, you know," says Tewkesbury about the early eighties. "Any woman I knew who had any aspirations of directing or getting into it was not working."

Ironically, Tewkesbury, Weill, and Silver had been among the lucky ones.

In 1979 six members of the Directors Guild of America—all with experience directing TV—got together to discuss why they weren't working more. The six—the Emmy-winning producer-director Joelle Dobrow, the Oscar-winning documentarian Lynne Littman, Susan Bay, Nell Cox, Delores Ferraro, and Victoria Hochberg—received permission to go through thirty years of Directors Guild deal memos to develop employment statistics.

In June 1980 the new Women's Committee released their results to the public:

- Of the 7,332 features made between 1949 and 1979, only 14 were directed by women.
- From January 1, 1978, through July 1, 1979, only one of 78 features released by the major studios was directed by a woman.

The committee called for a voluntary affirmative-action program among the studios—with such specific demands as at least one woman to be hired per thirteen television episodes and at least two interviewed for other Directors Guild positions.

With great fanfare all the studios sent representatives to a Voluntary Resource Committee to screen and recommend Directors Guild women for employment. Over the next year the committee held sixty interviews, although the stature of the studio representatives attending steadily decreased until the prospective candidates found themselves talking to secretaries and then labor-relations lawyers. The guild focused primarily on TV because the movie studios were, if anything, more resistant. The studios claimed the agencies had the power in the era of packaging and the agencies failed to advocate women clients. Conversely, the agencies argued that the studios never asked for women. To the women of the Directors Guild committee, the few, scattered female executives and agents seemed almost entirely unhelpful. The whole charade came to an abrupt end when not one of the industry representatives showed up for the crucial meeting at which they were supposed to make employment recommendations.

Angered by the studios' lackadaisical attitude, the Directors Guild national board in February 1981 filed charges with the federal Equal Employment Opportunity Commission, the first step in a class-action suit charging that twenty-one motion picture companies and television networks systematically practiced wholesale discrimination against women and minorities. The guild filed its first class-action suit against Warner Bros. in July 1983, and a second one against Columbia five months later.

The sticking point was quotas, which the guild and the government referred to by the less inflammatory title *goals*. The guild wanted the studios to agree to hire a certain number of women within a specific time frame. The studios fought back furiously, claiming that such restrictions would deny them their First Amendment rights to choose who should direct their pictures. Warners and Columbia countersued, arguing that the low number of women (and minority) directors was the result of restrictive guild practices.

In other industries female employees had banded together in support of class-action suits. In Hollywood, however, the women were scared and divided. Startlingly, few women would speak in favor of the Directors Guild action. Many were used to being the only woman in the room, dependent on the goodwill of a particular man for being there.

Although the studio system was long gone, the patriarchal attitudes remained in the new, smaller tribes that populated the town.

Finally, in 1984, a federal judge, a Reagan appointee, dismissed the case, declaring that the Directors Guild couldn't be a litigant in the suit because the guild itself was guilty of discriminatory practices. In film (but not TV), directors were responsible for hiring assistant directors. Moreover, although the individual plaintiffs could pursue their grievances on their own, the judge enjoined them from using the legal team with whom they'd toiled for several years because their lawyers were "tainted" by their contact with the guild. "It cast a chilling pall over the legal efforts at changing things," recalls one of the founding members of the guild's women's committee, Victoria Hochberg. The suit was never refiled.

THERE WERE NO WOMEN DIRECTORS
REALLY TO SPEAK OF

While one generation largely floundered in their attempt to establish viable directing careers, another followed such legends as Francis Ford Coppola and Martin Scorsese into the nation's film schools.

By the time Amy Heckerling started at NYU in the early seventies, filmmaking had become a kind of jihad that she pursued over a variety of inner and external obstacles. The daughter of a pair of Bronx accountants, Heckerling had always reveled in the old films she watched on TV. James Cagney, Clark Gable, and the Three Stooges had practically served as her baby-sitters during the long afternoons she spent alone as a latchkey child. At the age of fifteen, Heckerling realized that film might actually be a profession she could pursue when she heard a male classmate at Manhattan's High School of Art and Design read aloud a personal essay about how he was going to Hollywood to become a director. "I just got insanely jealous," she recalls. "I just thought, You said you can make movies. I love them more than you do. And besides, you cheat off of me on your tests, so I'm smarter, so I should do it." When she thought about it later, she realized that she was jealous "because this is what I want to do, but you just think it's too good to ask for, and there were no women directors really to speak of. It didn't seem like a reasonable thing to want to do."

Heckerling's parents were skeptical when she announced she wanted to go to film school. She could point to only one other woman working in film: Elaine May. "It was hard to justify me spending all that time learning to do something that only one other person was doing," says Heckerling, who worked three jobs and borrowed money to pay for her tuition. Her first year, she vowed to become a director.

After graduation Heckerling followed her film school boyfriend, Martin Brest (who went on to direct *Beverly Hills Cop*), out to L.A. "I'd always been like the little girl behind him going, 'What do I do next?' " she says. Like Brest, she applied to the American Film Institute graduate program and was one of only two in her NYU graduating class to gain admission. Brest and Heckerling looked like twin leprechauns with dark tumbles of hair and limpid brown eyes, and thick Bronx accents. They lived in a shabby apartment with a TV set, and Heckerling rode buses around L.A. because she couldn't afford a car. She supported herself by syncing the sound on *Jaws, Paws, and Claws,* which she describes as "a kind of *That's Entertainment!* but with animals." She matched audio woofs to screen images of dogs barking. Martin Scorsese was editing *Taxi Driver* in the editing bay next door, and every time he'd leave to go to the bathroom Heckerling would rush out to try to run into him, to little avail.

Unlike those of Tewkesbury, Silver, or Weill, Heckerling's sensibility was comic and broad. It was well-suited for mainstream Hollywood comedies except for the fact that she often liked to put girls at the center of her stories. Her AFI thesis film, *Losing It,* was nominated for an Oscar in the short film category. Heckerling both wrote and directed the *Mad* magazine take on a girl's right to sexual self-determination. "She's got eight hours left before she turns twenty, and she's determined to lose her virginity while she's still a teenager" is the way Heckerling describes the plot. Her Oscar competition consisted of NASA footage from the moon, a Canadian film board documentary on a crippled girl, and a short Steve Martin had directed for Paramount. The cripple won. Yet Heckerling was launched.

In the years that followed, Heckerling expanded her humorous exploration of female sexuality with her screenplay "My Kind of Guy," a kind of female version of *Carnal Knowledge.* Pretty and engaging, Heckerling set the film up at Warners, although it soon drifted into development hell, moving first to Universal, then to the studio of last resort,

MGM under David Begelman, who gave it the green light. "I was real excited because I would have been as young as Orson Welles doing a picture," says Heckerling. Three weeks before her start date, the Actors Guild went on strike. In the interim MGM picked up *Rich and Famous*, a different kind of tale that also focused on two women friends (Candice Bergen and Jacqueline Bisset), to be directed by the legendary women's director George Cukor, and hence canceled Heckerling's film. "So, then I had to call a few hundred people and tell them they were out of jobs. Then I went to unemployment, and I kept bumping into all the actors there [who] had been reading for me." The failure of "My Kind of Guy" left her a bad legacy; it made her question her ability as a writer, as a teller of her own stories.

Heckerling finally got her break directing what would become the one genre permitted tyro female directors: teen comedy. It was the cinematic age of the male adolescent—the era of *Porky's* and *Risky Business*. The genre was cheap and relatively commercial, and it didn't require stars. Teens were not considered quite full people in Hollywood . . . and neither were women.

"I saw the AFI short that she did, and it was so dirty and sexy and down, and I was, like, 'Ooh, this girl really gets sex,' and, let's face it, *Fast Times at Ridgemont High* was a high school movie about sex and she really got it, and that's why we chose her," says the producer Art Linson, who'd met Heckerling on the Universal lot and been impressed by her advice about a script he'd been thinking about directing.

On the surface, *Fast Times at Ridgemont High* fit the genre perfectly— it featured high jinks and ogling and one of the most memorable wastecases ever to hit the screen in the form of the stoner-surfer Spicoli, so memorably vivified by an intense young Method actor, Sean Penn. The ensemble comedy happened to be based on a book, penned by a young *Rolling Stone* writer, Cameron Crowe, who had gone back to high school, undercover, to chronicle the youth of America. Crowe, who later came to fame as the writer-director of *Jerry Maguire*, unerringly caught the lingo of Southern California kids and imbued his protagonists with a poignant ignorance that goes hand in hand with their attempts at cool. The film highlights sexual embarrassment, although Heckerling's girls are hardly one-dimensional sex bunnies. Indeed, the relationship between her main character, the innocent Stacy (a young Jennifer Jason Leigh), and her nymphet best friend, Linda (Phoebe Cates), takes on the tone of a shopping mall Tom and Huck. Stacy is eager to discover the joys of sex but finds out that copulating with the too-cool school stud turns out to be a bumbling, alienating experience. Linda, meanwhile, memorably demonstrates how to give a blow job using a banana.

Heckerling ran the production much like a student film. Unaware of the etiquette of rehearsal, which usually started with a table reading, she and the young cast simply poured into Van Nuys High School, where they blended in with the real kids, went to lunch, and then held mock classes in an empty classroom, with everyone in character. "Sean brought Chinese food with him, and he was being disruptive," says Heckerling, who poured Penn's antics into the film. "It was just fun. We were making it up as we went along—the way it never could be again, [because it was] your first [time]. You are just so happy to be doing it, and you don't know what the rules are."

She was, however, a nervous first-time director, terrified of failing and with a current of pessimism that ran deep. When she couldn't get the right tone for a scene, she'd redo it again and again in different locations. The character-driven piece scared the studio. Most of the time the producer Linson buffered Heckerling from the studio's anxiety, but one day the director John Landis, then hot off *The Blues Brothers*, stopped by. Heckerling had met him only once and was baffled by why he was there. "He told me later, the studio executives didn't know what this movie was, and they asked him to check it out," she says. "And he told them, 'What's the problem? Give her a break. It's okay.' "

A heated battle broke out over the film's soundtrack. The movie had been green-lit in part to support a soundtrack to be released by the mega–record producer Irving Azoff, also one of *Fast Times*'s producers. But Heckerling led a war against Azoff, who wanted to use acts of his like the Eagles instead of edgier new wave music. At one point tensions grew so high Heckerling refused even to talk to the music supervisor. "I was still like a teenager really, [yelling at them], 'Put those songs in,' " she says.

The director's problems in postproduction were compounded by her deteriorating relationship with her husband, whom she had insisted on marrying one weekend during production, partly because she was determined to break her lifelong habit of sacrificing her personal life to pursue filmmaking. "My idiot husband thought that the whole idea of doing a movie was to annoy him," she says. "If I was working late shooting, it was because I wanted to stay away from him." Her husband took to calling her in the editing room: "Before long, he would be calling and calling so much we had to unplug all the phones in the cutting room. And one of those phones, I remember, couldn't unplug, so we took it off the hook and it was making this loud annoying noise. So we put it in a bin and covered it with trash," recalls Heckerling. "We tried to roll it down the hall to [the editing room] of *Psycho II.*" She laughs.

"One day he was ranting and raving and I just got in my car," says Heckerling. She had never given up her own apartment, "because it was not working that well all together. And Judge Reinhold and his girlfriend, Carrie Frasier, who was my assistant on the movie, they lived upstairs from me. So we all went out, got big steak dinners, something I never—I don't eat meat, but—it was just something to do, had to be eating flesh. So, that was the end of him. I never went back."

By the time *Fast Times at Ridgemont High* was completed, Universal had lost confidence in the project; the studio dumped the film, with scant publicity, into a tiny run of two hundred theaters on the West Coast. Kids lined up around the block to see it—prompting the shocked studio to rush the film into wide distribution. By that time it was September, and Universal had missed most of the crucial summer movie season. The amiable if slightly haphazard film went on to gross $27 million domestically, enough to qualify as a little hit.

"Years later when I met people that were at Universal, they'd go, 'Honey, you got screwed.' " Again Heckerling laughs. "Unfortunately I was too young to know what was going on."

IF YOU DON'T HAVE AN AMBITION, YOUR LIFE IS MEANINGLESS

Heckerling's experience was almost directly paralleled by that of Martha Coolidge. Earnest and ambitious, this descendant of Calvin Coolidge had applied to NYU's graduate film school, only to be told by the interviewer: " 'You can't be a director, you're a woman. You're wasting your time and your parents' money.' And little did he know it was *my* money," recalls Coolidge, who had worked her way through school mostly as a production assistant and an editor. "He said, 'You can't name five women directors in the world.' And, of course, I couldn't, because in the cinema study classes I had, nobody taught anything about women at all. I didn't even know about Ida Lupino. But

I did know Agnès Varda. We talked, and I got in." She graduated in 1971.

Unlike Heckerling, Coolidge wasn't a writer, so at film school she made a documentary, chronicling her actual rather than her imagined life. *A Portrait of My Brother* cost Coolidge $9,000 and documented her brother's drug addiction. She got a grant from the National Endowment for the Arts and raised money from private investors (mostly with the last name of Coolidge) to fund a portrait of her grandmother, *Old-Fashioned Woman*, which she sold to PBS, and followed that up with an unflinching documentary about her own rape, called *Not a Pretty Picture.*

Coolidge loved the freedom of the independent world but despaired over the constant economic pressures. Basically, she wanted to make mainstream narrative movies. She had raised $46,500 to make *Not a Pretty Picture*, which she was still editing, but she didn't know how she'd raise the $100,000 necessary to make a feature.

Providence arrived in the form of the director Francis Ford Coppola, who had seen her documentaries. His producing partner, Fred Roos, called Coolidge and invited her to meet him at his hotel, the Sherry-Netherland. "We talked about lots of things, and then Francis came in, and then we all went to a movie, and came back, and Francis said, 'We're looking for a woman director to work with. I really think you're it, and we'd like to work with you somehow. I'm starting this film, *Apocalypse Now*, but let's keep in touch, and if you want to come out to Hollywood, here are our numbers.'

"It was an incredible, incredible, pivotal, significant event, because to an East Coast independent filmmaker, Hollywood seems extremely far away," Coolidge gushes. "Particularly to a woman. I had no relatives in the business or [any] reason to think I would have an easy access."

The following January, 1977, Coolidge flew to California because *Not a Pretty Picture*, which had premiered at the Kennedy Center, was going to open in San Francisco. She called Roos and Coppola and through them met all the filmmakers in town, including Philip Kaufman and Tom Luddy. Armed with a list of Coppola contacts, she continued on to L.A. and met industry players like Mike Medavoy and Marcia Nasatir at United Artists, and the popular and well-connected art director Toby Rafelson, who introduced her around town.

The following year Coolidge drove across country to move to L.A. She lived in a decrepit hotel, interned on a Robert Wise movie, and pitched her feminist-oriented projects to little avail. Her desire to direct took on the dimensions of "a spiritual religion. If you don't have an ambition, your life is meaningless. And, believe me, I faced near despair every day," she recalls. For almost a year she looked for an agent.

Although Coolidge had made her name with feminist documentaries, she was wary about hooking up with other women. When a female agent finally asked to represent her, she refused because, as she says, "everybody advised me, Don't go with a woman agent. You're a woman. It was a time when women did not bond together with other women." Although she opted for the powerful Bob Bookman at ICM, her career went nowhere. She made a short, *Bimbo,* about a reunion of three male college roommates, which she hoped would showcase her narrative directing skills as well as dispel the potentially pigeonholing feminist aura surrounding her work.

Finally Coppola returned from filming *Apocalypse Now* in the Philippines and hired Coolidge to develop a girl-empowerment coming-of-age tale set in a run-down Pennsylvania mining town. The project died because the woman screenwriter refused to let Coolidge direct. "The reason was that she wanted to direct it, and she couldn't understand why I could direct and she couldn't." It was an all too familiar scenario to Coolidge. Once, an agent had suggested she meet with Nancy Dowd, the screenwriter who had been a mentor in Jane Fonda's feminist awakening. Coolidge later heard that Dowd had refused even to meet her: "I remember her saying, 'You're a director. I want to direct. Why should I meet you?' It was every woman for herself, and you only got your chances through men."

Coolidge was nonetheless devastated by the debacle of her proposed debut film. "I must have cried for four days," she says. "And I remember my boyfriend just couldn't stand it. I think it was one of the things that made him leave town." He moved back to New York. It would be one of the signature lessons of her life: Few men could bear the frustration— and disappointment—that accompanied a woman who wanted to be a director.

Coppola next hired Coolidge to develop a contemporary rock-and-roll love story, *Photoplay.* For two years she researched the film, clubbing five nights a week to catch exploding acts such as Tom Petty, Bruce Springsteen, and Talking Heads. Coppola's name opened doors, and he put her on the Zoetrope payroll. A small inheritance from her grandmother allowed her to buy a house, although, as the months passed with no movie, Coolidge was forced to take out a $5,000 bank loan against her salary just to live. She kept hiring and firing employees as the start date for *Photoplay* kept getting postponed. Coppola's studio was tottering on the brink of bankruptcy; finally *Photoplay* was definitively canceled.

Coolidge watched her life, her dreams, her ambitions, spiral into free fall. She floundered. One bad thing after another happened: A series of floods almost destroyed her house. Her car blew up. When she went to pitch a new idea to one of the studios, the studio president locked his door and chased her around his office trying to grab at her. Two days before Christmas she received a call from the Canadian distributor of *Not a Pretty Picture*, who had recommended her to a producer financing a movie as a tax shelter. He didn't have a coherent script, just $400,000 in loose cash that he needed to spend by the end of the year.

The project was virtually a soft-core porn film, but the producers were so desperate they were amenable to her proposal to strip the film of exploitation, and Coolidge rationalized that she could always take her name off the picture. "And the guy had lied, he didn't have $400,000, he had about $40,000, and he started bouncing checks on everybody, and the Teamsters, the drivers, went and bashed up his car, and later one of the actresses tried to kill herself. I had to shut the movie down in the third week." Coolidge took the dailies that she could afford to print and went to New York and L.A. to canvass potential investors. She crashed on the actress Colleen Camp's couch and made the rounds before Camp introduced her to the director Peter Bogdanovich, who had just finished *They All Laughed* and was starting his own production company, Moon Pictures.

"Peter really saved my ass. He said, 'I'll buy this movie,' " recalls Coolidge. But as soon as she finished the extra footage, Bogdanovich ran out of money. With the salary he'd already paid her, she paid the editor and the lab, and finished the picture. Yet no distributor was interested.

For a year Coolidge lived in a small room over a friend's apartment. She wrote a script with Camp and waited for someone to take note of her film. Finally, a pair of young producers, friends of hers, approached her with an offer to direct a script called *Valley Girl*. "And I sat there in shock, realizing that my first actual offer for a real go movie in Hollywood was coming from this guy who had this low-budget picture that he had written for this company, that his partner just didn't really want to direct it, because the partner is an action director, and this was about girls. And they offered it to me knowing that it was either me or a student."

She was surprised and relieved, when she read the material, that it could be more than exploitation dreck. She agreed to direct the film. Her salary was to be $5,000.

The two producers then had to sell Coolidge to Atlantic Records, which was financing the picture through foreign presales. Atlantic balked, worried that Coolidge was too much of an artist and that it would be, as one executive commented, "women-libbed to death." Slipping into a depressive funk, she took to her bed for two weeks.

Atlantic finally relented, although Coolidge had to audition with the head of the company. "I want you to know we must have naked breasts in this movie four times," she recalls him saying. "I said, 'Well, I don't have a problem with that as long as I can do it my way.' He said, 'I don't care how you do it, I just want naked breasts.' I said, 'Fine.' So we shook hands and then he said, 'Welcome to the team.' "

Coolidge managed to stick the breasts into the film in unusual ways. When a young buck tries to get back at the girl who dumped him by making it with an "easy" girl, she shows the despair of the buxom, bare-breasted vehicle for his revenge. In the middle of making out, the confused young woman asks, "Does this mean we're going steady?" and the would-be seducer recoils in horror and stalks out, leaving the girl with the realization that she's been used. The $350,000 film, which starred a winsome young Nicolas Cage, went on to garner $17 million. Coolidge was flooded with offers to direct teen sex comedies.

THEY LOOKED LIKE MEN'S FILMS

Resistant to enforced change, Hollywood was notoriously less resistant to new ways of making money. One of the major stumbling blocks to women directing studio films was the fact that the few films they had directed looked disconcertingly rough-hewn or simply bad. It was a popular assumption in Hollywood that women were visually inept, with the work of Elaine May or Claudia Weill as proof.

The film that went the furthest toward dispelling this stereotype was the Australian import *My Brilliant Career,* directed by a young film school graduate named Gillian Armstrong, the first woman to direct a feature film in Australia in fifty years. It arrived with tremendous fanfare—and standing ovations—at the 1979 Cannes Film Festival.

Assured both technically and visually, *My Brilliant Career* was a clarion call of female empowerment minus the trappings of current politics. It was the Australian author Miles Franklin's autobiographical tale of the willful Sybylla, played by Judy Davis, daughter of a poor, turn-of-the-century farmer who yearns to become a writer. Sybylla's rejection of a perfectly pliable, supportive, rich suitor (played by a young Sam Neill) in order to pursue her dream was considered revolutionary—a rejection of salvation by a handsome prince. Sybylla chooses self-realization over cozy domesticity, especially shocking because her suitor seems perfectly happy for her to continue to write.

Armstrong was the strong-willed daughter of a teacher who had given up teaching to raise a family and a real-estate agent–cum–amateur photographer who viewed with pleasure his daughter's interest in the visual arts. She emerged in the 1970s from a nascent filmmaking system that lacked established players or profit-driven entities, and she benefited from a government interested in promoting film not just as an industry but as a vital proponent of Australian culture. The various state film commissions were backing the emerging Australian new wave, the distinctive work of such renegade talents as Peter Weir, Bruce Beresford, Fred Schepisi, and George Miller.

Moreover, while overt American feminists—save for actresses like Jane Fonda—were marginalized from the levers of Hollywood power, Australian feminists had successfully banded together to lobby the government. The newly formed Sydney Women's Filmmaker Group—whose prime goal was to make politically oriented films about women's issues—was instrumental in the establishment of a government-backed women's film fund to pay for training women in technical areas. They also pressured the recently established national film school to publish its admissions records in order to ensure that the percentage of applicants who received positions was the same for women and men.

Armstrong graduated first from Swinburne Technical College, and later won a place in the pilot class of the Australian School of Film and Television, a class that consisted of ten men and two women. Although she benefited greatly from the calls for equality by the Sydney Women's Filmmaker Group, her main motivation wasn't politics but art.

From the beginning Armstrong startled audiences with her technical fluency, the graceful, intelligent composition of her films. At Swinburne she won the cinematography prize for her surreal study of suburbia, *The Roof Needs Mowing*, which featured women sitting on a clothesline. At the national film school the government paid for each student to make three films and provided an array of unusual short stories by prominent Australian writers that could be turned into scripts. Armstrong's first, called *100 a Day*, was about a backyard abortion at the turn of the century. Her second, inspired by a close friend, told the tale of a young man getting ready for a big night out, which turns out to be a gay dance—at the time a very radical notion.

The films won awards, and Armstrong took them to the newly emerging women's film festivals. "I was more advanced technically as a filmmaker. I actually had some of them criticize my films. They looked too slick. They looked like men's films. A lot of the women making films were very untrained and still learning. A lot of their films were very rough and sort of almost out of focus, and some thought this was women's special way."

When Armstrong finished graduate school, employment was readily available. She was an art director on several films and shot documentaries—one of which became *Smokes and Lollies*, about what it was like to be a fourteen-year-old girl in Australia, the first in a series of films that charted the development of these girls as they aged. With another government grant she directed an hourlong drama, *Private Dancer*, which won a slew of Australian awards for both her and the lead actress, and was eventually sold to Australian TV.

My Brilliant Career arrived in Armstrong's lap via the producer Margaret Fink, who had hired her as a prop girl on *The Removalists*, one of the first features to come out of Australia's new wave. Fink had taken an interest in Armstrong's career and three years later asked if she was interested in directing *My Brilliant Career*. Armstrong was leery—recognizing the challenges a complicated period piece presents for a novice director. But she figured it would take years to get the script right and hoped she would have a movie to her credit by then. It took Fink four years to raise the necessary $800,000 from a variety of sources, primarily the government.

They lost their lead actress when the investors demanded a screen test, and, to their own shock, she wasn't appropriate. Fortunately, they discovered Judy Davis, newly minted from drama school.

While doing the publicity for the film, Armstrong learned from Davis that "she never liked the part. All her friends said she had to do it, it was such a good break. I think some of it is because she admits that [Sybylla] was too close to herself and her own adolescence. She did not like having to play an adolescent again. She didn't like the character. She thought that she was sort of a show-off [with all the] up-front, out-rageous sorts of blabby things she had to do. She hates doing them. But she did them for me. I didn't realize until the whole thing was over how unhappy she was about the film. She thought it was like a kids' film. And then she never liked looking at herself. She didn't like the way I made her look either. So you have never seen those freckles ever again." Armstrong laughs.

Perhaps Armstrong was oblivious to Davis's unhappiness because she was obsessed with getting the film the way she wanted it. She was conscious of the whole country's eyes upon her—of the notion that if she failed it wasn't just the failure of Gillian Armstrong but the failure of all women in directing. Armstrong wasn't simply being grandiose: The mere start of filming was treated as a publicity stunt by the Australian media, alternately enchanted, skeptical, and dismayed by the sight of a pretty twenty-eight-year-old riding into the outback to begin making the most expensive Australian movie ever by a beginning director.

"There was terrible bitching in the industry because it was a woman producer and it was like women working together, they must be on to-gether," Armstrong, who isn't gay, recalls with a laugh. Later, in the editing room, all sorts of film folk dropped by, fascinated to see if her footage was cutting together.

Armstrong had to overcome the popular notion that directors were burly men with megaphones. For her, the strongest resistance often came from female crew members working the traditional female jobs on the set. "I had a hard time from women," she says. The flip side of Arm-strong's insecurity could be a slightly frosty exterior—a penchant for asking for what she wanted bluntly, unapologetically.

"There are some women who enjoy working for the great male di-rector," says Armstrong. "They sort of slave. We're used to the boss being that type of person they can always fantasize about being in love with or whatever. And then there's a script supervisor who also likes to work on sort of a flirtatious sexual level. But that wasn't going to work with me. So they were unhappy in that situation because they thought their role was to serve the great male God director. And there are some actors too who were used to the great male God directors that they could fantasize about."

Armstrong had little idea what it meant for her film to be accepted at the Cannes Film Festival. Its first public screening ever was on the

Croisette, at 11:00 A.M., and she spent her first darkened moments in the theater gripped with panic. "So any person that coughs, or wrinkles their face, [I thought], They are hating it, they're hating it. I finally could not stand it, and I said, 'I have to get out. Everybody hates the film, they're all bored by it.' " When she couldn't take her own anxiety anymore, she crept out early, only to suffer a fit of paranoia that her departure would encourage others to skip out. Later, a friend who had been at the screening ran up to her screaming: " 'Wasn't that wonderful?' and I go, 'What?' " To Armstrong's surprise, the crowd energetically embraced her film.

Yet Armstrong was disconcerted that the audience and the critics saw *My Brilliant Career* as autobiographical. They simply assumed that the young Armstrong was Sybylla. "They all thought I'm this passionate, struggling, angry young girl who the world's against," says Armstrong, "and actually I had fantastic parents who really encouraged me, and I had a really wonderful sense of my own talents, and my mother thinks everything I do is good. I didn't have to struggle like Sybylla at all. That's more what my producer's life [was] like."

The moment the film premiered in Cannes, Armstrong was beset by Hollywood. She thought William Morris was an advertising agency until someone informed her that it represented stars and directors. At the New York Film Festival, strangers pushed scripts into her hands. She was deluged with costume dramas about female achievers "climbing mountains or flying planes," and the nanosecond pigeonholing of her talent shocked her. Finally, she signed on with William Morris, hoping to meet more writers. "The next minute I was in L.A. meeting studio people, people offering me films with Dustin Hoffman and Sally Field to start the next week! I just felt honestly that was a huge step as a filmmaker, and I wasn't ready. I said no to everybody. I said, 'I'm still learning, and I think I should learn in the country I belong to and keep learning with the team I started working with.' I said, 'No, I am committed to [staying in Australia], thank you very much for the offers.' "

11.

THE ASSUMPTION OF POWER

FORMER MODEL TAKES OVER
HOLLYWOOD STUDIO

In the summer of 1979 the popular Fox studio production head, Alan Ladd, Jr., quit, taking with him most of his creative executives, including Paula Weinstein. The chairman, Dennis Stanfill, discussed the opening with, among others, Sue Mengers, but ultimately named the former Columbia chief Alan Hirschfield as the new chief operating officer of the movie division; Hirschfield offered head of production to his former lieutenant Dan Melnick. Melnick opted instead for one of the most lucrative production deals in town and set about convincing Hirschfield to hire Sherry Lansing.

The CEO wasn't easily persuaded. She was inexperienced. Then again, she was excellent public relations, with high visibility and good talent relations, which they desperately needed in the wake of Ladd's departure. Melnick promised to backstop Lansing as long as necessary, an avowal that soon became public knowledge.

Finally what she had long sought hung within her reach, yet Lansing hesitated. She worried about what the promotion would do to her private life, her vision of herself as a woman with a family and perhaps a child. "I always was as concerned about my personal life as my professional life," she says. "And then I was thirty-five. That's like not a kid. I always was afraid that I wouldn't have a life. I would just work. And I had seen all these guys that were doing these jobs twenty-four hours a day, because I had worked around them, and I didn't think it was that great."

Sherry Lansing poses by a bust of Darryl F. Zanuck,
the founder of Twentieth Century-Fox, at the
Fox lot theater, 1980.

Ron Galella, Ltd.

Hirschfield set about seducing her—presenting a sparkling vision of the future, a new team reinvigorating a great institution. Fox's publicity maven Bob Cort and incoming distribution chief Norman Levy, whom Lansing knew from Columbia, called her repeatedly. " 'What, are you crazy? This is a wonderful opportunity,' " Lansing recalls them saying. "Then they'd push buttons, like 'Don't you realize this is a big step for women? How can you be so selfish?' "

Lansing wasn't blind to the fact that Fox was a lions' den. She was twenty years younger than the rest of the management team, and she knew their egos well enough to wonder if she would have any authority.

Hirschfield repeatedly allayed her concerns, promising her all the freedom she needed and spinning out visions of autonomy. She would have to report only to him, and he'd back her to the hilt. When they talked about salary, Lansing floundered. She had no idea what to ask for, so she just added a healthy amount to her $75,000 salary as a vice president, bringing it to just over $100,000. Hirschfield chortled outright. "Alan said, 'That's not enough,' " recalls Lansing. " 'That's not what other people earn on the job, and I do not want this to be perceived as a token job.' " He upped her salary to $325,000, a figure that would be trumpeted in the press.

Lansing kept her meetings with Hirschfield a secret and continued to talk about a new deal at Columbia. "I had talked to her three times," recalls Frank Price. "Because there were rumors around that she was going to Fox. And I asked her in and said, 'What's going on? Is there anything to these rumors?' And she said no. I said, 'Well, can we close up the new deal then?' She said she'd talk to her lawyer—and the rumor persisted, and we still couldn't get the deal closed, so I called her in again and she assured me there was nothing to it and we shook hands. I think she was struggling with the whole thing. I had assured the board that we were okay because they were hearing the rumors too. I said, 'Sherry and I met, and all is well.' "

Finally, Lansing told Price that she was not going to renew her contract but declined to enlighten him about her future plans. He was enraged by what he considered a betrayal and locked her out of her office, refusing to speak to her.

Finally, she showed up one Saturday morning at his house. "She was really in tears because she was quite torn," recalls Price. She told him she just couldn't turn down the Fox offer.

While Lansing was thrilled to see the news of her appointment emblazoned across the front page of *The New York Times*, she was mortified by the headline: SHERRY LANSING, FORMER MODEL, NAMED HEAD OF FOX PRODUCTIONS.

"I was a model when I was twenty-two!" she fumes. "It negated three years working with Ray Wagner. Two years working with Talent Associates. Three years at MGM. Two and a half at Columbia, more than ten years of work. But that's the way it was all over the place." The headline seemed to crystallize the official mythology about Lansing's ascension: Doris Day Takes On Hollywood.

The next day the studio was inundated with media requests for interviews with Fox's newest star. Hirschfield teased, "I hope you can sell movies as easily." He joked that he felt like Branch Rickey, the manager of the Brooklyn Dodgers who had hired Jackie Robinson.

The board congratulated Hirschfield on his masterful publicity stunt—a woman, a beacon of progressiveness to wash away the stink of Alan Ladd's acrimonious departure. "It really caught me by surprise because everybody was saying, 'Wow, what a brilliant move; you really did raise the radar screen for Fox,' " recalls Hirschfield. "I said, 'You know, it sounds like a very corny answer, but after I looked at everybody, she really just seemed to be the best person, and it never occurred to me particularly that she was a woman or a man.' " But Lansing had come in with explicit wording in her contract that she could convert her deal to a producing deal within eighteen months if she so wished; Hirschfield begged her to stay longer so the studio wouldn't look foolish.

He also encouraged her to talk to the press, and they agreed on ten outlets that would be granted interviews. She spun journalists like a pro—warm, superficially accessible, unfailingly upbeat, Teflon-coated. Reams of flattering profiles appeared in such publications as *Time* and *Newsweek*.

But Hollywood savaged her with jealousy and malicious gossip. She was derided as a "geisha," a woman who served powerful men, like her former lover, Dan Melnick.

"There were specious accounts of how she fucked her way to the top," recalls Polly Platt. "Horrible. And I have known Sherry for a long time. And it simply is not true. I mean, you can't. There were horrendous comments made about her. I doubted her ability to function, they were so bad. And I worried about her."

"Sherry got the job very elegantly by 'father may I,' " says the producer Lynda Obst. "Sherry was the classic mentor of men, okay, which is the perfectly appropriate way to rise to the top, and it happens in every business in the world. But in this town, when you mentored your way up, it was presumed that you were sleeping your way up, because there are so few power positions that even the polite way of getting the job makes people say mean things about you."

Furthermore, Lansing quickly realized that her position was not much more than a shiny press release. She arrived to a studio full of empty suites and offices, and her wings were clipped to make necessary and fast hires. She discovered she needed Hirschfield's approval to get the money to hire big-gun talent and producers, as well as her own production staff. She left message after message at his home in Westchester, New York, most of which went unreturned. Hirschfield would soon prove maddeningly elusive when pressed about actual decisions. His waffling over the Begelman issue at Columbia repeated itself in a daily refusal to commit to either projects or people. Lansing had to abandon a movie or forge on without her boss's go-ahead, often sparking adamant second-guessing by Hirschfield, who would display his displeasure in a torrent of sarcasm.

Publicly, the tall, silver-haired Hirschfield was jocular and paternalistic to his production president. Driving into the studio with a journalist in his limo, he spotted Lansing and leaned out the window to yell: "Female executives suck!" Rumors circulated that Hirschfield was sleeping with Lansing. "She came to me once and said, 'Do you know what people are saying about us?' " he recalls. "I said, 'Yes, it's terrific. It's great for my ego and my reputation for people to even think you'd give me a tumble. I didn't think you'd give me a tumble.' "

While the Ladd regime had largely backed directors and talent, Hirschfield set up a number of deals with prominent producers—among them Zanuck-Brown, Stanley Jaffe, and Melnick. It was also announced that Lansing would have no authority over any of her former mentor's projects—a condition that Melnick had insisted upon, supposedly to protect her from criticism should the deal fail. Lansing was relieved that she would be seen as beyond reproach and that she'd never have to hear Melnick tell her that she owed him. Yet the arrangement could also be read as the demeaning assumption that a pliant Lansing would auto-matically rubber-stamp anything her former mentor wanted.

Despite the restrictions, Lansing attacked her job, as one friend joked, like little Miss Homework. The media waxed poetic about her graciousness: She's polite! She can say no without hurting people's feelings! Lansing worked at being accessible and unthreatening—attributes that alternately helped and hindered. Some of the powerful men who brought her their projects were able to leave with their egos intact—as one agent turned producer bragged to his poker buddies: "She turned down my project, but maybe I can still fuck her."

To some, Lansing's 1950s manner seemed jarringly out of kilter with that of the new emancipated woman, who had been bred on the women's movement or left-wing politics. She was often suspected of being fake, or at least disingenuous. Shortly after she arrived she wooed one studio executive who was contemplating leaving to little avail. "When I went in to quit, she was very sweet," recalls the executive, who says Lansing cooed, "Oh, hon, I'm going to miss you. You're so great. Are you sure?" By the time the executive had reached the door, the per-son overheard Lansing's assistant lean in to say, "Aren't you thrilled, you got what you wanted."

Lansing's agenda-filled cajoling was no match for the brass-balls politics of Fox. After only a month on the job, her tenuous authority was further undermined by Norman Levy's arrival. In his attempt to staff up the studio to his liking, Hirschfield had promised everything to everybody. Levy was told that within eighteen months he would as-sume charge of movie production—a detail that Hirschfield hadn't shared with Lansing. Likewise, Levy did not know that Lansing's con-tract stipulated that she reported to Hirschfield only. In fact, Stanfill, noticing that Levy's and Lansing's contracts conflicted, had refused to sign Levy's papers.

Immediately, Levy tried to boss Lansing around. "I just felt that he was out to get my job," she says. "I didn't know he had been promised it. And we locked horns all the time. He would get into my territory, and I didn't understand why he was doing it." Lansing was commiserating with Frank Price one day over lunch when her former boss (who had forgiven her, once he realized she was getting promoted) illuminated her. "I said, 'That's ridiculous, Frank.' And I didn't even believe it," re-calls Lansing.

"One day we had this huge fight, and Norman said to me, 'Why are you acting like this? How are we going to work together in twelve months when I take over?'

"And I said, 'What are you talking about?' " Levy told her about his contract, and she told him about hers. Levy immediately called Hirschfield in. "Alan just went, 'So kill me.' He just went crazy," says Lansing. "He just wanted us both, and he figured he'd work it out."

To compound the issue, Levy brought with him a cartload of bad will, having alienated topflight talent such as Steven Spielberg during his days at Columbia with his refusal even to entertain the filmmakers' thoughts about how they would like their movies distributed. Charged with buying films from independent production companies for distribution by Fox, Levy further undercut Lansing's ability to woo creative people by giving his pickups the prime release dates, at the expense of studio-produced fare. It was a charge he adamantly denied. "Norman would just divert her in every way," recalls Melnick. "[He'd say,] 'This movie can't be sold.' Then, when selling those didn't work, he never had to take responsibility that maybe his marketing and distribution wasn't good, and he always had someone to blame in that regard. Second, he would bad-mouth everything."

One of their biggest battles came over *Chariots of Fire.* Lansing had paid a million dollars for the script and foreign rights, with the potential to buy domestic rights for another million after seeing the movie. She had flown to England to see the film, and loved it. Producer David Puttnam brought the film to America to show Levy, who strolled out of the screening for twenty minutes to smoke a cigar. He refused to pick up the rights. Lansing appealed to Hirschfield, but he backed Levy, a decision that cost Fox Oscar bragging rights.

If Lansing's Achilles' heel was a penchant for catering to powerful men, the situation at Fox played on her weakness. "She really was kind of trapped between too many competing parties," recalls Robert Cort, head of Fox publicity at the time. "Sherry, I think, never truly was her own boss. She had Alan, she had Norman, she had Danny [Melnick], even though he was not an executive. It was the government in which too many people had a hand, and I think she never really had a fair shot at it."

Furthermore, in June 1981 Lansing lost one of her most stalwart allies when the Denver oilman Marvin Davis bought the studio. He promptly fired Stanfill. Straitlaced and patrician, Stanfill had at least listened to her opinions and taken her seriously.

I WANT JERRY LANSING!

At a charity benefit for Brandeis University honoring Sherry Lansing, the three-hundred-pound Marvin Davis bragged about his first meeting with her. When he took over the studio, he had asked his executives who ran movie production. He thought he heard "Jerry Lansing." He demanded to meet him, and a few moments later a pretty brunette wandered into his office.

"No, no, honey, I don't want any coffee right now."

The woman answered, "I'm Sherry Lansing."

"No," retorted Davis, "I want Jerry Lansing, the guy who runs the studio."

"No, it's Sherry Lansing," she replied, "and I run the studio."

The crowd gasped.

"In the oil business, we only work with guys," explained Davis. "I never worked with a broad. So I thought she was supposed to get the coffee."

Lansing laughed away Davis's clumsy attempt at a joke, just the most outward sign of her ongoing struggles at the studio. She had come to the dinner with Levy as her date to try to present a united front. Davis's buyout had made Lansing a couple million dollars. For Lansing, the payoff was to be blood money for a slow and steady diminution in stature.

It was not that Davis didn't like Lansing. He loved her. He regarded her affectionately as his "dollface," his "dolly," his "bushky," his surrogate daughter. At meetings with filmmakers he'd declare, "My dollface wants" or "She's the only woman who costs me more than my wife." Davis just didn't pay much attention to her business plans.

From her first meeting with the gargantuan-sized owner, Lansing knew she faced an implacable barrier of old-school assumptions about women and power. She complained to Melnick and Jaffe, "This is not going to work."

"You can get along with him," insisted Melnick. But she was pessimistic, because it was clear to her that on a business level Davis preferred men like himself and particularly Levy. She despaired that she was nothing like them. Whenever her enthusiasm for her job flagged,

Hirschfield would remind her that she was a symbol for all women—implicitly suggesting that her failure would be a failure for all women.

He was hardly the only one. Not long after Lansing had started at Fox, Frances Lear, the then wife of legendary television producer Norman Lear, gave a dinner in her honor and invited fifty high-powered women, everyone from Marlo Thomas to Joan Didion. Each woman was to stand and salute Lansing with an inspirational message or words of advice. The ritual started out friendly enough, but gradually the voices turned more and more hostile, until finally one woman, an official in the Carter administration, hectored Lansing angrily: You owe it to all women to succeed in this job! If you fail, we all fail! You have to do it for at least ten years! Lansing was mortified. At last, Marlo Thomas stepped in, and tried to calm the situation, pointing out that no one—man or woman—ever stayed in the president-of-production job for very long. Lansing went home feeling awful.

Many at the studio felt that Davis treated Fox as an expensive plaything. He didn't take much stock in hierarchy and would often call the production department with ideas for movies. "Dollface, why don't we do a sequel to *The Sound of Music?*" he suggested to Lansing, who had to point out that Rodgers and Hammerstein were dead, and that musicals of more recent vintage had flopped.

"He was not part of your life every day. But then word comes down that he loves Kenny Rogers. We end up making *Six Pack* with Kenny Rogers, so you know he has influence," says Susan Merzbach, a production vice president who had followed Lansing from Columbia. "He wants his son to learn the business. So suddenly his son is all over the studio. As far as I remember he gave [Lansing] for Christmas once this Piaget watch, a $20,000 watch."

"I remember sitting in a meeting with Alan Alda when [Davis] called me dollface, and Alan Alda said later, 'Maybe I should punch him when he does that.' And I realized that Marvin didn't mean anything. I didn't think calling me dollface was the worst thing in the world. The worst thing in the world was not having distribution report to you, you know what I mean?" says Lansing. "Call me dollface, let distribution report to me." In fact, Davis soon promoted Levy to vice chairman and made him a member of the board, de facto one of Lansing's bosses.

Lansing desperately wanted to do well, so much so that industry wags dubbed her "the princess who sits on the fence" for her cautious, defensive manner of assembling pictures.

"She had reticence about committing to a whole lot of projects. She just didn't want to make a mistake, and we tried to encourage her not to feel pressure," says Hirschfield. "That's why Norman was out busy picking up a lot of product to fill in. At a certain point you need the movies. But it takes a couple of years from scratch, and she really inherited an empty larder."

Lansing did not help herself by assembling a weak slate of pictures. Her choices tended toward middlebrow, safe adult comedies by the likes of Herb Ross and Neil Simon, sprinkled with issue-oriented dramas that could be politically risky and controversial. "She frankly did not have a successful production program," adds Hirschfield. "I think her taste was what I would call softer, in terms of not going for the kind of hard action, harder type movies, that, well, frankly was the only thing that was working back in the early eighties," says Hirschfield. "I think where we didn't do well was in the kind of action-adventure genre that the other studios were doing. She didn't put any of those together. And didn't have access to those at that point in time."

In the fall of 1981, Davis finally saw the first two films produced by Lansing's division. The first was the controversial *Making Love*, the tale of a man who leaves his wife for another man. It was one of the first gay-themed films to be made by a major studio. Melnick produced the $8 million picture. The first screening for Davis did not go well. "He jumped up and was shocked when the two men embraced," recalls Melnick. "You could just feel him squirming in his seat."

Later that same week, Davis was called in to adjudicate a dispute about Lansing's second film, *Taps*. The $15 million film, produced by Jaffe, was about a wrongheaded insurrection at a military school, and featured such up-and-comers as Tom Cruise, Timothy Hutton, and Sean Penn. Lansing loved the film and thought it had a powerful anti-war message. According to her, Levy had thought the movie was depressing and asked her to reshoot the ending, in which the National Guard mows down the teenage protagonists. She refused, and Levy threatened to sell off half of Fox's interest in the movie if she did not relent. (Levy denied doing this.) Davis agreed to make the decision. "We showed it to Marvin and he loved it," recalls Jaffe. Davis declared he wouldn't sell any of it.

When the reviews began to roll in—most of them negative—Davis waffled. He called his dollface in and demanded to know why she had changed the ending. He had remembered the kids living at the end, but the critics all claimed they died. Although Davis would deny this account, Lansing told him, "The kids were dead six weeks ago, four weeks ago, and now. Dead is dead." Levy, who was present, backed her up.

When she left his office, she fantasized about quitting, but decided to await the public's verdict.

The film's Manhattan premiere was a gloomy affair. "The audience were all forty, fifty, sixty years old and they were Republicans. They didn't get this movie," recalls Jaffe. Lansing pointedly did not hide her head in the sand, but wore a bright red dress and danced the night away with Jaffe, convinced she was about to get fired.

Taps turned out to be the big hit of the Christmas season, earning Lansing kudos and one more reprieve.

A COMPLETE LOSS OF MYSELF

As she had feared, Lansing's life turned into a twenty-four-hour-a-day blitz of work—breakfasts, lunches, dinners, parties, and events every evening, all of which she attended with indefatigable cheeriness. She hobnobbed with the likes of the Fox board member Henry Kissinger, who became a close friend and staunch supporter.

"She's like a politician. She can work a room better than anyone," says her close friend David Niven, Jr., who was often enlisted to escort her to various functions because her boyfriend, Wayne Rogers, hated them.

"I was one of the ideal types of escorts for her," says Niven, who made two poorly received films for the studio. "That's when we were great friends, and I also know almost as many people as she does in this town, so therefore, whenever she had to go to a function, I was kind of perfect, because she could go rolling off and do her thing and didn't have to drag along someone and then introduce them and go through all that. So she would head to the left, I'd head to the right, and then it was time for dinner, and then we'd sit down and sit next to each other."

The obsessive work took its toll on Lansing's relationship with Rogers, who had his own largely unrealized ambitions in the movie business and an aversion to Hollywood's schmoozathon. They were constantly breaking up and reconciling, brought together by a certain physical passion, torn apart by the pressures of Lansing's career. "The work becomes a way of life," says Rogers. "It's pervasive. The work is all around you. When you're in that job, if you go out socially, it's not social, it's work. You're going to openings and premieres and charitable events, so the work is constantly thrust at you. There is no escaping the work unless you literally leave the country. Rarely did we talk about the work, [but] I found it an enormous intrusion. And, if the truth be known, it's probably one of the reasons that our relationship did not work ultimately. We had some unpleasant times about that."

Lansing had used her Fox windfall to move out of her modest apartment. For $600,000, she bought herself a two-bedroom hide-away at the end of a long driveway in Benedict Canyon. (Unable to bear having a debt, she paid off the mortgage immediately.) Her home was still small by Hollywood standards, but she was able to turn the den into the screening room that her employers wanted her to have. "Jean Ad-cock did it for her, but it had a love seat, not a couch, so she could sit there with just one other person," recalls Gloria Stern. "It was almost like an office. She'd go in and watch her film, or watch dailies, but it wasn't a big social thing of having friends over. I've never known her to try to impress anybody."

Her friends teased Lansing about her no-nonsense personal presen-tation: tweed working-girl pantsuits, the merest dab of makeup, the same flip hairdo she'd worn in college. When she started her job, she bought a wardrobe of six evening dresses from Holly Harp that she wore until they were in shreds.

Lansing continued to fantasize wistfully about kids and even mar-riage. Although her mother finally seemed to realize that she wasn't ever coming home to Chicago, Lansing had internalized her mother's credo and still felt guilty about the choices she had made. "I had been programmed to get married and have two children, so as a good girl al-ways said, no matter what I was doing, I would quit everything if I could get married and have two children. But there's an old expression: Watch your feet, not what you say." In truth, although Lansing loved Rogers, she could never marry him. "I didn't want to marry anyone, be-cause I felt in every relationship that I was in a complete loss of myself. It is like I felt that my identity would never exist," she admits in retro-spect. "And I felt it even when I was dating." They tried living together. But the minute Rogers put a suit in her closet, Lansing began hyper-ventilating. "I couldn't breathe. I thought that the air had been sucked out of the room. It was one jacket." They tried a marriage counselor, but all that Lansing could do was suggest they buy a duplex and live in adjoining apartments.

All her family and friends indulged her, fretting about her ticking biological clock, but few believed her.

"I don't think she really wanted children," says Rogers. "Once again, I think that would have been a major change in her life, and an intrusion into what had been thrust upon her. Now you would have to say, Well, she must like this, because she doesn't rebel against this life. Yes, obviously she must."

"I'm sure being a mother is great, but I don't think I ever really wanted to do it, or I would have done it," says Lansing.

I CAN'T EXIST LIKE THIS ANYMORE

Lansing's frustrations, particularly with Levy, continued to mount, and for the first time in her life she felt the clammy tentacles of failure. "It was like a nightmare," she says. "And I was the person who wanted to make movies and was like a Ping-Pong ball thrown this way, that way, this way. I never had a sense of accomplishment. I was always putting out fires."

Lansing was dismayed to find that producers she didn't respect were able to bypass her to get green lights from Davis or Levy, yet she needed the approval of Hirschfield, Levy, and now Davis.

Even on calls when Lansing proved prescient, credit went to Levy. "I was in a room when [the executives] came up from the screening of *Porky's*," recalls Stanley Jaffe. "It was a pickup, but they hadn't seen it. [Levy] said he hated the movie. She walked in the room and said, 'I can't tell you it's got the highest taste quotient. I think that picture is a huge picture.' Levy didn't even want to let the Fox logo be attached to the picture. Hirschfield and Levy agreed to test the film in two obscure markets. They tested it to see if they could bury it," says Jaffe. *Porky's*, technically Levy's pickup, was a smash.

Lansing tried to adopt a strategy of letting her work speak for itself. "She kept going forward," Jaffe adds. "Instead of turning around and taking a stand, she just thought, All I have to do is make my movies, and make sure they're successful. Their agenda had nothing to do with movies. It was just control. Who was going to control the studio. She didn't care about it. She wanted to make movies, and half the time she spent defending herself." Increasingly Lansing used to joke that the only thing she was allowed to do on her own was sharpen a pencil. "I kept telling her that she should kick them back, she should push them back," recalls Jaffe. Occasionally, she'd make verbal jabs, which were largely ineffective.

Davis in turn was growing more and more dissatisfied with Lansing's slate, which continued to underperform in his assessment. Although *Modern Problems* and the caveman epic *Quest for Fire* had been modest hits, the more recent *Author! Author!*, the story of a single father played by Al Pacino, and Neil Simon's *I Ought to Be in Pictures* had flopped, leading the papers to be full of such unattributed innuendo as "She only likes domestic character studies that only play well on airplanes."

People made fun of her style. "I remember going to a screening of *Making Love* in the Little Theater, on the lot, where Sherry worked the aisles like an airline stewardess, hugging and kissing everyone she knew," one executive quipped to the press.

Lansing's disgust and frustration crested with Martin Scorsese's film *The King of Comedy*, "which I really, really loved," she says, "and no one, none of them came to the previews to see it, which meant that they were just going to bury it." The studio dumped the picture into only a handful of theaters. "I just thought, I can't exist like this anymore. I felt like he had made this gem of a film. Classic, and I couldn't protect it. And therefore I was useless. I was letting down the very people whose respect I wanted. I couldn't do my job, and therefore what was I doing?"

By contrast, Levy's pickups, like *The Cannonball Run*, seemed to print cash. In June 1982, Davis decided to give Levy a $125,000 raise. He also told the executive that his battles with Lansing would soon be coming to an end. He was fed up with his dolly; she would be allowed to remain at the studio only in a much more subordinate position. The trades were soon full of talk of Lansing's imminent professional demise.

She finally confronted Davis, who told her that when her contract expired at the first of the new year, he'd happily grant her an "indefinite extension," although she'd have to accept a de facto demotion to production vice president, reporting to Levy. Lansing knew that this was untenable.

As she stewed about her professional dilemma, her personal life exploded when her close friend the lawyer Norman Garey killed himself. Lansing was distraught. Another man had left her world without explanation. His suicide meant "none of us knew Norman Garey," she told *The New York Times*. "Our father, in a sense, betrayed us."

Garey's death seemed inexplicable, and Hollywood hunted for culprits. Lansing was dismayed and enraged when she heard the rumor that Garey had killed himself over a broken love affair with her. That innuendo paled beside the next one: that she had loaned Melnick a million dollars of Fox money interest free, and he had given it to Garey to save his law firm; when Davis demanded the money back, Garey took his life. Soon the amount Lansing was supposed to have loaned Melnick grew to $50 million, and then came the purported news that she and Melnick had embezzled money from Fox. When she went to Europe on business, gossips said she was stashing the money in a Swiss bank account.

In truth, Davis had been enraged by the size of Melnick's contract, and Garey had been negotiating for Melnick to sell his company back to Fox for $2.5 million. The lawyer had been despondent over his failure to win every one of Melnick's negotiating points.

Yet the press heard the roiling innuendo and assumed another Begelmanesque scandal was in the works, especially since a former employee of Melnick's had complained to the studio of financial improprieties at his production company. Finally, the Los Angeles District Attorney's Task Force on White Collar Crime launched an investigation, which ultimately cleared Melnick, Lansing, and everyone else who had been caught in the rumor mill.

NOW EVERYBODY THINKS WOMEN ARE EQUAL, BUT NOBODY DID THEN

"You think you're my *equal?*" Melnick raged at Lansing, little pieces of sushi flying out of his mouth. "Well, if [you don't think so], I wasn't to start with," she retorted. All she was doing was asking for 50 percent of any producing partnership they would establish. She was only asking for what a man would ask, for what she thought she was worth.

She was familiar with Melnick's theatrics. When she had refused to follow him out the door of Columbia, he had left a note pinned to the underside of his desk: "You have betrayed me." When she was unhappy at Columbia, Melnick, Jaffe, and she had tossed around the idea of setting up an independent production company together. They were going to allot her 10 percent of the company, and when she balked, they raised it to 25 percent. "Now everybody thinks women are equal, but nobody did then," says Lansing.

Now, as she plotted her escape from Fox, Lansing had several professional suitors. Ned Tanen, the former president of Universal, was one; the more adamant Melnick, another. She had been loathe even to discuss a co-venture with him, reluctant to subordinate herself to his ego, to his reputation and his personal idiosyncrasies, which were becoming more troubling. Yet Melnick was persistent, even coming back to her with an offer of 49 percent—a mere 1 percent less than half, that would nonetheless leave him firmly in control of their joint venture. Lansing refused, but, ever the dutiful daughter, she soothed his wounded ego, explaining how she needed to break away from his shadow to establish her own professional identity.

Instead of Melnick and Tanen, she opted for Stanley Jaffe, who now simply assumed they would split the company fifty-fifty. Jaffe, whose home base was New York, would operate from the East Coast, while Lansing would raise the company flag in the West. In later years she explained her decision to several colleagues: "Ned's and my tastes were too similar. Dan's and my neuroses were too similar. Stanley needed me the most." (Lansing denies saying this.) They were the best fit, and, in her mind, he was the strongest producer.

Jaffe, meanwhile, immediately flew to New York and secretly arranged for an independent production deal with Barry Diller and Jeffrey Katzenberg at Paramount. Paramount would have the right of first refusal over their projects, although the duo would have the unusual prerogative of being able to, essentially, green-light a certain number of pictures at a certain price.

Now the pair had to concentrate on getting Jaffe out of his contract at Fox. He had a key-man clause, tied to Lansing, meaning if she left, he was free to go. The catch was that Jaffe had just completed his directorial debut, *Without a Trace,* for Fox; it was slated for an early 1983 release. Both Lansing and Jaffe were worried that if Fox knew what they were planning, the studio would dump the picture.

Over Thanksgiving, Lansing went to Tucson to visit Niven, who was doing a movie for Fox. "I was then going out with a girl who I found there who was a very big, tall thing with an exceptionally well-endowed physique," recalls Niven. Over Thanksgiving dinner Niven's friend told Lansing she was a dancer. "Anyway, we had more and more to drink, and Sherry then wanted to go where she danced. Well, she was actually the number-one naked go-go dancer. I said, 'You don't want to do this, Sherry.' 'Yes, I do.'

"So we go off to one of these places, which is really a bikers' dive, and this table right in front is suddenly produced. We all thought we were going to get killed by these bikers with their tattoos and helmets.

"Sherry says, 'Well, David, you didn't tell me.'

"I said, 'I tried to, but you wouldn't listen.'

"And so this girl is just giggling and wiggling for Sherry's benefit, and it was hysterical. Sherry was clapping louder than anyone, [going,] 'It's fabulous.' "

The sojourn to the strip club was a welcome release for Lansing, who, at age thirty-eight, was trying to figure out what to do with the rest of her life. She and Wayne Rogers had finally broken up for good, and she swore to her friends that if she ever fell in love again she'd get married within three months.

Less than a month later, she quit her job, but refused to tell her employers what she was doing, so as not to imperil the release of Jaffe's movie. "I don't think they were particularly happy with me," she says. Davis was furious that she was beyond his control, that his dolly was leaving him. He flew in from Denver to try to convince her to change her mind. When she wouldn't budge, unflattering innuendo leaked into the press. Sources close to the billionaire told journalist Alex Ben Block that the mogul had in fact fired her. Board member Henry Kissinger purportedly leaned on the Fox executives to cease the war of vitriol against Lansing. Hirschfield and Davis had asked her to stay four months to ease the transition, but she remained for only one. At least one of her last movies, *The Verdict*, was a hit.

Niven had T-shirts printed up. On the front was emblazoned HI, HONEY; on the back, BYE, HONEY.

Paula Weinstein, vice president of production, Warner Bros. Pictures, 1976.

12.

WAR GAMES

I HAD TO COMPLETE THE CYCLE

Sherry Lansing's ascension pained many of her peers, women such as Sue Mengers, who saw her primacy eclipsed by someone younger and prettier, and Paula Weinstein, who had been the highest-ranking woman at the studio. Weinstein herself had toyed with going for the job. Both Melnick and Geffen urged her on. Her phone lines buzzed with busybodies asking, " 'Do you want it, do you want it?' " recalls Weinstein. She was discomfited by the men who offered to mentor her—and all that mentoring seemed to imply.

Forthright and brash in her professional dealings, Weinstein was nonetheless ambivalent about her own ambition, ambivalent about her transformation into a woman in the gray flannel suit, albeit the Chloé gray flannel suit. "You have gotten the fanciest title a woman has ever had, now the next step is this, and of course you can do it" is what she thought she should have said to herself, but "Laddie [Alan Ladd, Jr.], who had the job before, had been in the movie business for thirty years, and knew everything! I felt conflicted in my loyalty to Laddie."

She also felt conflicted by her loyalty to her mother, who had watched her daughter's steady rise through the studio system with partial trepidation. Paula had evolved into one of those executives whom Hannah usually loathed, who constantly devalued the need for intimacy, for a satisfactory personal life. Hannah gave her daughter conflicting advice, on the one hand urging her to "go for it," on the other, warning her, "You've got to have a personal life."

"That was the moment where I [could] have surpassed my mother in our mutual field," recalls Weinstein. "So I think there might have psychologically even been that playing into it.

"When it went to a woman, she was very upset for me. She was upset for herself in some odd way," says Weinstein.

Weinstein followed Alan Ladd, Jr., out the door and set up shop at the newly formed Ladd Company, where she supervised *Body Heat*.

Two years later Weinstein was offered another opportunity to become president of production when David Begelman resurfaced as the head of MGM/UA. "I knew I had to complete the cycle," she says in retrospect. "I said, 'Okay, it's important to go, and to now see how it is to run a team of people and really take that authority.' "

While she had been wary about the turmoil at Fox, there were reasons to be even more so about MGM/UA, which only two years before had gone through the withering debacle of *Heaven's Gate*. Kirk Kerkorian had spent almost fourteen years running the studio into the ground, then suddenly, in the middle of 1981, he about-faced and shelled out $380 million to buy United Artists—the company started by Mary Pickford, Douglas Fairbanks, D. W. Griffith, and Charlie Chaplin—and hired Begelman. Instead of collapsing the two entities into one, Kerkorian decided to keep them separate. Begelman hired his old partner (and Weinstein's former boss) Freddie Fields as head of production at MGM, and Weinstein at UA.

Despite his recent scandal, Begelman had breathed a heady rush of enthusiasm into the moribund and depressed company. Before UA had even been bought, he had green-lighted a number of risky and pricey pictures: *Yes, Giorgio*, Luciano Pavarotti's film acting debut; *Cannery Row; Whose Life Is It Anyway?*; and the surreal Dennis Potter musical *Pennies from Heaven*, which cost $27 million. He decided to resurrect the career of seventy-five-year-old Billy Wilder with a Walter Matthau–Jack Lemmon farce, *Buddy Buddy*. Legendary faces like Wilder's soon filled the commissary, and the new executives set about refurbishing their offices.

Before arriving, Weinstein had been warned about the tart-talking vice president of production, Anthea Sylbert, who had left costume designing to become a studio executive. "People told each of us that it was not going to work out: 'Women are so competitive,' " recalls Sylbert. "What turned out is I found a sister. It was a big surprise to everyone. We were not just able to get along but formed a friendship that is forever."

Sylbert would be Weinstein's biggest support when the situation at MGM/UA started to crumble. The studios began hemorrhaging money, and David McClintock's book *Indecent Exposure* resuscitated the Begelman scandal. By June 1982, Begelman had been fired. His departure left MGM/UA without clear leadership, a redundant management structure, and two production heads, neither of whom had the total confidence of CEO Frank Rothman, a former corporate lawyer who had served as Kerkorian's consigliere. Talk of layoffs and firings spread like fungus.

Almost immediately a power struggle developed between Fields and Weinstein. "Rothman was quite a brilliant lawyer. But he didn't know anything about movies," says Weinstein. "He was susceptible to all the passion and greed. It was like a court of a country that was in trouble, and nobody was telling the king the truth, and the king was somebody who didn't know anything. It was extremely ugly."

Fields immediately began attempting to consolidate his power. "We were in, I thought, and by description, equal jobs," says Weinstein. "But this man would call the director of the project and say, 'Don't talk to her, talk to me. I'm trying to put these companies together and I'm the real boss.' I was rendered completely impotent."

"It was insidious at first," adds Sylbert. "I remember the time Rob Reiner was doing *This Is Spinal Tap*. We had agreed to do *Spinal Tap* in the morning. By night, there were agents on the phone saying, 'Business affairs says you're not doing anything.' It was like *Gaslight*. But once it started, it was quite rapid."

Fields clearly had Rothman's ear, a fact accentuated by the proximity of their offices, but Rothman refused to adjudicate the situation. "What bothered me was that Frank didn't seem to want to make a decision. He wanted for economic reasons to keep the companies separate," recalls Weinstein. Rothman wanted Fields to look over Weinstein's projects without officially giving him that job.

The struggle came to a head over the film *WarGames*, about a young computer genius who inadvertently hacks into the Pentagon computer network and triggers a nuclear showdown. The script had been discovered years earlier by Paula's older sister, Lisa Weinstein, who was then working as a D-girl for the powerful production team of Leonard Goldberg and Jerry Weintraub at Universal. Several years older than Paula,

208 / IS THAT A GUN IN YOUR POCKET?

and with a shy, middle child's temperament, Lisa had convinced her bosses to option the material, and they gave her the privilege of producing it. The company hired a young hotshot director, Martin Brest, whose movie *Going in Style* had received kudos.

Universal deemed the $14 million budget too high, and the project ended up at UA, where the movie was cast and sets begun when "Fields came in," recalls Lisa Weinstein. "I was the producer, but I had never produced a movie before in my whole life. I was producing this hugely complicated technical special-effects movie, and I was really in way over my head. Fields hated Marty, and I think he wanted to put his imprint on the movie, and Paula unfortunately was caught in the middle of this. She and I had a couple of really hideous fights, because I was by then madly in love with Marty."

Lisa Weinstein and Brest had tried to keep their burgeoning relationship secret—unsuccessfully. "[Marty and I] kind of avoided each other for a long time," says Lisa. "It took around six months, and then it just happened. Neither of us wanted particularly to have it happen. Because I had always been very strict about never getting emotionally involved with anybody I worked with, because I thought it was too dangerous. And he was living with somebody then, and it just happened. We didn't stay together the whole time. There were periods during that experience where we weren't together, where he just went back with his girlfriend and tried to make that work, and it was a very volatile courtship."

Fields hated the first crop of dailies from *WarGames*. He had little experience evaluating rushes, having never run production, but he thought Brest's work was slow and clichéd. The Weinstein sisters' enthusiasm for the footage didn't sway him. Indeed, Fields's antipathy toward Brest seemed to stem in part from his growing antipathy toward Paula Weinstein, and he accused her of being partisan because of Brest's relationship with her sister. Indeed, Fields says that Paula Weinstein should have recused herself from the situation: "She had a personal tie. It's a conflict. She wasn't behaving objectively."

After several weeks Fields called over to United Artists to say he thought Brest should be fired and suggested a replacement, an obscure British horror director named Stewart Raffill. To placate Fields (although he putatively had no jurisdiction over UA), Sylbert examined Raffill's work and was horrified. Weinstein tried to save Brest's job, going so far as to cut footage together and show it to Frank Rothman, to little avail. Accepting seeming inevitability, Paula Weinstein and Sylbert solicited new directors, among them John Badham, of *Saturday Night Fever*.

Paula Weinstein called a meeting with their outside financiers; and, to her surprise, in strolled Fields. They began to discuss possible replacements for Brest, and Fields adamantly advocated for Raffill.

"I don't think he should be part of this discussion. Not only is he not experienced enough, he's not good enough," said Sylbert.

"You have no right to say that. You don't know who he is," countered Fields.

"I don't have to know who he is. I only have to know his work," Sylbert said acidly.

With that, an angry Fields retorted, "Shut your fucking mouth or I'll shut it for you."

"I got up from my chair and said, 'Let me say something to you. I have gone head-to-head with the best of them, but not even a disgruntled lover gets to talk to me that way. I'm out of here,' " recalls Sylbert. She stormed out.

When Sylbert returned from lunch, an ugly bouquet of flowers graced her desk, with a note from Fields: "I wish to apologize. Rudeness is my suit. I wish to explain."

"I took a piece of paper and said, 'Dear Freddie. Thanks for the flowers. I wish to explain,' " says Sylbert, and sent the note by interoffice mail. Two days later she quit the company.

The pressure was growing on the increasingly isolated Weinstein—pressure from the company and from her sister. "The day before Marty was going to be fired she actually called me and said they were going to fire him tomorrow," says Lisa, "and we tried to get his agent to call the Directors Guild and do something about it, but it was all too late. They had already hired surreptitiously this other director." Fields asked John Kohn, the head of production for one of the film's financial partners, to break the news to Brest on the set.

Lisa Weinstein's lawyer, Tom Pollack, had called begging her not to walk off the picture; the studio would undoubtedly fire her, but she would get to keep her credit, and the money. Yet when Kohn told her afterward what he had done, she couldn't control her feelings. "Because I tend to do things emotionally rather than sensibly, I shot off my big mouth and said, 'I'm going to resign,' and so they took that as an official resignation, even though I hadn't said that officially to anybody."

The next day, she received a telegram from the studio: "We accept your resignation."

"I really felt that I had the blood of Walter and Larry [the writers] on my hands, and the idea of having Marty's blood on my hands if I stayed. It was just impossible for me," says Lisa Weinstein. "I was so in love with him that I couldn't bear the thought of being in the movie without him. I felt it was so unjust and that he was never fired because of the work he had done, but rather because of politics and personality. And I couldn't go along with something I felt was wrong. Other people felt that I was the schmuck of life to give up a movie for a guy. But that's Hollywood."

Brest himself had told her not to quit a project that had consumed over three years of her life over him. Yet afterward, "I think he was thrilled," says Weinstein, "because I think he felt as I felt, that if I stayed on the movie our relationship would be over. We couldn't bridge that."

Fields attempted to straighten out the situation, by assuring Paula Weinstein that he really wanted her to continue to work for him. She responded with fury: "You have got the same title I have at a sister company. I don't work for you. Until somebody walks in here and makes you chairman of the board of this company, I do not have to report to you. It's not your project, so forget it."

Paula declined to come to work, stating that her contract, stipulating that she had to answer only to Rothman, was being violated. "And Fields was like Othello to the end," she says. "He had every person fired. He was like Iago in the ear of this man who was there to watch the money. He said terrible things every day and called me in the middle of the night. It was the most extraordinary display of female-hating, power-hungry behavior."

"Paula and I were mad at each other for a day," says Lisa Weinstein. "We can't be angry at each other too much. It's too important a relationship for us to allow anything, or anyone, to come between us."

Brest, however, stewed at Paula for years before all was forgiven. After the *WarGames* debacle, he and Lisa were treated as persona non grata by those in Hollywood who feared that failure was contagious. "Marty had been this golden boy in Hollywood, and then we would go to screenings together and people would literally turn their backs on us and move away from us as though we were pariahs," says Lisa Weinstein. "You could see people looking at him thinking, 'Gee, maybe we're wrong. Maybe he isn't that talented. Maybe it was just a lucky fluke what he had done before.' "

The couple wound up marrying and having a child. Two years after *WarGames*, Brest directed *Beverly Hills Cop*, one of the top-grossing movies of the 1980s.

Meanwhile, although Paula Weinstein had been at the studio only about a year, she decided to leave. "I think the people at MGM would have been very happy for me to have stayed, to have toed the line and said, 'Okay, great, sure I'll be your assistant.' So I left, and we went into arbitration over the contract."

It was a long, debilitating battle against Hollywood's ritualistic humiliation of out-of-favor executives. Weinstein and her lawyer tried to take a page out of the class-action suits waged against various manufacturing industries, where management had pushed people—usually minority groups or women—out of their jobs by systematically stripping them of duties. Such a suit had never been won by an individual.

Concurrently, it was and is frequent operating practice in Hollywood to isolate an employee so much that he or she would quit, and thereby forgo a hefty severance package. Weinstein tried to argue that the studio had taken away her duties—"what defined being president of a production, that was tantamount to a firing," she explains.

"They never went in and said, 'Hey, it isn't working out. We know we owe you two years on your contract, and we'd like to settle out if you get another job.' They always did this terrible but, I suppose, completely corporate responsible thing, which is to close the doors and close the doors until you have rendered somebody impotent. I've seen it happen to man after man after man. I've seen faces go from joy to such unbelievable pain and, finally, what's it over, a million bucks, $350,000, $600,000?"

Weinstein fantasized that she could set a precedent for the industry. A number of the town's most powerful players—including Frank Wells, one of the leaders of Warners, and the rising agent Michael Ovitz—came to testify on her behalf. Although Fields denies doing it, industry players recounted how they were told by other executives at MGM/UA not to do business with her, says Weinstein. At one point one executive even testified how Freddie Fields had called and threatened him with professional ostracism in order to discourage him from supporting Weinstein's position in the arbitration.

"It was an unbelievable show of support, and lots from women," says Weinstein. "A lot of women calling up and saying, 'Great, I'm really glad you're doing it.' "

In the end, however, she did not win. Weinstein recalls: "The arbitrator declared, 'It isn't really prejudice because she was allowed to stay with her title and all of that, even if she's not doing her job.' They said the corporation has the right to behave in any way they want." The arbitrator did agree, however, that there had been "some prejudicial behavior. Not enough to win me the money. But enough to not make me pay all the legal fees. It was, like, whoever lost had to pay the legal fees."

Looking back on the saga almost fifteen years later, Weinstein is chagrined by her own naïveté, her idealistic stand against the monolith of corporate America. "You can't win a lawsuit like that. This would be winnable if you were a black woman in the South—but as a white middle-class woman in the movie business, the chances of winning this are slim to none. There just isn't any [legal] precedent.

"So that was a mistake, and exhausting," she says philosophically. "I am sorry I just didn't say, 'Guys, I'm out of here.' "

13.

———

BROKEN BONDS

I CUT THE CORD

One hot August day in 1980, Polly Platt received a strange phone call: an almost incoherent man bellowed, "Where's Peter Bogdanovich? Where's Peter Bogdanovich?" Platt thought the man was a spurned actor, hung up the phone, and quickly forgot the incident.

That summer had been a psychic oasis. She and Tony Wade were remodeling their Pacific Palisades home, adding two bedrooms so that each of their four children could have a separate space. "We were very happy. It was like a storybook," says Platt. Antonia worshiped Tony, loved him. While he was at work, she and her sister and her stepsiblings, Kelly and John (who were around their age), would run wild. "The children were so *bad*. They were so *bad*." Platt laughs. "And then Big Tony would come home and they would be so *good*."

Platt and Wade had gotten married in 1979 in part because Wade suffered from a form of lupus, which had gradually worsened after *Pretty Baby*. He had fought the disease mostly by ignoring it. By the time of their wedding, however, his medications had transformed his once handsome face into a balloonlike orb. "The only thing you could do was suppress the symptoms," recalls Platt. "You couldn't treat the disease. He took cytoxin"—a drug used against leukemia—"which is very debilitating and you bleed from any mucous membrane of your body." They formalized their relationship so that Platt could theoretically take over the care of Wade's two children, who had been living with them for years, in the case of his death.

When the strange call came, Wade was working on a picture in San Francisco, while Antonia and Sashy—and Platt's loyal housekeeper—

Jodie Foster in Taxi Driver.

were off for several weeks with Peter Bogdanovich and his new girl-friend, Dorothy Stratten, *Playboy*'s Playmate of the Year. Bogdanovich had met the luscious Canadian blonde at the Playboy mansion and fallen in love with her, fantasizing that he could remold her into a movie princess. He had written her into his latest film, the romantic comedy *They All Laughed*.

Platt later learned from the police that the mysterious caller was Paul Snider, Stratten's estranged husband. A small-time hustler who had hurtled the two of them out of Palookaville on the strength of Stratten's blond hair and statuesque figure, he had grown steadily more enraged at his former wife's preference for Bogdanovich and his os-tracism from her increasingly jet-set life. When Hugh Hefner banned him from the Playboy mansion in early August, a furious Snider had waved his .38 outside the electronic gates of Bogdanovich's Bel Air mansion. A couple of days later Stratten told Snider she was leaving him definitively. After an irate phone call, Stratten agreed to see Snider again, and on the morning of August 14 she stole out of Bogdanovich's mansion to meet him at their former home. Snider shot her head off with a shotgun. At some point in the afternoon, he phoned Platt look-ing for Bogdanovich. Ultimately he turned the gun on himself.

Bogdanovich had spent the day frantically worrying about his girl-friend. Around midnight Hefner called and informed him that Stratten was dead. The children were still at the Bel Air house. "I was out of my mind," Polly Platt recalls. "I was horrified. I wanted to get the children out of there. I couldn't get Peter on the phone." Bogdanovich had col-lapsed in his bedroom, banging his head repeatedly on the floor.

"He won't see anyone. He won't see the children. I don't know what to do!" she wailed to Wade on the phone.

"Why don't you send him a subscription to *Playboy*?" joked Wade.

Platt was sucked into the whirlpool of grief and bizarre behavior that followed Stratten's death. The beauty's eleven-year-old sister, L.B., was also in the Bel Air house. Platt barely knew her—L.B. was simply an extremely shy, practically mute little girl whom she occasionally took for ice cream with Sashy and Antonia. No one, in particular her mother, who was thousands of miles away in Canada, wanted to break the news to her about Dorothy's murder. Peter's sister, Anna Bog-danovich, enlisted Platt to talk to L.B.

"As you know, your sister has disappeared," she managed to tell the little girl, "and they think maybe she was with her husband. It looks as if it could be something really bad. Your mother wants you to come home." Platt recalls, "She just seemed to be in shock."

Stratten's death—and the violence it brought to Sashy's and Antonia's lives—severed Platt's years-long umbilical tie to Bogdanovich. "It was almost as if the trap closed," Platt recalls. "Peter had always justified his behavior by trying to find fault with me, and he had a very good partner in that. I would always agree with him that it was my fault. The Dorothy Stratten thing proved that I was right, that he was *evil*. He had sinned. It really wasn't me. My family had never had a murder in it. I cut the cord.

"I blamed it all on Peter, which seems odd from an outsider's point of view because it's obviously not his fault that this horrible man did these horrible things. But because Peter lived only in celluloid, I always thought he was ignorant and insensitive to the effects of his actions on other people."

Bogdanovich was destroyed. He was a shell of a man in search of a personality. His orgy of grief enveloped the entire family. Platt recalls waking up one morning alongside Wade to find Antonia and Sashy dressed in their Sunday finest, standing by their bedside. They were going to their father's. "It's Dorothy's birthday," they told her. "There's a cake, and we're going to visit her grave."

Platt says, "I don't know why it bothered me so much. It seemed such a maniacal thing to be doing. You know, bury the dead and live for the living. I felt like E.T. I could feel my neck elongating and felt like I was going to explode. If you said, 'I don't think you should be doing that,' the children would go, 'No, Dorothy is wonderful. She's a white goddess.' So Big Tony sat up in bed and said, 'It's Dorothy's birthday, whatever are we going to buy her as a present?' The kids were *ahhhhh*. He made a shocking remark, and then they started laughing. It was the first time anyone had made a healthy joke. That kind of healed us all a little."

The bizarre pall of Stratten's death took its toll on Platt's relationship with Wade. "It was almost as if Tony and I didn't have a chance, in the sense I worried so much about my children. I did well with Kelly and John [her stepchildren]. You could talk to them forever. There was no way I wasn't the greatest mother to them. I was not as great a mother to my own children, in the sense that I didn't know how to deal with it all. I don't think anybody would have."

Bogdanovich plummeted into a free fall that included an ill-advised, publicly excoriated paean to Stratten, the book *The Killing of the Unicorn*, which engendered a feud with Hugh Hefner, whom Bogdanovich blamed for Stratten's death. "I finally became very angry with him at that time, and we didn't speak for about three years," says Platt. "But it was not because of her murder, it was because of the way he fell apart over it, and the effect on my children. And he became obsessed with Dorothy's little sister, L.B., who is really a nice girl. But at the time, she was only eleven."

Bogdanovich used to bring L.B. to Platt's house. The child was afraid of the dog, afraid of the water, of seemingly everything, and would cling fiercely to Bogdanovich. Platt used to tell people L.B. was like a koala bear. She grew more and more horrified by her ex-husband's ministrations to Stratten's little sister. Hefner publicly accused Bogdanovich of sleeping with L.B., who was underage at the time, but the Los Angeles Police Department could find no evidence that a crime had been committed.

"I was deeply offended by his affection for this little girl. She's the same age as my children," says Platt, who hated how the children felt slighted by their father's fawning over L.B. "I felt that he should be paying attention to our daughters. So we quarreled over that, big. And I really thought I would never talk to him again."

She was infuriated that Bogdanovich bought L.B. a BMW and jewels and paid for her elaborate dental surgery, but balked at giving Platt child support. He married L.B. when she turned twenty. His life became steady fodder for *People* magazine.

In 1985 Bogdanovich declared bankruptcy. "He was unable to support the children. Of course, that was the best thing that ever happened to me, because I said, I better get my act together," recalls Platt. "I always thought Peter would be able to send them to college. It never occurred to me that it would be me."

I WAS VERY AWARE OF BEING A WOMAN ALONE

After *Pretty Baby* there had been many writing deals—a script for Streisand, a coveted writer-producer deal at Paramount, for which she wrote a rock-and-roll remake of *White Christmas*, and then a more personal screenplay about a distraught man who jumped off the top of the Brooklyn Bridge, "and when he survived he became a sort of mini-hero for the summer." The studio system—the need to validate herself as an artistic authority in her own right—overwhelmed and baffled Platt.

When a writers' strike put a crimp into that steady revenue, Platt returned to the familiar and comfortable world of production design, an enormously influential role on the movie, but one that clearly serves the great master auteur. Insecure about her position now that she was no longer intrinsically linked to the director, she adopted a stance of strident advocacy. She could be an aesthetic Stalinist—exceedingly vehement about her ideas, and sometimes she threatened to upstage her directors.

"I definitely was fighting all my life to be recognized as an artist in my own right, for sure. I felt that my accomplishments with Peter were erased. I wanted to be someone. Not to be famous, but I wanted my peers—I wanted to have the authority and power to make movies, which I had.

"It was very hard to adjust to being a working girl in a profession that's all men. I was with men all the time," says Platt. "I traveled all over America with different men—male construction coordinators, directors—and they would have adventures in hotels, pick up women and take them to their rooms, and the next morning they would tell all their stories. Maybe not even bragging, saying, 'She wasn't too attractive but she seemed so needy.' 'I nailed her.' Whatever. I would sit there and look at them and have these thoughts: 'Why don't I do that?' 'Why don't I pick up the guy at the bar, and take him up to my room and sleep with him?' 'Why don't I do that?' Because I don't want to. They want to. I was very aware of being this woman alone."

"She was my mentor. My film-directing mentor," says Garry Marshall, who worked with Platt on his directorial debut, *Young Doctors in Love.* "She was the first one who really tried to help me. She had come on as the production designer, but really to teach me about directing. I can't tell you she's this wonderful warm, nurturing person who takes you under her wing and walks you around and talks to you. That's not Polly. Polly cuts to the chase. She used to stand on the side and when I was setting up a shot I would kind of glance over to her, and she would put her finger in her mouth and make believe she was gagging, which simply told me that it was not going to be a good shot, so I immediately changed the shot. She was very quick and blunt—this is good, this is bad—and she could do it from twenty feet away. She designed it so it would be easier to shoot. I'd say, 'You got to make a sign with an arrow.' She'd say, 'You don't need a sign. I'll do it with colors. When you see another color you know you're in a different place.' She said paint is cheaper than signs.

"Then she sat with me and told me how important it was to stick up for things that I believed in. She helped me differentiate between which were petty, egotistical arguments and which would break the picture."

Platt had taken a cut in salary because the film was low-budget but filming in L.A., and she wanted to stay home with her children. "And years later he sent me a check for twenty thousand dollars because the movie did so well he felt that I should participate in the profits," she says.

Platt designed *Young Doctors in Love* entirely sober. She had quit drinking with Big Tony, but he wouldn't stay sober, and couldn't stay faithful, so they broke up in 1982. For a while Antonia moved in with Wade and his kids. "I didn't blame her, you know. I just wanted him to be nice to her," says Platt. When the film was over, however, Platt was so lonely that she began drinking beer on the weekends. "The children hate me not only for Peter. Now they hate me for Big Tony," she says she thought to herself.

MY BODY JERKED IN PAINFUL CONVULSIONS

On March 30, 1981, John Hinckley, Jr., a paranoid loner from a wealthy family in Denver, fired six bullets at close range as President Reagan left the Washington Hilton after having addressed a group of trade unionists. One bullet lodged in Reagan's lung. Others hit a Secret Service agent, a police officer, and the president's press secretary, James Brady, ultimately paralyzing him.

It was an uncanny real-life enactment from *Taxi Driver*, in which Travis Bickle attempts to assassinate a political candidate in order to win the notice of a campaign worker played by Cybill Shepherd. Hinckley had seen the movie in a theater in Lubbock, Texas, when it debuted in 1976—although instead of Shepherd he'd become obsessed with the teen prostitute played by Jodie Foster.

For months before the fateful shooting, Hinckley had stalked the actress, now a freshman at Yale. He made several visits to New Haven, hung out around her dorm, and followed fifteen feet behind her with a loaded gun in his pocket. In the fall and spring, he barraged her with letters, several even pushed under the door of her dorm room. "After tonight, John Lennon and I will have a lot in common," he wrote in one. "Jodie Foster love, just wait, I'll rescue you very soon," he wrote in another—a missive very similar to the one that Travis Bickle sends Foster's character in *Taxi Driver*. Three weeks before the shooting, Foster had given a package of his notes to a Yale administrator who gave them to the campus police who searched for their author—in vain.

Later, in Hinckley's Washington hotel room, police found tapes of phone calls he had placed to Foster, which consisted mostly of him begging to be allowed to call her again. Her roommates can be heard giggling in the background. "They're laughing at you," Foster tells him, then says in an aside to her friends: "I should tell him I am sitting here with a knife."

"Well, I'm not dangerous. I promise you that," Hinckley interjects. "Can I call you tomorrow night?"

"That's fine," Foster replies tersely. Although later in the conversation, her bile and frustration bubble over: "Oh God, oh seriously, this is really starting to bother me. Do you mind if I hang up?"

"Oh, Jodie, please . . ." Hinckley can be heard moaning.

In the hotel room police also found photos of Foster and a letter—written but never sent—in which the would-be assassin beseeches his elusive object of desire: "Jody [*sic*], I would abandon this idea of getting Reagan in a second if I could only win your heart and live out the rest of my life with you. . . . I will admit to you that the reason I'm going ahead with this attempt now is because I just cannot wait any longer to impress you."

Hinckley's obsession and its unfortunate consequences torpedoed the normalcy that Foster had tried to establish for herself at Yale. She had gone off to the Ivy League college in an almost quaint search for a life she could call her own. She was thrilled to be among what she perceived to be the best and brightest of her generation. "It was really important for me to be someplace where my achievements were my own achievements, and where they weren't mixed up with anyone else's and it wasn't about the movie, and it wasn't about my mom, and it was just about what I did and what I do," she recalls years later. "Just [to have] my own life that I had built, and to be able to succeed or fail in those parameters."

Some of Foster's newfound freedoms were poignantly ordinary. It was the first time she had been allowed to decorate her room away from Brandy's strict aesthetic dictates, the first time she could eat with impunity, or not brush her hair if she didn't feel like it. She dabbled in collegiate partying and frequented the New York nightclub Area. (In 1983 she was arrested at Boston's Logan Airport for carrying cocaine and fined a hundred dollars.) Perhaps most important, it was the first time Foster was able to develop sustaining relationships with members of her peer group. "I really had not spent that much time with people my age. I didn't have a lot of friends, and I wasn't very social, and L.A. is different. People don't really talk about what's bothering them. They just go to the beach. I don't remember anybody having long conversations about anything in Los Angeles. But the second that I got East, it was like a whole different culture of people sitting in coffee shops while it was raining, you know, pouring out their life stories. That's just not part of L.A. Oh, I loved it."

Hinckley shattered Foster's newfound playfulness, the carefully constructed anonymity she had built for herself. Her first public reactions were those of a well-trained child actress who knows the show must go on. Against the advice of many, Foster organized a press conference and read a statement—in a kind of hopeful bargain that if she told the press what they wanted to hear, they would finally leave her alone. "I felt very sad, frightened, distressed. I acted badly. I guess I cried," she said, describing her response, adding pointedly, "I'm not here to answer questions about *Taxi Driver.* In no way have I ever been sorry about any film I have done."

Although Foster quickly moved out of her shared dorm room into a single, she continued to march through the constructs of her life. She went to classes and went on with her part in a student production of *Getting Out,* Marsha Norman's prison drama about a former prostitute who serves eight years for murdering a cabdriver. It was Foster's first theater experience, and she played the woman—Arlene—as a young girl. It was directed by another child of Hollywood, and a close friend at the time, Tina Landau, the dark-haired, clever, outspoken daughter of the film producer Ely Landau.

If Foster had backed out, the play would have had to have been canceled, and she wanted to prove that Hinckley didn't run her life. The Yale police frisked every member of the audience. Foster asked that all cameras be confiscated because the whirring of the motor drives unnerved her. (One of the producers let one in, without telling her before-hand, which infuriated her.) The five-dollar tickets were scalped for fifty.

Two were bought by a would-be Hinckley copycat, Edward Richard-son of Pennsylvania, who caught Foster's attention during both per-formances. He sat in one of the front rows and seemed fixated upon her, staring relentlessly without a trace of emotion. His plan was to shoot Foster, but when he actually saw the actress, his resolve crumbled, be-cause she was "too beautiful to kill." He later phoned the New Haven police, claiming to have planted a bomb in Foster's dorm, which he would detonate if Hinckley wasn't freed. In the middle of the night, the dormitory was evacuated. He wrote a death threat to Foster, and an-other to Ronald Reagan, which he left in his New Haven hotel room. Soon after, the Secret Service arrested him in New York's Port Author-ity Bus Terminal.

In the public consciousness Foster quickly transmuted from the brightest child star into the world's most famous would-be victim, and then into a punch line on late-night TV. "Why did Israel bomb Lebanon? . . . To impress Jodie Foster." Fortunately, the court ruled she didn't have to testify against Hinckley in person. A videotape would suf-fice. Unfortunately, an agitated Hinckley was nonetheless present at the taping. He threw a pen at Jodie and screamed, "Jodie, I'll kill you," be-fore he was taken from the courtroom.

For months after the attack the actress was shadowed by security guards. On occasion Foster was forced to move around via freight ele-vators and the trunks of cars. The guards more than embarrassed her. They humiliated her. They were pointed reminders of how different she was from other Yale students. "I felt like a pariah," she said at the time.

Foster says she was depressed most of her teen years, a depression that had just begun to lift when she arrived at Yale. Now she sank back in. She gained twenty pounds and wore the same clothes for weeks at a time. She saw death lurking in every corner. A fellow student sent a dis-patch to *People* magazine about her state—an awful reminder of how everybody was forever watching her.

She shut out many and became testy when the unwanted tried to get close. "She was very flip about Hinckley," recalls Harry Ufland, her agent at the time. "I tried to warn her to take it seriously. She was very shaken up by it, but wouldn't talk about it." She ultimately retreated into the embrace of a handful of friends.

Twenty months after Hinckley's attack, Foster released what would be her definitive statement on him—an essay entitled "Why Me?"—published in *Esquire*, at the behest of her friend and mentor, the editor Lee Eisenberg, with the intention of once and for all answering the dreaded questions. As would become her way, Foster could be more revealing in print, in the abstract—in art—than she could be in daily relationships where she adopted Teflon bravado. "My body jerked in painful convulsions. I hurt." She was not thinking of Reagan or the assassination attempt or the circling press. "I was crying for myself. Me, the unwilling victim. The one who would pay in the end. The one who paid all along, and, yes, keeps paying," she wrote. There was an undercurrent of martyrdom in her statements: "People were punishing me because I was there." They were hurting her intentionally, without even making physical contact. "They were manifesting a need to wound, and I just happened to be the victim."

"It was a shattering of the bubble for me," Foster says in retrospect. "A big moment in my life. Everybody's got their one moment where suddenly all their illusions become clear to them."

IT'S NOT EASY FOR ME TO SHOW WEAKNESS

The summer after the Hinckley episode, Foster returned to L.A. and threw herself into a TV project, *O'Hara's Wife*, a silly fantasy about a workaholic lawyer who's goaded into giving up his mania for the rat race by the ghost of his late wife. Foster played his wisecracking daughter. She returned for another semester at Yale, then took time off to do a TV film, *Svengali*, in New York. It was a vehicle beneath her talents about a rock singer who fears she can't perform without the help of her Svengali, Peter O'Toole, with whom she has an affair.

The attention she had received in the aftermath of the Hinckley incident was perhaps the only kind of attention that Hollywood didn't relish. Nor did the unflattering paparazzi shots help. Foster's relationship with her agent, Harry Ufland, was fraying. Ufland had left ICM to set up his own shop and Foster had followed him but felt that she was receiving less and less of his attention. "He just wanted to do the boys," she recalls. "I was the only woman he had, really. At one point he had Liza Minnelli, but only for one year. He just wasn't very interested in me. Mostly because I was living on the East Coast, and he was a Malibu guy. . . . So I went to Sam Cohn. He's the only person that I knew in New York at ICM, and I thought he would get me some parts. And for whatever reason we didn't really click. He wasn't interested in me, because I primarily wanted to be an L.A. film actor. And he was very upfront about, theater is everything, and New York is everything, and why do you wanna go out there and be an L.A. brat, and you should really learn your craft. So, he just pawned off everything onto Joe [Funicello] anyway. And since Joe had been my subagent with Harry, and now he's my subagent with Sam, and he did everything anyway, finally one day I said, 'You know what? We're gonna have my papers changed, and now you'll be my agent.' And he's like, 'Okay, well, great.' And I don't even think Sam noticed."

Ufland's and Cohn's perceived reactions weren't all that surprising, given the coolness that was rapidly descending on Foster's career. Cohn had been particularly blunt about her weight—telling her she'd have to shed those extra pounds if she wanted to work. In truth, Foster was not so sure she did. She was growing more and more ambivalent about acting. "Let's just say that I did what I used to do when I was five years old, which is like sell dog food as an actor. You know, do a dog food commercial or toothpaste, or this or that. Basically, what I would be is a body and a face and gestures for advertising. Which is what most actors can hope for. I just was like, I don't think I'm courageous enough to take the risk and then wake up when I'm sixty and say that I sell dog food."

"At the time she was very disillusioned with acting," recalls Natasha Richardson, daughter of Tony Richardson and Vanessa Redgrave, who met Foster on the set of her father's film *The Hotel New Hampshire* in the summer of 1983. "I think she found it too easy for too long. I think when something comes naturally to someone, it's very easy to denigrate it in some way. She had this talent and facility, and she wanted to just kick it away."

The Hotel New Hampshire was based on John Irving's bestseller about an eccentric family of innkeepers who are drawn into a whirlpool of seriocomic disasters. Foster plays Frannie Berry, who gets gang-raped at the beginning and spends the rest of the film recovering, through an affair with her brother and a young woman with a penchant for wearing a bear suit. She received a career-high salary of $500,000. It was one of the first times she played a victim on-screen.

Richardson conducted freewheeling rehearsals. "Jodie had a streak of anarchy about her in those days," recalls Rob Lowe, who played her brother, "and Tony was nothing if not the ultimate anarchist. So they sort of fed off of one another. Tony took great glee in the more tempest that was going on around the set and the drama and the high jinks."

Indeed, the precarious nature of the project fostered a sense of camaraderie. Foster cottoned to Lowe, as well as to Nastassja Kinski, the rising German starlet who graced the cover of *Time* during the shooting. Foster had convinced a wavering Kinski to commit to the movie. "Nastassja, I think, worshiped Jodie at that point," says Lowe, "and I don't think *worship* is too strong a word. She just was completely overwhelmed with Jodie."

For the first time, perhaps ever, Foster seemed to enjoy making a movie. The day he met her, says Lowe, "She had been on the plane with Brandy and she had tried to bite the top off a canister of Krazy Glue, and, of course, she did bite it off and got it all over her lips and mouth—she looked like a burn victim. It was just a horrible, horrible scar she had, this sore." He laughs. "I thought, Oh my God, are we going to be able to shoot? She's got that side to her that's sort of really goofy, funny, playful, a side that I don't really see represented a whole lot in public. She has seen every episode of *Bewitched* and loves *The Wizard of Oz*. She and I would sing 'Midnight Train to Georgia' in the makeup room."

For all her intellectual airs, Foster relished a retreat into calculated immaturity, the cocoon of the seventy-person movie set. "I remember on the set she turned to me one day and said, 'This is so much fun,' " says Lowe. "I said, 'Yeah, isn't it?' And she said, 'But it's never been fun for me before now.' I just don't think that there was any levity to her experience on movie sets."

Foster balked at taking off her clothes or even appearing in the rape scene. "I sat down with Tony Richardson, saying, 'I can't do this, I can't do that,' " says Foster. "I remember him saying to me, 'You won't be a real actor until you realize your body is part of who you are and what you do. If you can't share that, I don't know what you're doing being an actor.' At the time, I thought he was really an asshole for saying that and I stuck to my guns. Now I see the wisdom of what Tony was saying. Your body is part of who you are. At the time, I really wanted to hit him."

When the film was over, she flew off to Paris to shoot Claude Chabrol's *The Blood of Others*, based on a Simone de Beauvoir World War II novel about a dress designer's assistant and her doomed affair with a resistance fighter, played by Michael Ontkean. Since Foster had started college, Brandy had been living in France most of the time. Foster dubbed her own part in both French and English. "If the Hollywood phone isn't going to ring, how fabulous is it to go off to Paris and work with Chabrol and do a movie in two different languages?" Lowe sighs. "That's what Jodie Foster does when the phone doesn't ring. When the phone doesn't ring for other actors, God forbid what they do." While she was in Paris, Foster received word that the jury had deemed John Hinckley not guilty by reason of insanity.

Even the wounds of Hinckley began to fade, transmuted through will into fodder for black comedy. Foster moved off-campus with her friend Jon Hutman, another born-and-bred Angeleno, who teased her about her Brandy-like pretensions, nicknaming her Miss Authoritiva and decorating their apartment with ironic eighties kitsch, an inflatable child's swimming pool, and bad fuchsia lawn furniture. Although Foster kept her own room an ascetic, spartan lair, she did contribute to the overall decor: On the wall of their kitchen hung a huge blowup of the famous photograph of Reagan getting shot: "an ironic thumbing of your nose at the absurdity of life in the public eye," says Lowe, "and how Fellini-esque it truly can get through no fault of your own."

"That picture had been given to me by the Secret Service," says Foster. "I was full of defenses, and I think that definitely"—she pauses— "I'm not somebody that's comfortable being emotionally available. It's not easy for me to show weakness. I have such a hard time with it," she says. "Just to prove to myself that I could handle it, I would read every horrible letter sent to me, every disgusting thing, and laugh at them and say, Ha ha, like I can cope with this, and that's a really complicated, tortured psyche."

14.

THE DAWN OF A NEW AGE

OH SHIT, NOW WHAT DO I DO?

By the spring of 1979 it had become clear to everyone on the Paramount lot that *Star Trek: The Motion Picture* was a disaster in the making. Launched in quick response to such successful sci-fi epics as *Star Wars* and *Close Encounters of the Third Kind*, the big-screen version of the cult TV series was far behind schedule, with a script in constant flux, special effects that weren't working, and a budget climbing to a then unheard-of $44 million. Paramount's president, Michael Eisner, had instructed the merchandising department, then a studio backwater mostly devoted to purveying *Happy Days* and *Mork and Mindy* paraphernalia, to raise guarantees from potential licensees that could cover part of the cost of the film's production. All the potential licensees were invited to a presentation at a Paramount studio theater, which had all the charm and finesse of a stage at sleep-away camp.

"I was a desperate person," recalls Dawn Steel, then vice president of merchandising in charge of *Star Trek*. "There was no product because there was no movie to show anyone. So I had to do this razzamatazz bit onstage so I could convince the people to make pajamas and toys and Coca-Cola and McDonald's to do the tie-ins." With the aid of a special-effects expert, she says, "I figured out how to do this laser thing. I beamed myself onto the stage. *Nobody else* was going to beam me onto the stage."

The crowd gasped, then applauded as they caught sight of her, an animated elflike woman with a tumble of thick brown hair. Before they could completely recover, she snapped into her spiel—a kind of running commentary with a HAL-like computer as a sidekick. Then the rest of

Young Dawn Steel with her mother, Lillian Steel, 1952.

the *Star Trek* cast, Leonard Nimoy, William Shatner, James Doohan—
not seen since the series went off the air in 1969—materialized. Steel
then leapt like Phil Donahue into the audience and lobbed *Star Trek*
trivia questions at the representatives of the fast-food chains and the re-
tailers. The audience went nuts.

It was a characteristic Steel entrance, a triumph of showmanship, a
never-before-seen infusion of sales dazzle into a virgin market, a victory
over long odds, and a platform from which she could launch the myth
of Dawn Steel.

Steel arrived in Hollywood just as studios were discovering that ancillary markets like merchandising or soundtrack could generate revenue streams equal to or even surpassing the ticket grosses. Movies
were no longer just the national escape; they were transmogrifying into
the national marketing juggernaut, whose reach included clothes, toys,
fast food, and records.

"Dawn took the ball and ran with it. In many ways, she really defined the idea of movie merchandising and brought a real P. T. Barnum
sense of salesmanship to what had basically been a kind of [sleepy]
business at hand," recalls Jeffrey Katzenberg, then the Paramount vice
president responsible for the production of *Star Trek*.

Steel appeared just as marketing was consuming the movie business, and her greatest product was herself. Unlike the baby moguls, who
were just reaching their apex in Hollywood, Steel was neither book nor
film literate. She was not an intellectual, nor was she politically conscious. She was drawn to Hollywood not for love of movies but for love
of money, and glamour, and the opportunity to become a member of
the American aristocracy. Hollywood could provide the outsize success
that would soothe her outsize insecurities. To those who observed her,
Steel's defining characteristic was unapologetic ambition, a consuming
desire to make it, to fit in, that seemed to rise off her like heat in the
desert. "She was severely touched by the fact that she was going to
make it. She had a severe urge," recalls the costume designer Marilyn
Vance, one of Steel's first friends in Hollywood. Unlike Sherry Lansing,
who cloaked her drive with girlish ingenuousness, or Polly Platt, who
channeled hers into a series of male mentor-partners, Steel zeroed in on
what she wanted with up-front ferocity. "Dawn thought she could do
anything, which was both great and horrifying," recalls Platt.

In later recountings of the story of her life, Steel always claimed
that, unbeknownst to her, Michael Eisner had been in the audience for

that *Star Trek* presentation. "And he said to me the next day in the commissary, yelled across the room, 'Dawn, I want to see you in my office tomorrow morning at eleven.' " She feared that she was about to be fired. "And the next day I went to see him and he said, 'What do you want to do with your life?' I said, 'Well, I am interested in television, Michael.' And he said, 'Forget what you want to do. This is what I've done. Congratulations. You're the production vice president of features.' I was speechless. And he said good-bye, good luck, and break a leg. And I remember standing out in the hallway. I got ushered out of his office. He clearly didn't want to sit there and talk about how scared to death I was, you know. And I walked out in the hallway and stood there and said, 'Oh shit, now what do I do?' "

No matter how much Steel promulgated this version of history, Eisner would always deny it. "There was no incident where we said, 'Oh, my God, it's the second coming,' " he groused. "She was creative, and we decided maybe she could learn the motion picture business."

Furthermore, it was almost a year before Steel switched departments. She did generate a *Star Trek* merchandising bonanza, convincing McDonald's and Coca-Cola to spend millions of dollars to feature Klingons chomping on Big Macs and swilling soda, as well as pony up tens of millions more to pay for network advertising to run around the release of the movie. She flew to New York to show top executives the commercials. She was talking to Paramount's CFO, Art Barron, outside his office on the thirty-third floor of the Gulf + Western building when the elevator arrived, and she stuck her hand in to hold the door open. "While I was finishing a sentence to him, I hear this very thick Viennese voice," recalled Steel. "This was such a defining moment in my life. In the elevator was Charlie Bluhdorn [the chairman of Gulf + Western]. And I hear him say, 'Ms. Steel, do you think you can close the elevator door?' It had been clanging like this, clanging, and I turned around and said, 'Oh shit, Mr. Bluhdorn. I'm sorry.'

"And on the way down, he recited to me every single thing I accomplished on the *Star Trek* merchandising and the Coca-Cola tie-in, which was this big thing. Because Coca-Cola bought all this network time to advertise our movie, and it hadn't been done before. This is thirty-three floors down, he is telling me everything I've ever done in my short career in the movie business. How did he know? And I was so flustered that, when the door opened, I looked at him and I said, 'Now will you buy me Bloomingdale's?' He thought I was cute. That elevator ride kept me going for twelve years."

EVERY SINGLE ONE OF US BEHIND
THE CAMERA STILL NEEDS THE LOVE
OF TEN THOUSAND PEOPLE

Steel wasn't naturally introspective, and her rapid-fire success in al- most every business she touched was often offset by a remarkable blind- ness about the ramifications of her actions. "Dawn was a complete mixture of being incredibly shrewd and incredibly vulnerable at the same time, which is why life was so hard for her," recalls her close friend Amy Pascal. "Because she was both things equally, and it is hard to know which one it is, if it's what you are doing, or what is being done to you."

Therapy helped her construct a narrative of her childhood. To Steel, her vaunted drive was the unintended by-product of a youth marred by downward mobility and emotional deprivation. Until well into middle age she was furious with her parents. "I always had a theory that really successful people in our business came from dysfunctional families. And I'll bet you anything it's true," said Steel in 1992. "It really was a Dickensian childhood. My parents were both very critical of me. But their point of view was that they were pushing me further and further to do better. But the way a child sees that is [that] I was being criticized."

She was born in the Bronx in 1946, descended from Russian Jews on both sides. Her father's family name had been Spielberg, but her fa- ther, who participated in weight-lifting tournaments, changed it to Steel, after his stage moniker the Man of Steel. Dawn arrived by ce- sarean section, leaving her mother with a scar that ran the length of her abdomen and the permanent joking admonishment to her daugh- ter, "Look what you did to me. I almost died." A year later Steel's younger brother was born. Her mother perpetuated a mythology: Larry was the pretty one, Dawn the smart one.

Her father sold zippers to the military, then started a business con- verting yarn into fabric. They moved from the Upper West Side of New York to Long Island, to a house that reminded the young Dawn of Tara in *Gone with the Wind*. She idolized her father, who would throw her up in the air and tell her he was "the King of the Giants." In later years

Steel would attribute her success in the business world to the fact that "I was always comfortable with men. It comes from the relationship with my father. And I was very fortunate to have that, and a lot of women don't."

But when she was nine, Dawn's father suffered a nervous breakdown. His business partner had embezzled funds from their company and thrown it into bankruptcy. The IRS came after Steel for the stolen money. He moved into his bedroom and essentially didn't emerge for two years, although shock treatments and therapy eventually returned him to a functioning state.

With his disability the family quickly slipped down the economic pole, settling in a damp, rented house in Little Neck, Long Island, the hamlet adjacent to the much more affluent Great Neck. (In Steel's retelling the house was a hellhole of embarrassment; in actuality it was firmly middle-class.) Her mother—enraged, bitter, and terrified—went to work as a bookkeeper for an electronics firm. According to Steel, she was exceedingly demanding, and caustic toward her daughter.

Steel would later describe her willpower as the search for her mother's approval. When she worked for her mother one summer, she turned herself into the perfect little helpmate, unable to tolerate mistakes, especially from herself. She was "the best calculator, switchboard, and mimeograph operator in the Western world," she said. Indeed, Steel described her voracious need to make it in Hollywood: "Every single one of us behind the camera still needs the love of ten thousand people, and the approval of ten thousand people. And the biggest [accomplishment] for me was to finally grow out of that."

From a very early age Steel equated masculinity with success. As a nine-year-old she wanted to be a boy. She hated dolls but was the pitcher on the softball team and a competitive swimmer. As a teenager she was perpetually ashamed of her mediocre grades and hauntingly aware of the fact that she was a poor girl in a rich town. Huge reservoirs of energy went into maintaining a presentable front. She was consumed with a desire to be like everybody else. "I wanted great clothes. I wanted to go to Florida on spring break and ski on winter break. I wanted a nose job," she wrote in her autobiography. Early on she learned that whatever she wanted she'd have to work for. When her mother refused to buy her the Pappagallo shoes so popular among the soigné set, Dawn went to work in the Pappagallo shoe store and bought them herself. She spent weeks practicing a dance routine to the music of *The Bridge on the River*

Kwai in order to make it as a cheerleader—called a kiltie—and hence gain entrée into the in-crowd. Her success in this endeavor "was the biggest personal triumph of my life," she later wrote.

After graduating from high school in 1967, Steel spent a year studying marketing at Boston University. She relished the fact that she was often the only woman in her business classes but felt isolated and lonely. She supported herself as a go-go dancer and a waitress, complete with fringed miniskirt and fake white Courrèges boots. She flunked calculus twice and transferred to NYU. She still lived at home in Long Island and worked every afternoon as an assistant bookkeeper. She watched from afar while her peers staged love-ins and protest marches.

After two years Steel quit college for good and took a job as a receptionist at a small sports book publisher, which she called "a dream come true for the kid who was out there to make it as a man." She eventually became a researcher for books like the *NFL Digest*. Although it wasn't an actual sportswriting job, it did provide her with press credentials. However, when she showed up at Yankee Stadium to cover a Giants game, the male sportswriters refused to let her in. Steel raised "a stink," and the stadium management created an alternative press box in a turret over the fifty-yard line.

Around the time ten thousand women marched down Fifth Avenue arm in arm with Betty Friedan and Gloria Steinem to celebrate fifty years of voting, Steel got a job at *Penthouse*, which, she said, was "perfect for me because it was the locker room." She assigned articles, wrote copy, devised the first advertorials—eventually handled all aspects of the magazine except photography. After four years Bob Guccione made her head of merchandising, entrusted with launching a product line with the *Penthouse* logo and a novelty mail-order operation to hawk off-color gimmicks. It was a perfect job for someone who spent a lot of time thinking about how other people lived. Her first success was a handknit garment she called a "cock sock," which was to be worn over the penis. She sold it in red, white, and blue—all marked extralarge.

Steel soon started her own novelty business on the side with her boyfriend—and later husband—Ronald Rothstein. Steel had noticed that amaryllis plants looked exceedingly phallic before flowering, so she had dreamt up the idea of Penis Plants, sold under the tag line "Grow your own Penis. All it takes is $6.98 and a lot of love."

She then decided to parody the growing merchandising mania by printing the Gucci insignia on toilet paper. It was a quintessential Steel idea, clever, mocking of pretensions, and vulgar. Six months later Steel was sued by Gucci for copyright infringement, a lawsuit chronicled in the *New York Post* as "the Gucci Toilet Paper Caper," with Steel as an appealing David versus the Gucci Goliath. While the lawsuit eventually ended the Gucci rolls, Steel started a new company she christened Oh Dawn, for what people said when they heard about it. She went on to other gimmicks: toilet paper imprinted with excerpts from bestselling books on the theory that eight out of ten people read in the bathroom; kitchen towels with recipes from James Beard's cookbooks; soap in the shape of a fortune cookie that came in a Chinese take-out container.

Despite the success of her various businesses, Steel had grown depressed and went into what would become years of therapy. Her marriage had broken up after only ten months. What had started out as an amicable parting had turned into a courtroom slugfest over the division of the business, although after five months of not speaking, Steel and Rothstein had a cup of coffee and resolved their differences.

She was pulled to Hollywood more by the social whirl than by the movies. At a dinner party in L.A. held by Robert Finkelstein, then a manager in Jerry Weintraub's company, Steel met a crew of up-and-coming Hollywood people, among them the Paramount executive Craig Baumgarten and the not yet famous Richard Gere. "We all thought it was hysterical that she invented Gucci toilet paper. We ended up sitting around, playing poker with matchsticks," recalls Baumgarten. "She always kind of had this I'm-as-good-as-anybody attitude. There was no— nothing coquettish about Dawn, or girlish in the sense that she gave you any ground. She was always comfortable in the boys' club. She was like the first woman you knew who knew as much about pro football as any of us."

"She had a ponytail on the top of her head that went off to the side, and she was a little doughy," recalls Joan Hyler, who also met Steel around this time. "There was something about her that was so friendly and open and lovely. The great thing about Dawn in those early days is she was game."

Several months later Steel ran into Gere again, and they began a torrid but unfulfilling fling that ended within a couple of months when she flew to London to surprise him for his birthday on the set of *Yanks*. She called him from the airport, only to have another woman answer. She took the first flight out, which happened to be going to Italy, and spent two weeks traveling by herself. When she got back to New York,

Gere's movies—*Bloodbrothers* and *Days of Heaven*—were just coming out, and his face was all over the magazine stands. Steel couldn't take it. She went back for more therapy, mostly about why she was attracted to unavailable men. The doctor forced her to look at her relationship with her father and to forgive him for his failure. She kicked around for something new to do with her life.

"I just kept saying to her, You've got to come out here," recalls Baumgarten. He told her if she could merchandise smut at *Penthouse* and toilet paper, she could certainly handle movies. A week later she had packed up and moved to L.A. On her first night there she went to the Playboy mansion, in her words "a brothel for foreplay. If someone had tried to invent a Hollywood purgatory for me, they couldn't have done better than this lavish place full of playmates with huge breasts and has-been actors and no one paying attention to me."

Baumgarten and Finkelstein introduced her around, most significantly to Richard Weston, who was running Paramount merchandising and angling for a better Paramount job. She was also vouched for by her lawyer in the Gucci case, Sid Davidoff, an official in the Lindsay administration, who happened to be a mentor to Weston, as well as a former roommate of Jeffrey Katzenberg. Weston hired her as his assistant; six months later he left to run Paramount TV, and Steel was promoted to vice president in charge of the department.

For most of her time in merchandising, Steel was stuck in a cubbyhole far from the action. Her introduction to the rest of the company was a divisional retreat at La Costa, a resort near San Diego. She drove down with Laurence Mark, a friend from marketing who'd just been promoted to vice president of production. Both were anxious—less about their presentations than about the legendary "new ideas" meeting, where each participant was expected to pitch an idea for a movie. The fact that Steel would be the only woman in a room of seventy-five was simply a given. "She was actually a tad shy about the whole thing," says Mark, "and she would always come on strong, but there was a little girl beneath it all, which was indeed coming out in that car ride."

On the way down they practiced their spiels, role-playing that they were themselves and then Michael Eisner. Mark christened Steel's movie "Eve's Rib." It was a reverse Pygmalion tale of a talented young woman executive in an automobile company who can't get promoted. All the men around and below her simply rise through the corporate ranks, but she is stymied. She makes a bet with a friend that she can turn a guy from the mailroom into an executive who gets promoted faster than she does. She grooms him, teaches him the business. He succeeds wildly, and they fall in love. The pitch went over extremely well.

After days of being locked in together, the Paramount executives were allowed outside for a lunch break. "Finally we were getting outdoors to sit under an umbrella, and there was sun happening. She looked up at the sun for about maybe thirty seconds, looked back down, and said, 'Am I brown yet?' " Mark laughs. " 'Why aren't I brown yet, I am Dawn Steel for heaven's sake.' "

SHE WOULD OUT-BOY THE BOYS

"She definitely made herself over. In the beginning she wore crocheted shawls," recalls the former Paramount executive David Kirkpatrick. "She had that little red Fiat, and she had these clogs, which had two-inch heels. And you could literally hear her coming down. You could hear from your window the fact that she had stepped out of her car, because that clogging sound was her."

When Steel was officially named vice president of production in May 1980, Paramount was at its peak, built largely in the image of its brilliant, bullying, irascible chairman, Barry Diller, a Beverly Hills High graduate whose modus operandi was constantly to see how far he could push people. He detested the foolish, the unprepared, the unctuous.

In 1974 Paramount's chief, Charles Bluhdorn, had hired Diller, then the programming chief of ABC, where he had helped invent the movie of the week and the miniseries, as chairman of Paramount. In 1976 Diller hired his protégé, Michael Eisner, ABC's chief of prime-time programming, as president. Starting with *Saturday Night Fever* in 1978, the Diller-Eisner team turned Paramount into the most successful studio in town.

While other studios acquiesced to the rising power of the star agents, who sold them expensive, fully assembled packages—a script, director, and stars—Paramount balked at paying the agent's price or ceding control over their product. Executives were expected to assemble their movies piece by piece, and to cull not only the right star but the right story. There was increased emphasis on getting the right script.

Moreover, Diller operated the studio on the advocacy system, turning his executives into gladiators in an arena of ambition. Whoever screamed loudest and fought hardest would win a green light for his or her proposed picture. The underlying subtext was death to the competition. "There was no support except for your own interest in getting something made. Your colleagues never supported you in what you wanted to do," recalls Kirkpatrick. "The old line at Paramount was we'd green-light a picture and then we'd dare you to make it."

The movies that most easily made it through the gauntlet were the ones that could be explained most quickly. Paramount soon devolved into the home office of what Hollywood called the high-concept film, one that could be described in two sentences or less, simple melodramatic premises such as fish out of water (*Beverly Hills Cop*) or underdog makes good (*Top Gun, Flashdance*). "The zeitgeist of the second floor of the administration building was, If you can't pitch it in one sentence, it's not worthwhile," said Steel.

Diller would often play the cynic, Eisner the enthusiast. Diller had more sophisticated taste, while Eisner was viewed as the champion of the masses. Balding, with broad shoulders, penetrating blue eyes, and a taste for white, handmade shirts under beige suits, Diller traveled with stars and the gay elite. Eisner—tall, preppy, with features that looked as if they were made of Silly Putty—preferred to spend time with his wife and three children. Both men could be detail-oriented and excruciatingly hands-on, at least from the point of view of filmmakers and producers, who behind their backs referred to them as "the chic and the shit."

Steel's immediate boss, Don Simpson, added a high-testosterone, rock-and-roll, bullying gloss. Keenly intelligent, he had a penchant for black leather jackets, bimbos, cocaine, and outrageous statement. He told the troops: "I'm looking for commando players who can get behind enemy lines and get it done."

It was into this environment that Steel arrived, ballsy, insecure, and almost completely ignorant of not only the movie business but pictures themselves. "It was overwhelming. I had not been a movie buff," she explained. "You know, I had to work. And there wasn't a lot of time and money to go to the movies."

"I remember one of my first days when I got in there, there was a pile of cassettes, videocassettes on her desk, and she said, 'Oh these were movies somebody told me I should see. Do you think I should see any of these?' " recalls the former Paramount executive David Madden, who worked with Steel for several years. "And I looked at the cassettes of movies she had never seen, and they were like *Maltese Falcon* and *All About Eve*."

Steel recalled, "But the whole thing about those Paramount years was that I read and read and read, and I had never read a script. I went and saw as many movies as I could see, and I remember the first time I went to meet a director. It was Tony Bill, and he had just done *My Body-guard*, and he was getting every offer in town to do a movie. And I said, 'I don't know how to talk to a director, what am I going to say to a director?' I had no vocabulary. And I went out to meet him in Venice at his place on Market Street, and he was about as generous as anybody could be."

Despite the competitive nature of the studio, Baumgarten took Steel to every meeting with writers, directors, or agents that he could. "I used to always tell her, 'You are in a great position at the studio, because you can say in every meeting the following sentence, "I don't know anything, but I think . . ." and you could say *anything* then. No one will get mad at you.' She did that for years," says Joel Silver, then an assistant to a producer who targeted Steel, ultimately speaking to her every day for the next decade. He filled her ears with the logistics of filmmaking (" 'The grippers?' she'd say. I said, 'No, Dawn, grips and gaffers' "), the perks of the executives ("Whenever you hear the word *traveling*, Dawn, say you want to go first-class."). "We used to have a lot of fun. She wanted to know about the process of picture making, about the way the studio works. The politics."

Silver was hardly Steel's only daily phone call. In fact, she was perfectly capable of calling her peer friends (among them women like Marilyn Vance and Tova Laiter) fifteen times a day to solicit their advice on the minutiae of her life, a kind of ongoing neediness that bonded people to her. Like a heat-seeking missile, she also sought out powerful men and submitted herself to their tutelage. "I remember trying to get Dick Zimbert to explain to me what *rolling point break* meant, which to this day I don't understand. But I would know that it was a specific kind of deal making. And, by the way, the years before me, Jeff Katzenberg was asking Dick Zimbert the same questions. Women have mentors. I think you need to want them. You have to instigate the questions." Art Barron, Paramount's chief financial officer, guided her through the political shoals of the studio. Jeffrey Katzenberg, then Simpson's assistant, became one of her closest mentors, as did David Geffen, the record mogul.

As Steel recalled, "I needed people's approval constantly. I needed it for the psychological filling up. But I also needed it to get promoted. You know, I needed people's approval. That's the difficulty with working in a corporate environment. You cannot succeed unless someone else approves of you. So that's the Catch-22 of the whole thing."

While Sherry Lansing's cultivation of mentors sparked legions of sexual innuendo, Steel was never presumed to be sleeping her way to the top because she went out of her way to present herself as one of the guys. She was determined to swagger. If the guys were out drinking, she'd outdrink them. If they were making raunchy remarks, she'd out-raunch them. Nothing could offend her. No topic—however sexual or profane—was out-of-bounds. She was perfectly capable of walking into a bar and declaiming, "Look at the rack on that woman." "She would out-boy the boys," says Mark. "And kind of be just as brash and just as ballsy as they." She swore profusely, including frequent use of the word *cunt*, which still held its ability to shock. The producer Dan Melnick used to call her "my favorite truck driver."

"I do have at times a mouth that is somewhat foul," Steel explained. "It's funny, because I do call people I like assholes. It's a term of affection to me. I have also in my life called people fuckhead or fuckface—but never motherfucker. Look, if the worst thing they ever say about me on my tombstone is that I had a foul mouth, then fine. I'm not ashamed of it.

"It did stop people, and some people thought it was hilarious," she added.

Steel, who later admitted that she had never cultivated a woman friend until the age of twenty-six, relished being the only woman in the pack. "She really loved being around men," recalls Craig Zadan, a producer and friend from her early Paramount days. "She did not like being around women. She really felt that another woman in the room was competition. And it was also very important that she be accepted as an equal. It was a very, very important thing for her that she wasn't treated as the girl. That is probably where a lot of the stuff she said came from. Because if a guy talked like that, no one would notice."

To some degree, her tactics worked. "To some extent, they were scared not to [treat her as one of them]. Scared at the fuss that would happen," says Mark. "She would not let anything lie. She certainly wouldn't let the status quo lie. And she certainly did get everyone's attention."

Still, no matter how high she rose, Steel didn't feel like a bona fide member of the boys' club. She begged, pleaded, badgered, and cajoled Katzenberg to let her go on the annual all-male rafting trip he organized for executives, agents, and stars. "I think that she had more fun teasing me about it than actually having a genuine ambition for going," he recalls. "Every time she said, 'Well, the girls want to go.' And I said, 'Well, okay, so have the girls have a trip, and I'll organize it for you.' Nobody ever called me to ask me to put it together. There are things that the girls don't do, there are things that the boys don't do. It's not sexist."

Despite her macho behavior, Steel's ace remained that she was all woman, potent and sexual. "She drank with the best of them. She fucked with the best of them. She told the same bawdy stories. It was like being with a guy. But she was very sexy," recalls her close friend Howard Rosenman. "She had beautiful legs, big tits, a great mane of hair. She was electrifying."

When she started at Paramount, Steel was cautious about whom she dated, in part because Katzenberg specifically told her, "'You can't have relationships with any men that work in this business,'" recalls Baumgarten. "He really freaked her out. She really thought, My God, what am I going to do? For like two years, if she had a relationship with anybody, it was completely clandestine. She thought that Jeffrey was giving her good advice."

"She wanted to be part of the boys' club, not the girls' club," adds writer Katherine Reback, who worked on *Flashdance*. "She felt she had to be careful about mixing her two lives. But there was a period of time where dating was on the back burner, where work was everything." Steel was fond of telling an anecdote about a married agent who came on to her over the phone and asked her out—she was game for the affair, but less game when they both consulted their calendars and couldn't find a free meal until six weeks later.

When she did have affairs, they seemed to be more notches on her belt than relationships. Everybody came to know about her escapades with Gere, Richard Dreyfuss, Don Simpson, supposedly Charlie Bluhdorn himself. She wrangled herself into the wrap party for Richard Pryor's film *Some Kind of Hero*, held at Pryor's house. The star had turned his tennis court into a rolling rink, and his girlfriend at the time, the actress Margot Kidder, had taken a spill and gone home early. Steel disappeared upstairs with Pryor for a while. When she returned, her hair was all mussed, and there was strange glop on her face. When someone asked her what it was, she burst out that it was Pryor's semen. Steel, in thrall as ever to power and charisma, developed a mad crush on Barry Diller, and consistently tried to discern the nature of his relationship to the designer Diane von Furstenberg. But this was a Don Quixote tilt at an elusive windmill, considering the fact that Diller was gay. Steel's friends teased her that she was "power-fucked."

"She used those relationships to make her management take her seriously," says Silver. "She then was able to perform on a level playing field."

"She was in life lust," recalls the agent turned manager Melinda Jason. "I think that she was like a starving person who was let loose in the food court of life where every single restaurant was a designer restaurant."

Despite her vaunted conquests, Steel hardly viewed herself as a femme fatale; in fact, she was riddled with insecurities over her perpetually failing romances. "I remember one night I was sitting at home, and she called," says Silver. "She was hysterically crying. She was in Westwood, and she was going out with some below-the-line guy [a member of a film crew]. Someone had dropped her to go to the movies, and he just didn't show up, and she was like, 'What's wrong with my life? I don't have anybody, and this idiot doesn't even show up,' and I said, 'Dawn, shut up, stop crying, I'll come get you.' I went and got her and we had dinner and I said, 'Dawn, relax, who gives a fuck? He didn't show up, who cares?' But I remember how she was upset that, again, like most women at that time, she felt that she needed a man to validate herself."

Adds Reback: "One night we had gone to the Palm for dinner. She was a very sexy woman, and we were walking out of the restaurant. You know how you have to walk through all of those booths. And all these guys are looking at us, and she says to me, 'Is my fly unzipped?' And I said, 'No, you jerk, you look fabulous. You're a hot thing.' She was often unself-conscious. Not always, but often. There was an innocence that at times was surprising given the powerhouse that she presented herself to be."

A SCHLEPPER WITH A DREAM

In the years before she emerged as a Hollywood supernova, Steel had precisely one transcendent moviegoing experience: *Rocky.* When

Sylvester Stallone grunted "I just want to go the distance," Steel related completely. "The moment he ran up those steps in triumph, arms raised in victory, I wanted it to be me on those steps," she later wrote. "Not a male model or a female model, a universal model for a schlepper with a dream."

It was the movie that first inspired her to think about going to Hollywood, as well as the movie that she would make and remake throughout much of her career. It was the mantle of myth in which she wrapped herself.

For her first year and a half in the production wing of Paramount, Steel didn't have much to show for herself. She had worked hard, practiced what Katzenberg used to call reeling in the tuna, cajoling talent— and their representatives—to bring their projects to her. She often followed Katzenberg around the office, going to his meetings, or sitting with him as he did reel-by-reel examinations of the rough cuts of movies like *Going Ape!* Like many junior executives, she served as punching bag/chum for her bosses. Once the marketing chief, Frank Mancuso, asked her to tell Steven Spielberg the release date of one of his movies; Spielberg immediately retorted, "Who are you to tell me when the release date is?" Steel often walked around telling herself, "I won't cry." She felt frustrated and excluded. "I was just not part of the boys' club," she recalled. "There were many, many, many meetings that I was not privy to."

She was particularly distressed by the fact that she had not been able to initiate a single project. Everything she had brought up in the group meetings had been shot down, and she privately resolved to make her pitches one on one.

Finally, in 1981, she received a phone call from a young literary agent, Melinda Jason, hawking a "hot" script that belonged to Universal but was teetering on the edge of turnaround, in which a project is canceled by one studio and available to be bought by another. The project was so secret that she couldn't let Steel keep a copy of it. It was the High Holy Days, and Jason was having a post–Yom Kippur breakfast at her mother's. Steel drove there and read the script in her little red Fiat by her cigarette lighter.

The script was *Flashdance*, the improbable tale of a young working-class woman (a welder in later versions) who at night transforms into a spectacular, and spectacularly erotic, nightclub dancer but dreams of a better, classier life. "*Flashdance* for me was about *me*. That girl was *me*,"

recalled Steel. "I was in Hollywood. I didn't know anybody. I was just beginning to find out what my talent was. So I was completely caught up in this fictional scene that was me."

Steel was not the only young woman caught up in the fantasy of *Flashdance*. The piece had been developed for two years at PolyGram by a young D-girl, Lynda Obst, initially under the aegis of her boss, Peter Guber, who was joined by his new partner, Jon Peters, Streisand's former paramour. "I think what is signature about it to me was that it was a female entitlement piece. It was taking *Saturday Night Fever* and *Rocky* and the man's entitlement piece and turning it on its head and saying women have dreams, and women don't want to be given things from men," recalls Obst. "Women want to earn stuff by themselves, and they won't sell out for a love." While Obst cottoned to the feminist subtext, Peters fancied the opportunity to have young, scantily dressed women writhing in front of the camera.

Steel pitched the idea in a production meeting. "*Flashdance* is a female *Rocky*," she announced. Katzenberg liked it, but everyone else, in particular her immediate boss, Don Simpson, simply ignored her. She couldn't even get him to read it.

"They had that kind of love-hate thing," recalls Baumgarten. "She didn't understand the rules, and sometimes that frustrated Don. He absolutely loved her, and at the same time Dawn didn't really give a quarter to people. She didn't just sit there in a corner and keep her mouth shut until she got smarter, according to Don.

"Don, I think it is fair to say, especially at that point in time, had trouble with women in these kinds of roles. He expected Dawn to not challenge him in a way that he didn't think was right to be challenged, especially by a chick." (Indeed, at one corporate retreat Simpson pulled his girlfriend's bathing suit bottom down and gave her a smack, and Steel scolded him as if he were a wayward boy.)

Steel began to despair that she'd never get a movie going. She sought out Art Barron's advice. "Could it get any worse?" he asked her.

"No," she told him.

"Quit. What do you have to lose?" he said.

Simpson had in fact begun to complain to his associates about Steel's ineffectiveness, and even talked about firing her.

After talking with Barron, Steel went to dinner with Simpson at Le Dome. Before he could express his displeasure with her performance, she announced she was quitting. "I said that if you don't want to pay

any attention to this, if you don't want to read this script, you'll never, ever want to pay any attention to anything I ever do, so I may as well not be here," Steel recalled. "He just thought, Well, here's a chick with balls."

"What movie?" he asked her. Her boldness had finally gained his respect. Simpson read the project and became a champion. Jerry Bruckheimer, who had produced *Cat People* and *American Gigolo* for the studio, was assigned to produce. Shortly after, Simpson was fired because of excessive drug use and became partners with Bruckheimer.

Obst found herself cut out of the loop once the film got the green light. Her bosses, Guber and Peters, who had ignored the movie, received executive producer credit, while she got the lowest possible credit, as an associate producer. Obst was enraged and blamed Steel, mostly, she says, because "we were very competitive with one another, and because she was my friend and I don't expect Don and Jerry to take care of me, but the fact is, she was swept by the process into doing that."

"There was not enough for both of us," recalled Steel. "The pie was not big enough for all of us. I don't remember thinking about it consciously, but I'm sure on some level I did think about it. It's possible that I was less than conscious during that time. I was less than conscious for most of my life."

Steel felt guilty about selling out her putative friend. It was true that she loved being the only woman in the room, but it was also true that how she'd acted was fairly standard operating procedure in Hollywood. She was more obsessed by her own debilitating affair with the original writer of *Flashdance*, Tom Hedley, a witty, hard-drinking former *Esquire* writer. It was her first real affair since she had arrived in Hollywood: monogamous for her, pointedly not so for Hedley. The relationship, she said, made "my sexual self-confidence, which always served me well, [desert] me"; it plunged her back into crisis therapy.

Despite her personal setbacks Steel attacked her first project with the zeal of someone with something to prove. Hedley was fired from the movie, and Simpson and Bruckheimer hired the already pricey Joe Eszterhas to rewrite the script almost from scratch. Simpson, Bruckheimer, and Steel then went hunting for directors; they were turned down twenty-seven times, until Steel hounded Adrian Lyne into accepting, asking him no fewer than eight times. She was less impressed by his debut, *Foxes*, than by his commercial reel, his abundant, sunny charm, and his patently clear obsession with sexy women. She clinched

the deal by taking him into an expensive lingerie store and announcing, "Here's what the movie feels like." The irony of selling her woman's em-powerment piece on the basis of lacy slips and scanty thongs escaped her.

Finally, in September 1982, the movie—budgeted at a measly $7 million—received a green light at a meeting that took place in San Fran-cisco with Bluhdorn, Diller, Eisner, and Katzenberg. No one was partic-ularly excited, but the studio needed product for April, traditionally a slow time in the film business. *Flashdance* would have to complete film-ing by the end of the year, a very quick schedule.

But before they could start, the *Flashdance* team needed two essen-tial elements—a girl and a script.

The production team had scoured the country, auditioning hun-dreds of women in cattle calls for the part of Alex, the break-dancing welder. The field was narrowed to three, who were screen-tested. (An out-of-work actor named Kevin Costner fed them their lines.) Only ex-ecutives—who all happened to be men—were invited to view the screen tests, earning them the in-house nickname peter-meter screenings.

Lyne wanted Jennifer Beals, a strikingly beautiful half-black, half-white nineteen-year-old from Chicago who had come to an open call. The studio had trepidations about her race, and "everybody had a dif-ferent choice, so it was a mess," recalls Bruckheimer. Steel advocated a more typical blond-haired, suburban-looking actress for the role and talked about forcing Lyne to hire her, a tactic that Simpson and Bruck-heimer discouraged. Finally, recalls Bruckheimer, "Michael Eisner took a bunch of secretaries into a room with himself and screened the three candidates, and all the women picked the same one Adrian did."

Even after Beals was chosen, some members of the production team opted for every opportunity to ogle her. Although Peters had barely been present for the preproduction, he showed up for the wardrobe fit-tings, along with Lyne and the other men.

"Dawn made it a point to be there, because she knew all the guys were going to be there," Beals explains, "and she knew the nature of some of the wardrobe, and she made it a point to be there so that I would be protected. She made it a point to say to me, If you ever want me to be there with you, if you ever feel uncomfortable, call me and I will be there for you."

As the script was being developed, Steel invited a new friend, the fledgling screenwriter Katherine Reback, to Palm Springs with her for the weekend. As they lounged around the pool, Steel tossed her *Flash-dance*. She knew Alex's inner life wasn't particularly realistic, but she didn't know how to fix it.

Reback quickly identified what had been an ongoing concern for all involved in *Flashdance*. In both Hedley's and Eszterhas's versions, Alex "didn't seem to want anything for herself. And, of course, *Flashdance*, as it turns out, is a little, tiny idea: girl has dream, girl is afraid to pursue dream, girl pursues dream. And so if you don't have a dream, where are you going?" recalls Reback. "Dawn identified with that completely, because that's what she was about." Reback suggested that Alex should dream of becoming a ballet dancer, a goal seemingly out of reach of her blue-collar roots. Months later, Steel gave Simpson Reback's unproduced script "The Receptionist" (about her time working for comedian Alan King), which he liked, and later she convinced the producers to hire Reback for a last minute polish. "I remember Jerry distinctly saying she was like a mother hen, and she was," recalls Reback, "and I was her chick."

Steel emphasized that Reback would be able to write authentic "girl's dialogue," but Reback and Simpson fought bitterly over "how girls talk," says the writer. "There were previous scripts that were grittier in their writing, that were 'fuck this and fuck that, and his dick is this big,' and I would say to Don, 'I don't like that line.' And Don would say, 'Put the line back in the script,' and I would say, 'No.' We almost had a fist-fight one day." Reback had balked at reinserting Eszterhas's vulgar quip, "The smallest penis ever measured is an inch and a quarter long," but the line ended up in the movie anyway. Reback also inserted bits of her girls-in-arms chatter with Steel into the script. "For years Dawn would have a date with somebody over Saturday night, and she'd say, 'He didn't call.' I would say, 'He'll call.' It's in *Flashdance*. There's a whole scene 'He didn't call, he'll call.' I took it from our lives, because it was ongoing," she says. Reback and Steel later fought bitterly—not speaking for several months after the writer refused to secretly slip Steel her new pages.

Although she knew little about the mechanics of filmmaking, Steel hovered over the production like a pint-sized bobcat. The studio wasn't particularly confident in Lyne and rode him fiercely. Steel carried decrees back from Eisner, who declared after several days of dailies that Lyne was using too much smoke. Steel planted herself firmly on the set one morning to prevent the dry ice machines from whirring, but she returned from lunch to find a grip running around blowing on the dry ice to make whispers of white smoke.

"When you start from scratch, you don't know what you're doing and you don't know what you can't do. So I did all sorts of things that I shouldn't do," said Steel. "I looked at dailies of the first couple of days, and I remember thinking that this place [where] the Jenny Beals character was living was filthy. The windows were dirty. The floor was dirty. There was this big stain on the couch. It was disgusting.

"And I go marching down there. And I basically said, 'Adrian, she wouldn't live like this. This is disgusting, you know.' And he was really pissed. He said, 'If you know so much, here is the production designer, you tell him what to do.' You don't tell a production designer what to do, but I basically said, 'Could you clean the windows and clean the floor and get the stain off the couch, and how about a tree, you know?' I was completely intimidated. I could barely get the words out of my mouth."

"So Don and I went down there and looked at it. Just needed a little paint job," says Bruckheimer. "She was going to shut the movie down. She was mad."

News of Steel's tantrum quickly circled the studio: "People were making fun of her for doing it, but she wanted to have it be good," says Silver.

In her later years Steel would claim that she had picked Lyne for his MTV sensibility, but in truth, Simpson, Bruckheimer, and Lyne discovered the look that would make them all famous during a scouting trip to Pittsburgh, where MTV happened to be test-marketing itself. Lyne shot the women discussing "Will he call?" to images of them working out, which were then cut together in a splice-and-dice montage. "Dawn looked at this footage and couldn't make head or tail out of it, and wanted us to reshoot it," says Bruckheimer. "Because she was a neophyte at the job, and didn't realize that all these little pieces, you can make a little story with music. So I said, 'Dawn, relax, let me cut it together and you'll look at it.' We cut it together for her, and she flipped. She loved it."

Despite her penchant for theatrics, Bruckheimer and Simpson relished Steel's forthrightness. "Everybody is so politically correct, and doesn't want to hurt anybody's feelings, and says, 'This is wonderful,' then they start tearing it apart in a very subtle way. Dawn would never do that," says Bruckheimer. "Dawn would say, 'Look at this shit. What are you guys doing to me?' It was never, Let's sit down and talk about this. Her emotions would flow immediately."

The rough-cut assembly of the film went badly. "It was a disaster when we showed it to Michael [Eisner]," said Steel. "He thought it was a complete and total mess, and restructured the movie in the meeting. We all sat there very quietly. I was mesmerized, because I had never seen anything like this, ever. Michael said, 'Well, if you put this scene here and you put this scene here, and you do this, and you do this, it'll—it'll be fine.' And he was right."

Afterward, Steel immediately ran over to Dan Melnick's office and began to cry. He consoled her with tales about Bob Fosse, who vomited after every rough cut. "Calm down and let's think about what works and what doesn't work with your movie," said Melnick. "Then you can throw up."

One of Eisner's demands was that they reshoot the ending so the film built to an exciting finale, namely Alex's successful audition for the elitists at the ballet academy. It appears to be Beals dancing, but in truth it was a montage of professional dancers: the best leaper leaping, the best pirouetter twirling, the best break dancer—who happened to be a man decked out in a wig and makeup—spinning wildly on his back.

Despite the efforts to fix the ending, Paramount had so little faith in *Flashdance* that it sold off 33 percent of the film to a Texan consortium a few weeks before opening. Even so, the $7 million film grossed $90 million domestically, a pop culture phenomenon that spawned a best-selling soundtrack, a workout craze, and legions of sweatshirts with their necks ripped out. Paramount made a video for MTV of Irene Cara's Oscar-winning theme song "What a Feeling"—the first time a film was marketed on MTV. Indeed, the soundtrack's singles became hits one after the other.

Perhaps not surprisingly, the critics hated the film, seeing it as a vacuous exercise, with little real plot and thin to nonexistent characters. Pauline Kael was particularly harsh: "For this picture the producers have put together a prime collection of rumps: girls' rumps, but small and muscular and round, like boys'. The picture is a lulling, narcotizing musical, the whole damn thing throbs. It's soft-core porn with an inspirational message, and it may be the most calculating, platinum-hearted movie I've ever seen."

———

Steel followed up her *Flashdance* success with another music-driven teen picture—*Footloose*, about a bunch of progeny of fundamentalist Christians who angle for the opportunity to hold a dance. The picture had landed on her desk via her friendship with the up-and-coming producer Craig Zadan, who worked for Dan Melnick. While Melnick was working out the details of his divorce from Fox (then still in the Hirschfield-Lansing regime), Zadan slipped Steel the script with the proviso that she would have to tell Melnick she got it from CAA. She not only convinced Melnick to set up *Footloose* with her but landed one of her biggest mentors, a savvy insider with whom she consulted frequently on everything from the logistics of filmmaking to the ornate intricacies of studio politics.

The movie almost fell apart in casting. The filmmakers needed someone who could dance and proposed Kevin Bacon, who'd just made an auspicious debut in *Diner.* Steel balked.

"She said, 'No, I don't want Kevin Bacon. He's not fuckable,'" recalls Zadan. "And I said, 'By whose standards?' I said, 'Dawn, come on.' She said, 'No. No. No. I don't find him sexually attractive.' "

There was no backup to Bacon. Tom Cruise, whose film *Risky Business* was still unfinished, even brought a boom box to his audition to demonstrate that he could dance. The filmmakers kept insisting on Bacon, and Steel kept refusing to approve him. Tempers boiled. At one point Steel ran around the halls of Paramount with a mug shot of Bacon asking all the secretaries if they thought he was "fuckable." Although the typing pool was pro-Bacon, Steel still refused to change her mind.

Finally, director Herb Ross threatened to walk off the picture if Paramount wouldn't approve Bacon. Moreover, Bacon was going to go star in the John Carpenter film *Christine* if an offer for *Footloose* wasn't forthcoming immediately. The filmmakers decided to screen-test Bacon "to prove to them at Paramount that he was fuckable," says Zadan. They hired a stylist from *GQ* to cut and style Bacon's hair in the windswept cut that he sported in the film and brought in fancy, expensive clothes for what was turning out to be a fashion show cum audition, with Bacon playing the scenes, then twirling around for the cameras to the music of Michael Jackson.

The screen test was shown to Eisner, Diller, Katzenberg, and Steel, who announced just as the lights were going down, "I hope you have someone in your back pocket because I'm never going to approve him." When the lights came up, Eisner, Diller, and Katzenberg loved him, and Steel was forced to relent.

"She was the only one who always told the truth," recalls Zadan. "We would be at a meeting with Barry Diller, Michael Eisner, Jeff Katzenberg, and they'd say something and she'd go, 'Oh no, well that's stupid.' She would go, 'I don't want to do it that way, I want to do it this way,' and they'd look at her like, 'How could you talk to us in front of people like this?' She had no sense of politics. I don't think anyone has ever spoken to that group of people like that."

As with *Flashdance*, the rough assembly screening of *Footloose* pointedly did not wow the studio. As the lights rose on a roomful of dissatisfied executives, Ross's wife, the ballerina Nora Kaye, succinctly summed up the problem: "Herbert, you old fart, you made a really good movie but the end sucks."

This time Steel didn't need Eisner to tell her what to do. She secured another $250,000 from the studio to shoot a dancing finale.

Steel fought vociferously with her bosses over the soundtrack. She wasn't senior enough to merit a sound system in her office, so the songwriter-screenwriter Dean Pitchford and Zadan and Steel would pile into her car to play her the tracks from the emerging rockabilly album.

"All we had going for us was Dawn Steel," recalls Pitchford. "Dawn Steel would dance around. I'd see her in the cafeteria, and she would sidle up next to me, and she would sing a song that I had played her the night before. I had left the tape with her, and she would have listened to it seventy-five times. She would know the words backwards and forwards, and she would know how to sing it to you."

The studio had little faith in Steel's taste, even secretly commissioning an alternative disco soundtrack without her knowledge. When Columbia Records, which was putting out the *Footloose* album, showed unprecedented enthusiasm for the Kenny Loggins rockabilly tracks, Paramount quickly quelled the disco version. *Footloose* ended up grossing $80 million in the United States, and the album went platinum.

Columbia gave a party for everyone in the movie. Melnick introduced Steel to Walter Yetnikoff, the president of Columbia Records. "Baby, do you know how I define success?" he asked.

"No," she responded.

"By the size of my erection," said Yetnikoff.

In the spring of 1983, Steel was sulking on the Paramount jet to ShoWest, the annual dog and pony show at which the studio made presentations of its upcoming lineups to the exhibitors. The jet was filled with Paramount's current luminaries, not only Diller and Eisner but also Steven Spielberg and Harrison Ford, about to start *Indiana Jones*, Eddie Murphy, John Travolta, and Jack Nicholson and Debra Winger, stars of the upcoming *Terms of Endearment*.

All Steel could think about was the fact that Frank Mancuso, the newly promoted president of the motion picture division, was barring her from sitting on the dais with the other Paramount bigwigs. As would be her way throughout her life, Steel was extremely sensitive to all the subtle and not so subtle trappings of Hollywood hierarchy. She was obsessed with where she sat at restaurants, and whether she was on the list for a hot party.

She was consumed with her anger and impending shame when Frank Marshall, Spielberg's producer, introduced her to Martin Scorsese, who was about to shoot *The Last Temptation of Christ* for Paramount. Steel was giddy and elated, even more so when Scorsese sneaked off the dais ten minutes into the Paramount presentation and suddenly materialized at her side. "Want to have a drink?" he asked. They went gambling and later drove up the coast together. He stayed in her art deco apartment when he was in L.A., which was increasingly more of the time. "She was like a little kid. She really, really was crazy about him," recalls Marilyn Vance. "She was smoking, and Scorsese was totally allergic to it, and because she cared so much about him, she completely stopped smoking. She had that will, that determination, I'll sacrifice for what I want. When she wanted something she would do whatever it took to get it."

"Marty was all about old movies," recalls Howard Rosenman. Scorsese gave her a poster of *L'Avventura*, but Steel had to call a friend to ask who Antonioni was. "Dawn was very hungry for knowledge. She learned an awful lot from Marty Scorsese," says Rosenman. "And that was I think what part of it was about. He taught her."

Scorsese used to stay up all night watching old movies. He made Steel watch *Touch of Evil* over and over and over again, to show her how the opening shot—one single camera move made without cuts—was done.

He introduced her to his friends, including Gabriella Forte, who ran Armani. Steel began to wear Armani suits, with her trademark T-shirt, a uniform she popularized among female executives in Hollywood.

Through Scorsese she socialized with Steven Spielberg, Brian De Palma, George Lucas, and Francis Ford Coppola, the cream of the film school directors. "She was in her office one day, and this was around the time when she was dating Marty Scorsese. And she said, 'Come in, come in, come in.' This was at the time when Trivial Pursuit was really big. And all over the floor were spread the Trivial Pursuit cards," recalls one former Paramount executive. "She was memorizing all the answers to Trivial Pursuit, because she was going over to play Trivial Pursuit at Steven Spielberg's that night. And she didn't want to come across looking like a dummy. I spent four hours with her tutoring her on it."

As Scorsese's girlfriend, Steel debuted in the gossip columns, a scrutiny that became even more intense when *Flashdance* opened and she became the "It" girl. Six weeks later she went with Scorsese to Cannes for the debut of *The King of Comedy*, then to Tunisia, on what was to be half vacation, half location scouting for *The Last Temptation of Christ*. She also prevented Isabella Rossellini from getting a part in one of the movies she supervised because Rossellini had once been married to Scorsese.

To those who saw them together, it was a relationship of seeming opposites: the *Flashdance* princess and the *Raging Bull* director, an aesthete who lived and died by art alone. When they went to Paris together, Steel didn't want to go to museums. She wanted to shop. Their disparate attitudes toward the movie business brought tension to the relationship. Scorsese tended to call studio executives "you people," which he pronounced in one long disgusted slur, "youpeople," the enemy of everything creative and true. As Steel once explained, "He would sputter, for example, 'Youpeople have no idea what you're doing. Youpeople have never made movies.' "

Scorsese's disdain for Hollywood was only magnified by his ongoing problems with *Last Temptation*, the story of Jesus based on Nikos Kazantzakis's novel. While Steel had been fighting about whether Kevin Bacon was "fuckable" or not, Scorsese was trying to explore the religious questions posed by the Kazantzakis novel and its extremely controversial portrayal of a deeply human Christ, racked with doubt about his mission.

It had started out budgeted at $11 million, little even in those days, but had quickly risen beyond $14 million. Moreover, the studio thought the new script revisions were too arty, too difficult to understand. They told Scorsese they were worried they were moving "from a green light to a blinking yellow light." He replied that this movie was "like praying to me."

In November 1983 a group of Protestant women called the Evangelical Sisterhood put out a newsletter asking people to protest the movie and threaten a boycott of the products of the studio's parent company, Gulf + Western. Gulf + Western began to receive five hundred letters a day, letters with declamations like "'God invented syphilis to kill free love or VD. God invented AIDS to kill homos. If you make this movie God is going to kill you. Love Joe,'" recalls one former Paramount executive. The studio sponsored a theological seminar drawing religious figures from across the spectrum to discuss the issues raised.

Inside Paramount, Steel tried to stay out of the fray. "I was the executive on *The Last Temptation of Christ* because she was dating Marty at the time," recalls David Kirkpatrick. "She really felt that in terms of her own relationship with Marty that she had to keep her distance from the project, which was very right for her politically."

"She never had any involvement in one way or another," says Katzenberg.

It was probably not the right thing for her romantically, however. "She knew it was a volatile situation, she tried to stay out of it, but I think with very limited success, because I don't think Marty gave a shit about those kinds of niceties," recalls Craig Baumgarten, a friend to both of them. "His attitude was, Get involved, save my movie, you're my whatever. You're supposed to be there to help me, and it was a real conflict, and I think it was really difficult for her, and I think it speeded what was probably an inevitable end to that relationship."

The couple began to bicker. Steel felt more and more excluded from Scorsese's creative life. Her fury was often directed at his assistant, whose job it was to protect him from interference. Scorsese was slipping into a depression, becoming more and more remote to Steel, a turn of events that only reminded her of her father's depression. She felt that her bosses were trying to use her to get to Scorsese.

That November, Steel was promoted to senior vice president of production at Paramount. On Thanksgiving morning, Barry Diller called Scorsese at her apartment and asked him to come to a morning meeting. The studio (at the direct urging of Gulf + Western's chairman, Martin Davis, although this was not told to Scorsese) was putting the film into turnaround. From Thanksgiving to almost Christmas, Scorsese tried to figure out a way to save the project, cutting the budget to $6 million, including the $4 million they had already spent. Finally, on December 21, Diller killed the project unambiguously. "She felt terrible about it, but there's no way to tell the person you care about that you tried everything," says Vance.

The movie was turned down by every other studio in town, although in 1988 it was made by Universal. Soon after, Scorsese broke up with Steel and went home to New York. "He could not forgive her for not being able to get that movie made," recalls Baumgarten. In later years Scorsese would always deny to his friends that the relationship was as important or significant as Steel made it out to be.

15.

WOMEN DIRECT

I TOOK IT AS A SIGN
TO MAKE THE MOVIE

Of all the movies Streisand could have chosen to make her directorial debut, *Yentl* was probably the most quixotic. The studios were all dying to be in business with the biggest female star in the world, but no matter how she described *Yentl*—as a classic sex comedy, or a Joseph Campbell hero quest, or a belated coming-of-age story—they were nervous about the subject matter. They couched their reserve euphemistically: "It was a movie that only played in New York and L.A." Or, more pointedly, "Would Middle America buy the story of a singing shtetl Jewess (played by a middle-aged woman) who yearned to do, of all things, study?" Streisand intuited the problem. *Yentl* was too Jewish. "I think there's a lot of Jewish anti-Semitism in our business," Streisand says. "A lot of Jewish self-hatred. The original German Jews who started the movie industry were embarrassed by the Polish Jews. They didn't want a Jewish subject. They didn't want to be made fun of."

Streisand identified increasingly with Yentl's plight. "The same problem I was having getting it made was going on for Yentl, so it was a very truthful parallel in our lives," she says. If anything, the pitch Streisand *didn't* make about *Yentl* was what the movie truly embodied. It was a home movie of Streisand's psyche that tapped into the issues that obsessed her: gender politics, unrequited love, a woman's search for expression and power. Yentl's male disguise could easily be seen as a metaphor for celebrity, the cloak by which people knew the surface Streisand, though not the real one.

Barbra Streisand on the set of YENTL.

In fact, most of the important creative decisions in Streisand's career have emerged out of an unusually strong psychological connection to material. She was first struck by the Isaac Bashevis Singer story because of its first four words, "After her father's death," which evoked memories of her grief at the untimely death of her own father.

"It appealed to me," she says. "I was so molded by the fact that I didn't have a father." Her father, Emanuel Streisand, a high school teacher, had died when Streisand was only fifteen months old. Her mother told her that he'd been killed by a cerebral hemorrhage caused by overwork, although she learned as an adult that he died from an improperly treated epileptic seizure. She'd always been angry at him for abandoning her to grow up in her grandparents' crowded three-room apartment in Bedford-Stuyvesant, and later with a stepfather who didn't like her.

As she brewed over *Yentl* in the fall of 1979, she went to visit her father's grave for the first time. She asked her brother to take a picture of her next to her father's tomb, a photo she later showed to her staff. "Rusty, my assistant at the time, says, 'Look at the tombstone next to your father,' and the name is Anshel, and it's not Irving or Sam but Anshel," says Streisand. Anshel is the name of Yentl's dead brother, and the moniker she adopts when she assumes the guise of a man. "I took it as a sign to make the movie," Streisand says.

Like many who have been showered with outsized fortune, Streisand could be superstitious; she believed that the universe sent her omens—confirmations—of her own desires. Her brother, whom she regarded as a realist, had told her about a strange encounter with a Jewish medium who had put him in touch—or so he believed—with their dead father. Streisand asked to meet the woman, who came the next night. They sat around a table with their hands on top, and suddenly, according to Streisand, the table started to move. Each bang corresponded to a letter in the alphabet, one for *A*, two for *B*, and so forth. The table spelled out M-a-n-n-y, and then B-a-r-b-r-a. When the medium asked if he had any message for his daughter, the table banged S-o-r-r-y and then S-i-n-g P-r-o-u-d. "It scared me a lot. I never wanted to do it again," says Streisand, who remains convinced that her father's spirit was in the room that night. "How would anybody be that brilliant to know to say to me 'sorry' or 'sing proud'?" she insists with conviction. " I had always taken my gift of singing for granted. I was kind of embarrassed about having to be a singer at first. I wanted to play Medea, Hedda Gabler, and

I had to sing in a nightclub to get noticed, because I couldn't get noticed as an actress."

Although Streisand had initially conceived of *Yentl* as a straight drama, she knew that her voice always opened doors, even when her will failed her. She recalled an incident when she had wanted to do *Romeo and Juliet* on TV: "The network said, 'If you do it as a musical.' I thought, 'What?' But that kind of stayed in my head. I felt it would be easier to get *Yentl* made as a musical." Music would also accentuate the fantasy element of the story and help soften the fact that Streisand, on the cusp of forty, was a little old to be playing a naive ingenue. "I was getting older, and if it's kind of a realistic fairy tale and a musical, you buy it more," she explains. For the score, Streisand reunited with her close friends the lyricists Alan and Marilyn Bergman and the composer Michel Legrand, who had done her *Je M'Appelle Barbra* album. Despite the fact that the film was set in 1904 Poland, there was to be no klezmer ethnicity. Instead, she opted for dreamy French melodies, which only she would sing. The songs were to serve as Yentl's interior monologue.

Streisand was growing increasingly consumed with *Yentl*. She re-immersed herself in Judaism. It was all very familiar. She had been raised in a kosher home; her grandfather, a tailor by trade, used to double on occasions as a cantor at the local temple. "This is why it was so easy for me to play Yentl, and to understand the whole world of the film. I remember that my grandfather took me to shul and I sat in the section with the men because I was four, five, six years old and the women sat up above. I sat with the men and I could read Hebrew. I didn't know what I was saying, but in yeshiva we learned how to read Hebrew," says Streisand. She attended the yeshiva from kindergarten through second grade. "In yeshiva, I always had A's in scholastic studies, but I got a D in conduct because I would talk during [class]. If I knew the answer I was so excited, I would just say it. If [the teacher] didn't call on me, I'd just say it anyway. I was just excited by learning. I had a 93 average in high school, [and was] a member of the honor society called Arista. They couldn't believe I wasn't applying to college. They even called my mother in."

Streisand's interest in Judaism was marked by the same omnivorous impatience she employed in her career. She spoke to dozens of rabbis, and torpedoed through a series of different synagogues, including a Venice Beach congregation where the rabbi bar mitzvahed her son (amid great publicity) and the UCLA Hillel. Ultimately she embarked on biweekly study sessions with the feminist rabbi Laura Geller and donated to Hillel a Jewish performing arts center that drew Jewish superstar speakers such as Elie Wiesel and Cynthia Ozick. After the lectures, speakers would often find themselves whisked away to receptions at Streisand's Holmby Hills mansion, where they would meet the star herself.

Every visit to the synagogue became grist for the script, which had already gone through eight different incarnations by writers as diverse as Isaac Bashevis Singer, the author of the original story, and Ted Allan (*Lies My Father Told Me*). Streisand wrote three versions herself. "I didn't put my name on it because I didn't want people when they read it to be affected by the fact that it was me writing it," she says. "I didn't want them to prejudge it. That's why I put my name as a director *after* the film, not before." Streisand raised Yentl's age from sixteen to twenty-eight, and transformed her from a naif to a spinster who'd been shut off from life. The new Yentl stops resenting men once she enjoys their prerogatives, yet when she marries her would-be love's ex-fiancée, Hadass, she learns to see beyond the girl's docile, feminine passivity.

While Streisand liked to garner ideas from everyone, regardless of their status—her driver, her dresser, the soundman, a grip—she solicited script notes from a long parade of A-list writers such as Elaine May, Paddy Chayefsky, and Bo Goldman. Sometimes, she wasn't seeking advice so much as a warm ear. "Telephone conversations with her about the script tended to go on rather longer than it took to lay the Atlantic cable and rarely required more than the occasional 'uh-huh' from me to indicate I was still listening," wrote Steven Bach, the studio executive assigned to the project, who nonetheless enjoyed Streisand. Streisand's work habits could be so consuming that in later years, such as on *The Prince of Tides*, she even moved writer Becky Johnston into her home to have her on call twenty-four hours a day.

At times, even writing was a step too removed from her creative process. To understand Yentl, Streisand literally needed to be Yentl. She'd don Yentl's trademark hat and coat, and act out bits of the movie in an almost continual workshopping of the material. "We'd have members of her household staff and friends play parts," recalls coproducer Rusty Lemorande. "She would have her little boom box, which would play back the songs, and I'd tape them and then we'd edit them. There would be actors who would come in and read the script, and we'd tape that and cut that and make a little radio play." As she scouted locations in Czechoslovakia, she wore her costume and strolled through the cobblestone streets much as Yentl would have, all the while being filmed on super-8 tapes by Lemorande. By the time she was ready to shoot, she had put together almost a mini-version of the film, combining super-8 and video.

When the writer Chaim Potok approached her about an interview, she agreed, with the tacit understanding that she would be able to pick his brains about the constantly mutating screenplay. Potok, a rabbi, was surprised to find that "in matters Jewish, Barbra's knowledge is confused and rudimentary. Yet she asks questions, unself-consciously and with no hint of embarrassment, and takes notes with the assiduous concentration of one long-committed to learning." He and his wife meticulously corrected the errors they found, and even wrote a draft for a new ending, though Potok was a little dismayed when Streisand read through their work almost flippantly, "words skipped and blurred, passages intoned mechanically as if from a telephone book. She appears unimpressed and unmoved."

Still, he was awed by her commitment: "At times it is difficult to determine where Barbra ends and Yentl begins; the edges of the two personalities blur into each other. She seems filled and possessed by the work."

I HAD TO GIVE UP ALL MY SO-CALLED POWER

In 1981, Streisand submitted the latest version of the script to Sherry Lansing, the newly installed president of Twentieth Century–Fox. She hoped that Lansing, another woman, would be different from the male studio executives who'd bragged about turning down the biggest female star in the world. According to production sources, as well as at least one biography that quotes the director, Streisand went to discuss the project with Lansing, bringing along her super-8 footage to show that she could pass as a man, and a cassette of the songs to underscore the fact that this was a Streisand musical. Excitedly, she discussed her passion for Isaac Bashevis Singer's determined heroine. Afterward, she appeared expectant and optimistic. Several days later, however, Streisand heard that Fox had passed too. "I couldn't believe that a woman wouldn't understand how universal this story was," Streisand said in an interview. Twenty years later, neither Streisand nor Lansing remembers an actual meeting; still, the supposed encounter has acquired a certain mystique. The fact remains, though, that even Lansing didn't want to make *Yentl*.

Orion's rejection of *Yentl* had been a devastating blow for Streisand. No other studio stepped into the breach. She ultimately set the project up again with Jon Peters, who had moved on to running the small film division of the music giant PolyGram. For Streisand's team, it was a comedown. PolyGram didn't have enough office space for the production, so the company installed the director and her team in the basement of a dingy former old-age home across the street. Chinese folding screens had to be brought in to prevent people from staring at Streisand. Moreover, the Dutch company was willing to put up even less than the $13 million Orion had originally offered. While Peters and Streisand were still together, Peters was increasingly consumed with his burgeoning professional relationship with Peter Guber, and Streisand with *Yentl*. The couple butted heads.

Finally, in frustration, Streisand pulled the plug. It was a business rift that foreshadowed the couple's ultimate parting. For several months she funded the production out of her own pocket, a figure that grew to more than $500,000 as she hustled for a more prominent backer. Time was of the essence. The longer it took, the more it would look like *Yentl* was simply a vanity production. At one point during a location scout of Eastern Europe, Streisand grew so despairing that she talked of making *Yentl* a TV movie. When a new version of the script was finished, her associate Lemorande (who had replaced Peters as coproducer) secretly submitted it to low-level executives at three studios simultaneously, telling each that an offer was imminent from another place. In the end, Barry Diller at Paramount offered to put up $1 million to develop the movie further, while Bob Daly and Terry Semel at Warner Bros. said they'd make the movie—but only for $10 million (essentially requiring Streisand to give up her salary). United Artists, still reeling from the *Heaven's Gate* fiasco, offered to put up $13 million and to start funding the production immediately.

The studio's resolve to actually make the movie was further strengthened when studio vice president Lois Smith brought her boss, studio president Norbert Auerbach, to have tea with Streisand in New York. Streisand took the opportunity to present *Yentl*; she unleashed her voice and gave Auerbach a personal concert of the songs. When she explained that she wanted to shoot in Czechoslovakia, Auerbach, who'd been raised in Prague, began to reminisce excitedly. He later told his vice president Steven Bach that he was "in love with Yentl," the movie and the woman, and that Streisand had even asked him to play her father in the film. On March 31, 1981, United Artists announced it had a deal to make *Yentl*. The studio was in desperate shape, and wanted to say it had a Streisand musical.

Several weeks later, Auerbach and several of his executives took Streisand to dinner at Ma Maison. Auerbach again began to talk fondly of his childhood in Czechoslovakia.

Streisand looked up quizzically. "I didn't know you were from Prague," she commented. An increasingly flummoxed Auerbach went into a full recitation of everything he'd told her weeks before in Manhattan, and ended with a flourish. "That's why you asked me to play your father, remember?"

Streisand was shocked. "Morris Carnovsky is going to play my father," she gasped.

In the end, TransAmerica, the corporation that owned United Artists, put the kibosh on the whole idea and Nehemiah Persoff wound up with the part. United Artists asked for a rewrite, and Streisand brought in the British writer Jack Rosenthal, author of *Bar Mitzvah Boy*, a kind of English *Portnoy's Complaint;* Rosenthal shared final credit with her on the screenplay.

For her costar, Streisand chased Richard Gere, hot off *American Gigolo*, but he was skeptical about the star's ability to juggle her various tasks. "He said he'd act if I didn't direct, or he'd let me direct if I didn't act in it," remarked Streisand afterward. Rebuffed by Michael Douglas, after much hand-wringing Streisand finally settled on Mandy Patinkin, who'd just won a Tony for playing Che Guevara in *Evita*. For Hadass, the woman Yentl marries, Streisand wanted Carol Kane, but the studio balked. "They said she was too Jewish. They said, You have three Jews now, Mandy Patinkin, me, and Carol Kane. They allowed me to have Amy Irving," Streisand says, before chuckling. "I don't even think I told them she's half-Jewish."

Streisand would later complain that in order to make the movie she had to "eat shit" every step of the way. "I had to give up all my so-called power," she groused. In exchange for what was now a $14 million investment, United Artists, now run by Streisand's former agent David Begelman, had extracted from its star/director a stringent deal: $3 million to star (a million less than she had made on *All Night Long*) and Directors Guild minimum, $80,000 to direct. If the film went over budget,

Streisand would have to return half her salary. The studio had script approval, star approval, and final cut. For someone long accustomed to controlling everything, from her negatives to the lettering on the covers of her albums, this was a bitter pill.

Despite all her concessions, nothing could assuage the studio's nagging fear that Streisand, the well-known perfectionist, would go out of control. The day before principal photography was to begin, the studio added one more proviso: They insured, or "bonded," the picture, meaning that if Streisand went just 10 percent over budget, a completion bond company would take it over. To pay for the bond, they took $700,000 out of her budget.

"I was so dismayed," says Streisand. "The thought of a woman *actress* directing a movie, I think, scared them. They couldn't imagine that I could be financially responsible."

THEY CAN'T HANDLE A WOMAN HAVING THIS MUCH CONTROL

Streisand's obsessive attention to detail continued through the production. She insisted that Amy Irving wear real antique petticoats under her dress. "No one is going to see them," explains Streisand. "But the actor will know she's wearing them. That helps the performance . . . and the feeling for the period."

Streisand's attitude toward her actors was a curious idiosyncratic blend of deference and possessiveness. They were at once fellow artists and tools of her vision. Unlike Elaine May, Streisand didn't like to do endless takes. She made a point of first asking what the actors wanted to do in the scene before guiding them into what *she* wanted. "I touch my actors. I comb their hair. I watch their haircuts," she says. "It's like Hadass. Amy Irving was like the female aspect of the film. She was my doll. I wanted her hair to be backlit." She wanted Hadass to be the beautiful one, and would fuss with her clothes and hair, making sure that her lipstick matched the fruit on the table.

"I didn't pay that much attention to myself in that film. My scenes were at the end of the day, because I didn't want the actors to feel I was serving myself," says the director. With the prodding of her cinematographer, Streisand even relaxed her famous dictum that she wanted to be shot only on the left side of her face, theorizing that her putatively less-pretty side should be used for her masculine persona.

The major confrontations on the set came from her male costar, who bristled under the demands of his female director. By the time shooting began, Mandy Patinkin had already spent a month holed up with Streisand in intense rehearsals, and seemed to chafe at the many hats she wore and the control she exerted. "If Barbra was just a co-actor making the requests of Mandy, and not the director, he would have had every reason to feel the demands were extraordinary, but I and all the crew members felt Mandy was being unreasonable and difficult," says Rusty Lemorande.

Early in the production, Streisand grew so frustrated that she considered firing Patinkin. She didn't seem to find him attractive; he thrashed about in front of the camera, unwilling or unable to be still. His Method theatrics could be irritating. While preparing for the scene in which Avigdor turns in fury on Yentl after she reveals her true gender, Patinkin raged around the set screaming "Cocksucker! Motherfucker! Shit!," spewing hostility the meaning of which was not lost on anyone. During the filming, he pounded his fist on the wall, and Streisand looked fearful that he might actually hit her. "Take it down. Take it down," she urged, switching into her directorial mode. She kept the cameras rolling.

If there was one thing that was unnerving about Streisand, it was her ability to switch from acting to directing with almost freakish ease. "She can go from being the winning, appealing actress to the commanding director. People got nervous when those switches occurred," says producer Lemorande. "She is this soft innocent Yentl who adores Avigdor, and then suddenly she becomes the director. Remember, film is a monarchy, not a democracy."

Much of the time, Streisand was anxious, terrified about directing, convinced she was getting psychic payback for all the times she wouldn't stop her questioning. "I was worried I couldn't do it," she confessed to one production staffer. "That's why it took fifteen years." While her demeanor was generally calm on the set, the tension showed on her face, the dark shadows and swelling under her eyes. "Jeez, I look awful," she could be heard muttering under her breath as a makeup man would be called to brush away the fatigue. At night, she hounded her retinue of advisers with questions. As one staff member recalled, "Hers was not the cautious scholar-at-the-feet approach; it was Brooklyn, straight-up-front 'I wanna know.' " She routinely called the camera operator at three in the morning to discuss shots. She was determined in her belief that everything reflected on her. Sometimes Streisand didn't seem to be listening, although she would later incorporate others' ideas, not remembering where exactly they'd come from. "She wants all the attention, all the compliments" is the comment of someone involved in the production. "Just about when you want to wring her neck, she sings." The crew talked among themselves of how she got sick on the way to the set.

Yet she was equally convinced that her faith in *Yentl* was righteous. Every day, she walked around Czechoslovakia with a Jewish-star pin affixed to her cap. Although the Holocaust had decimated the country's Jewish population, she insisted that those Jews they could find be used as extras, because "I had to have Jews play the part of Jews in the synagogue. I can't teach other people how to *daven* [pray]," she explains.

At times, her belief in her own powers was startling. She had dreamed that it would be sunny the day that Yentl makes her first foray—a river crossing—as a boy. The first day, however, dawned overcast. "My vision was to have sunlight," explains Streisand. "It couldn't be a gray day even though David Watkin [the cinematographer] was saying, 'Well, the gray light was pretty.' He's right, except it wasn't my vision."

Streisand decided to gamble, waiting to shoot the scene the following day. But the next day, the sky remained cloudy. "I prayed and used every bit of willpower that I ever had and said, 'I *must* have sparkles on this water.' It was to be a joyous time, that first crossing. It was those moments when I prayed to God and to my father to open the skies and let there be sun, because that was my vision. Sure enough, the skies opened up and the sparkles were on the water."

After nine months in Europe, Streisand finished filming in October 1982. As her completion gift for her cast and crew, she gave everyone specially crafted pink boxes with a collection of her autographed albums, as well as sterling silver pins in the shape of books with a tiny pair of glasses on top.

By April of the following year, the bond company threatened to take over the picture unless Streisand finished editing and scoring and delivered the final picture within six weeks. She'd gone a million dollars over budget. She begged for an additional four weeks. "I'm going to die from the pressure," she told them, but the bond company refused to budge. She worked round the clock to finish, and in the end UA didn't change a frame.

Yentl debuted on November 16, 1983. Streisand went to a Hollywood theater to check the sound and picture, and then went to the nearest candy store she could find and bought "all the candy I could find and all the cookies I could find and a ham and cheese croissant and everything fattening and stuffed my face, just trying to feed that fear that nobody would show up."

There's no doubt that *Yentl* was a bold and deeply personal directorial debut. Once a viewer adjusted to the alternate universe in which Streisand was playing a naif in forelocks, the picture was an enjoyable Barbra Streisand feminist tale.

Reviews tended to split along the lines of whether the reviewer bought into the myth of Barbra Streisand. *Time* and *Newsweek* raved about the picture. Pauline Kael in *The New Yorker* cheered Streisand's effort, particularly the fluid naturalness and intimacy in the scenes between Streisand and Irving; the doyenne of film critics commented that "the whole movie has a modulated emotionality that seems distinctively feminine. . . . There is something heroic in the mixture of delicacy and strength that gives this movie its suppleness."

Other critics charged the director with narcissism. The film featured several pointed shots of Yentl looking into the mirror, imagery that fed her detractors. Janet Maslin in *The New York Times* wrote that *Yentl* "resembled a vanity production from afar (or at close range, too, for that matter)," while Isaac Bashevis Singer lambasted the actress publicly: "I must say that Miss Streisand was exceedingly kind to herself. The result is that Miss Streisand is always present, while poor Yentl is absent," he wrote in the *Times*. Some critics scoffed at the ending, a veritable replay of "Don't Rain on My Parade" in *Funny Girl*, although this time it's Yentl singing aboard a boat headed toward the freedom of America.

To Hollywood's surprise, *Yentl*, the movie nobody wanted, went on to earn $40 million domestically, just about enough for UA to get its money back. Streisand won a Golden Globe for directing, though the film was shut out at the Oscars, save for minor categories, igniting a media storm over whether the Academy was sexist or merely anti-Barbra (although undoubtedly some members of the Academy were neither). As the Oscar-going stars wound their way up the red carpet at the Dorothy Chandler Pavilion, they were greeted by rabid pro-Barbra protesters who bore placards reading, OSCAR AT 56—IS HE STILL A CLOSET CHAUVINIST?

Streisand herself was philosophical about her Oscar omission: "I don't necessarily think I deserved it. I don't think that way. I was thrilled to get the Best Director award at the Golden Globes, and then I thought, Jim Brooks's movie [*Terms of Endearment*] was fantastic. He deserved it. I don't think I was being snubbed particularly. It did shine a light on the woman issue. It would have been nice just to be nominated."

Yet the bad reviews infuriated and ultimately wounded her. Despite the massive self-confidence it took to get the movie made, Streisand retreated afterward. "I didn't direct for eight years because I didn't feel passionate about any other projects. I also hated the reviews that were mostly written by women . . . being put down with superficial comments," says the director. "I was trying to celebrate women and all they can be—childbearers and thinkers. The women's comments felt competitive and petty. They didn't see the overall theme. It was too much for me. Who needs this crap? I'm only interested in the creative process. And all this other nonsense is just really aggravating to me.

"I was looking at a movie the other night. Kevin Costner has huge close-ups, from over his eyes to under his mouth. His company produced it. He's never attacked for having big close-ups. I don't have one big close-up like that in any of my movies. None. And these people call me an egotist because they can't handle a woman having this much control . . . I guess."

WE'RE GIVING THIS PURPLE-HAIRED BITCH HER BIG BREAK

It was several years before Hollywood seduced Gillian Armstrong. After the triumph of *My Brilliant Career,* she retreated to Australia, where she quickly dispelled her brand-new reputation for refined period fare by directing a splashy rock-and-roll musical, *Starstruck.* In the years that followed her Cannes debut, Hollywood had continued to court her. She received what she jokingly called a Ladd Company fellowship—a short development deal that gave her an office in Los Angeles and a stipend to explore the country without asking for anything in return. She traveled around America and went to film festivals, and one of her most persistent admirers, Diane Keaton, flew into Minneapolis expressly to meet her. "Before I met Gillian, I had a big crush on her," Keaton later said. "Like everyone else who had seen *My Brilliant Career*, I wanted to do something with her, anything with her. Naturally I phoned her. I pursued her with my agent and my managers and the promise of doing a big American film, her first. I even flew to the Midwest to try to seduce her. Even though she was extremely charming, she turned me down. Like any rejected admirer, I kept pursuing her."

While Armstrong was in America publicizing *Starstruck*, a young producer, Scott Rudin, had better luck. He bore *Mrs. Soffel*, a script by Ron Nyswaner. Set in 1901, it was based on the true story of a middle-aged warden's wife, Mrs. Soffel, who falls in love with a handsome young prisoner, Ed Biddle, convicted of murder. Biddle adeptly preys on her attraction to him, convincing her of his innocence. She engineers Biddle's and his brother's escape and goes with them, abandoning her puritanical husband and her children, and becoming a heroine to the women of the community, until the trio are hunted down by a vigilante posse keen on containing this threat to God-fearing law and order.

Although he was only twenty-four, Rudin played Armstrong beautifully. Once a painter, Armstrong responded viscerally to visual stimuli; she liked to storyboard her movies herself in elaborate pen-and-ink drawings. Rudin brought her pictures of "an enticing image of this jail that looked like a medieval church, and [got her] to think of these people who were kept in a jail that looked like a church which they break out of with a woman who's deeply religious." He also knew of Keaton's pursuit of Armstrong, and dropped the fact that the star was interested in playing Mrs. Soffel.

The movie was set up at MGM, which in the years since Paula Weinstein's departure had continued to struggle under extreme financial pressures. *Mrs. Soffel* had risen through the ranks at MGM mostly on the passion of a young woman development executive, Ileen Maisel, a former assistant to Freddie Fields, who was given unusual leeway to develop what she wanted free from much of the bureaucratic routine. Yet almost from the beginning the top executives were in total disagreement about what the film was about. According to Peter Bart, a former MGM vice president of production, the studio head Frank Yablans thought *Mrs. Soffel* was a steamy love story–cum–chase picture, a blend of two recognizable commercial genres; for the studio production president, Freddie Fields, *Mrs. Soffel* was *Bonnie and Clyde* redux.

For Armstrong, it was an erotic love story, told from a feminist point of view, of a repressed woman fighting a restrictive society. "Exploring that sort of passion, that sexuality of somebody who was not a great beauty," says Armstrong. "She was a very ordinary middle-class woman. What made her give up her husband and her children and run off with two thieves?" To Armstrong it was clear that Biddle hadn't simply cynically used Mrs. Soffel but had stuck with her long after her usefulness evaporated and her presence hindered his and his brother's escape: "What was it that was going on between those three people that made them stay together? [It was] something that was going to slow them down, going to make them much more obvious targets, and not only put his life in jeopardy but put his brother's life in jeopardy."

From the beginning Rudin wanted Mel Gibson, another newly minted star out of Australia, who had just done *The Road Warrior* and *The Year of Living Dangerously*. Gibson was familiar to Armstrong, so familiar that he wasn't exciting. "There must be another Mel in America. There must be a million Mels," she said. She screen-tested all the rising young stars, from Tom Cruise to Kevin Costner, and soon concurred with Rudin that Gibson was unique. Fortunately, he wanted to work with his fellow national—and to make a provocative film unlike the usual studio fare.

From the beginning almost everything about Armstrong—from her inexperience in big-budget filmmaking to her engaging but slightly cool manner and her punk-rock haircut (quickly abandoned after an airport official mistook her for Linda McCartney)—had raised flickers of apprehension within the MGM power structure, apprehension that was swept aside once Keaton and the nova-hot Gibson signed on.

Armstrong attended a meeting with the head of physical production, Lindsley Parsons, Jr., a strict, formal, blue-suited old-schooler with the demeanor of a high school principal. Parsons emerged from that meeting in a panic about the rising budget and about Armstrong's seemingly presumptuous demands for authentic wardrobe and a long shooting schedule, which included a proposed twelve-day stint in Pittsburgh, which had the real period prison. Inside MGM it had been supposed—somewhat arbitrarily—that the budget could be kept to $10 million. Now it appeared to be climbing to $13 million. When Armstrong's demands were later conveyed to Yablans, the head of the studio raged: "We're giving this purple-haired bitch her big break, in return she can cut the budget."

"I actually had no sexism in all my early upbringing, or my early career in Australia. It was really only meeting an elder generation of very conservative men in Hollywood. What I was naive about is that every studio has somebody who is head of production," says Armstrong. "You have got to be looking after the money in the budget, and very often in that situation it's a conservative older man. I think a bit of this goes on with any director. Me and them, it's this battle, and I'm trying to rip off their money or whatever. But when it was a woman who could hold them over for an extra day, or didn't get the shot that night, when it was a woman that had the power of the money, they were very, very upset."

For Armstrong the battle seemed nonsensical. As she understood the situation, the movie had been budgeted at $12 million and was now coming in at $13 million because they had cast Gibson. "Everyone kept forgetting we had also signed up Mel, and the film had never been budgeted for two stars!" she says. "When I look back now, I had an innocent confidence. I had never dealt with the studios before. On an independent film, you work in a great position of trust. There's a certain amount of money; when it runs out, everyone comes together and goes, How are we going to finish the film? When I came to America and they started chopping at my script—when they started saying, Can't you shoot a jail wall and not have a real jail?—it was like I got $12 million, why can't this money be on the screen? The only reason I'm here is I'm hoping I can make a better picture."

As the movie proceeded toward production, budget tensions escalated; MGM said they would pull the film unless Rudin was fired. "It was an absolute freak-out for me," says Armstrong, "because I had come from an independent industry where you form a relationship with a producer. You do the film together. You never think of a producer going away. It was definitely studio politics. They felt like he was an upstart."

Edgar Scherick, the film's powerful executive producer, who had set up the film at MGM, flew in to counsel Armstrong. The former head of production at ABC, Scherick had a reputation for screaming tantrums directed at underlings, although on *Mrs. Soffel* (as, ironically, he had years before on *The Heartbreak Kid*) he threw his considerable weight behind his director. The studio was also demanding that Armstrong fire her production manager, who happened to be a woman, one of the only female production managers in the business. "They could not cope with the fact that a young woman was responsible for that much money, and to have *two* of us," says Armstrong. "Ed Scherick gave me the advice. [The production manager] understood as well, we were just going to be beating our heads against the wall. We had to have a man that they trusted about the money, because they didn't trust me and there was no way they were going to trust her. It was a sad thing to save the film." For years that firing filled Armstrong with guilt.

MGM succeeded in whittling down the budget, but once filming started in Toronto the production quickly veered off schedule, though only by a few days. Some difficulties were simply endemic to shooting in the winter, in the snow, which kept melting and ruining their shots. "The grips were moving things around in the snow, and you have to wipe out footprints between every take," says Armstrong. The director was also a perfectionist, precise and hovering over every decision, like a painter carefully stroking her palette. Like any number of male directors, Armstrong would do take after take to etch out her vision. In the seduction scene, where Gibson and Keaton were supposed to kiss through the bars, Armstrong kept the stars' lips locked together so long that Keaton took to assuaging her mouth with Blistex and tea. "Thank God you're the world's best kisser," she whispered to Gibson.

What seemed to gall the executives was that not one of them was able to communicate with Armstrong, who appeared to be withdrawing from anyone who was not in her tight Australian coterie, primarily the cinematographer Russell Boyd and her live-in boyfriend, who was working as an assistant editor. The studio felt she refused to rely on her veteran department heads or even show her shot list to Scherick, who remained one of her biggest supporters. Armstrong is by nature aloof, but her added chilliness was not surprising given the lack of support emanating from the executives. "I think they were all harder on me," she says. "Like they had to come up and check on me. Somehow, maybe physically, I was slow in the cold. And it was sort of like, excuse me, I am just standing here waiting. We had trouble with the snow." (The former MGM production executive Peter Bart had a different take, describing how it once took almost four hours to light a simple interior shot because Armstrong was never satisfied.)

Armstrong was perfectly aware of the pervasive threat (briefly realized and quickly rescinded) to take away her ten-day shoot at the real Pennsylvania jail, whose image had enticed her to do the film. "People were calling me at night and so on," she recalls. "My agent was fantastic in fighting and saying, Just lay off her. So I have to say that he took the abuse." Armstrong didn't hesitate to threaten—"Tell them I am going home."

She was aided by the support of her stars. Off set Gibson indulged in wild drinking sprees, even destroying a house in a tantrum, a stunt that cost the studio $50,000. On the set he was indefatigable and professional. Yearning to direct herself, Keaton followed Armstrong around with "this little black notebook in my hand. I would write down her elaborate shots as if I was suddenly going to get her imagination, and the more dutifully I wrote down her camera angles and her way of approaching the scene, the more of a mystery it became," Keaton later explained. She joked, "The more I actually became aware of how unique and special her talent was the more I wanted it for myself."

In the end Armstrong's obstinacy and ultimately her vision won out. She won almost every battle. While Frank Yablans continued to carp about the budget—even broaching the possibility of firing her—Freddie Fields took to championing her work, declaring, "She's getting great stuff on film. That's what matters." Armstrong ended eleven days over, but "on budget," she insists.

She edited the film in L.A., where she conceived her first child. Her boyfriend had become the postproduction supervisor. She spent her nights throwing up and her days working at her film. "I checked the first answer prints—I was six months pregnant—and got on the plane to go back to Australia," says Armstrong. "I learned over the years that the filmmaker has a really bad time if the studio is over the edge. They're losing money. The week *Mrs. Soffel* opened, Frank Yablans lost his job and they all went. . . . I later realized they were all worried about losing their jobs."

16.

OWNING YOUR VOICE

YOUR HORRIFYING
INELUCTABLE DESTINY

"Not only did I have the only working mother but it was just an industry where there were almost no women," says the writer-director Nora Ephron, daughter of the screenwriters Phoebe and Henry Ephron, authors of *Desk Set* and *Carousel.* "Many of the women who worked in the industry worked with men. My mother; Frances Goodrich. Fay Kanin did a lot of scripts with her husband."

Ephron, a well-known journalist and writer before moving into film, is taking a break from editing *Sleepless in Seattle,* a romantic comedy that will cement her position in Hollywood as not only a top screenwriter but a top director. Dark-haired, with asymmetrical eyes and a clever, knowing smile, she is a woman who prides herself on knowing what she wants—whether it be the appropriate slipcovers for a couch or an Oscar on her mantel. She doesn't believe in whining; her weapon for eradicating life's sorrows is the satirist's pen. Pointed but politic on the record, cutting and more forthright behind the scenes, Ephron adeptly spins the mythology of her own life.

"I had this very clear sense my mother led a different life from other women," she says. "I was always talking about how she wore suits. She was out of a Tracy-Hepburn movie. She had an offbeat, tomboy great look. They went off to Twentieth Century–Fox in separate cars, which was about 3.5 minutes from the house. My mother had a 'forty-seven Studebaker, which when she traded it in eight years later for a Thunderbird had twelve thousand miles on it. They worked there as contract

Nora Ephron (looking away), husband Carl Bernstein,
and an unidentified woman, 1977.

writers, and they wrote one movie after another after another, and what they wrote got made.

"I think if you grow up with a working mother, your horrifying ineluctable destiny—you can paddle as hard as you can—it's amazing how many of us either literally or metaphorically or figuratively end up being our mothers. In addition, my mother was a truly adamant person about working. She had contempt for women who didn't work. There was none of that stuff which is fashionable now which is to pretend to respect any choice that people make. My mother did not respect the choices that most women had made. We all grew up knowing that she expected us to work, and, of course, there was no sense in our house that [that] excluded getting married and having children. She had done that too."

Born in 1941 and named for Ibsen's feminist heroine in *A Doll's House*, Ephron grew up in a household where her mother's favorite maxim—which she repeatedly ground into her four daughters—was "Everything is copy." At the age of two Nora provided the fodder for her parents' first big Broadway success, *Three's a Family*, which ran 495 performances and played for a year and a half in London. Her mother was the writer of the pair, pounding out the scripts at the typewriter while her father paced and edited.

When Nora was five the family moved to L.A. so that her parents could go into the movie business, a traumatic event about which Ephron repeatedly says, "Everything had gone downhill as a result. I had been in a place that I knew was welcoming and safe for smart women, and I had a very clear sense that Hollywood was not that place. It was very clear from my own mother's sense of alienation from the regular community and her defensiveness about the choice she had made even though it wasn't even a choice for her. It was just what she was going to do."

Although Phoebe Ephron disdained such conventionalities as the PTA, she was fanatical about keeping a certain decorum, making sure her daughters took two years of Latin, three years of French, and refrained from sororities. She was full of idiosyncratic life lessons: "Don't eat leftovers," "Never buy on sale," "Never marry a man with fat ankles."

"She was so strangely religious about dinner," recalls Ephron. Phoebe and Henry arrived home every day at four-thirty, and at five-thirty the whole family assembled in the den for cocktails and crudités, before a dinner cooked by "this amazing cook. You would die to eat this food," Ephron gushes. "And then at seven-fifteen, we would all go our separate ways. But it was very civilized, though. Very, very civilized, and very sweet, and we all had fun."

Mealtime was a competitive derby for the best bon mot and cleverest witticism. "You were supposed to tell little stories, and funny was better than not funny," Ephron says. She thought it was great, because she always won, but her younger sisters thought it was grotesque. "I really felt like a favored child," recalls Ephron. "I was like a parent's dream. I got good grades and I never did anything . . . we didn't even have anything you could smoke then, except cigarettes, and I didn't even do that."

It was a household long on accolades for achievement and short on sympathy. "When I was little, my parents went away to do a play. I sort of remember that. In fact, I remember it to the extent that it cost me about twenty thousand dollars to remember it even better," jokes Ephron. Uninterested in anything that wasn't a success, her mother controlled her daughters by withholding approval. She was remote, fictionalized in Ephron's novel *Heartburn* as a "washout at hard-core mothering; what she was good at were clever remarks that made you feel immensely sophisticated and adult and, if you thought about it at all, foolish for having wanted anything so mundane as some actual nurturing."

"I always envied the girls whose mothers helped them with stuff," Ephron adds. "My mother just—it was like"—Ephron claps her hands with a thunderous clack—"Figure it out. She was very, very laissez-faire in many ways.

"When you look at those women who do well, their fathers all made them," adds Ephron. "I mean, my father took us to football games, took us to baseball games, played tennis with us, did not treat us as if (a) he wished we had been boys or (b) we were sort of little princess girls. And the other thing was that, as weird and as deranged as they were, there's no question that they spent a huge amount of time with us in a way."

Outside the household there was a different kind of pressure. Although she was voted "most likely to succeed" in her high school class, Ephron was stunningly aware that "I was completely different from everyone I went to Beverly Hills High School with. Completely," she says. "Yeah, there were lots of dark Jewish girls at Beverly Hills High School, but I wanted to get out of there and I didn't want to go to Berke-

ley and join the AE Phi and marry a ZBT and get married at Temple Em-
manuel and, and live in a house north of Santa Monica. I mean, nobody—nobody wanted to have a career in 1958 who was a girl."

She bristles at the suggestion made by former high school mates
that it might have been difficult to have been skinny and flat-chested—
not a great beauty—in a land that worships the pert-nosed, shiksa
blonde. Yet her own feelings of physical inadequacy informed some of
her earliest writing, from the title of her first collection of essays, *Wall-
flower at the Orgy,* to her teenage quest for bigger breasts, which included sleeping on her back for four years, buying a Mark Eden Bust
Developer, and splashing "cold water on them every night because
some French actress said in *Life* magazine that was what she did for her
perfect bustline."

By the time Ephron was in high school, her parents' perfectly done
lifestyle had begun to disintegrate. Henry was offered a producing deal
at Fox. He and Phoebe began to work separately. "They were very competitive when my father started producing. My mother was very angry
about that. Very, very angry about that," says Ephron. "It was the beginning of the trouble, and I think she felt that he was— I think he was
being unfaithful to her in every way, so . . ." Her voice trails off. Phoebe
went to New York for several months when her first solo playwriting effort, *Howie,* was produced. It flopped. "She really began drinking when
I was in high school, but then it got really bad when I was in college,"
says Ephron. "And it went from being a sort of occasional thing to an
almost chronic thing. And Delia and Hallie and Amy [her sisters] really
had the worst of it. I got out," Ephron says, although when she came
home from college the household was filled with her parents' screaming matches. Their father had also begun to drink, although none of his
daughters acknowledged this fact until after their mother died. He was
later hospitalized for manic-depression.

"It was horrible," Ephron says, before downplaying the black lining
in the silver cloud of her youth. "Kids are so strange and resilient about
things like this, even . . . I mean, it's easy for me to say, 'cause I didn't
have the bad part, but—but really, you do cope. There were many kids
with alcoholic parents who had much worse times than we did."

Phoebe used Nora's letters home from Wellesley for her next play,
Take Her She's Mine, which became a hit on Broadway, with George Ab-
bott directing and Elizabeth Ashley starring. "This adorable person was
playing someone who people thought was me, and I would have killed

to be Elizabeth Ashley," says Ephron, who pooh-poohs any notion that her parents' ready use of her life was exploitative. "It never would have crossed my mind to say, 'Oh please, please, please, don't write a play about me.' Because I didn't think of it as a play about me particularly. I thought it was more about them, and I thought it was more sort of fiction. It wasn't really what had happened. It was all kind of innocent and heady.

"It was an absolute given in my house," says Ephron. "I think we all grew up knowing that they wrote a little bit about us, and someday we were going to write about them. Who is it that said, 'Writers are predators'? *Everybody* knows that. It's just a question of who do you prey on?"

Ironically enough, Phoebe was unhappy one of the first times Nora put *her* in a piece. "I wrote in this story about how they had to have their house done over in Beverly Hills by the head of set decoration at Twentieth Century–Fox. And it was kind of a funny thing . . . and it really hurt my mother's feelings," recalls Ephron. "She never told me. I didn't find out until after she died. I think she understood that it was fair, it was like"—again, Ephron claps her hands to denote a thing that has been done and cannot be questioned—"they had done it and it was fair game."

Phoebe was hospitalized for the last couple of months of her life, and she died at fifty-seven of cirrhosis of the liver in 1971. When Nora visited her on her deathbed, Phoebe turned to her and commanded, "Take notes, Nora, take notes."

Years later Nora played Phoebe's excruciating death scene for laughs in *Heartburn.* "One day her stomach swelled up like a Crenshaw melon and they took her to a very fashionable hospital for rich people with cirrhosis and the doctors clucked and said there was nothing that could be done. . . . She lay there slowly dying with my father impatiently standing by, 'Pull the plug,' he would say to the doctor . . . suddenly she opened her eyes and looked at me. 'I just screwed Darryl Zanuck on the remake,' she said, and gave a little croak . . . and died."

It was only after Phoebe Ephron died that the sharp-tongued, ironic voice readers associate with the professional Nora Ephron began to emerge, mostly in a series of essays on the women's movement written for *Esquire.* Ephron had already spent ten years as a journalist, the culmination of a fantasy she had as a teenager of being Dorothy Parker.

"When I went into journalism, I thought it was a rebellion," she jokes. "I wasn't going into the horrible movie business, living in horrible Beverly Hills with all the horrible strawberry blond ladies. That was not going to be my life. I was going to go back to New York.

"Who wouldn't become a journalist?" she asks. "It's the greatest job there is. I knew very early on, I knew in a subconscious way that I was never going to have a specialty. I was never going to know anything about anything in a deep way, nor was it interesting to me. The idea you can do a little of this or a little of that, like Lois Lane, Brenda Starr, and his girl Friday."

It was also the era of New Journalism, when journalists like Tom Wolfe were becoming stars and the profession retained a glamorous air. Ephron started out doing fluffy "women's page" work at the *New York Post*, where she capitalized upon her parents' friendship with the daughter of the owner, Dorothy Schiff, to present her fellow journalists' complaints about the *Post*'s stunningly dirty and decrepit working conditions. Schiff ignored her, and years later Ephron deftly decapitated her former boss in an essay for *Esquire* as the Marie Antoinette of the newspaper world.

Her essays on the women's movement—written during the years 1972 through 1974—are widely considered her best journalistic work. Ephron served up for *Esquire*'s largely male readership the concerns of the movement largely filtered through her own psyche and experience— essays on breast size, and vaginal perfume, the Pillsbury Bake-Off, consciousness raising, and the phenomenon of *Deep Throat*. She showed feminism not in theory but in practice—pointing out, without any of the movement's cant, the difficulty of "women pulled between the intellectual attraction of liberation, and the emotional, psychological, and cultural mishmash it's hard to escape growing up with." Her politically incorrect admissions—such as a rape fantasy or the notion that "sisterhood is difficult"—occasionally enraged more hard-line feminists.

Ephron moved on to become an acerbic media critic, the great deflater, the self-anointed enemy of cant, the scourge of bathos, self-righteousness, and faux profundity. Her scalps grew to include those of the historian Theodore White, *Passages* author Gail Sheehy, the *New Yorker* writer Brendan Gill, and the feminist godmother Betty Friedan.

Ephron quickly established herself at the top. "I certainly remember when I was coming up, knowing who the other women journalists were, and the other women magazine writers," she says. "But, at about the time I sort of was starting, things got much more open for women in journalism, so it wasn't that thing where there was only room for so many of us. So, you don't have that thing you have in Hollywood where there's only room for one token woman and who is it going to be? And, of course, it plays into all the stuff that women grow up with, the competitiveness with the mother and all that stuff. I do remember that Sally Kempton was writing for magazines when I started in, and she was awesome. She was unbelievable. And then she retired to become a disciple of Baba Ram Dass, and I went, 'Phew, thank God she's out of the way and the coast is clear for me.' I did have that moment of that."

While Ephron was lauded by many of the women who read her, she polarized the women she actually met—dividing the world into two camps, women she'd later call "one of us" and those who pointedly weren't. The "one of us" women were often her biggest supporters: her first writing partner, Alice Arlen; her sister and second writing partner, Delia; such bright, tough Hollywood women as Lynda Obst and Dawn Steel; and, later, rising executives like Amy Pascal. The others were women toward whom she felt jealousy, or who didn't even merit her attention.

Ephron freely admitted in one essay that she was jealous of women who took advantage of men because it was a skill that escaped her, and that jealousy—said her critics—could turn to venom, with targets including the lithe feminist avatar Gloria Steinem, who once appeared at a Hamptons party in a backless dress only to have Ephron hiss, "Did you see the fat rolls on her back!" When her close friend the director Mike Nichols married the blond newscaster Diane Sawyer, Ephron gave a toast on "How to keep Mike happy" to Sawyer; it walked the line between funny and mean—focusing on food, although Sawyer is pointedly uninterested in cooking, and the fact the marriage was performed in a church, although Nichols was Jewish. Everyone there knew what was not spoken—that Ephron is a terrific cook and that she happens to be Jewish.

Of course, Ephron is far more famous for her antipathy toward certain men, in particular the two ex-husbands who betrayed her. A New York tabloid once featured her as one of the "Ten New York Women Who Make Men Nervous," a moniker that mostly stems from her book *Heartburn*, the screed of all women scorned.

Heartburn is a roman à clef about the demise of Ephron's second marriage, to the Watergate hero journalist Carl Bernstein. Married in

1976, the pair were the toast of the media world until Bernstein commenced a steamy affair with Margaret Jay, the wife of the British ambassador, while Ephron was pregnant with their second son, who was born two months prematurely after Bernstein confessed to Ephron his passion for the other woman. Stung by the rejection, with the added humiliation of feeling like a dupe, Ephron pointedly did not retract into victimhood. She called the New York gossip columnist Liz Smith and announced the marriage was through.

Ephron took her mother's credo, "Everything is copy," to heart, and, unlike Phoebe Ephron, spun her humiliation into gold. In her bestseller *Heartburn*, she characterized her ex-husband as callow, narcissistic, and cold: "The man is capable of having sex with a venetian blind" was the most famous line in the book. Ephron's first husband, the humorist Dan Greenburg, who had sex with her best friend, didn't get off so lightly either—he was transmogrified into a stingy neatnik, so obsessed with his four hamsters that when one died he had it cryogenically stored.

While some critics have dismissed *Heartburn* as simple revenge, the book remains one of the most memorable artifacts of the sexual revolution, a pop female answer to Philip Roth's *Portnoy's Complaint*. "I think in some way my writing that book was a certain kind of nightmare come true," Ephron told *Vanity Fair*. "Glenn Close in *Fatal Attraction* was one kind of male nightmare: 'What if I slept with a woman and she got pregnant and ruined my life?' I think I was some other form of male nightmare: 'What if I got involved with a woman and told her all my innermost secrets and she went off and wrote a book about it?' "

In later years Ephron took a certain offhand pleasure in her reputation for intimidation and her ability to instill fear by wielding her powers of social humiliation. Male studio executives often adopted better behavior when dealing with Ephron—much to the amusement and chagrin of the other women who populated her production teams.

"I don't mind if people are afraid of me," she says. "When you're a director, people are kind of afraid of you, and if it works for you, it's okay. Nobody who knows me well is particularly afraid of me. And most of the people who work with me know that I work in a very blunt way. I mean, I'm very"—she claps her hands—"it's like, that doesn't work, let's find something else. And I'm as horrible about my own work as I am about, you know, if we're working out what the room should look like. I think you pass through a period when you worry a lot about what people think of you. And then, you discover that people think things about you that really don't have anything to do with reality, and there really isn't much you can do about it. So you might as well relax."

In some ways it was inevitable that Ephron would turn to screenwriting—less because she was the child of screenwriters than because it was the mid-seventies, and "everybody wrote a screenplay," at least everybody Ephron knew. She was dating Bernstein when the first draft of the movie *All the President's Men* came in, and she and Bernstein revamped it themselves, "which is of course something we should not have done," she says. "I always tell everyone who asks me how to learn to write a screenplay, 'Just rewrite a screenplay by William Goldman, because he's a great screenwriter. Second of all, he does things so economically that you can't believe it.' "

Goldman was not amused by Bernstein's and Ephron's presumptuousness and stopped talking to Ephron, but not to Bernstein or his partner, Bob Woodward, which Ephron found "interesting." Only one of their scenes made it into the final script, "a really nifty move by Bernstein where he outfakes a secretary to get in to see someone," says Goldman in his book *Adventures in the Screen Trade.*

Their draft nonetheless made the rounds in Hollywood, and Ephron was hired to write a TV movie, *Perfect Gentlemen,* a female caper picture with Lauren Bacall and Ruth Gordon. "It was terrible, but it got made and I thought, Everything I do is going to get made," she says. "That turned out to be one of the great delusions of all time." She wrote a rock-and-roll musical for Paramount about the daughter of a singer who outdoes her mother by becoming a rock star and a draft of the suburban satire *Compromising Positions,* but the rights reverted to the author, Susan Isaacs, who did the screenplay. Like her parents, Ephron and Bernstein even tried to write a screenplay together—not terribly successfully—Ephron wound up doing most of it.

When her marriage broke up, Ephron returned to New York with her two sons—both under fifteen months—quickly set up a household, and took up screenwriting with a vengeance. "The truth was screenwriting saved me from destitution," says Ephron. "One of the reasons I started writing screenplays was I had just had a baby. It was really hard for me to imagine how I was going to go off and do these long reporting pieces that I liked to do with the baby. I needed money desperately," she says. "I was basically supporting all of us by writing screenplays. In the middle of one of my screenplays I wrote the first forty pages of

Heartburn in a burst, and so what would happen, I would work on screenplays for eight months, and then it would buy me enough time to spend four months on *Heartburn.*" After about three years she had a novel.

Ephron's name as a cult journalist gave her some entrée in Hollywood. Yet she was treated with all the respect—or lack of it—afforded to a screenwriter without much of a track record. "I *had* to do the screenwriting or the household was going to grind to a stop," she says. "And I wanted to do *They're Playing Our Song* and I knew how to do *They're Playing Our Song.* It was a Neil Simon musical [but]—Neil didn't want to do the script."

After pitching to the producer, Ephron went to pitch to the head of the studio. "So I go in. He was the head of the studio, and he had just started having an affair with his associate. And I went in to pitch this thing in a room that had this big L-shaped white couch, with a huge amount of room on it." Unfortunately, the studio head and his associate sat right next to each other on the couch. "They were lighting each other's cigarettes and they were basically fucking except that they weren't. It was so unbelievable. It was humiliating. I mean, there you are, going on and on—is anyone listening? It was so awful." The meeting was a microcosm of what had happened with Bernstein.

"I left the meeting—I missed the only plane I have ever missed, I was so rattled by the whole thing. The next week they did the same thing to Hannah Weinstein, and Hannah actually said something to them like, 'Do you mind paying attention to me and stop doing whatever the two of you think you're doing?' I remember everyone was talking about it because it was so shocking."

One day Ephron, an ICM client, received a phone call from the agency powerhouse Sam Cohn, asking if she wanted to meet Meryl Streep. Cohn's girlfriend, the ICM agent Arlene Donovan, had read Ephron's version of *Compromising Positions* and, knowing her background as a journalist, suggested her for a project that interested Streep. It was the life story of Karen Silkwood, the blue-collar nuclear power plant worker who had turned antinuclear activist.

The meeting with Streep went well, but ABC Films, which owned the project, balked at hiring Ephron. The company head, Robert Bookman, a former ICM agent who had ironically enough represented

Ephron in her TV deal, insisted that her only skill lay in comedy. But Streep—and Cohn—persisted, and Ephron was offered the deal.

Nervous about how she was going to manage Oklahoma research with two small babies, Ephron asked her friend Alice Arlen to collaborate. Arlen had written one screenplay for Robert Redford, and, more important, she had followed Silkwood's case because she knew the first lawyer. "The original impulse was she was going to help. She'd go out to Oklahoma and do all this research, but as it turned out, it was a completely equal collaboration," says Ephron. They outlined the piece, then each took scenes, then revised and edited.

The real Karen Silkwood had been a contradictory character, a plant worker whose life was imploding when she was mysteriously killed in 1974 on her way to meet a *New York Times* reporter, purportedly with a cache of papers proving poor safety conditions in the Kerr-McGee plant, which made plutonium rods for atomic weapons, as well as evidence suggesting a secret, and illegal, diversion of plutonium from the plant.

But Ephron's way into the script wasn't strictly political. "You're always looking for a moment when you can connect to somebody, or in some way, go"—she claps her hands—"oh, that's who it was." For Ephron that moment came while reading transcripts of a long interview Silkwood's boyfriend Drew Stephens had done with the executive producer. Amid pages and pages of transcripts, Stephens suddenly told how when he warned her to be careful, Silkwood ripped open her shirt and flashed him her breast.

"I knew exactly who she was at that moment," says Ephron, "She was a provocateur."

As she had filtered the tenets of the women's movement through her idiosyncratic *Esquire* pieces, personalizing power politics, Ephron and Arlen set Karen Silkwood's emerging activism amid the pungent domesticity of Silkwood's life—the loving but fraught relationships with Drew Stephens (Kurt Russell) and their lesbian roommate, Dolly Pelliker (Cher), the pain of having lost custody of her kids to her ex-husband, the growing tensions with her factory mates, an extended family in the midst of fracturing. "The fact that a person who does a thing like this still has to get out of bed in the morning and fight with people over who does the dishes is very much how I [and Alice] come at things," says Ephron. In bed one night, Karen asks, "Drew, do you feel different about me since I got cooked?"

Despite the initial hurdles in getting hired and ABC's subsequent trepidation about the film's political content (overridden by the fact that they couldn't *not* make a movie that starred Streep and was directed by Mike Nichols, for fear someone else would win an Oscar with the material they'd developed), Ephron relished her *Silkwood* experience. The screenplay didn't diverge enormously from how she wrote it, mostly because "Mike [Nichols] identified with Karen," says Ephron. "Usually on a movie, the director, who is usually a man, identifies with the male character and you constantly have to fight to preserve the line with the female character. This is a movie about waking up. He felt that he had been through an experience that caused him to wake up." Nichols, who hadn't directed a movie since the 1975 failure *The Fortune*, had recently recovered from a debilitating depression. "Therefore it wasn't this thing where he was suddenly trying to make the Kurt Russell part, the part that drove the movie."

I TOTALLY IDENTIFY WITH SALIERI

The first time Polly Platt met Jim Brooks to discuss *Terms of Endearment*, she was distinctly unimpressed. "I was infuriated that he was that late," she recalls. "Fifteen minutes or half an hour, who cares, but to be a whole hour late." She waited for him at Gladstone's, a tacky tourist joint on the Pacific Coast Highway. "I just remember I didn't like him . . . I just didn't like his turn of phrase . . . I didn't like the way he referred to the people. I didn't like the people he was talking about working with." It was still the era when TV was TV and movies were movies, and Brooks's creation of both *The Mary Tyler Moore Show* and *Taxi* carried little weight in the world of film. He spoke in a curiously elliptical fashion and seemed to know nothing about filmmaking. Moreover, his enthusiasm for her—once he got there—was suspect. Deeply engulfed in her struggles to raise her children and her relationship with Tony Wade, Platt was distrustful to the point of obliviousness of the success that had accrued to her in the wake of *Pretty Baby*. "I had my miserable life and I didn't get it," she says. "I didn't know there was a momentum, that people respected me."

Passionate, insistent, Brooks had tracked Platt down because he wanted to make a movie version of Larry McMurtry's novel *Terms of Endearment*, the story of a self-involved, wildly controlling southern widow, Aurora, who discovers her humanity when her free-spirited but accepting daughter, Emma, develops cancer. McMurtry had borrowed elements of Platt's relationship with her daughter Antonia to create the dynamic between Aurora and Emma, elements such as "parents who love their children too much and the devastating effects upon them," explains Platt.

Says McMurtry, "I wouldn't say they had nothing to do with *Terms*."

More salient perhaps was the fact that Paramount owned the rights to the book. At the behest of the actress Jennifer Jones, who wanted to star, the studio had asked Platt to adapt the novel, but she had gotten stymied. While on one level she thought Brooks was "dopey," there was something about him that appealed to her. "He wanted to put his whole life on this movie, and I thought it was an odd film for him to make, about two women and cancer. This was a mother-daughter thing, and he had done *Taxi*, which was all guys. I introduced him to Larry, and I know I was helpful in getting Jim the rights to the book."

Six months later Brooks sent Platt the script, which impressed her greatly, especially considering that she had taken a stab at the material herself. She arrived at their next meeting armed with script notes and practical filmmaking advice: "He thought he could shoot it for some three million dollars, and in his script I counted out the number of costume changes and the number of cars. And I said there were sixty-four costume changes for Aurora, because it went from 1960 to 1980."

Brooks just remembers that the day after their second meeting Platt had arranged for him to meet some cancer patients. It took him four years to raise the money, and for much of that time he pursued Platt to produce. She kept turning him down, in part because she thought he would never get the money to do it properly, in part because she was awash in family crises and self-loathing. One day, "she came to lunch wearing a sweater covered with little furry balls," recalls Larry Mark, the executive at Paramount overseeing *Terms*. "She'd worn it because that was what Aurora [the mother] would wear. We knew we had to get her." Brooks spent most of the lunch fingering the balls, cajoling, begging, and seducing. He wrote out a personal check and told her to fill in the sum. "Finally I said, 'I'll help you as best I can,' " recalls Platt, " 'I'll come, I'll design the movie, and I'll take half my usual salary,' because I kept having to go home to see the children.

"With Jim I formed this kind of relationship that I had with Peter," Platt says. She was enchanted by his verbal brilliance and his keen—

occasionally corrosive—intelligence, his insight into the human psyche; she was willing to devote herself wholeheartedly to his aims, often
indulging his narcissism. They were also bonded by intelligence, arrogance, and a pool of self-disgust that motored a steely perfectionism.
Platt says, "I understand Jim, which is a thrill in itself. I know Jim better than I know myself."

For Brooks, a writer who came from the three-camera world of sit-
coms, Platt was key in helping translate his ideas into the language of
film. They worked symbiotically—in a private code of nuances and
looks. She helped him *see* both literally and metaphorically. "I think
she's an Indian guide," says the *War of the Roses* screenwriter Michael
Leeson.

"Something in her does believe that a director must be protected.
Something deep in her believes that, in a religious way," says Brooks.
"There are times when that really comes in handy. She used to say she
had a rule with me where she'd say things three times. If I didn't listen
to her the third time, she'd drop it. Well, she rarely drops it. The amazing thing is she will get on board an idea that is maybe antithetical to
one that she thinks—without resentment."

Brooks threw himself into research, spending weeks in Texas exploring cancer wards, women with cancer, women from Texas. He realized that Houston was less longhorn prairies than "Andy Hardy
country" and took inspiration for the look of the film from Norman
Rockwell. "It was great for all of us to literally be on the same page, to
be outside ourselves looking at [Rockwell's] models, looking at his representation of America, having these conversations, it was great," says
Brooks.

As was her way, Platt burrowed into every aspect of the production,
designing all the clothes and sets. She took Brooks to a bedroom she
wanted to use as a prototype of Aurora's lace-and-ruffle-festooned
boudoir, and when Brooks lay down on the bed, he began to giggle at
the thought of Jack Nicholson under such frilly covers. She also over-
flowed with practical advice: "I understood production because it was I
who taught Jim. He didn't understand a company move, you know, if
you shot half a day in Houston and had to move across town, you'd lose
half a day, and Jim didn't understand any of those things because he'd
just done television." She'd build sets in the back of Shirley MacLaine's
house to obliterate the need for a time-and-money-consuming company move.

"One of the things he says is that I had a tremendous amount of patience with him," Platt recounts. "I believe it's because he wrote a good script . . . he made so many mistakes. I mean, he literally fell in love with Debra Winger, and I could see that Debra Winger was trouble from the word go, and Debra was trying to get rid of Shirley MacLaine. We were in preproduction and she was just doing everything she could to get him to fire Shirley, everything, and I don't care if she hears it. She was so manipulative. She was so out of control."

A huge star coming off *An Officer and a Gentleman* and *Urban Cowboy*, Winger had thrown herself into the movie during preproduction, even helping Brooks lure her friend Jack Nicholson to play the crucial part of the astronaut who moves next door and romances Aurora. "There was a time in the preproduction of the picture when she was like the greatest associate producer in history," says Brooks. "Just with passion and intelligence and a first-rate mind living, breathing with her soul and everything and giving all of it to the movie for six months before we started shooting. You bet I liked it. And then when we started rehearsals, things got different.

"The dynamic changed, and I was able to use the great gift of being naive, being stupid. Because of what was in their own minds, Shirley and Debra were using their power in a lot of different ways. It was all fiery and volatile. When they were in my apartment in New York, I could never get them to rehearse what was on the page, because there was so much being played out and acted out, I would just observe that and would call that a rehearsal. At times I felt like I was auditing the course, instead of being the professor."

The tension was so bad that a week before principal photography was to begin, Brooks contemplated firing MacLaine. "I said to him, 'Believe me, believe me, halfway through this picture, it's going to be the other way around,' " says Platt. " 'You're not going to be able to bear this girl, and you're gonna thank your lucky stars you cast Shirley MacLaine in this part,' 'cause I could just see it all."

According to MacLaine, on the first day of actual shooting, Winger flipped her skirt over, leaned over, and literally farted in MacLaine's face. MacLaine had enough savoir-faire to riposte, "Do you always talk with your mouth full?" Winger's behavior continued to be hyper and unpredictable. During MacLaine and Nicholson's post-making-love scene, she secretly climbed into bed with the two actors and began licking their legs. On another occasion, she bounded up and down the aisles during dailies, carrying a Coke with brandy in it. Joyful at what she saw on screen, she threw her arms around MacLaine, and then yanked her right breast. MacLaine responded by ramming her elbow into Winger's stomach, and Winger ran from the room in tears. Soon after, Brooks banned MacLaine temporarily from dailies. He let her back in when a passel of studio executives arrived to see what was going on, only to insult her after she proclaimed the dailies were great. "That's why I don't want you in the projection room," he fumed. MacLaine tried to walk off the picture, and Brooks apologized for having a "weird and warped sense of humor."

Throughout the nightmarish shoot, Platt continued to be racked with problems with her children. "I kept having to go back home," she says. "All I know is that at some point we were looking for locations in some college town. We were in somebody's house in this little podunk town, and I had a call from Sashy, who was then thirteen. Antonia and Sashy were home with a new housekeeper in my house in Pacific Palisades, and Antonia was never home, and Sashy called me up and said, 'Mom, guess what? Kathleen Turner's staying with us,' and I said, 'What? What?' She just came by and she was in a limousine and she said, 'Is it okay if I come stay?' because she had stayed with me after *The Man with Two Brains*. I enjoyed her as a houseguest very much, but I was just out of my mind. Like somebody was moving into my house with my two children without me. She moved in there, and she lived there for a couple weeks. We've never spoken of it. It was a bad time in Kathleen's life.

"Jim was like, 'You're a riot.' He just kept laughing at it. I was out of my mind. I flew back. I didn't confront her, because she'd already moved in, and I just said to the housekeeper, 'Next time, would you let me know?' "

On the set Platt's nighttime drinking was so common as to be unremarkable, especially considering that almost every major *Terms* participant save MacLaine partied heavily. For better or worse, Platt functioned at work.

Home was another story. Platt flew back and forth constantly. "I would come home. I was living on Valium and beer, and I would come home, and I'd have my Valium on my bedside table. I only used it to go to sleep, and on weekends, I would have like three beers for lunch and take a Valium and sleep all afternoon so that I wouldn't have to cope," she says.

Platt was constantly mystified about why there always seemed to be less Valium in her vials than she thought there was. "I didn't abuse it. I didn't take it for my nerves. I took it to sleep, and I would say, 'Isn't this odd, I thought I had more. Where did it all go?' and I'd wander downstairs, and see Sashy and Antonia, and her boyfriend, and I'd say, 'I don't understand, I have to order some more Valium.' I was that naive. I knew I wasn't abusing Valium. I just didn't understand what happened. Was I taking more than I thought? At any rate, they were selling it. Antonia's boyfriend was taking my Valium and selling it, and he was getting thirteen dollars a pop for whatever, ten Valiums."

Soon, other possessions began to disappear from the house. "The money out of my purse and the silverware off my mantelpiece, and the Tiffany cup that Big Tony gave me that said 'Mama Bear.' My jewelry, my watch, things just kept disappearing. In retrospect, it's hilarious," she says. The first big item to go was a brand-new VCR, which Platt had bought herself for her birthday. She bought it on Friday. When she came home from work on Monday, it was gone. "I remember saying to everybody, 'I don't even care about the VCR. The rug was worth more.' The rug was worth four thousand dollars, and then the next time, they took the rug. I really did think I was losing my mind, and I finally did realize that it was Antonia's boyfriend. Antonia feels terrible about this, terrible."

While Brooks had begun *Terms of Endearment* intent on fashioning the first comedy about cancer, the end product was a soggy but effective family drama, a throwback to a 1940s weepie. The film featured two strong, vivid female characters (no small feat in a town increasingly geared to the fifteen-year-old boy), but feminist critics chafed at what they viewed as its conservative, old-fashioned nature with Emma, a paragon of female virtue made all the more virtuous by her suffering, and Aurora, a classic overbearing mother.

"I remember people got upset about it, even though it was like two incredible females," says Brooks. "It brought up a lot of ambivalence about women's roles." Pointing to Emma's acid rejoinder to the career women's lunchtime gossip, "I can't talk about my little tumors," Brooks says, "I think it was a fair comment about, say, what her attitude is towards those career women. I think it was a fair representation of *that* young Texas woman. I think it was in character. When I was doing *The Mary Tyler Moore Show*, Gloria Steinem once got me booed by an audience of twelve hundred women at the University of Texas because Mary called her boss Mr. Grant."

Most important in Hollywood terms, however, was the fact that the movie was a box-office hit. It went on to win the Oscar for Best Picture in 1984. Platt was also nominated for an Oscar. "I certainly don't think it's my best work," she says, "although I was thrilled to be recognized." She took her two daughters to the ceremony.

The success of *Terms of Endearment* buoyed Platt. "Women were so racked by that movie that they just wanted to get close to anybody who had made it," she says. "With Peter, I was the wife who was left behind, so I didn't get to experience it. So *Terms* was the first experience of having people call me, talk to my office, offer me deals. Everyone was after me because Jim was going around saying, 'She's a genius.'" Don Simpson and Jerry Bruckheimer hired her to write and direct a movie about a man who develops a computer with the capacity to think, which folded after MGM came out with the similarly themed *Electric Dreams*, which flopped. "It wasn't a picture that I would have chosen to direct. I was very torn. But I was [over] forty, and I thought, Maybe I should do that, because I didn't know what else I was going to do besides be a production designer. I didn't think I was good enough as a writer."

Platt rewrote the script. She heard about a new young actor, Kevin Costner, who would be perfect for the lead. She went out to see him on the set of his first starring role, in *Fandango*, but Paramount refused to let her cast an unknown in the lead. Platt quit the film. "Everybody said, 'You're completely crazy.' And it was the smartest thing I ever did. I just knew that if they would fight me on that I'd never win anything—I knew that from talking to Henry Hathaway and John Ford and Howard Hawks. I figured when I quit they'd give in and I'd win, but they didn't give in, much to their regret, years later. I lost my gamble."

But Platt had found a project she wanted to do more, the black comedy *The War of the Roses*, which she viewed as "a modern horror story," a battle of the sexes about a divorcing couple who literally fight each other to death. Platt had optioned the Warren Adler book with her own money and had brought it to the Warners production president, Mark Canton, the son of a friend of hers, who had lived in her house for several months when he started out in Hollywood. Both husband and wife die at the end of the book, a finale Platt adamantly wanted to keep and Warners adamantly did not. Distraught that the studio was pressuring her to compromise, Platt left the book on Brooks's desk with a little note explaining what it was and went off on vacation to Hawaii with her kids. Platt figured Brooks would side with her on the ending and, with his status as the darling of Hollywood, would be able to nudge Canton on her behalf.

To her surprise, Brooks called Platt in Hawaii and announced that he wanted to produce *The War of the Roses*, making it his first movie under his new lucrative production deal, Gracie, set up at Fox.

Although she was thrilled to find herself working with Brooks, Platt soon began quarreling with the screenwriter Michael Leeson over tone. "Jim and Michael would sit there and talk about their wives and how they spent money and how they hated this that their wives did and that that their wives did and what women do and how awful women are, and I started to get offended because all the really funny, mean things that were being done were being done by the woman character," recalls Platt. "I felt that the balance was being lost. The only way the movie would work was if they were equally idiotic and awful, and did terrible things to each other. Finally they put back in him sawing off all the heels of her shoes. In the book he puts diarrhea food in her pâté. He does a whole lot of stuff to try to sabotage her, and so we argued over that."

A more serious issue arose over money. Platt was getting only a $25,000 development fee. After two years of not earning money, she began to panic. She had moved into a big new house in Santa Monica. The kids were running wild, and Antonia had ended up in a serious car accident. She was drinking again, and Big Tony was dying.

After a year apart they had begun to see each other again. They were growing closer. Once he was on his own, Wade stopped blaming Platt for the problems with the kids. He was supposed to be her line producer on *The War of the Roses*.

If the putative issue was money, the truth was that as Platt grew closer and closer to actually directing she began to lose confidence. She says, "I didn't think I could direct a movie anymore. I was beginning to lose control." She was slowly withdrawing from the picture. She stopped going to script meetings. She stopped even going to the office. Finally, she agreed to do the production design on George Miller's *The Witches of Eastwick*. "I knew that when I left that would be the end of my life with Jim. I knew it was a big deal. I was home here in this kitchen, and Jim called me and he tried to get me not to leave and he fought harder than I've ever seen anybody fight. He kept saying that it was a really big deal if I left—in *Broadcast News*, when she won't go with him on the plane, he keeps saying, 'It's a big deal.' And I remember when Jim just kept saying to me, 'It's a big deal if you leave.' He means it's over. He's threatening me. He's telling me it's over, and I knew that I would be destroyed if I stayed on."

Brooks called all day long, begging Platt to meet again with Leeson. The operator interrupted one of their conversations with a call from Big Tony's agent. Wade was in Florida working on *Miami Vice*, but he hadn't shown up for work in three days. Platt told them to break down his door.

The operator interrupted a second time. The company had found Wade on the floor in a coma. Platt left immediately for Miami.

When she arrived at the hospital, Wade was in the ICU. The doctors were baffled. When Platt walked in Wade opened his eyes. "He looked at me and his eyes got really big. 'Now I know I'm really in trouble if you're down here.'

"The bed was jacked up. He was sitting up, but he looked terrible. He looked like an old man. His hand was really shaking as he was trying to put this egg into his mouth. He looked me up and down. I didn't have a change of clothes because I had flown down there without clothes. He didn't get the egg into his mouth, but he said, 'I guess you'll have to get my credit card and buy some clothes.' He was very funny. He said, 'I don't know how many more recoveries I have in me.' He was a man who should have never been sick. When the nurse gave him a shot, his heart would escalate so much this little alarm would go off. He was this big, thick, strong man who was terrified of the shots. He was just terrified of the pain, but he never complained. He just kept making jokes." Platt insisted that Wade see his children. He died two weeks later.

"Big Tony's death was the thing I could grieve about more than anything else—especially because his children were young and I really related. I just felt much worse, worse than anything I could describe. I think I cried over his death more than for my divorce, my parents, everything.

"I think about him, and I think I never really let him know me. I never let go of Peter. Until now, I think if I met him now it might be possible, but I just didn't let go.

"One of the reasons I didn't fight harder to do *War of the Roses*—one of the things I knew for sure—without someone completely on my side,

294 / IS THAT A GUN IN YOUR POCKET?

I wouldn't be able to do it. Without Tony, I couldn't have done it. It felt
to me that the last person who really loved me was dead. I always
thought he was the only man who ever really loved me."

Without Wade's support, Platt says she wouldn't have been able to
stand up to "the pressure of the way Jim [Brooks] thinks movies should
be made as opposed to the way I think movies should be made. It isn't
that he's wrong. I just know that I'm a different kind of a filmmaker
than he is. I thought, I can serve Jim, but Jim ain't going to serve me,
because he only knows one way and that is his way. I don't how to explain it without criticizing a person I love very much."

Nonetheless, when Brooks called Platt in her *Witches* hotel room to
tell her he was sending out the script to other directors, she began to cry.
(She ultimately took an executive producer credit on the film.)

The Witches of Eastwick turned out to be, she says, her best production work—part New England WASP, part sybaritic fantasy. The movie
is the tale of a contretemps between the devil (Jack Nicholson) and
three modern-day beauties (Cher, Susan Sarandon, and Michelle Pfeiffer) who learn they have the power of witches. As Pauline Kael points
out, "The film wavers between satirizing a hypersexed male's misogyny
and reveling in it." When George Miller asked Platt to do something
that would show Nicholson trying to win the approval of the witches'
children, Platt came up with "this one image of Jack Nicholson holding
a pink balloon." It blossomed into a deliriously silly sequence in which
Nicholson twirls the three witches around on a medical gurney in an
opera-house-sized hall filled with 13,000 pink balloons. The production itself was a nightmare of ego conflict between the director, George
Miller, who wanted a witty social commentary, and the producer, Jon
Peters, who was angling for a special-effects extravaganza.

The three actresses felt particularly maltreated in the fracas. At first
Miller promised Sarandon the part of the sexy sculptor but was pressured by the studio at the last minute to hire Cher instead, forcing
Sarandon to play Witch Number Two. After an initial mistrust, the
three banded together, frustrated that the script depicted them as inter-
changeable, and said they would quit unless it was amended. The production, which was throwing zillions of dollars into special effects for a
number of scenes that were cut, chintzed on their costume budget, forcing Cher to supply both her own and Sarandon's wardrobes and Pfeiffer to raid secondhand stores. Peters had particular contempt for
Sarandon. He once threw a chair in a meeting with her and barred her

daughter from visiting the set, although he brought a group of onlookers, including Barbra Streisand, during a particularly sensitive scene.

At the end of the production, Platt was worn out emotionally and physically. "I quite literally went to bed when the movie was over, like my mother." She stayed there for weeks. Richie Marks, the editor on *Terms of Endearment*, took her to dinner. She recalls, "He knew I was falling apart. He said, 'Don't do this to yourself. Don't cut off your nose to spite your face.' He was the only person who came."

After sending an emissary to test the waters, Brooks eventually took Platt to dinner and asked her personally to produce *Broadcast News*, his morality tale set in the Washington bureau of a major news network, featuring a young, hotshot producer (Holly Hunter) who can't decide between her brilliant but intensely neurotic best friend and co-worker Aaron (Albert Brooks) and the studly but intellectually limited newscaster (William Hurt) who embodies everything she hates, namely the relentless dumbing down of the news. Platt always felt that Brooks borrowed from her life, in this case Hunter's character's mania for giving directions right. The woman news producer ends up alone, refusing to sacrifice her journalistic principles for the possibility of love.

Platt reluctantly agreed to help Brooks and brought her meticulous attention to detail. Brooks wanted *Broadcast News*'s key color to be red. As he was shooting the school yard scene in which the young Aaron gets beaten up, he looked up to see the woman who fifteen years before had removed the *ex* from *Texaco* on her hands and knees painting a red accent line on a staircase. Despite her willingness to do whatever needed to be done, Platt bristled at her secondary position. Her usual truth telling took on a slightly abrasive edge. She says she was hostile and abusive to people whose work wasn't up to her vision. "I felt like I was a shill for Jim. A shill is basically somebody who pimps for somebody, somebody who's used. Sometimes he said to me, 'You didn't have to be so rough on me,' and I said, 'Listen, people think I'm your yesman,' and he just roared. He just said, 'I hope people don't have that impression.' I said, 'I don't want to be perceived as somebody who's there to kiss your ass.' He said, 'Boy.' It's true. I don't kiss his ass. I do adore him, there's no doubt about it. I hate him too.

"I've discovered that just because you're the greatest teacher in the world doesn't mean you can play the piano better than your students. There are times when I hear Jim talking about work for a script . . . I experience something that is so much worse than the jealousy that I felt towards Cybill. It's not evil. I am so envious of his ability to think and express himself that I think I'm going to die. I just feel like Iago or something. I totally identify with Salieri, because when he picks up Mozart's music and starts talking about how brilliant he is, I feel like that's me. I really feel like that, but I don't have any desire to destroy Jim or Peter or anybody."

In the year after *Broadcast News*, Platt wrote an adaptation of the Charles Bukowski novel *Women* for the director Paul Verhoeven. It was a tale she knew well, that of a priapic poet who attains a smidgen of critical success and can finally score with all the women he wants. "We'd meet in the Bel Age Hotel and discuss our sexual lives," says Verhoeven. "It was a good thing it was at breakfast." Yet as Platt got close to finishing, she couldn't bear the weight of her own high expectations. She leased her Santa Monica home to Billy Crystal and rode off in an RV to travel around the Southwest. She returned to L.A. and parked her trailer on the Universal lot, living there until the guards threw her out.

Not long after, Platt wrote an adaptation of Larry McMurtry's *All My Friends Are Going to Be Strangers*, the story of a self-loathing writer who gets his first novel published but fails miserably in his search for love and lets his child fall into the hands of her maternal grandparents. As the screenplay ends, he systematically drowns the only manuscript of his second novel. "It's his punishment," explains Platt. "He did not rescue his child from the mother. He's doomed to live a miserable and unhappy life.

"That's his acting out," she says, tacitly acknowledging the parallels to her own life. "The alcohol. The destroying of the art."

Her own mother abandoned her. It's a painful truth that Platt hates to acknowledge. Her eyes narrow. She is wary. "I broke the circle," she finally says. "No matter how uncomfortable it is between Antonia and me. I didn't abandon my kids, although I did leave them. My shrink once told me, 'Bad mothering is better than no mothering.' "

17.

GO-GO YEARS
AT PARAMOUNT

I'M NOT GOING TO TELL YOU
THAT I AM MARY POPPINS

Ned Tanen's arrival as the new president of the motion picture division at Paramount exacerbated Dawn Steel's feelings of desperate ambition and creeping anxiety. The unthinkable had just occurred. The gridlock of executives above her had suddenly dissolved. In September 1984, Barry Diller quit Paramount to take charge of Twentieth Century–Fox. Ten days later Michael Eisner was named CEO of Walt Disney, and on October 1, Jeffrey Katzenberg was anointed president of motion pictures and TV at Disney. The diaspora would change the Hollywood landscape, leading ultimately to the creation of the Fox network and the revitalization of the moribund Disney company. Although a herd of executives trooped after Eisner and Katzenberg, Steel wasn't invited. The slight stung badly, but she was realistic enough to see that her long-cherished fantasy of becoming president of production suddenly was within her grasp. The highest-ranking executive remaining, Steel quickly assumed the duties of acting head of production.

She felt confident about her relationship with Frank Mancuso, the former head of marketing, who had, to the surprise of the entire community, trumped Eisner out of the top job at Paramount. Soft-spoken, Italian, with a penchant for big, pointed shirt collars, Mancuso gave the sometimes misleading appearance of a benevolent patriarch. He also happened to be Steel's first boss at the studio. The night *Star Trek* had

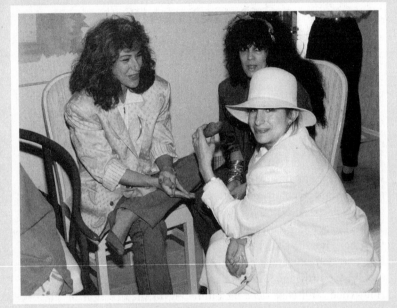

Dawn Steel (left) and Barbra Streisand
at Steel's wedding shower, 1985.

opened, the pair had driven around New Jersey joyously watching the lines snake around the theaters.

In fact, Steel initially welcomed Tanen with a sigh of relief. Years before, Steel and the longtime president of Universal had gone on an infamous date at Morton's, the watering hole for the executive elite. That day Steel had undergone minor surgery for hemorrhoids, and during dinner her stitches burst and she discovered blood coursing down her backside. Tanen wound up taking her to the hospital, and by noon the next day Steel had regaled fifty of her closest friends with the tale—her usual tactic for dispelling embarrassment. At their first official lunch, at Mr. Chow's, she gaily told him, "Boy, am I glad I didn't sleep with you." The gambit fell flat; as Tanen made clear, their relationship was now to be purely professional. Pointedly, he didn't offer her the job of official head of production, and he later told the press that reports of Steel's ascension were premature and without merit.

Steel was alternately pissed off and uneasy. "She said, 'They're going to fire me, they're going to fire me,' " recalls Joel Silver, who spoke to her ten times a day. "I said, 'Steel, they can't fire you. You're the only one that knows what's going on there.' " She felt that she had long ago proven her worth, and moreover that Mancuso had indicated she was going to get the job.

For five and a half months she waited for her coronation, doing everything she could to charm Tanen, prove her competency, and win him over. She stewed when she heard rumors that he had tried to hire Sean Daniels, an executive from Universal, and then Bruce Berman from Warners, for the slot. Tanen insists that he initially admired Steel's verve but had to overcome his boss's reluctance. "Martin Davis in New York really didn't want her in the job at any given time, and she knew it as well as I knew it," explains Tanen in retrospect. Indeed, it was unclear if New York's animus was personally targeted at Steel or just residual anger toward one of the few remaining members of the Eisner regime.

Finally, one day Tanen called Steel into his office. "Congratulations. It's yours," he told her, adding, "I'm going to try to give you this job when I leave, and I'm not staying that long." Indeed, he talked about leaving within a year and a half. Afterward, Steel claimed that his disenchantment was palpable.

Nonetheless she was thrilled. She was only the third woman ever to run production at a major studio. That night she attended a political fund-raiser at the home of Lew Wasserman, the chairman of Universal Pictures and the most powerful man in Hollywood. It was the first time she had ever been invited to his home. She lasted only fifteen minutes, walking around the house by herself, looking at all the people ahead of her on the power ladder, people she didn't yet know. She left.

As Steel waited outside for the valet to bring her car, she spotted Robert Daly, the chairman of Warner Bros., coming toward her, hand outstretched. Finally, someone knew who she was.

"It's a white Mercedes," he said, as he handed her his valet ticket.

That weekend Steel celebrated by going to the Hagler-Hearns middleweight boxing match in Vegas, an event that all of macho Hollywood attended. She was sitting so close to the ring that blood splattered her. She hated it.

Steel attacked her new job with the zeal of a true believer. Her religion was the high-concept film, the gospel according to her former mentors, Eisner and Katzenberg. She spelled it out in almost scientific detail for all who worked for her—if the movie had a strong core idea but just average execution it would turn out fine. If a movie had a mediocre idea and brilliant execution, at best it could be *Tender Mercies,* the 1983 Robert Duvall drama, which Steel despised and used as an example of all that was wrong with the movie business.

"She'd say, 'I hate *Tender Mercies.* Don't ever mention it. It's the worst movie we ever made,' " recalls her close friend Howard Rosenman. "She hated anything that she thought was pretentious or arty. Subtitles, she didn't like. Fifteen minutes into a movie, if it was too arty, she'd be out of there."

Steel preferred action to thought. She loved chasing down talent but hated long story meetings and the details of script analysis. If her staff wanted to pitch her an idea for a movie, they'd have to stand poised by her desk while she was rolling phone calls and make their pleas between hang-ups. "You had about two or three sentences to get her hooked, and if you didn't, then you would see her glaze out," says David Madden, one of her former executives.

"To her, a lot of the time there was very little difference between a good movie and a successful movie," adds Lindsay Doran, another one of her vice presidents. The Paramount staffers often saw completed films available for distribution. "She would think of something as a bad movie, another studio would pick it up and it would do really well, and then she would think of it as a good movie. If a movie worked, then it was good creatively and good commercially. And if it didn't work, then there was something deeply wrong."

Steel's management style was often imperious and loud. The eighties was Hollywood's most furious decade, when business was conducted at maximum decibel and a sign of power was the ability to inflict an opinion at ear-deafening volume. The most famous power players—Don Simpson, Joel Silver, Barry Diller—yelled, and Steel adopted their style with impunity. She was fueled by a battery pack of anger, which she clung to as a righteous fury, a scourge against incompetence and fear. She clothed her percolating insecurity in permanent attack mode, constantly reasserting that she was top dog.

"She always thought whatever she wanted she should get, and she just didn't understand why she wouldn't get it," recalls her friend Jim Wiatt, then a prominent agent at ICM. "She would pick up the phone and say, 'You *better* get this for me, you *better* tell an agent that works for you to make this happen. You *better* tell the director he better do it.' Her style was to get right in your face. And if you didn't get things, she'd get pissed."

The decibel level of Steel's tirades became legendary. She treated her staff with her own version of tough love. She was at once intensely loyal and demanding, willing to take the blame from her superiors if something went wrong, yet hectoring her vice presidents incessantly, checking up on them as if they were children, and furious with them if they didn't treat her with filial obsequiousness. She would delegate her authority but then not fully trust anyone, riding her underlings vehemently to make sure their work was up to speed. "She had a really hard time with people who allowed themselves to seem weak," says Doran. "If she got angry with somebody and they played the victim, then that made her even angrier. I think she responded to strength. If somebody said, 'Let me tell you why you're wrong,' she'd listen. Or if you said, 'You know, you're absolutely right, I did that wrong and I won't do it again,' that was the end of it. But if people whined or people sniveled, or people cried, that was harder for her."

"Look, I'm not going to tell you that I am Mary Poppins," explained Steel a number of years later, using her favorite rejoinder. "But some days were really bad, difficult days. There were some days where the stress and the anxiety and the palpable fear for me was so high that I could barely contain the top of my head. I would feel that it just was going to shoot off, you know, with the steam that was under the top part of your head. And there were days when I was less than compassionate, and there were days that I lost my temper, and there were days that I yelled. And what can I tell you, I'm a human being. Other people who run other corporations have those same personality characteristics because they are very stressful situations.

"And by the way, there were times when it was completely legitimate that I was upset. It is a very frustrating thing to constantly push people to get the best out of them. [To have to say] 'This isn't good enough, this isn't good enough, this isn't good enough.' "

"I did seem to feel that it was harder for men to be yelled at by a woman than it was for them to be yelled at by a man," recalls Doran. "I could see the expression on certain men's faces when it happened to them, and they were furious." Doran refers to ancient Greek warriors emblazoning their shields with the most terrifying images they could think of: "It was the picture of the angry mother. And they could give it snake hair, and they could give it everything else, but basically in Freudian terms, a [Medusa] is just your angry mother. And I have a feeling that that's partly what went on."

While Steel was proud of what she saw as her unflinching honesty, her commitment to tell it like it was, her emotional ballsiness, she could be completely, willfully oblivious of its effects. She was so wrapped up in her own dramas that she didn't often notice the sparks she sent out. "I don't think she was mean," says another former Paramount executive. "At that point she was just so focused on making it in her career that she wasn't big on empathy. She couldn't stand outside of herself."

"She and I often talked about how angry she was," recalls David Geffen. "It was many conversations over a long period of time. Steel would end up in trouble with people, and she'd wonder why, and she tended not to see her own response."

She was at once obsessed with being a good person and brutal to the people who worked for her. "She would not really make the connection between the two," says Marcelle Clements, who ghost-wrote Steel's book. "And I imagined she operated in the same way vis-à-vis herself. She was very insecure, but she knew that she owed it to herself to be very ambitious, at the same time that she was so mean with herself on little things, flaws of performance."

Steel often could not stop herself from belittling others, particularly her secretaries, on whom she took out the brunt of her simmering rage and feelings of powerlessness. She employed two secretaries at a time; most of them lasted about four months. She was a frequent user of the c-word epithet and treated her staff's flaws as betrayals of trust.

"She had no patience, so if somebody was slow, to the point where you or I might get aggravated but just kind of simmer, she would explode," says Madden.

"God knows, the secretaries—if a man treated them that way, he'd be incarcerated," says Tanen, although he points out, "She ended up being rougher on herself than anyone else." Tanen, as well as a number of her allies, advised Steel to try to restrain herself, so she would often warn new hires up-front about her volatile behavior. She managed to keep one assistant, Gerri Barton, for several years.

"She yelled at everybody. I mean, who wasn't yelling at anybody?" says Barton. "We had Ned Tanen next door, who was yelling at everybody, including Steel. She has always said that it's not personal. Yet she could be very personal. She threw me a bridal shower at the Ivy. She gave me a thousand dollars cash, rolled up in Fred Segal socks for Christmas. She was very guarded, but she let some people see her that way."

Also, Steel could be fantastically charming to movie stars, blunt, bawdy, self-mocking, and riotous. She took pride in her burgeoning friendships with divas like Debra Winger and Barbra Streisand, with whom she discussed mutual man problems.

"She was at least a colorful personality," says Madden. "And since I never worked for people like Harry Cohn and Darryl Zanuck and Louis B. Mayer, this is as close as I got to that kind of personality."

WHAT SHE HAD TO TEACH WAS WHAT I NEEDED TO LEARN

For women in Hollywood, Steel became a signature figure—for some, an icon of aggressiveness and entitlement, for others, a woman who'd become a man in high heels. She was the stylistic opposite of the only other woman who had ever achieved significance in the studio system, Sherry Lansing, and people compared them incessantly. While Lansing had been pejoratively called a geisha, a woman who served men, Steel was often derided as the biggest ball breaker in town.

"The first time I met Dawn was in an elevator in Chicago when we were sneak-[previewing] *Heartburn*," recalls Nora Ephron. "And she was at Paramount. Anyway, she was already a legendary terrifying human being. I think that Dawn's reputation for saying what she thought had given her a reputation of being terrifying that was probably way in excess of the reality. . . . She had the most terrifying name. It was like a Jacqueline Susann kind of a name. It is almost impossible to think that she didn't cook it up herself in the process of sort of myth-making, because it was just a name that struck fear in everyone's heart. And then, of course, she turned out to be a perfectly nice-looking person, who seemed very friendly. And I remember thinking that I was probably going to end up being friends with her."

Steel herself was slowly waking up to the potential of a kind of professional sisterhood—not, of course, with the secretaries but with other women like herself, smart, aggressive, bumping their heads against a glass ceiling. She claimed the seminal event in her thinking was her rapprochement with Lynda Obst, her onetime *Flashdance* cohort. After *Footloose* debuted to great fanfare in the spring of 1984, Steel had received a congratulatory note from Obst, who had been warned by her new boss, David Geffen, that she had to get over her thing about Steel. The note read, "Okay, you're really good. I really commend you. This is not about me, this is not about you, this is about talent, and you've got it." Moved, Steel invited Obst to be her date at the Crystal Award luncheon honoring Barbra Streisand.

"And we sat so far in the back of the room, Dawn and I were so insignificant, that the waiters were slamming their doors on our faces," says Obst. "We were watching Barbra talk about women going after men, and that the meanest reviews Barbra had ever received were from women. It was very important for Dawn and me to sit there and listen to this, because we had almost been victims of the same kind of divide-and-conquer sensibility, and if one woman succeeds, all women fail is the game that they set up."

In a gust of optimism Steel declared, "Within a year I am going to be married and the president of Paramount." Obst looked bemused and asked, What about Katzenberg? What about the fact there wasn't a date on the horizon? "It moved me because Dawn [did] not have entitlement problems, and that's why she's been such a signature girlfriend to me. I do have entitlement problems," says Obst.

Indeed, Steel had deeply conflictual relationships with almost all her woman friends, a lack of personal boundaries and an occasionally high-handed attitude that inspired alternately closeness and fury. "We fought like animals, the two of us. It was love and hate all the way," says Marilyn Vance, who befriended Steel soon after she arrived in Hollywood. "You'd be shocked to realize how really sensitive she was. Her demeanor was sort of strong and sharp, and then you'd say something and it would trigger this reaction that was ridiculous. Sometimes she would hurt my feelings so much by assuming something like 'Well, I thought this would work, so I just told them to call you and I think you should work together,' without even asking me. She was a very controlling person. And I am a controlling person."

While some of her friends chafed at Steel's desire to stage-manage their lives, her impulse was often generous. Steel helped Obst throughout her career, putting her together with her first producing partner, Debra Hill, and later giving them a production deal. She made Nora Ephron's first directing deal.

"She tried really hard to make other women succeed," recalls Lindsay Doran. "There was another woman executive who she felt for one reason or another wasn't working out. And rather than just letting her go, she had her camp out in her office all day long, to watch her on the phone, to watch her have meetings, to watch the way she did it."

Doran herself was one of Steel's first protégées, and her polar opposite. While Steel draped herself in the accoutrements of power—the shoulder-padded Armani suit, the famous helmet hair, the terrifying reputation, Doran was soft-spoken and sweet, with a hippie-intellectual air. While Steel loved the game, Doran loved the word, and at Embassy Pictures she had developed a reputation as a woman with a fantastic ability with scripts and writers, nurturing such scripts as *Stand by Me.*

"I always compared myself to Wendy and the Lost Boys," says Doran. "Every now and then when people would call me for a job, I'd say, 'You want a Wendy.' And they would say, 'Yeah, you're right. I want someone to come home to at night, and who will make pockets for us. And we'll build a house for you.' I think Wendy is an archetype. That sort of nurturing presence who is proud of her boys. And boys go out and fight pirates all day, and then they come home, and you say they did great."

After the Paramount shake-up, almost every studio in town came chasing Doran. Rob Reiner had recommended her to Steel. "This was after the great diaspora, so everybody was looking for a cheap girl, remember. And so I had offers from several places, and the truth is it was a very competitive atmosphere at that moment. Everybody was trying to get executives, so what really made her different from everybody else was this determination. Everybody else was saying, Well, you know, maybe our lawyers will talk. And she was like, How do I make this happen? What do I need to do? How fast can I make this happen? And it made a huge impression on me, that determination. It makes you feel great for one thing."

"The truth is, what she had to teach was what I needed to learn," says Doran. "Before I went to Paramount I was much more passive as an executive. I tended to sort of wait for things to happen. The idea that it was my responsibility to make things happen as opposed to just report to her what was going on was a brand-new way of thinking for me."

Doran's key lesson in assertiveness came during the casting of *Blue City*, a teen thriller starring Ally Sheedy and Judd Nelson, which was directed by a twenty-three-year-old woman, Michelle Manning, who had been Ned Tanen's assistant and protégée. "David Caruso had come in to read for the third lead, and he was absolutely great. And Michelle Manning had called me and said, 'If we don't green-light the movie, we're going to lose David Caruso,' and at that moment we were in the middle of a budget crisis," says Doran. She went in to see Steel and repeated verbatim her conversation with Manning. Steel asked her if she thought they should green-light the movie at the proposed budget. And, says Doran, "I went, 'Oh no. I guess not.' And she said, 'But you really want to hang on to David Caruso?' And I said, 'Yeah.' And she said, 'Well, what are you doing about it?'

"And I said, 'What do you mean?'

"She said, 'What are you doing to make sure that David Caruso stays in this movie until we work our budget problems out?'

"I said, 'Nothing.' "

Steel told Doran to find Caruso's home number, call him, and "tell him that you really want him in the movie and you hope that he will stick around until we can get our budget problems worked out. It was a revelation. It was the deciding moment for me," says Doran.

"Dawn left Paramount before I left Paramount," adds Doran, who went on to run United Artists. "Right after I went to work for Mirage there was some dinner for Jane Fonda where Sydney Pollack invited me to sit at the Mirage table. And I saw Dawn. It was the first time I had seen her since I had the job. And she came over and she stood behind me and she put her hands on my shoulders, and she looked across the table at Sydney, and she said, 'I invented her.' My mother was like, 'Hello, I think maybe I had something to do with it.' The instinctive part, I guess I knew how to do. But the other half, the part of being proactive, I learned from her."

IT'S ABOUT FUCKING TIME

"I was a workaholic. I was truly a workaholic, and I had some dates, you know, sometimes. But the higher up I got, the less men asked me out," Steel recalled in 1992. "And when I got to be president of something or other, no one asked me out. It was a nightmare. It was like the end of my social life. It didn't have to do with the workaholic part of it at all, it had to do with the title. It had to do with the perceived power of it all. And that the more powerful you are, perceptually to some men, the less attractive you are."

One man Steel had heard a lot about was Chuck Roven, an arbitrageur turned movie producer, with one respectable movie under his belt, *Heart Like a Wheel*, the true-life story of Shirley Muldowney, a professional race car driver. He wasn't nearly as powerful as she, or even in the top rank of producers, but their mutual friend Marilyn Vance had filled Steel's ears with talk of him. "It's just so funny how I flashed on these two together," recalls Vance. "And I was telling her about it, and she was really into it. 'Well, when am I going to meet him?' I said, 'Well, he's going with someone, but it's not working out, and so sometime in the future.' "

A little while later Steel, as acting president of production, was hosting a Writers Guild screening of Stanley Jaffe and Sherry Lansing's first film, *Firstborn*. She was working the room when a CAA agent, Laurie Perlman, tapped her on the shoulder and asked if she knew Chuck Roven.

Steel spun around, looked at the lanky six-footer in front of her, and announced, "It's about fucking time." He laughed.

Steel started off their first date by announcing that she was passing on his project *Johnny Handsome*. Roven was unfazed, even when he found out later that she hadn't read the script, merely the coverage. Steel, who was entranced by all things New Age and health-oriented, had been watching an Herbalife convention on cable when he arrived.

People were giving testimonials on how Herbalife had helped them shed those extra pounds. Roven was amused by her preoccupation, and the pair jumped in the car, drove to the convention in Santa Monica, and spent the day listening to Herbalife testimonials.

The second date went badly. They went to an industry charity event, and Steel spent the whole time proving how much more in the know she was than he. They fought. He didn't call afterward.

For several weeks Steel talked with her psychiatrist about the fact that Roven wasn't calling. Her psychiatrist finally suggested that he sounded like the first appropriate man she had dated in a long time. Perhaps Steel should call him.

Steel waited some more and finally relented.

Roven was thrilled that she called. Steel asked him, "Would you have called me if I hadn't called you?"

"No," he said. "You never would have forgiven me."

Within months they were engaged. Roven came from a wealthy family and knew more than a little about strong-willed women. His mother, Blanca, had escaped the Holocaust, walking across Czechoslovakia carrying his older brother. Blanca was skeptical that Steel was Jewish. She suggested that Steel was merely pretending to catch her son. Steel was enraged, even more so when Blanca hired a private investigator to find out whether she had secured a Jewish divorce and later to track down her parents, whom Steel had cut out of her new life in Hollywood. Still, Blanca's meddling brought her back in touch with her father and mother, both of whom came to the wedding.

Lynda Obst, Katherine Reback, and Rosalie Swedlin, the senior woman agent at CAA, gave a shower for Steel, which Obst loved to call the first "power shower" in town. Thirty women were invited, including Barbra Streisand, who lost the address and wandered Bel Air ringing doorbells looking for the shower.

Steel orchestrated the entertainment herself, calling Polly Platt, a pal, and asking her to put together a video of all the men who had been in her life, giving her a list of names including Richard Dreyfuss, Fox's president, Larry Gordon, and Don Simpson. "She told me it was all the men she slept with, although I couldn't personally believe that she slept with some of them," recalls Platt. "Scorsese was not on the list." It was to be called "The Crack of Dawn," although they later toned it down to *Men of Steel.* Streisand sang the score, a rewritten version of the Julio Iglesias song "To All the Girls I've Loved Before."

"Oh, you can't imagine what went on in that video." Melinda Jason laughs. "Don Simpson was holding an Uzi and pretending it was a penis, and rubbing the gun up and down, and I'll never forget Sherry Lansing's face at that show, she was appalled."

"It was much more like being at a bachelor party," adds Doran. "There was a level of bawdiness to that gathering that was just not how I was used to being. I was really kind of shocked. A lot of the women there were shocked, and the other half went, What? That was the only time that I felt that I sort of saw a side of her that I just really hadn't seen before. I think other people would have been appalled at the idea of showing a film with all your ex-boyfriends. And she just loved it."

Jodie Foster at Irving "Swifty" Lazar's Spago Oscar party, 1989.

PSYCHES ON-SCREEN

I'D GO FOR NINETY TIMES

Sherry Lansing was thirty-eight years old when her mother, Margot, was diagnosed with malignant ovarian cancer. Margot was only sixty-two, and during the next two years she died a slow and lingering death, furious at what had happened to her and refusing all pity. Lansing lied to her mother and told her that the studio had extra first-class tickets, in order to get Margot (who was wealthy in her own right) to stop taking circuitous Supersaver flights and throwing up in the bathroom during layovers. For almost two years Lansing veered between doggedly canvassing the medical world to find a cure or treatment and feelings of hopelessness. Watching Margot suffer, she swore that if she ever became that ill, she would stockpile drugs and put herself out of her misery. "It was just horrible," says Lansing, who went back into therapy. "And I would go a lot of times to talk about it. It was like so many mixed feelings."

Her years in analysis had helped Lansing come to terms with Margot's controlling nature. She once confessed to her mother that she couldn't remember one compliment from her during her childhood years. "Her mother was shocked. She said, 'What do you mean?' " recalls Gloria Stern. "Later, Sherry would call her mother and she'd say, 'Hi, Mom, how are you?' And her mother would say, 'And how is my talented, beautiful, wonderful daughter?' And then Sherry would say, 'Fine. I've got a blind date with ———,' and Margot would say, 'Well, that's the luckiest man in the world to go out with you. You're such a bright, warm, charming person.' "

Yet there was still vestigial guilt over the way Lansing had opted to lead her life, work-focused, without a child or a man. "When she was dying, I wanted to say to her, 'Mom, don't worry. I'll get married,' " recalls Lansing. "She said to me, 'No, it's okay if you don't. You have a wonderful life, maybe you shouldn't get married.'

"All she wanted was for me to be happy," says Lansing.

"I am telling you, I swear when my mother died, as sad as I was, there's also something that happens that's freeing, and it allows you to choose what you want. The little woman who was on my shoulder, who's still there sometimes, was gone and I didn't embarrass her anymore," says Lansing. "And I am telling you, I am really happily married now, and I chose a man that I love, that's for me, which years of analysis teaches you to do." Still, for almost a year after Margot died, Lansing felt "nonfunctional, . . . guilty any time I laughed."

Her producing partnership with Stanley Jaffe had not gotten off to a rousing start. Their first two films, *Racing with the Moon* and *Firstborn*, were both low-concept character dramas that flopped at the box office. In the first four years of Jaffe-Lansing, the pair saw so little success that Lansing was surprised when Paramount's chairman, Frank Mancuso, renewed their deal.

Personally, she drew support from Jaffe, who, along with her friend David Goodman, showed up at her mother's funeral in Chicago. He handled almost all the duties on *Firstborn* because she was taking care of Margot. "We served as a married couple in a strange way without the sexual or competitive nature of the marriage," says Jaffe. For the first seven years of their partnership, neither of them was married. "And that may have fed off of each other, by the way," says Jaffe. "I think my getting married allowed her to get married to Billy in a strange, subconscious, convoluted way. Not for any reason that she was holding out for me, or I'm holding out, but she took care of every need I had from a woman except sexual, and vice versa. She knew I was always going to be there. If there was a problem I'd get on a plane and go. If there was a problem she got on a plane and came. That's the way it was. And there was the bonding of a male and a female to talk about things the way a husband talks to his wife. So it provided us with a cocoon family without the marriage."

They shared a taste for classic liberal melodrama—character-driven pieces that imparted a moral message. In the beginning they developed the movies together, although eventually each supervised a personal slate, then they produced the pictures together. Their styles and strengths largely complemented each other. In the beginning Lansing knew next to nothing about physically producing a film and spent most of her time observing Jaffe, who, despite his background as the scion of one of Hollywood's ruling clans, seemed to prefer the minutiae of filmmaking, where he could obsess (to some directors' chagrin) over everything from location scouts to editing decisions. He also negotiated the monetary aspects of their deals.

Jaffe, however, hated the supplication inherent in producing. He hated to sell himself, or his projects, both tasks that soon evolved into being Lansing's forte. She relished the P. T. Barnum aspect of show business. She liked packaging films and navigating studio politics, hawking their wares to executives, and later to the world, as veritable extensions of her personality. Her seeming need for approval transmogrified into a need for approval with an agenda. Lansing schmoozed. She played phone jockey. She cooed and cajoled, willing and able to work the industry with unflagging determination. She often doled out honey and hugs like Santa at Christmas. While her 1950s good-girl persona struck some as disingenuous, it disarmed others. Her girlish manner often belied a relentless will. "I would never take no," says Lansing. "I just couldn't believe that someone didn't want to do it. Perhaps maybe after fifty nos, Stanley would say, 'Are you sure they don't want to direct?' 'No, they're still going to do it.' I'd go for ninety times."

"I said, 'Sherry, you can't take yes for an answer.' " Jaffe laughs.

Whereas Lansing's nonconfrontational style had hampered her at Fox, Jaffe conducted a veritable tutorial in aggressiveness. Lansing deeply admired the fact that Jaffe didn't seem to care what people thought of him. Pugnacious, abrasive, he relished a good fight. He didn't want an acolyte, he wanted a sparring partner, someone with whom he could debate heatedly without the discussion escalating into an ego-driven mano-a-mano, as well as someone to listen to his ranting. He tended to yell—often, if not always delivering his opinions at a high decibel level, which alienated many, but which Lansing pooh-poohed to herself and defended to the world at large. "That's just his way of talking. And after a while you don't hear it," she says. "My mother was a screamer. I don't mean that she was nasty. But we had a healthy, 'I don't want to do that.' Nothing was that upsetting for me. You get used to the rhythms of your partner, just like you do in a marriage. It's a platonic marriage.

"Stanley and I would argue all the time. When people first would be exposed to the dynamics of it, they would try to like get in the middle, and then they would soon realize that arguing didn't mean anything to us." On their first movie, *Racing with the Moon*, the director Richard Benjamin tagged them the Bickersons.

While Lansing often had the job of sweeping up Jaffe's debris, playing reasonable to his irascible, the town tended to view the pair as a classic good cop–bad cop routine, split along traditional gender lines. Stanley screamed. Sherry soothed. Stanley ruffled. Sherry unruffled. Sherry said yes. Stanley said no. Sherry played the carrot, Stanley the stick. "She kind of brought him down a few notches periodically in a gentle way, or managed to be the intermediary. [She'd say,] 'Stanley didn't really mean that when he called you the stupidest son of a bitch he's ever met in his life.' I would just look at her and say, 'How do you do it? More importantly, why do you do it?' " recalls Ned Tanen, who ran Paramount during their producer days. "And then she would tell me he's not really that bad. You just look at her and start laughing, saying, 'My God, you're going to be canonized.' " Privately, however, Lansing pressed Jaffe not to blow up at filmmakers and scream such well-chosen epithets as "your dailies suck."

Moreover, Jaffe's belligerence allowed Lansing to maintain a front of sympathetic femininity without having to displease or alienate or forgo her agenda. Jaffe was always around to draw fire. "You need to succeed on your own terms in a world where you think you've got to be really ruthless and tough to succeed. On the other hand, you need, for your survival, to be able to perceive yourself as well as have other people perceive you as this wonderful, good, supportive person. And the truth of the matter is, a person like that is capable of the most brutal, ruthless behavior as long as there is someone to deflect it to," says one who worked closely with Lansing.

Even when Lansing pointedly said no to a director or a project, she often left the impression that she wished it could have gone another way. "The perception was sometimes that Stanley didn't like it but I did." Jaffe laughs. "I used to come into restaurants, people would kiss her. They would be annoyed with me on spec.

"And a couple of times I said, 'I'm tired out here being cast as the villain,' " recalls Jaffe. " 'You're not doing it purposely, but all the no's aren't mine.' "

Despite her usual pattern of soothing, Lansing does have "one of the great tempers around when she wants," says Michael Douglas. "You want her as a friend. You don't want her as an enemy. I've seen her a number of times when people have misunderstood her going along with something, or if people have gotten carried away, or have gotten dismissive, or abusive—her eyes get as big as saucers, her voice doesn't raise, and she lets people have it. She has a cold, undermining ability when she wants to."

Lansing knows the power of withholding. "Her normal way of really getting to you is being disappointed," says Douglas. "And that's the one that just devastates you. What you take for granted in her is generosity. The take on Sherry is 'It is a ten, it is a ten, it is fantastic,' " says the actor mimicking, as many do, Lansing's occasionally over-the-top enthusiasm. "Her effusiveness is clearly seen when she withholds. When she withholds her ability to give, it's devastating because she gives so much."

No Jaffe-Lansing project was less popular with studio executives than *Fatal Attraction.*

Based on a forty-five-minute film, *Diversion,* by the British writer-director James Dearden, it is the story of a writer whose wife and child go away for a weekend. As soon as they're off, he calls a girl whose number he has in his little black book, takes her to dinner, and beds her. He thinks that's the end of the affair, but the next day she calls him. He spends Sunday with her, and, when he tries to leave, she slits her wrists. He stays another night and arrives home the next morning, just before his wife. The phone rings. It's the girl. He brushes her off. The phone rings again, and the wife goes to answer. The audience is aware that he's about to be found out, and the screen fades to black.

"The short film probably was evenhanded, not even a judgment, it just told a very simple tale, the one-night stand that went wrong," says Dearden. "And there was a certain amount of sympathy for the woman, because in a sense she'd been used for the physical gratification of the man, and then discarded. It's obviously quite a complicated issue, but she didn't become this sort of harpie."

Jaffe and Lansing disagreed on which character's predicament was the most compelling. For Jaffe it was the man's, while Lansing was taken by the woman. The two flew Dearden to L.A. to discuss his film ideas, none of which appealed to them. "I kept coming back to this woman that just fascinated me because she seemed so together in the beginning of this little short, and was in such pain. I think that at any given time in a producer's life, the movies that you choose to do are a Rorschach test for your own personality," says Lansing.

Indeed, the parable was like a prism of Lansing's life, reflecting every ambivalence she felt about being an independent career woman, a single woman searching for love. "I was fascinated by these countless men and women that I knew that when their boyfriends or girlfriends left them, their lives crumbled. I had seen over and over again my friends, or even traces of it in myself, that if somebody left you, you felt like part of you was gone. You felt less. Maybe they would take half of your soul away. And I wanted to do a movie about that.

"And having seen myself pick up the phone once—" She was working at MGM and had been dumped by her boyfriend, a real-estate lawyer, the first and only time in her life a man had left her. "He picked up the phone, and he went, Hello, and I hung up the phone. It was like two in the morning. I said, What, am I crazy? I mean, what does this prove? I was fascinated by what would drive you to do that." In fact, she drove by where he used to play basketball just to get a glimpse of him.

Underlying that neurotic behavior was a long-ingrained fear that without a man Lansing was at sea. She worried desperately about being able to take care of herself, yet, she says, "I never wanted to get married for somebody to take care of me. So it was like this dichotomy. I was just always frightened that I would get married."

"For a very long time she had an image of herself scrounging in garbage pails," says Jaffe. "And she had money. There wasn't the male figure in her life at night, so when the doubts are there and you're lying in bed, somebody can soothe that. And it was tough."

Lansing was also irritated by the cavalier way men could treat women. "For years I've heard men say, 'Oh, I had a great weekend.' I'd go, 'Oh yeah, are you going to see her again?' 'Oh no!' The guy is not going to call her again. You mean you had a great date and you are not going to call this girl? Well, your actions have consequences. What goes around, comes around. There is somebody else in the bed." Lansing continued to dwell on Dearden's short. Jaffe was dubious, but finally told her, "Well, if you're so fascinated, why don't you and James see if you can make it into a movie?"

The pair holed up together for a couple of days, hashing out ways to expand the short. "The wife reaches, picks up the phone and . . . freeze-frame. Where do you take it from there? Most people don't end a ten-year marriage because somebody had a one-night stand. I mean, some people do, but that's not a movie," says Lansing. At one point, Lansing wondered aloud what would happen if the Alex character ended up pregnant. "It's another thing if your lover or husband says to you, 'I had a one-night stand, I think there's going to be a child there.' That's a real thing to deal with."

Sparking to her suggestion, Dearden quickly spun out what would become the essential plot of the film *Fatal Attraction.* Shortly after Dearden completed his initial passes, Michael Douglas became attached to the project. Lansing was one of Douglas's most ardent fans. When she was president of Fox, she had purchased such Michael Douglas projects as *Romancing the Stone* and *The Star Chamber.* The pair were so close that some involved in *Fatal Attraction* believed they were having an affair (which Lansing adamantly denies). In any event, Douglas was not only a star, but also a strong-willed producer who had won an Academy Award for *One Flew over the Cuckoo's Nest.* "I think when Michael came on board, obviously he had a desire for his character to be more sympathetic, as every actor always does," says Dearden. "That was obviously a major influence. A lot of the final shading of the character came from Michael."

Indeed, according to Dearden, "The blame, if there is blame, was shifted more and more onto the Glenn Close character." In her account of the development of *Fatal Attraction* in *Backlash,* Susan Faludi described how Dearden was pressured to shift the onus for the affair from the male character (now a Manhattan lawyer) to the female character (a career publishing executive) with each revision of the script. The man became softer and more sympathetic, and the woman turned more predatory and aggressive. Ultimately, Dearden abandoned the little black book, and made the female the instigator of the illicit liaison.

"[Lansing's] imprint must be on the character too," adds Dearden. "I didn't consciously model Alex in any way on attributes of Sherry. But I think she, just having been a very prominent career woman and Alex was a career woman, she had ideas about the character and what it was like to be a kind of high-powered woman in a man's world."

Lansing and Jaffe paid Dearden out of their own development fund, and kept him plugging away at *Fatal Attraction,* periodically hiring him for other scripts, which kept him employed and yet still available for *Fatal*. They would fly the screenwriter to L.A. for three-day brainstorming sessions where they'd lock themselves in a room for marathon eight-hour story sessions, and bring in food so no one would leave. "Stanley is very logical, and Sherry is very intuitive," says Dearden. "So they made a good soft cop–hard cop team. And Sherry has a great instinct for the way a story should go. It's very helpful if you're a writer, because a lot of people when they're developing a script can just say they don't like something, but they often aren't able to point you in a different direction or give you suggestions that are actually helpful. Also Sherry can have that kind of quality or attention that makes you feel so intelligent no matter what you're saying."

In 1985, Lansing and Jaffe submitted both a copy of *Diversion* and Dearden's new script to Dawn Steel and her boss Ned Tanen at Paramount. Neither was enthusiastic. In her inimitable fashion, Steel threw the script at Lansing and barked at her for submitting such an apocalyptic vision of connubiality when she herself was newly married and so happy. The project went into turnaround, and the producers proceeded to be turned down by every studio. Douglas wasn't considered hot enough, and the various executives—all male—told them they couldn't relate at all to a man who cheated on such a nice wife.

The producers set about trying to find a director to make the project more attractive. Douglas had vetoed Dearden as director (and indeed had at one point insisted on the hiring of the writer Nicholas Meyer to hone his character, transforming his home life into a paradigm of yuppie bliss). A long list of directors passed, until finally Brian De Palma signed on. Unfortunately, Lansing and Jaffe hated his rewrite of the script, and balked at his suggestion that they fire Michael Douglas. Six months later, an agent at ICM sent the script to Adrian Lyne.

In the years since *Flashdance* Lyne had directed the controversial *9½ Weeks*, a glossy examination of sadomasochism whose most notorious scene features a once-proud art dealer, Kim Basinger, groveling for money at the feet of her Wall Street boyfriend, Mickey Rourke. The film barely made a dent in America but was an overseas blockbuster. The director had grown dramatically in confidence and assurance. By turns ebullient and energetic, willful and manipulative, Lyne had a penchant for coaxing performances out of actors by any means necessary, and his technique ranged from almost jovial adoration and devotion to a kind of Method directing, springing little surprises on his performers to draw out "real" responses.

Lyne's proposed participation turned an uninterested Steel into the project's most avid fan. "I think once Adrian got into it, that gave her a kind of personal vesting in the project," recalls the former Paramount executive David Madden, who was in charge of *Fatal Attraction.* "It was a movie Dawn was very determined to make, and Ned sort of went along with the flow."

Steel was keen, however, to make sure that the audience's affinities remained with Douglas. "And, yes, we made Michael more sympathetic," explained Steel. "Now let me describe this movie to you. Here is this asshole guy, and he has screwed around on his wife over and over and over again, and then he has this affair with this really horrific woman and she wants to kill him. Who gives a shit about either one of them?"

Lyne set about pushing the script from the realm of Hitchcockian melodrama into myth. He sent Dearden back to further sharpen the characters, in particular to render the wife and the mistress into polar opposites, the "Dark Woman and the Light Woman," as the writer told Faludi. The wife, Beth, had originally yearned to return to her job as a teacher; now she was simply a housewife, a vision of 1950s domesticity, with added 1980s sexual allure. She was beautiful, tenderhearted, a paragon of homey loveliness.

The part of the Dark Woman became even darker, a venomous, virulently sexed career woman who Lyne decided should wear her hair in a Medusa-like tangle of blond tentacles, and should seduce her victim in a cool, modernist loft in Manhattan's deserted meat-packing district. It had been a particularly difficult role to cast. Actresses ranging from Debra Winger to Jessica Lange to Susan Sarandon had turned it down flat. The producers flew Judy Davis in from Australia because they had heard she was interested in the part, but Davis told Lyne that the movie was "a piece of shit" and tried to talk him out of doing it.

By contrast, Glenn Close's agents hounded the producers about the part. Close was keen to break out of the good-girl perfection that had been her persona and straitjacket in both *The Big Chill* and *The Natural.* She even agreed to screen-test, unusual for an actress of her stature, and came wearing a svelte—and sexy—black dress. After she was cast, she threw herself into making Alex into a viable creature, consulting three psychiatrists. When it was time for her big seduction scene, Close blunted her inhibitions with several margaritas.

While Lyne succeeded in whipping Close up, he worked just as hard at keeping Douglas toned down, and impotent. "I had an ongoing—not a fight, but I would have endless conversations with Michael during the course of the movie. Michael would say literally, 'You have to let me do something,' " recalls Lyne. "And I said, 'You can't, because in the end you're guilty.' God knows she was torturing him, but I sympathized with her for a long while in the movie. He picked her up and then dropped her like that."

Ironically, Jaffe and Douglas hated the Alex character, while Lansing and Lyne found her sympathetic. "The movie when we conceived it, we thought was a very strong feminist movie," insists Lansing. "We thought that it was a movie that said, Your actions have consequences. And you are responsible for what you do." If Lansing felt any qualms about turning what was originally a tragic heroine into a villain, she kept them to herself. The Dark Woman and the Light Woman were almost caricatures of her id, a harsh, nightmare rendition of who she was, and a golden, sanctified vision of who she had been raised to be.

Lyne's relations with Lansing and Jaffe were close but contentious, with Lyne, a meticulous and perfectionistic shooter, wanting more shots, more days, more money, and Lansing and Jaffe trying desperately to control his more outrageous impulses. The dynamic among them often resembled an adored rambunctious child and his controlling parents. "We would argue and practically roll around on the floor or both," says the director. "I've always felt that any movie was kind of like going to war. The producer is the enemy. The producer's point of view is, anyway, part economic. My job is always to pull them screaming in the opposite direction. I think I must drive people mad. If you come at it from a point of view of total paranoia, that everybody is your enemy. That you're getting fucked up at every juncture. If you assume that, you will be wrong maybe a third of the time."

The differences between Lansing and Jaffe often aided Lyne's case: "I would say more often than not Sherry and Stanley would disagree, which kind of helped me sometimes, because one of them would tend to agree with me. They would argue endlessly, and I would argue with both of them."

The two men often resorted to belligerence. "She separated us about four times," says Jaffe. "We came very close to going at it. Adrian is Adrian. And it just so happened I was the male of the group. So I'd take Adrian on and she would jump in. Don't forget that Adrian likes you for doing it."

When he wasn't bickering with Lansing, Lyne tended to treat her like his comforting teddy bear, his gal pal, making her sit next to him on the set. One day, he even convinced her to refashion her hair like that of Close's character, Alex. The film's hairdresser washed her hair and styled it with gel, turning her slightly dowdy hairdo into a soft tumble of curls. "She doesn't have a sense of her own dignity, which is nice," says Lyne. "Sometimes she doesn't know whether something is good or bad. And I think that she has the honesty to say that. She allows herself to be vulnerable."

Perhaps no battle was more heated than that over the ending of *Fatal Attraction*. There were four test screenings, two in L.A., one in Seattle, one in San Francisco. The scores were in the low seventies out of a possible 100. The film played fantastically until the last ten minutes; at three of the test screenings, the audience was so mad they hissed.

Originally, Dearden had devised a denouement in which Close kills herself to the strains of *Madama Butterfly* with a knife bearing Douglas's fingerprints, framing him for her death. But the studio didn't want to end the picture with Douglas languishing in prison. Lyne added a coda in which "Anne Archer would find this tape in which she hears Glenn's voice saying that if Michael doesn't come through for her she'll kill herself." Yet the finale remained dissatisfying to the preview audiences, who were expecting blood, especially after the notorious scene in which an unbalanced Close boils Douglas's child's pet bunny. They viewed Close's character as evil rather than damaged; there was no mass catharsis in Alex's self-abnegation, which was at best a Pyrrhic victory.

The whole filmmaking team was resistant to changing the ending, but the studio chief, Ned Tanen, was adamant: "I couldn't get anybody to listen to me, and finally I said, 'Okay, let me make it easy, we're going to change the end of this movie. The audience wants this bitch terminated with extreme prejudice, and that's what we're going to give them.' "

"I called a really good friend of mine, a psychoanalyst, and said, 'I don't want to do a slasher movie,' " remembers Lansing. " 'And I know what the audience wants, and I need you to help me and tell me what is psychologically true. Does this make sense?' " Lansing fretted about being a total sellout, but less so after her analyst friend reassured her that Alex in a murderous rage was a realistic premise.

So Lansing took on the role of indefatigable expediter. "Of the production people, Sherry was the one who got it," adds Tanen. "She knew it had to be changed, and it was not as easy with anybody else connected. And she worked on Michael, and worked on Stanley and Adrian. There was a lot of criticism, and everybody was in love with the movie, and nobody wanted to change their work."

Throughout the film Lansing had served as the prime mediator between Lyne and the studio, a tricky negotiation that on at least one occasion had caused the director to accuse her of promising one thing to him, then selling him out to the studio. Now she pressed Lyne and Jaffe to accept the inevitability of the situation, and the trio had a three-way screaming fight outside the Mayflower Hotel in New York. "It became patently clear we could either stay with this picture, release it, and have a modest success or do something dramatic," recalls Jaffe. "We were all looking for answers. Were we prostituting a picture for the possibility of a hit?"

"It was tough to ignore the fact that it didn't work with the audience, and in the end you're making a movie partly for yourself, but you're also making it for an audience," says Lyne in retrospect.

Manic to fix the problem, Jaffe peppered Lyne with suggestions, most of which irritated the director, but one caught his attention. "I remember Stanley mentioning Anne Archer, maybe the possibility of her doing it, and then kind of dismissing it as being kind of not right or silly," says Lyne. "And I remember then getting incredibly excited about that, because she in the end was the only kind of blameless one." Archer, the protector of home and hearth, was the only one in the film who hadn't brought misfortune upon herself.

Lyne then ignored Jaffe's beseeching to set the finale at a fairground and, after holing up with Dearden for several days, devised an ending that borrowed elements from Henri-Georges Clouzot's masterpiece *Diabolique*. On a homicidal tear, Alex attacks Beth as she is drawing her bath; a struggle ensues; Dan hears the commotion, rushes in, and overpowers Alex, throwing her into the bathtub, but she springs back. Dan is ultimately saved by his wife, who shoots the other woman through the heart. The wife destroys the other woman. The family survives. It was an ending that would satisfy the audience's bloodlust, although no one seemed to be concerned about the death of Alex's unborn child. The proposed finale enraged Close, who aptly saw it as a betrayal of her character. She adamantly refused to film the reshoots.

Lyne went to Close's house to work on her, spinning a vision of the finale that was more than simple monster movie gore. He stressed the underpinning psychology when Alex appears in the bathroom, dagger in her hand, so oblivious that she wouldn't notice when the blade jabbed against her thigh, cutting her. Tanen and Steel, meanwhile, made their case to Douglas, who hadn't attended any of the previews. "Michael had a very legitimate concern about, 'Jesus Christ, it's not bad enough I've destroyed my family in this movie, and now I have to have my wife save me by killing this bitch,' " says Tanen.

"Yet when Dawn and Ned took him through why it didn't work, he understood it," says Madden. "I think it was two or three days before the reshoots, and Glenn said she wasn't going to do them, and nobody chose to believe her, but she kept saying, 'I'm not doing that, I'm not doing that,' and then finally Michael got her in a room and talked her into it."

Douglas pressed Close on the "responsibility of the character to the movie," he says. "It's not to yourself, to what fulfills you as an actor. As a producer, my history has always been that an actor's responsibility is to make the best movie, and so we talked about it, and the last conversation I had with her, she came over and agreed."

The studio spent $1.5 million to shoot the extra scenes, and Lyne went over by three days. On the eighth day Tanen demanded that they finish that day, period. Lyne wailed to Lansing and Jaffe that if he didn't get some additional footage the scene wouldn't cut together properly. They squabbled. Finally, Lansing proposed that the three of them pay for one more day (about $100,000) out of their own pockets. She worked on Jaffe first, shaming him into agreeing. When she presented this solution to Lyne, however, the director blanched. "Fuck it, I'll make it work," he told her, and called a wrap.

The weekend before *Fatal Attraction* opened, Lansing went to see her friend Dan Rissner in a panic that the film would flop and she would turn into a homeless person. "I said, 'Danny, I'm so nervous,' and he said, 'You're not going to be a bag lady.' "

Indeed, *Fatal Attraction* turned into a smash sensation, the nation's zeitgeist primer on sexual relations, number one for seven weeks, grossing $150 million domestically and sparking a legion of press and talk shows about the issues it raised. "During the film's grisly finale, grown-ups cry out, 'Don't trust her! Don't trust her!' Men leave the theater shaken, silently or openly reaffirming their marriage vows; women leave resolving to make their husbands see it," gushed *People* magazine before a feature devoted to real-life *Fatal Attraction* scenarios. Critics tagged the film a post-AIDS thriller, a morality tale that enforced conservative values by shoving fear down the audience's throat.

Others saw a male screed about the threatening power of women. While Alex was the latest in a long line of Hollywood femmes fatales whose sexuality rendered them man-eaters, feminists rightly took umbrage at the depiction of the career woman as homicidal maniac. Marsha Kinder, a film professor at the University of Southern California, told *Time* magazine: "In this film, it is not sexual repression that causes psychosis. It is sexual liberation. For men, Alex's sexuality is a succubus; it saps a man's strength. *Fatal Attraction* is also about how men fear women. Because in this movie, women have the power positively and negatively. When Alex hears Dan threaten her, she doesn't take it seriously. But when Beth tells Alex she is going to kill her, Alex trembles. And the final battle is between the two women. . . . The movie cleverly plays to both sides of woman. And even though it's hateful politically, it is appealing to women. The film itself has a fatal attraction."

Indeed, the film's main audience was women, attracted to the bold display of female fury and strength. It highlights women's power, then does everything possible to tame it, to push the genie back into the bottle and reaffirm the status quo, in this case, the moral superiority of the nuclear family.

Ironically, the film turbocharged the careers and lives of its two most significant female players. Close emerged a major star (although she pointedly chopped off her Alex curls after the film), and Lansing was transformed into a power player.

Because Jaffe hated the publicity mill, Lansing became the producers' point person with the press. Attractive, accessible, and quotable, she veritably wrapped herself in the mantle of *Fatal Attraction*. She honed what would become her main PR tactic, providing snippets of personal information that relayed to audiences everywhere her intimate involvement in the film, which was but a projection of her own psyche. "*Fatal Attraction,* c'est moi" could have been her credo when she told a TV audience her own tale of calling an old boyfriend in the middle of the night, then hanging up on him when he answered.

Lansing braved the feminist backlash with a front of cheery denial, adamant that it never crossed her mind that anyone would demonize Alex or view her as an icon of the career-girl shrew. During preview screenings she professed surprise when the audience laughed at what she considered one of the most poignant scenes in the film, a distraught Alex compulsively flipping the lights on and off in her apartment. "When I started out, it was painful to me when it was perceived as antifeminist," she says in retrospect. "It really hurt. Of course I didn't understand it. I literally balled up one review and said, 'Can I explain what I'm saying?' My life is about being independent, doing things on my own. I supported every woman's cause. I don't get it. [A friend] explained it to me, as working woman versus [mother]—I didn't understand what she was talking about. Now I do understand the criticism. That's not what we wanted to do. It's the way it was interpreted. To me, the Glenn Close character said, 'I will not be ignored.' She makes trouble. She won't just fall down. And *that* I felt was strong. I still think that people identify with her pain. And then, because she goes too far, they say, 'Well, thank God, that's not me.'

"You do the movies that you want to make, because you believe in them, and they get interpreted by people, sometimes incorrectly and sometimes correctly, and it's their right," says Lansing. "And you might be puzzled, and you may question it, but you can only deal with what you believe in."

She recalls watching the Anita Hill–Clarence Thomas hearing with her husband, William Friedkin, who directed *The Exorcist.* "One guy is reading from *The Exorcist,* and he is talking about this thing with the pubic hairs, and the Coke, and then he says, 'Let me talk about *Fatal Attraction.*' We were both sitting there going, 'I don't get it.'"

Lansing's attitude about the backlash was certainly more tolerant than those of some of the other participants. Douglas (perhaps unwittingly recapping the theme of the movie) fumed to one journalist, "If you want to know, I'm really tired of feminists, sick of them. . . . Guys are going through a terrible crisis right now because of women's unreasonable demands."

Lyne, meanwhile, repeatedly told a story about a strident female movie producer (most assumed it was Lansing, given that she was the only female movie producer he had ever worked with): "The other day, I saw a woman producer who was really quite powerful, and she railroaded, walked all over this guy, who was far less successful and powerful than her. And it was much more disconcerting because it was a woman doing it. It was unfeminine."

The truth of the matter was that, to some people's surprise, Lansing loved all the hoopla. "She looks like a person and sounds like a person who doesn't, but I think she loves controversy," says Tanen.

Indeed, while Lansing had subverted and molded every one of her initial impulses to get *Fatal Attraction* through the studio system, its resounding success led to her own emancipation. After years of fending off backbiting and innuendo, Lansing relished the film's indisputable success. Moreover, both she and Jaffe had taken modest up-front fees in return for gross points in the movie. (After the studio recouped its investment, their take zoomed up to close to 30 percent of the box-office revenues.) She now had what they call in Hollywood fuck-you money, enough money that she would never have to work again. "It was really *Fatal* that made me know that I was secure for the rest of my life," says Lansing. "And I think it was extraordinary for me, given my neuroses and previous experience, and I felt free. I wasn't scared anymore. I wasn't worried about taking care of myself."

Not long after *Fatal Attraction* came out, she felt free to date whom she wanted. "I was always being fixed up with guys that people thought were very appropriate for me. They were very rich—millions, billions. And they were very nice, but I had no attraction to them, and they didn't make me laugh. Yet I'd always go out with them a second time, to give them the benefit of the doubt. I thought, Maybe this is what I should marry. After *Fatal Attraction*, I didn't have to go out on second dates.

"I think one of the worst things would be, must be, to marry someone you didn't love, so they would just take care of you. I think that would be like a prison. Now, you didn't need to ever think about that. You didn't need to worry about dying alone, because you could take care of yourself. It was very freeing, and it allowed me to feel self-confident in my decisions, not to be afraid of being unpopular. The bag lady dreams went away."

IF IT'S ONE FUCKING PENNY OVER, YOU'VE SCREWED ME

Dawn Steel's tenure as president of production at Paramount was marked by record grosses and films that embodied the status quo conventional wisdom of Hollywood, few of which portrayed women characters in a particularly flattering light. The launching point of the hit *Three Men and a Baby* is a single ambitious career woman who abandons her baby at the doorstep of three bachelors. She is joined by the lawyer girlfriend of one of the bachelors, who is repulsed by the mere touch of an infant. The film's humor stems from the inversion of the natural order that Mom cares for a baby, and the men are depicted as merry, overgrown adolescents (happy caricatures not of real men but perhaps of the new breed of Armani warriors just then taking over Hollywood). In *The Untouchables,* another prime Paramount hit, Eliot Ness is defending, among other things, the sanctity of the home (his most obvious feat of derring-do involves saving a wayward baby carriage), although the film's only female presence, his screen wife, occupies mere moments of screen time.

While Paramount's Don Simpson–Jerry Bruckheimer films offered token nods to women's power—giving them cartoonish supporting roles as *Beverly Hills Cop II*'s platinum blond killer bimbo or *Top Gun*'s strapping, sexy flight instructors (indeed, Steel had been the one to insist the woman lead be transformed from an airhead to an egghead)—their films of this period were largely paeans to testosterone. Steel liked to say that *Top Gun* was simply *Flashdance* in the air. Pauline Kael agreed, in the sense that it was a "self-referential commercial," but also pointed out: "When Kelly McGillis is off the screen, the movie is a shiny homoerotic commercial featuring the elite fighter pilots in training at San Diego's Miramar Naval Air Station." She added, "It's as if masculinity has been redefined as how a young man looks with his clothes half off, and as if narcissism is what being a warrior is about."

The few Paramount films that dared to feature women as active participants were the John Hughes teen oeuvre, including such films as *Some Kind of Wonderful* and *Pretty in Pink*, which featured Molly Ringwald coming of age in upper-middle-class Chicago. Steel, however, had relatively little to do with these efforts, because she had alienated Hughes. Nor was she deeply involved with Randa Haines's *Children of a Lesser God,* which featured the memorable Marlee Matlin as an angry deaf woman, because it was a pet project of her boss, Ned Tanen.

Steel was later horrified when Susan Faludi, in *Backlash,* cited as examples of Hollywood's misogynistic attitudes toward women films that she had worked on. "Faludi takes all these movies that I worked on apart. I was devastated reading this. Here I have worked for all these decades in the movie business thinking that I had to have some consciousness, and she thought I had no consciousness."

While Steel had, to this point, spent most of her adult life concerned with making money rather than statements, she viewed *The Accused* as her "protest march." "That was the movie that I was most invested in in my entire career, from a personally creative place," she said.

The Accused was inspired by a notorious 1983 incident in which a twenty-two-year-old woman, Cheryl Araujo, wandered into Dan's Tavern in New Bedford, Massachusetts, for a pack of cigarettes. On the way out she was tripped by a man's jutting leg, then found her jeans ripped off by more than twenty pairs of hands. She was dragged at knifepoint to the back of the bar, where she was gang-raped on a pool table. A group of men cheered on the rapists. The ordeal scandalized America, and several hundred women held a candlelit protest vigil outside the bar. At the trial the rapists claimed that Araujo had "asked for it" by dancing provocatively at the jukebox. Four were ultimately convicted of rape, and the two who held Araujo down were acquitted.

Steel first heard about the attack while watching CNN one night with her then boyfriend Martin Scorsese. "I said, 'These people, they witnessed this rape. They egged these men on,' " she recalled. "They're as guilty as rapists, as the people who raped her, how could this be that they're not being tried?

"Marty looked at me and he said, 'Make a movie about it.' "

Steel pitched the idea to the Katzenberg-Eisner regime and hired Tom Topor, a former New York *Daily News* reporter, to write a first draft. When Katzenberg asked her to assign the film to one of the producers on the lot, Steel broached the subject with Stanley Jaffe, who wasn't wildly excited about it but dutifully relayed the idea to his partner, Sherry Lansing.

Over the years Steel and Lansing had circled each other as warily friendly allies. They had lunch once a year and commiserated about why everyone in town was constantly comparing them as the two polar examples of how to be a woman in Hollywood. In truth, Steel copped to her friends that she was competitive with Lansing, although Lansing adamantly denied that any such feelings existed.

Like Steel, however, Lansing was drawn to the rape drama, but she didn't want to focus specifically on the Araujo case. "What I wanted to do was a movie about the people who stood by and watched," she recalls. She met with Topor and explained, "I want to do a movie about the culpability of the bystander." It was another step in Lansing's personal exploration of the meaning of guilt. *The Accused* was the flip side of *Fatal Attraction.* Here the passive man, the bystander, is roundly punished. The angry woman is not the villain but the hero.

Publicly, Lansing characterized her interest in the film as second-generation Holocaust survivor guilt. "My mother had grown up in Nazi Germany. And I had always thought, What would I have done in those situations? Would I have hid the Jews? Would I stand up? I remember reading about Kitty Genovese. And reading about the people who stood by, thirty-six people, while she was beaten up. And so I remember always being curious, fascinated by that, and always hoping that I would have the courage if I saw someone beating somebody up, to stand, to step in and do something about it."

At the time Lansing related the violence to incidents in her own life. "Sherry talked about an incident where she was [driving] somewhere and she saw a man slap a woman, and then pull the woman behind some trees, and she thought to herself later, Was he a killer?" recalls Susan Merzbach, who worked as Lansing's development person. "It became an inquiry into all of our responsibility in terms of the violence around it."

Despite her interest, Lansing knew relatively little about rape: "I became totally aware of the heinous crime of rape, about how the victim becomes the accused. How the victim is guilty. I knew all these things before, but to a much greater level, because we researched over 150 rape cases to get this compilation."

The script spent five years in development limbo. A plot was concocted involving a working-class rape victim and her upper-middle-class lawyer, who winds up bringing to trial all the men in the bar who had eagerly watched the rape, doing nothing to prevent it. It attacked the viewpoint that if a woman is provocative, she gets what she deserves. After Topor's first draft, their initial director, Harold Becker, had suggested saving the actual rape until the end of the movie and playing it in flashbacks during the courtroom finale, essentially structuring the film as a kind of mystery. Jane Fonda was interested but refused to approve Becker as a director, so he withdrew. Fonda further insisted on hiring a female screenwriter for a polish, and that turned out to be Joan Tewkesbury, who had written *Nashville*. Unhappy with the Tewkesbury version, Fonda then quit the project. Forty directors turned down the assignment until Steel sent it to Jonathan Kaplan, who had directed her husband's film *Heart Like a Wheel*.

Kaplan discovered that Topor had "walked away from the class conflict. He had changed it into a careerist dilemma story about an upper-middle-class lawyer. The rape victim had gone from being the central character to the MacGuffin." Tewkesbury had written "great scenes between the two women, which were buried amidst all the stuff about the lawyer." According to Kaplan, Steel informed Lansing and Jaffe that hiring him was the only way their now moribund project was going to get revived. After listening to Kaplan's ideas about the script, Lansing told the director what he wanted was really already in Topor's second draft. "She said, 'Ethically, I think we need Tom,' " recalls Kaplan. "Tom was feeling dumped because he had a penis. Sherry without a doubt is as close to a great politician as you'll ever get. She can make you say thank you as she fires you. She was able to coax Tom back to the project. Joan kept working on the specifics of the relationship between [the lawyer] and her sister and between the [lawyer] and [the rape victim]."

By this time the regime at Paramount had changed. Tanen was not impressed by the project. "'This is horseshit, who gives a shit?'" he fumed, according to David Madden. " 'It's a TV movie. There's no male role in it. It's about rape. It's not even about a rapist, the witnesses to a rape. This is so esoteric.' And he just hated it. And ninety-nine people out of a hundred, and I think most of the people who are working in the studio today [would say], My boss doesn't want to make the movie. Well, I've just got to put this away. And Dawn would not. If she loved something she would not take no. And at the time, what got that movie green-lit was Kelly McGillis."

The sultry, blond McGillis was one of Paramount's rising stars, having just come off *Top Gun* and *Witness*. The filmmakers sent the script to McGillis on location in Israel. She didn't want to play the rape victim, because she herself had been raped (a fact Lansing didn't know until after the movie). Yet she very much wanted to see the movie get made, so she offered to play the now less showy part of the lawyer.

Steel convinced Tanen to okay the picture by shaving the budget down to $8 million, a figure low enough that the studio felt it could easily emerge unscathed if the film flopped. "She was very tough with me," says Kaplan. " 'You got to do it for eight million,' [she said]. 'If it's one fucking penny over, you've screwed me.' "

IT'S OKAY FOR YOU TO FEEL PAIN, BUT GOD FORBID A MAN SHOULD CRY IN THE PRESENCE OF YOU

In the years since she had graduated from Yale, Jodie Foster thought frequently of giving up acting. Her Hollywood career was cold. She found work in the quasi-independent realm, quirkier films where the experiences "were okay, but disappointing," she says. Her parts included a witness to a mob killing in *Backtrack*, directed by Dennis Hopper, a miserable experience in which Foster felt mistreated by Hopper (ultimately, the film was released only on video); a repressed husband-killing wife in the New Zealand costume thriller *Mesmerized*, another disappointment; and a looped Sloane Ranger in *Siesta*, an artsy surreal romance by the music-video director Mary Lambert.

Stealing Home was a saccharine drama about a failed baseball player (played by Mark Harmon) who is given the ashes of his childhood idol, played by Foster and seen only in flashback. While critics derided the film, Foster defended it as at least ideologically progressive: A young woman plays the hero to a boy. Brash, confident, she teaches her young ward how to smoke and how to look sexy for girls: "She is what he would like to grow up to be. I've always wanted to be a hero for someone—and that's someone I've always wanted in my life too," she explained.

Five Corners made an attempt to be an authentic American art film. Based on the first screenplay by John Patrick Shanley, who later won the Oscar for *Moonstruck*, the film, set in the 1960s in the Bronx, eerily recycled the Hinckley-esque subtheme of Foster's public life. Foster played a working-class girl who is stalked by a newly released ex-con (John Turturro), whom she whacks with a board, momentarily winning her freedom. He catches up with her, and, in a send-up of the usual great male protector who comes in to save the day, it takes an army of cops and neighbors to save her. "I get knocked over the head and carried around unconscious in John Turturro's arms for about forty percent of the movie. Very King Kong," she told one journalist at the time. "It never occurred to me until I started shooting it that there could be any comparisons in my own real life. Even my mom didn't think of it. When I read the script I laughed at some of the scenes." Ironically, the production began receiving threatening letters from a would-be Foster stalker and had to hire extra security.

The film's financiers, HandMade Films and Cineplex Odeon, had balked at casting Foster. "At the time, she was definitely out of favor with the establishment, as it were," recalls the director Tony Bill, who knew Foster slightly from when he was involved with *Taxi Driver.* "And they made all sorts of claims that she was overweight, and that she was not attractive enough. And so actually with a bit of subterfuge I managed to get some photographs that had been recently taken of her, which were sort of undeniable proof that she wasn't overweight. It was a real battle. And I just refused to take no for an answer."

It was a similar struggle for Foster to land the part of Sarah Tobias, the furious rape victim in *The Accused.* Disillusionment and self-doubt had begun to gnaw at the actress.

"I couldn't see spending my life working with bad material. Sometimes as an actor you just wear the grape suit and be the best grape you can possibly be. My ego is too huge to not do something that has an impact on the culture," she later explained.

"See, *The Accused* was my last try," she says. "I sort of felt like I'm just going to give it one last try and I'm going to take my GREs."

Scores of young actresses trekked to Paramount to audition for the part, including Demi Moore, Rosanna Arquette, and Meg Tilly. "A lot of actresses didn't want to do the rape scenes," recalls Jonathan Kaplan. He knew Foster, whom he calls an "actor's actor," from when they almost worked together on *Ladies and Gentlemen, the Fabulous Stains* in the early eighties.

"Jonathan begged and borrowed and stole to get me the audition, 'cause they wouldn't audition me," says Foster. "Jonathan was a for-hire guy, so he was vulnerable too. These were big producers, and it's a big deal. So he wasn't in any position to be championing me at all. But he knew me and he wanted me to be included in the audition process and they said no. And I wasn't allowed to get the script.

"Of course I already had the script. I had all the scripts. And nobody was allowed to tell me what the audition scene would be because I wasn't allowed to be auditioned. So basically I had to fly into New York the day before and meet Stanley Jaffe. So that he could look me over and make the decision about whether or not I was good-looking enough." Jaffe allowed her to audition the next day, so she didn't have time to memorize the material.

"So I did the best I could, and I felt like this was the characterization that I wanted. I thought she was a tough, broken girl, and I had a little cut-off black T-shirt on, and a pair of jeans or something. I felt that was the character."

Kaplan thought she was great. Lansing quipped, "The envelope please." Yet the studio resisted. Lansing conveyed to Kaplan, with a look of potent disgust, that the studio thought "Foster wasn't 'rapeable enough,' " says the director. In typical fashion Paramount as well as Jaffe questioned whether she would be sufficiently sympathetic.

Says Foster, "They said, 'She's too urban. And we think that's really bad. She's too tough.' So Jonathan called me back in a panic and said, 'Well, that's it. They're gonna go with somebody else, but I would like to bring you back in [for the final screen test].' I thought, Back in for what? He said, 'Look, let me just give you a hint: Just don't be urban at all. Just be as California as you are. Wear something really nice and come in and be soft.' So I said, 'But, but, but, but that's not, you know, that's not [the character].' And he said, 'We'll worry about that later.' And I said, 'Well, okay.' And it was probably the worst performance I've ever given. And they hired me after that."

Kaplan and, probably more important, Kelly McGillis, then a major star, threatened to quit unless Foster was given the part. In truth, Ned Tanen had mandated that other actors be tested. His girlfriend at the time was Meg Ryan's manager, so Ryan was dutifully auditioned. "I don't think Stanley, Sherry, or Jonathan Kaplan had any real interest," recalls David Madden. "I think they were kind of humoring him." Indeed both CAA and William Morris honored Kaplan's unofficial request not to send over any more candidates, but Foster's own agency, ICM, continued to present other actresses. Although the filmmakers had promised Foster a quick decision, she waited for weeks to hear.

"Well," she says, "let me put it this way, they waited until a week before I was supposed to go shoot. So they could have enough time to see if someone else better came along."

As the movie progressed toward shooting in British Columbia, Lansing and Jaffe devolved into their usual division of tasks, Lansing ministering to the script and Jaffe ministering to the logistics of filming. "Sherry doesn't like to schlepp to location," says Kaplan. "Jaffe is the least elitist person. He loves to be on set with the crew and the Teamsters. He picked all the locations except for two. He's a great line producer."

Ironically, Foster turned out to be one person who wasn't susceptible to Lansing's honeyed charm. "She reminds me of the Dianne character in my movie *Little Man Tate*," said Foster several years later, comparing Lansing with the fussy, controlling, but well-intentioned specialist in child genius played by Dianne Wiest. Foster does a little sample interplay between herself and Lansing.

"She's, 'Well, we're all fine,' " recounts Foster, in a high-pitched, singsong voice.

"I'm really sick," counters the actress, as herself.

"[Sherry goes], 'Oh! No you're not. You only have a little allergy. You're not sick,' " relays Foster in the disingenuous voice.

At one point Lansing grew so frustrated at her inability to connect with her star that she called a mutual friend, who counseled, "Let Stanley handle the relationship."

Foster responded to people who were straightforward and blunt. She liked Dawn Steel and Jonathan Kaplan, another former child actor, who spent more than a little time directing the film at the top of his lungs. The first day of shooting, Foster walked on the set and Kaplan yelled, " 'Stop it. What are you doing with your hands? Do you have any idea how stupid that looks?' " recalled Foster. "Nobody had ever said that kind of thing to me, but you get used to it after a while."

"Jodie, Dawn, and I all have reputations for being abrasive," says Kaplan. "Jodie Foster can be bloodcurdlingly honest. The volume's not as loud, but it can take your breath away." Foster also grew close to her costar Kelly McGillis. McGillis, Foster, and Kaplan spent hours hashing out the film.

In looking back on the making of *The Accused*, Foster repeatedly calls the experience "a real unconscious moment in my life. I have no idea why I was so obsessed with it. I think all my friends would disagree, they'd say, 'Oh no, you say you were unconscious but you weren't. You never shut up about . . .' But I don't experience that at all. I sort of feel like I jumped into that movie with that absolutely-not-knowing kind of thing. I did no research, at all. The only thing I did was I met with some rape crisis center people and said, 'Well, I wanna be like that!' " She laughs. "I never read the script more than once. I would just think of these excuses to not read it. It really wasn't until I got there that I realized what I had gotten myself into. I just completely avoided it."

Kaplan planned to shoot the rape sequence first. The first week on location he drove Foster to the bar set and walked her through the storyboards of the scene. "She got really quiet. She had wanted the part so badly that she hadn't allowed herself to think about what it entailed," says Kaplan. They rehearsed for several days, and Kaplan gave Foster the choice of shooting the scene over time or all at once using a number of cameras. She opted for the whole shebang, although even that way the sequence would take five days to shoot. On the appointed day she arrived and announced, "Let's rape." She told Kaplan, "Now, Jonathan, don't worry about me. I won't be all right, but I'll be okay. I'll tell you if I'm not all right." She asked McGillis to be present. Lansing and Jaffe stayed in the trailer.

"From the screen test to the filming, the element that was added was the depth of her rage," recalls Kaplan. "She could access that depth from going through the rape. She wasn't penetrated, but the sequence was ninety percent the same as in real life. She had to do it over and over again.

"I felt, at times, that [the crew] were so ready to leave that film, and that some of the reason why they stayed was they felt sorry for me," says Foster, who cried so much during the scene she broke the blood vessels in her eyes. "They felt protective of me."

The men playing the rapists and the guys cheering them on also started to cry. Foster handled her fears by taking care of them. "That's what obsessed me, actually thinking, I don't want those guys to feel bad; I don't want them to feel guilty." Says Foster, "A year later I said, 'What do I care what they think!' Why was I so worried that somehow they were gonna feel bad about themselves?

"It's a pretty strong, feminine trait, which is, it's okay for you to feel pain, but God forbid a man should cry in the presence of you. It's your responsibility, 'cause men can't handle it, to make sure that they're taken care of. But, you know, forget yours. You can survive. It's interesting for the part because somewhere down the line you think you deserve it. Whatever pain you go through, it's okay because basically you must deserve it. And that movie really made me examine that in myself. That I've kept it so focused on everyone else. In my film where I went through so much. But I didn't wanna think about what I was going through. I had to take care of everyone else."

Foster's mother visited for several weeks during the time they shot the rape scene. "That was the last—really the last picture that I went to with her. Because I felt that it was a reference that she had not experienced," says Brandy Foster. "And I knew it was going to be kind of devastating, that rape scene. And we talked about it, but I didn't hit on it too much. But I was there back at the hotel waiting when she'd come home at night. And we'd have dinner or I cooked something—I kind of stayed out of the way. I knew that she was exhausted and it was very devastating for the guys. They were all really nice guys. And so she would say, 'Well, that's all right. You know, it's a job.' And she was bruised and it hurt and it went on for a week and a half. And it was kind of an untalked-about thing. So I just felt it was important that she have somebody around."

"This is how I recovered: I went to a club every night," says Foster, laughing. For three months she danced as Sarah Tobias was punished for doing. "I've never done this since. All I wanted to think about was what cool black dress or outfit I was gonna wear, and I wanted to go to, like, really cool clubs and hang out with really cool people and drive around in really cool cars. It was as if I was a model. It's so not like me. I want to be as superficial as I can possibly be. I just want to not think about it. Not feel too much. I was really depressed at the end of the movie because the end of the film was incredibly difficult. And I was sure that I'd stunk, and that was it. I thought, Well, I basically am going to have to give up this business.

"I still look at the film and think I'm really over the top. But I couldn't do it any other way. I've never been so—entrapped?—that I couldn't change my performance.

"One of the big revelations about *The Accused* was that I was not able to follow directions. And I thought, 'Well, this is it. It's the end of my career. I'll never work again, because I can't tailor my performance to be what they want me to be. I can't do it. I guess because I suck.'

"And years later, finally, I think Jonathan said, 'You dummy. Don't you realize that you couldn't play what wasn't real? What wasn't true.' And there's a great bonus having won an Oscar for that movie."

———

The Accused went a long way in defining the grown-up iconography of Jodie Foster. If the motif of the films of her youth was a child sexualized by the world of adults, the theme of The Accused was a reclamation of self. The key moment of the film occurs before the rape when Foster dances confidently, sexually in the bar, watched by men and ultimately violated by the rapists. She dances for herself and is punished for it. For the rest of the film she fights back, a lone, vulnerable woman with righteousness on her side. She chops off her hair, throws out her unsupportive boyfriend, invades the dinner party of the defense lawyer who plea-bargains her case demanding angrily the opportunity to be heard, rear-ends her car into the vehicle of one of the rape witnesses. She pointedly rejects victimization and muteness. As she tells her lawyer from her hospital bed, "I never got to tell nobody nothing. You did all my talking for me." In the end, the legal system saves the day, perhaps not a realistic ending but certainly a Hollywood one.

But it was another bumpy road getting the film into theaters. When The Accused was previewed, it got "the single lowest score in the history of Paramount Pictures," says Lansing. The audience believed exactly the opposite of what the message was supposed to be—that Sarah Tobias was asking for what she got. Lansing pleaded with Tanen for another $180,000 to reedit, and she and Jaffe supervised a new cut because Kaplan was sick in the hospital. "They didn't crumble. Stanley and Sherry have enough self-confidence and experience not to let the movie turn beige," says Kaplan.

The film went on to make more than $75 million worldwide. According to Barry London, the Paramount marketing chief at the time, the studios devised a two-tiered marketing campaign, one tier that appealed to the p.c. crowd, the other that appealed "to the lowest common denominator, people who found the rape titillating." Hence it wasn't surprising that in some theaters the rape scene elicited whoops of excitement and glee. Still, Lansing trumpeted it as a vindication for her feminist credentials: "If anyone thinks this movie is antifeminist, I give up," she told the press. "I doubt that you will ever, ever think of rape the same way. Those images will stick in your mind, and you will be more sympathetic the next time you hear of somebody being raped."

Again, Lansing had handled the lion's share of the publicity chores. To get a better handle on the marketplace, she hired a jet to fly the filmmakers and stars to cities across the United States to talk to local media. Foster herself was taken to task for playing yet another victim, a charge to which she responded: "Someone said to me, 'You call yourself a feminist and yet you play victims in movies.' But can you tell me that being a victim is not part of womanhood? If I portray a victim, does that mean I'm not Wonder Woman? Well, I'm not trying to be. You can't censor art through political correctness."

Foster won an Oscar for the part. Dressed in an aquamarine satin gown, she gazed out on Hollywood's assembled elite and thanked her mother, who, she said, "taught me that all my finger paintings were Picassos and that I didn't have to be afraid." She added, "Cruelty might be human, and it might be cultural, but it's not acceptable, which is what this movie is about."

I DEFY US TO FIND ANY WOMAN WHO DOESN'T HAVE HUGE RESCUE FANTASIES

In the months after getting bounced out of her job as head of production at United Artists, Paula Weinstein floated through life, doing nothing much but shopping. She was thirty-eight years old. It was the first time in over a decade that Hollywood didn't occupy twenty hours of her day, that there weren't phone calls to return, deals to do, dramas to resolve, a legion of personal assistants to facilitate her every whim. "For me work was everything. I was completely involved in and obsessed with work, and when I finished work then I wanted the drama of a boyfriend, or a romance, or to be swept off my feet," she recalls. "And I defy us to find any woman who doesn't have huge rescue fantasies when work isn't going well and things are troubling. The big issue is, is there going to be some fabulous guy who is going to sweep me off my feet and all the problems are going to be solved, and won't that be great? And I want to be rescued."

It wasn't a particularly realistic fantasy, but for years Weinstein didn't want a particularly realistic relationship. "Everybody always says, 'Oh well, I'm always attracted to guys who are unavailable or unattainable, even if they're available.' The truth is that women who go for men like that don't really want to have a relationship. I don't think I would have lasted married to any of them," says Weinstein of her old boyfriends. "If any of them had actually said, 'Okay, I'm yours,' I would have taken for the hills."

Unsure of what to do for the rest of her life, Weinstein fell in love—with Mark Rosenberg, her oldest and closest friend, the man she had always dismissed because he was too familiar, too safe. A huge, Rabelaisian figure with a limitless appetite for food, booze, grass, fly-fishing, and music, Rosenberg was abrasive, outrageous, loud, and fun, the kind of guy who hopped from tabletop to tabletop in Havana's Tropicana nightclub, organizing a three-hundred-person conga line, and shouting, "Viva Fidel," all the while explaining to Weinstein and their close friend Harry Belafonte the promise of reconciliation between Cuba and the United States. He kept a poster of Che Guevara behind his desk at Warner Bros., where he was president of production and responsible for such films as *Risky Business, The World According to Garp,* and *The Killing Fields.*

"Enough people I trusted said, 'Don't you see, when you and he are in a room, and there are fifteen other people, he's the one who makes you laugh, you're the one who makes him laugh. You're always looking at each other. You play every scene to each other," says Weinstein. They had circled each other for years, intimate when both were single, less close when each was involved with another person. They had once even toyed with getting married, but Weinstein balked. In fact, Rosenberg was married to producer Lauren Shuler when he decided he was in love with Weinstein. He flew to Italy, where Shuler was on location, and broke up with her in order to start a relationship with Weinstein. The scandal burned up the phone lines in Burbank.

"The minute sex entered into it, it became male-female in another way, other battles that had never emerged in all of our years as friends came up," says Weinstein about her marriage to Rosenberg. They battled frequently for control of the relationship and the limelight, which was hard because Rosenberg could vacuum-pack a room with the force of his personality. "[It was always] 'Who was dominating the situation?' Whereas, as friends, Mark could be with me, and I could be talking for two hours, and be the center of attention, and he would enjoy it, or say, 'This is boring, I'm leaving.' As my spouse, it would be like, 'It's enough already.' " Rosenberg used to frequently bang on the table, and jokingly say, " 'Who's the boss?' And we fought it out. I mean, we had huge battles, huge."

While theirs was the only union between studio production chiefs, peer marriages were on the rise as women entered Hollywood in growing numbers. Lives commingled personally and professionally. While the UA debacle had blackened Weinstein's professional reputation, Rosenberg helped her land a production deal at Warner Bros. Rosenberg himself was fending off an attack on his job by the vice president Mark Canton (ironically enough, a former boyfriend of Weinstein's), who seemed to embody the types of low-brow films engulfing Hollywood, schlock comedies like *National Lampoon's European Vacation* and *Caddyshack.* Bantam-sized and irrepressibly (often unrealistically) optimistic, Canton and his friends Jon Peters and Peter Guber hounded the Warners chiefs Terry Semel and Robert Daly about Rosenberg's job. Soon Canton's bride-to-be producer, Wendy Finerman, and Weinstein joined the fray, in a widening war of recrimination.

Weinstein would call agents, only to be told that they'd just gotten off the phone with Finerman, who had told them that Rosenberg was being replaced. Weinstein and Rosenberg fought as she tried to make him face the reality of the situation.

In a surreal Hollywood moment when personal interplay accurately reflected political power plays, Peters threw a lavish engagement party for Canton and Finerman, decking out his Bel Air mansion like Tara and installing a chimpanzee with a Warner Bros. T-shirt on a tree. As Semel and Daly and all the industry stood around drinking champagne, Rosenberg had the misfortune of falling into the pool, an event made all the more embarrassing by his extreme girth. "Mark fell into the pool! Mark fell into the pool!" cried Canton and Peters with glee, in a moment of ugliness shocking by even Hollywood standards. As Rosenberg went inside to dry off his clothes, Weinstein purposefully stayed outside with the rest of the party. Afterward, they fought bitterly. He was enraged, but she passionately defended herself by saying it was better to behave nonchalantly.

Several months later *Variety* announced Canton's promotion to head of production and Rosenberg's departure to form an independent production company with Sydney Pollack at Universal. Rosenberg went on to produce such films as *White Palace* and *Presumed Innocent.* Weinstein's first producing effort, meanwhile, failed miserably. In partnership with Gareth Wigan, a close friend from the Ladd days, she made the anemic *American Flyers,* a maudlin *Brian's Song* on bicycles, written by *Breaking Away*'s Steve Tesich and directed by none other than Martin Brest's replacement on *WarGames,* John Badham.

———

Weinstein's precipitous fall from power also resulted in a renewed commitment to politics. Her steady rise through corporate Hollywood had left her little time for her previous activism, save for a minor role in Tom Hayden's 1976 senatorial campaign (Jane Fonda was then her biggest client). Nonetheless, Ronald Reagan's election in 1980 had made a dent in her apathy. She felt guilty that neither she nor anyone in her generation had done anything to stop it. She wondered if in their obsession with material success they had inadvertently paved the way for a resurgent right wing.

Weinstein was not the only woman with a hankering for meaning in her life and money to burn. In the spring of 1984, the producer Julia Phillips was invited to a dinner of showbiz women to discuss what they could do about the potential demise of the California chapter of NOW, as a result of insufficient funds. Taking a cue from Hollywood honchos like the Universal chief, Lew Wasserman, who used his money to buy clout in the Democratic party, Phillips offered to throw a fund-raising brunch on her front lawn. If Michael Eisner and Jack Valenti could network the town for money, why couldn't they? Why did they need to wait for another guy to tell them where to relieve their checkbooks? The brunch netted four thousand dollars.

The next day Weinstein (who hadn't attended) called Phillips about organizing a political group, and soon a dozen women met at the producer Barbara Boyle's house to form the nonprofit Hollywood Women's Coalition. They included the Oscar-winning songwriter Marilyn Bergman; Columbia Pictures Television's then president, Barbara Corday; and Weinstein's close friend Anthea Sylbert. They hated the fact that Reagan had become the poster boy for all Hollywood. "There was that sort of personal thing," recalls Sylbert. "We wanted to make sure that everybody knew that there was this other Hollywood."

More than a few of them—Weinstein, Phillips, Sylbert—had had their heads thwacked by the glass ceiling, and within a few years others, such as Corday and Boyle, would receive similar head bangings. They had money, ambition, intelligence, a healthy measure of professional success, but little real power in either Hollywood or Washington.

They decided to throw a fund-raiser at the Hollywood Palladium to collect voter registration funds for the National Organization for Women. They enticed Jane Fonda and Sherry Lansing to act as cochairs, Melissa Manchester and Whoopi Goldberg to entertain, and sold tables for fifteen hundred dollars apiece. "After the first event, we were sort of giggly that we pulled it off," recalls Sylbert. "It was like, we got by by the skin of our teeth."

They were also pumped up, although the burst of excitement was dampened by the fact that simply raising money for voter registration still left the women on the sidelines of the political process. When the Democrats tapped the New York Representative Geraldine Ferraro to be the first woman on the national ticket, Andy Spahn, a young Democratic aide organizing Hollywood, enlisted the women to work on a major Democratic fund-raising dinner, and they fanned out looking for checks. Right after the Democratic National Convention they opted for the power afforded by cold, hard cash and formed a political action committee, the Hollywood Women's Political Committee, to participate directly in partisan campaigns. Although Walter Mondale's prospects for election were rapidly dwindling, the women raised $300,000 for the dinner, about half of the total collected that night.

The HWPC had arrived, and soon it evolved into a quintessential Hollywood liberal institution, which "allowed its members to reaffirm their militant ideology without repudiating their comfortable lives," as the historian Ronald Brownstein points out. As if in a modern-day temperance movement, women networked under the guise of a higher moral purpose, their ambitions channeled into a self-important do-goodism, their checkbooks wielded like swords.

The HWPC was elitist, sifting real women players from the Hollywood wanna-bes. One had to be nominated by two members to join, and the fee was high, $2,500 (later reduced to $1,500) a year. Throughout 1985 the founding mothers, as they called themselves, selectively recruited their friends to join. Weinstein and Bergman were soon hosting sellout recruitment lunches, as membership grew from twelve to seventy within six months. They held a fund-raiser at Spago, the hip Sunset Boulevard restaurant, for the Democratic Senatorial Campaign Committee and soon after hammered out an unabashedly liberal manifesto: "We are committed to the belief that the ultimate defense of the United States of America lies in the immediate dismantlement of the global nuclear war machine. . . . It is time to expose and penalize as criminals those who knowingly destroy the balance of nature. . . . We are committed to an economic policy based on every citizen's full participation in our country's economic wealth."

The women of the HWPC wrapped themselves in a shroud of ideological purity and announced that they would give money only to candidates who passed their self-devised litmus tests. As Weinstein bragged to the press, "We are not consensus democrats and are never going to be." While Washington politicians griped about what they perceived as the HWPC's abrasive self-righteousness, they nonetheless made pilgrimages westward to suck for dollars.

In 1986, the organization presented the most glittering fundraiser–social event of the Hollywood calendar. That was the year the Soviet nuclear power plant Chernobyl exploded, the year Barbra Streisand, dormant in politics since she sang for George McGovern in the early seventies, joined the HWPC. Newly concerned about the environment and the nuclear arms race, Streisand was lured into the HWPC by her close friend Marilyn Bergman, who also helped the singer educate herself about the issues (by setting up dinners with leading nuclear analysts like Marvin Goldberger, then president of the California Institute of Technology). Bergman and Weinstein also convinced Streisand, who hadn't sung in public for five years, to give a HWPC fund-raiser to benefit the Democratic Senatorial Campaign Committee. Weinstein spent two months working on the event: "I did nothing else but that."

On a Saturday night in early September, a hundred and fifty couples—who had paid $5,000 each—showed up at Streisand's secluded Malibu ranch to hear the reclusive star warble seventeen songs and tweak the GOP. She was vibrant and masterful, and left her audience, which included anyone who was anyone in Hollywood, from Jack Nicholson to Goldie Hawn, in raptures. The event raised $1.5 million, far more than President Reagan managed the next night in L.A.

"I remember getting a call from Frank Wells, president of Disney, when the invitations went out for $5,000 a couple. He said to me, 'You're off your fucking rocker,' " recalls Weinstein. Four weeks later, Wells called again looking for tickets. "He said, 'I have to eat crow.' "

Sue Mengers and Milton Berle, Los Angeles, 1988.

PETER BORSARI

A LEGEND RETURNS

I FELT I NEEDED MORE MONEY

It was in 1988, two years after the legendary William Morris agent Stan Kamen, the linchpin of the agency's motion picture wing, had died of AIDS-related lymphoma, that the West Coast administrator Roger Davis finally capitulated to the beseechings of his staff and placed the call to Sue Mengers. In the months following her retirement, Mengers and her husband, Jean-Claude Tramont, had been enjoying a second honeymoon. They had cruised along the south of France with the Sidney Poitiers and Leonard Goldbergs, visited Gore Vidal in Italy, toured Israel. They had reconnected in a way they had never been able to when she was working all those hours. "It was like the courtship we never had. Those two years were glorious. We were together all the time," says Mengers. This is not to say she wasn't tempted, seriously tempted by what Davis had to offer—namely the position of head of the William Morris Motion Picture Department.

Kamen's death had struck Morris hard. The antithesis of Mengers (with whom he had shared a kissy-kissy friendship), the relentlessly low-key hand-holder had represented everyone from Jane Fonda to Steve McQueen. When he died, Morris began to wither under the blistering heat of the new industry powerhouse, Creative Artists Agency. Led by the former Morris agent Michael Ovitz, CAA was on a permanent raiding mission; they wanted stars at the pinnacles of their careers.

On the surface the CAA agents resembled the office from which they sprang; conservative, buttoned-up, indistinguishable in a panoply of well-cut suits. They eschewed the flamboyant individualism of a Mengers or a Freddie Fields. Ovitz was all about business. As the costs and profits of movies continued to skyrocket, the deals afforded stars became infinitely richer and more complicated. There were new ways to get the talent bigger slices of the pie, and Ovitz promised to maximize their portion of each potential revenue stream. He had a business plan, and a team of well-trained lieutenants eager to implement it ("foot soldiers marching up and down Wilshire Boulevard" he infamously was said to call them). Ovitz picked Morris's cherries one by one: Robert Redford, Burt Reynolds, Sylvester Stallone, Jane Fonda. Within four months of Kamen's death, almost all his former clients had switched to CAA. The rest of the agents were clinging to their most lucrative meal tickets and begging for a new leader.

Roger Davis scouted candidates, focusing first on such former competitors as Mike Medavoy and Guy McElwaine, who had bailed out of agenting in the mid-seventies to take studio jobs. Davis was offering a million-dollar salary and stock in the company, but there was dissension among the board members about whether the new worldwide motion picture chief—Kamen's title—could join their exclusive club. Few were anxious to take the job without some promise of autonomy. Leonard Hirshan, Clint Eastwood's agent, was appointed West Coast head of the Motion Picture Department as a stopgap measure. By the beginning of 1987, a consensus had formed among the upper-echelon agents: They wanted Sue Mengers.

For months the former star agent had received solicitations from her contacts at Morris, from Boaty Boatwright, a genteel southern belle who represented Norman Jewison and Alan Pakula, whom Mengers had known since they both started out in New York in the sixties; from the lively, self-professed *tummler* (Yiddish for one who stirs the pot) Toni Howard, who had been a secretary at CMA when La Mengers arrived in the business. In those days Mengers had liked Howard, frankly because the younger woman had simply worshiped her; now she cooed that she hadn't known how smart she was.

If Mengers had ignored Howard in the early days, she had been dismissive of Ed Limato when he arrived at ICM's Los Angeles headquarters in 1979 as a former theater agent from New York with scarcely a client list. She had heckled him in staff meetings about his parties— "Boys' Towns!" she decried. "You can never have stars come to your house." He had lasted at ICM only eight months before Kamen wooed him to William Morris, where he wound up representing Mel Gibson, Michelle Pfeiffer, and Richard Gere. Now he too joined the voices beckoning her back to the business. At first there was even talk that the two would share the post of head of the Motion Picture Department, but Mengers flat-out refused.

She was tempted, however, by the job. She was bored with retirement. She and Jean-Claude had sold their fabulous Zsa Zsa house during the real-estate boom and bought apartments in New York and L.A. They had just decided to stay west after all, and Mengers had recently seen a precious little house in Beverly Hills that she fancied. The million-dollar salary began to look enticing. "I wanted more money," she says. "I felt that I needed more money, because I never made big money, never. And it caused a problem with my husband, because he felt that we could live on less. He was not happy about me going to work again." If money was one reason, regret was another. "I think unconsciously I wanted to make sure I hadn't made a mistake. Had I done the right thing? It seemed so easy to me being an agent. I thought, Well, let me try it for another three years, big deal. I'll make this money and how hard can it be?"

The six men who filled William Morris's board were loath to put a woman in the job. They had tolerated Kamen's penchant for hiring women, but a number of them still had difficulty envisioning agents in skirts. One board member had gone so far as to quip, "Wouldn't it be nice without any female agents?"—a line that quickly reverberated through the halls of the agency.

It took months for Morris to make Mengers's deal, in part because each point had to be vetted by six board members on both coasts. She was warned that the board still wielded great power, although they seemed like a bunch of fuddy-duddy old men to everyone outside Morris. Yet Mengers was so confident in her ability to handle them that she didn't insist on a seat on the board, nor did she demand the right to put agents under contract, thereby binding them to Morris. She did, however, ask for Kamen's old title, head of the Motion Picture Department worldwide.

As the board dithered, the troops, in particular Ed Limato, became impatient. Limato had a long-simmering resentment at how he had been treated at Morris and genuinely felt threatened by the outside agents circling his stable of superstars. Jeff Berg, the chairman of ICM, had been calling at regular intervals, and now Berg and his cohorts Jim Wiatt and Sam Cohn began to look like men Limato could rely on. Limato broached the topic with his clients, like Gibson and Pfeiffer, all of whom were willing to go with him. He didn't tell Mengers. He felt guilty about it, but not that guilty.

Limato disappeared from William Morris the last week of March 1988. Even his close friend Toni Howard didn't know where he was; when she found him he broke it to her that he was going to ICM. She was crushed and begged him to let her tell Mengers, still finessing the finer points of her deal. Limato reluctantly agreed, but the news didn't appear to rattle Mengers, who never seemed to have really understood what the big deal was about Limato. "Now they'll really need me," she said.

On the morning of April 8, 1988, Ed Limato tendered his resignation to William Morris, sending panic and dismay through the Morris halls. By 4:00 that afternoon, Mengers had arrived to take charge of the motion picture company. She was horrified by what she was beginning to realize: that the town would view Limato's departure (with major clients in tow) as an indictment of her. Yet she stuck it out with bravado—loud, brash, indomitable—declaring to anyone who would listen the difference she would make.

Dressed in a Chanel suit, a jaunty scarf around her neck, Mengers held court in Stan Kamen's old office as the graying padres of William Morris strutted around, proud of their newest acquisition. One by one the agents were brought in to meet her. She wanted to meet all their biggest stars right away and warned agents with desirable clients that their prized possessions were very vulnerable. She told Mike Simpson that he could lose Tom Hanks if he didn't add another presence to his representation.

For JJ Harris, who was shocked to find herself suddenly facing not only Mengers but much of the Morris board, it was all about her one star client, Kevin Costner. Mengers wanted to know where he was.

"And I said, 'Well, right now he's having lunch with Ed Limato.' He asked Kevin to have a meeting with him upon him going to ICM, and Kevin honored that, because they had a relationship and they were friends, and I felt zero threatened by it. But I was telling her the truth," recalls Harris. "And she made this most crass, crude comment, 'Oh, so right now you're here walking around the halls and Kevin Costner is at the Ivy getting a blow job from Ed Limato.' "

Harris was repulsed by Mengers's attitude. "And Kevin knew who she was, and he had no interest in meeting her. I had to live with this

nightmare of her being up my butt—'I have to meet Kevin. It is to protect you'—and Kevin saying, 'I ain't going to meet Sue Mengers.' And
me trying not to hurt her feelings."

At the end of the day Mengers went off to the set of *Tequila Sunrise*
to try to save both Mel Gibson and Michelle Pfeiffer for Morris. It was a
fool's mission. Both followed Limato to become the latest jewels in ICM's
crown. Costner, meanwhile, ended up at CAA.

Carrie Fisher and Penny Marshall, Los Angeles, 1983.

PETER BORSARI

20.

CULTURAL ICONS

DON'T BE ASHAMED OF YOUR TALENTS

"I know all their names." Penny Marshall laughs as she surveys her Beanie Baby collection, tiny stuffed animals that line the walls of an entire room in her Hollywood Hills mansion. "It's sick, isn't it," she says. Each animal is carefully placed in a pocket of a hanging shoe bag. There are more than five hundred plush alligators, bears, ocelots, and moose, and dozens more, doubles, that she keeps in the room next door, carefully filed in plastic Ziploc bags. Marshall lives alone in the spacious house, which is almost how you would imagine Laverne De-Fazio, her famous TV alter ego, would live if she ever struck it rich. Her home is a cornucopia of American kitsch, a hymn to abundance. It is the lair of an obsessive collector. There's not one hooked rug hanging on the wall but more than a dozen, a collection of World War II bullet art, and assorted pillows embossed with homilies. The kitchen sports what must be almost three hundred refrigerator magnets, in all shapes and colors.

It is a balmy Friday evening in the summer of 1999. The fifty-six-year-old director is exhausted, almost chronically so, from months of insomnia, although she's coming off three good nights' sleep, courtesy of a doctor's aid. She's wearing pajama-style pants and a beat-up, oversize T-shirt, her hair slung back in a ponytail. The features are softer and rounder than they played on TV; the campy homeliness that defined her screen persona is gone. She's chain-smoking again, after having managed to quit for three months. "I hate people watching me eat all the time, that's why I don't go anywhere," she says, in her famous Bronx whine. "I like everything to come to my house. I don't think I've been to my offices at Universal for months."

She did venture out today. After a two-and-a-half-year hiatus, Marshall, the first woman to become an A-list director, the first woman to make a film that grossed over $100 million, is finally beginning a movie again. She ate a late lunch with Drew Barrymore at which she offered her the lead in *Riding in Cars with Boys*. She had wanted to take Barrymore to a WNBA game this weekend, where she was going to have "Drew, you got the part" emblazoned on the scoreboard, but Barrymore couldn't make it. It's been a long haul for Barrymore, who was offered the part by the producer, Jim Brooks, before Marshall signed on, then essentially had to reaudition, because Marshall hadn't known she'd been officially cast.

In person, Marshall has a talent for intimacy. She sits close, inches away, with the boundaries blurring, evincing a disarming vulnerability. With men, she can be extremely flirtatious. That openness can also be turned off; the drawbridge snaps shut, leaving Marshall frosty and distrustful. She often conducts interviews in the persona of Laverne, the daffy, insecure, unthreatening Milwaukee brewery worker she played in the 1970s sitcom *Laverne & Shirley*. It's both a Teflon wall and easy shtick for her. Jokes are funnier in the Laverne voice—it's a "rhythm" delivery, she explains. Getting a laugh makes her feel safe. "I'm not that great an actress, and I could go into her at any moment. It's not that big a stretch," she says. "Half the people call me Laverne, so I can pretend I'm her. On *Jumpin' Jack Flash* [her first film], they'd say, 'Laverne,' so I'd be Laverne directing. The same words are going to come out."

Of course, the Laverne-does-Hollywood story has a kind of unbeatable upbeat trajectory, a natural populist appeal. Marshall has always taken solace in the fact that, no matter what the reviews (and critics savaged her sitcom), "they liked me in Idaho, so what do I care?" She hasn't made really personal films, or, as she says, "sophisticated theater." She prefers to make movies with "universal themes," which she has often boiled down to inspirational mantras that she repeats to herself during filming. For *Big*, it was "Don't give up your childhood"; for *A League of Their Own*, it was "Don't be ashamed of your talents." For most of her career she has studiously rejected the label of woman director, for which she was the poster child, at least in other people's minds.

Ironically, *Riding in Cars with Boys* has the potential to be Marshall's most autobiographical work. It is about a teenage girl who gets pregnant and keeps the child, a boy whom she raises into manhood. "This is Penny's life" says Brooks, one of Marshall's closest friends. Indeed, Marshall wound up pregnant herself at the age of twenty. "She was a young teenage mother of ambition [who] suddenly had that happen to her at a time when there was no community for anything and no options open."

"I identified with her," says Marshall. "I hope I can get in the feelings I know." Already she's been hashing out the character with Brooks. She doesn't want her to be weepy or pitiable, or a one-dimensional hellion. "I have Jim saying she's a bad girl," she groans. Marshall doesn't like his tone of parental censoriousness. "It's like my mother," she says. "I had to let my mother's shit go past me. 'Cause that's *their* opinion." Brooks was the one who gave her *Big*, and now has coaxed her back to work after two disappointments, *Renaissance Man* and *The Preacher's Wife*, which made her lose faith in her instincts, and definitely in the studios that employed her. She talks with passion about how people don't like to tell you the truth once you become so-called powerful.

"I was immobilized for the last year or so. I just didn't want to do anything. Nothing jazzed me. Fear drives me sometimes. You're so scared so you keep moving. I'd say things out of fear because I was scared and they laughed. Half my humor comes from I'm afraid. Just jumping in and doing it—you don't know what you're doing, so you're scared. But then there's another depression, fear of not trusting anyone. It's a different fear that will immobilize you, one, me. It's really not a good feeling." She sighs. "It really sucks."

THE BAD SEED

When Marshall was a child, her mother used to call her "the bad seed."

"[My mother's] mother always said she was so wonderful and it drove her crazy and so she wasn't going to do it to any of her children, and she succeeded," says Marshall, unable to keep a touch of acid from her voice. "Maybe I was. I liked boys. I was athletic. I wasn't pretty so I played ball with them. Anything for attention. I could hit and run. My diary from when I was thirteen is very sad: 'So-and-so hit me in the face with a snowball. I think I like him.' Any sign of attention, I was in love."

It was the fifties, and Marshall was growing up in an apartment on the Grand Concourse in the Bronx, on a block that spawned Neil Simon,

Paddy Chayefsky, Calvin Klein, and Ralph Lauren. She was the youngest of three born to Tony and Marjorie Marshall (formerly Marscharelli). Her father, a director of industrial films and commercials, "had the personality of a lamppost," she says. Her mother ran a dancing school in the basement and routinely dragooned her youngest daughter to perform in her shows. Hers was the only mom in the neighborhood who worked, who wore pants, and who hated to cook. Marjorie talked so fast it was as if she were on speed and kept a suicide jar in which she deposited one of every prescription ever written for any member of the family, so she could put herself out of misery if she ever ended up like her mother, who was blind and lived with them throughout Penny's childhood. Her mother was the one with the talent and the big mouth, the one who specialized in sarcasm. She told Penny, who had buck teeth, that her overbite "could open a Coke bottle." (Indeed, she once demonstrated this exact skill on *The Tonight Show*.)

"That was just her way. 'Oh, you're going to wear *that*,' " says Marshall, with a dismissive intonation. "I find myself doing it. I don't drive, but [I'll tell who's driving], 'This is the way you go.' Just needling. I just don't realize that I'm doing it."

Her parents fought ferociously. In another era they would have been divorced. Penny spent her youth rebelling, testing people and limits. As her sister Ronny has noted, "If someone told her, 'Don't go into the gutter,' she'd go in the gutter."

"I was wild," Marshall says, then immediately modifies. "I wasn't wild. I was just very athletic and ran around. I didn't want to be in the basement with my mother with the dancing school. I wanted to be with my friends and the boys. My mother always said, 'Don't be better than them. They don't like it if you beat them.' I wasn't even thinking about that. I just wanted their attention. I didn't want to be better. It wasn't a contest. I just wanted to be part of them. Even in college, I hung out with the football team, so I could bask in their glory. I'm okay in that position."

Marshall didn't want to think of herself as smart, or different, going so far as to get her mother to wrangle her out of high school honors classes. Her siblings went to Northwestern; she attended the college of her mother's choice, the University of New Mexico in Albuquerque. At least it was far away.

The second time she ever had sex, Marshall got pregnant. "I got nailed," she says. "Thank you. A one in a million chance. What are you going to do? You make your bed, you sleep in it." She quit school after three years and married the father, a football player named Michael Henry; to support them, she found a job as a secretary, and later taught tap dancing. "I didn't know dick. I was in New Mexico. I got fat. When my water broke, I'm sitting on the toilet. 'Where's the book? What do we do?' I worked, and he went to college, and [the baby's] great-grandmother took care of her. When [the baby] got sick, we could call his parents. 'Oh, we'll come get her because you have to get up for work and you have to get up for school,' [they'd say]. So they'd take her and we'd go 'Yeah! You want to play?' We were too young."

The marriage broke up two years later. "My mother and his mother got custody. They made us both out to be so inept. We never went to court, so they could have made it all up because my mother was good at making things up," Marshall says, recalling how her parents and in-laws took control of the situation, and of her child, who for a while went back and forth between her parents. "It could have been a lie. [Michael] came over and we cried. I gave him half the pots and pans. There's no alimony. There's no child support. I took it for granted [that the parents would get custody]." She assumed that was right because, she says, she believed, "I'm no good. He's no good. So we're fucked."

In 1967, Marshall packed her belongings in a suitcase and headed to Los Angeles to join her older brother, Garry, who was a writer on *The Dick Van Dyke Show*. She didn't know him well. She'd been only nine when he went off to college, but at least she wasn't going home to her parents'.

Marshall didn't know what she wanted to do with herself. After her brother henpecked her into deciding on something, she admitted that she had enjoyed performing as Ado Annie in an Albuquerque production of *Oklahoma!* Garry suggested acting classes, and ultimately Marshall began to audition. For someone so insecure about how she looked, trying to make it as an actress was often an exercise in ego decimation.

One of the first jobs she landed was for Head & Shoulders shampoo. She was hired to play the girl with stringy, dandruff-infested hair. Far-rah Fawcett played the girl with thick, bouncy hair. As the director was lighting the set, Fawcett's stand-in wore a sign that said PRETTY GIRL. Marshall's wore a placard that said HOMELY GIRL. When Fawcett saw this, she ran over, crossed out HOMELY with a pen, and replaced it with PLAIN.

It was a nice gesture, but Marshall still came home that night, as she did many others, crying. Her brother tried to help, hiring her for bit parts in forgettable movies like *How Sweet It Is!* Marshall's brother ultimately hired her to play Jack Klugman's hangdog secretary on *The Odd Couple*, a part that kept her going for four years, although Paramount took advantage of her relationship to the producer. When all the supporting players got hundred-dollar-a-week raises, Marshall was passed over.

In the meantime, however, her personal life had also turned around. At Barney's Beanery she had met Rob Reiner, son of the comedian Carl Reiner. He was abrasive and ambitious and determined to best his father. They both auditioned for *All in the Family*, but only Reiner was cast; he went on to great success as Meathead, Archie Bunker's son-in-law. During the show's hiatus in 1971, the couple married. Marshall, who was twenty-seven, vowed not to make Reiner, twenty-three, nervous. In the years since she'd left New Mexico, Marshall's daughter had moved in with her ex-husband, who had remarried. "She'd come out and go back and forth, but it's hard when they're little. A wall goes up. There's a guilt factor," says Marshall, who now brought her daughter to live with her and her new husband in their Encino home. Tracy took Reiner's name.

Their household fast evolved into the hangout for the young comedy crowd, a haven for a group of gifted but anxiety-ridden young male talents like James Brooks, Albert Brooks, Richard Dreyfuss, and Charles Grodin. Marshall served as den mother: "I kept quiet. I knew how to keep quiet. They were bouncing off each other. It could be very intimidating. I learned. I laughed. It was just like this salon. We were the only ones married. We had a stability. They would come over. They were like our children. We fed them. They entertained us, and they went home, or they stayed. I'd go to sleep and they still hung."

The only other women were occasional girlfriends. "Louise Lasser—they all jumped up and performed for her because she was Woody [Allen]'s ex. She once said, 'I think there's a definite and strong correlation between a man's sexuality and his sense of humor.' Well, you never saw guys jump up and perform." Marshall laughs. "The girls weren't encouraged to talk. I knew how to do needlepoint. Anything to keep my hands from my throat. Rug hooking. I would roll the grass. I listened. I could say a line here or there from the kitchen. I didn't make the stuff, but I was a good cleaner-upper.

"I was very happy," she says. "Rob was the kind of guy who was going to work all his life. He was a driven man. I felt very secure that he would work so I was cool. At times I felt bad because everyone was working all the time so there was no one to play with. I acted like a kid. I still do. I wanted someone to play with. He would go off to work, and by the time he came home, there were fifty people in the house."

"This was a time when all her strengths and all her intelligence had no practical utilizations in the world," Brooks once reminisced. "She was sort of a housewife, and it was great for all of us who knew her then because all her marvelous talents were available for your life. Any problem you had, you got this great force of energy from her. I enjoyed it while I had it, but I saw it slipping away, because she had to go out and be a whole person."

There were times when Marshall was so depressed she'd spend all day in bed, rise at night, and pretend she had been up all day. She went back into therapy, which she had tried when she first came to L.A. For thirty dollars a day, she worked as part of a team of performers—among them Steve Martin and Harry Shearer—who were writing sketches for a Zoetrope film about the bicentennial.

Her brother called one day while Marshall was working with fellow actress Cindy Williams on a skit about inventors. For an episode of *Happy Days*, Garry Marshall had written in a pair of fast girls who go on dates with Richie and Fonzie. Running behind on casting, Garry asked Penny and Cindy to help out, and play the tough talkers with kerchiefs and hickies on their necks: Laverne and Shirley. The casting had an inside joke: Williams had played Ron Howard's girlfriend in *American Graffiti*. The pair were a hit with the studio audience.

The next season Garry spun them off into their own series, which debuted at number one. "We went from being easy girls on *Happy Days* to virgins on *Laverne & Shirley*." Marshall laughs. The critics were merciless. *Time* magazine derided the show's sheer "witlessness" and declared that Marshall had "chosen not to characterize her role but to do an imitation of the inimitable Judy Holliday." Still, when the women made their first public appearance, at the Macy's Thanksgiving Day Parade, they were mobbed. "We were blue-collar heroes. In New York, I'm the safest person in the world."

Laverne & Shirley ran for eight years. It was a wildly dysfunctional family affair, with a bevy of malcontents and two battling sisters at its center. Williams's and Marshall's agents immediately took to fighting

over billing (settling eventually for "equal staggered billing") and then
over money (settling for a "most-favored-nation" clause, meaning what
one got the other did). The press soon filled with accounts of the actresses fighting over the number of their respective lines, and throwing
scripts against the wall if one part was bigger than the other. There
were days, indeed entire weeks, when the pair didn't speak, except in
character.

The show's cabal of Marshalls—which included Penny's father and
her sister—threatened Williams. "Cindy felt she was being slighted because Penny was my sister, and in a sense I overcompensated. I was so
attentive to Cindy's needs that Penny started thinking about how Cindy
was getting all the attention, and then Penny started to get weird and
nervous," recalls Garry Marshall. He also hypothesizes that despite the
popularity of their show, the two were embarrassed among their high-
powered friends by the show's lowbrow quotient and its dependence on
broad physical comedy. Indeed, John Belushi regularly referred to her
show as "crap." Marshall felt that her male friends were irritated by the
fact that she couldn't be there for them in the way she used to be. They
hated it when she was the one who whined about overwork.

Success also wreaked havoc with Marshall's marriage. The moment
Laverne & Shirley debuted, it knocked *All in the Family* out of first place
in the ratings, which, she says, "didn't go well at home. I was apologizing. Then I got embarrassed instead of having a sense of pride. It got to
where I knew it would cause trouble." Reiner did encourage her, says
Marshall, but "it's hard for any of us. I didn't want to make more money
than he did because I knew it would be a problem. So I negotiated lower
and he said, 'What, are you crazy?' Five years after we broke up, he did
an interview with *Playboy* saying, 'Penny said it would cause problems,
and I said, "No," but she was right.' "

They were both working, and the tension between them worsened
when Reiner quit *All in the Family*. Says Marshall of Reiner, "He should
have known better because he grew up in the business. How fleeting it
is. One minute one person's hot, the next minute, the other person. It's
a seesaw. We were younger. It was very easy to separate," she says, with
what sounds like a twinge of regret. "I'd probably feel secure if I knew
he'd be pushing and working all these years and then I wouldn't have
to worry at my age: 'I have to work still?' "

They split up after ten years. Marshall moved from rented house to
rented house because, she recalls, "I didn't know how to spend money

on myself." When she finally bought her current house, she stockpiled it with friends and family, who came and stayed. Her daughter lived in the bottom half. Jim Belushi stayed for two years, Joe Pesci for three. "I was afraid to be alone," she recalls. "I'd come home after six months and [Joe]'d go, 'The thing's broken.' I'd go, 'What, your finger's broken? You can't call someone to fix it?' Him and [Jon] Lovitz were here at the same time." She told all the boarders that their girlfriends weren't welcome to stay over because she didn't want to talk to them in the morning.

Marshall found herself deep in the Hollywood party scene (although she tried in vain to curb the excessive drug use of someone like John Belushi, who once spilled so much cocaine all over himself and her house that she told him to take a shower). As Steven Spielberg quipped, "If Penny could wring out all the tears cried on her shoulder, she'd flood Encino." She dated ferociously, and promiscuously. She was squired around Hollywood by the actor David Dukes and later went out with the singer Art Garfunkel for five years. They rode motorcycles through Europe; Garfunkel complained when she sang the theme from *The Sound of Music* as they toured the Alps.

Marshall had met Garfunkel through her friend Carrie Fisher. The two women had bonded over, among other things, their status as slightly embarrassing cultural icons. Every fall they gave a joint birthday party, which evolved into one of Hollywood's prime social events, a mecca for the famous. It was their consecration as hip social doyennes, the coolest girls in town. As Albert Brooks once wisecracked, "If a bomb dropped on this party, Anson Williams would have a career." (Williams played Ron Howard's hapless sidekick on *Happy Days*.)

Marshall wasn't keen on going back to work, especially to the kind of "swinging from chandelier" parts that were offered to her. She was happier just hanging out with Garfunkel. "I wanted to rest, and I was in love, so that cures a multitude of problems," she says, adding, "Everyone kept saying, 'Whatever you want to do.' " The world was her putative oyster, if she could only make up her mind. "Like I'm going to say, 'I know I want to be a judge.' I don't know what the fuck I want to do!" recalls Marshall. "Show me something! When they give you 'whatever you want,' you get very scared. I do. Other people might love it. I go and hide. 'Whatever you want' is not what I want to hear."

"She always loved men. She always loved men," says Jim Brooks about Marshall. "She's a groupie at heart. That's her femininity."

It's an assessment that Marshall agrees with. Her latest passion has been the Chicago Bulls, and during Michael Jordan's last year she spent much time simply following the Bulls from game to game. "It was great! I'm looking up to these guys. I'm cheering. I'm very good. I go to every game. I'm in Chicago. I'm in Utah. I went back to the locker room when they were in Utah. MJ [Michael Jordan] is being cool. He says, 'I hear they booed you out there, but you handled it great, Penny.' The man's in a time-out and he's aware of what's going on.

"I love that shit," she says enthusiastically. "I love being around people doing their best. I'm happy to be out there. That's why this part of directing, when they think you have the power and you don't—and I don't know who to look up to except I have to look to myself—I find it difficult to do."

It's a conundrum for Marshall, who once aptly described herself this way: "I think I have a massive insecurity complex combined with a very huge ego. If I could ever just trust my instincts, which I'm told are good, I'd be all right. But I never say, 'Do it this way because I want it this way.' I just mumble and make people keep asking me my opinion until they get it out of me."

"She's a brilliant woman, but maybe you don't want to *scare* people, because some people can be *afraid* of a brilliant woman," Robin Williams once explained. "It's a great *smoke screen*! That way she *gets things done*, and you don't even know they've been done!"

Marshall doesn't describe directing as something she sought out for herself. She insists it's been a series of serendipitous occurrences, "little adventures that I was having. I never volunteered. I never said, 'I got to make it,' and knocked on people's doors. Someone would come ask me to do something."

Laverne & Shirley had proved fertile training ground. Although the show became well known for its Lucy-like pratfalls, it hadn't started out that way. "It became so because we didn't like certain scenes. Instead of putting on the party hats, which was the signal we didn't like the scene, we put physical stuff in," says Marshall, who excelled at devising impromptu bits of business. "Even in my movies, if I don't like the dialogue, I'll say, 'Let's keep the people moving at all times, doing all sorts of stuff, so you never hear the dialogue.'"

Unlike on *Happy Days*, there was no regular director on *Laverne & Shirley*, and many cast members tried their hand at directing. For Marshall, it came at the behest of David Lander and Michael McKean, who played Lenny and Squiggy. " 'You're the only one who comes out and watches our scenes when you're not in them,' they said. I did. I was always watching," says Marshall, who says her first foray behind the camera "wasn't like 'Oooooooh, this is something.' It felt right. I could improvise."

Marshall was a comedy logician, a stickler for ensuring that every joke made sense, that the humor, although broad, wasn't sloppy. "She used to cut film in her head while she was acting," adds Jack Winters, one of the sitcom's directors. "When I directed, I'd go, 'Oh God, we've got twelve new pages out of twenty-six and they'll never learn it!' And Penny was out there, and not only had she learned her lines, and was doing something new to get a laugh, but she was already going, 'Okay, we've got C camera on this, so we can cut that and go to close-up and then cut to the master.' " Marshall used to memorize her lines according to whatever staging she'd devised. She directed two episodes of *Laverne & Shirley* and a pilot called *Working Stiffs*, starring Michael Keaton and Jim Belushi.

Unlike other women trying to break into directing, Marshall had high-powered encouragement, from her brother, from Jim Brooks, from Steven Spielberg, who had cast her in a small part in *1941*, where she spent a lot of time watching the director of photography, William Fraker, and learning how the Luma crane worked. Spielberg saw how she had nurtured the TV aristocrats at the Reiner-Marshall salon. She recalls, "He'd see me talking to all these guys, listening. He said, 'Directing is baby-sitting. You do it for free. Why don't you get paid for it?' " He noted her famed facility at jigsaw puzzles and said, "That's editing."

There was also her agent, Mike Ovitz. Marshall had been one of CAA's first clients. "Mike Ovitz always said I should direct because Steven Spielberg told him I should direct," says Marshall. And she was a valuable client, able to launch a TV series with a flick of her wrist should she choose to do so. Some of Marshall's old TV compatriots, such as Ron Howard of *Happy Days*, had started directing, as had her ex-husband Rob Reiner. It wasn't surprising that someone who had always wanted to play baseball with the boys would try their new game.

Her first offers came from those who were perhaps hoping to cash in on her strong relationships to talent. Paramount, which had owned

Laverne & Shirley, gave her *The Joy of Sex* to direct, in the hope of turning it into an *Airplane*-like parody. The studio was pressuring Marshall's friend John Belushi to star, although he was nervous about the material and wasn't sure he wanted Marshall, a close friend, to direct. Still, Marshall held a reading at her house, with friends such as Carol Kane and Ed Begley voicing the parts and Steven Spielberg taking pictures.

Perhaps not wanting to tread on their friendship, Marshall didn't confront Belushi directly. The night before Belushi was to meet with Paramount to decide on hiring Marshall, he died from a heroin overdose. It was a stunning blow for Marshall. The one time he'd brought heroin to her house, she'd grabbed it and flushed it down the toilet. "I always had thought if I had approached John, and we had been talking that night, he wouldn't have died. Everyone feels their self-importance in their bizarre way when somebody dies," she says. Her plans to direct fell apart completely when Cindy Williams walked off *Laverne & Shirley* in a fit of pique, and Marshall was forced to finish the season alone.

She next flirted with directing *Peggy Sue Got Married,* which was produced by Ray Stark. Marshall related to the story of a young mother who gets the opportunity to live her teen years again. After a tiff with one of the producers, Marshall was fired. "It was all politics. They never wanted me. They wanted Debra [Winger, a close friend]. Debra wanted me, so in order to get Debra, they hired me, and once they had Debra, they let go of me," says Marshall. "Then they said it was too big a movie for a first-time director and did I want to direct *Annie,* the musical? I turned them down. It's 'too big a movie.' "

Still, the blow was devastating. "I ran away," says Marshall, to New York, where Garfunkel lived and where she had landed a role in an Off Broadway play, *Eden Court.* She bought an apartment in New York and came home to get winter clothes. Then she got a call from Lawrence Gordon, head of production at Fox. Gordon knew Marshall from the days when they all had offices at Paramount, and he asked if she was interested in directing a movie called *Jumpin' Jack Flash.* It had started shooting ten days earlier.

"This thing that directors have power is a crock of shit," says Marshall. "Like Steven [Spielberg] said, *Baby-sit.* You'll make the movie in editing, and you got to compromise every day of your life. That's one of the things my brother always said, I'm a good adapter. I can talk to any crowd. I also knew how to be quiet and learn and be whoever they thought I was supposed to be. It's a compromise. The thing you need to keep is perspective. I think that's why they thought I could direct on *Laverne & Shirley.* I just didn't worry about my part. I worried about the whole show."

Jumpin' Jack Flash was a troubled production that needed a lot of compromise. In a part originally conceived for Shelley Long, Whoopi Goldberg starred as a young computer programmer ensnared in international espionage. Unfortunately, the script was a disaster. The studio hated the footage shot by the director Howard Zieff, and Zieff and Goldberg hated each other.

One person whom Gordon and his cohort Joel Silver thought could manage Goldberg was Marshall, who knew the new comedy star through both Mike Nichols, who had directed Goldberg's Broadway show, and Paul Simon. Gordon and producer Joel Silver had seen them eating dinner together. "[Whoopi and I] hung out, and I think the producers saw. 'Oh look, they're talking to each other. They must be friends. Let's make her do it.' And I swear to God, I think that's what happened."

To remove a director requires the utmost finesse. Silver also knew that Marshall had been flirting with switching agencies to ICM, going so far as to give CAA official notice—added impetus for the agency to get her a job, even at the expense of another of their clients, Zieff.

Gordon and Silver presented their plan to the studio chairman, Barry Diller: Shut down the movie for a few days, relocate everyone to L.A., hire Marshall. Diller signed off, with the provisions that Goldberg agree and that it not cost the studio any more money. In other words, that they finish the entire movie in what remained of the original schedule. Ovitz interceded with Goldberg's manager to convince them to accept Marshall, and Gordon called Marshall with the offer.

She wavered. Start shooting a movie in three days? "I called my brother and I called Jim Brooks, and I said, 'What should I do?' " recalls Marshall. "And my brother said, They pay you to learn in this business, which is one of the great phenomenons. And Jim felt, you've got nothing to lose. If it gets finished and on its feet, then you're the Lone Ranger. If it doesn't do well, then it's not your fault. So I figured, what the hell, let me try it. I didn't know what preproduction was, so I thought I was just cutting a class."

On the morning of the third day, Silver arrived looking for Marshall. He heard that she was in the makeup trailer. He assumed she must have been talking to Goldberg. "I go over there, and she is there getting made up," says Silver. "I said, 'What are you doing?' She said, 'I felt really that I needed to get made up.' I said, 'Penny, you're the director of the movie.' She said, 'I can still look good. I just need to feel better.' I said, 'Penny, get the fuck out of here and get to the set.' She said, 'When I'm finished being made up then I'll go to the set.' "

Despite their social acquaintance, Goldberg was distinctly unhappy to see Marshall on the set. "By the time the movie was going, she hated her," says Silver. " 'She is a television actress. What does she know about comedy?' She was horrible to her during the whole course of the movie."

"I think Whoopi was so shocked," says Marshall. "It's an uncomfortable situation. The producer, the director, and the camera guy were gone and here I am.

"She was stuck. She wasn't mean, per se. She was confused. She was upset. And then *The Color Purple* opens and everyone's calling her. Do you think she wants to get up at five in the morning? She's flavor of the month. She wasn't mad at me. She was mad at her situation. Everyone goes through their freshman year of fame, and there's no stopping them. Everyone gets crazy. Everybody wants you. They're blowing smoke up your ass like you know something, and you start to behave in a certain way that's stupid, but you don't know what else to do. You don't know who to trust. I was probably an asshole too [when it happened to me]. She was stuck on this movie that wouldn't end because they kept changing the schedule, changing the dialogue, changing the directors, changing everything. It was frustrating to her. It was frustrating to me."

If there was one thing Marshall felt confident about, it was performance, particularly comedy, but it was difficult to get Goldberg to listen to her ideas. "She didn't want to do this. She didn't want to do that. She wasn't willing to be collaborative," recalls Silver.

Marshall tried to mediate with her, by changing the bit or by attempting to goad Goldberg into what she wanted by turning to the crew and saying, "What do you think?" "I'd try to lighten it up. 'We're taking a vote, Whoopi. Okay, how many think that's good? How many don't? There you go. We voted. *Democracy*.' Some days she was great, fantastic, terrific. Some days she'd say, 'I don't feel so good,' and I'd say, 'The words are right there on the monitor.' She was at the fucking computer forever, and all the lines were written there. Some days, she was testy." Polly Platt ran into Marshall at the Gracie Christmas party and the new director seemed in muted despair.

If Goldberg was recalcitrant, Silver could be famously bossy, often standing directly behind Marshall's director's chair barking out orders and curbing her desire for more coverage or more takes, which couldn't be done on the schedule. "Penny was and all the way to this day continues to be very methodical, almost to the point of insanity," says Silver. "She is very thorough, and I guess she approaches this thing from an actor's point of view."

At night Marshall worked with cinematographer Matt Leonetti to block out the next day, often forcing him to act the scene because that was how she could figure out the staging. "Then he'd draw pictures and little *x*'s which way you could come [with the camera]." She surrounded herself with friends in the supporting roles, comedians like Jon Lovitz, Phil Hartman, and Carol Kane, who could flesh out the dialogue with funny business and gags. Over the weekend, Marshall huddled with Silver and the studio executives to cut and paste a new version of the script from all the existing drafts.

"I was on the set of *Jumpin' Jack Flash*, and it was so clear that she was just making a picture out of mayhem, the mayhem that she inherited with every problem you could have, and to me there was no mistaking her ability," says Jim Brooks. "She just sucked it up and did it. It was bizarre—rewriting as she was shooting. A guy following her around pitching jokes to her. Joel Silver wanting to have all those explosions taking place that she didn't want but she had to live with, because he was the producer. Somehow she did it."

The end result was a mediocrity, and a box-office fizzle, but at least it was a real movie; it showed that Marshall could competently tell a story. "There are things in it that aren't tasteful that aren't mine and things that are mine that are awkward," she later remarked. "But I think Whoopi's more likable in it than in her next five movies." Still, Marshall knew that there were problems and that she'd "better do something fast."

Marshall's unease was not hers alone. Most of her female counterparts knew that they weren't going to get a lot of chances, that failure, even simple mediocrity, was a privilege afforded only men. As Marshall struggled on *Jumpin' Jack Flash*, Elaine May was in the midst of creating one of the most famed box-office bombs of the decade, a $50 million fiasco called *Ishtar.*

Despite the notoriety of *Mikey and Nicky,* May had revived her career by winning an Oscar for cowriting *Heaven Can Wait.* She had gone on to polish such high-profile films as *Reds* and *Tootsie,* refusing to put her name on any project she didn't initiate but enjoying an increasingly burnished reputation as a script doctor. Finally, her friend and *Heaven Can Wait* cohort Warren Beatty convinced Columbia to put up the money to finance May's return to directing.

Ishtar is a comedy about a hapless song-and-dance team who play a gig in Morocco, find themselves ensnarled in international intrigue, and wind up in May's favorite existential plight—betraying each other yet still bonded. The conceit was to have two of the biggest stars in the world—Beatty and Dustin Hoffman—play the feckless losers. The production was vastly larger and logistically more complicated than anything May had previously attempted, and almost immediately it went awry.

One of May's first demands was for sand dunes, not just any dunes but dunes in Africa near a luxury hotel, where cast and crew could stay and not have to trek several hours to location. She sent her production designer, Paul Sylbert, on a multiweek location scout to find the appropriate terrain, which he did in the Moroccan Sahara. Yet once she arrived and took a look, she "revealed she really thought of the desert like Brighton Beach, and there were no dunes in her mind. She couldn't cope with sand dunes," says Sylbert, who hired a crew at union wages to flatten the dunes. They spent ten days scraping away all the piles of sand in a square-mile radius in order to give May her flat desert.

"The story of *Ishtar* is that Elaine reduced us all to ineffectuality. [Vittorio] Storaro [the Academy Award–winning cinematographer], myself, Beatty, who is a good director. We were all nullified by her fears. People who are frightened get really defensive, so nobody could help her at a certain point. Beatty was so angry. His control is magnificent. He knew if he blew up it would all stop and nothing would happen, so he backed off," says Sylbert.

While May's free fall was the most spectacular, many of the other women directors were struggling too. Amy Heckerling hated being pigeonholed as a female director. "Give me a break with this woman stuff," she recalls thinking. "I didn't want to be like a girl, doing a girl movie. So I kind of rebounded and did a very boy movie, which was probably, in retrospect, a very big mistake." Indeed, after *Fast Times at Ridgemont High*, she took two studio assignments, both horrendous experiences with producers battling for control; at least the second one, *National Lampoon's European Vacation* (starring Chevy Chase), had performed okay. Martha Coolidge also took lowbrow studio assignments, which flopped, while Kathryn Bigelow, a Columbia Film School grad with a bravura visual style, had yet to make a film that connected to audiences.

The most successful female directors were Susan Seidelman, who garnered a commercial hit and nice reviews for the amusing comedy *Desperately Seeking Susan*, a feat that she could never repeat, and Randa Haines, a former script supervisor who had directed a screen version of the play *Children of a Lesser God.* The movie was nominated for five Oscars, including Best Picture, although pointedly not Best Director. Yet Haines had barely survived its making. Almost everyone on the set seemed to hate her, including a producer who fomented disrespect for her among the crew, and a star, William Hurt, who was contemptuous, and with whom she engaged in heated screaming battles. No one would eat lunch with Haines save the cinematographer. As she explained afterward, "You win the war, but you saw people die. Some part of you died when you were out there fighting." She didn't direct again for five years.

Fortunately, Marshall, like May, had a powerful benefactor and friend. During the postproduction of *Jumpin' Jack Flash*, Jim Brooks had strolled into her office and slapped a script down on her desk, announcing, "This is your next movie." She was the last in a very long line of directors (among them Spielberg and Nichols) he had tried to entice to direct the movie. The script was *Big.*

Written by Gary Ross and Anne Spielberg, *Big* is a fable about a twelve-year-old boy who wishes he were "big" and wakes up the next morning to find himself in the body of a thirty-five-year-old. He goes to New York, where he lands a job in a toy company, ultimately impressing the owner with his insight into what toys are fun and winning the hand of a jaded career woman (Elizabeth Perkins), who is moved by his childlike innocence.

"I thought, Well, it reads like an afternoon special," recalls Marshall, but she recognized that "everybody has had the thought, What [am I] going to do when I'm big?" She pointedly did not attach any political significance to what she chose to direct. "I didn't think about [being a] girl doing a boy thing. Those things didn't enter your mind."

She ignored the fact that there were two films with the same premise already going into production and began casting. But she quickly got turned down by her first choice, Tom Hanks, whom she knew from her sitcom days, then Kevin Costner and Dennis Quaid. In an effort to differentiate hers from the other projects, she tried to rethink the part, envisioning her lead as a more macho man, someone like Clint Eastwood or Robert De Niro. Brooks was leery, the studio leerier, but they permitted her to make an offer. De Niro said yes.

This time, Marshall put her preproduction time to good use. She fiddled with the script. Some critics in the frenetic career-obsessed eighties saw the film as a woman's yearning for a less driven, more emotional man, and Marshall encouraged the screenwriters to accentuate her desires and fears: "I got in a scene in which she asks him, 'What do you feel about me,' because girls always want relationships defined."

Marshall spent months working with De Niro, who read with various costars as they auditioned. He practiced his skateboarding in her driveway. De Niro told her to study his films, so she knew what he could and couldn't do, and could refer to past performances in directing him. It was a technique she adopted for all her subsequent movies.

Preproduction started in earnest in New York, but Fox now balked at closing De Niro's deal at the designated price, a standard ploy to get rid of someone a studio doesn't want. Brooks and Marshall agreed to chip in money out of their fees to make the difference, but De Niro refused to take their money, and pulled out. "Once Bobby wanted to do it, then Tom [Hanks] wanted to do it. Bobby gave me believability or credibility," says Marshall. Yet Hanks wouldn't be available for several months, and so the production shut down to wait for him.

Brooks gave Marshall two Tracey Ullman TV shows to direct while she waited. She also shot videotape of David Moscow, the twelve-year-old who played the Hanks character as a boy, performing all of Hanks's scenes, to show the star how a real child responded in those situations. Marshall used the video to "keep Tom down. Keep it real." She wanted the scenes played without self-conscious irony, and sometimes her instructions were alarmingly simple. "There were so many scenes [that were] the same. He was scared for twenty-two scenes. He was confused for twenty-two scenes. He was happy for twenty-two scenes. 'You're sad. You're not as sad as you will be but sadder than you were,' " Marshall says, recalling her directing notes.

Hers was not an economical way of shooting. Unlike Elaine May, who was searching for authenticity in acting, Marshall was accumulating coverage, systematically stockpiling as many options as possible, from as many angles as possible, for when she retreated to the editing room to really make the film. Sometimes she didn't even yell cut, just to see what the actors could come up with if they were forced to improvise. One of the most humorous moments in the film comes when Hanks attends the office Christmas party. Dressed in a spangled white suit fit for Liberace, he ventures into the realm of too many martinis and bad office affairs. He stands by an array of fancy grown-up food, takes a piece of baby corn, and tries to eat it like it's corn on the cob. To achieve that moment, Marshall hauled in a variety of food and shot Hanks chowing down in every childlike way they could think of, eating olives off his fingers, licking cream cheese out of celery. She didn't laugh much, constantly worried about how she was going to cut it all together.

Her method was intensely slow, and the days could turn long and dreary, particularly on occasions, such as one of the first days of shooting, when she couldn't decide if she wanted Elizabeth Perkins to be a blonde or a redhead, and so shot her with one color of hair until 3:00 in the morning, and then redid all her scenes with Perkins sporting different tresses.

The crew often treated her as if she were nuts, and didn't know what she was doing. Nobody thought they were working on a big hit movie. "She was up against a tremendous amount of male chauvinism on that film," Brooks remarks. Marshall spent almost an entire night shooting Hanks and Perkins's first night together, which ends with the pair jumping on a trampoline. "Barry Sonnenfeld [the cinematographer] ridiculed Penny like crazy because she wanted to go across the street and get a shot of them from the outside. And she just wouldn't be deterred. And that's the shot that makes the scene," says Brooks. "It was a different time. You can meet Penny and think that everything is going to be fun, and you would be able to do your act, but she is going to do *her* act. She's a rock. You don't move her. Maybe he didn't get that."

Sonnenfeld ultimately relented at five in the morning when he finally understood what exactly Marshall wanted and why. Marshall had been frustrated and disappointed in him from the first day, because she hated how Sonnenfeld kept trying to stylize the film. "Barry was hard on me because he wanted to make the schedule and wouldn't do coverage," says Marshall. "He didn't like lighting the women. Elizabeth Perkins. He was coming from the Coen brothers, and I had to make it look nice." To make Perkins look glamorous required extraordinary patience, and taping white cards all around her body to prevent unseemly shadows. "To light her properly takes time and he didn't want to waste the time.

"I do know what I want," adds Marshall. "I just don't verbalize it."

"People don't get Penny," says Sonnenfeld, who says he tried to give Marshall what she wanted. After *Big*, he fielded all sorts of calls from studio executives who assumed that Marshall hadn't really directed the movie. "Everyone says Penny can't make up her mind. It's just that Penny knows [you] don't make up your mind until someone makes you, which is in postproduction. She would cover her bases every way she'd be allowed, which, if you can do it, is profoundly secure. To not go, 'Oh, everybody is looking at me. I want to do another take of Tom eating corn but everybody's looking at me.' That's the thing that people don't get. Penny has the self-confidence to keep shooting when everyone is telling her not to."

She was aghast when she saw the first assemblage of the film. The first cut of *Jumpin' Jack Flash* had looked like the movie, but *Big* looked like a horrible, confusing stew of characters and story lines. She couldn't bear her failed expectations. "I went into a depression. My editor said, 'Go home. You're depressing me,' " says Marshall, who later realized that she'd never be able to handle seeing the first cut of her movie. "It got to where I'd take Prozac as soon as I'd yell 'wrap.' I'd start the Prozac so the first assemblage wouldn't put me in the toilet. I could edit on it, but I can't cast and shoot because your feelings are numbed. It takes the bottom end off so you don't cry."

Big debuted in June 1988, with a two-thousand-person party on the Fox lot. The reviews were largely enthusiastic. "Penny Marshall has turned into an adroit director—the first two thirds of *Big* are an utter delight, full of sharp things to say about men, boys, and corporate life," wrote *Newsweek*. While *Big* never occupied the number-one slot in America, it played for weeks and weeks, ultimately racking up $115 million of business. Suddenly Marshall was inundated with scripts.

Success turned out to be great for her ego, not so great for her heart. "Yeah, that sucks the big one," says Marshall, who now lives alone in her expansive hacienda, surrounded by her obsessively collected totems of childhood and ordinary folk. "When you're an actress, they think you're ditsy so they're not afraid. Directors they think are too powerful. What power do I have? I don't have power. I'm trying to keep the movie in my head."

"It's hard to date because you're never free once you start a movie," she adds. "You're totally obsessed with your career. You don't have time. When you come home at night, you have to choose whether you're going to eat, make a phone call, take a bath. You can't do everything. You can't. You have no time."

WHAT PERSON DO YOU KNOW THAT GOT ENOUGH LOVE?

"I was in a rehab," says Carrie Fisher, "and while I was in there Crown Books offered me to write a book of nonfiction based on an interview I had done in *Interview* with twenty questions, which was pretty crazy stuff, given that also I had probably done this interview about the same time as I was ready to go to rehab, which, as I said, could have been at any moment from about age twenty-two to twenty-eight, when I went in."

The 1985 *Interview* interview, conducted by her close friend Paul Slansky, featured Fisher's musings on her favorite bumper sticker (LOVE IS THE LIBERACE MUSEUM) and the difference between New York and L.A. (three hours). The initial book proposal was for a series of essays—à la Fran Lebowitz in Hollywood. The working title was "Money Dearest," and she hired Slansky to edit, then lost interest, because she didn't feel she could comment on L.A., on the industry, with any sort of moral authority. "I felt in it but not of it, but that doesn't mean that I feel like I can take this supercilious stance on the community," she says. She was emotional rather than analytical, still a die-hard romantic about the industry of narcissism.

She found her focus after reading Dorothy Parker's short story "Maybe Just a Little One," about a woman's losing battle with alcohol, and decided a novel about drug addiction could update that nicely. Parker seems to hover over Fisher's imagination, as both the woman she wishes to be and the one she fears she may become.

At least she knew how to start the book. " 'Maybe I shouldn't have given the guy who pumped my stomach my phone number, but what the hell, he'd probably never call me,' " she says, quoting one of the first salvos of an incisive, ironic, Holden Caulfield–like rant about trying to survive as a woman in Hollywood. "I knew that was funny. And I know anything that you're not supposed to say (particularly if it relates to you), I'll always say. I'm a product of this sort of public life. I was photographed when I was three hours old. I was sort of a prop in a way. And what I had learned to do from the first book was to perfect this material in public."

It's been more than ten years since *Postcards from the Edge* spent fifteen weeks at the top of the national bestseller charts and Fisher transmuted herself from *Star Wars'* Princess Leia to Hollywood chronicler, screenwriter, and pricey script doctor, called in to punch up relationships and girl-speak as films hurtle toward production. Her books, comedies that delve into the whirlpool of heartbreak and romantic anhedonia, have generally tackled her breakups: with drugs (in *Postcards from the Edge*), with her first husband, the singer Paul Simon (*Surrender the Pink*), and with the CAA agent Bryan Lourd (*Delusions of Grandma*). She plumbs the eternal question of whether unconditional love can exist in a culture of self-interest.

On this weeknight Fisher is nursing a soda, dressed in shapeless earth-colored clothes, her hair short and pixielike, her face knowing way too much. One of the first things she says by way of introduction is "Yes, I'm fat," pointing out what a viewer might think but never say, ergo dispelling any backstage whispers concerning her loss of de rigueur Hollywood svelteness. She seems exhausted, cosmically so, her speech slowed. Her patter has been described in countless interviews as turbopitched, comedic spew, doomed to be recounted by would-be Boswells in capital letters, with heavy emphasis on irony. Yet now, while the wit continues unabated, the fizz is absent, almost as if a forty-five record is being played at thirty-three. She conducts at least one interview from her bed under a blue ceiling painted with gold stars.

Her toddler, Billie, has gone to spend the night with her father, Lourd, and his boyfriend. That breakup was bitter, chronicled in the gossip columns as a kind of nineties-style replay of Fisher's parents' split when her father ran off with Elizabeth Taylor, who had been a family friend. By way of reconciliation, Fisher has pointedly invited her former husband's new partner to her daughter's birthday jaunt to Disneyland.

In a gesture to reclaim one of the bitterest memories of her youth, Fisher is going the next day to Elizabeth Taylor's Fourth of July party. "I did this thing for amfAR where I was the cochair. And on the day of it I got some flowers from Elizabeth Taylor, and I thought, It's just too funny," recounts Fisher. "So when I got up to make my speech that night I said, 'You know, before I say anything, I want to say that I got flowers from Elizabeth Taylor today, and I cleared everybody out of my room to read the note in anticipation of calling my therapist knowing that it was the long-awaited apology for stealing my father thirty-seven years ago. But, in fact, it was just a note to commemorate my work of this evening. I could read an apology between the lines if I wanted to.'

"So she heard about it. She wasn't there. But I would have done it if she was there. And she thought it was funny. So she has invited me to her Fourth of July party, and I'm fucking going because I smell closure." Closure, and an opportunity to permanently remind Taylor of her presence, a self-anointed defense against verbal gibes Taylor has purportedly made about Fisher's mother, Debbie Reynolds. Fisher will be attending the party with Sharon Stone, who can't help but draw attention to herself. "If you lived in a small town and this stuff had happened, you would cross the street. But I'm not real interested in crossing the street. So hooray for Hollywood."

"Cora had adapted herself to her mother's brand of kooky, cockeyed optimism by always fearing the worst, looking over her shoulder." So Fisher described her literary alter ego in *Delusions of Grandma*. "Her voice had acquired its sharp tone early—it was designed to wrest people from dreams, to train their eyes on how it was and not how it was going to be when they got through with it. In counterpoint to her mother's buoyant optimism, she was cautious, ambivalent, pessimistic. She wandered through her mother's lifelong dream with dread."

Fisher debuted in public in a spread in *Life* magazine, an angry two-year-old bundle in her mother's arms, a footnote in a story about the breakup of America's sweethearts, Debbie Reynolds and Eddie Fisher, after which she never saw her father much. She was fierce and introverted as a child. "Lucille Ball used to come over and say, 'Why is Carrie mad at me?' " she's quipped. Her mother said her first word was *hi*, her second, *why*.

"I worshiped my mother because she was as much in a way Debbie Reynolds to me as she was for everybody else. She was beautiful. And she was loving and I felt for her because I knew stuff was difficult for her. But it was, yeah, difficult to feel . . . really like . . . " She pauses and closes down the self-pity. "Let's put it this way, it don't matter. My mother had to work. She wasn't getting any alimony from my father. So I was sort of lonely. My father was gone before I was conscious. And I had known that there was someone there that I cared about that I had lost, so I was heartbroken." Again she skirts away from wallowing. "What person do you know that got enough love?"

Fisher's mother would often arrive home from the studio with body makeup, wigs, furs, the works. One of her earliest memories consists of putting on her mother's wig, looking at herself in the mirror, and bursting into tears, because Mom was so beautiful and she was so ugly.

"I decided so early that I wasn't good-looking, but you lead with your strength. And unfortunately my strength is verbal," says Fisher. "I'm sort of competitive that way. I think that comes from Mom. Not that competitive is a bad thing. It will get me through work, but it won't get you through relationships."

When Fisher was thirteen her mother put her in her nightclub act. While Reynolds paraded around in gold lamé, Carrie wore antique lace and sang a song from the musical *Purlie* and "Bridge over Troubled Water." "I did what I needed to do to be with my mother," she says, "but I really killed myself over it. I was a complete perfectionist, so if I hit a note that wasn't perfect I would go berserk," recalls Fisher, who'd often vomit before performing. "It wasn't something I could do. Plus, I was listening to music I wasn't singing, so it didn't jive." She was listening to pop music and singing Judy Garland. She says Paul Simon said to her once, " 'You have an old Broadway voice,' and a week later I said to him, 'But it's a good old Broadway voice.' My big rebellion in my family is not that I've done drugs or anything like that, it's that I had refused to sing."

Her relationship with Reynolds was complicated and entwined. When Carrie was four, Reynolds married Harry Karl, a shoe magnate, compulsive womanizer, and gambler who went broke and ultimately brought his wife to financial ruin. "As soon as I was old enough, which was when I was an adolescent, she started to tell me all the troubles," says Fisher. "I tried to take on her pain as a means of taking care of her. And I knew she needed me as a sort of pal. So I knew things were shit, and my brother was protected and I was the strong one. Well, it was sort of too late for me to say after a certain amount of information, Wait a minute, I'm not the strong one. I was very upset when my mother sort of broke down when I was about fourteen. I didn't have anybody else. So I needed for her to be okay."

Fisher went into therapy, a psychological odyssey that has lasted over twenty-five years. "I started writing when my mother was missing for a little while. She was in such trouble," says Fisher. She mostly wrote poems and assiduously kept a journal. A few years later she would write comic prose poems, from which she'd extract certain lines and make other poems. Her friend Joan Hackett helped her get one of them published in *Interview*. "I was very ashamed of saying that that's what I wanted to do, because I was not in a family that was geared towards that," says Fisher. "It's just sort of embarrassing. I was a reader, and who gives a shit, because like seventy-five actresses come out and say they're voracious readers, and you want to shoot yourself." She quit high school in eleventh grade to join the chorus of her mother's show *Irene.*

At age seventeen Fisher started acting. Through her mother's friend George Perth, she met Warren Beatty, who cast her in *Shampoo* without even bothering to have her read. The part uncannily reflected Carrie, a neglected but ironic Beverly Hills teen, dressed in tennis whites, anger bubbling underneath the placid surface of wealth and puppy fat. It has become apocryphal legend that her first line on screen was "Wanna fuck?" uttered to Beatty, although in truth that was one of her later epithets, which followed "You're here to see my mother" and an in-your-face interrogation, "Are you queer? . . . You can tell me. Don't be afraid."

"I liked being around sets. I didn't necessarily like being an actress. I didn't like the way I looked and so forth," recalls Fisher. "Going into acting wasn't based on a lot of ambition. I went into the family business, how hard was that? But who wouldn't have gone along with it? You met great people. You traveled a lot. You make a lot of money." Fisher was always wary of celebrity as a mirage constantly threatening to disintegrate. "I had watched my parents' career on the slide when I got old enough to see what was happening. So I could never fully enjoy because I could see what it had done and was doing to me."

She applied to the Central School of Speech and Drama in London but had decided not to go, until she and her mother got into a fight that lasted almost a week, the first fight of their lives. It ended with Fisher on a plane to London and a rift that lasted several years. For a year Fisher savored normalcy.

At nineteen she was cast in *Star Wars*. "So then I was Princess Leia, and then I was typecast. Well, how do you get typecast as that? How many other roles are there to do that?" she quips.

Fisher began contemplating screenwriting by watching Harrison Ford adjust and rewrite his dialogue. George Lucas's script was fine on the page but impossible for an actor to make real, particularly "a female one," says Fisher. "I started to watch Harrison, then I would want to do that. And Mark [Hamill] would get very upset and said, 'You know the novelization of this stuff isn't going to work because certain people are rewriting the dialogue.' I did a great one, one time and they didn't let me do it."

By the time she was twenty-one, Fisher was the "It" girl for everyone who was cool and trendy. She ran with the *Saturday Night Live* crowd, dated Dan Aykroyd. She met Paul Simon at the L.A. Film Critics Awards in 1978. "I was there for *Star Wars*, and he was there to pick up, I think, a writing award for Woody Allen and *Annie Hall*. He was there with his girlfriend, Shelley Duvall, and I was there with Mark [Hamill] and Gary Kurtz and all that.

"And then we all went to dinner at [Richard] Dreyfuss's hotel, and [Paul] and I got into a fight. Not a bad fight, but I told him that I was going to go to Sarah Lawrence, which I had been accepted into. He said, 'You won't do well. You've got a show business family.' And he was right, but I was like 'Well, fuck you.' I was inspired by 'Fuck you.'

"And so we met and then we remet at a party after *Saturday Night Live*, where everybody always met, at Studio 54. I was very popular then. I was the new girl in town, though I didn't know it. I was very fast and very verbal and cute. I'd always been a huge fan of his. I had sung 'Bridge over Troubled Water.' And he had done the score to *Shampoo*. I think we danced together or something. I guess he asked me out on a date. Because other people were sort of after me too there was this push. And he seemed the least interested. He's not enthusiastic in terms of his demeanor. So at some level I obviously was interested in him. Another level I thought, Well, he's not going to push for this because I'm twenty-one years old. He had broken up with Shelley by then. I don't know who he was going out with.

"I was going to Japan to promote *Star Wars*. He was going to Greece. And I was so stupid geographically. You might find this hard to believe, with all of my education. And he said, 'Why don't we link up in Greece?'

And I said, 'Okay.' And I got on a plane in Japan, and I said to the stewardess, 'How long is it to get to Greece?' And she said, 'Twenty-three hours.' And I got off the plane and I said to him, 'Link up?'

"Buck [Henry] had said to me, 'If you go on this trip, you are in a relationship. *A relationship.*' It was off and on for a really long time.

"When I got with Paul, I apprenticed myself to something in him that I understood, a way of using words that there was a rhythm in. Given that I had refused to sing, and that I had an almost instinctive percussive relationship to how the words were used rhythmically, I could do a certain kind of prose. But it had to be this particular way. I was really nuts about it, the same way that I was nuts about 'you can't sing the note wrong.' But it makes it unpleasant a little bit. Not with writing, though, it's very pleasurable with writing, because you have more control," says Fisher.

In her twenties Fisher was diagnosed with a form of bipolar disorder. "I didn't like the diagnosis at all. I was told when I was like twenty-three or twenty-four. I didn't like it. Skipped that," says Fisher, who understands how the disease probably sparked some of her behavior. "The shopping lust," she points out. "I said to my doctor one day, 'So what's the deal? So rich people have manic-depressive disorder, right?' They travel all over the world. Too much traveling is in the mix. All this stuff I had where you just say, 'Hey, I should go to India,' and you're gone for three and a half months." Her illness was compounded by drug abuse. "I'd had a lot of bad brushes with narcotics" she says. "But it was a way of self-medicating, and I was also a junkie. I used to call drugs taming the beast. But here's what I heard, the statistics of fifty percent of manic-depressives are on dope or alcohol, and fifty percent are not. But I want to meet the ones that are not.

"There's nothing in my life that I could say is more shameful than my appetite for narcotics. Any need that you don't have control over is humiliating. You're admitting that you are out of control. So a way to control that is to verbally attack it. This does work for it. If you can own it again with humor, you do not [feel shame]. I always said that *Postcards* was the long version of walking in the room and saying, 'Okay, I'm back.' "

Even after she was sober, it was six years before Fisher really addressed her manic depression, "because," she says, "to me it was something humiliating." Recently, after a particularly bad episode, she was hospitalized. Indeed, "It took a stint in the mental hospital before I dealt with the manic depression." She ultimately went on medication for it.

In any event, mania has been good for her creative process. "It's great for writing if you catch the wave right. Whenever I was in a vivid state, abstracting it was a very good solution to kind of escaping it. And then you get something out of it rather than just trampled."

Postcards was written on a manic jag. Fisher spoke the tale of a not-so-young woman trying to find herself into a tape recorder in only four months. The ease of it embarrasses her a little. Paul Slansky helped her paste the book together. She's never spoken a book since, but she fantasizes about it.

Mike Nichols paid several hundred thousand dollars for the movie rights and supervised Fisher as she turned the largely interlocking narratives into a coherent script, which focused less on recovery than on the actress's relationship with her alcoholic mother, who had been a singing star.

Fisher had kept notes on things her mother had said to her when she was in rehab. In the screen version, the former star arrives and announces to her daughter, "I don't know how you stand this. The color here is so blah," and then the two begin talking at the same time, at each other. Fisher says the dynamic is an atavistic one, a throwback to adolescence.

"I wrote a lot of it, and they saw that. And they said, 'Write down more of their relationship,' and I said, 'How?' So we made up this completely idiotic thing where I had to stay with her because of the insurance company, so that she can watch over me."

While the book carried the ring of authenticity, the film is pure Hollywood, the realistic, desperate quality eradicated in no small part by the casting of such bright stars as Shirley MacLaine and Meryl Streep. MacLaine does a kind of *Terms of Endearment* retread while Streep—around whom Nichols had packaged the film—seems curiously ill-suited to irony, like a beauty queen who's slumming it.

After five years of on again, off again, Fisher married Simon; she split up with him two years later, around the time *Postcards* became a movie. "He needed someone who was really devoted and who was going to stay in New York. . . . And we had a competitive relationship," says Fisher. "But when I went onto *Postcards* I stayed too long away. I loved New York, but uninterrupted New York. I moved around for a year. There wasn't anything to save." She didn't take any money.

Sue Mengers gibed Fisher that she had lost Simon because she was so infatuated with Meryl Streep. Indeed, the pair did become close, so much so that Nichols complained they were ganging up on him. One of the most true, poignant scenes of the movie occurs during a welcome home party the singer holds for her returning daughter. Everyone asks the daughter to sing, and she does so in a quavering voice, only to be outshone moments later by her mother, whom she watches adoringly. It's hard not to hear echoes of Fisher and Reynolds.

Fisher began writing *Surrender the Pink* during the production of *Postcards*, and Streep and Richard Dreyfuss read pages out loud to her. Although she went on to write another book, Fisher has not had an original screenplay produced since *Postcards*, nor has she written many, in part because of her child and her breakup. "It's difficult to maintain mothering and working and managing this house. It's like I'm my own wife and I want a divorce," she jokes. Doing rewrites was easier and lucrative (at an estimated $100,000 a week), and she was asked to add her brand of irony to a number of films.

She started with Steven Spielberg's *Hook*, spending weeks making Tinkerbell less mealy. She added more panache to the tough-kicking, self-sufficient Rene Russo, Mel Gibson's latest love interest in *Lethal Weapon 3*. She zipped up Whoopi Goldberg's *Sister Act*. She script-doctored more than two dozen scripts, some more successfully than others, often at the behest of friends, although she later felt guilty about disappointing Warren Beatty on *Love Affair* and Barbra Streisand on *The Mirror Has Two Faces*. She worked on an update of *Two for the Road* for her friend Meg Ryan, and took a stab at cowriting a script with Streep that fizzled.

"I was brought on to make the woman smarter and do love scenes," she says about her script doctoring. "Because *I have fantasies*. I have a fantasy about it and how they talk, deal with it. Vivid. Because I was brought up by *her*—I can create. She showed me every old movie that existed. And so I was a romantic, plus from reading all these old books, and I knew the right way they should speak to you, so I freaked out when men were like really sexual, because that's not how it was in those days, how it was presented to me."

When it came to men, Fisher wrote them as she wished they were: "I do these guys that I've never seen, and then I do ones that I have seen that are duplicitous, but I know how to make them that. I know how to make them the perfect guy who then turns. Maybe that's my life too.

I'm easily fooled because I want that other thing to be true. Because my father sort of fooled me. Because he's so charming, and then he disappears. That's very disappointing. But every time I see him I believe it."

THE TRUTH IS THE DIRECTOR HAS ALL
THE POWER AND YOU HAVE NONE

In a town that often banishes the screenwriter from the filming, Mike Nichols let Nora Ephron and Alice Arlen into the process, permitting them to attend casting sessions as well as to stay on the *Silkwood* set during the production. Ephron soaked up the apprenticeship, studying at Nichols's side like a prizewinning student.

In the years that followed Ephron and Arlen wrote three more scripts together, one called *Cookie,* an airy comedic riff on the Mafia directed by Susan Seidelman. Ephron hated the film, which she felt had been vulgarized, a confection turned into a tart. Solo, she wrote the screenplay for *Heartburn,* but the movie was a limpid rendition of the book, champagne lacking the gossipy fizz. It was directed by Nichols, and although Ephron had initially envisioned someone like Goldie Hawn as her screen alter ego, Meryl Streep, perhaps inevitably, was cast, or rather miscast. Ephron's ironically enraged first-person viewpoint was dropped in favor of a more neutral, neutered third-person view. Her ex-husband, Carl Bernstein, then spent almost five years in court battling Ephron's right even to make the movie. Although his chief concern seemed to be how he was going to appear, Bernstein characterized his wrangling as a defense of the couple's two sons against their exploitative mother. The divorce settlement was intertwined with the battle over the screenplay, which was severely amputated in the process, and Ephron was legally enjoined from ever writing about Bernstein or her children again.

"Nora told me she wasn't pleased with *Heartburn,*" explained Carrie Fisher. "I guess it was the restrictions imposed by her ex-husband [prior to the movie]. His character couldn't scream, 'You know why I fucked someone when you were pregnant? I was terrified!' A lot of men do that.

"She married a man not known for his fidelity. A known hound. She was thirty-nine. She needed to have children. Nora never copped to that. It was implicit."

Ephron's next film, *When Harry Met Sally . . . ,* released in 1989, grew out of a 1984 invitation to lunch by Rob Reiner, who had just directed his first film, the rock-umentary spoof *This Is Spinal Tap*, and his producing partner Alan Scheinman. She announced at the beginning of the meal that she had no interest in the project they were trying to talk her into, so the three spent most of their time in a rollicking discussion of Scheinman's and Reiner's bachelorhood (the latter had long ago broken up with Penny Marshall). A month later they had lunch again, and Reiner suggested doing a movie about a man and woman who opt for being friends rather than lovers, vowing to abstain from sex because "sex ruins everything"; then they have sex, and ruin everything.

Ephron was keen on the idea, and a couple of months later Reiner and Scheinman returned to New York and gave her several days' tutelage in male-relationship anxiety—from a man's inability to stick around for postcoital intimacy to his inability to maintain amity with a woman because, as Harry ultimately says, "He always wants to have sex with her." Ephron decided to model her male protagonist on Rob, who was funny but extremely depressed, and to formulate a female protagonist who was his polar opposite, perky, controlling, and relentlessly optimistic, a kind of sunnier version of herself. "In the beginning plans for *When Harry Met Sally . . .* , she was Jewish and he was Gentile," says Ephron. "And then Rob fell in love with [Elizabeth McGovern], so Elizabeth McGovern was going to play it. So we had to change it because there was no way that she could play . . . so I switched their last names. And we made him Jewish and her . . . you know."

Originally Harry and Sally weren't meant to end up together, and Ephron wrote a first draft in which the pair nurse each other through the breakups of their first big relationships to the beginnings of their second. Reiner went off to direct *Stand by Me*, and when he returned they decided that Harry and Sally had to end up together. Ephron wrote a second version, Reiner directed *The Princess Bride*, and then they sat down and together hammered out five more drafts.

Ephron characterizes the development process: "The director is constantly trying to screw the writer out of the things that mean the most. Every script I've done, my favorite scene was on the floor, except of course for the ones that I have directed. Part of the development process—the director is squeezing you and squeezing you and squeezing you because you have no leverage. There is the pretense that there is a collaboration, but the truth is the director has all the power and you have none." A way for the screenwriter to protect her work is "to make the script as personal for the director as it is for you. You have to invest the director in it as much as you are."

What made *When Harry Met Sally . . .* different was that each creative participant had a character he or she owned. Reiner had Harry; Ephron had Sally. And many of Sally's best lines came out of sessions in which Reiner and Scheinman probed Ephron on the intricacies of women's minds—prompting diatribes on sex fantasies and faked orgasms that wound up in the script.

"It was as much fun as I've ever had," says Ephron. "Rob's so funny. He's also very combative. We fought bitterly about lots of stuff that's in the movie, and, as a result, the fights are in the scenes." Ephron uses as an example the New Year's Eve finale, in which Harry and Sally reconcile. "We had a huge battle about this. Rob wanted him to say basically, 'I've been thinking it over and I love you.' I wanted him to talk about her. I said, 'This guy has been a narcissist for the entire movie. It's time for him to talk about what it is about her that's important.' It was a gigantic fight, and the result is a scene that has both of those things in it."

Again, Reiner invited Ephron to be a part of the production. Despite what turned out to be an erudite script, it was exceedingly difficult to cast the movie, particularly Harry's part. Because the male part was presumed to be the financial anchor of the film, they were looking for a star, but a long list of actors turned the part down: "Everybody, one after another. Tom Hanks, Richard Dreyfuss, Albert Brooks, Michael Keaton, I'm sure there were more," says Ephron. "These scripts—you have to believe in them. They're like gossamer. It's all in the playing. There's no net, there's no plot to save you if it doesn't work, there is nothing but performance and is it funny."

Hanks turned it down because when "*When Harry Met Sally . . .* starts out Harry's so miserable because his marriage has ended," says Ephron. According to her, Hanks couldn't relate to the part because he had been happy when his first marriage ended. "I don't think Tom ever regretted not doing it, because he just never knew how to play it. That part really was very much out of Rob's own kind of Jewish self-obsessed thing that I don't think Tom has a clue about.

"Richard Dreyfuss turned it down in front of me," recalls Ephron. "Richard—who is a nightmare, a total nightmare—said to Rob, 'God, it's too bad you don't want to direct the movie I really want to do'—*Let It Ride*. He said, in front of me, 'It's the opposite of this situation. That has a great script and no director.'

"It was just—it was an amazing moment. What am I going to say, 'How dare you say that, Richard?' I will love Rob forever for this. Richard said, 'I want to know more about these people's jobs.' Well, Rob and I had been through this a million times, and that was not what we were doing. We were doing a thing about friends. And it wasn't about work. There is no director living on this earth who wouldn't say to an actor, 'Hmm, that's an interesting idea, we'll think about that.' And Rob said, 'Well, I don't.' It was like a man on a white horse. It was just great the way he stood up for it."

The film wound up with Reiner's close friend the comic Billy Crystal as Harry (although he had never successfully carried a film) and the blond, up-and-coming Meg Ryan as Sally. Reiner believed that Harry was the bigger part, although Ryan came flush with ideas on how to flesh out her character. At the first actors' read-through, she suggested that she fake an orgasm in the delicatessen scene. To which Crystal suggested that an onlooking patron could quip, "I'll have what she's having." It became the most famous scene in the movie.

While Ryan went on to a long career in comedy and played Ephron's alter ego in three movies, she ended up odd man out on the set of *When Harry Met Sally . . .*, pointedly excluded from what many perceived as a Castle Rock boys' club, the close-knit fraternity of middle-aged Jewish men. While Ephron was amused and content enough to watch the often humorous banter between Reiner and Crystal, Ryan couldn't seem to find a niche for herself in the film's pseudofamily. Crystal incessantly beseeched Reiner to give him encouragement ("How did I do? Did you see my dailies?"), and Reiner stroked his ego assiduously, often ignoring his leading lady, says one close observer. Ryan, who has a reputation as hardworking, self-sufficient, and extremely professional, was often left to figure things out on her own. "I felt like I was doing my work in my trailer," acknow' lges Ryan. Rapport between the costars quickly degenerated. On occasion, they were barely talking.

Said Ephron in the aftermath, "It was a big shock to [Rob] that the movie was as much Sally's as Harry's. Harry had more jokes, but he was a less complex character. I knew this when I wrote it, but [Reiner] didn't know it, so when Meg began to work in the movie, they were all stunned since she kept stealing scenes. But those scenes were all there in the script, ready to be stolen by the right actress." *When Harry Met Sally . . .* became a major hit, as well as a template for the urban, romantic comedies that made Ephron's subsequent directing career.

Dawn Steel in her office at Atlas Entertainment, 1995.

SOFIA COPPOLA

STEEL IN THE FURNACE

I NEVER THOUGHT OF MYSELF
AS A VICTIM

Wild success papered over the initial differences between Dawn Steel and Ned Tanen. Their first year together spawned such hits as *Top Gun, Crocodile Dundee*, the Eddie Murphy vehicle *The Golden Child*, and the John Hughes film *Pretty in Pink*. Soon thereafter, however, their relationship began to deteriorate.

Unlike the days of Eisner and Katzenberg, Tanen didn't thrive on turning his executives into gladiators forced to fight things out among themselves. He was known in-house as the "Angel of Death" for his soothing bedside manner when a film failed. Alternately, he occasionally suffered what he called "green-pea-soup days," after the infamous scene in *The Exorcist*. He preferred discussion to advocacy. Steel felt he was burned-out, and claimed that he threatened to quit whenever he was asked to take on more corporate responsibility. Steel bonded through head-on clashes, and she found her new boss, despite his own whiplash temper, to have exactly the personality type that suited her least—the king of withholding, the pasha of no, the man who infamously told those who came to pitch him, "I'm in the movie business. I make movies. You're not. Give me a reason to put you in the movie business."

Their personality differences soon translated into the studio's management style. "Ned never wanted to play bad cop. So any unpleasant conversation, any conversation that would have the word *no* in it, he would leave to Dawn," recalls David Madden. "Dawn, not being an idiot, saw that this was the way the game was being played, and she didn't have a problem saying no to people, but she recognized that Ned was coming off as the filmmaker's white knight, while she was the person who was slashing their budgets, or saying, 'You can't do that.' "

Despite tacitly designating her the studio hatchet woman, Tanen grew to despair over Steel's aggressive style. According to a former Paramount executive, he kept a foghorn in his office, and whenever Steel strode in, he'd blare the horn to drown out her voice. (Tanen denies this.) "He thought she was being too hard on the staff. He felt she was being too hard on the filmmakers," recalls Lindsay Doran. "He felt that she was abrasive and that it was really costing us business, and costing us relationships. And I think she felt set up. She felt like she had been put in the job to do the hard thing, and then to be penalized for that felt wildly unjust."

The antipathy soon engendered rivalry and quickly enveloped the entire staff, as the vice presidents scrupulously avoided the appearance of taking sides. Films were divvied up as Ned's projects or Dawn's, Ned's relationships or Dawn's. Tanen implored underlings to come directly to him, yet Steel was acutely sensitive to being bypassed. She read Tanen's schedule regularly; once she accused a staff member of arranging a meeting for Tanen with the director James Cameron without her knowledge. "I get in one morning and it's eight-fifteen, eight-thirty, and my intercom button is ringing. I pick up, and it's Dawn and she's ballistic. She's yelling so loud that I don't even need the intercom, I can hear her from my office," recalls the executive, who placated her by swearing he wasn't the culprit and promising to arrange a Cameron meeting for Steel.

Soon it became clear that détente was impossible: "Dawn would simply try to win the war, because that was Dawn's methodology," says Madden. "It was all coming from her own perspective of being emotionally honest. If she thought somebody hated her, she was going to say, 'Why do you hate me?' She was incapable of being inscrutable."

Steel also trumped Tanen in the publicity game. He hated to give interviews, while she doled out colorful bons mots to the journalists who called, a tactic that raised her profile even further. Although Tanen was the executive who handled the lion's share of the duties on *The Untouchables* (indeed in the homestretch one active participant on the project claims that the director froze Steel out completely), Steel ran around town taking credit; she later did the same in her autobiography. She bragged about hiring Armani to do the costumes; in truth, the principals wore almost none of Armani's clothes because the designs arrived not in the predesignated period-looking fabrics but in the materials of the designer's fall line. In one interview Steel said that she had conceived of the assassin Nitti wearing only white, although that had been Brian De Palma's contribution.

In March 1987, GQ ran a story on the "thirty-five most important people in Hollywood." Steel was cartooned on the title page with Diller, Ovitz, and Spielberg. Tanen wasn't even mentioned. Frank Mancuso pointedly told her that "Ned's jealous of your attention in the press."

Nora Ephron recalls, "One day I called Dawn, who told me that Ned Tanen had tried to run her over with his car." Ephron laughs. "I used to race cars. If I was going to run her over, I would have hit her," Tanen quips. Ephron sent Steel a large photograph of John Gotti, smiling beneficently as he left the courthouse during his most recent murder trial. "There is no way you would ever look at this picture and think this is a man who is on trial for murder. And I felt that Dawn might find it useful to stare at it now and then because it had an important lesson, which was, Don't let them know what you're really feeling. When I first met Dawn, there was absolutely no question that that message had never been uttered to her."

By her own admission, Steel's anxiety and anger intensified when she became pregnant in 1986. She felt fat and ugly, unable to don her Armani armor, or even drown out her sorrows in the great comfort of shopping. She was exhausted. She was scared. "Dawn was not particularly happy with those nine months, you know," says her husband, Chuck Roven. "They were rough on her. They were rough on *us*."

Steel's war with Tanen was also taking its toll. She felt constantly criticized and undermined, a replay of her childhood with parents whose approval she could never attain. "He just tortured her, tortured her, tortured her," says Joel Silver. She lashed out more and more at her staff and the filmmak :s, which further angered Tanen. "She called John Hughes one day and just started screaming at him, and he said, 'I don't know what you're talking about' and hung up," recalls Tanen, who got the call from the *Pretty in Pink* director saying he refused to speak to Steel anymore. Her edgy bluntness had also made an unnecessary enemy of Frank Mancuso, Jr., a producer whom no one took seriously but who happened to be the son of her boss. "Phone calls were coming in from all over the place that she was difficult to work with and extremely abrasive to people. There were shots in the L.A. *Times* about her being nastier than Sid Sheinberg and Ray Stark," says Tanen. He urged Steel repeatedly to rein in her caustic manner. "You'd say, 'What the hell are you doing? Why are you doing this?' There were moments when she was like General Haig in the White House [after the assassination attempt on President Reagan] with Dawn going, 'I'm in charge here.' "

Complaints poured in to Tanen, ranging from the head of physical production, whom Steel had tried to force to report to her when his contract stipulated that he reported only to Tanen, to members of the production staff. The last straw finally came when Tanen found Doran sobbing after a withering Steel outburst. "I had one of the woman's executives come to me in tears saying, 'I can't do this anymore. I can't sit there and just have her abuse me in this way,' " says Tanen. "They didn't have any choice! We began having to work around her."

Steel immediately noticed: "I was beginning to be excluded from meetings, meetings that I should have not only attended but led." She confronted Tanen, saying, " 'What's wrong? What am I doing wrong? You are clearly unhappy with me.'

"Ned said, 'Go away. There's nothing wrong.' And then he told me a bad joke," recalled Steel.

Ironically, Tanen had given the green light to Chuck Roven's film *Johnny Handsome* (the project Steel had passed on on their first date). Given their subsequent relationship, Steel was barred from having anything to do with it, but this didn't stop Tanen from needling her about the film, announcing periodically, "I'm going to put your husband's picture into turnaround and throw him out of his office," just to see her blanch.

Steel also felt a chill in her all-important relationship with Mancuso. She believed he had indicated that she would get Tanen's job after a few years of seasoning as head of production. Now she was watching almost ten years of support trickle down the drain. Some of her ardent friends claimed that her pregnancy put the final kibosh on her relationship with Tanen: "In terms of the whore-madonna complex, I think the minute she became pregnant she ceased to be one of the boys," says one.

Steel struggled increasingly with depression. The flip side of her rage was shame, and a genuine desire to improve herself, to mold the product that was Dawn Steel into a better, brighter, more humane version of herself. "She was her own worst critic, but she also listened to criticism, and whether or not she was defensive at the moment," says Roven, "she would definitely worry it like a dog worries a bone."

Steel constantly searched for panaceas in New Age enthusiasms, trying out channeling, psychics, and the I-Ching. None, however, caught her enthusiasm as much as Creative Visualization, based on a book by Shakti Gawain. While Christianity stresses the afterlife and Buddhism advocates the renunciation of ego, Creative Visualization focuses on self-empowerment. Followers are told to visualize their fantasies, in effect to harness their conscious energies to make their fantasies reality. Steel threw herself into visualizing a happy, healthy baby standing in a stroller: "It was an image that defined bliss itself for me," she noted. Daily Creative Visualization sessions became a Steel staple, and she plied all her friends with copies of Gawain's book.

Increasingly alienated from her mostly male colleagues, Steel reached out to the only other top-level industry woman who was having a baby. "She actually called me up and said, 'I know we hardly know each other, but we should become best friends because we're both pregnant,' " says Lucy Fisher, then a senior vice president of production at Warner Bros. "We didn't have anything in common. I was a sort of hippie, rock-and-roll-lady type, and she was herself, but sure enough, she decided and we became really good friends. We ended up doing Lamaze together.

"Dawn is so motivated. She would say, 'Okay, now we do Lamaze, now we do this, now we do that,' and then we had all these talks about what it would be like after we had the kids. She was only going to take a week or two off, and I was going to take three months off."

Steel felt more and more destabilized by the increasing whispers of her professional demise, completely unaware what she might have done to cause it. "My husband was convinced that I was hormonal," she said. "He kept saying to me, 'You're imagining it.' It didn't occur to him that it could be true that they were trying to hire someone around me or over me." Steel heard that Tanen was courting the CAA agent Jack Rapke for her job, and she confronted Tanen; he heartily denied it. Tanen offered David Kirkpatrick all the duties of president of production, including direct reporting to Tanen, but without the title; he told Kirkpatrick they were wary about firing Steel outright because doing so while she was pregnant could leave them vulnerable to a lawsuit. Kirkpatrick opted instead to leave the studio. "I had heard about it and heard about it and heard about it, and it was never confirmed to me," Steel said.

Steel's anxiety lessened slightly when Frank Mancuso's wife, Faye, her daughter Maria, and her daughter-in-law, Becky, threw a baby shower. Steel knew that a lot of agents and producers came to pay homage to her position, but she was pleased by the star turnout—Bette Midler, Barbra Streisand, Diane Keaton. As is typical in Hollywood, the presents were so lavish that she didn't have to buy her baby a thing for the first three years. Steel hadn't felt so included since she was a cheerleader in high school.

Three weeks later, on an evening in March, Steel gave birth to Rebecca Roven, by emergency C-section because it had been discovered that the baby's umbilical cord was wrapped around her neck.

"When I came out of the morphine, the first phone call was Ned Tanen saying congratulations," recalled Steel. "The next thing that happened was my husband walked in with the trades and showed me the front-page story that Gary Luchessi had been hired over my head by the very person who had just called me to say congratulations.

"Paramount didn't say they fired me, because to fire someone while she is in labor is actionable. It was a very careful plan; they hired someone to report directly to Ned Tanen—it was a production executive who should have reported to me based on how the corporate organizational chart was drawn."

According to Steel, Tanen insisted that it wasn't he but his superiors who had demanded her head. Yet it was his boss Mancuso who came to visit several days after Steel got home from the hospital and pleaded with her to come back.

"You must be kidding. How could you want me to come back?" she screamed at him. "You let Ned torture me. You let him humiliate me."

Mancuso told her he didn't know how to handle Tanen when he got in these moods, but he would make it work out. Steel never heard from Mancuso again.

"I've never thought of myself as a victim," she said. "I pulled myself up and got on with my life. What was my choice? And what was much more important than that was the fact that I was not going to let them take away from the joy that I was feeling with my daughter for more than a minute," she added adamantly. "And they got their minute, and that was all I was going to give them."

With her practical bent Steel knew that if she was going to be fired, this was as good a time as any. She would be able to focus on and enjoy her child. "She would call up at six-thirty and say, 'Well, let's go to the park, in the morning,' and I'd say, 'It's not light out yet,' " says Lucy Fisher, who also had a baby girl. " 'Well, so what,' [she'd say]. So we would get up and the sand would still be wet at Holmby Park. She was always looking for something to do. She wasn't good at just relaxing."

Fortunately, Steel didn't have to relax for long. She took the golden parachute for fired executives—a lucrative production deal on the Paramount lot, which she was going to share with the actor Michael J. Fox. Yet, as the plans were being formalized, she received a call from the seventy-something producer Ray Stark, the long-standing power behind the throne at Columbia Pictures. With a lengthy track record for mentoring rising power brokers, Stark had first called Steel after reading about her and *Flashdance* in the *Los Angeles Times*. Over the years Steel had assiduously paid homage to him, amusing the veteran with her bawdy humor and stroking his ego.

Her canny politicking was now paying off. Stark announced, "I've been discussing you for the Columbia job with Victor Kaufman [chairman of Columbia], Mike Ovitz, and Herbert [Allen]." The job in question was president of Columbia Pictures, and Stark happened to hate the current seat holder, David Puttnam, the British producer of such high-minded fare as *Chariots of Fire* and *The Killing Fields*. Puttnam had arrived with grand pronouncements that he wasn't going to purvey the same overpriced Hollywood crap as all the other studios but would concentrate on more modest, socially conscious films with true artistic merit. His tone of self-righteousness quickly alienated much of the Hollywood establishment, as he clashed with stars like Bill Murray (of the studio's *Ghostbusters* franchise) and the longtime Coca-Cola spokesman Bill Cosby. Yet all hubris would have been forgiven had Puttnam not committed the great Hollywood sin: commercial failure. His films sank at the box office. In the fall of 1987, Coca-Cola merged Columbia with its sister studio TriStar and dubbed Victor Kaufman chief of the joint entity. Kaufman left TriStar's president, David Matalon, in place, but Puttnam was out. It was to be the fifth administration change in as many years, and Columbia now ranked second to last in market share.

As the industry wags began to discuss who was on the shortlist for the Columbia job, Steel despaired over why no one was mentioning her name. She wasn't sure she wanted the job—mostly because of how badly she could behave under pressure—but she wanted to be asked. "I didn't say to her, 'I'm going to get you on that list,' " says Roven. "I didn't know what the fuck I was doing, but I was hoping that I could accomplish something through Todd Smith," a friend at CAA. Roven made it clear that the Paramount deal notwithstanding, Steel was definitely available and suggested that Smith talk to his boss Mike Ovitz, stressing that "she'd be a big splashy name to have. Everybody else on the list was a nobody. And that's what Todd did, that got Mike to call Ray, and Ray to call Victor, and Victor to call a meeting."

Steel's allies rallied to her cause. Dan Melnick also worked on Stark. "Ray and I, because we had a strong ongoing relationship with Columbia, were anxious to have someone simpatico to picture making," he says. Kaufman had hoped to hire someone with more experience than Steel and had offered the job to Terry Semel, the president of Warners. The Hollywood cognoscenti assumed that whoever took the job would be kept on a short leash, having to answer to a kitchen cabinet of Kaufman, his number-two man Lew Korman, Stark, and the investment banker Herbert Allen. Nor was there job security, as rumors continued to swirl that Coca-Cola was simply going to sell the studio. As with the promotions of Sherry Lansing and Paula Weinstein, the Columbia job was hardly ideal for Steel, but it was the only opportunity that would open up for a woman. Steel made it clear that she was willing to play by Hollywood rules. "I thought she would be a strong leader who would have a true commercial sense, and that she would get tremendous support in the creative community," says Kaufman.

Steel embraced her new boss. "Victor Kaufman was someone who looked at *me*—there was no gender issue. It wasn't about male or female. He made me feel that I was the one person he wanted for the job," she said. Kaufman promised her a measure of autonomy over her slate (as long as she kept him apprised), as well as whatever help she needed to make her life as a working mother easier, namely a nursery next to her office for Rebecca. The über-agent Michael Ovitz negotiated her deal. Ironically, Frank Mancuso refused to let her out of her contract until Kaufman paid several hundred thousand dollars in reparations. Steel's new boss also offered her the opportunity to take less in salary and more in stock. She took the stock.

She was to be the first woman to run an entire motion picture corporation, both the business and the creative side. "She was thrilled," says Steel's friend Craig Baumgarten. "No woman had ever done this before, and she was keenly aware that if she did it well, it would bury the boys' club a little bit more."

Steel rhapsodized, "The first time I looked at the Columbia symbol, which is the only female symbol in the history of the movie business, I thought, Wow, look where I am."

SHE WHO DOTH PROTEST TOO MUCH
SOUNDS LIKE AN ASSHOLE

Excited by her ascension into the true power circle, Steel didn't sleep at all the night before her new job was to begin. The next morning she got lost on the way to the Burbank studio, then ran out of gas. When the security guard at the gate ushered Steel to her new parking spot, she was so happy she hugged him. As another guard escorted her to her new office (laden with welcome gifts from the power establishment), her employees lined the halls like soldiers awaiting the general's inspection.

In one of her first acts as president, Steel summoned the production staff to comb through all the remaining Puttnam projects. "I remember thinking to myself, Oh shit, what do I do now?" Steel said. "Because David Puttnam and I have tastes that are diametrically opposed. I had to start development all over again from scratch. It was a huge blow. There I was, ready to sprint out of the block, and there was no writing."

Steel did everything she could to send out the message that she was willing to make movies the old-fashioned Hollywood way. She spoke to Ray Stark every day. She green-lit *The Karate Kid Part III* and wrangled all the stars together to make *Ghostbusters II* by giving them hefty chunks of the back end. "They gave away the whole fucking store," fumes an executive who was intimate with the deal. "Although I don't think Dawn recognized it at the time, the truth is Victor and Lew were only interested in selling the studio. So the idea of having made *Ghostbusters II* was going to look very attractive. It didn't really matter if the company made money on the movie." Steel announced to the creative community that she could also be serious by picking from the Paramount turnaround heap the relatively expensive ($25 million) *Casualties of War*, Brian De Palma's gritty tale of a young G.I. who witnesses the rape of a Vietnamese girl by another G.I. It starred Sean Penn, and Michael J. Fox in an uncommon dramatic role. Two weeks after she started her job, Steel's former boyfriend Martin Scorsese called her about the restoration of *Lawrence of Arabia*, which had begun under the Puttnam regime but had been halted because of legal complications. Within a week, Steel had cleared the way.

"It was so moving to be able to take David Lean into the theater [for the premiere]," remembered Steel. "There were fifteen hundred people sitting there [among them Scorsese and Steven Spielberg], and you have to sort of walk him down the aisle so that people could respect him. And they did. He finally got the respect and the adoration that he, in my opinion, was entitled to and had been for a very long time."

Steel slashed the Columbia workforce by over 10 percent and spent a lot of money on wooing production deals for actors, among them Michael Douglas, Cher, Sean Penn, Kevin Bacon, Emilio Estevez, and Molly Ringwald—all of whom, except for Douglas, were neophyte producers. Some of the deals cost as much as $1 million each. In her first six months, Steel spent more money than in the rest of her two-year tenure.

Publicly, she often performed a dazzling one-woman show. "She was completely electrifying in the staff meeting. She would walk in with those Armani suits, and she always wore these hilarious shoulder pads, and a white T-shirt. It was so eighties," recalls Amy Pascal, one of her vice presidents. "She would crack jokes, and she was really funny. She just knew how to turn it on. She was more like a performer than any other studio executive I've ever seen. She was like a star. In her own mind more than anywhere. But because of it, she was brilliant. When I used to go to screenings with her, she would walk down the aisle, you know, and all the reporters would scream her name." She appeared all over town, often with three young male executives in tow, all of them vying for the position of production chief.

Steel was also a very high-profile mom, setting up Rebecca's nursery next to her office, making a point of spending time with her daughter in the early morning and going home for two hours of Rebecca time before going out again for a business dinner. When she was out of town for more than two days, she took Rebecca with her. When the instructor of her Mommy-and-me class changed the meeting from the weekend to a weekday and then banned "caregivers," a fuming Steel staged a parental walkout and orchestrated a different class.

Steel did her best to release the thirty-three Puttnam films she inherited, although ultimately his slate, which included such nonstarters as the Cyndi Lauper psychic comedy *Vibes* and an unreleasable film in Serbo-Croatian, cost the studio $100 million in write-offs. Providentially, Puttnam also left behind Bernardo Bertolucci's *The Last Emperor,* which won nine Academy Awards. The night before the Oscars, Steel held a lavish party in her new Beverly Hills home for the director and the film. She asked Bertolucci's legendary cinematographer, Vittorio Storaro, to light the house for the event. It was her arrival on the Hollywood A-list. The president and chairman of Coca-Cola flew out for an evening that featured Arnold Schwarzenegger, Robin Williams, Sean Connery, Kevin Costner, Madonna, Richard Pryor, and Tom Hanks. The hostess surveyed the crown jewels of Hollywood with deep satisfaction; little Dawn Steel, the girl who dreamed of being a cheerleader, had finally made it.

Away from the klieg lights, however, the bloom inside Columbia was already fading. Five months into her administration, just weeks before the big *Last Emperor* win, the Writers Guild went on strike, halting all script work and thwarting Steel's goal of filling the Columbia pipeline with new commercial fare. Steel purchased what she could, even if it meant hiring scabs. In a notorious move that angered the union, she purchased a half-million-dollar script titled "Pincushion," a futuristic tale involving a female action hero, and lured Cher to star in it.

"These rumors seemed to surface right after the writers' strike. The rumors would say, Columbia was being sold, and not only was Columbia being sold, but I was out of a job. I began to feel like Job, or Sisyphus," recalled Steel. "So let me tell you how difficult it was trying to bring talent to Columbia Pictures, when they didn't know if I was going to be there. It made it very difficult to say to the creative community, artistic community, Come and work with me. I'll nurture you. And it's hard to defend yourself, because she who doth protest too much sounds like an asshole. There was nothing to do but keep my head down and keep working."

Steel's first movies underperformed at the box office. *Ghostbusters II* grossed $112 million, a hefty chunk of which went to the myriad gross players, while *The Karate Kid Part III* churned out only $39 million. To her dismay, *Casualties of War* bombed. Steel continued to plug away, picking up *Awakenings*, a directing vehicle for Penny Marshall based on an Oliver Sacks book, when it went into turnaround at Fox. For Michael Douglas's company she bought a Brat Pack karma picture, *Flatliners*. She also paid top dollar for the Mike Nichols–Meryl Streep ICM package *Postcards from the Edge*, based on Carrie Fisher's autobiographical tale.

"She called one night from her car screaming that *Postcards* was there and it belonged there," says Fisher. "It was the female of it. She used to talk a lot about women sticking together."

While early in her career Steel had done everything she could to be one of the boys, she now extended herself to other women trying to make it, not all women, but to her compatriots, giving production deals to her friends Lynda Obst and Melinda Jason, as well as to Wendy Finerman, who was married to Warners' president of production, Mark Canton, and her former employee Laurie MacDonald. She hired Nora Ephron to direct *This Is My Life.*

"There was a part of her that was very self-conscious, especially after all the negative press," recalls Joan Hyler. "She would call us constantly, me and Katherine [Reback] and Tova [Laiter] and Lynda [Obst] and just make sure that we knew that no matter where she was going, there was always a place for us in her royal court. Now that probably offended people. I thought it was funny."

As the pressure rose at Columbia, Steel became more agitated, resorting again to chastising her staff. She had a recurring dream that all her former assistants went on the tabloid TV show *Geraldo* to bad-mouth her. Negative stories filtered out of the studio. Even so, she often failed to grasp her impact on others, and she was truly shocked when she appeared as the cover girl for a *California* magazine article naming the worst bosses in the state. She was crowned the Queen of Mean. The magazine described how one of her assistants had to be taken out of her office on a stretcher—which happened to be true—though Steel later vociferously denied the contention that she had leaned down and screamed at the woman, "You haven't finished your calls." According to Steel, the woman, who had suffered a medical emergency, later wrote to the magazine stating that Steel had simply asked if she wanted her to call her father.

Steel was devastated. "I never saw her so upset," recalls Amy Pascal. "She locked herself in her office and cried. She had no idea how she came off to people. She never forgot it, she never got over it. She didn't see herself that way at all. She was shocked." She was horrified that Rebecca might one day hear about it.

In later years Steel would explain that the editor of the magazine had demanded a woman CEO for the cover, putatively because a woman fire-eater would trade on antiwoman fears and sell better. "There was this guy in there who had stuffed two migrant workers into a refrigerator and tried to flush another one down the toilet," she said. "But I was [supposed to be] worse than him."

The article was a wake-up call for Steel to reevaluate her pent-up anger. It became one of the turning points in her life. "If there was something in that criticism that resonated with her, she would go after it to try to get rid of it," Roven says. "As she needed the anger in her own mind to get where she got to in terms of her career; she used [anger] to give her power, but she ultimately realized that that was limiting. The *California* magazine cover hurt her deeply. But it did make her recognize that she had to deal with it."

While Coca-Cola had had a policy of not speaking to the press, Steel, with the aid of her head of publicity, Mark Gill, now devised a rehabilitation of her image, which questioned the sexist assumptions behind her vilification in the press.

"It was pretty easy to say as a man, 'Hey, look, you know, you don't think every other guy who is running a studio doesn't do the same thing? How come she gets a different standard?' That worked really well," says Gill. "I've worked for a lot of these guys who have run companies, and I'm telling you, the guys get away with a lot more than the women do. Anything that she did to punish somebody, or any time she had to discipline somebody, it would always get out as this god-awful story, usually dramatically embellished. This was the kind of thing that went on every single day of the week at every other studio, but because the guys were dishing out the punishment, it didn't really make news.

"The good news is, the perception turned around within about a year," says Gill, who pressed Steel to go out and meet the town, and to brandish all the warmth and earthy charm she was perfectly capable of. His handiwork resulted in positive pieces in *The Wall Street Journal* and *New York* magazine, the latter including a hairdresser raving about Steel's lustrous tresses.

Steel's image was further burnished when she won a long-desired Crystal Award, given to the most prominent women in the business. Coca-Cola hired a speech consultant to help her practice public speaking, which terrified her, and her friends impressed upon her the need to appear humble, self-mocking, and accessible—in a distinctly womanly way. "I had her do the Women in Films speech, where she showed some vulnerability talking about the guilt she feels going into the office and leaving her baby behind—these are very human, identifiable things, and nobody expected them to come from *her*," recalls Gill. Her pals Lynda Obst and Katherine Reback helped Steel polish her speech. Nora Ephron introduced her. She calmed herself by visualizing everyone cheering for her.

"This is the second award I've gotten this year," Steel told the crowd of 1,500, which included Victor Kaufman, Barry Diller, and Jodie Foster. "The first, which was given to me by *California* magazine for being one of the worst bosses in the state, is shared with nine other persons, one of whom received it for trying to flush two of his employees down the toilet. I didn't deserve that award, and I don't deserve this one. But getting this one makes me feel a whole lot better about getting that one."

B y the end of Steel's first sixteen months in office, earnings at Columbia were down 53 percent, to a mere $2 million, but already the studio had begun to rebound. Soon after, Kaufman put both TriStar and Columbia in Steel's domain. Although Steel had intended to dump TriStar's woman-centered comedy *Look Who's Talking*, a lawsuit threatened by its stars, Bruce Willis and John Travolta, scotched the plan, and that film, along with Castle Rock's *When Harry Met Sally . . .*, turned into bumper hits. By 1990 Columbia would move from eighth studio overall at the box office to third, a fraction away from the leading contenders.

But it was too late for Steel. In September 1989, a mere two years after her arrival, Kaufman called and announced that the rumors were all true. The studio was being sold to Sony for an exorbitant $5 billion. Steel recalled, "My first question was, Are you staying? Because I knew if he stayed I would have to stay. But if he left he would have freed me."

Kaufman recalls with a laugh, "I think she was so excited about the worth of her stock." For her toil Steel garnered $7 million on her stock options (Kaufman made more than $22 million). Her windfall allowed Steel the psychic freedom to evaluate whether the job was worth all the trouble. "I think she felt very good about the fact that she finally had what she called fuck-you money, and that she did not have to depend on the next job to support herself," says David Geffen.

The security of the bonus proved increasingly useful in the days to come. Ten days later Kaufman announced his resignation. After preliminary talks with Michael Ovitz, Sony hired the producing team of Peter Guber and Jon Peters, Steel's erstwhile cohorts from *Flashdance*, to run the studio and paid a price estimated at close to a billion dollars to extract them from their Warners contract.

Peters announced his presence with flash and circumstance. His first day on the lot, he strode into Steel's office unannounced, interrupted her meeting, and threw her over his shoulder, demanding with the effusiveness of an imperious puppy dog that she come with him to see Guber. They trekked down to a conference room where Guber was meeting with accountants. They all kissed and hugged, and Guber and Peters announced that they wanted her to stay. Steel had remained friendly with the pair since *Flashdance*, particularly with Guber (who had been executive producer on one of Roven's films) and his wife, Lynda. Now the duo spun out a fantasy for her of a reinvigorated leadership that was firmly committed to the movie business (unlike Coca-Cola, which was ambivalent at best). They sent her flowers every day. Finally, Steel relented and began negotiating a new deal.

By the time the team attended their first production meeting several weeks later, the honeymoon was kaput. Without consulting Steel, who was supposed to still be running Columbia, Peters paid a phenomenal $700,000 for *Radio Flyer*, a script about child abuse, and promised the screenwriter, David Mickey Evans, another $300,000 to make his directorial debut. The normally fast-talking Guber kept his mouth shut during the meeting, while Peters tore to shreds Steel's upcoming slate, which included *Flatliners*, *Postcards from the Edge*, and *Awakenings*. When the topic turned to "Skirts," a Debbie Gibson musical Steel was developing with her girlfriend Lynda Obst, Peters was dismissive, particularly of her plan to hire the choreographer Kenny Ortega to direct. No choreographer will ever direct at this studio, Peters declared.

"What about Bob Fosse?" someone asked. Fosse, who had directed the Oscar-winning *Cabaret*, had died several years earlier. "I don't want him either," retorted Peters. He later killed "Skirts," outright. Steel was beyond humiliated. She was furious.

Despite his own larger-than-life reputation, Peters bragged to his staff that Steel was meaner than he was. At first schadenfreude swept through a legion of her ill-wishers, but as it became more and more apparent that Steel was subject to Peters's whims and tirades, the ballast of sympathy swung toward the diminutive studio chief.

Not long after the production showdown, while Steel was in the New York office, she received a phone call from an enraged Peters: "Dawn, I want to make something really clear. You report to me, and everyone in the company reports to me."

"Read my contract," she told him. She might report to him, but everybody else reported to her.

"And he said, 'I don't give a shit, you all report to me,' and he hangs up," recalled Steel. "In a minute or two, he calls Tom Pollack, and he's screaming at Tom, 'You tell Dawn Steel she reports to me. You tell her that everyone reports to me.' And Tom asks, 'Why are you telling me this, Jon?' Jon says, 'Aren't you Dawn's lawyer?' He said, 'No, I haven't been her lawyer in ten years. I'm the chairman of Universal Pictures.' So I called my lawyer, Jake, and I said, 'He's in breach, everybody doesn't report to him, they report to me.' I said, 'You've got to get me out of there.' "

Steel's lawyer devised a speech calculated to get her out of her contract without damaging her financially.

Steel called Guber to request a meeting, which the partners decided to hold at Peters's Beverly Hills home. Although she was perfectly capable of tirades, Peters's demonstrated potential for violence scared Steel. In his den the warring parties traded small talk; then Steel began to deliver her set piece. Peters erupted. "Who the fuck are you to tell me you don't want to do this job!" he fumed. "What have you done in your career to tell me that?"

Peters advanced toward her, quaking with rage. Steel thought he was going to hit her, and she looked for help at Guber, who merely watched passively. In fear, she tore out of the house and jumped in her Jaguar. As she sped out of the estate, she called friends from her cell phone. By the time she arrived at her doorstep, her phone was ringing. It was Guber, who quickly apologized.

Another meeting was held to see if the relationship could be mended, but it was over. Not long after, Guber called Roven to tell Steel that he would release her without fuss.

But there was one last skirmish. Steel's contract was finally settled out in January 1990. In the interim Peters came by, trying to take over her office. Her secretary stood guard and refused to budge until Peters finally relented. That year, *Awakenings, Postcards from the Edge,* and *Flatliners* all became hits. Given the fact that only Michael Douglas was a gross-point player (and that Julia Roberts was still inexpensive), *Flatliners* was one of the most profitable films in Columbia's history.

THE DEMISE OF SUE;
THE RISE OF THE SUE-ETTES

GO TO CAA, RONNIE MEYER
JUST WANTS TO FUCK YOU

Sue Mengers returned to William Morris like a conquering general striding home from the battlefield. Unlike during her tenure at ICM, where she ran her own private boutique, Mengers was now management, and she took it upon herself to give the younger agents a badly needed dose of Agenting 101—returning calls with dispatch, insinuating yourself into a client's life, discerning which offers to take. Funny and brash, she held court in her second-floor office, near her troops but pointedly not on the first-floor power corridor where the board members had their lairs.

For a number of the women agents, Mengers was a godsend, an authority figure who took them seriously. As late as 1980 women were generally not allowed to work in the Morris mail room, the vaunted training ground for every male agent and the launching pad for such power players as Mike Ovitz, Barry Diller, and David Geffen. Women started out as secretaries and hoped to jump the fence. By the late eighties a number of young women had begun to make their mark—Elaine Goldsmith and Risa Shapiro, with such rising clients as Julia Roberts, Andie MacDowell, and Tim Robbins; and the lanky JJ Harris, with Morris's most recently minted superstar, Kevin Costner. Stan Kamen also had made a number of prominent female casting directors, among them Toni Howard and Boaty Boatwright, into agents. Despite thriving careers, however, many of the women felt cut off from the arena in

Sue Mengers at the premiere of
Bob Roberts, Beverly Hills, 1992.

which men helped men. (This was, after all, a company that hosted an annual charity event for Big Brothers, to which women were pointedly not invited.) Bobbi Thompson, who had discovered both James Cameron and Tim Burton, had to bulldoze John Ptak into teaching her the subtleties of foreign financing, while Risa Shapiro just gave up the idea that she would ever receive mentorship or encouragement.

Shapiro, a leggy former model and teacher from Baltimore, had endeared herself to Mengers by resolutely standing up to her. On Mengers's first trip back to New York, she had culled through every agent's client list and pointedly told Shapiro to drop the unknowns, railing that you couldn't build a business on the backs of nobodies. Shapiro thought Mengers's attitude was "from another world," unrealistic about the possibility of a young agent signing superstars in a world dominated by CAA. Indeed, the only woman ever to sign a superstar had been Mengers. Shapiro knew that her power would come from being able to find diamonds in the rough. She told Mengers that her clients were so talented, they would be stars and refused to shed a number of them. When two of her discoveries—Julia Roberts and Andie MacDowell—proved prescient, Mengers moved Shapiro from the New York office to L.A., where the action was. Mengers personally found the young agent an apartment in a building near the office. Says Shapiro, "She acts like she's very tough, but she's very motherly."

Elaine Goldsmith, an overweight, dark-eyed girl from the Valley with an insouciant, brash charisma, spent hours in Mengers's office, discussing her clients' careers and soaking up Mengers's many bons mots. She recalls negotiating Julia Roberts's deal for the screen test for *Pretty Woman*: "Sue asked, 'Haven't you closed this deal yet?' " recalls Goldsmith.

"I said, 'No, no.'

" 'Why?'

" 'Well, Julia doesn't do nudity,' which she doesn't.

"And Sue said, 'Honey, it's about a hooker.'

"Julia said, 'Well, I don't know if I want to show nudity.'

"Sue said, 'We're not talking beaver here.'

"Julia blushed seventeen shades of red. Then she said, 'What am I going to tell my mom?'

"Sue said, 'Tell her you're in a Disney movie. She won't know the difference. Honey, if I had your body, I'd be shopping nude down the aisles at Gelson's.' " Goldsmith laughs.

"She was harder on the women than on the men," recalls Toni Howard, whom Mengers had ignored when she was a secretary at ICM but now embraced. Mengers reminded her women agents that it was imperative to "get close to the wives," enlisting them as allies instead of potential competitors. She dismissed pregnant women as "breeding cows" and chastised all the women about their appearances, often pointing to the pretty Paula Wagner at CAA as a yardstick of perfection.

"I used to walk into her office and she would look at me and she would say, 'Those are absolutely the wrong colored socks for that skirt,' " recalls Joan Hyler. "I remember once I had a permanent and she said, '*Velda chai, velda chai.*' It means in Yiddish 'wild animal.' I was wearing a pair of dangling earrings, and she said, 'Those are not the earrings I would wear to lunch with Shirley MacLaine as a friend. Those are not Shirley MacLaine earrings.' She pulled them off and gave me hers."

"She believed women had to be conservative to compete with men. She used to criticize my appearance every day," recalls Bobbi Thompson. "It was like my mother criticizing me every day." Mengers hated Thompson's asymmetrical haircut and wild clothes, and hounded her into getting rid of them. "She got a lot of the women to cut their hair. Risa, Elaine. She tortured us. I spent more money on clothes, and I looked great."

Mengers was a yenta—in a town increasingly populated by MBA's and Armani rangers. Her distinctive style—her ability to play on an actor's insecurity with vulgar in-your-face truth telling—seemed suddenly as antiquated as bell bottoms and love beads. "Go to CAA," she derisively told the starlet Valeria Golino, who was vacillating about William Morris, "Ronnie Meyer just wants to fuck you." Others were subjected to amusingly told tales of her sexual escapades, not uncommon among men but still unsettlingly frank for a woman. While Mengers was aggressive about salary demands, she was perceived as not possessing the financing savvy of the town's newest dealmakers, preferring that business affairs negotiate the finer points of a deal. Her past sins came back to haunt her: her elitism, her penchant for negativity. Mengers hadn't simply refused clients or turned down requests, she had annihilated beseechers—people such as Jessica Lange, Dudley Moore, and Al Pacino. All the people she had been mean to in her waning days at ICM were now in positions of power. All the stars to whom she had complained about agenting were still stars.

Mostly, Mengers had lost her once-unquenchable yen for agenting. Gone was her infallible belief in the power of stars, in the religion of celebrity; gone was her unfailing ability to charm stars. "It was a nightmare," she recalls. "I couldn't sign Peter Coyote. I found out that I had lost it, because I no longer had the mental balls to want to fight. I had a husband at home with whom I'd had fun traveling for two years. If these people didn't realize how good I was, I didn't want to play. The hardest thing was the not caring anymore, because the old me would have worked through it. But I think that taste I had of two years of no stress, two years of having something that I had never had in my life [made me look at things differently]. I mean, all those years that I was young and working, I never had a guy. I never lived with anyone. I never had a boyfriend. I was good old Sue."

Within weeks of her arrival, the weekly Wednesday staff meeting devolved into an exercise of hope versus humiliation as Mengers would declare sarcastically, "Let me tell you who turned me down this week," rattling off names of former clients such as Barbra Streisand, Goldie Hawn, Sylvester Stallone, Michael Caine, and Jonathan Demme. She accompanied her most cutting remarks with a profane hand gesture denoting jerking off. She'd quip, "The good news is I signed Richard Pryor; the bad news is he can't work." Sometimes she appeared to the troops to be lost in her own reveries, so much so that one agent commented, "She's channeling Freddie Fields." Since Hollywood hates anyone with the stench of being on the downslide, the Morris movie department assumed the aura of an untouchable.

"The one quality I have that attracted clients was they sensed my real enthusiasm," she reflects. "It wasn't faked. I was psyched. By the time I went back to the Morris office, I was no longer that girl. And many times I would go into signing meetings that my associates wanted me to come into, and my heart wasn't in it. I really didn't care if we signed that particular client. And I think actors' sensitivity is such they know when you are really, really hot for them. I regret that I lost that thing that I had. I missed that."

Mengers began to realize the gravity of all she had given up when she had made her deal with the Morris board. Like King Lear, she had believed that she was inherently powerful; in fact, she had opted for the dollar over any real power. She couldn't hire or fire, reward or punish, set salaries or bonuses, or put agents under contract, ensuring their loyalty to William Morris. Six months later, when Morris promoted four new men, including the film agent Lenny Hirshan, to sit on the board of directors, Mengers was conspicuously absent.

Yet Mengers didn't fade away without a fight. By the start of the summer, a mere two months after she arrived, she had devised a battle plan centered on the few jewels left in the Morris crown, namely material, created by writers such as Susan Isaacs, who had spawned *Compromising Positions*; Buck Henry, who had written *The Graduate*; and the newcomer Carrie Fisher, in the midst of writing her first screenplay, *Postcards from the Edge*. The agency divided the town into fiefdoms, those for them, neutrals, and those against them, the last group, the so-called CAA apparatchiks—like Castle Rock and former Morris clients like Jane Fonda and Herb Ross—to be summarily frozen out of their cache of material.

Moreover, while the women vaunted her, Mengers still seemed to dote on the rising young men, bucks like Cary Woods, Stan Kamen's former protégé, who handled the young Uma Thurman. "She was close to the women but thought the power resided in the men," recalls Joan Hyler. Like a jealous daughter, Toni Howard used to berate Mengers about her Woods fixation. When William Morris celebrated its ninetieth anniversary, Mengers held a special cocktail party, but invited mostly male agents. On her wall she kept a picture of herself as the belle of the ball, surrounded by young male attendants.

In November 1989, Mengers was pushed out of her job the way people (such as Dawn Steel and Paula Weinstein) in Hollywood are always pushed out of their jobs—others were hired around her to assume her duties. John Burnham and Mike Simpson were named coheads of Morris's West Coast motion picture office (although not to the William Morris board). Mengers had seventeen months remaining on her contract; she stormed in to see Roger Davis, enraged. It was another year, however, before she finally left.

Mengers's final departure was a blow to her female acolytes, a form of corporate matricide. She was the only person in the agency to whom they felt loyalty, the only reason in fact to stay at William Morris. Moreover, her replacements were simply their contemporaries, who had been promoted over them. They weren't in the league of Ovitz or Berg. A number of the women groused that Simpson hadn't even signed his most important clients, Tim Burton and Tom Hanks; he had inherited them.

In any event, it seemed that Morris hardly cared whether women stayed. Four women were pushed out of the New York office alone. In California they canned one fourteen-year veteran who hired the out-spoken feminist attorney Gloria Allred and filed a wrongful termination suit against Morris. When a popular agent lost Richard Grieco, of the TV show *21 Jump Street*, to CAA, she too was let go. Howard, Goldsmith, Shapiro, and four others lobbied the board unsuccessfully for the woman's job.

"We thought if we work in a company and we're supposed to be a part of the company, you should listen to what we have to say and it should mean something," recalls Shapiro. "It should be taken to heart in some way. And they said, 'I'm sorry, it's already done.' So we had no voice ever."

Morale continued to spiral downward. All the women had gripes. For Shapiro, it was the fact that management refused to give her an as-sistant. For Goldsmith, it was the fact that the board demanded she try to inject another, "more senior" agent—namely John Burnham—into Julia Roberts's life in a flat-footed attempt to forestall what had hap-pened when Kamen died.

Everything about Morris's outdated management seemed encapsu-lated in an exchange Goldsmith had with one of the board members: "We were talking about a young male agent, who had started after me, who didn't have the clients I had, and I said, 'Why does he get to go to the Cannes Film Festival and I don't?' And the board member said, 'Be-cause you two'—meaning my female agent friend and I—'are the fu-ture; he's now.' "

And then there was the money issue. A number of the women sus-pected that they were paid as much as 40 percent less than their male counterparts, and it rankled.

For a year and a half ICM's chairman, Jeff Berg, had been calling Goldsmith every month with the Zen pitch "There are no finite choices in life." Ed Limato had joined the seduction, calling Goldsmith and Toni Howard.

Howard was bristling at Morris's culture of disrespect. Three months after she arrived, she had flown to New York and signed Joanne Wood-ward, returning home to find a note from the board thanking her and stating that they would deduct forty dollars from her expenses for tak-ing a limo. She knew she didn't have any superstars, but she knew what she was doing, and her clients were eminently respectable—Anjelica Huston, James Spader, and Jason Robards. She was plugged in. She knew the value of teamwork.

She became enraged at the end of December when she saw her bonus. All year the agents of Morris had fretted about the size of their bonuses, which, unlike at CAA, were not the bulk of their annual paychecks but did account for at least a third of their pay. It was the time of year when the daddies of the business decided which of their children had been naughty and which had been nice, summoning them one by one before the board and presenting them with computer readouts that summed up their clients' earnings. If an agent shared a client, her or his participation was assigned a percentage value.

Bonus time that Christmas was bloody. Howard's close friend Boaty Boatwright resigned on the spot when she saw what they were offering her. They told her she didn't really represent Alan Pakula and Norman Jewison because she hadn't signed them. It took a week for Howard and John Ptak to convince her to stay.

Howard herself was enraged to find her bonus fell about $15,000 short. She thought she deserved a six-figure cherry, a $100,000 bonus instead of $85,000. She went to see the agency's president, Norman Brokaw, who waxed on about his client Gerald Ford but proffered no more money.

The women of William Morris held court at the Golden Globes of 1991. Their clients were awash in nominations: Anjelica Huston for *The Grifters*, Joanne Woodward for *Mr. and Mrs. Bridge*, and Goldsmith and Shapiro's supernova Julia Roberts for *Pretty Woman*. That night Howard told Goldsmith that she was leaving for ICM the next day.

Howard spent the week working on her girlfriends, Boatwright, Goldsmith, and Shapiro. "Toni definitely did sign us," recalls Shapiro. "She took us out. It was like a romance." Within a week the trio had departed for ICM. The four women brought with them about $25 million worth of business, including Julia Roberts, Rosie O'Donnell, Samuel L. Jackson, Anjelica Huston, and Alan Pakula. The women's salaries zoomed into the half-million-dollar range.

William Morris had just lost most of its stars. The press portrayed a company that had been surgically gutted. "Now, they can really call us the c-word," Howard gaily told the circling reporters. "That's right, competitors."

23.

LEADING-LADY BLUES

THE CHIEF OCCUPATION OF WOMEN ON EARTH WAS HOOKING, AND I DON'T MEAN RUGS

"I'm barely able to contain a guffaw when a reporter asks me what drew me to a role, as though there is a rainbow of well-written female leading roles," declared Meryl Streep, standing before an audience of several hundred women at the Screen Actors Guild's first National Women's Conference, held in the summer of 1990. "There's very little work for women. And when we do work, we get paid much less than our male counterparts. And what work there is lately is odd." Pointing to the crop of movies that had appeared that year, which included *Total Recall*, *Dick Tracy*, *Die Hard 2*, and *Pretty Woman*, Streep suggested that one might assume "the chief occupation of women on Earth was hooking, and I don't mean rugs."

It was a rare public outburst for Streep, for any actress really, let alone the most respected actress of her generation. Yet the occasion was a somber one. The Screen Actors Guild had just completed a report showing that in 1989, 71 percent of all roles in feature films and 64 percent of all roles in TV went to men. The combined income of all male actors was $644 million, more than double the combined income of all female actors ($296 million).

"If the trend continues, by the year 2000 women will represent thirteen percent of all roles. And in twenty years we will have been eliminated from movies entirely. But that's not going to happen, is it, ladies?" joked Streep, adding that women over forty had practically disappeared from the cineplex. No matter who they are, they "face the age police, who want to see your passport or driver's license.

Carrie Fisher, Meryl Streep, and Shirley MacLaine at
a party for POSTCARDS FROM THE EDGE, 1990.

Streep railed against the Hollywood blockbuster, targeted at young males; against the power of the overseas market, in which Hollywood decision makers believed that only muscles and gunpowder traveled well. She decried the fact that Jack Nicholson, her costar in several movies, earned twice what she did, elaborating later that she didn't "feel greedy," but "when Rick Moranis makes what Michelle Pfeiffer makes . . ." she trailed off. "It's all the way down the line until you hit scale—women make forty to sixty cents on the male dollar.

"Hollywood is run by some stupid and greedy people," she added later. "Too often the studio marketing men think only of men, regarding the choice of the movie as just his. They seem to think that people want to go see violent films or films with Arnold Schwarzenegger."

Everything Streep said was true, although her palpable frustration made the industry see her as petulant rather than heroic, a Cassandra-like figure spouting verities that no one wanted to hear. Other actresses distanced themselves. They weren't paid equally, but they were paid well.

Streep maintained an odd role in the industry, at once the most respected actress of her time and suspect for her steadfast refusal to pander to popular taste, mistrusted for her acting pyrotechnics, her love of pageantry and costumes. Early on she eschewed stardom for art, despised the cult of celebrity, balked at playing sex symbols. There was no fixed Streep persona; each role was a further unveiling of her psyche. Often she didn't even play the beauty card.

"In her willingness to forgo easy identification, Streep brings to dramatic point something that has been nosing its way to the forefront of consciousness for some time: the whole issue of a woman's lovability," commented the critic Molly Haskell. "As women in real life and on-screen choose roles that exude toughness, strength, obsessiveness, ambition, secretiveness, power, and self-interest, as opposed to the traditional (and often hidden) female qualities of openness, vulnerability, and surrender, do they automatically risk losing their 'sex appeal,' hence acceptance? Do they risk losing their marketability?"

Streep certainly seemed devoted to challenging the norms of female behavior. Indeed, throughout the decade she was a one-woman rehabilitation machine for a host of difficult women, rebels, mothers ambivalent toward their children, activists angry about the government, ordinary women furious at their lot in the world. Her women showed no feminine resignation, from *Out of Africa*'s Isak Dinesen, the prototypical self-created female adventurer, to Susan Traherne, the heroine of *Plenty*, whose glory days were in the World War II resistance and who afterward drowns in a tsunami of unwanted domesticity.

Indeed, the part in which Streep seemed to take the most perverse glee was Lindy Chamberlain in *A Cry in the Dark*, the true story of an Australian woman who was accused and unfairly convicted of murdering her baby on a camping trip. The subsequent trial had riveted the country, where the people were eager to believe the worst of Chamberlain because she and her pastor husband didn't conform to the sanctified image of motherhood. She was ugly and stoic; she accepted her child's death with the philosophic resignation espoused by their Seventh-Day Adventist religion. She spent three years in jail, until exonerating evidence was discovered.

"I loved the problem set up in that, which was the woman was vilified by how she appeared," recalls Streep. "That interested me because it was like if she'd only been a better actress, then people would have thought she was innocent. And I wanted to defend her from the inside and not change a thing about the outside of her." Indeed, the worse her circumstances, the more sympathetic Chamberlain became, mostly because she seemed to adhere to her own code of morality, of suffering without sentimentality.

Unfortunately for the actress, *A Cry in the Dark* was for her the third in a series of box-office bombs. In her commitment to being an artist, Streep had forgone much of the power that comes with being a star. She began to tell friends she was tired of the whole seriously suffering Meryl Streep persona and in the late eighties embarked on a series of comedies. She didn't want to be out of touch with the way films were being made.

Ironically, it was the funny women who had survived the decade with their stardom intact. While Kathleen Turner had first caught Hollywood's attention as the manipulative sexpot Matty Walker in *Body Heat*, her biggest hits were the romantic comedy *Romancing the Stone* and the black farces *Prizzi's Honor* and *The War of the Roses*. The unlikely star Bette Midler had torn up the box office in a series of outsize genre pieces—*Ruthless People*, *Outrageous Fortune*, *Big Business*—which capitalized on her brash, domineering persona. The newly revitalized Disney, under Katzenberg and Eisner, liked to bet that they could turn undervalued talents into superstars, and Midler was exhibit number one.

Streep's efforts were less successful. While *Defending Your Life* (and Streep's hilarious lampooning of herself as the perfect woman) had been charming, it performed negligibly at the box office. Her three other comedies, *She-Devil*, *Postcards from the Edge*, and *Death Becomes Her*, all touched on feminist concerns, presenting some of the issues that concerned Streep through a new prism. Unfortunately, the last turned outright woman-hating in its execution.

"*Death Becomes Her* was in advance of its time." Streep sighs. "That's about the desperate, desperate desire for women to stay young. I liked what it was going to be about. I didn't like making it at all." Indeed, she loathed the meticulous mechanics required by F-X filmmaking. "And I don't know if it ended up being about that. I read somebody said it was misogynistic. Oh, no, no, no," she utters playfully, and laughs. "It's the truth!"

Surprising many, Streep moved with her family to L.A. and left her longtime agent Sam Cohn (after a fight over *The Remains of the Day*) for CAA, and her close friend Carrie Fisher's then boyfriend, Bryan Lourd. Critics accused her of trying to shore up her fading commercial appeal (as if ambitiousness on her part was a bad thing). The accusation, especially when wielded in *The New York Times*, enraged her, particularly because no one seemed to believe her when she stated that she had made a number of career decisions based on the welfare of her four children (whom she raised without the requisite Hollywood platoon of nannies).

"I went out there to make *Postcards*. We rented a house. And while I was there, Albert Brooks offered me the role in *Defending Your Life*, which I thought was a hilarious script, and so I said, 'We've gotta rent the house another time.' But we couldn't get that lease, so we rented another house. And we moved everybody. And I made *Defending Your Life*, and then I took another job with Jack Nicholson, and I got pregnant and I couldn't do it. This was after we had rented the house. So then we had enrolled the kids in school, so we stayed there while I was pregnant. And, you know, we had our children in school there. And that's why we did it.

"And [*The New York Times*] thinks that I stayed there because I was desperate to revive my career that was flagging. Believe me, I don't think about this. If it was flagging, I didn't know it. No one told me, because I was getting paid a lot of money and I thought they were good movies that I was in.

"Being actors' kids, [my children] have been moved around. My son Henry went to seven schools. He went to prekindergarten in England, kindergarten in Africa, first grade in Connecticut, second grade in Australia, third grade in Connecticut. Oh, he went to another preschool in Texas. I mean, he's really been jerked around a lot, and by the time he was seven, he said, 'Mom, I don't want to move anymore.' And I really hurt him. I thought, Yeah. Okay. We're not gonna do that anymore."

Streep ultimately moved back to Connecticut. She had found L.A. lonely. "I hate being there," she says. "I really require a great deal of privacy. I don't like to be out and dressed up and seen."

24.

INDECENT PROPOSAL

I'D JUST LIKE A LIFE

In 1989 Sherry Lansing was photographed by Annie Leibovitz for an American Express advertising campaign featuring icons of modern American life. Amid a panoply of heroes such as Ella Fitzgerald and Tip O'Neill, Lansing appeared as the putatively ironic personification of old Hollywood glamour. She was dressed in a long satin gown, standing against the Paramount back lot, her head tossed back in faux abandon, her eyes shaded by a pair of dark glasses—the suggestion being that the modern-day producer, one of the top businesswomen in her field, was really Gilda at heart. She justified the self-promotion by donating her fee to cancer research, although the Paramount wags gossiped that her latest media coronation must have rankled her partner, Stanley Jaffe.

In truth, if there was dissatisfaction in their partnership, it was increasingly Lansing's. She resented more and more that the nonstop work marathon (the latest being a six-month stint in Japan on the set of their Michael Douglas police yarn, *Black Rain*) deprived her of any real personal life. Lansing always had dates with a string of prestigious bachelors—ranging from fl. ations with Pierre Trudeau, the former prime minister of Canada, to serious relationships with the architect Richard Meier (who went on to design the Getty Center) and Count Giovanni Volpi (who presided over the Venice Film Festival), but no relationship endured. "I wondered if perhaps the reason I was alone was because I never had the time to really take more than two days off," says Lansing. She fantasized more and more about quitting the movie busi-

Stanley Jaffe and Sherry Lansing on the set of BLACK RAIN, 1989.

ness for good, maybe devoting herself full-time to her pet cause, the fight against cancer.

Eventually she confessed to Jaffe that she wanted to take a break from the business when her contract expired in two years. " 'I'll be forty-eight, and I just don't want to wake up one day and all I've done is made movies,' " she told him. " 'I have this fantasy, and it's a real fantasy, that if I take time off, that I will finally have a personal life.' I didn't care if I got married, that wasn't it. I'd just like a life. I'd like to come home to something. I'd like real intimacy."

Being Lansing, she asked if he was mad at her. "I'd thought you'd wait until you were fifty," he quipped.

Ironically, it turned out to be Jaffe who ended the partnership. While Lansing had been dithering on *Improper Conduct,* a Harold Becker film that she eventually let wither away because it seemed like nothing more than a *Fatal Attraction* retread, Jaffe was deeply immersed in his second directorial effort, *School Ties,* an old-fashioned exploration of anti-Semitism at a 1950s boys' prep school, which played like a 1950s Sidney Poitier movie where the hero is smarter, better-looking, and more talented than everybody else, and just happens to be not black but Jewish.

Jaffe was squabbling with Paramount's production president, David Kirkpatrick, over the film's budget. The studio was in a box-office slump, and Paramount Communications' chairman, Martin Davis, was under pressure from shareholders to improve the stock price and line up a successor.

In January 1991, Jaffe took a meal with Davis, ostensibly to talk about *School Ties,* although several weeks later he met Lansing at New York's Carlyle Hotel and admitted he'd been offered the job as president of Paramount Communications, which included not only the studio but properties such as Simon & Schuster and Madison Square Garden. She was stung that her business partner and putative best friend had kept such a secret from her, especially in light of the fact that the pair had devoted the last several v. eks to making Jaffe's dream of directing a reality, scouting locations, filling their movie with a bevy of new talent, including the newcomers Matt Damon, Ben Affleck, Brendan Fraser, and Chris O'Donnell. Jaffe apologized, explaining that Davis had sworn him to secrecy. Lansing felt as if he were almost asking her permission to take the job, that he needed reassurance that their relationship would be fine. She told him if he was even thinking about taking the job, he should just do it.

It had been one of the biggest differences between them. Jaffe always wanted more, while Lansing more and more thought she had enough. The driving ambition that had brought her to the heights of Hollywood seemed to have topped out. For Jaffe, who lived and breathed in New York's mediaocracy, running a multinational corporation was the pinnacle of success. For Lansing, Davis's offer provided a neat way to end their partnership. Jaffe could run Paramount, and she could quit the business with a clear conscience.

Jaffe asked Lansing if she wanted to run the studio, but she refused, as she had four other times since she left Fox. She never wanted to be a studio executive again. She told Jaffe that she'd finish out *School Ties* and then, "I'm going to hopefully find a life."

"There is nobody that doesn't love Sherry," Billy Friedkin, Lansing's husband for nine years, sighs. "If there is, I've never seen it. She has more friends, more acquaintances, than anyone I've ever met—people who are in some way emotionally dependent on her almost on a daily basis. She has never cut anyone out of her life."

The Academy Award–winning director of *The French Connection* and *The Exorcist* is sitting in his cluttered office on the Paramount lot. A former Hollywood wunderkind, the Quentin Tarantino of the early seventies, he is now in his mid-sixties dressed in muted colors—leisure pants and Izod shirt with a Boston Celtics logo. He is pudgy with close-set, animal-like eyes whose wary examination peers out from under a veneer of well-honed charm, a onetime arrogant bad boy who has been tamed by maturity, two decades of professional disappointment, and a recent spate of bad press about the exploits of his youth.

On the wall across from his desk are a number of framed, professional glamour photos of Lansing that Friedkin took from his wife. On the wall of her office (in the building next door) are a set of Francis Bacon paintings that she took from him, violent, sexual images, "which she took because she thought they were pretty," jokes Friedkin.

Their marriage surprised almost everybody in Hollywood, a Beauty-and-the-Beast pairing that continues to be mystifying, particularly to those close to Lansing. "I was very surprised, because I found them a very unlikely pair," says the producer Richard Zanuck, who ran Fox when Friedkin made *The French Connection* and has been a friend of

Lansing's for decades. "I've never seen Sherry happier. Billy is Billy, but it seems to be working great. She seems to be just so in love with him, and taken by him, and almost mesmerized by him."

"She has a need for harmony in her life, and I perhaps have a need for chaos," philosophizes Friedkin, the latest in a string of bad boys who caught Lansing's fancy. "I will often try to communicate every side of the experiences I have, and she's only interested in the bright side of it. Does not want to dwell on negatives. She can't have negativity around her."

Friedkin's reputation is certainly one of the most checkered in Hollywood: the early brilliance, the controversial, wildly successful early films, which went hand in hand with extreme arrogance, manifesting itself in both contempt and outrageous posturing in relations with rising studio executives such as Barry Diller, as well as a penchant for the firing of good portions of his crews in fits of bad temper. All would have been professionally forgiven if his films had continued to make money, but after *The Exorcist* they did not; even the critics savaged such efforts as *Cruising* and *Rampage* for misogyny, homophobia, or for simply being extremely ugly views of mankind. Like those of his contemporaries Bob Rafelson and Peter Bogdanovich (with whom he once shared a production company), his career floundered.

Friedkin's track record with women was equally volatile. "The first sex I had was with a black hooker, five bucks a pop, and for years I would just see hookers," he told one journalist. While he installed his beloved mother in Beverly Hills and took care of her until her death, he cut a swath through the female population, spawning persistent rumors of tempestuous liaisons, an illegitimate son, whose relation he would acknowledge only after a paternity test, and three marriages, to Jeanne Moreau (for eighteen months), the L.A. news anchor Kelly Lange (two years), and the *Upstairs, Downstairs* actress Lesley-Anne Down (three years). The last marriage produced a son, Jack, and a vicious custody battle.

"I think I was sort of unconscious during my other marriages," says Friedkin. "None of it really meant a lot to me—the whole idea of making it work. I was more involved with other things during the time of my other marriages. I used to play basketball for like twenty years and travel on the road with the Boston Celtics, and go to the rookie camp. I was married, but it didn't matter. I love spending time with Sherry. I find it very entertaining. I don't go out on the road with the Boston Celtics anymore. One of the reasons is they're a lousy team too."

Friedkin was on his way to a Chinese gambling club in Gardena in 1991 when Tita Cahn, the wife of his close friend Sammy Cahn, dragooned him into accompanying her to an Academy Award party given by the real-estate investor Richard Cohen. She introduced him to Lansing, an acquaintance, after which, says Cahn, "Billy leaned in and said to me, 'I had no idea Sherry Lansing was such a fox,' and a bit later Sherry said to me, 'I had no idea Billy Friedkin was so young and sexy.' "

Soon after the party they began dating. "They were totally smitten with one another," says Cahn. "And, in fact, it became a running gag. He would be holding her hand and saying, 'If you love her, you have to protect her, don't let me marry her,' because Billy had been married several times before. He said, 'I'm like the Drake Hotel murderer' [referring to a famous murderer in Chicago during Friedkin's youth], who would write in lipstick, Stop me before I kill again. He would say, 'Stop me before I marry again.' "

Three months after they met, Lansing skipped a budget meeting on *School Ties* (perhaps the first skipped meeting of her life) to secretly marry Friedkin in Barbados.

Friedkin looked up the number of a synagogue in the phone book and found out it would take three months to get a rabbi up from Venezuela. They decided to try a nondenominational clergyman who they had heard conducted interfaith weddings. An elegant black man, he invited them to watch him perform a ceremony, after which, "Sherry said, 'Look, we're both Jewish and you have this cassock and you are wearing a cross and you're using a Bible.' She said, 'I could never have the words Jesus Christ in our ceremony,' " recalls Friedkin. "And he said, 'Oh that's not a problem. I'll just go through the text and I'll omit any reference to Christianity or Christ.' She said, 'Great.' "

They were married at their rented beach house, the only witnesses the compound's two domestics. The minister began referring to Christ in the ceremony. "And he did this a couple of times, and Sherry said, 'Hold it, wait a minute,' in the middle of the ceremony, and he said, 'What's wrong?' And she said, 'You said you weren't going to mention Jesus.' And he then said, 'Oh yes, I'm sorry,' " says Friedkin. "She made him take off the crucifix he was wearing. And so then he went through the ceremony and he started to sight-edit it. And when she first stopped it she was very upset and irate, and she pulled me aside and said, 'Did you hear what he said?' And I said, 'Yeah.' She said, 'Didn't it bother you?' And I said, 'No.'

"So then after the ceremony we were talking, and I said, 'Sherry, I have to tell you something. I am not a Christian, but the mention of Jesus Christ really doesn't bother me. In fact, I'm fascinated and interested by Christ.'

"And she said, 'Do you believe in him? Do you believe in Jesus?' And I said, 'I guess I do.' And she said, 'How could you believe in Jesus?' I said, 'Sherry, for two thousand years hundreds of millions of people have believed in Jesus.' And she said, 'Do you think he was a god?' And I said, 'Well, again, for two thousand years there's millions of people who've believed he was the son of God, and I can't say that he wasn't.'

"And she said, 'Well, I don't.'

"And I said, 'Well, what do you think about Jesus?'

"She said, 'I think he was a nice guy, that is all. But he's not a god.' "

"Billy is what I need and want, and I don't know if I would have recognized Billy when I was in my twenties either," says Lansing. Despite his vivid past, Lansing saw Friedkin as a true aesthete, like her father, a fierce intellectual with a passion for Proust and classical music, a superb eye for art, and a resulting collection that includes Picassos. He was a Chicago Jew like her, yet he seemed to possess the quality she admires most: He was an iconoclast and a provocateur. "Billy is definitely out there. I can watch Billy at a dinner party when nobody's very lively. I can watch his eyes and he's getting bored and he'll just say something to make everybody go, 'What? He's kidding.' And he's not. And then he'll get energized. It stimulates him." And it amuses Lansing. "It really does," she says. "I never would do that."

Almost every man Lansing had seriously dated had proposed to her, and many of the relationships had ended when she refused, although she assiduously maintained a friendship with every former flame. "I didn't want to marry anyone because I felt in every relationship that I was in—and it's not their fault—a complete loss of myself," she says. "It's like I felt that my identity would never exist." Given her relationship with her mother, it was not surprising that Lansing was attracted to men who could be controlling, to rich men used to getting their own way. Nor was it surprising that people misread her seeming desire to

422 / IS THAT A GUN IN YOUR POCKET?

please, her need for social harmony, as a desire to transform. It was a common misconception, even after *Fatal Attraction* had made her so much more confident. "I just felt like nobody let me be myself. Billy was the only person who said, 'I'm not asking you to change.' It was non-judgmental, unconditional love for the first time.

"Of all the men I've ever been with, Billy was the only man who didn't seem to put restraints on me," she rhapsodizes. Friedkin didn't seem threatened by the vortex of her work life and her ambition. "It was like he was the only man who didn't seem to pout when I was late, do you know what I mean? If I called up and said, 'I have to work,' he seemed to say, 'Oh, no problem.'

"I remember when we were shooting *Indecent Proposal,* and it was probably like a year into our marriage, and we were shooting all night. Lots of times I would call and he would say, 'Don't worry, honey, I understand. Just stay there as long as is necessary.' He was just very supportive. And so was Jack, I never had a stepson who would say, 'But you said you'd be home.' He was a kid who understood it. He didn't complain."

They had radically different philosophies toward films, imbued perhaps by Lansing's recent successes and Friedkin's recent misfires. "She genuinely loves movies, which I don't anymore," says the director. "I don't like these movies that are being made. She has a fabulous feel for it, and I think it stems from the fact that she emotionally is like part of the public. I was. When I did *The French Connection* and *The Exorcist* I used to ride the subways, and I was not rich, and I lived very much like the people that I was making movies for. I knew exactly what films they would want to see in that period because they were what I wanted to see. Now I feel almost totally disconnected from that, and she's very connected to it still. Her tastes are, well, obviously the tastes of the average person, but mine are definitely not. My tastes are much more acquired."

How does he handle their discrepancies in taste, not only in what makes a good movie but in how one arrives there? Citing Christian scriptures, Friedkin quips, "*Render unto Caesar the things that are Caesar's.*" He neglects to finish the quote: "And to God the things that are God's."

In the fall of 1992 ShowEast, a convention of theater exhibitors, named Sherry Lansing producer of the year. When the ceremony was

over, Stanley Jaffe took her hand to lead her through the packed Atlantic City convention hall. He beamed like a teenager escorting the
prom queen. For a contingent of Paramount onlookers, it was clear that
Lansing was coming to take over the studio.

The following week, Jaffe begged Lansing to come to his rescue and
replace Brandon Tartikoff as chairman of Paramount Pictures. Not
only was the former NBC programming whiz distracted by a personal
crisis (a major car accident involving his daughter) but he seemed unable to put pictures together expeditiously. Paramount was supposed to
be making twenty pictures but was making only nine. As he lost faith
in his chairman, Jaffe began to micromanage, green-lighting projects
without consulting Tartikoff and terrifying the production staff with
his explosive temper. Some in the studio workforce were further alienated by Jaffe's displays of wealth in magazines such as *HG* at a time
when he had pink-slipped close to four hundred employees.

Jaffe promised Lansing that it would be nothing like her misbegotten tenure at Fox. She would have complete support and total authority over marketing and distribution. He and later his boss, Martin Davis,
stressed that the first year would be relatively easy because there were
so many sequels in the works, such as *Addams Family Values, Wayne's
World 2,* and *Beverly Hills Cop III.* He neglected to enlighten her about
his problems with Tartikoff.

Both Jaffe and Davis promised Lansing that the chairmanship would
be a boon to her personal life. For the first year and a half of her marriage, Lansing had been on location half the time, shooting *Indecent
Proposal,* another Adrian Lyne special about a wife (Demi Moore) who
agrees to sleep with a mogul (Robert Redford) for a million bucks. Jaffe
waxed on about how she could spend more time with her new husband
and stepson. "[Stanley] wanted Billy to feel comfortable," adds Lansing.
Indeed, Jaffe, trying to reach Lansing through her husband, invited
Friedkin to sit in on the job discussions. Friedkin refused to lean on her
one way or the other. "He said to me, 'I don't care. Do it or don't do it,
either way, it doesn't make any difference,' " says Lansing. "I asked Jack,
and he didn't care one way or the other. Jack didn't even know what I
was talking about."

She solicited the advice of Michael Ovitz, who was not only her
agent but at that time the godfather of Hollywood. While it's unlikely
that he would have asked about her spouse if she were a man, Ovitz too
wondered what Friedkin thought of the opportunity. Billy just wanted

her to be happy, she assured him. Ovitz stressed that the relentlessness of the job would play havoc with her personal life. If her family didn't care, it was up to her. She admitted she wanted to do it. He made her promise not to talk to Jaffe until he made her deal.

In November, it was announced that Sherry Lansing had been made chairman of Paramount Motion Picture Group. Her responsibilities were less than Tartikoff's because she didn't want to run the TV department, of which she knew nothing. In the press attending her promotion, she reiterated that she was probably the first studio chairman who took the job so she could be home for dinner. Any sense of her own ambition was carefully veiled, as was the primary reason she agreed to take the position—she could never have refused Jaffe. "Truly, she took the job for Stanley. He said, 'I really need you to do this,' " says Friedkin. "I think part of her motivation was to succeed in it for Stanley. She didn't want to do the job again, and I don't think she would have done it for a stranger." Indeed, other friends hypothesize that Lansing entered the Paramount fray precisely to dispel the lingering stink of failure from her Fox debacle.

When she went to see Tartikoff about the transition, she thanked him for making it so easy for her, for putting all these projects into the pipeline. He looked at her blankly and informed her that none of those films—*Wayne's World 2* or *Addams Family Values*—had a script. They were just titles. Intentions for movies. In actuality the Paramount cupboard was so bare that the studio could conceivably stop distributing movies for an entire year—that or radically slash the normal postproduction time on the films they did have.

She called Jaffe. "There's no script for *Beverly Hills Cop III*! There's no script for anything! What did you do? There's nothing."

"You didn't expect me to tell you everything, did you?" he retorted, and laughed.

A GIANT LEAP

HAD I HAD A GUN IN MY HAND, I VERY LIKELY WOULD HAVE JUST SHOT RIGHT AT HIM

Callie Khouri was walking down the street in West Hollywood when two men pulled up alongside her in a Mercedes and one—who was old enough to be her grandfather—screamed, "I'd like to see you suck my cock." Khouri was in her early twenties, strapping and athletic, with tumbles of blond hair and a wide-open face. Here I am, I'm working this shitty waitress job. I'm just walking to put my thirty dollars of tips in my crummy little bank account, and I have to take this shit? Khouri thought.

Moments later she snapped. She whipped off her sunglasses, stalked toward the car, and leaned into the convertible. "You don't know who you're talking to," she purred with clearly honed malice. "The unmitigated nerve of that guy just absolutely short-circuited me. I realized at that moment, What if I had a gun? Had I had a gun in my hand, I very likely would have just shot right at him."

It was a moment that crystallized in Khouri's mind, the taunt that ignited her simmering frustration into a fire of rage. She couldn't bear the discrepancy between who she wanted to be and who others thought she was—between this private vision of herself and what she could effect in the world. She was high-spirited but impatient, with a big mouth, a crackling wit, and an underlying vulnerability. She was an idealist, with a streak of naïveté that made her disappointments exceptionally heartfelt. Khouri had spent the last several years floundering,

Callie Khouri and Harvey Keitel at the premiere of
A LEAGUE OF THEIR OWN, 1992.

PETER BORSARI

imbued with the sense that "there was something I'm supposed to be doing, but I just can't figure out what it is."

In truth, she had never been able to stay with anything. She was a doctor's daughter from Kentucky; her father had died when she was sixteen. Khouri majored in drama at Purdue University but skipped out after only five semesters and detoured to Nashville, where her widowed mother lived. She had apprenticed at a local theater and waitressed before making the pilgrimage to L.A., ostensibly to act. She studied with the acting gurus Lee Strasberg and Peggy Feury but flailed at auditions. "I wasn't one of those people who could really drag myself into an agent's office and do all those things I knew other people were doing to get parts," recalls Khouri. "Part of the reason, I wasn't seeing anything out there that I wanted to do. I always said half-jokingly that Debra Winger got my acting career. The roles she got were the ones I saw as really attractive." The roles offered to Khouri were usually prostitutes.

In 1984 she landed a job as a receptionist at a music video production company and worked her way up to producing videos for Robert Cray, Alice Cooper, and the Commodores. Order made her feel good. She liked the certainty of putting numbers in a column and was adept at bossing people around. "I loved production, but I hated the result," says Khouri. She was embarrassed by the inherent mediocrity and ashamed of the roiling misogyny. "As antiwoman as I feel those things can be, the women never failed to show up in droves. The consciousness that was out there was as depressing as the fact that I was out there participating in making them. There was only one time that a girl said to me, 'I can't do this. I'm dressed like a whore. I can't go through with this. You guys say you need a dancer. I'm not here as a dancer. I'm here looking like a prostitute.' All the other times, it seemed like the girls were willing to exploit the shit out of themselves."

Mostly Khouri despaired that she wasn't doing anything creative. As a kid she had secretly fantasized about being a writer, although she'd never done much about it aside from a few poems scribbled in a journal. "To me being a writer was always the highest calling, and one that I always thought was well outside my own abilities. I kind of revered the process to the point of going, 'Oh lowly me, you should never even attempt such a lofty thing,' but then after living out here for a few years, and seeing what passes for work, and the amount of really bad writing that gets made, I just thought, Jesus, who am I kidding? I could do this with one hand tied behind my back."

One night she was pulling up to her Santa Monica apartment when, recalls Khouri, "This idea just popped into my head: Two women go on a crime spree." It was the genesis of *Thelma & Louise*. "It was like a bolt of lightning thing. I just went, 'Oh, my gosh. I just had an idea, and I think it's going to change my life.' And it is like I saw the whole thing in a flash. I saw the transformation."

Starting in February 1988, Khouri spent six months sketching out the script in longhand, writing whenever she could fit it in around her work schedule, and often traveling back to her office in Hollywood late at night to input her work on a computer. Thelma's and Louise's voices filled her head. "I wanted [the characters] to be people who you could understand and relate to," says Khouri. "I didn't want them to be like power executives. I wanted them to just be the kind of women you see in a grocery store, the kind of women that you don't notice. You have no idea that there is this incredible person in there."

Thelma evolved into an eager but innocent housewife who is kept in a state of childish dependency by her husband, a stupid, bullying carpet salesman named Darryl. By contrast, her neat, precise, in-control friend Louise, a waitress, lives with the nice but feckless traveling musician Jimmy, a man who can't commit. Louise entices Thelma to shed Darryl for a long weekend and join her at a friend's vacation home. On the way, the fun-loving Thelma convinces Louise to stop for a drink at a roadhouse, where a local womanizing thug mistakes her naive and drunken flirtatiousness for seduction. He tries to rape Thelma in the parking lot, but Louise rescues her at gunpoint. When the rapist is unrepentant, and taunts Louise with "suck my cock," she shoots him, in an echo of what went through Khouri's mind during the incident in West Hollywood. "I didn't know that people would cheer when it happened," says Khouri. "And that really freaked me out, because I wanted them to be making this huge mistake. She just inalterably changed the course of their lives." Convinced that the authorities won't believe them, the pair decide to make a break for Mexico, and the rest of the film riffs on classic outlaw films, chronicling Thelma's and Louise's psychic emancipation as the long arm of the law hunts them down. The film ends with a *Butch Cassidy and the Sundance Kid* homage: The outlaws drive off a cliff into the Grand Canyon, a last gasp at freedom, a kind of giant fuck-you to male authority.

Writing the script was "the most joyous experience I have had in my life that doesn't involve my relationship with my husband," says

Khouri. "It was the defining experience of my life so far. It is the time I felt the most full, the most complete. Like I was actually doing what I was put here on Earth to do."

Khouri let her roommate read her pages as she went along, and when she was done she gave the script to several friends, including her fellow video producer Amanda Temple, wife of the rising video director Julien Temple. Amanda Temple was going to produce, Khouri direct. "I knew I could convince somebody to give me a few million dollars. Whether it took one, five, ten, or twenty years, I could get the movie made with me directing someday. And that's what I wanted to do," says Khouri. Temple sent the script to Mimi Polk, head of Ridley Scott's production company, for advice on raising foreign financing. Scott, the talented director of *Blade Runner*, wanted to buy the property initially just to produce. It was a fork in the road. "I knew I was giving something up, but I also knew I was going to get the movie made," recalls Khouri. "Amanda got pregnant too with her first child, and wasn't going to be able to produce it for a while. She was pretty adamant that it was the right thing to do."

Scott pitched the film to a number of studios, where development executives despaired that the women weren't sympathetic enough. Despite Scott's stature, only MGM, by far the weakest studio in town, was game to let him make the movie exactly the way he wanted. (Ironically, MGM was now run by Alan Ladd, Jr., who when he was at Fox had backed projects such as *Julia* and *Nine to Five*.) One of Scott's development people slipped the script to the ICM agent Diane Cairns, who immediately signed Khouri. Khouri had sold the project to Scott and MGM for $500,000. Polk told her gaily that she could buy a house. Scott eventually opted to direct, although he could secure a budget of only $17.5 million, far less than he would have gotten with two male protagonists. He stipulated in his contract that the ending would remain as written: The women go off the cliff.

In the beginning Khouri was thrilled with the process. She spent several weeks with Scott finessing the script. Mostly the goal was to shorten it, and they ended up paring several scenes that showed the complexity of Thelma and Louise's relationship. In the most poignant one, each woman confides what she fears most in the world, essentially, growing older. For Thelma, it's spending the rest of her life with her husband, who doesn't love her; for Louise, it's spending the rest of her life alone. The project was offered to a bevy of actresses, including

Meryl Streep and Goldie Hawn, who turned it down, before the film-makers settled on Susan Sarandon and Geena Davis. Khouri's opinions were never solicited, although later Davis took the writer out, plying her with question after question about Thelma's character.

Once filming started, Khouri was relegated to being persona non grata. "It was weird to go from spending every day with Ridley to being completely and utterly excommunicated," she says. Even to be allowed to visit the set took several days of negotiation. "It was humiliating, and it changed me forever, because I was treated like a nonbeing. I think it was because of Mimi. Mimi actually said to me, 'Darling, that's always how it is. The writer never gets to do blah blah blah,' " says Khouri. She wasn't invited to any preview screenings. (They did test an alternative ending, which failed miserably with the audience.) Khouri paid her own way to New York to attend one screening, then watched as Scott, Polk, and the studio brass went off to discuss the results. She wasn't invited to the New York premiere. "It was the closing-night film of the Cannes Film Festival. I was prohibited from going," says Khouri. "It is the way writers are typically treated. I had a typical experience, and it made me vehement that I would never go through it again. After the movie came out, everybody wanted to talk to me. Before, they all pretended like Geena and Susan and Ridley made the whole thing up."

At least Scott was a talented director, and Khouri recognized it. The taciturn Brit had inadvertently created the first female superhero with 1979's *Alien*, a script that featured a male protagonist until the producers, Walter Hill and David Giler, decided to play a mind game with audience expectation; they rewrote the part of Ridley, the lone surviving member of the space crew, to be played by a woman, Sigourney Weaver. Scott ensured that the character, while imperiled, showed grit and mettle. Recalls Weaver, "They gave me this costume that was light blue with a little pink trim. And Ridley came in, and he said, 'You look like fucking Jackie Onassis in space.' And we went into this room, and we were pulling things around, and he threw me this flight thing from NASA, and I put it on and it fit perfectly."

A stunning visualist, Scott painted *Thelma & Louise* in mythic terms, outsize characters hurtling in a bright blue convertible across the American West, a landscape that is part desert, part industrial waste-land, a land where minimalls alternate with the otherworldly vistas of Monument Valley. Thelma's and Louise's passions are given grandeur. When a loathsome oil-tank trucker hassles them with sexual taunts, they blow up his rig with a burst of firepower and a boom loud enough to shatter public consciousness. Davis and Sarandon turned in spectacular performances, and Scott alternated the vistas with close-ups of Davis's unkempt giddiness and Sarandon's tightly withheld fears, the drama inside the car as exciting as that outside. He carefully preserved Khouri's conceit—that the relationship between the two women remain paramount.

Unlike a legion of male buddy movies in which the relationship seems like an exercise in joint narcissism, an avenue for each partner to achieve autonomy, *Thelma & Louise* presents sisterhood over all. "I have a lot of friendships that have good points and bad points that fit together really well. Our weaknesses are compensated by the other's strengths. I wanted them to be like that, to be a real team," recalls Khouri. "And that is the kind of relationship I wanted to have, and I wanted it to be nonsexual."

As the movie progresses, Louise's remorse over what she's done, and fear of the consequences, erode her take-charge persona, leading her to cede control to Thelma, who's discovered freedom for the first time in her life. Empowerment is eroticizing as Thelma tastes her first orgasm with a young hitchhiker they pick up; unfortunately, he absconds with Louise's life savings, although he instructs Thelma in the finer points of armed robbery. After she holds up a convenience store, Louise tells her, "You've always been crazy. This is just the first chance you've had to express yourself."

Thelma's joyous embrace of the outlaw life, coupled with the fact that the film avoids any explanation for Louise's descent into violence, other than an allusion to a traumatic experience in her past (presumably a rape), seemed most to enrage a certain kind of viewer. Unlike in most movies of the week, Louise's action isn't succinctly justified by gang rape, incest, or any tabloid TV staple. The film implies that her murderous response is the effect not of a lone, aberrant victimization but of a lifetime of sexual exploitation, the kind that most women suffer, the taunts one hears walking by a construction site, or in one's own home. Furthermore, the film offers an array of deeply flawed male characters: a chauvinistic husband, a sexy but snaky drifter, a guy who can't commit, and Harvey Keitel as a well-meaning cop who's sympathetic but only from afar. This led some critics to label *Thelma & Louise* a man-bashing rant.

The film debuted in the spring of 1991 to a torrent of controversy, the first movie to inspire such table pounding since *Fatal Attraction*.

Thelma & Louise landed on the cover of *Time*, was discussed on *Crossfire*, and was dissected in editorials across America. "A paean to transformative violence . . . an explicit fascist theme," decried John Leo in *U.S. News & World Report*.

"It justifies armed robbery, manslaughter, and chronic drunken driving as exercises in consciousness raising," fumed Richard Johnson in the New York *Daily News*; he added that it was "degrading to men, with pathetic stereotypes of testosterone-crazed behavior."

"Call *Thelma & Louise* anything you want but please don't call it *feminism*," roiled Sheila Benson in the *Los Angeles Times*. "As I understand it feminism has to do with responsibility, equality, sensitivity, understanding—not revenge, retribution, or sadistic behavior."

An equal number of critics championed the film as breathtaking and gender busting, decrying those who found female violence upsetting while blithely watching Schwarzenegger and Stallone blast their way through film after film. "Its heroines are thoroughly independent. No wonder they've ruffled a few feathers," wrote Janet Maslin in *The New York Times*. "It's exhilarating, that ride, during which Thelma and Louise aim their ire, and a pistol, at a lifetime of sexist indignities. When they're finally halted, at the edge of the Grand Canyon, they've no place left to run. Even so, Thelma and Louise keep on running—and if their leave-taking is tragic, it is also triumphant." "Divested of all their worldly goods, and all their worldly fears, they're not carrying any baggage when they go," added Mary Cantwell in an editorial in the same paper.

While the debate centered on the film's violence, perhaps the line that resonated most with viewers was Louise's credo, "You get what you settle for." It was more a call to self-assertion than a call to arms.

Suddenly attention was showered on Khouri, who thrived in her moment in the limelight, although she took umbrage at the gender-based criticism, particularly the charge that the film was man-bashing. The week *Thelma & Louise* went into production, Khouri had gotten married in a big poufy dress in Nashville to the writer-producer Dave Warfield. "After that initial period of being totally stunned by that criticism, it really made me angry," says Khouri. "I had gone into movie theaters and watched women be treated completely as shit for as long as I can remember, and they can't take a little good-natured jab. Oh, a rapist got shot. Bad guys get killed in every goddamn movie that gets made, and that guy was the bad guy and he got killed. It was only because a woman did it that there was any kind of controversy at all. If a guy had come out and saved their asses and shot that guy and said, 'Run, quick,' do you think there would be a fucking moment of controversy?"

Khouri also chafed at those who perceived Thelma and Louise's relationship as homoerotic: "Everything about women in films and literature, they're so sexualized anyway. And that was something that I was actually trying to make a point about. These were two women who were not going to conform to the expectations, and a lesbian relationship is one of those expectations."

The film wound up grossing $43 million domestically, a respectable figure but less perhaps than it would have had it been released by a major studio. Khouri won that year's Oscar for Best Screenplay. In retrospect, she was sure of one thing, she had never intended Thelma and Louise to be literal role models: "I heard a conservative type on a talk show say, 'Well, what are we saying here? Are we saying we should give all women guns and they should then kill themselves?' " recalls Khouri. "If that's the literal interpretation you walk away from a movie theater with, then perhaps you should not be allowed to go into a movie theater. If you're really taking everything you see on a movie screen at face value, then you're stupid."

I CAN'T REALLY GO OUT ALL THE TIME AND FEEL OKAY ABOUT WHAT MIGHT HAPPEN TO ME

In October 1991, Jodie Foster landed on the cover of *Time*. She appeared to be sitting in a screening room, the glow from the projector casting a golden halo over her head, the light from the off-camera screen highlighting the earnest scrutiny of her porcelain features. The headline blazed, A DIRECTOR IS BORN.

No other female director had ever received such hosannas, no male director been cheered for such a modest directorial effort. At age twenty-eight, Foster had directed *Little Man Tate*, a lovely, well-told tale of a young mathematical genius torn between the affections of his intellectually limited but nurturing blue-collar mom, Dede, played by Foster, and his mentor, Jane Grierson (Dianne Wiest), an emotionally crippled former child prodigy who runs a school for gifted kids. *Time* compared Foster's work with Louis Malle's legendary exploration of childhood, *Murmur of the Heart*, and trotted out Malle to praise it. "Jodie's film is basically about the profound loneliness of childhood, and she's dealt with it head-on," he said, adding, with a touch of condescension, "I would be very happy and proud to have made the film she did."

The film was nowhere near as challenging or provocative as a host of films she had made as a child. It was nice, sincere, a counterpoint to the suburban fiction of such writers as Ethan Canin and Amy Bloom. Foster's rapturous acceptance as a director (a number of other magazine covers followed suit) seemed not only a surefire way to sell more magazines but a mass confabulation between actress and star, endowing her small, middlebrow tale with the strength and moral vigor of her screen persona.

Indeed, Foster was coming off her first blockbuster hit, *The Silence of the Lambs,* in which she played the FBI trainee Clarice Starling, a role she claims most parallels who she is in real life—a woman with a mission "to save the women she's been taught to disrespect. She needed to love them in order to respect them, to not find repulsive their commonness, their fatness, their anonymity. It's examining what she's so goddamned afraid of becoming that finally gives her the answer."

As she did for *The Accused,* Foster campaigned for the role in *Silence.* She had initially tried to buy Thomas Harris's book herself. When it was too late for that, she kept in contact with the writer Ted Tally as he worked on the script, lobbied Orion for the part, and later flew to New York to convince the director, Jonathan Demme, to consider her should his first choice, Michelle Pfeiffer, pass, which she did, turned off by the darkness of the material.

Silence is a feminist twist on the serial killer genre; the hunted becomes the hunter. Starling rescues the maiden from the clutches of Buffalo Bill, who chases women not simply for their sex but literally for their bodies, their skins, with which he hopes to make a "woman suit." Unlike in the typical slasher fare, where sex and violence are commingled in a toxic stew, Demme rigorously stripped Buffalo Bill's actions of sexual frisson.

Moreover, whereas the Foster of *Taxi Driver* and *Bugsy Malone* wore a kind of pasted-on sexuality, like a little girl in her mother's high heels, Starling's attempt to dress like a woman—she dons a skirt when she goes to see the psychopathic psychiatrist and serial killer Hannibal Lecter in prison—earns her verbal abuse from the other prisoners and scorn from the mad doctor.

The Foster of *The Silence of the Lambs* is a virginal woman warrior whose ambition renders her solitary. In the book, Starling seeks advice from both the bad father, the serial killer Lecter (played so memorably by Anthony Hopkins), and the good, her boss, the head of the FBI serial killer unit, with whom she has an unconsummated romance while his wife lies dying. Demme removed the Oedipal subplot and depicted Starling as wary, even with members of her own team, who use her as bait for Lecter. Her boss sends her to tease information out of the mad psychiatrist, although he warns paternalistically, "Whatever you do, Clarice, don't tell him anything about yourself."

It is advice soon discarded; Starling must forge her own path. She is not merely a Rambo-ette figure but a woman who uses her vulnerability to solve the mystery. Her famous confrontations with the psychopath—shot in a series of riveting close-ups—play like a psychiatry session gone mad, in which Lecter goads her into personal revelation as the price of information.

"The way he tortures her is by feeling sorry for her, which is probably the worst thing you could ever do to Clarice," recalls Foster. "He was in the middle of something, and then he started imitating my accent. The first time he did it, I wanted to cry or smack him. I just was so upset. You're in a scene, so you sort of feel those things, but as an actor, having somebody imitate your accent—it just killed me. It was the perfect thing for Lecter to do, because Clarice has been hiding her rural accent, trying to speak better, escape her origins in a certain way. And here's a guy who nails her." As Starling struggles to maintain composure, Foster's reactions are marvels of economy and pathos.

Ironically enough, while *The Silence of the Lambs* earned Foster her second Oscar, it sparked a vocal backlash from gay activists who perceived Buffalo Bill as a negative stereotype and targeted Foster (rather than Demme or anyone else involved in the production) in an "outing" campaign. "Jodie Foster, TIME'S UP," wrote Michelangelo Signorile in *OutWeek*. "If your lesbianism is too sacred, too private, too infringing of your damned rights for you to discuss publicly, then the least you can do is refrain from making movies that insult this community. Is that too much to ask of you? You want to have your cake and eat it, too. No way, sister." Another group posted flyers around New York City with pictures of celebrities they claimed to be gay. Under Foster's mug was the caption, "Absolutely queer. Oscar winner. Yale graduate. Ex–Disney moppet. Dyke." Activists protested at the Academy Awards as the stars strolled up the red carpet.

For years John Hinckley, Jr., was a taboo subject for those who interviewed Foster. Now she was the target of questions about her private life, queries that she fobbed off with pointed coldness. Her lawyers were vigilant in protecting her privacy.

"The problem is, I can't really go out all the time and feel okay about what might happen to me," says Foster in the autumn of 1994. She is curled up in a big, comfortable chair in her offices at Egg Pictures, her production company. Her sister Connie designed the decor—soft, white couches with kilim throw pillows, elegant black-and-white photographs on the walls, rows of dog-eared books. Out in the hallway, a security guard stands by the elevator, not far from the bolted waiting-room door—an ever-present legacy of Hinckley and the paparazzi who hound her about her private life. "I don't get to go out like other people do. I can't go to McDonald's or a coffee shop."

Foster is decked out in Hollywood armor—a suit, hair cropped to the chin, horn-rimmed glasses. She's gracious but tired, suffering from nights of bad dreams and sleeplessness because, she says, she doesn't live anywhere anymore. Foster bought a house in the Valley near her mother a couple of years ago, when she was in an "L.A. is a scuzzy Hollywood town" mood, but now she thinks it's too far from town. She's having trouble finding a new place; she can't bear what an ugly doorknob or badly designed light switch might imply about her. She has a fear of being trapped. She's been camping out at a friend's long enough, and she's planning to move into a hotel on Friday. It's a depressing thought.

Foster seems at once intensely vulnerable and intensely defended, fragile but on guard. "I'm not somebody that's comfortable being emotionally available. It's not easy for me to show weakness," she says. Her world is a circumscribed one, by both natural inclination and necessity. She has few friends, she mentions—"the five guys in my life all know each other and get really jealous of each other," she says, "and I would die for them. If it was three in the morning and they said, Quick, get $100,000 and get on an airplane and go to Tehran, I would be there. They're some of the most solid feelings that I have in my life." Her personal life—and Foster has relationships—is kept under tight wraps.

"She's meticulous and calculating about everything. Everything's geared towards self-protection and not getting abused," recalls one friend. "She's so well-defended, I'm not sure she knows who she is anymore. She's thrown away the key."

Foster has a frequent dream of herself as a member of a band of hooligans who commit "bad, horrible crimes," leaving destruction in their wake, with nary a thought of guilt or remorse. In her dreams she's often in a movie. "I'm somebody who in some ways really does see the world through my head," she says. She sees acting as a kind of therapy, formerly a way of acting out what is not allowed, now a way of having a life she's often not permitted. "I tend as an actor to choose lives that I never had to be, or that I never got to be or that I never was allowed to be, and it's a way of ritualizing that kind of shadow side of yourself. Whereas the directing in movies is about who you are. Totally about *who you are.* Not about who you aren't, or who you could have been, or who you might have been had this happened; it's not about hypothetical scenarios at all, it's totally about who you are, what your personality is, what your sense of humor is, what your tone is, who you like, who you don't like."

As a filmmaker she's gravitated not to the mythic but to the superordinary—obsessed with family bonds, the drama that can happen inside a single house, the search by "outsiders trying to figure out a subset where they fit in—an incredibly complicated psychological family of sorts," as she explains.

Foster had wanted to direct ever since she was a child: "Well, it's obvious when you're a little kid and you're on a movie set and you work with eighty-five people, and you say, 'Well, what am I gonna be when I grow up?' You look at the director and think, That's what I'll be. At five or six years old, that's really obvious that that's the power place."

As a teenager she directed a short film for the BBC, *The Hands of Time,* based on a painting her father had given her mother, one in a series by John Wilby that depicted a man's life through his hands. "It showed the progression of man from being a baby. And then it took it to a boy's hand playing with a blue marble. Then it goes on to a boy's hand with a peach, which symbolized puberty. And then a woman's breast—touching the nipple of a woman's breast, and then an old man's hands," recalls Brandy Foster. "I would love to have had all of the paintings. But at that time the painting was almost a thousand dollars, and that was a lot of money in 1957. But my husband did buy me the one with the woman with [the breast]. And so we always talked about that painting. And I had a picture of the brochure that came from that show. And we talked about how I would like to have had the series. And so she took it from that. She used her nephew as the baby, and she picked up an old man in the park in Santa Monica who had very gnarled hands for the old man, and she ran through a man's life through his hands."

Foster leveraged her Oscar from *The Accused* into an opportunity to direct *Little Man Tate*, a script that had languished in Hollywood for almost a decade, at one time attached to the director Joe Dante, then passing into the possession of Scott Rudin. When Dawn Steel asked Foster what she wanted to do after her post-*Accused* Oscar blush, Foster, who had fished the script out of the slush pile, mentioned *Tate*. Steel was mystified by her choice—" 'Why do you want to do that? It's such a small movie,' " she asked.

"I said, 'Well, you know, it's a real small movie but it's great,' " recalls Foster, who was eager to play the mother, Dede, mostly to help get the film into production. Looking back on the completed film, it's easy to see the appeal of the story for Foster; it seems to encapsulate so many themes from her life: the child prodigy, set apart from his peers, with an unusually close and closeted relationship with his single mother. Foster mulled over her involvement: "Finally I said, 'Well, I'm going to direct it, so ha ha ha,' and they didn't really want to think anything more about *that*."

Foster persisted: "There are two people who should direct this, Louis Malle or me." Malle wasn't available. "Finally I said, 'Well, knowing that you're having all this trouble . . . I think I can get the setup with Orion [the studio that released *The Silence of the Lambs*] if I'm directing.' " Foster flew to New York to meet Eric Pleskow, Orion's president, to make a pitch for her directing.

"I was totally nervous," says Foster. "I was in my salesman rap, and Pleskow said, 'Shhh. Shhh. It's okay, you don't have to sell me.' He said, 'We like you. You're a first-time director, chances are your movie is never going to make a dollar. We know that going in. So, don't try and tell me how it's gonna be *Star Wars*, because chances are it won't. We hope we'll be in business with you when you make your second one.' Which I was just, like, that's the greatest thing I've ever heard. But just to be in that room . . . ," says Foster rhapsodically. "Bill Bernstein, Arthur [Krim], and Eric just talking about all the old stuff. 'Remember

I had *Last Tango* for the weekend read and we couldn't get . . .' It was just like about the House Un-American [Activities] Committee and who was turncoat for McCarthy. . . . It was great! They had learned all of the lessons of goodness, I think. And it's an era for me, it represents an era of a certain business morality and to be like you were the young buck that in some way is gonna take that philosophy and run with it."

Foster filmed *The Silence of the Lambs* during the day and labored over the script for *Tate* at night, even flying the writer, Scott Frank, to Pittsburgh for a week. She sat next to him in her pajamas as he worked on the computer to polish the script. Indeed, Frank's initial conception was more of a surreal black comedy, à la Tim Burton, about the "nightmare of being a social anomaly. Fred had the unfortunate ability to be seven and to recognize that it was absurd and wear the weight of that," explains Frank. By contrast, Foster, perhaps because comedy isn't her forte, was drawn more to the two women characters and the idea that "they both had something to offer. This whole notion of alternative parenting was big to her," says the screenwriter.

While Frank labored to give Foster what she wanted, Rudin became increasingly enraged. "I was angry," says the producer, whose reputation for volatility was growing. (He once putatively went through twenty assistants in three months.) "I felt like if she had wanted to make a movie that was that different from the script, I would have liked to have known it. I thought there was a more commercial movie in it." Frank became the object of a tug-of-war between the two, ultimately opting to serve Foster, although Rudin warned him repeatedly that he was ruining his script. The director and producer brawled again when Rudin refused to approve Harry Connick, Jr., for the role of Tate's collegiate hero unless Foster screen-tested him.

The then twenty-seven-year-old Foster arrived for production hyperorganized, every page of the script storyboarded, every prop predetermined, all her thoughts for the film encompassed in one large book, a bible. BLT—bossy little thing, her nickname from *The Accused*—was stitched onto her crew jacket. Foster surrounded herself with compatriots. Her best friend from college, Jon Hutman, designed the film. Another former child actor, Randy Stone, was the executive producer and became one of her closest friends. Stone's relationship with his mother had dramatically influenced Frank when he was first shaping the material. Indeed, the Fred-Dede relationship was less Jodie-Brandy than Randy and his mother.

For those in Foster's camp, the film was an idyllic experience, one of those rare times when people are working not for money or glory but for a kind of love, united in their devotion to Foster, who, as on *The Accused,* took to looking after them. "You're awash in her maternal vibe," says Frank. "She is incredibly maternal to everyone she works with. You fall under her protective umbrella. She is taking care of you at the expense of herself. On *Little Man Tate,* that crew would have killed for her, would have done anything for her. They adored her because she was Mom."

Foster had found Adam Hann-Byrd, who played her son, through an extended casting search and broke the ice with the intensely shy nine-year-old with a series of karate moves. Cognizant of her own hatred of cosseting ("When I'm treated preciously I can't perform"), Foster told the boy, " 'Just pretend really well.' " She fared less well with Connick, whose performance she ended up almost totally excising in the editing room, although initially he had anchored the second half of the movie.

There was also friction with Dianne Wiest, who not only is from a different generation but is a different kind of actress from the highly technical Foster, the kind who likes to discuss motivation. Wiest requested a private meeting to try to work out their conflicts. "First-time directors tend to be very controlling, which makes me feel suffocated," commented the actress afterward. "In the end, I was glad for some of her strong-mindedness."

"I'm not a pain in the ass," says Foster. "I'm bossy, but I'm not a pain. And anything I demand is always about the movie. It's not about comfort or vanity. I don't like people who are afraid of me. It bugs me to have people who are obsequious. If someone's humoring or manipulative, I won't have it. The truth I can handle. I can't handle not knowing what they're thinking or feeling."

One person who pointedly didn't try to humor or manipulate her was Rudin, and the tensions between the two escalated. Foster was moving quickly and was so determined to be fiscally responsible that she came in a million dollars under budget on a film that cost only $9 million. Rudin begged her to slow down, shoot more coverage and more punctuation for each scene, good practical advice perhaps, but it was delivered in such a high-pitched manner that Foster responded as if he were questioning her ability as a director and trying to take control of the production. Seeing the dailies for one scene he suggested, "We need a single [close-up] here," to which Foster cracked, "Why don't you get Mary Lambert to come in?" (Lambert, who had directed Foster in *Siesta*, caught wind of the remark and sent Foster an acerbic note.) Within days Foster threw Rudin off the set. "She never threw me off," insists the producer. "I didn't want to be there, to be honest with you. I was only ever going to be there for a couple of days. But we were not getting along. I did not enjoy the relationship, and I know she didn't either."

In the end Foster made the movie she wanted to make, a movie that elegiacally depicts the kind of romance that occurs between a single mom and her child and the pain of being different. As the critic David Thomson points out, it is a generous "bow to mothers like her own."

"When I saw the film the first time I just absolutely broke down," says Brandy Foster. "And it's the scene that touched everybody, and I didn't realize it until I saw it on-screen. It's when she was sending him off with the woman, and she said, you know, if I could be born again I'd want to be just like you. And it was just something that I used to say to all of my children. Just at the time, you're just my favorite person in the world."

Foster was readying *Tate* for theaters when Orion went bankrupt. Several of the company's executives suggested shelving the film for a while because they didn't have the money to release it properly. By this time she had made up with Rudin, whose belligerent fortitude was now a plus, and the pair lobbied to get the film released as scheduled. "I said, 'But wait a minute. I've got four [magazine] covers,' " recalls Foster, explaining why she couldn't wait. Rudin threatened legal action. The film arrived in theaters as scheduled and earned a respectable $24 million domestically. Foster saw none of the profits, or any money at all, because Orion's creditors ate up the revenues.

She rebounded from the experience hell-bent on controlling her future products, at all costs. She turned down a variety of studio offers to set out her own production shingle. Instead, Jeff Berg, the head of her agency, introduced her to Michael Kuhn, president of PolyGram's reemerging film division, who was trying to establish a U.S. movie presence. Foster made it clear that she wasn't simply looking for a vanity deal and walked away with a state-of-the-art production company, $110 million in financing, and the authority to green-light six pictures over the next three years, three in the $12 million range, three in the $25 million range. PolyGram would have no creative control (although each picture would be vetted with foreign sales agents to ensure the star power was commensurate with the proposed budget). Foster also had the unheard-of right to choose her own distributor. No other actress (and few actors) had ever been handed such ostensible power. The deal was announced with great fanfare, and soon afterward Foster explained, "The people in the industry I have known over many years that I consider actually 'the old boy network,' that for some reason I kind of belong to, were really helpful and very, very supportive. They want me to do this."

The actress turned director described the kinds of films she wanted to make. "I really want to do good and progressive things, and I want to maintain a kind of independent flavor, and I want to do dangerous types of movies that people haven't done before, but I'm not really interested in alienating the public completely. As I always say, if you're dead, you're no good to the revolution. And I think that the way to change the system, in a lot of ways, is to get inside of it and change it from the inside, not necessarily from the outside.

"The one thing that we are not," she said adamantly, "is a 'woman's movie studio.' "

HOW WAS I GOING TO DO
IT WITH MY KIDS?

Nora Ephron was fifty years old when she directed her first movie, *This Is My Life.* "I didn't really always want to direct," she says. "It never crossed my mind for a long time. First of all, how was I going to do it with my kids? When I wrote *When Harry Met Sally . . .*, I knew that I could direct it. That was a simple movie, a logical first-time director movie. There was this little fly buzzing around my head: If Rob [Reiner] doesn't make this movie, maybe somebody would let me make it. Then I saw it and I thought, Well, thank God I didn't direct it, because Rob did a hundred times better job than I would ever have done on it. Then I did *My Blue Heaven,* and it was completely destroyed by Herbert Ross. Destroyed. And I looked at it and thought, Well, I could have done just as terrible a job as he did.

"You get to a certain point, especially if you keep writing—there were good parts for women in it—it is a nightmare finding guys to direct them. And you might as well do it. The point is that men don't want to direct movies about women," says Ephron, reeling off the names of the few standard-bearers who will: "Jim Brooks. And then who? Mike Nichols. And then who? Tell me who the third one is?"

Dawn Steel, then at Paramount, was the first studio executive to suggest that Ephron test her hand at directing. In Steel's inimitable fashion, she had called Ephron out of the blue and announced, "Lynda [Obst, a mutual friend] says we should have lunch, and Lynda says we should be friends." A lunch was had, a friendship decreed, and when Steel became head of Columbia, she called again and said, "You know, I told you I wanted you to direct a movie, and I want you to do it. And I put Lynda in charge of finding you something to direct." Three days later Obst called Ephron with a proposal: a screen version of Meg Wolitzer's book *This Is Your Life.* It is a double coming-of-age story about a mother who yearns to be a stand-up comic and her two daughters, who in a sense raise one another. It was fertile territory for Ephron, with autobiographical overtones as both the child of a working mother and the working mother of two small boys. She knew that the cost of a woman's intellectual fulfillment is high, particularly for the children. Moreover, like Phoebe Ephron, Dottie feeds on the lives of her young.

Nora sent the book to her younger sister Delia, the author of several highly regarded humor books such as *How to Eat Like a Child.* "We sort of got rid of the last vestiges of the bad sibling stuff ten years ago," says Ephron. "For me working with Delia is having someone whose truth is the same as mine. When you get notes from someone, one of the hardest things to evaluate is whether they're right. The most horrible thing of the movie business is getting someone to tell you the truth, by which I don't mean what they thought but some more abstract existential thing. When [someone] tells you what's wrong with a script, it has to be 'what's wrong' in a way that makes sense to you, and not just to them. If you write a magazine article and show it to your friend Abigail, she'll say it's great because she loves everything you do. If you show it to your friend Sarah, she'll hate it because she's jealous of you. Everybody comes at everything from their own point of view, from their own craziness, and you're always trying to find the person whose craziness meshes with yours, so if they say that scene isn't working right, it's true, and you've got to deal with it. Delia is that person for me. She's very tough.

"It's hard to know the truth about a movie you're working on. You basically fall in love with it in some very damaging way. You fall in love with your actors, meaning you think they're great even if they're not. You fall in love with that scene that works only for you. It doesn't cross your mind it can be altered." Moreover, whenever Delia and Nora fought, Delia deferred, because, after all, Nora was the director. Nora also trusted her sister to do the on-set rewrites because she found it difficult to write and direct at the same time.

By the time the Ephron sisters turned in the script for *This Is My Life*, Steel had been replaced by Peter Guber and Jon Peters. One afternoon, Ephron received an unexpected call from her executive at the studio, Amy Pascal, who announced she was driving around Manhattan in a limo with Peters and his latest girlfriend, the blond supermodel Vendela. As Ephron waited on the line, she could hear Pascal explaining to the Sony Pictures chairman who she was, and then she was asked to meet the trio at their hotel at 4:00 P.M.

"Jon Peters told me in that meeting many things. He told me about his shrink who was trying to help him get in touch with his inner child, which I did not think was going to be much of a stretch. And he told me quite a bit about Peter Guber's marriage, and he told me that he had made sixty-eight, I believe it was, movies, and he had never read a script and he didn't need to read a script. And what was my movie about?" says Ephron. "So I told him what the movie was about, and he and Vendela then had some things to say about the subject of working mothers. Vendela said that someday she hoped to have children and go on working. It was that kind of thing. And I walked out into the street afterwards and, while I didn't cry or anything, I just thought, It can't get any worse than this.

"We found ourselves in almost a year of sadness. Columbia was horrible. They weren't going to make it. They didn't know what it was. They didn't care about me. They just weren't going to put it into turnaround." Ephron's agent, Sam Cohn, slipped the script to Joe Roth, head of Fox, and, after much haggling, Columbia's president, Frank Price, let the project go. "I don't think women have been more helpful to me than men," said Ephron in the mid-nineties. "It is true that Dawn thought of my directing, but it's Joe Roth who gave my movie a green light, not Dawn. In the movie business, I have been helped enormously by women but also by men. If you're not helped by men, you don't get anywhere in this business, because they run it, women don't."

While Penny Marshall and Elaine May developed reputations for indecisiveness, Ephron impressed all with her ability to make fast judgments; indeed, there seemed to be little that Ephron liked better than deciding, choosing, arbitrating, presiding, or dictating, whether the choice involved something as insignificant as what color tablecloth to use or something as major as which actor to cast. She did not lack opinions, or faith in her own opinions. She didn't get mired in perfectionism.

According to Lynda Obst, Ephron, famed for both her food acumen and her Sally-like penchant for ordering meals with the precision of a field marshal, convinced Roth of her ability to direct by ordering lunch at the Russian Tea Room. "Nora said to Joe, 'You should try the chicken Kiev. Roger [Birnbaum, Roth's number two], you should have the beef Stroganoff. I'm going to order the chicken salad but without the mayonnaise,' " explains Obst. "Joe sank back in his chair and said, 'I know I have a director!' "

Initially, Fox mandated that they cast a star—namely Cher or Michelle Pfeiffer—as the Jewish woman from Queens. Dawn Steel had suggested that they change the mother from a comic to a singer, which was how the Ephrons initially wrote it. Bette Midler wanted to do it, but Disney wouldn't let her out of her contract. Again the project's fate looked tenuous. Ephron cajoled Roth out of his star fixation and convinced him to let her use someone who was right for the part of Dottie Ingels, someone like Julie Kavner, most famous for Brenda on the TV show *Rhoda*, the voice of Marge Simpson, and numerous small parts in the films of Woody Allen. Afterward, Ephron was stunned, and relieved, that Roth had agreed. The tiny $10 million budget meant that she could make her directorial debut in peace, without the scrutiny and pressure attendant to a more high-profile venture.

Before setting off for Toronto, which was to sub in the filming for New York City, Ephron went to see all the directors she knew to solicit their advice on directing. She picked Mike Nichols's brain about acting. "One of the things I said to him was 'What if you give someone a note and it makes the performance worse?' Which I was very worried about, because it does happen. He said, 'Then you just walk up to them and say, "Ignore everything I just said to you." ' Now he couldn't have been more matter-of-fact about it, but do you know, I didn't know the answers to those questions." Rob Reiner spent an afternoon with Ephron combing through the script, making recommendations for cuts (which she ignored but recognized afterward were correct). "I remember very clearly he said that making a movie was like having a party. And that he was the host at the party, and he had invited all these people to come to the party and it was up to him to make sure they had a good time." (Ephron had the crew audition six caterers and vote on who should get the job.)

During filming Ephron left her prepubescent sons in New York with their father and stepfather. They visited, and she visited. In the film Kavner's character jokes (or partly jokes), "You give your kids a choice, your mother in the next room on the verge of suicide versus your mother in ecstasy in Hawaii, and they will choose suicide in the next room."

Ephron rationalized, "I waited until they were—you know—old. They were eleven and twelve. But they didn't feel particularly old, and they had had this very bizarre experience, because even though I was a working mother, I was never out of the house. So they didn't really understand that I had a career in any real way, which is to say it affected them, until the moment I went off to do this movie. On the other hand, they were really, really proud of me, and really happy I was doing it, and they took enormous pride in my career, but then suddenly it cost them in some way. I wasn't there. And that was difficult for them.

"You worry about it, and then you say to yourself, But this is what I want to do. You're making that choice, which is that for three months the thing you're doing will take priority, and that on some level is a cold decision. You delude yourself into thinking that they had eleven or twelve years with you, and they will be fine."

This Is My Life debuted to mixed reviews and negligible box office. In truth, it wasn't in quality or subject matter very different from Foster's film, which did well on the strength of her name as a star.

"I did realize, when I got done making it, that I probably had better make a commercial movie if I wanted to go on making movies that meant something to me," says Ephron. "I better do this, or I'm going to be in big trouble."

A QUEEN'S PREROGATIVE

**I DON'T BELIEVE IN DICTATING TO ARTISTS
WHAT THEY SHOULD DO, AND I DON'T BELIEVE
THAT I KNOW THE ANSWERS**

The minute Sherry Lansing ascended to the chairmanship of Paramount, the ugly but persistent innuendo that she had slept her way to the top ceased. It was a relic from an earlier time, a tale repeated by people who didn't know whom it referred to, although it appeared to encapsulate her soft, man-pleasing persona. Over a decade after her tenure at Fox, the town was willing to accept Lansing for what she now was—a chairman of a major studio. Her gender was noted but officially glossed over, her appointment relegated to the business pages instead of the front pages.

More important for the agents, producers, and directors around town, Lansing was now a buyer, a powerful one, and she quickly announced her presence to the town with a few splashy script purchases that reflected an atavistic grasp for things she knew had worked for her in the past—movies that reeked of sex. Within days of being in office, she paid $1.1 million for *Milk Money*, the story of three young boys who pool their milk money to buy a prostitute. Days later she paid *Basic Instinct*'s scribe, Joe Eszterhas, $2.5 million for a two-page outline for a project called *Jade*, a kind of *Belle de Jour* meets *Jagged Edge* about a San Francisco psychologist who moonlights as a prostitute.

Lansing arrived with twelve years more experience under her belt and the knowledge that she could produce a hit movie herself, and she sought to spread that confidence around at a studio collectively in need

Sumner Redstone and Sherry Lansing, New York City, 1997.

Ron Galella, Ltd.

of a pat on the back and a kick in the pants. She combed through the development slate and picked out the future tent-pole projects; she reassured her major staff—including all of Tartikoff's production team—that their jobs were safe but pressed them to be both more assertive and more responsive to the myriad sellers pounding on Paramount's door. "We were in Las Vegas for ShoWest, and she was like, 'You're not returning your phone calls,' " recalls the then president of production, John Goldwyn. "Return every single phone call. Own your decisions. Don't pass it upstairs. I don't want to hear you liked it but Sherry didn't."

The second day on the job, she asked the techno-producers Mace Neufeld and Robert Rehme to take over the troubled production of *Beverly Hills Cop III*, whose proposed budget was spinning out of control in part because Stanley Jaffe had mandated an accelerated production schedule to meet an August release date. Lansing quickly abandoned that idea, ultimately shutting down the movie and laying off more than a hundred crew members so that a new script could be fashioned and the ultimate budget brought back to the stratosphere. On *The Firm*, the big-screen version of the John Grisham novel set to star Tom Cruise, she convinced the director, Sydney Pollack, and Jaffe not to pursue their plan of turning the film's corrupt lawyer villain, Avery, into a woman (ostensibly Meryl Streep) so she could romance Cruise. She argued that they should not alienate the book's numerous fans.

The studio was starved for product. Lansing acquired the South African drama *Bopha!* and *What's Eating Gilbert Grape*, both relatively small films (that ultimately did little business). Moreover, she asked a number of directors to tighten their postproduction schedules, which normally last twenty-two to twenty-three weeks. Adrian Lyne was given only seventeen weeks to finish *Indecent Proposal*. He used four teams of editors and complained vociferously at what he perceived as Lansing's abandonment of the project because she could only stop by at night to check on her own film. (With Jaffe gone, Lansing stepped up to be Lyne's sparring partner, a tumultuous relationship that resulted, on one occasion, in her spitting at him in frustration.)

The job of head of the studio has been described as that of a maître d' at a large hotel restaurant. Unfortunately, Paramount hadn't been able to entice any patrons to its dining room, or even to establish a strong food court. A strong believer in a producer-driven studio (as opposed to the centralized management of Katzenberg's Disney), Lansing nailed down crucial producer deals, calling Scott Rudin five times a day until he desisted from his intended plan to shift his shingle to TriStar. She signed Cruise/Wagner, the new production entity from Tom Cruise (abetted by the fact that Jaffe had cast Cruise in his star-making role in *Taps*), the director Barry Levinson, as well as Kathleen Kennedy and Frank Marshall, the husband-wife duo who had produced most of Spielberg's films, for whom she shelled out one of the richest deals in town, $1.5 million per picture as well as 5 percent of the first-dollar gross.

It also fell to her to inform Tom Clancy, the author of the Jack Ryan books, that despite his vociferous objections (and vehement public attacks), the studio was going ahead with Phillip Noyce as the director of the third installment, *Clear and Present Danger.* It was a corporate decision that had gone all the way up to Martin Davis, although Lansing served as the honey-tongued hatchet woman. Yet almost immediately after the rift Lansing spent seven months wooing the author back to the Paramount fold, in the hope of making another Jack Ryan film.

"It was Sherry who very consciously was responsible for Clancy and I making up," says Neufeld. "She had many, many conversations with him. She finally got Tom to agree to meet with me, and the two of us flew down to Baltimore at his invitation to see a ball game." The whole ride across the country, Lansing kept reassuring Neufeld that things would go smoothly, which they did, and later the pair returned for another ball game. Not long after Viacom purchased Paramount, it was announced that the studio had bought *The Cardinal of the Kremlin*, the fourth installment in the Ryan series, a book that Clancy had sworn he was never going to sell to them.

One of the ugliest messes left to Lansing was Jaffe's bitter fight with David Kirkpatrick, the former studio executive who had the bad fortune to try to cut the budget of Jaffe's film *School Ties.* In a lawsuit against Paramount, Kirkpatrick claimed that Jaffe had sought to end his production agreement as part of a "pattern of irreversible hostility" toward him. It was Lansing's job to break the news, and she performed masterfully, her eyes seeming to fill with tears as she dolefully announced that "it wasn't working out" at Paramount: She promised him a dignified exit, then determinedly steered the shocked producer into the office of Bill Bernstein, the head of business affairs. According to the lawsuit, when Kirkpatrick asked about settlement, the studio evicted him from his offices and threw his furniture onto the lawn.

"Fuck 'em!" yelled Robert Evans. "Let's just go for NC-17."

Lansing looked blankly at the legendary producer of *Chinatown*, an expression echoed on the faces of the screenwriter, Joe Eszterhas, the director, Phil Noyce, and Jaffe. Evans's enthusiasm to *épater le bourgeois* might have gone over well in the seventies, but it was hardly something that Lansing or Jaffe could embrace, given how such a rating would restrict the audience for *Sliver*, a $30 million studio investment. The group was huddled in the Paramount executive suites trying to ascertain how to respond to the Motion Picture Association of America's demand for 117 cuts to secure the necessary R rating. It was the latest blow for a troubled production that featured not only two stars, Sharon Stone and Billy Baldwin, who despised each other but a well-known instance of putative husband snatching (Stone went off with the married coproducer William Macdonald) and several cases of near death (a helicopter crashed into a volcano). Jaffe, who had revived Evans's career after Evans's misdemeanor cocaine conviction and a damaging association with the Cotton Club murders, suggested they take a breather. Moments later Evans was rushed to Cedars-Sinai, diagnosed with a massive anxiety attack, and admitted for recuperation.

While Evans's panic attack was flamboyant, Lansing's anxiety was less palpable; she had presided over a far graver problem than the tentative ratings (the cuts would simply have to be done): mass rejection by the preview audience. When Evans ran Paramount, he had brandished his opinion with vigor. Now the people who truly mattered were the unknown, often teenage masses who attended the recruited screenings on the lot.

Fatal Attraction had taught Lansing several things, namely that films are fixable, and that it's best to give the audience what it wants. Although Hollywood had used test screenings starting in the forties, the practice flourished in the eighties as the studios sharpened their marketing strategies. The numbers became of do-or-die importance in the nineties, since the cost of an average film doubled between 1993 and 1998 to a range of $50 to $75 million. Lansing seemed to view Joe Farrell of the National Research Group as an unimpeachable Virgil, a guide to bring the studio closer to box-office success. One director who worked at the studio recalls seeing her awaiting the test results of *Wayne's World 2*: "She was standing around with the executives and the filmmakers and Mike Myers, and Joe Farrell came in and announced the results. She was ecstatic. She didn't hug the director or the star. She hugged Joe Farrell as if he was a doctor who had just looked at someone's X rays and announced the patient would live."

Creative types tended to view the research with skepticism. Powerful directors such as Steven Spielberg wrote into their contracts that they would not be subjected to the process, while others groused that while perhaps the research could forecast how an audience might respond to a film, it couldn't predict whether an audience would go. For Lansing, research was an objective way to slice the Gordian knot of power dynamics. It wasn't the studio that mandated changes in a film, merely the facts. "The preview process is a process that you can use destructively, or you can use it constructively," she says. "And it is very healthy to say to a filmmaker, if you have any disagreement, 'Maybe you're right. I don't know. I think you're wrong, but I'm not a genius. Why don't we put it in front of an audience? I don't even have to come. And why don't you see what happens?' "

Given her experience making movies, Lansing was more aggressive—and more confident—than many of her peers in rolling up her sleeves if the scores were bad. When Evans returned to the editing room, he found Lansing and Jaffe editing the film themselves, he claimed in the press—an allegation denied by the director, Phil Noyce. In fact, to placate Evans, Lansing had given the onetime pasha of Paramount his own version of the movie to edit in one bay, while Noyce worked on the official version in another. She promised the director that he'd never have to look at what Evans was doing, and that she would tell him if there was anything usable, and at the end of the process, she showed him one shot, which found its way into the final version.

Based on a novel by Ira Levin (author of *Rosemary's Baby*), *Sliver*, which was green-lit by Brandon Tartikoff, concerns a shy book editor (Stone) who falls for a handsome young man (Baldwin) with a penchant for voyeurism who secretly videotapes all the occupants of the apartment building in which they both live. In the initial cut of the film, he is also secretly murdering their neighbors, and she marries him knowing this. The last sequence shows the two taking a helicopter ride into a volcano—the danger of death being the ultimate sexual high. Audiences hated the film's dark, ironic ending, and the arty flourish with which it was shot.

Lansing made a policy of telling filmmakers her opinion before there were numbers so they would know what she truly thought. After each preview the directors, producers, and executives would retreat to her office. "We would go around the room, and everybody, usually starting with the lesser executive, would talk, all the way up to John Goldwyn, and then the filmmakers. I would speak last, so that nobody could ever say, 'Well, Karen is just agreeing with you because you're the boss,' " says Lansing. At this juncture, Lansing's comments were often couched as suggestions: "Usually it was 'I love this movie, but we're not getting the response. . . .' "

For those who had primarily seen Lansing in social situations, her candor inside her lair often came as a surprise. "I find her very frank in those meetings, very frank," says Richard Zanuck, whose film *Deep Impact* was significantly reworked by Lansing and company after bad initial previews. "When it really comes down to the crunch, she is very specific. Some of the personal, wonderful charm gives way to a much more controlled manner. It really is all business."

Yet her style was not bulldozing but a carefully thought-out strategy of advance and retreat, rewarding and withholding her favor. A psychological tactician, she would suss out what she thought the filmmaker needed to go forward in a way she approved, all the while trying to avoid the appearance of a crass bottom-liner or an authoritarian jerk. She made calculated appeals to a filmmaker's desire for a hit. "It wasn't that as soon as we got a lousy score on *Sliver* she said, 'You've got to change it,' " cautions Noyce. There were other test screenings. Noyce spent hours with Lansing trying to figure out what was wrong. "She would push, push, push, push, push. Then finally, virtually when the posters were going up, it was sort of like, we're not getting it to where we want, what are we going to do now?

"Sherry is very, very persuasive. And, because she is very smart, she argues incredibly logically, and after she's swayed you on the point, you sort of feel like you just spent five minutes with some supersalesman," says the director. "You think back over the conversation and you realize yourself, What a brilliant opening statement. She has a real schmoozer's ability to put someone at ease, make them feel good about themselves and about their relationship with her, about the world, and so she structures her conversations or confrontations quite brilliantly at that. She also has an innate understanding of psychology. She can convince you that what she thinks is what you think.

"At the same time, more than any men that I've seen, she has this ability to project 'I'm the boss. Yes, you're the director, whatever you say, but I'm the boss,' " adds Noyce. "So she says, 'Okay, you can do what you like. It should be what you've done already. I'll give you the money to do that. But, this is just my advice,' and it is cast in such a way, so you are thinking, Father, father, I know you love me, I know that you have only got my best interests at heart. My best interests and the family interests are the same thing. We have to face the world together and make these hard decisions. And the part of it that is true is, of course, that a parent will never turn on you having done that. And will always then see it through."

After much hand-wringing, the *Sliver* principals finally agreed that it was the last five minutes that failed. Eszterhas, Noyce, and Lansing hashed out various options. At first Eszterhas made a big plea to ignore the preview results; then he attended a preview, listened firsthand to Farrell's spiel, and underwent a conversion, calling up Noyce in a panic to say that something had to be done. Tossing around possibilities, Eszterhas suggested making Tom Berenger's character—who had been the red herring—the killer. Essentially he proposed a radical face-lift, eradicating the putative point of the film, namely that the taboo was exciting.

The sets were exhumed, the actors brought back. About ten days before the film was released, the filmmakers tested two new endings. The deadlines were so tight that reviewers didn't get an opportunity to view the picture before it was jammed into theaters, a lucky break given the fact that they ultimately savaged it.

The night of the premiere, Lansing hawked *Sliver* with her usual indefatigable energy and over-the-top gushing. "Sherry was right there, absolutely supporting the picture," says Noyce. "She organized this charity screening for one of her charities, one of her cancer societies. And she hasn't even seen it. She's calling the whole fraternity to buy tickets and she's making a speech. That takes courage." (Courage that Noyce didn't have—he skipped his own premiere.) Afterward the studio sent Noyce on a vacation to Jamaica as a small thank-you for making his deadline. The film opened huge and quickly dropped off, earning only $36 million in America but going on to be a great international success ($80 million) on the strength of Stone's name, new trailers, and an additional four minutes of sexually provocative material.

Lansing's tenure was filled with films that had been reshot and re-edited, usually under her guidance—everything from success stories like *Congo, Deep Impact,* and *The Truman Show* to disappointments such as *Beverly Hills Cop III, Jade,* and *The Saint.* (At the end of the first screening of *The Saint,* Lansing had sobbed copiously at the death of the heroine, Elizabeth Shue, and declared, "It's a masterpiece." After the cards were handed in, she mandated that Shue live.) The numbers could often be used to thwart power plays by big stars. Harrison Ford was so appalled when he first saw *Clear and Present Danger* that he demanded all the reels be sent to his home in Wyoming so he could recut the film himself. He was rebuffed by pushing forward the preview screenings, which showed the film to be a huge hit.

Still, auteurist directors complained bitterly about Paramount's strong-arm tactics, while producers grumbled at Lansing's unshakable allegiance to the numbers. "I think they pay too much attention to test screenings," says the Paramount stalwart Mace Neufeld. "And while they're a useful tool, I don't think that the tail should wag the dog."

"I don't use research as a Bible," Lansing insists. "I believe in the process. I don't believe in dictating to artists what they should do, and I don't believe that I know the answers."

I HAVE GOT TO RIDE THIS BULL

Forrest Gump was precisely the kind of project that made Sherry Lansing nervous. It was both pricey and risky, two qualities she generally tried to keep separate. Based on a novel by Winston Groom, *Gump* is a picaresque tale about an idiot Candide who traverses the totems of the baby boom generation with unparalleled success—a football star at the University of Alabama, a Vietnam War hero, a Ping-Pong champion, a running phenomenon, and an accidental millionaire courtesy of an investment in Apple Computers. It was easy to justify to Lansing's bosses a film like *Mission: Impossible,* with Tom Cruise, less easy to explain the commercial potential of a world-class idiot. Unlike his stance with Tartikoff, Jaffe was adamant in his support of Lansing, telling all involved that she was the one running the studio. She had the authority to green-light whatever she wanted, yet she purposefully solicited Jaffe's opinion, whether the project cost $10 million or $50 million. She was less insecure than cautious, with a fervent desire to avoid mistakes, which sometimes gave the impression of foot dragging. She was ever the diligent student searching for an A-plus.

If Lansing had an Achilles' heel, it was her conservatism, a preference for almost old-fashioned dramas, with clearly sympathetic, recognizable stereotypes facing moral quandaries. Paramount even eschewed the kinds of merchandising juggernauts, such as *Batman* or *Jurassic Park*, that served as tent poles at rivals Warners and Universal and brought in millions in ancillary revenue. While Lansing recognized the value of camp (particularly family-values romps such as the Brady Bunch movies, which she insisted on making over the objections of her staff), she was less attuned to harder nineties irony, embodied by such movies as *Pulp Fiction* and *Men in Black*.

"I think Paramount tends to make a more conservative slate of movies than I think they should make," says Scott Rudin, the studio's leading producer. "Like *Congo* and *The Saint*—they feel like they're behind the curve instead of setting the curve. And I have frequently had this conversation with Sherry about you can safe yourself out of business. She agrees. But she's under a tremendous amount of pressure, and I think studio executives make decisions to make movies for two reasons: How is the movie going to be if it succeeds, and how can they defend it if it fails?"

Gump's prime champion was a young female producer, Wendy Finerman, who after eight years of nursing the project had secured the services of director Barry Sonnenfeld, who had in turn lured his former *Big* cohort Tom Hanks. The package had elicited the gung-ho enthusiasm of then studio head Brandon Tartikoff.

Unfortunately, by the time Eric Roth had finished writing the script, Tartikoff was gone. Moreover, when Lansing first read *Gump*, she liked the script but thought it needed work. Lansing was in fact plying Sonnenfeld with offers of obscene amounts of money—three times the amount he'd earn on *Gump*—to make the sequel to his highly successful *Addams Family*. Sonnenfeld was torn. He wanted to do both, and asked his agent to see if he could push *Gump* back a year. Finerman panicked that she'd lose Hanks if they waited. She screamed and pressured Sonnenfeld to let go of *Gump*.

"I said to myself, I have to find inner strength. I have got to ride this bull, all these agents and megapeople and directors and stars. If I didn't hold on, it was going to fall apart," recalls Finerman. For Sonnenfeld, Hanks, and Lansing, *Forrest Gump* was just another movie in their long, successful careers. For Finerman, it was her life and her self-respect all wrapped up in relentless yearning. At age thirty-three, the curly-haired, obsessively thin producer had all the jumpiness of a thorough-bred racehorse who had never been allowed to race. What was her only credit? Associate producer of *Hot to Trot*, the tale of, yes, a talking horse. What did everyone in town know her for? Her marriage to the ebullient, glad-handing Mark Canton, now chairman of Sony, who kept his oeu-vre, including *Pee-wee's Big Adventure* and *Batman*, lined up in leather-bound editions on his bookshelf. Indeed, when she had married Canton, Finerman, a Wharton School graduate, had said to herself that it was okay that he was the one with the career in the limelight. She was in-tensely proud of the fact that she had raised two kids after all (three by the end of *Gump*), although her marriage collapsed soon after. All she wanted was a little respect of her own.

Michelle Manning, the one Paramount vice president who shared Fin-erman's passion for *Gump*, counseled the young producer to get another director fast or the film would slip back into the netherworld of develop-ment. Hanks felt that he had to send it first to his *Big* director, Penny Mar-shall, who dithered. Over Christmas the Canton-Finermans borrowed the director Robert Zemeckis's vacation house in Jamaica, and when Finer-man returned to L.A., she submitted *Gump* to Zemeckis's agent at CAA. Within twenty-four hours Zemeckis, the director of *Romancing the Stone* and *Who Framed Roger Rabbit*, was in. He later described his vision of *For-rest Gump*: "It's Norman Rockwell painting the baby boomers."

With its episodic flashback structure, the script of *Forrest Gump* didn't adhere to any easily classified genre, although in truth Roth had given Groom's book a classic Hollywood face-lift, ridding the material of the slightest edginess. Roth changed Gump's acerbic first line of the book, "Let me say this bein a idiot is no box of chocolates," to the far sweeter "Life is like a box of chocolates because you never know what you're going to get." Roth's Gump is a pure innocent, no longer dab-bling in drugs or sex, where, according to Groom, he had Kama Sutra–like skills. As in *Fatal Attraction*, anything negative or controver-sial was foisted on Forrest's love interest, Jenny, who grew to embody the underbelly of the sixties and seventies. She is not only a victim of child abuse but a druggie, an antiwar political activist, and a Hollywood wanna-be. In a marked departure from the book, Roth even kills her off, making her an AIDS victim. The dramatic tension of the story now comes from whether Jenny will allow her noble idiot knight to save her. (Indeed, the only sex Forrest now sees is a once-in-a-lifetime coupling with Jenny.)

Still, Lansing announced that she wanted even more romance at the first meeting with the newly reconfigured *Gump* team. Her demand for script revisions was a shock to the second most commercially successful director in Hollywood, who was used to getting what he wanted and had started the meeting demanding millions up-front to begin preproduction. Zemeckis described his vision of using Industrial Light & Magic's new technology to insert Hanks into old newsreel footage, to show *Gump* interacting with such real-life figures as Lyndon Johnson and Johnny Carson. Unlike Zemeckis, Lansing didn't romanticize special effects. A compromise was reached in the form of what Lansing called "a blinking green light"; she would allot funds to begin production; in return the filmmakers would revamp the script and come back in three weeks.

Lansing's original reserve concerning *Gump* would eventually rebound in the form of a whispering campaign perpetuated largely by the *Gump* team that she didn't "get" the film. Unlike Finerman, Zemeckis, or Michelle Manning, Lansing was not perceived as a true believer in the mystical power of *Gump*, which to her seemed a silly distinction, given that she signed the checks. "I wouldn't have made it if I didn't get it," she fumed. "You can't be indifferent to something and green-light it for forty million dollars. You have to love it." Indeed, three weeks later Lansing pronounced the new script "perfect," although, in the view of the filmmakers, the changes were negligible.

Any wariness between the two sides was immediately accentuated by a brewing budget battle. The studio had agreed to a tentative preliminary budget of $40 million—$39,999,999.99, joked the director. Paramount's budget didn't make a provision for Zemeckis's special effects; now Steve Starkey (Zemeckis's line producer, who had taken over much of the day-to-day producing chores from Finerman) submitted a real cost breakdown, which, according to a Paramount source, was $59 million.

In a theatrical gambit Lansing declared she couldn't go back to Jaffe, Davis, and the Paramount "board" and ask for so much more money. In subsequent press accounts she reiterated this version of events, a slight exaggeration that both positioned her as the production's besieged advocate and accentuated the fact that more money would be hard to come by. In actuality, it wasn't Lansing's practice to ask the Paramount board for more money on a particular movie. Budget discussions were between her and Jaffe, and, at the end of the day, she was totally responsible. Yet Lansing didn't want to look like she couldn't control her productions, and Jaffe was, in the words of one Paramount executive, "psycho" on the subject of a $59 million budget. *Clear and Present Danger*, the studio's other summer tent pole, came in huffing and puffing at $53 million, and that was part of a proven franchise. A few days before production was scheduled to start, Lansing agreed to meet the filmmakers halfway, bringing the total up to $49 million.

Hours later the filmmakers submitted the real ILM budget, $4 million, double the initial estimate. For Lansing the only answer was to make the filmmakers share the risk. As she had so successfully done with Robert Redford on *Indecent Proposal*, she asked the principals to defer a portion of their up-front paychecks for increased back-end participation. Despite her own precedents, her risk-sharing penchant was a rarity in a Hollywood where star salaries were exploding and Columbia was paying Jim Carrey $20 million to star in *The Cable Guy*.

Lansing's suggestion went over badly. Zemeckis's CAA agent, Jack Rapke (who later became his partner), tried to find another studio to partner with Paramount, and although Universal seemed mildly interested, they wanted to own domestic rights in return, which Paramount refused to relinquish. Zemeckis and CAA then demanded that Paramount put the movie into turnaround so they could take it somewhere else, but Lansing balked, a move that was seen as particularly gutsy given the firepower involved.

The filmmakers were left with the ultimatum: defer or no picture. They deferred. It was a decision that ultimately netted Zemeckis and Hanks in excess of $30 million each. Zemeckis nonetheless dragged his feet about signing his deferment. John Goldwyn, the president of production, whom Lansing forced to be her hatchet man, called the director and told him if he didn't close his deal they would shut down the picture. Zemeckis refused to talk to him. Goldwyn, who had placed the call from Lansing's office, handed the phone to her, and while she didn't back down, Lansing opted for the soft touch, patiently explaining the reality of the situation. "Look, Bob, Stanley's beating me up," she said, which although both she and Jaffe publicly deny it, seemed to both her Paramount staff and the *Gump* team to be the truth.

Relations between the studio and the production team continued to deteriorate, particularly when *Gump* began to soar over budget because of weather delays and the unpredictable nature of cutting-edge special effects. To compound the problem, Paramount's physical production department was in disarray, and the studio couldn't accurately keep track of the money as it was going out; according to its records, *Gump* went $1 million over budget in one week. Although the total figure would ultimately run to about $10 million, not an outrageous amount considering such recent $100 million productions as James Cameron's *Terminator 2, Gump* was rapidly turning into the most expensive movie of Lansing's tenure. The studio reacted as if it had a runaway production on its hands.

Based in New York, Jaffe wasn't even seeing the dailies but was growing increasingly unhappy about the cost overruns, as was Martin Davis, who called him practically every day about it. At one point, Jaffe barked at Lansing: "When they [the *Gump* team] get back from South Carolina, I want you to go down and stomp on their faces." Lansing periodically sent members of her production staff as skirmishers in the battle of the budget. Zemeckis refused even to see Goldwyn (although he was allowed to spend several hours with Starkey going over the budget). The director dragged Michelle Manning, his most loyal studio backer, out of a bar to yell at her. Both returned to tell Lansing that, although the filmmakers were making a more expensive movie than the studio had intended, the Zemeckis team absolutely knew what it was doing. When Jaffe was scheduled for a Los Angeles visit, Lansing told Manning to stay away from the office so Jaffe wouldn't know that she'd come back from Savannah.

By the time shooting wrapped at the end of December, the film's budget had hit close to $59 million, and Paramount was so furious that it refused to allow the production the $20,000 initially allotted for a cast party. Hanks, Zemeckis, Finerman, Starkey, and the coproducer Charles Newirth paid for it out of their own pockets (although they were eventually reimbursed). In postproduction Zemeckis took to fighting with Jaffe directly, particularly when he needed an additional few hundred thousand for the editing. "It felt like it became a punitive thing," complained the director afterward. "You've spent millions and millions of dollars and now you're gonna quibble over, like, two hundred thousand dollars?"

I'LL DO ANYTHING

THE MINUTE HE NEEDED TO BE THE BOSS, I NEEDED TO BE THE BOSS

For almost the entire year in which she was in production on *A Dry White Season*, Paula Weinstein barely saw her husband, Mark Rosenberg. "I said, 'I'll be back in two weeks,' and I came back eleven months later," says Weinstein. Rosenberg came to visit her twice in Europe, but not at all during the three months she spent on location in Zimbabwe, which was fine with her because she didn't have time anyway.

The film had been an ambitious attempt by Weinstein to put her ideals on the big screen. Based on the South African novel by André Brink, it tells the story of a naive Afrikaner schoolteacher, Ben du Toit (played by Weinstein's former client Donald Sutherland), who is enlisted by the school's black groundskeeper to gain the release of his son, who was arrested by authorities during the Soweto uprising. Imagining he can obtain justice for the victim's family, the teacher is awakened to the reality of police brutality, and his enlightenment costs him his job, as well as the support of his family and his community.

Weinstein had spent four years trying to get the movie made and ultimately hired Euzhan Palcy (*Sugar Cane Alley*) to be the first black woman ever to helm a studio picture. In a casting coup she wrangled the reclusive Marlon Brando, who hadn't been in a film in almost a decade, to play du Toit's defense attorney for scale, $4,000. Unfortunately, she fought with Palcy in the editing room over several key scenes in the movie. Weinstein finally convinced Brando to take a look at the film; he wanted to go into the editing room and work on the sequences himself, but he couldn't do it for a couple of months because he was shooting in

Polly Platt in her office at Gracie Films/Sony, 1995.
STEVE BANKS

Canada. The studio didn't particularly want to spend the extra half million or delay the release of the movie. It all ended very badly when Brando publicly trashed the film. "He wanted me to go on his side and publicly denounce it and do all of that and I wouldn't do it," says Weinstein. "It was upsetting to me that Marlon was critical of me and upsetting to me that I thought he was right on the things that I had given in on that I shouldn't have." Brando's few moments on-screen enlivened what is an earnest but didactic effort. The film died at the box office.

Discouraged, Weinstein decided she didn't want to produce anymore on her own and set up a new production company on the Warners lot with her husband. "Part of the motivation for starting this company together—our joke version of it—was, we'd be working together so much in development all day long at work, and at home every night, that by the time we got a green light, we'd be so thrilled for four months away [from each other]," says Weinstein.

The power issues of coupledom multiplied exponentially. "The first year was extremely competitive and combative," says Weinstein. "I needed to be an equal partner. He needed to be the boss. So, the minute he needed to be the boss, I needed to be the boss. And it was hard going. There were slammings of doors. Raging around. The truth is, it is extremely hard for two high-powered, driven control freaks to be married to each other. And then there's sex. How do you feel not beaten down so that you're feeling feminine and enjoying it and how do you have a dance that's fun, and sensual and exciting, and at the same time, be business partners?"

The resolution was simple. They decided they "would never produce together"; each would have a separate domain in which he or she could be boss. "It was spectacular. We began to see each other's strengths and weaknesses and fill in rather than compete." She was a pessimist, he an optimist. Weinstein provided a cautious counterbalance to Rosenberg's impulsiveness, while he provided a healthy reality check against her tendency to moodiness and depression.

"One of the things that I really learned from Mark, is that he wasn't my girlfriend. For a long time once we were married, I expected him to be like my friends. I would call up and go, 'Oh my God, you can't believe what's going on.' " And they would address the emotions at the moment. "Mark would say, 'Don't be ridiculous. Get the fuck out of bed.' He was not going to indulge any view of myself that was insecure. And his way of doing it was to say, 'Of course you can do it.' And I did."

In their off hours they took pains not to let work consume them, changing their clothes for Friday night dates and spending weeks between films at their ranch in Montana. For almost seven years they tried to have a child, spending tens of thousands of dollars on fertility treatments in what they came to call the "baby derby." When Rosenberg was forty-four and Weinstein forty-seven, they finally decided to adopt a child, opting for an open adoption where the parents to be support the birth mother both materially and emotionally until the child is born. "I thought it would be nice for my daughter when she becomes curious for me to be armed with information, and not just a blank sheet of paper. And while it was more painful for me potentially in the short run, in the long run of her life, it meant that I could really talk to her about her birth parents. For a child's sake it would be better."

Their first candidate had been a disaster. Billed as a woman they should snap up before she got taken by someone else, the birth mother had repulsed Weinstein, who realized within half an hour that "I could never look at this woman's child and not see the behavior of this woman in it. This woman was so clearly disturbed and difficult."

They switched to a lawyer in San Francisco, where Weinstein was shooting *Fearless*, Peter Weir's 1993 existential drama about a man (Jeff Bridges) who survives a plane crash. Both Weinstein and Rosenberg had films hurtling into production. Rosenberg was prepping *Flesh and Bone* in Texas. They expected it would be six months before they found a new candidate. They would both be safely in postproduction. Within two weeks the new lawyer sent them someone else. "She walked down the hall of the hotel, and I liked her immediately," says Weinstein. It was September, and the baby was due in November.

They still wavered, ostensibly because the logistics were difficult. "Even the logistics of Mark being able to meet this birth mother, it seemed like, No, let's not do it, and [the birth mother] said, 'No, no, I'm not going to let you say no.' She had seen stacks of pictures of people, and letters that you have to write describing what your life is, and she just felt intuitively that of all the people she had seen the photographs of and read about, that we were the people. So she said, 'No, I'm not giving this baby to anybody else. And by the time she's born, if you don't want the child . . .' Well, of course, we wanted very much to have her child.

"It is intense because you do become involved in the birth parents' lives. There's a reason people do not casually give up children. So they're in some emotional state as it is, so it's very hard not to become a kind of parent figure to them in that period." The birth mother moved to L.A. for the last weeks of her pregnancy, and Weinstein took her to the doctor, ate dinner with her, spoke to her constantly on the phone. She tried not to fear that the birth mother would change her mind at the last minute and keep the baby. Every day on the phone she recounted for Rosenberg in Texas the progress of the pregnancy. If anything, she says, he "had more anxiety. We kept talking about, 'What happens if suddenly she goes into labor and the baby comes, how are you going to get here from Texas in time to be in the room when your daughter is born?' "

Rosenberg's health also worried Weinstein. He smoked incessantly, drank far too much. He was dangerously overweight. He happened to be a diabetic with a food addiction, happiest when chowing down snacks like fried chicken and tubs of butter. Dinnertime often roiled with tension as Weinstein watched him consume foods that could kill him. "Everybody would have a great time, and I would be enraged. So you feel like 'Oh what's the matter with me?' But every night was like that for us. Food addiction is the hardest addiction to break. You have to sit at a meal three times a day. And I think he was coming to it. But, frankly, Mark said, 'You could exercise for two hours a day and eat Pritikin, and have your life—it's not that you live longer, it just feels like you do.'

"I had a feeling that Mark might not make it, and I could have stopped the thing with the birth mother, and there was plenty of opportunity the three months before he died to say, 'Mark, you get your health in shape or I'm not going to do this.' And one of our last conversations was that, with me saying, 'I don't want to be a single parent.' He said, 'Well, then you better give up having the baby, because I don't know that I can do it. I'll try.' And I said, 'I'm not giving it up, because if I don't have you, I want to have her.' "

Weinstein was driving in the car with her sister and a friend when she got a call on her cell phone that Rosenberg had had a heart attack on the set of *Flesh and Bone*. He died instantly.

"I'm told from those who were in the car the first thing I said was, 'I'm keeping the baby,' " she says. "I don't remember that, because certainly in the next few days I pondered whether it was fair to her, and whether she was coming into a life of such turmoil. Mark's dead, three movies going, learning how to be a parent at forty-seven, fearful that it wouldn't work out, and that my sadness about being a single parent would affect my relationship with her." Everyone kept telling her she had to keep the baby—"obviously my own emotional instinct is I'm going to do it. But I was a little messed up by everybody saying you have to, because I thought, Oh wow, great, this is a great Hollywood story. The tragic heroine keeps the baby. It's like the tragedy of the year. And I didn't want to be seduced by that as if it were a play and not my life."

Weinstein's sister Lisa informed the birth mother that Rosenberg was dead, and later Weinstein told her she would understand if she rescinded the adoption because she wanted the baby to have two parents. "There's a Jewish expression *bershert,* which means, 'it's meant to be.' [The birth mother] really felt that her determination for us to be the birth parents came from some instinct and that this was meant to be. I was supposed to have Hannah, and Hannah was supposed to have me."

Rosenberg was buried in New Jersey three days after he died. Weinstein flew back to L.A., where the following week passed in a haze of people, the house filled with friends and fellow politicos from all over the country. "Friday was the memorial, and then I remember awakening Monday morning thinking, Okay, all I have to do is to go to the set if I have the energy. And otherwise I can sleep today.' And my sister took the birth mother to the obstetrician and said, 'Her water's broken, come right now.' "

Weinstein, her two sisters, Rosenberg's brother, her niece, a close friend, and the birth mother's mother were all in the room when Hannah Mark Rosenberg was born ten days after her adoptive father's death. "A lot of my closest girlfriends said, 'Don't expect to take a baby in your arms and have it feel like your own. Mine came out of me and I didn't,' " says Weinstein. "I felt like, Who is this creature? I cut the umbilical cord. I slept in the hospital with her that night. I took her home the next day, and then the next day I had to go to the set to see something, and I realized the minute I walked out of that house, My life has irrevocably changed. I felt a part of my brain there in the house worried about her, I was now responsible for her."

It took Weinstein almost two years to recover from Rosenberg's death. She didn't sleep for most of that time, although she forced herself to go to work every day. She had anxiety attacks, stomachaches, every hypochondriacal disease listed in the medical manuals. She suffered from what she calls "strong woman's disease," a willed blindness in the face of adversity. While she was the type of person who, she says, "takes Prozac when I'm happy," now she refused to take antidepressants because "I have a reason to be depressed. . . . When your husband dies at forty-four on the set of a movie, your conscious mortality hits you in the face pretty deeply," she says. She vacillated between guilt and resignation over Rosenberg's death. Some days she blamed herself for not taking him on in a stronger way, forcing him to stop eating. "I just knew that Mark would be so angry, and I wasn't willing to expose him that way." Other days she philosophized that "this was Mark's destiny. He fought against mortality. And I think that's what people do who are consumers of life. I think really it's a dance with death. They're defying it. And you don't win that battle."

Whereas before she had been a drama queen, tempestuous and outspoken about the littlest problems, now Weinstein retreated into herself, unable to communicate with anyone but her closest friends. She couldn't bring herself even to visit the set of *Flesh and Bone,* and on *Fearless* she would drop in for a couple hours a day, a far cry from her previous dawn-to-dusk ways. She spent Christmas in New York, working on the script of *With Honors,* about the friendship between a Harvard student and a homeless man. Distracted even in the best of times, she found herself hovering above her life watching, removed from almost everyone "with the exception of my daughter, who I could focus on and knew I had to make her feel safe. But even that was hard for us until I talked about Mark.

"The day I started to talk to her about Mark we became a family. She was six months old. She didn't even know what I was saying." Weinstein was putting Hannah to bed one night. "I was wearing a red necklace that Mark had gotten from the Indian reservation, and she was always playing with it. So I said, 'Okay, come and look, this is Papa Mark's picture,' " recalls Weinstein. "I told her the whole story of the beads. I took her around and showed her the picture of everybody in the family. There was something about saying, 'Papa Mark died.' It didn't mean anything to her, but we stared in each other's eyes as I told her the story, and then it was fine for me to be able to be sad with her." In all her mania to make Hannah feel loved, Weinstein hadn't ever really been herself, a woman who was grieving. "I'm sure she must have felt it. All babies are intuitive, but mine is the best intuitive. I'm in love."

She still reels with the irony that after years of therapy she has ended up with her mother's life, a single woman with a daughter to raise. "I came to understand all of that so I wouldn't repeat it, and here I am," she says. "I'm conscious when the phone rings now to turn it off when I'm at home with her for the hour or two we're playing together. But it took a great deal of discipline, because when you're as old and as selfish and as self-involved and as used to doing what I wanted to do, or as important, as a producer, being used to being at the beck and call of a director, meeting other people's needs, being there for adults—forget the pleasure one gets from it oneself—you have to say, 'I'm not going to do it. The adult can wait. She can't.' And it was a big deal the first time I said, 'Tell them I'll call back, I'm playing with Hannah.' "

IF I HAD ANY GUMPTION,
I'D GO OFF ON MY OWN

On August 7, 1993, Polly Platt attended the first preview of *I'll Do Anything,* James Brooks's ambitious attempt at an old-fashioned musical about life in the entertainment business, with Nick Nolte, Julie Kavner, Tracey Ullman, and Albert Brooks, incongruously warbling songs by Prince and Sinéad O'Connor, and twirling around to choreography by Twyla Tharp. Platt, who was producing the $40 million picture, had begged Brooks to take the preview out of town, away from eyes that were focused on Sony, mired not only in a losing streak but in the Heidi Fleiss prostitution scandal. Yet Brooks was superstitious—he had always had his previews in town, and the studio chairman, Mark Canton, had promised him that they would carefully vet all the attendees at Sony's Cary Grant Theater. The studio brass wouldn't even come.

Over the years, Platt had filled Gracie with new talent. She introduced the work of cartoonist Matt Groening to Brooks, which resulted in *The Simpsons.* She brought in Callie Khouri for a two-picture deal, to include her directorial debut as well as *Bottle Rocket,* by Wes Anderson and Owen Wilson. She produced Cameron Crowe's charming paean to first love, *Say Anything,* but she and Crowe stopped speaking for several weeks after she tried unsuccessfully to sway—some say bully—him. Platt was disappointed in what she perceived as Crowe's refusal to buck Brooks and how Brooks wanted the movie to be. Crowe was furious because he believed she didn't understand or support his intuitive directing style. Amends were made after she saw the movie.

Gracie had continued to grow by leaps and bounds, raking in profits from *The Simpsons* and a string of Brooks-produced hits—*Big, The War of the Roses.* In 1994 Brooks had signed one of the most lucrative production deals in town with Sony, which had offered $20 million more than its nearest competitor, as well as $100 million in production financing.

Platt had spent almost three years helping Brooks on *I'll Do Anything.* The director insisted on proceeding in his own idiosyncratic fashion—hiring actors instead of singer-dancers, more crucially perhaps, deciding not to work with a composer from the inception, the way musicals are traditionally done, although Platt had begged him to do so. Although he met with forty-odd music professionals, Brooks couldn't find anyone with the right chemistry.

Platt seemed as involved as ever, participating in long script sessions with Nolte and Holly Hunter (which she videotaped), giving her usual advice about all visual matters, hiring planes to fly around the country to look at choreography, holding discussions with Prince, who wound up contributing most of the songs. Yet she felt her influence over Brooks was dwindling. "He lost respect for me. Jim loves me as best he can. But [our initial battle over the composer] definitely strained the relationship—everything that I asked for him to do, he would do the other." Compounding Brooks's sensitivity was the fact that *I'll Do Anything* was in a sense his most autobiographical work. Set in Hollywood, it is the story of an out-of-work actor, a single father, who finds a measure of personal redemption and love through raising his difficult daughter.

Platt sat next to Brooks during the preview, and when the audience seemed to get through Albert Brooks's big dance number, they thought they were home free—"I remember we kind of looked at each other, and grabbed each other's hands," she says. Yet, when the little girl began to sing, about a dozen people walked out, and when Julie Kavner began to sing, there was a mass exodus, with loud snorts heard throughout the auditorium. The back exits were shut because of construction, so those who fled had to walk in front of the screen, casting shadows on the still-projecting movie. "It was hideous, and we sat there in shock," recalls Platt. Brooks wouldn't let her run any of the planned focus groups.

The brain trust retreated to the Gracie offices in the restored Jean Harlow Building, and Brooks broke out the bourbon. It was the worst night of his work life, the first augury of professional debacle in a career until then blessed by critical kudos and commercial hosannas.

Over the next couple of days, Brooks holed up with Platt to discuss plans for editing some of the musical numbers and retesting. Monday morning, however, Platt received a call from a reporter at *Variety*, who had heard about the terrible test screening. Soon after, the *Los Angeles Times* planned to run an item. Brooks brokered a deal by which the article was killed, but he was forced to allow a *Times* reporter to attend two other screenings, as well as to interview him. Over the next couple of weeks, Brooks continued to test the movie and ultimately wound up cutting out the musical numbers.

Platt fretted about her deteriorating relationship with the director. Not surprisingly, he was depressed and harder to reach. In the past Platt had never been the target of his lacerating wit, but she had seen its sting. Now she felt its bite. Brooks made jokes at her expense, and her daughters (two of whom she had found jobs at Gracie) noticed, which made the insults even more painful. She was aware of people like Jerry Belson, once Brooks's best friend, to whom he no longer spoke after a lawsuit over the revenues from *The Simpsons*. Platt's drinking didn't help. When Platt had too much, her normal brand of vehemence took on an unpredictable edge, which irritated the director. He seemed further concerned that Sherry Lansing at Paramount was pursuing Platt to produce the sequel to *Terms of Endearment, The Evening Star,* which he had turned down but she was considering.

Suddenly the situation boiled over. In the middle of the preview dramas, Platt's agent at ICM called to inform her that Brooks wasn't renewing her two-year contract. When she asked her business counterpart at Gracie, Richard Sakai, about it, he informed her that Brooks wasn't renewing anybody's contract. "And I felt that it was a slap in the face," says Platt. "I was on the phone desperately trying to keep the press off Jim's back. I was killing myself. I just was enraged.

"I think he already knew about *Evening Star.* He has, as he put it, issues of abandonment." Brooks had long told her she had "issues" with money. She resented his psychologizing, although later she would admit that though she wasn't particularly materialistic by Hollywood standards, money had grown to symbolize for her everything from respect to love. Although her salary—$600,000—was hefty, it was a drop in the bucket compared with the tsunami of cash that flowed through Gracie or the millions of dollars someone like Brooks earned.

When she actually confronted Brooks about the contract imbroglio, she says, "he dismissed it as unimportant. It didn't mean anything, and

I had nothing to worry about. And I said, 'Yes, but why are you doing it? It's not as if it isn't important to me. I have children.' " Indeed, Platt was still helping both her twenty-something daughters and stepdaughter, one of whom was still in college, and furthermore had lost a significant sum of money because of a bad business manager. "He said something like 'Oh, yes, your children starving in the streets.' And I completely lost my temper at him, and said, 'How dare you make any disparaging remarks about me having money worries, you rich son of a bitch?' " She banged her fist on the table. He banged his fist on the table.

Their screams echoed down the Gracie halls, unnerving the underlings in the office, as if Mommy and Daddy were fighting. Platt tried to grab control of the fight by forcing Brooks to admit that, given his exalted status in the industry, he couldn't begin to understand her financial worries. "He said, 'All I can admit is that I should have been smarter than to get in an argument with somebody who is clever, more clever than I am.' And I went, 'Oh shit, don't jive me. Don't try to manipulate by pretending that you think I'm more clever than you.' " Although Platt knew that they had already negotiated a deal for her to produce *Bottle Rocket*, she announced that she was going to leave Gracie. She'd get another job.

Brooks stalked out of the office, only to return a little later with a note for Platt, stating, "I do within human limitations want what most makes you happy and fulfilled."

All Platt could think of was that, ever since she could remember, she'd been "serving somebody. I was always somebody's handmaid. I was always honoring these great directors and worshiping them, genuinely worshiping them, so there was a sense if I had any character or gumption I would go off on my own. And then it became diverted into this economic issue, where I then wanted my stated deal. I was the only one who brought any pictures in. Everybody else was gone, and I was being treated as a pariah. So I was furious."

Soon after, her agent called, announcing that Brooks was willing to renew her contract, but it was too late. Acceptance had superseded her fury. She decided that after *Bottle Rocket* she would produce *Evening Star* as her ticket out.

"It was upsetting to me that she didn't quite cop to it being her choice [to leave]," says Brooks. "That if those circumstances hadn't happened, she would have stayed. I don't think that's the case." He turned around and became quite supportive, telling Platt she should try to direct *Evening Star* herself.

She knew that segueing from Jim Brooks's world to producing *Evening Star* was taking a step down, but she says, "I needed to go out there in the cold world." She begins talking about herself in the second person. "When you work with Jim, it is such a rarefied atmosphere, and creatively it is so exciting—it is in the family that you were never in, and you're always wanting to please them. You're always wanting to come up with something that makes them laugh, and there's something so weird about the dynamic, and that is not his fault."

"I just know that I approved of her. I approve of her," says Brooks in retrospect. "That's the only thing you have to get to with Polly. She had to play out some dramas with me, and I approve of her need to do that. Because with Polly, if you start judging what she thinks of you and taking offense, you're going to be in trouble."

In truth, the fight with Brooks helped solidify feelings that had been brewing in Platt since the early summer, when she won a Crystal Award. When her friend Barbara Boyle had called her to announce her selection, Platt had thought that she was making a joke, that the selection committee must have run out of worthier candidates. Flattered, thrilled, she finally was being offered the moment of approbation for which she had longed. "I realized that I had a fulsome career, and that it was worth noting." Again, she can't quite speak of herself in the first person: "You kind of had a sense that you owed something to what you had become with or without your permission, or with or without your intention. You had become a kind of a symbol of certain accomplishments, and you owed something to what you had achieved.

"It kind of changed my life. I had spent my whole life serving people like Jim, Peter Bogdanovich, Carl Reiner, Garry Marshall, Michael Ritchie, George Miller. I had loved them all, and I just realized that it was kind of time for me to go out and just do something on my own. There was something inside of me that felt like I hadn't accomplished anything, that it was really *them.* And so I said, 'Do you want to go through your whole life feeling like everything that you have done, really all the awards and all the respect that you have gotten, really deserves to be given to somebody else?' That is no way to live your life. So why don't you just take the lead, and go off by yourself, and do something? The good reason would be, what if I fail? That is more terrifying than death."

THE WORLD NEEDS
A REWRITE

DO YOU REALLY WANT ME CALLING
YOU TWENTY-TWO TIMES A DAY?

Sherry Lansing's promised land at Paramount quickly disintegrated into Poland on the eve of World War II. In the fall of 1993 a heated takeover battle for the studio emerged between Sumner Redstone, chairman of Viacom, a conglomerate that included the country's largest privately owned theater chains, as well as the cable stations MTV, Showtime, and Nickelodeon, and Barry Diller, former Paramount chairman, media darling, and now head of the QVC Home Shopping Network.

With Lansing's arrival the studio finally had begun to act as if someone was manning the tiller, although there was precious little she could do about the 1993 slate, which produced two bona fide $100 million hits out of only fifteen major releases, a fourth fewer than its rivals. Its market share had tumbled to 9.3, a nadir, making it sixth out of all the studios.

Lansing tried to stay sanguine about the acrimony swirling about her and refused to read the papers, "which trashed [the studio] daily." She signed off on *Losing Isaiah*, a drama about a custody battle between a poor, black birth mother and her child's rich, white adoptive family, as well as the comedy *I.Q.* (although the script was nowhere near ready), and a remake of Billy Wilder's *Sabrina*, directed by Sydney Pollack. Still, many agents groused about gridlock at Paramount, while others were simply wary of taking their best material there, given the precarious-

William Friedkin and Sherry Lansing at a party, 1996.

THE WORLD NEEDS A REWRITE / 475

ness of the studio's future. In December it appeared as if Diller would win, and the studio teemed with gossip that Jaffe would be out. Several of the lot's bigger-name producers quietly renegotiated their contracts, installing "key man" clauses so that if Jaffe and Lansing, or in some cases just Lansing, were forced out, they too would be free to depart.

By February, however, Redstone, a seventy-year-old who according to legend had survived a major fire in a Boston hotel by climbing out a window and clinging by his fingers to a ledge for ten minutes, won Paramount by bidding nearly $10 billion (almost $2 billion more than the price offered in the initial friendly merger). To raise the necessary cash, he also agreed to buy Blockbuster, the video store chain, for $8.4 billion.

Both Jaffe and Lansing made millions from their Paramount stock, although Jaffe was quickly forced out. (Indeed, Lansing's Paramount stock is now worth tens of millions of dollars.) Rumors ran through the Viacom hallways that Redstone was going to bring in his longtime friend the troubled Robert Evans to take Lansing's job. Rival Hollywood players—self-anointed power brokers as well as potential heirs apparent for her job—clamored to fill the new owner's ears with all Lansing's weaknesses. "I can't tell you how many people would call up and tell me how bad Sherry was," recalls the former Viacom CEO Frank Biondi, reiterating the litany of complaints against Lansing: "She just can't say no. All she does is return phone calls. No taste. Her people are weak. Yada yada yada." Biondi surmised, "In my experience, a lot of it comes out of the agency community, and how friendly you are toward them or not. If you're a little bit tougher, and you don't package, you somehow find yourself characterized as not a player. . . . It turned out the people were much better than advertised."

Soon after the takeover, Lansing was taken to dinner at the industry hot spot the Ivy by her new bosses: Redstone, Biondi, and several of their lieutenants. Jaffe urged her to stay, and she had never really considered leaving, although she knew she was on trial. At the dinner the Viacom team told her that they weren't going to bring in anyone over her, that she would report directly to Biondi. "I think they were under the impression that if they brought someone in I'd be upset," recalls Lansing. "I didn't care. And I said, 'That's okay, Frank, and that's okay, Sumner, but do you really want me calling you twenty-two times a day, because that's what I do.' "

In the end, the Viacom people were satisfied for the time being with Lansing creatively but decided to hire a strong numbers cruncher to back her up, ultimately choosing a former Fox cohort of Lansing's, Jonathan Dolgen, president of the Sony Motion Picture Group, to oversee both the film and TV divisions. Dolgen, whose nickname at Columbia was Repo Man, was known throughout Hollywood as a hard-nosed bottom liner. Unlike Jaffe, however, Dolgen would be based in L.A. Lansing was not upset at all that her bailiwick was changing. In fact, her one disappointment with Jaffe had been that he often ignored the studio, preferring to spend his time on Paramount's sports team and other ventures. She felt perfectly able to handle it; the financial side just didn't interest her. Indeed, as she watched the jockeying for political position in the aftermath of the Viacom buyout, Lansing quickly stressed to her new boss that she wanted not more authority but less. For instance, she would be thrilled to get rid of theaters that reported to her (no such luck).

Just days before Dolgen was officially installed, Lansing and her marketing staff saw their first cut of *Forrest Gump*. The filmmakers timed the screening to occur soon after Tom Hanks won the Oscar for *Philadelphia*. Lansing was rapturous, even turning to Michelle Manning afterward and admitting, "You were right."

To those around her Lansing's attitude toward *Gump* seemed to transform instantly. Her support for the project, which had been subtly withheld as a measure of control, now gushed. She called Zemeckis and cooed. "She went into Sherry seduction," recalls one who witnessed the display: " 'You are the brightest, the greatest!' She crawled on her belly to this guy, hurled herself, seduced him without being sexual, prostrated herself without being unctuous. She gets you in her sights and traps you in the high beams. She says what you've always wanted to hear from a person in power and has you feeling like you're a million dollars, like you're walking on a cloud of air." Afterward, Zemeckis seemed giddy with Lansing and the reception of his film, all his insecurities vanished under her barrage of congratulations. Lansing threw herself into marketing the film, authorizing rare one-minute TV commercials, the length necessary to convey the picaresque scope of the film.

The personal cease-fire was, however, brief. At one of the previews held on the lot, the director wanted to use his own specially devised cards. Lansing wanted to use the ones the studio always used. Both Goldwyn and Manning had been sent to convey this message to Zemeckis, but it never got through. When the lights came up, one of Joe Farrell's workers began passing out cards. Immediately, Zemeckis's producer, Steve Starkey, tore down the aisle trying to retrieve them.

Zemeckis jumped up to confront Lansing. Soon they were yelling at each other. He didn't want cards. She did. For those who had never seen her this way, Lansing in fury was a shock, the mask of niceness ripped away, her chest huffing and puffing in her tailored suit. Who was Zemeckis to tell them what they could do? Paramount had $60 million invested in this film. He didn't have to look at the cards, but they were going to get them. Dolgen, who had been on the job just weeks, tried to calm Lansing down. "Okay, okay, okay," he told her.

"It's not okay," she snapped at her new boss. "Don't tell me how to do my job."

Finally one audience member stood up and yelled to the pair, "I don't know why you're fighting. You have a wonderful movie here."

In the end there were cards, and the scores were uniformly excellent. *Forrest Gump* turned into not only a hit movie but a cultural phenomenon, earning more than $300 million at the domestic box office alone, as well as a slew of Oscars, including Best Picture.

That summer boasted another $100 million Paramount hit in the form of *Clear and Present Danger*. In 1994 the studio rebounded spectacularly at the box office, zooming up to number three in market share, behind Disney and Warners, although it released almost ten fewer films than either behemoth. The new owners were ecstatic about Lansing's performance. As Biondi admitted to her, their attitude changed from "Shall we let her stay?" to "How can we get her to stay?"

On the eve of the Oscars, Lansing's final victory in her comeback year, she faced one final indignity in *Vanity Fair*'s much-hyped Hollywood issue, which featured a bevy of young actresses sporting underwear on the cover. Inside was a five-year-old outtake from her old American Express photo session depicting her wearing a white bathing suit poolside. "I started to scream when I saw it," she told the *Los Angeles Times*, a breach in her usual speak-no-evil policy. "I thought it was totally inappropriate. It diminishes the accomplishments of all women, not just in our business."

By the time Lansing had settled into chairmanship, it had become apparent that her much-vaunted niceness, her desire to be liked, was at once genuine and her sharpest political instrument: a cheery front behind which she increasingly played hardball, determinedly molding her realities into a Lansing reality. "Sherry has an ideal vision of the world, and that's when everybody is agreeing with everyone, especially her," says her husband, Billy Friedkin, who was shocked to hear his own wife praise films in public, or even semipublic, that she abhorred in private. She acted as if each of her own movies was her most-beloved child.

"It is very hard to get Sherry to say an even quasi-negative thing about something," says Biondi, recalling her performances at internal Paramount presentations as "a little bit like Kabuki: 'This is the greatest slate that has ever been produced by mankind.' You know it's not going to happen, and she knows it's not going to happen. It's almost like a ritual." He laughs.

Ironically, Lansing had inherited that exact quality of her mother's that drove her nuts as a child—a vigilant belief in her own reality, sometimes blocking out all evidence to the contrary. Although she adopted a professional stance of womanly empathy—and pointedly refrained from the de rigueur Hollywood rites of humiliation—she ignored realities that didn't conform to her vision, a personality quirk that led detractors to accuse her of lying. From Lansing's perspective, the biggest contretemps usually occurred over budgets, and other people's inability to believe she meant what she said.

"She has a desire to see things a certain way like anybody does, and I think sometimes the people around her have a hard time—they're not always eager to go and say, 'Wait a minute, this thing you think is happening, this is not happening,' " says the producer Scott Rudin. "But you can call her and say, 'Excuse me, you're on Pluto, and come back to Earth with the rest of us.' "

Lansing's friends, such as the producer Lawrence Gordon and William Morris's president, James Wiatt, chided her that she terrified her staff into submission, a charge she professed not to understand. Says Wiatt, "I don't think Sherry's aware that the staff is frightened of her. She's such a strong personality. They're very deferential to her: 'Let me see what Sherry thinks.' They look to her for her opinions and then they try to execute what she wants. No one operates autonomously." Wiatt points out that the particularly small Paramount production staff—most of whom were inherited by Lansing and had been at the studio for years—hasn't produced any rising stars, the kind that get the community buzzing.

Paramount produced no junior stars in part because Lansing was so accessible. Agents often tried to bypass the chain of command to push their projects through by calling directly to the top. Some, like the ICM hotshot Ed Limato, could rail at Lansing without fear that it would be held against them in future dealings. Unlike in a corporation like Warner Bros., where the president of production typically assembled packages for the chairman to ratify, Lansing could often be seen doing not only her job but those of everyone below her. Unlike most studio chiefs, she read every draft of every script. She was both obsessive with details and controlling, happiest with her staff when they sweated the minutiae.

"I think there is a side of Sherry that likes to do every job. I said to her once, 'You would be so much happier if you were head of production than if you were the chairman of the studio,' " says Rudin. "She likes all that little detailed stuff, and it's hard for her to let go of it, but her staff's not afraid of her. I just think they sometimes will maybe feel preempted by her. She's a big personality, and she is the court of last resort."

"It's normal for me to hear from Sherry ten times on the weekend," says the president of the motion picture group, John Goldwyn. "I hope that Jack has a Little League weekend or Billy's in town. You pray and hope." Goldwyn recounts the usual routine. Saturday morning at 9:00 often brings the first phone call. " 'Hi, hon, have you done the reading?' she asks. [Over a weekend most studio executives will read as many as ten scripts.] 'I've finished them all,' says Lansing. 'You read them all and then let's talk.'

"She won't tell people what she thought. She wants to know what you think. She'll call again on Sunday. You've only read half, but she's already talked to so-and-so and so-and-so, various executives [about the material]. By Sunday night, what should be Monday morning's staff meeting is already done."

Lansing often took a script with her wherever she went, reading during classical music concerts at the Chandler Pavilion (where Fried-kin, a music fan, had a subscription) or during her stepson Jack's Little League games, and called in script notes during breaks. On the week-end of a film opening, she'd talk to Dolgen and the marketing team Friday night to see how the film was doing, then spend the rest of the weekend refining the advertising spots. In a surefire grasp of Hollywood political etiquette, she would apprise every relevant member of the film's creative team on how it was faring in the marketplace.

Sunday afternoons were not infrequently reserved for nailing down directors to Paramount pictures, calling people at home, and flattering them with offers of her favorite script in the Paramount cupboard (all the scripts were her favorite script). "It means a lot to these people that she tracks them down," says Goldwyn.

"I don't think [my staff's] afraid of me. I'd feel really bad if [they] were all afraid of me," says Lansing. "On the other hand, I'm their boss. They don't like to disappoint me. The very nature of the job is something I'm not aware of. The nature of leadership is that one person has to make the final decision. Not often, but several times, no one on my staff has liked the movie and we've made it. Again, not much but several times, everyone has liked the movie and I haven't and we've gone ahead and made it. To the outside world, no one would know. Once the decision is made, we all march forward and make it with great possessiveness. I don't think that's being afraid. That's good leadership. You try to get your view so that it looks like a consensus thing."

All of Lansing's indefatigable people skills were necessary, because Paramount was fast transforming into one of the most difficult studios for producers and agents to do business with, mostly because of its new cost-sharing philosophy.

The one thing Lansing had learned from Alan Hirschfield in her misbegotten experience at Fox was protect your downside. Six months before the takeover battle, at a corporate retreat in Northern California, she presented a series of charts that showed how the studio would profit in the long run by sharing the cost on each film with either equity investors or other studios, especially because the budget of the average movie had climbed from $30 to as much as $75 million in the past five years. One flop could wipe out a year's profits. They could dramatically cut their downsides, but also their upside. It was an idea regarded by most top-level studio honchos as anathema, and Davis and Jaffe vetoed it but gave her a twenty-thousand-dollar brooch in appreciation for what she had done at the studio.

By contrast, Dolgen, keen on reordering the studio's finances, had not only made each film's profit-and-loss statements public knowledge to the staff, he positively embraced cost sharing as his new mantra. One of his first highly publicized acts as chairman of the Viacom Entertainment Group had been to seal a production deal with the actor-producer Michael Douglas and his partner Steve Reuther, who would cofinance

Paramount movies with millions in backing from the German company Kirsch. Intent on leaving his imprint, Dolgen also trimmed the staff 10 percent, as well as bigfooted other films long hurtling toward production. On Labor Day weekend, the producer Kathleen Kennedy received a call from Lansing, who was with Dolgen and the *Forrest Gump* contingent at the Venice Film Festival. Kennedy was due to start principal photography on the $40 million *Indian in the Cupboard* in ten days. Lansing now informed her that Dolgen had decreed the producers would have to find a financial partner to shoulder half the film's cost.

Kennedy, who had produced such films as *E.T.* and *Jurassic Park*, as well as built Steven Spielberg's production company, Amblin Entertainment, into the industry gold standard, was shocked. Paramount's action was brutal by Hollywood standards, an almost certain death knell for the movie. Given her stature in the industry, Kennedy was able to reach all the major studio heads on the phone that night, and by the end of the holiday weekend Columbia had picked up the other half of the movie.

Another person in Lansing's job might have taken umbrage at Dolgen's actions, which seemed to undercut her authority on a variety of fronts, but Lansing turned keel, embracing him as her partner. She had never been interested in domination, only in coexistence, with the uncanny ability to adapt herself to powerful men without truly subverting her ego. She made their professional marriage work. "For Dolgen, every crisis seems to be the end of the world," says Friedkin, who has spent much time with Dolgen and his wife. "That's how [both he and Jaffe] deal with it, and they communicate a lot of that to Sherry. They use Sherry like a shrink in a sense. That is why she succeeded with Stanley and with Jonathan where others have failed. They just lay it all out there. It is usually 'This is a fucking disaster. I want to kill that motherfucker.' That's not their real nature, but that's how they have to function to perform. Sherry knows about the need to vent."

For her part, Lansing was thrilled to find someone who shared her hypercautious approach to the business—while success was wonderful, only failure was certain. "Jonathan's the only person that worries as much as I do," says Lansing. "He's the only person that I can call at eleven at night and say, I'm really worried about this, do you think we can do it? I mean, he'll talk."

Despite her love of the limelight, Lansing had an ego that encompassed not just herself, but the bigger picture, the whole studio. She and

Dolgen were forced to work increasingly close together given the new cost-sharing philosophy. She was cognizant of the fact that her skills and Dolgen's complemented each other. Dolgen was largely content to leave creative decisions to her, and she was happy finally to have a partner who, unlike Jaffe, would focus on the studio and really loved to sweat the financial options. As she and Dolgen settled into a comfortable working relationship, he used to joke that Lansing would inevitably find an excuse to get out of every financial meeting after only twenty minutes. "Can't you even pretend to look interested?" he'd quip. To which she would retort, "I'm not interested, so why do I have to look it?" While Lansing and Jaffe always made a point of celebrating their joint birthday together, several years into their tenure she and Dolgen were taking vacations together, talking shop while their spouses relaxed in various vacation spots around the world.

While both Lansing and Dolgen began to bill themselves as an inseparable partnership, old perceptions persisted, namely that she had simply shifted her good cop–bad cop routine to Dolgen. With his fierce, deep-set eyes, blunt manner, and sardonic sense of humor, he was the dark cloud to Lansing's silver lining, a characterization that increasingly smacked of chauvinism. "It never ceases to amaze me that sometimes I can deliver the worst news in the world to somebody and they'll blame it on Jonathan and he wasn't even in the room," fumes Lansing. "Some of that's style. Some of that's sexist." As she grew in the job, she more freely took on talent and dispatched her bad news herself. "I have seen her be tough on people, but it's usually been pretty appropriate," says Rudin. "She doesn't like to be bullshitted, and I think she doesn't have a lot of patience for people sort of blowing smoke, so I think when somebody does that she'll definitely take them on."

As Lansing and Dolgen solidified their relationship, producers and agents increasingly complained about Paramount as the land of the "blinking green light." No one knew if a movie was actually going to be made because the final definitive go seemed contingent on finding outside sources of financing. (Although Lansing insists she green-lit the movies first, and then worried about how exactly they would be financed.) Besides Douglas-Reuther, Paramount lined up other financial partners, such as Rysher, Lakeshore, and Mutual, independent production companies that brought their own financing to the table. Within four years almost every Paramount film that cost more than $25 million was cofinanced with equity investors or other studios. Most Holly-wood insiders assumed the new philosophy was due to a cash shortage caused by Viacom's enormous $10 billion debt load, a contention that the Paramount brass heatedly denied.

While Paramount continued to make far fewer movies than Warn-ers or Disney, Viacom announced its intention to increase the Para-mount production slate. Lansing filled that slate with risky midbudget films, mostly generic thrillers that lacked major stars, further indication to the cognoscenti that the Paramount coffers were empty.

"What I found was there was never that kind of united confidence that you feel where everyone would step forward and say, Okay, yes, we want to make this movie," recalls Kathleen Kennedy, who used to be based on the lot. "It was always like roadblocks going up, that we had to figure out how to get beyond, and then the minute you get beyond that, it seemed like another one would come up. And there may be something I don't entirely understand involved in the complications of their financing expensive pictures that didn't allow them to give a 100 percent green light until they knew that the picture had been 100 per-cent financed. But I've never encountered that kind of stop-start kind of process before. I found it psychologically debilitating."

Moreover, after the banner *Forrest Gump* year, in which Paramount took in a profit of $120 million on gross revenues of $1.4 billion, Lans-ing's wing fell into another slump. It was a particularly inauspicious time, because Viacom was under intense pressure to raise its stock price. In order to buy Paramount, Viacom had promised investors that the stock would rise 25 percent by May 1995; if it didn't, Viacom would be compelled to pay shareholders a penalty in cash or stock of between $1 million and $1 billion. To raise the stock price, Viacom had to prove that it was a growth company, increasing its cash flow and showing bet-ter-than-expected earnings, particularly in the first two quarters.

In his ongoing push to increase investor confidence, Redstone exu-berantly trumpeted the summer's tent-pole release, *Congo,* as the next big hit to come from the studio. Based on Michael Crichton's book about a breed of killer apes, *Congo* was produced by Kennedy and directed by her husband, Frank Marshall, whose credits included *Arachnophobia* and *Alive.* Lansing begged Redstone not to place such outsize expecta-tion on a film they hadn't seen. While she had no problem with hyping her products afterward or internally, she was wary about creating expectations in the marketplace that might not be met. In any event, Redstone mandated that Lansing present *Congo*, complete with a "killer ape" (a man in an ape suit), to the Wall Street analysts.

Lansing's worries about *Congo* were warranted. The studio had started production with a brilliant merchandising strategy devised by Kennedy and fantasies of another *Jurassic Park*. It had a summer release date and an accelerated postproduction schedule. It was the most expensive movie green-lit in the Stanley Jaffe era. It just didn't happen to have a good script or, consequently, any stars.

While Lansing was away, Dolgen had gone ahead and allotted Kennedy and Marshall $4 million more (bringing the budget into the sixties) to shoot a new grand finale: the eruption of a volcano.

The first cut had been horrifying; the second a bit better. At the next preview the audience filed out in droves. Those who remained chortled at the spewing lava sequence. By this time, Lansing had left for New York for her big presentation to the analysts. Her deputy, John Goldwyn, told Joe Farrell not to tabulate the numbers, as if this screening never happened. Goldwyn faxed Lansing at the Sherry-Netherland with a cryptic message: Please call me about numbers. He arrived home at two in the morning and told his message service to put all his phones save one on hold. At three, Lansing began calling him, and she proceeded to call every fifteen minutes until he picked up the phone at 5:00 A.M. He told her that at least thirty people had walked out of the screening. He could hear her shuddering on the other end of the phone.

As Lansing grew in stature, she lost her temper more freely. It usually manifested itself in declamations such as "I'm confused," or, if she was really mad, "I'm fucking confused." She also had anxiety fits where she would spin out her worries like sparks jetting from a flame.

Under real stress, however, Lansing completely calmed down. In this case she didn't scream. "We'll go over the film reel by reel and do what it takes to fix it," she told Goldwyn decisively. Paramount had after all pretested the concept—the film would work if they could make it presentable.

Still, the moment she walked into the analysts' meeting, Dolgen could tell from her expression that something was very wrong. She confessed about the preview, and they fretted over whether to tell Redstone, ultimately opting to let the Viacom owner know that *Congo* looked to be a full-fledged disaster. Redstone advised Lansing to ignore the subject during her spiel, but, if asked point-blank, not to lie.

The presentation started with a man in an ape suit cavorting through the meeting hall. Lansing spoke positively about *Congo,* and when asked about its box-office potential, she demurred, saying they didn't know, they were still working on the movie.

Afterward, she had dinner with Jaffe. She was burned out and tired, unusually depressed. She questioned herself and her abilities. It was the beginning of what would be a six-month losing streak, a time when she would wonder if she was doing the right thing.

Several days later Redstone called to give her a pep talk: "You were right to buy the book. You hired a good team. You did everything right. Don't be down on yourself."

Afterward, the studio brought in Neil Travis, who reedited several sequences of the film frame by frame. According to both Goldwyn and Lansing, they, along with Michelle Manning, haunted the editing room, riding Marshall to fix the picture. (Kennedy calls this version of events "total bullshit.") The scores rose, and Lansing was particularly heartened when her stepson, Jack, came to a preview and loved it, running up afterward to ask to see it again. At least adolescent boys liked it. *Congo* opened to a surprising but bang-up $25 million box office and a critical dunning, which helped stunt its domestic profit to $80 million, a far cry from *Jurassic Park.*

The usually politic Lansing was unusually open in her fury toward Kennedy, whom she perceived as having abandoned not only the picture but, worse, her husband. Kennedy had gone off to Kansas to produce *Twister* for Amblin and flew back only every eight days or so to supervise postproduction on both *Congo* and *The Indian in the Cupboard.* Lansing was mystified and enraged at the hold Spielberg still had over Kennedy, a loyalty born out of decades of working together (not to mention the fact that Spielberg had made her career).

"What does he have on you, pictures?" she fumed at the producer. In truth, Kennedy was contending with a nightmarish production situation on the tornado picture. Still, she missed her husband's film's premiere, leaving Marshall alone to hawk what seemed to be a certain disaster.

Lansing's anger at Kennedy seemed to carry an unusually personal twinge, because she had done everything in her power to bolster Billy

Friedkin's flagging career at an increasing cost to her reputation and increasing personal distress. As one Paramount insider recalls, she was "shameless" in her advocacy of his talent. Although Friedkin had made only critical and commercial disasters for at least a decade, Paramount green-lit two of his films, *Blue Chips* and *Jade*.

Publicly, Lansing defended the obvious nepotism with cheery nonchalance. "Here's what I think about husbands and wives working together. First of all, I think it's great. I think husbands and wives, boyfriends and girlfriends, or whatever should be free to work together. And I think nobody should be penalized because they're married to someone, man or woman. I'm all for hiring people's sons. I'm all for hiring people's daughters. I'm all for hiring husbands and wives. I don't think you should be penalized because of that."

A month after Lansing took over as chairman, Friedkin replaced Michael Apted on *Blue Chips*, a Ron Shelton (*White Men Can't Jump*) morality tale about college basketball that had been knocking around for twelve years. Indeed, it had recently been put into turnaround by Lansing's deputy John Goldwyn. Because of Paramount policy, she recused herself from directly handling her husband's project. Jaffe personally oversaw *Blue Chips*, a task made slightly trickier not only by the fact that Lansing was off the project but because Shelton, who was producing, hadn't forgiven Goldwyn for previously spiking the film.

"I did as much as I could from three thousand miles away," recalls Jaffe. "To the extent that Billy was involved, if there was a major thing, then I would be referee. I tried to function in a way as a buffer between Sherry and Billy, because it would not have been good if there was too much direct contact between them. Pillow talk I can't control." There wasn't much Lansing could do when Jaffe and Friedkin had their inevitable battles but hover on the sidelines.

Still, the Hollywood smirk machine went into overdrive when Paramount agreed to pay $7.5 million for Nick Nolte to star, a career high for a fine actor who had never opened a movie in his life. The film was filled with real-life basketball figures, including the superstars Shaquille O'Neal and Larry Bird. Friedkin darkened Shelton's script considerably, and the resulting film played on one level as a career mea culpa for the director, the tale of an honest coach, once the best in the country, who falls on hard times and sells out everything he believes in to keep on winning. At last, he admits his wrongdoing in a burst of career-ending integrity.

Blue Chips garnered decent reviews and opened to a healthy $10.2 million weekend, although it quickly fell off, with viewers alienated by Friedkin's moral gloom. The official budget was $20 million, although the film wound up costing $30 million. *Blue Chips* wound up grossing only $22 million domestically.

Friedkin's next film, *Jade*, proved far more problematic to both the studio and his marriage. In one of her first buys as studio chairman, Lansing had paid $2.5 million for *Jade*, based on a two-and-a-half-page outline that Robert Evans had passed on to his close friend Stanley Jaffe. Joe Eszterhas proposed a story about a sexy psychologist, who moonlights as a high-class hooker, and her hotshot attorney husband, who believes he's so skilled that he can frame his wife for murder but get her acquitted. In a typical Hollywood confluence of improbabilities, the investigating police officer happens to be the wife's old flame, and the husband's best friend.

When the high-profile script was finished, Friedkin was the only director to whom it was offered. Not only was he close to Evans but at the time, says the producer Craig Baumgarten, "everyone thought *Blue Chips* was going to be a hit."

"Sherry has never asked me to do a picture, nor have I ever asked her to do a picture," insists Friedkin. "Eszterhas and Evans wanted me to do *Jade*. I liked it, and I always felt it was unfortunate they both happened to be at Paramount."

His second day at Paramount, Dolgen green-lit the *Jade* cast contingent. Officially, Dolgen would take over Jaffe's position on Friedkin's film. "No one was nuts about [doing *Jade*], but we were okay with it," recalls Frank Biondi, then Dolgen's and Lansing's boss at Viacom.

Friedkin says he generally refrained from talking specifics about his film with Lansing, although he did solicit her advice on casting. From the beginning, the highly derivative *Jade* had trouble attracting the kind of A-list talent the filmmakers had envisioned. Lansing unsuccessfully tried to get Mel Gibson attached, to fulfill a commitment he owed the studio in return for Paramount backing *Braveheart*. Warren Beatty wanted to do it—if he was promised 10 percent of the gross. The studio ultimately opted to scale down its expectations, casting the hot newcomers David Caruso and Linda Fiorentino instead of established stars, bringing the potential budget down from $75 million to $34.7 million (Friedkin was to receive a $1.25 million salary), a figure that Friedkin initially balked at signing off on, because he thought it wasn't realistic, and he knew, given his relationship with Lansing, he'd be "crucified" if he went over.

As production moved forward, Lansing's recusal became more and more difficult to maintain given the naturally adversarial relationship between studio and director, and a film that went over budget by several million dollars. "She did the very best she could to level the playing field. And the only way that she could do that was to remove herself from the decision-making process. But you have still got people who have got to make decisions about what Billy can and can't do, and what he could and couldn't spend, and they still have to report to Sherry," recalls one *Jade* insider. There was little upside for her staff in taking on their boss's husband, who wanted what he wanted and could be dismissive to people he thought were stupid (an attitude that alienated some crew members).

More troubling for Lansing were Dolgen's weak creative skills. He would ask for advice from Goldwyn, who in turn would ask Lansing, leaving her in the precise position she never wanted to be in: her husband's boss. "The head of the studio and a director are often on opposite sides," recalls Lansing. "You respect each other, but, by the very nature, you're the authority. You're fiscally responsible, and you have to say no. And that puts a strain on a marriage, you know, because it's like, 'What do you mean I can't shoot that?'" From her perspective, the studio was so keen on not showing favoritism that people tended to treat Friedkin worse than other directors.

The situation was further complicated when *Jade* previewed badly. A consensus was reached that the last twelve minutes didn't work, although no one—not Lansing, Dolgen, Friedkin, or the producers (Eszterhas had moved on)—could devise an appropriate ending. The couple fought. "We made a lot of changes based on the preview. Do they help the film? I don't know. They were certainly different," says Friedkin. "I think [test screening] is all bullshit, because if the other elements aren't there, if the audience really doesn't care about the actors who are playing those parts, about the story that you're giving them, about the concept behind this story and its theme, you can reedit a film four hundred times—" He stops himself. "Again, I must say that Sherry has taken certain films here, changed them considerably, and turned disaster into gold. She has a great feel for how to use that process."

Despite her outward cheeriness, Lansing seemed increasingly sensitive to the fact that everyone in Hollywood was scrutinizing the film because of her and Friedkin's relationship. "It just eats her up," recalls

Wiatt, who had become Friedkin's agent. "Every day she was calling. She felt like she was being watched by everyone, and that people wouldn't tell her what they felt because he was her husband." To some inside Paramount, she seemed obsessed with the *Jade* marketing campaign, although she denies it. She rode the staff incessantly, personally fretting over the trailer and the precise shade of green to be used on the background of the poster; her production staff barely saw her for almost a week.

Jade was a financial debacle for Paramount, earning less than $10 million, and garnering withering reviews. Most of Lansing's production staff hadn't even seen the film until the premiere, from which Friedkin departed early, leaving Lansing alone to cheer it on and to wave both the corporate and the connubial banners. In retrospect, she would blame the country's new puritanism for the failure of *Jade*, which in fact came on the heels of another Eszterhas disaster, *Showgirls*.

"When the picture didn't work, everybody kind of said, Let's not visit this place again," says Biondi, recalling Viacom's attitude. "I'm not sure anybody ever told [Sherry] per se. I just think everybody understood it. He's not banned from Paramount, but he doesn't work directly for Paramount. It's hard. That picture did go over budget: What do you do, go running back to your husband and beat on him?"

In retrospect, Lansing believed that *Jade* was a misguided attempt by Friedkin to make a Sherry Lansing–type movie, a piece of mass entertainment, and that he would be better off "[following] his own muse and [not having] the pressure of his wife, who is running the studio."

She herself wasn't keen to work with Friedkin again, at least not in the same capacity. Says Lansing, "[We said] let's not do this for a couple more years. You'll go do your picture someplace else, and I'll just be a supportive wife for the process rather than . . ." (Since *Jade*, Friedkin has completed a TV remake of *Twelve Angry Men* and the feature *Rules of Engagement*, and as of early 2002 is filming *The Hunted*.)

Still, *Jade* was one of five Paramount films in a row that flopped, culminating in the massive disappointment of the major Christmas release *Sabrina*, starring Harrison Ford, a film that was as fusty and old-fashioned as the original had seemed spry and romantic. The failures depressed Lansing. Redstone decided to slash the number of films for the next year. Rumors circulated about her demise, although Lansing would never have quit while the studio was in a slump. The only high point of the year was *Braveheart*, on which Lansing herself had negotiated a fantastic deal (a mere $17 million investment for domestic rights). The film ended up grossing $80 million in the United States, as well as winning Paramount its second consecutive Oscar for Best Picture.

While Lansing was swimming in the Caribbean over Christmas vacation, a little boat sped out to inform her that she had to take an urgent phone call from the States. It was her lawyer, Bert Fields, announcing that Viacom was desperate to renegotiate her contract by the first of the year.

According to Biondi, Geraldine Laybourne, the head of Nickelodeon, had received an offer from Disney, and Viacom had countered with a matching offer, which would have made her the highest-paid division chief at the company. Although Laybourne wound up going to Disney anyway, Redstone and Biondi decided to raise the salaries of all their division heads—Dolgen, Lansing, Tom Freston at MTV—to bring them more into line with their counterparts'. In return, each division was asked to extend their contracts several years.

Ironically, only Lansing's deal was trumpeted in a banner headline across *Variety:* $20 million for a five-year pact. Lansing claims that she didn't know how *Variety* got that information, although she saw it as their way of reaffirming that women could make big money in Hollywood (and put to rest the rumors of her demise). She could earn another 100 percent in bonuses. Still, what both she and Dolgen were making was a far cry from the compensation received by Warners heads Robert Daly and Terry Semel, whose salary estimates ran as high as $15 million a year.

Immediately after the announcement Hollywood wags bruited the rumor that Redstone was distancing himself from his floundering division chiefs, supposedly calling the new deal "the immaculate conception." His intentions soon became clear: One month after all the division heads sealed their deals, he fired their boss, Frank Biondi.

29.

___

THE BUTTERFLY CHASERS

THE GOOD NEWS IS SHE WON THE ACADEMY AWARD, AND THE BAD NEWS IS SHE WON THE ACADEMY AWARD

Thelma & Louise transformed Callie Khouri into an icon, a spokesperson for all that was wrong and right with women in America. It was both exhilarating and unnerving to find herself the object of adulation by young women who took to heart Louise's credo, "You get what you settle for." She was offered speaking engagements, showered with awards, quoted in the papers, and deluged with offers from Hollywood. At times her displays of heartfelt emotion seemed extravagant, as when she sobbed receiving the *Glamour* Women of Distinction Award.

Creatively, the heat was paralyzing. "I was totally freaked out," Khouri says. "*Thelma & Louise* came so easily. I never had a moment of doubt. It would be like, if you always dreamed about playing the piano and then you were in a car accident and you wake up and you think, I can play the piano, bring me a piano. Somebody brings you one and you can play.

"It was not just a single cause, like writer's block, I think it was everything. It was fear of the second project. Then having a story that was complicated at best," says Khouri, who isn't the kind of disciplined writer who can just sit down every day and pound it out. She's a social animal. As she says, "My preferred method of communication is interacting."

"Who would want to be Callie? You write a script as—you are in a closet somewhere borrowing somebody's computer. You sell it. You

Nora Ephron and John Travolta on the set of MICHAEL, 1996.

win the Academy Award. You become this feminist heroine, you're feted everywhere, and now you have to sit down to write your second script that is an idea that you happened to rework and now you want to make it your own, and everybody is still calling you saying, Come out, speak at this graduation. That's a lot of pressure on somebody," says Paula Weinstein, repeating an oft-told Hollywood adage—"The good news is she won the Academy Award, and the bad news is she won the Academy Award."

Weinstein and her close friend Anthea Sylbert happened to be the producers who landed Khouri's project. Indeed, they had hired her for a studio rewrite on a project called *Sisters* before *Thelma & Louise* even debuted. When Weinstein met Khouri, she was taken with the writer's girlish enthusiasm. "There's a very sweet, simple, direct, open quality about Callie that is so different from Anthea and me—you know, two really urban fashionista women," recalls Weinstein. "I was fascinated because she was getting married, and she was also telling me about sitting with her family, and showing us the wedding dress; by the time I got married I was thirty-eight years old, and [my mother and sisters] would no more allow me to wear a wedding dress . . . It was just out of the question. I had to go buy Mary McFadden. All I wanted was a wedding dress, and I thought, I can't have it. And there was Callie talking about the wedding plans, and she loved David."

Sisters had started life in the mid-eighties as a vehicle for Goldie Hawn and Barbra Streisand, with *Nine to Five*'s Patricia Resnick as the initial screenwriter. "We had one meeting that was Paula and Anthea and Streisand and Goldie and myself at Streisand's house," recalls Resnick. "Streisand put on this great spread, and had hot and cold running servants, and hors d'oeuvres. Even if you work with stars, she's still *such* a star. So it was very nerve-racking. I feel pretty comfortable with Goldie, but Streisand kind of fires a lot of questions at you very rapidly. And if you don't immediately have the answers, you kind of get knocked off balance. But then it ended up being a lot of fun, and she and Goldie ended up discussing food and exercise and men."

Unfortunately, Cis Corman, who ran Streisand's company, wasn't enthusiastic about Resnick's first draft. Moreover, "Barbra thought Goldie's part was better and Goldie thought Barbra's part was better," recalls Resnick. Streisand dropped out, and eventually so did Hawn, who came back after Resnick wrote yet another draft.

Khouri's pitch was to junk the script they had; she regaled Weinstein and Sylbert with tales of her southern upbringing and a story about a southern family of horse breeders. At the heart was a feminist, or perhaps a postfeminist, issue of how to have it all, and how to be true to oneself. If *Thelma & Louise* was the quest for self-empowerment set in the genre of the outlaw road movie, *Something to Talk About* (*Sisters*'s new title) was supposed to be the quest for self-empowerment set in the family saga. "We talked a lot about the socializing of women, what they're faced with as they compromise their way through their life," says Khouri. "I don't have kids. I have a lot of friends who do. And at some point it always comes down to they're failing. They're failing their kids, but they're not spending enough time with them because they have careers. They're failing in their careers because they're not focused. They're failing in their marriages because they're so fucking tired. And so it's like all these incredible women walk around feeling like failures all the time. I think that's probably one of the defining issues of the nineties for women, it's just feeling like they're not enough. But that's not interesting to make a movie on. It's interesting to have as an aspect of a character."

Khouri's story concerned Grace, a thirty-five-year-old mother, a southerner who was raised to serve others and who did everything she was ever expected to do: marry the right guy, work for her father, raise a little girl. Unfortunately, she isn't quite present in her own life. Grace is constantly leaving her daughter places and has lost interest in sleeping with her husband. She nonetheless goes into shock when she discovers that her husband is cheating on her. His infidelity pushes her into belated adulthood and forces her to live not simply for other people but also for herself.

Grace's life in some ways mirrors that of Khouri's mother, a southern wife and homemaker, yet from the beginning the writer found herself judging her main character's plight harshly; hence she was stymied. "I kept not being able to feel any sympathy for the woman who had made the choices that she'd made. She had just always been the good girl, and I could never imagine wanting that.

"I called Anthea one day and said, 'I can't do this. I feel nothing but contempt for the choices this character has made.' And she said, 'Well, what would it take for you to not feel that?' I said, 'For her to rebel against these choices,' and she's like, 'There you go,' and I was like, 'Okay, I've got to go.' "

Khouri spent three years laboring on the script. She fretted over the ending. She didn't want Grace and her husband simply to get back together. She was drawn to an *Unmarried Woman*–type finale in which Grace goes off on her own, but Weinstein felt that solution was too old-fashioned.

Still, she wouldn't abandon the project. "I had to finish it," she says. "That's always been the issue in my life. I never finished school. I didn't graduate from college. I've never finished anything in my life except *Thelma & Louise.* And now this. My whole life I know is going to be just made up by proving my value through my ability to actually complete a project, which is kind of pathetic in a way."

Repeatedly, Sylbert and Weinstein offered to let Khouri out of the deal, but she refused. Opportunities crowded her horizons. Polly Platt introduced her to James L. Brooks, and Khouri landed a deal to make her directing debut at Gracie, his production company. She began running out of money. Studios pay writers working on assignments in installments, start of writing, first draft, completion of writing, yet Khouri kept not finishing. She was to receive $250,000 for the script, and another $150,000 if the movie was green-lit, a total that was less than she had received for *Thelma & Louise* and a fraction of what she could now command as an Oscar-winning screenwriter. She and her husband lived off residuals and the income from his writing assignments; in the end, they borrowed money. When she turned in the script, however, she angled to be paid an extra sum that befit her status in the industry. The studio caved in to her demands, in part because she could have brandished the woman card so effectively in print. "It would have been humiliating, I think, for the studio," says Khouri. "I would have talked about nothing else had they not come up with that. When guys are out there getting three million dollars for shit they jot down in a few seconds—you know, welcome to lots of tits! I think it would have been really ill-advised not to just give me the money to make it fair. And they did."

While the writing of *Something to Talk About* was torturous, at least Khouri had some measure of control as long as the script was in her hands. The minute it was done, however, market forces took over. Immediately Weinstein and Sylbert slipped it to Julia Roberts, at that moment the biggest female star in the world. Roberts's participation would

mean an automatic green light for a movie termed by the studio difficult material, primarily because it was a woman's story, with a largely
female target audience. Both Weinstein and Sylbert were coming off a
series of flops. Sylbert was coming out of a series of Goldie Hawn disappointments. Despite Weinstein's high-minded intention to make
challenging fare, *Fearless, Flesh and Bone,* and *With Honors* had all failed
to do business at the box office, and she felt guilty about it, particularly
because Semel and Daly had been so supportive when her husband had
died.

Of course, Roberts was too young for the part, in her mid-twenties
as opposed to her mid-thirties. She was at the height of her beauty,
rather than a woman beginning to feel her age and the weight of ten
years invested in a marriage that has stopped working. "The part was
written for a woman who is not drop-dead gorgeous," says Khouri. "I
suggested someone like Emma Thompson, who, you don't look at her
and just think, Oh my God, that's the most beautiful woman on Earth.
Well, after you're around her for a couple of minutes you start to go,
'Well, she very well may be the most beautiful woman on earth, but it's
because of what comes from inside of her.' But a woman that when she
sees her husband with a woman who's younger and more beautiful, it
has a completely different kind of impact than it does if you're already
looking at somebody who is way more beautiful than 99.9 percent of
the people on the planet. It dilutes it. It's very hard as the writer to sit
there and be the one to go, you know, 'I don't want a big movie star in
the movie, because [then] the movie doesn't make any sense.' Everybody looks at you like you're out of your fucking mind.

"The game of making a movie for a studio is about making money.
It's almost impossible to do anything with integrity, if that's the point.
Integrity becomes accidental. You can be sold down the river at any
point during the process."

Roberts signed on for $12 million, then a record price for a woman,
and, as suddenly the most powerful person aboard, she had director approval, as well as approval over the actress who would play her wisecracking sister, Emma Rae. The film's proposed price tag skyrocketed
from $20 million to $40 million.

Again, Khouri had a fantasy of directing the picture herself. Sylbert
seemed leery, Weinstein seemed enthusiastic, but only if they were
turned down by their entire list of big- and medium-named male directors, and they were, by everyone from Sydney Pollack to James Brooks.

"It went to men in their fifties. And they thought it was about a woman who was frigid. They didn't get it," says Khouri. The last name on the list, however, agreed to direct the picture. The Swedish director Lasse Hallström was a curious choice for a rococo and comic southern family epic. His best picture, *My Life as a Dog*, was a lyrical but sad exploration of a boy coming to terms with the death of his mother. His American films, *Once Around* and *What's Eating Gilbert Grape*, had earned mixed reviews and negligible box office, although they were both family sagas, set respectively in Boston and the Midwest.

Khouri's experience on *Something to Talk About* differed dramatically from that on *Thelma & Louise*. Now, she was a welcome member of the production team, with her own trailer on the set. She found her producers sympathetic and loved Paula Weinstein. "I had total freedom to be myself all the time," she says. "I felt respected. I didn't have to explain the woman thing. We laughed about how other people didn't understand it sometimes. Because everything is qualified. It's always 'As a woman what do you think?' Everything I think was as me. 'As a woman' as compared to what?"

Unfortunately, there was only so much Khouri could do to influence the production. Hallström was generous to the writer, yet they often disagreed on fundamental interpretations of scenes. And while Khouri was nothing if not vocal about her feelings, he was still the director and she the lowly writer. "It was an oddly painful process, because to be that close to it and that far away from it at the same time was really, really strange," she says. "To be there every day and yet have no control, other than what I was able to exert through sheer force of will."

The production was, by several accounts, nightmarish. While Hallström was skilled at bringing out the reality of the situations, he was at a loss about the piece's theatricality. To several members of the production team, the director seemed not to understand the nuances of the script's distinct southern milieu. He seemed weak and so infatuated with the coquettish and attention-grabbing Roberts that it impaired his ability to direct her.

Early on, antipathy set in between Roberts and Khouri. "The bottom line was Julia was rude and Callie took it personally," recalls one on-set observer. "Julia didn't give her enough credit for what she had done." While Hallström was entirely focused on Roberts, Khouri befriended both costars, Kyra Sedgwick and Dennis Quaid, and spent hours discussing their characters with them. But Roberts treated her with disinterest. Khouri simmered, not discreetly, and her attempt to ameliorate the tension between them backfired. Khouri brought Roberts a gift and made a plea to the superstar about how much she could help her with her character if they could only talk more freely and regularly. "That night Julia said, 'She doesn't think I'm good in the movie.' If anything she was even angrier," recalls one observer.

Mostly, Khouri despaired as she watched the film derail. Roberts played the scenes for anger rather than vulnerability, skilled when the situations called for broad comedy but at a loss when they called for complex emotions. Khouri also fielded a call from Roberts's agent, Elaine Goldsmith, who was worried that Kyra Sedgwick's character might steal the picture from her client and made suggestions on how to make Emma Rae more pathetic. Goldsmith then lobbied Weinstein, who neatly deflected the advice.

Khouri could often be seen crying on the sidelines, and although Weinstein explicitly asked Hallström if he wanted the writer to leave, the director seemed perfectly happy to listen to her input. Khouri herself was more than a little aware of how her intransigence contributed to the tension. "I have an 'I'm right' complex," she says. "That's my biggest flaw. I have to be right. And the hardest thing in the world for me is to hear somebody first of all say that I'm not right and, second of all, to be right about the fact that I'm not right."

The situation came to a head over the most pointed scene in the movie, which was supposed to be the husband's impassioned explanation of why he had sought comfort in the arms of other women. "She was not totally without blame in what happened in that marriage," says Khouri. "She totally cut him out of her life, which I think is something that's pretty typical for married couples. You have heard the joke, How do you paralyze a woman from the waist down? Marry her." Khouri had envisioned a scene that was brutal but honest. When the husband suggests the wife might be frigid, Grace is supposed to retort angrily, "I have orgasms all the time. You just don't happen to be in the room." When Quaid was cast, Khouri decided to try to polish the scene to give him a real acting showpiece. As shooting day approached, Quaid was having problems with his half of the scene.

Coincidentally, Jane Fonda was visiting Weinstein on the set, and as she watched the actors struggle with the scene, she suggested they try an improvisation. Right before the improv was to begin, Khouri was disinvited. Afterward, she was given a version of what had transpired that completely gutted the point of the scene—sexual dysfunction. Roberts's orgasm line was out. Indeed, any mention of sex was deleted. Furious, Khouri confronted Weinstein and Sylbert. In all the months they had spent talking, they had always agreed that this was a movie about sex, and suddenly the sexual smoking gun was gone. Khouri threatened to take her name off the project, and Weinstein and Sylbert quickly recognized their folly. In the end the scene was shot exactly as written save for several lines of Quaid's dialogue.

Other fights broke out during the editing. When Khouri saw Hallström's first six-week edit, she was horrified that her southern family epic had been turned into bad Swedish TV. Hallström invited her to join the edit. She worked in one room, Hallström in another. Two weeks later the director went home to Sweden for a month. His wife, the actress Lena Olin, was about to give birth. Khouri was left to reedit the film by herself, and she completed several more edits.

Ironically, the test-screening audience prevented the movie from being totally eviscerated. Khouri had originally ended the movie with Grace alone on her father's farm but with her husband walking toward her, a hint of reconciliation in the air. The studio demanded that the husband be explicitly redeemed and the couple reconciled, the proverbial happy ending. "I kept saying, 'As soon as she walks back into that house, I hate her,' " says Khouri.

The test screening went horribly. "The audience hated it. They felt completely ripped off, because here they have watched this whole story about this woman who was going to change, and then what happened? She ends up with the husband on the couch," says Khouri. The audience wondered why after the character made such a big deal about going back to school she never did so.

Khouri wrote a new ending in which Grace and her husband make amends but don't sleep together, and Grace goes to veterinarian school. The last scene features her going on a date with her husband, the first tentative step to reconciliation. Hallström came back for the reshoots, although he initially suggested that Khouri just do them. With encouragement from Weinstein, Roberts made an effort to be nicer to the writer.

At the end of the day, Khouri felt intensely disappointed by the experience, and by a film that had charm but no pathos. Roberts was luminous on-screen, but seemed to have little feel for her character's plight. Even her vaunted commercial clout fell flat. The film grossed only $50 million in the United States, far less than the $100 million everyone assumed Roberts could knock out with one flash of her megawatt smile.

"Ultimately I felt it was soulless," says Khouri. "And that really bugged me. It was all pretty on the outside, but there was no there, there."

She rebounded by taking a rewrite job on *A Simple Wedding* for Sony, about a lesbian couple who decide to marry. She spent a year polishing the script, with fantasies again of directing, although few screenwriters ever get that break from a major studio, and when they do, it is almost always on a script they originated. Khouri was nonetheless crushed when the producer refused to give her the opportunity; indeed, she was fired from the project. "They just didn't want to make it, they didn't believe in me, they didn't believe in the script, and it turned out to just be a huge, heart-wrenching waste of my life, and I walked away feeling like I don't want to do this anymore," she says. "I really was just emotionally, and in some ways creatively, devastated by it."

On any given day, Khouri's discouragement alternates with a pulsating, fundamental optimism, a kind of genetic imprint that keeps her bounding back. She still has dreams of directing her own movie. "It's just really bizarre that I'm thought of as a screenwriter. I don't have any intention of just doing that. Screenwriting is just the first part." Moviemaking still holds a magical allure for her. "I love how hard it is. I love all the unexpectedness of what happens when you try to make that moment of theater when the film runs through the camera and you capture something. It really is like chasing butterflies."

IF I WAS NARCISSISTIC, THIS IS WHAT I'D CHOOSE?

"It makes no difference to me," Jodie Foster resolutely tells the director, Michael Apted, when he asks her where she wants to start the upcoming scene. "I see an orange mark and I stand on it. A Pavlovian reaction." On a hot summer night in North Carolina, Foster is standing in a remote forest enclave, a hovel as envisioned by Ralph Lauren with a dozen dried gourds dangling noisily from a tree out front, a fireplace for cooking, a spindle, a lathe, and carved stars-and-moon designs in the stone wall and floor. It is the screen home of her character, Nell, a wild child discovered in the backwoods of Appalachia speaking no known language, just a mysterious babble of her own. The film, *Nell*, is a modern-day Christ myth, in which Foster plays the one type of character that she's never been allowed to play on-screen before: an innocent—moreover, an innocent with transforming powers of purity.

Foster lost almost twenty pounds to play Nell, and the result is that she is spare and sinewy. Her pointed face is sharper; her hair, dyed ruddy brown, hangs lankly down her back. She wears thick, no-nonsense, steel-rimmed glasses, and a blue flannel shirt over her threadbare dress. The hair on her legs has grown long. As she stands still for the makeup people swirling around, a light from behind delineates her newly pared physique, an unexpected nakedness. Either Foster is oblivious to this or, more likely, she doesn't care.

Her preparation takes all of thirty seconds. She seems to move into a state of Zen relaxation, then suddenly grasps her hands, swings her torso out, stretches her arms overhead, and then curls back, pulling her limbs inward, swinging out, and curling back. Foster's face goes slack, abandoning its ironic archness, the quality she calls "defendedness." She would look dumb except for the feral intensity of the eyes. Her body stands awkwardly rigid, then suddenly explodes, as she hurls herself into the scene, slapping the table in rage, frustration, confusion, and panic. In a sense this is Nell's idiosyncratic version of a love scene, when she recognizes the doctor played by Liam Neeson as what she calls her "ga'inja"—Nellish for guardian angel.

It is the first moment of connection in the movie, and in a series of takes Foster tries a number of approaches. In one take she dances as if in a bacchanalia. In another she jerks to a halt midway, forgetting where she is in her lines, although, to anyone listening, she's just speaking gibberish. Her voice is high and breathy, younger and less assured than usual. In yet another take she seems to zero in on Neeson, taking his hand in hers and caressing her face with it.

In her trailer Foster seems both giddy and relaxed. She spends a lot of time here, alone, hunkered down at her PowerBook, writing business memos and E-mailing and faxing her friends. She's wearing her lucky shirt—red with a cowboy motif—and her FBI sweatpants, part of her designated set wardrobe, which she packs up in a suitcase between movies. When a journalist enters, she snatches down a photo of a famously narcissistic diva, which Mel Gibson just faxed to her along with some pithy bons mots. She and Gibson, who recently filmed *Maverick* together, have been faxing each other several times a day. She thought playing Nell would really take it out of her and told all her friends not even to bother calling her on location: "I really thought that this was going to be so hard for me. And what I found out is that it's kind of stressless."

Indeed, Neeson and his wife and costar, Natasha Richardson (who plays his real love interest), arrived at rehearsals expecting to explore and experiment; they were surprised to discover that Foster had already determined exactly what she wanted to do. She had tossed out most of the assiduous research she'd done so she could "just have the experience." She explains, "This has been really different for me. I've had to go look at the [methods] that other people use to become actors. They go to acting class and learn to melt like an ice cream cone. They act like a tree. That kind of stuff makes me roll my eyes, but there isn't any other way around [the part of Nell]." She laughs self-deprecatingly. "I mean, I have to be able to melt like an ice cream cone."

Indeed, working with a movement teacher, Foster devised a kind of gesture, almost a dance, to signify Nell's solitary state. It is a dance meant to be done with another person, namely her twin, who died during childhood, one of the key elements of the backstory. She demonstrates the motion again—pull forward, release back—"Every time I would do this, I would start to cry." In the movie Neeson's and Richardson's characters introduce Nell to the "human world that's filled with disappointment that people go away and that love in adults is conditional," says Foster. "That's a big, nasty disappointment for somebody who believes in utopia and unconditional love."

"I have a feeling there's a loneliness in Jodie," remarks Richardson, who plays a psychologist, "and a loneliness in Nell that she connects to."

If Foster sounds idealistic, and a tad New Age, the effect is all the more shocking when one considers that she is also producing this $30 million film, her first venture from Egg Pictures. She is receiving $4.5 million to act, another $500,000 to produce, and it's evident that she's the primary motivating force behind the project. She personally lobbied Chairman Peter Chernin of Fox, which owned the material, to let her new partner, PolyGram, participate in the financing of the film and take most of the foreign rights (which turned out to be a bonanza for Poly-Gram because the film's foreign sales were twice its $34 million domestic gross). Foster ran a tight financial ship, refusing actors' blandishments for more money, valuing fiscal responsibility as the best way of keeping her independence. Like *Little Man Tate*, *Nell* came in under budget.

She was introduced to the material by the producer Renée Missel, whose other main credit is *Resurrection*, also a tale of a female Christ figure. Missel introduced Foster to Mark Handley's play *Idioglossia*, right after *Silence of the Lambs*, offering her partnership in the film to ensure that the actress stayed attached. The pair sold the idea to Joe Roth, then head of Fox, and eventually hired William Nicholson (*Shadowlands*) to rewrite the script. In the play the Neeson character actually falls in love with Nell, which Foster wanted changed: "The play is about a male fantasy of the woman in a cave who understands me better than anyone else." In the new version Neeson and Richardson fall in love, while Nell is the innocent, otherworldly presence who winds up alone, different but beloved.

By the time she entered her early thirties, Foster was clearly cognizant that the half-life of an actress, even a double Oscar winner, was short. She seemed torn between the Meryl Streep and Sharon Stone poles of the business, a high-minded inclination not to pander and a simmering desire to project the requisite sexual heat, chasing down—unsuccessfully—the part of the seductress in Louis Malle's *Damage* and making pronouncements like "I believe women should be sexual. And why not? What a great thing to be: a sexual woman, coming of age and discovering sensuality and the intoxication of it. I've seen so many movies about women who don't like sex and really don't want to have sex, or have that posy stuff in the Calvin Klein ads. I'm sick of that myth being out there."

Her next movie, *Sommersby* in 1993, featured Foster in her first full-blown screen romance. Set in the South in the era of Reconstruction, it was an American remake of *The Return of Martin Guerre*, about a man (Richard Gere) who arrives at a plantation claiming to be the owner. His wife falls in love with him, despite the fact that he might be (and turns out to be) an impostor. Several people associated with the film billed it as a kind of Foster goes sexy, yet Foster was horrified when asked head-on if this was a bald-faced attempt to change her screen image; she saw the movie as a parable in which a woman finds personal authenticity while living a public charade.

While Foster earned good reviews for her work in *Sommersby*, she and Gere seemed to inhabit different movies. The romance didn't really work, and the question of Foster's sexiness surfaced repeatedly when she was up for parts. When Meg Ryan dropped out of *Maverick*, a western comedy from William Goldman about a group of gamblers starring Mel Gibson, the Warners head Terry Semel lobbied the director, Richard Donner, to hire Foster. Donner was nervous, worried that the Oscar winner wasn't sufficiently hot. Gibson's producing partner, Bruce Davey, dragged out photos from a recent studio photo session to prove otherwise.

Perhaps one of the most unusual aspects of *Nell* is that Foster appears nude in the film. Indeed, the first day of shooting Foster—as Nell—lifted her dress high above her head and spun around naked in a pool hall full of teenagers. The scene echoes *The Accused*, the young men taunting her sexually, but Nell doesn't understand their innuendo and responds joyously. In another scene, a bare Nell swims across a lake, moonlight shimmering off her luminescent figure. The woman psychiatrist taunts the male doctor about his interest in Nell—"Not exactly a grown woman, is she?" she asks, cognizant that Nell's lack of sexual guile is what makes her so appealing.

It's as if Foster is making an unconscious nod to the prevailing wisdom of the early nineties that nudity is necessary to prove an actress's Hollywood worth (indeed, not long after *Nell*'s debut, Demi Moore hit the record for female paydays—$12.5 million to play a stripper in *Striptease*). Yet Foster was determinedly shifting the meaning of the nudity, from fulfillment of a male fantasy to a state of childlike innocence, almost a kind of presexuality, Eve before the apple. "Ten or fifteen years ago, the idea of showing this much of my chest made me so insane that I could not possibly do it," Foster said before the movie's release. "But Nell wasn't looking at somebody and taking a shirt off, which is really uncomfortable." Her attitude had certainly changed since she had balked at disrobing for *The Little Girl Who Lives Down the Lane*. "I didn't know who was going to take advantage of it. There was a certain amount of control that I couldn't give up. Now I'm a little bit ready for it."

Foster recalls a moment when Nell remembers her childhood dance with her sister as "probably in terms of my acting life, the biggest, most important moment in my life. Just sitting on a rock watching that little girl spin around. It was one of these bittersweet moments that I think we live in our lives where we realize there was somebody that we used to be that will never be again, and we have to be accepting enough to say good-bye to who that was."

The reviews for *Nell* were decidedly unenthusiastic. Accustomed to a long string of hosannas, Foster was stung by the media's maligning of her motives, those who viewed the part of Nell as shameless Oscar pandering by an already overpraised actress. "I didn't care about the money," she says in retrospect. "The thing that hurt me the most were people who questioned my self-interest. If I was narcissistic, this is what I'd choose? Just the questioning of my ethics—it completely paralyzed me. It was the worst blow that anybody could ever deliver me. I don't think I've ever been as 'naked' emotionally as I was in *Nell*, and that's not an easy thing for me to do. And I'm not somebody who can do that and then kind of go, 'Oh well, whatever. That's the process and like who cares what everybody thinks?'

"I mean, *Nell* really, really, really, really hit me. I was so exhausted by the experience of acting in it and the experience of producing it, and then having to go on the road [to publicize the movie], all the while prepping [her next directorial effort] *Home for the Holidays*. By the time the reviews came out, I just wasn't in any shape to be getting them.

"After the third horrible review I just pretty much didn't want to hear about it anymore. I called up Fox and I said, 'Look, I just want you to know that Stuart [Kleinman, head of her company] is going to be calling you because I just get too emotional about it."

She sobbed all the way through the preproduction of *Home for the Holidays*. "I couldn't talk without crying," Foster says. "Like every time I'd say something like, 'I have to go to the bathroom,' if I started talking, then I would just start weeping again. We were in casting sessions, and the person would be doing a comedy scene, you know, and I'd start trailing off, and big tears were coming down my eyes. [Producer] Peggy Rajski and Avy Kaufman, who [is] my casting lady, would have to take me aside and go, 'But it's okay.' I'd try to make jokes, but it didn't help.

"It's not very normal for me. It's just not the kind of person I am, so it definitely threw me for a loop. And definitely Peggy and Avy were looking at each other and going, 'Whoa boy, we never see Jodie like this.' "

She took a break. "I went away, and I went to sleep for five days, and I didn't do anything, and I just ate food and I read books, and then I was better. And *Home for the Holidays* helped too, because I went off and did that film that I loved." The movie concerns the Thanksgiving of a normally dysfunctional Baltimore family. "I actually got to kind of download some of the things that I really feel, and I also got to be really parental and nurturing with all these actors, and that really saved me. To be able to go, 'Just show me what you want to do.' Just to be free with them, to not judge them and to not criticize it and to watch them go out on limbs, it was really curing."

I HATE HOW COMPETITIVE I CAN GET

Unfortunately, *Home for the Holidays* failed miserably at the box office (and fizzled with critics), a fact thrust into Foster's face when in January 1996 she attended *Premiere* magazine's annual women in film luncheon right after the film's debut. Foster was rigid and tense, dressed in a curiously prim brown plaid Armani suit, her mood not helped by all the power brokers who came to offer condolences about the lack of commercial acceptance of her film. "[People came] up to me and were going, 'Oh, I'm so sorry about your movie.' That's so mean. Why, because it wasn't *Dumb & Dumber* on the first weekend?" she fumes in retrospect. "I'm not a producer. I'm an artist, and the only reason I produce is to try to protect the projects, so that's not my identity," she says, though she admits, "I hate how competitive I can get. I shouldn't be worried about *Dumb & Dumber.* But there's a side of me that can't help it, I get eaten away."

Foster had come to the luncheon, in part, to give an award to Sherry Lansing. Despite her wariness toward Lansing after *The Accused,* it had been Lansing, as head of Paramount, who had bought *Home for the Holidays* in an unusually lucrative deal, even ceding the all-valuable home video rights to PolyGram, where Foster had her deal. Whereas she once mistrusted Lansing's enthusiasm, Foster now wallowed in it, finding herself one of many to feel Lansing's loyalty comforting in defeat. "If we do something together and we miss, I kind of like her the best," says the producer Scott Rudin. "Sherry is not big on blame the way other people can be."

"I'm sure that Sherry, under different circumstances, like every other good business executive, is very different. Under our circumstances we could not have had a better champion," states Foster, who says Lansing was the primary reason she sold the film to Paramount. "She loved it, and it wasn't a false enthusiasm. She never asked us to change an actor; she never asked for any rewrite; she never asked for a cut." Lansing came in on weekends to work on the trailers. "The moment that we showed it to Sherry, she said, 'I think it's perfect,' " Foster recounts, echoing a classic Sherry-ism. "I'm sure you guys will continue working on it because that's who you are. I wouldn't change a thing."

By the early nineties women directors had made small but distinct inroads. In the decade between 1983 and 1992, they had directed 81 of the 1,794 features released by the studios. The percentage of days worked by women Directors Guild members had grown from 2 percent in 1983 to 7.8 percent in 1990 (although women directors constituted 12 percent of the DGA membership). By 1994 it grew to 9.6 percent, but in 1997 it fell to 5 percent, a gap that most knowledgeable sources were at a loss to explain (although the overall numbers were so small that the addition or subtraction of one woman could alter the statistics). Only two women had ever been nominated for Best Director Oscars, and neither had won. Women writers fared better; in 1997 they constituted 17 percent of working feature writers. Fourteen women had won sixteen Best Screenplay awards. The figures worsened slightly when one considered only the one hundred top-grossing films. In a study commissioned by Women in Film, the San Diego State University professor Martha Lauzen determined that 20 percent of these films were produced by women, 5 percent were directed by women, and 13 percent were written by women. (She also noted that when a woman served as executive producer, the average number of women working behind the scenes doubled.)

The most high-profile women directors—women like Penny Marshall, Nora Ephron, Kathryn Bigelow, and later Betty Thomas and Mimi Leder—made films that didn't differ dramatically from those of their male peers, although their gender often affected how their films were viewed. Streisand's film *The Prince of Tides* was nominated for several Academy Awards, including Best Picture, but, again, not Best Director. Bigelow and Leder were both singled out for their putatively unfemale willingness to tackle the action genre, the ultimate boy bailiwick, although Leder proved more financially successful. In her review of Leder's *Deep Impact*, *The New York Times*'s Janet Maslin singled out the director's female touch as evinced by the fact that the film "emphasizes feelings over firepower whenever possible," though the film's kinder, gentler quality (which drew a heavily female audience) could as easily have been attributed to the influence of Steven Spielberg, or to the craft of its cowriter, Bruce Joel Rubin, whose other major credit was *Ghost*, the ultimate female fantasy film. Leder's first film, *The Peacemaker*, foisted on the capable Nicole Kidman one of the more insulting female parts of the year, a classic shrieking girl sidekick who was constantly being upstaged by the street-savvy Army colonel, played by George Clooney, although she happened to be a nuclear physicist.

Indeed, the prime difference between most American female and male directors seemed to be that the women had a higher propensity to put a woman at the center of their stories, or at least make women viable characters. (This was particularly true if they wrote the films as well.) The only material Penny Marshall ever developed on her own was *A League of Their Own*, a comedy about a true-life 1940s women's baseball league. While the film's prime message seemed to be a celebration of female talent, the director nonetheless shied away from calling it a feminist work (although its star, Geena Davis, seemed to take great delight in brandishing the f-word, to Marshall's obvious chagrin). Even Gillian Armstrong, in the interviews after *Little Women*, the ultimate female empowerment tale and a wonderfully crafted valentine that rehabilitated her Hollywood career, pointed out that the all-woman filmmaking team worried about the film "being portrayed as a feminist film" because "feminism has had irreparable amounts of bad press that has led men to assume it's about women rejecting men."

"I don't think we have a clue what kinds of movies women will make when many more women are making movies, but my guess is that except for the fact that more of them will be about women, they'll be pretty much the same," says Nora Ephron. "I'm not one of those people who believe that if women run the country we'll have no wars. I don't believe that if women direct the movie, you'll have a better time on the set or that women are necessarily better to work with. They aren't. Some women are good to work with. Some women are not. The only thing I know for sure is that when more women make movies there will be more good parts for women because when you're a woman filmmaker you look at these underwritten female parts and say, 'Who is this person? Let's make this part work.' Men look at movies with no parts in them for women and they don't do anything. You see one movie after another made by men and the woman's part—she doesn't have a tic. She doesn't have anything that tells me who she is."

Ephron's new credo about filmmaking might be summed up in a line from her second film, *Sleepless in Seattle*: "You don't want to be in love," the Rosie O'Donnell character tells the lead woman, played by Meg Ryan. "You want to be in love in a movie." In the wake of the commercial failure of *This Is My Life*, her second intensely personal film about a Jewish heroine (*Heartburn* being the first), Ephron began making what Hollywood insiders sometimes call movie-movies, old-fashioned fairy tales that exist largely in the province of soundstages and collective fantasy, populated by major stars who pose as ordinary citizens, imbuing so-called normal lives with megawatt charisma. "When you're making a comedy, it's only about having the audience like the movie," says Ephron. "That's the first thing you have to do with a comedy is make them laugh, and make them happy they came. So, if you don't do that, you can't delude yourself into thinking that there was something that you succeeded in in some other way, because the primary way you had to succeed, you didn't."

Ephron remained obsessed with the chasm between men and women but wrapped her irony in a happy Hollywood glow and sentimental, big-kiss endings. While her characters speak with Ephron's trademark urbanized wit, their dilemmas usually boil down to a sentimental search for true love; essentially she updated the kinds of films her parents used to make, like *Desk Set*. She tended to steal from herself, retreading *When Harry Met Sally . . .*, first in *Sleepless in Seattle* and later in *You've Got Mail*, down to the one-sheets where Billy Crystal and Meg Ryan, and later Tom Hanks and Meg Ryan, stare out from their respective sides of the poster. Moreover, she tended not to work from original material, either Ephronizing old films, like *The Shop Around the Corner*, or Ephronizing other people's scripts. She also benefited from her friendships with rising female executives like TriStar's president of production, Stacey Snider, and Turner-turned-Columbia president Amy Pascal, each of whom advocated two of her projects.

Sleepless in Seattle had originally been simply a rewrite job, arriving on Ephron's doorstep while she was still mixing *This Is My Life*. She kept the original premise of Jeffrey Arch's script, in which a young woman on the East Coast becomes entranced with a widower from the West

Coast, whom she hears talking about his dead wife on a radio call-in show. Ephron punched up the dialogue and made the characters more specific (including yet another female journalist), turning the woman's journey into a kind of comic spoof of *Fatal Attraction*. The producer, Gary Foster, was pleased with her work, although the director, Nick Castle, felt that in deleting some of the project's over-the-top sentiment she had undercut the script's emotional impact. Castle was soon off the film; Ephron proposed herself as a possible replacement and agitated vigorously.

Unfortunately, Ephron had been so successful in her rewrite that the script metamorphosed into a hot property, drawing interest from a number of stars, notably Julia Roberts, still in *Pretty Woman* afterglow. The Columbia producer Ray Stark had an option on Roberts and hovered as a producer; he preferred the more experienced Garry Marshall as a director. "I think that Ray Stark thought [*This Is My Life*] was too Jewish. It's that weird thing where it's sort of like, well, she can make a Jewish movie, but can she make a Gentile movie?" recalls Ephron. "I actually called him, and he said to me, 'You don't have a master shot in that movie.' I thought, What is he talking about, a master shot? I think what he meant was that I didn't have a big outdoor panoramic thing. But, of course, a master is not an outdoor panoramic shot. And I thought, Well, you asshole, this is the movie that was shot in Toronto instead of New York." Roberts let it be known that she preferred Ephron for the film, crushing the institutional opposition toward her. When Roberts dropped out several weeks later, Ephron remained, suddenly at the helm of a $25 million movie, now with the megastars Tom Hanks and Meg Ryan.

Ironically, while Ephron had often been brought in to beef up the female role, now Hanks insisted that his part be made three-dimensional. "We sat with him for many, many days, some of them fairly difficult, until he finally committed to the movie, and then it was much easier after that, where we just went through his scenes and he would say, 'Here's what I could do here. Here's what I could say,' and we would just write down what he said, because he's a great writer," says Ephron. "He didn't want the kid to be the only funny one in the scene. He wanted the father to have balls, and to be charming."

Sleepless in Seattle went on to garner Ephron an Oscar nomination for Best Screenplay. It also earned $115 million at the domestic box office, certifying her as a major Hollywood director.

A PRIMAL STORY ABOUT WOMEN
WHO ARE REPLACED BY YOUNGER
VERSIONS OF THEMSELVES

While conventional wisdom continued to hold the line that teenage boys drove the market, the maturation of the baby boomers, demographically the biggest segment of the population, changed who actually went to the movies. Unlike their parents, boomers still attended movies. Indeed, while a Motion Picture Association of America survey of moviegoing habits suggested that older men and women attended films at comparable rates, a number of industry market researchers believed that women over twenty-five controlled more movie-ticket dollars than anyone else, both because they tended to go with their friends to the new Cineplexes springing up in every suburban outpost and because they largely determined which films their kids saw. The children of baby boomers were another growing market, driving the success of the Disney animated films and *Home Alone* series. Even the vaunted theory that men decided which movies a couple saw soon became a myth of the past. "Today, the older female is the strongest moviegoer around," said Ed Minz, whose firm Cinemascore tracks filmgoing habits, in 1998.

While popcorn movies like *Batman* and *Jurassic Park* still constituted the studios' high-profile tent-pole pictures, female-oriented products—when they were made—often constituted serious profit centers, especially because they tended to cost less than action blockbusters. *Ghost* cost $20 million and grossed $218 million domestically; *Pretty Woman*, a $14 million movie, made $178 million; the $8 million *Driving Miss Daisy* made $107 million; *Fried Green Tomatoes* and *The Hand That Rocks the Cradle* both cost $12 million and made close to $90 million; while the $20 million *Sister Act* raked in $140 million and spawned a sequel. Studios ignored women at their own peril. The Oscar-winning western *Unforgiven* appealed only to men and earned half the amount in ticket sales of the Oscar-winning, female-friendly *Dances with Wolves*, which earned $184 million domestically. Even the foreign market proved more hospitable to romance than previously believed: *The Bodyguard* was one of the highest overseas grossing films in Warner's history.

What constituted a woman's film proved to be a difficult question to answer because, according to Ed Minz, women formed the main audience for such disparate films as *A Few Good Men* and *The Last of the Mo-*

hicans. The theory was that women like character-driven pieces and relationships, although the relationships don't necessarily have to include females. Indeed, while the female audience curiously didn't augur particularly well for individual female icons (after Julia Roberts, it took four years before the birth of another female star: Sandra Bullock), it did bestow its favors on a new kind of male star, preferring softer, gentler men like Tom Cruise, Brad Pitt, and the paragon of nineties male humanity, Tom Hanks, whose appeal as a romantic lead was burnished by both Penny Marshall and Nora Ephron.

While Paramount continued to churn out typical testosterone studio fare like *Mission: Impossible,* more than a few of its films appealed to primarily female audiences, such as Amy Heckerling's *Clueless,* a charming retelling of Jane Austen's *Emma* set in Beverly Hills. Perhaps the most personal film of Lansing's Paramount career was the 1996 sleeper hit *The First Wives Club,* a glossy, gleeful revenge comedy about three discarded middle-aged first wives who band together to exact vengeance from their former spouses. Starring a trio of over-fifty actresses—Goldie Hawn, Bette Midler, and Diane Keaton—the film grossed $18.9 million its opening weekend, the highest-grossing debut of a female-driven film ever.

"It was a primal story about women who are replaced by younger versions of themselves. I had seen that so often," says Lansing. "At first they want to get even, and then they realize that revenge isn't the answer, that you have to find your own self-esteem. I always knew I wanted it to be a comedy, but I didn't know the extent, because that sort of shapes as you go along. And then I took the job, and I remember saying, 'Okay, this is like an obsessive project of mine, let's do it.' "

As an independent producer, Lansing had discovered the novel in manuscript form after it had been turned down by a number of publishers. She beat out both Dawn Steel and Paula Weinstein for the rights. She hired the screenwriter Janet Roach and went through a number of unsuccessful drafts for the Tartikoff regime. When she became head of Paramount, she initially tried to interest Weinstein in taking over as producer before asking Scott Rudin.

If her relationships with Jonathan Dolgen and Stanley Jaffe had taken on the tones of a platonic marriage, her relationship with Paramount's most important producer had gradually assumed the quasi-familial tone of a matriarch and her brilliant, petulant dauphin, a prince who tended to throw tantrums every time she went on vacation, particularly when she took to vacationing on cruises with Dolgen, the paterfamilias figure at Paramount. Although they didn't discuss personal matters, Lansing often spent an hour every morning on the phone with Rudin, often calling before she arrived at the office. It was hardly surprising, given that at one point the producer had eight Paramount movies going simultaneously. Lansing's deft hand-holding had already resulted in the most prosperous time of Rudin's career, and the most surefire, productive deal on her lot. She believed in him totally, usually letting his petty rages roll over her, except for one earthquaking flare-up over *A Simple Plan*, which resulted in a six-week standoff in which neither spoke to the other. Lansing watched Rudin with the scrutiny of a shrink, trying to figure out what he really wanted under all the brash and brio. Says the producer, "It is hard to think of what more I could get from the studio than I'm getting from her. I'm talking support that's not just making movies, but emotional support—knowing that you're going to get taken care of."

Rudin and Lansing viewed *The First Wives Club* through slightly different prisms. "She was really interested in making a revenge movie," says Rudin. "I was more interested in making a movie about a sort of female friendship. My idea of it was that these were women who had been completely interested in the lives of the men they were with, and had no friendships, and had no relationships outside of their marriages." Rudin also pushed to make the film more and more comedic. "She thought it was a more serious problem than I did. To me it was three rich white women get dumped. This is not a big problem. To her it was Bosnia. She was right in a way. The grosses proved it."

While enlisting Midler, Hawn, and Keaton to play the wives wasn't especially difficult, Lansing hadn't been able to secure a financial partner for the film, and finding a director for the material proved problematic. Lansing really wanted a female director and offered the film, as one Paramount executive quips, to "every female in the DGA." Indeed, while the studio head's record on hiring female producers and writers was about industry average, Paramount did seem to make an effort to improve the statistics of working female directors. It came in second in a 1997 study of the major studios' hiring practices for the top one hundred films; Paramount, New Line, Fox, and Disney had each hired one female director, although that one constituted a higher percentage at New Line and Paramount, which had smaller slates. Still, the Lansing regime had given breaks to Betty Thomas, whose only prior credit had gone straight to video, and the neophyte Bronwen Hughes, both of whom went on to good careers.

Lansing lobbied Penny Marshall and Randa Haines, while Rudin pressed Nora Ephron and begged the *Private Benjamin* and *Father of the Bride* screenwriter, Nancy Meyers, who hadn't even directed a movie. "They said it was mean. In a way I think a lot of the women thought it was sort of lightly antifeminist," says Rudin, who disagreed. Close to thirty directors—male and female—passed on the material, until Rudin finally called Lansing to announce that Hugh Wilson, the director of *Police Academy* and Rudin's *Guarding Tess*, had agreed to take on the assignment. There was a long pause. "There's no one left," Rudin informed Lansing.

Indeed, Wilson, who had previously butted heads with Rudin, had only agreed to direct the film at the behest of his wife, who had read the book and was convinced it would strike a chord in the culture. Wilson personally revamped the script, written by Robert Harling, whose credits included *Steel Magnolias.* Hewing more closely to the dark tone of Olivia Goldsmith's book, he added back Diane Keaton's handicapped child, and, he hoped, a kind of Jim Brooks bittersweetness. While Lansing and Rudin approved the take, Midler balked outright.

"Bette said, 'I signed on to do a comedy, and you're taking this thing in another direction. And it's also taken on a feminist thing,' " says Wilson. "I said, 'That's good, my wife will be happy to hear that. Because nobody has ever accused me of being a feminist, although I do have four daughters.' I think she meant, I don't want you to turn it into a political thing, or a dark thing and all that, and I was saying, 'I'm trying to put some meat on the bone; they'll laugh harder if it's about something.' "

As the $30-plus million film hurtled toward a start date, Rudin brought in the funny screenwriter-playwright Paul Rudnick (*In & Out, Addams Family Values*), who polished the dialogue, conferring intensively with each of the three actresses about their parts, as well as with Rudin. But he pointedly did not once confer with Wilson. Rudnick continued to write, the script mutating on a daily basis throughout production. Several of the actors, such as Maggie Smith and Mandy Patinkin, were shocked when they arrived for the read-through to find the film so radically different from the one they had signed on for.

Wilson started shooting before Christmas with just Midler. About three weeks before production, Hawn began to show some nervousness about playing the part of an aging Hollywood screen queen, a role that ran dangerously close to self-parody. Lansing sought to reassure her, but over the Christmas break Hawn decided to drop out of the movie, frustrated, she says, because Paramount had not fixed the script as promised. Now Lansing got mad. "Does the name Kim Basinger mean anything to you?" fumed the studio head. In a notorious Hollywood incident, Basinger had lost an $8 million lawsuit after breaching her contract to make the film *Boxing Helena*. Hawn backed down after extracting a promise to make the women less angry and shrewish; soon after she showed up for work, cheerful and professional as ever.

"She went ahead and let them shoot her with collagen in the lips. I couldn't believe it," says Wilson. "It looked like Donald Duck. And I went over to her, and I said, 'My God, what's happened?' She said, 'Well, I'm ready for you.' And I said, 'Does it hurt to do that?' And she said, 'Are you kidding? Of course it hurts.' "

The three female stars got along throughout the production, except for one spat in a recording studio, but Rudin and Wilson brawled constantly. Wilson encouraged the actresses to improvise as much as possible to improve upon the script, which he hated, while Rudin insisted on reshooting scenes against Wilson's wishes. When the director called Lansing to arbitrate, she told him to indulge Rudin's desires. The fighting continued into the editing room, where the first cut, at close to three hours, played disastrously.

Rudin showed the rough cut to Lansing, in part to convince her that the film would never be ready for its scheduled summer release date. "I thought she was going to probably jump out a window after she saw it in such a mess," says Wilson, "but she said, 'Well, there is a movie lurking around in there somewhere,' which is kind of a cliché, but I thought that was a great thing for her to say." Wilson wound up writing a voice-over, as well as excising huge chunks of the movie. Afterward, Rudin retouched the film. The overly cautious Lansing had to be talked out of cutting the infamous scene where the three divas go to a lesbian bar.

In the end, the stars carried the day, sparkling through a film long on sight gags and short on character development, reeling off barbed one-liners such as Hawn's oft-quoted line, "There are only three ages for women in Hollywood. Babe. District Attorney. And *Driving Miss Daisy*." Their fury is hilarious. "This isn't about him—this is about my lips," Hawn screeches at her plastic surgeon. "You're very happy. You don't need self-esteem," Diane Keaton's screen mother says after Keaton's husband leaves her for her therapist. The ending sags, however, when the women opt to abandon their anger for sanctimony, opening up a women's crisis center, dancing around in white designer duds, and singing "You Don't Own Me."

While Paramount had struggled to get prerelease publicity, given the pointed lack of interest in three over-fifty female stars, the media swept down on the finished product, embracing the frothy comedy as social commentary and seizing the opportunity to ride its coattails. *Time* magazine put the three women on the cover and ran an article bemoaning the plight of the first wife, complete with stories of enlightened audience members attending the film with sixty of their closest friends and sidebars on famous spurned wives. Men's groups picketed the film in thirty-two cities. "It's one of the most blatant examples of sexism we've ever seen," griped Stuart A. Miller, legislative analyst for the Virginia-based American Father's Coalition.

The film historian Jeanine Basinger, who studies the image of women in film, took a more sober view of the *First Wives* phenomenon: "Maybe this is a problem that exists mainly around power bases in Hollywood, New York, and Washington, . . . but the media hype is presenting it to us as a meaningful event in terms of women's lives. I'm not sure that's the case."

LIFE IS NOT MADE UP OF CAREER CHOICES

Ironically, the most dazzling female writer-director (indeed one of the finest minds of either gender) turned out to be not American but from New Zealand: Jane Campion, a film school graduate and the auteur of films such as *Sweetie, An Angel at My Table, The Portrait of a Lady,* and, most notably, 1993's *The Piano,* for which she won an Academy Award for Best Original Screenplay. (Besides Lina Wertmuller, she was the only woman ever to be nominated for Best Director, but she lost out to Steven Spielberg.) Campion's style is sumptuous and cryptic, idiosyncratically selecting visual information that mirrors the uniqueness (bordering on insanity) of the central figures, almost always outcast young women with fierce personal visions and unexpected reserves of strength and self-acceptance. In both *The Piano* and its dark shadow, her adaptation of Henry James's *The Portrait of a Lady,* Campion was veritably obsessed with the power of sexuality to both unleash and annihilate, and its impact on the relations between men and women. Yet she skirted the madonna-whore ethos that still riddled American films.

"I have always been a pretty frank person and have a frank interest in how you reconcile your sexuality with your intellect," she recalled in 1996, over lunch at a London restaurant. At age forty-one she has deep-set blue eyes, shorn blond hair, and an antipodean lack of pretense. "How leveling sexuality is. You've got to be at a pretty earthy level to appreciate it. And it humbles us all. Look at how many politicians have been caught up in it.

"I think it is a really important issue for women today or men and women today, [to realize] that life is not made up of career choices. One of the most important things is to participate in relationships and friendships and, particularly, in the mythology of love. It's such a powerful myth in our society and a reality. I have a deep need for intimacy. Almost every human being has it, and how you reconcile that with everything else in your life is a problem that comes up."

Campion wrote her first draft of *The Piano* in 1984, right after film school, and five years before she shot her first film. She then spent almost eight years developing the nineteenth-century Brontë-esque tale of a mute-by-choice Englishwoman, Ada (played by Holly Hunter, who won an Oscar), with an illegitimate daughter who enters into an arranged marriage with Stewart, a land-hungry settler in New Zealand. She worked on the script with both the producer, Jan Chapman, and her then boyfriend, Billy MacKinnon, and, unlike in studio development, which often waters down the premise to least offend the most people, Campion grew progressively bolder in her approach.

Ada embarks on a transformative affair with her neighbor, Baines, a primitive-seeming man caught between white and Maori culture. Yet as Chapman has pointed out, what made the film modern as opposed to sentimental was the transference of Ada's erotic focus from Baines to Stewart. "Ada actually uses her husband, Stewart, as a sexual object—that is the outrageous morality of the film—which seems very innocent but in fact has its power to be very surprising," Campion once explained. "I think many women have had the experience of feeling like a sexual object, and that's exactly what happens to Stewart. The cliché of that situation is generally the other way around, where men say things like 'Oh, sex for its own sake.' But to see a woman actually doing it, especially a Victorian woman, is somehow shocking—and to see a man so vulnerable. It becomes a relationship of power, the power of those that care and those that don't care."

The Piano was financed by the French company CIBY 2000, and was later acquired for release in America by Miramax. Campion seemed pleased by the ultimate critical and commercial acceptance, although not unduly head-spun. "People would say to me, 'Oh, it's done so much.' And I just said, 'Is that good? Or does that mean I get any money?' Fortunately I know more about the box office now than what I knew at that time," she says. "Someone at the chemist would say, 'I really loved your movie,' and that was very touching to me when people—who I wouldn't have expected—had a real connection to the movie; it made me feel less lonely. I somewhat expressed myself in that movie, and people got it. I just didn't think it would be nearly that popular. I thought it would be an art movie somewhere. Don't get me wrong, there's a part of me that wants to be popular too or I wouldn't have existed very long in this business at all. I want to be loved. I sort of envy John Malkovich [the star of *The Portrait of a Lady*] because he seemed to just be happy to be hated too. He doesn't give a damn. He's very free of it. He really seems very unattached at that level."

Unlike some of her Australian counterparts, people like Peter Weir, George Miller, or even Gillian Armstrong, Campion generally refrains from going Hollywood, neither shooting in America nor accepting studio assignments, preferring to pursue her deeply personal imagination. She does, however, cast American stars and has ultimately accepted studio money to make her films. "It's scary how box-office-driven the ecosystem is there. I think [Hollywood] makes [films] for a very specific reason, and it's nothing to do with why all of us got interested in cinema in the first place," she says. "You say McDonald's is food—it's hard to believe. But occasionally you go there. Occasionally or not so occasionally I find myself there. So you need it."

30.

FADE TO BLACK

A FIGHT WITH EVERY SINGLE MAÎTRE D' IN TOWN

In the years since she had left Columbia, Dawn Steel floundered, searching for a new incarnation of herself. She could no longer be Dawn Steel, the hardest-charging woman in Hollywood, her anger wielded like a justified battering ram against the boys' club and the glass ceiling. Anger worked more effectively when she was in power, less so when she was just another beached mogul. "It turned out to be a very difficult two years," said Steel, difficult not to "have anything after your name, when you are used to having that façade." She became very depressed.

She had responded to her professional decapitation by running home to those she described as "Mom and Dad," Katzenberg and Eisner, setting out her shingle at Disney, because her old bosses "made her feel safe." The analogy turned out to be not only naive but seriously misguided. Almost immediately, contract negotiations turned acrimonious, and Disney began whittling away at her demands. "Dawn kept caving," recalls her husband, Chuck Roven. "She said, 'I don't need puts [the ability to automatically green-light pictures]. Jeffrey's my best friend. He's going to take care of me.' " The negotiations were so protracted that in the interim David Hoberman was given more authority over the motion picture division. These appointments set off a new round of problems because Steel wanted to report only to Katzenberg, and Hoberman wanted respect paid to his new position. Katzenberg tried to soothe all parties, declaring to Steel, "This is all about architecture. Tell me the house you want me to build for you and I will build it here at Disney."

Chuck Roven and Dawn Steel on a cruise
in Vancouver, 1990.

For several years she wallowed in her house at Disney. Her deal was lavish, her offices extravagant; she had all the accoutrements of power, masking the fact that she lacked any real autonomy. Steel didn't want to be just another producer to whom the studio assigned projects. She wanted to develop the movies she was interested in. She chafed at her sense of impotence, surprised by the glacially slow development process, and impatient with the hoops of bureaucracy she now needed to jump through to get anything done. She had to curry favor with the low-level studio executives she used to dispatch with a wave of her manicured hand. Steel's "I-Used-to-Be-Chairman" presumptions alienated many on Katzenberg's staff who handled her daily business. She fought constantly with Hoberman over what constituted a good picture, and, says Roven, "Jeffrey would have to play Solomon."

"I don't think Dawn ever really got the kind of support from the day-to-day troops that really gave her the kind of opportunity you need," says Katzenberg.

"[Katzenberg] was giving over the motion picture area to the people he was giving it over to," says a Disney executive. "He just let her swim in it, and she felt deserted. The relationship was with him, and she came in relying on that relationship. She didn't have that relationship because he didn't provide her with that access or that protection." Steel's relationship with Katzenberg became very strained.

It took her more than two years to get one of her movies into production. As the time ticked by with nothing to show, her confidence dwindled, her neediness and insecurity rising to the fore. "She was in a fight with every single maître d' in town," recalls one friend. "There was like no restaurant she could go to. She just had fights with everybody. Dawn wanted things to be done in a certain way. And when they weren't that way, she liked to say it was unacceptable to her." Her passion for New Age remedies seemed to intensify. "She believed," recalls Katherine Reback. "She would drive you crazy with her woo-woo stuff, but she believed." Every day a desire for calm struggled against her neuroses, as Steel could be found alternately meditating in her office or lashing out at her staff.

Like an Energizer bunny that never quits, she bolstered her flagging self-esteem by throwing herself into Hollywood's two biggest sidelines, politics and charity work. Steel and her husband, Chuck Roven, threw Hollywood's first fund-raiser for Bill Clinton, with whom she shared a birthday. She relished her F.O.B. status, attending the Winter Olympics with Hillary Clinton, sleeping in the Lincoln Bedroom at the White House.

In an effort to help channel her restlessness, Lucy Fisher introduced Steel to the AIDS activist Elizabeth Glaser, wife of the actor Paul Michael Glaser, who ran the Pediatric AIDS Society, one of Hollywood's most popular charities, with the intention that Steel could help Glaser produce a TV special to go along with an upcoming charity album. Almost immediately, however, Steel and Glaser began wrestling for power, fighting vociferously. Fisher pleaded with Steel to back off; after all it was Glaser who was dying of AIDS.

Like many in Hollywood who were taken by the stunning success of the producer Julia Phillips's memoir, *You'll Never Eat Lunch in This Town Again*, Steel decided to write her autobiography, a breezy rendition of the basic Dawn Steel Rocky-in-high-heels myth, targeted at young women who wanted to make it in the trenches, and sold under the catchy title *They Can Kill You . . . but They Can't Eat You: Lessons from the Front*.

She went through several ghostwriters; one, Marcelle Clements, was installed in her guesthouse for weeks. Not particularly reflective, or even cognizant of anything other than her own primal drives, Steel solicited from her friends and colleagues stories about her life. Some, such as Joel Silver and Tova Laiter, sat down with the ghostwriter, although one close friend who had told the unvarnished truth about Steel found herself almost totally cut out of the book. Ever a showman, Steel upgraded events for publication. Craig Baumgarten found a trip they had once made to Plato's Retreat, a sex club in New York, transmuted into an excursion by Steel and Richard Gere. "She remembered it was Richard, and she decided it was a better story with Richard, and it probably was, because who would give a shit if she went with me?" Baumgarten laughs.

Baumgarten, along with a squadron of friends such as Lynda Obst and Nora Ephron, read the manuscript and offered suggestions. "She didn't have enough trust in her own judgment, so anyone could influence her, especially if they were negative," recalls Clements. Notably, Steel toned down her mouth, omitting almost anything that would be offensive to people in Hollywood, except for a pointed salvo at Ned Tanen and Frank Mancuso. Gone was the refreshing, up-front sauciness that endeared Steel to her friends, replaced by a nicer, brighter, less angry, mass-market version of herself.

She also softened the portrayal of her parents. Not long after reading the manuscript, Steel's mother fell into a coma and died. Her relationship with her mother had improved dramatically after the birth of Rebecca. Her mother's death left Steel practically inconsolable, a feeling that deepened when her father died barely a year later. "I think that Dawn never recovered from her parents' deaths," says Howard Rosenman.

Ironically, Steel was on location in Jamaica when her mother died. Afterward she flew in her daughter, Rebecca, to stay with her on the island. As her Disney deal wound down, Steel went into production in December 1992 on *Cool Runnings*, a kind of *Flashdance* on steel drums, the true-life tale of the Jamaican Olympic bobsled team. She had argued vociferously with Disney over the script, which slowly transmuted from a ganja-filled comedy to a squeaky-clean Disney empowerment piece. "I remember at one point when Disney was really beating up on her, and she gave the script to me to read, and said, 'Am I crazy?' " recalls Nora Ephron. "And I read it and called her and said, 'This script is a mess and you've got to get it fixed, because it's going to be a huge hit.' "

The film, which boasted no stars, was put into turnaround twice, one time weeks into preproduction. At one point Hoberman took Steel to lunch and announced he had good news and bad news for her. The bad news was they were putting *Cool Runnings* into turnaround. The good news was that she owned a script, the Iris Stevenson story, that they wanted to use for *Sister Act 2*. Steel was incensed, pointing out that it wasn't terribly politically savvy to cancel her favorite project just when he wanted to extract a favor from her. "She said, 'Fuck you,' and left," says Roven. "By the time she had gotten back to the office Jeffrey had called." Katzenberg announced that the company would be making *Cool Runnings* under a different division, Walt Disney Films, as long as Steel conceded the rights to the Stevenson story.

At least she enjoyed making the movie, and developed a close bond with Jon Turteltaub, the director. "I always believed that Dawn was looking out for me," says Turteltaub. "It's funny, people talk about how tough she was, but as soon as you challenged Dawn and sort of pushed her away, she would shrink, because it was important to her to feel part of the process. One day, we got into some discussion, not an argument, and I wanted things my way. And I said something that hurt her feelings. Instead of yelling at me, which everyone said she would do, she just disappeared for a little while. And I realized that I had lost my partner, that I needed Dawn. She fought the battles. Dawn was my partner and my teacher, and, in some ways, my mother."

Disney remained distinctly unenthusiastic about *Cool Runnings.* "In my opinion, the studio not only thought it had a flop but probably hoped it had a flop. It wasn't very supportive of Dawn," says Turteltaub. The night the film opened, Steel and Turteltaub drove from theater to theater to watch the film play to empty houses. They stood around morosely in the lobby. "Dawn was saying, 'Hey, this happens.' She was very up, very positive—look, it's the way it goes, you can't have a winner every time," says Turteltaub. "And we get a phone call the next morning saying the movie's a hit, and we just happened to go to the theaters that nobody else went to. We just thought we were the losers of the century, and it turned out we were wrong."

In the days after, Turteltaub continued to fret that their good luck wouldn't last, but Steel kept reminding him to savor the moment. "She kept saying, 'Jon, you have to learn how to celebrate your victories, and you need to feel really good about yourself, and you need to feel real good about this movie,' " says the director.

Back in her own lair, though, Steel couldn't maintain the optimism. The Monday after the film opened, she arrived at the office in a foul mood. Although *Cool Runnings* was a hit, and her book was number one on the bestseller list in L.A. (but not in New York), she began barking at her staff as if everything was going wrong. At midday one person who saw her anxiety tried to talk some reason into her, pointing out that this was supposed to be a time of joy, not panic. She calmed down, but two hours later her bellows could again be heard down the halls.

In 1995 Sherry Lansing and Dawn Steel found themselves seated next to each other at Jake and Ruth Bloom's post–Yom Kippur breakfast, and they began talking for the first time—really—in all the years they had known each other. "Something like three hours later people said, 'Are you two going to talk to anybody else?' And we just bonded. We just sort of looked at each other and said, 'God, why haven't we done this more often?' " recalls Lansing. "And for the next three years, once a month like clockwork, we would go to this little restaurant on Beverly Drive, Balducci's, where nobody in the business went, so we could go in our sweats. And we just would get there at noon, and neither one of us is a drinker, but we'd have a glass of wine, and sit and have pasta and come home at four-thirty in the afternoon. We just became best friends in the last three years. All we did was talk about life and philosophy and what's important and what is not important. We never talked about the business."

For almost a decade the two women had been held up as rival poster girls of how to be a woman in the industry, decried as the Geisha and the Ball Buster, the classy, self-sufficient seductress and the omnivorous power junkie, one encased in Teflon coating, the other lacking all personal boundaries, a magnet for outsize loves and hates. One carried ambition as a battle-ax, the other as a carefully hidden stiletto.

For years Steel had felt competitive with Lansing, pointing out to anyone who would listen that she had been the first female studio chief. Lansing, by contrast, always denied any competition with Steel. At Lansing's fiftieth birthday party, not long before the flowering of their friendship, one guest had toasted Lansing as "the first woman to run a studio, not Dawn Steel," an improvident salutation that left the guest of honor grimacing and vaguely embarrassed. Indeed, throughout her career Lansing's large circle of women friends consisted of startlingly few other industry women, a conscious attempt to escape the all-encompassing embrace of Hollywood and an unconscious attempt to avoid competition directed at her.

"We were not competitive," insists Lansing. "That bothered both of us. At a lunch that we had eight years ago, we would say, 'Why are they doing that?' " Indeed, despite their stylistic differences, both were middle-class Jewish girls, raised primarily by their mothers, who had made it in the man's world of Hollywood. Their rise had now given them the confidence to pursue relationships with other women.

By the mid-nineties Steel was no longer in a rivalry with Lansing or with anyone, really. She had grown disillusioned with Hollywood. "She used to wear a T-shirt [that said], 'Out of Here in Two Years,' " says Lansing. "She talked about how she wanted to retire."

Steel had been shaken by the death of her former mentor, Don Simpson, who had overdosed on drugs in the spring of 1996. Not long before he died, Steel had run into him in the lobby of the Turner building. He was almost unrecognizable, grossly fat but stuffed into an Armani suit. "I was standing there with Chuck, and it was like a magnet. I went *Vmmm.* I was so glad to see him even though he had gained some weight and all of that. And I literally ran up to him, put my arms around him, and started to kiss him all over his face. I was so happy to see him, and he held me close and whispered in my ear, 'I am so depressed. I don't know what to do,' " Steel recalled.

If anything, Steel's own soul-searching had intensified after *Cool Runnings*, which turned out to be Disney's most successful movie of 1993, earning $140 million worldwide. She had toyed with running a studio again when Ted Turner approached her about starting his Turner Picture label. She was ambivalent, and her reluctance provoked Turner to sweeten the deal. Negotiations were started and ultimately only one sticking point remained on the table: To whom would she actually report? Steel decided to mull it over Christmas vacation. She came back and refused the offer but lobbied and secured a slightly diminished position for her protégée and close friend the Columbia executive vice president Amy Pascal.

Steel then established a new production company, Atlas, for herself and her husband, and his business partner, Bob Cavallo, at Turner. Steel wanted to be in business with her husband. "I think that she saw how much fun Bob and I were having, and she said, 'Let me, I want to be part of that,' " recalls Roven. "Bob was worried that because Dawn and I were married we would gang up on him since it was majority rule. But I told him he didn't have to worry, that probably he would be constantly sorting it out between us. Dawn and I always had that kind of in-your-face kind of relationship. And that turned out to be the way it was. Bob was always Solomon." In fact, Roven and Steel's relationship began going through a rough spell as Roven's career improved and hers deteriorated, altering what had been the balance of power in a way that Steel resented and handled badly. She wanted to be the only diva in the household.

Steel's first and only film for Atlas was a debacle, perhaps the worst experience of her professional career. *Angus* is the tale of the class geek who gets elected prom king as a joke. It was conceived ostensibly as a *Wonder Years* piece of nostalgia, targeted for older audiences. From almost the first day of shooting, Steel despised the director, Patrick Read Johnson, but Pascal, who was supervising the release of the film for Turner, prevailed upon her not to fire him, mostly because such an incident could adversely affect Steel, whose despotic reputation still made some talent wary. Steel and Pascal fought bitterly about it, with Steel accusing her protégée of not taking her side. After a terrible preview, it was decided that the audience was now teenagers. Although Steel was insecure about her abilities in the editing room, she insisted on changes, wielding her power over the final cut like a scythe. The protagonist's gay father was excised, which enraged the director. Steel also slapped on an ultrahip soundtrack. It was all to little avail. *Angus* flopped miserably, both critically and commercially.

If anything, failure hardened Steel's desire for real change. Her last illusions—that the movie business could provide yet another quick fix—were shattered. Her whole raison d'être had been achievement. Now she didn't know where to put all that drive.

In August 1995, Steel decided to take a trip alone. She kept telling Roven, "I need to go play," and drove up the West Coast for several weeks, wandering where she wandered, with tentative plans to end up at a New Age clinic in Idaho. "Most women would be afraid to do that," says Lucy Fisher. "I would have wanted to when I was like seventeen, and I had the spirit and the confidence then to think nothing could hurt me. Now I'd be too worried about too many things that could go wrong. But she took her portable phone and she just went."

Steel was going to miss Rebecca's first day of school, but she nevertheless insisted that now was the time. Roven outfitted a Range Rover–like tank with every electronic gadget on the market. Steel refused all offers from friends to help plan her journey in any way.

"She said, 'I'm tired of being spoiled. I'm tired of everybody doing things for me. I'm tired of never relating to people on a human level, having eight assistants do this and that,' " recalls Melinda Jason. "She said, 'I want to do my laundry with quarters in my pocket in little laundromats. I want to read magazines. I want to be unstructured. I want nothing to do.' "

Steel showed up unannounced on Jason's doorstep near Bend, Oregon. They went to see *The Brothers McMullen* and ate hot dogs at the local theater. Steel tried Watsu, a kind of New Age water therapy, which was supposed to facilitate interpersonal bonding. "These ex-hippies were doing it in a flotation tank full of leaves and crap in the backyard of a house that probably used to cultivate marijuana in the sixties," recalls Jason. "But she just jumped in at night. It was freezing cold, and afterwards she had leaves and stuff all over, it was really funky. She just needed to drink life. She needed to do that.

"She was so moved to want to do something in her life, and every single time something came up about the entertainment business, every time like I mentioned to her, 'Oh, you know, Jeffrey Katzenberg is doing this or that,' she'd go, 'I love him, but shut the fuck up.' It was like she became allergic to it."

"It was some desire to go inward," says Reback about Steel's solo quest. "It was like a yogi's thing to go inside. At Kansas she would be driving and I'd get this call, 'Bud, you won't believe it, I'm driving by corn. There's all this corn.' "

When Steel arrived home she announced to all her friends that she wasn't interested in the movie business anymore. She flirted with a variety of ideas to empower women, like starting a line of rape-counseling centers in shopping malls or a national chain of day-care facilities. She talked about buying a ranch in Oregon and getting out. Roven had finally had his own big success in Hollywood, producing the Brad Pitt movie *12 Monkeys*.

Four months after she returned, Steel began complaining of dizziness. Her legs were numb. Her jaw felt funny. "We had some meeting up in her pool house and she said, 'You know, I get this weird sensation in half of my body,' " recalls Amy Pascal. "She goes, 'Yeah, it kind of comes and goes, but it's like this weird thing.' I didn't say it, but I thought she'd had a stroke."

"And when she first felt these symptoms, she thought they were psychosomatic from not knowing what she was doing. The sickness seemed to her to be a symptom of feeling a little lost," says Lucy Fisher.

Steel went from doctor to doctor trying to figure out if she had an inner ear infection, temporomandibular joint disorder from clenching her teeth at night, or multiple sclerosis. Finally she was diagnosed with brain cancer, a malignant tumor located on the brain stem, which meant it couldn't be removed without destroying all her abilities to function. "The doctors told me that she's got the worst type of cancer at its most aggressive stage, in the worst possible place you could have it. And that they expected she had somewhere between four and six months to live. And I told her everything except the four to six month part," recalls Roven. She cried for a couple of minutes. "And then she said, 'Has anybody ever beaten it?' And I said, 'Yes.' And she said, 'Good. Then we'll beat it.' " She told her eight-year-old daughter that she had "schmutz" in her head but that she was going to make it go away, no matter what. At first she and Roven told everyone—even some of their closest friends—that the tumor was benign, but the truth eventually seeped out.

Steel blamed her years of rage for causing the cancer. What had
been her suit of psychic armor had turned into a hair shirt, and she set
out on yet another ardent course of self-reinvention, assiduously ridding herself of any vestige of negativity. "I think that she felt that anger
contributed to her getting the tumor," says Roven. "And as soon as we
found out what it was, she did her best to focus on a number of things,
one of which was to go to those people that she had a lot of residual
anger toward and just let go of the anger. She didn't want the anger to
be there inside her, because she thought it wasn't healthy for her." Steel
called many people to make amends. Her intense self-involvement
seemed to melt. When she asked how people were, she seemed genuinely interested. "She called my husband just for twenty minutes to
ask him how his teenage son was doing, and every time he'd say to her,
'Well, what about you, Dawn?' She'd go, 'Fuck me, there are other people in the world,' " recalls Melinda Jason. She practiced her Creative Vi-
sualizations every day, trying to will away both the anger and the
tumor. Her friends all told her that she was the one to beat the odds—
that was her formula, and she shouldn't screw it up now.

"I remember walking into that hospital room, and she looked at me
and she said, 'Kath, I've lost my anger,' " recalls Katherine Reback. "And
I don't think that was true by the way, but at that moment it was true.
She would say, no matter what condition she was in, 'I'm going to beat
this, I'm going to beat this,' and she considered it the way she considered
her whole life, a failure if she didn't. When she would go through very
bad times, and very weak times, it was as if she was failing herself."

"I knew what the statistics were. I knew no one had ever survived,
and she made me believe she was going to lick it," recalls Lansing.
"Dawn was such a strong personality. She made you believe that she
was going to be the only person that did it."

Steel underwent a series of operations, as the doctors removed what
they could of the tumor and tried to shrink the rest with steroids and
radiation. "She would have a drill sawing into her brain, and the next
day or two days later, she'd be home," says Fisher. Sensitive about how
she looked, Steel refused to see many people. A voice-mail line was set
up to receive messages, although she rarely called people back. She still
loved to hear the day's gossip, and, even during the times when she was
discombobulated and diminished, she demanded that those who saw
her treat her the same as ever, with respect, but not pity.

Despite the marital tensions that existed before her illness, Roven rallied to Steel's side, and the power women of Hollywood (along with her intimate friend Howard Rosenman) circled the wagons. "She really didn't let a lot of people in," says Roven. "I think she let the girls in because she was close to them, and I think she let the guys in very carefully and slowly not because she wasn't close to them, but because, I think, she was vain. She was always a dame, and she didn't like the way she looked and she didn't want men seeing her that way." It was women like Lucy Fisher, Sherry Lansing, and particularly Lynda Obst who persisted in the maintenance of Dawn Steel on a daily basis. Lansing called every day and haunted the hospital ward. She was the one who knew the most about cancer, from her charity work. Fisher took Rebecca when Steel went into the hospital. Obst corralled others to call Steel, to make time for her.

They watched her plight with a mixture of horror and admiration—horror at the physical ravages on one so young, on someone who had always prided herself on looking her best, on taking care of her body. This was, after all, a woman who brought her hairdresser to the hospital after she gave birth, and now her trademark tresses were gone, as were her neurotic posturing, her flying-off-the-handle theatrics. "There was none of that out-of-control, I'm-falling-apart thing that the woman I had first met, who was sort of a chaos junkie, would have had," says Nora Ephron. Yet the mere fact that Dawn, of all people, could get sick meant that any of them could be smote. Almost all her relationships with women (save for later ones like those with Fisher and Lansing) were fraught. For more than a few, Steel incarnated the shadow self—insecure, indomitable, supportive but omnivorous. Indeed, as word of her illness filtered through Hollywood, there were legions who thought that she had gotten what she deserved, and were nasty enough to say it.

In the summer of 1996, Steel suddenly seemed asymptomatic, as if she had succeeded in the ultimate act of will—making her tumor vanish. She insisted to both the inner and the outer circle that she had licked the cancer, calling people she hadn't seen in months to announce, "Okay, that's done. It's over." No one challenged her assumption; to do so seemed cruel.

"Even in her dialogue with me she said that she had beaten it. She knew the tumor wasn't there because she had visualized it away," says Roven. "What was I going to say? I said, 'Great, it's gone.' But in my heart of hearts I never believed that she believed in it." Steel began appearing around town, looking drawn and ten years older, her famed hair chopped off because of the chemo, but determined, and alive. She attended the L.A. premiere of Nora Ephron's picture *Michael* on the arm of Larry Mark. "For about six months, maybe eight months, from about July of '96 to February of '97, she was definitely on a recovery path," says Roven. "I don't think that anybody but maybe myself knew the difference between what she had been and what she was. The differences were so slight. She had recovered almost 100 percent. She drove. As things got bad the second time, she started bumping into things. We started calling her car living art, because every day she'd come home, there would be another new, wonderful paint mark on it [from some other inanimate object]."

One night Reback, Obst, and Steel decided to show *Flashdance* to Rebecca. "We were all lying there on the bed, right with Rebecca, watching *Flashdance,* and I'm reciting it from memory, and we're rolling our eyes. 'Oh, I can't believe we thought that was a good scene.' Rebecca really enjoyed it. There was a very poignant moment that evening. Remember the old woman, Hanna, who was a dancer, and Jennifer Beals goes to the ballet with her? Don Simpson used to say [during filming], 'Why does this woman exist?' And I would say, 'It is very simple why the woman exists. She exists to die. We need two scenes with her, then she dies, period.' We had a good laugh over that. Well, anyway, we're watching the movie, and suddenly there is this music that is very somber as Jennifer Beals is riding her bike over to Hanna's. Rebecca whirls around to me on the bed and she says, 'Uh-oh, uh-oh, is Hanna going to die?' And I looked at Lynda and I said, 'Gee, Rebecca, I really can't promise you otherwise.' And she said, 'Is Hanna her mother?' And I said, 'No, baby, Hanna is not her mother, and, yes, she's going to die.' "

Throughout the summer, friends—like Barry Diller and David Geffen—made pilgrimages up to Coldwater Canyon to see Steel. According to one close friend, Diller had been charming and attentive, but Geffen's nervousness and inability to slow down enervated Steel. In August, Lansing threw Steel a little birthday party, inviting only her closest friends—Howard Rosenman, Obst, Fisher, and her husband, Doug Wick. "I had seen her all the time, and so I was prepared for the changes," recalls Lansing, "because the steroids distort the way you look. No one else had seen her. She was nervous because she had gained weight, and her hair was like not the way it used to be. And she couldn't walk. Rebecca and Chuck and Billy and I—we were just talking before the other people came, and she said, 'Oh, I'm so fat, and my hair doesn't look good.' And Rebecca took her face in her hands, and she said, 'Mommy, you are so beautiful.' "

That August, Steel, Roven, and Rebecca went on a long trip to Cape Cod and took a cruise along the coast of Alaska. During the last days of the trip, Steel started to feel sick again.

When she returned home, she began a last campaign to forestall the inevitable. Most notably, she volunteered for an experimental gene therapy treatment at UCLA, run by a pioneer in the field, Dr. Keith Black. The doctors attempted to grow a kind of anticancer vaccine from her own cells. "It hadn't been done on a human," recalls Fisher. "It was called the Dawn Steel vaccine." Through their foundations, Ray Stark and David Geffen donated $500,000 apiece to Black's research.

Ultimately, however, Black could do no more. In a last-ditch effort Steel flew to Texas for six weeks to undergo a controversial treatment (not even approved by the AMA) that supposedly would boost her immune system by running an antineoplasty solution through her bloodstream. She couldn't walk, so Lansing flew her in the Paramount jet. When she returned, Steel nearly went into the hospital because her resistance was so low.

"At the end she was almost unrecognizable," says Lansing. "I still have this image of this smile that she had on her face. She would always take my hand. She'd reach up and just grab your hand and put it next to her cheek, then she'd kiss you."

It became increasingly difficult to communicate with Steel. "I would tell her different stories about work, just get her pissed off at people, because she always enjoyed that," recalls Fisher. "You know, what a jerk some producer was, because that would always distract her and get her in a good mood. And then I knew when she was getting really sick, when she would go, 'Oh, he's not so bad.' I'd say, 'Dawn, where is my Dawn?' We, her friends, saw her anger slipping away; it was almost like part of her essence was slipping away too. We loved that she wasn't in pain anymore, but it was like, 'Where's Dawn?' "

Said Reback, "We had this visit that was probably the last, best visit I had with her, and we were sort of tripping down memory lane, and I said, 'Remember fifteen years ago when you told me not to buy the Anne Klein outfit.' She looked at me, and I said, 'Remember, it was very hip, it had a navy blue skirt, and a blue and black sweater. You said, "Do not buy that," and I bought it. And a couple of days later you came to pick me up, and I walked out of the apartment in my navy blue skirt and my blue and black sweater, and you rolled down the window and you said, "You look like a bruise." ' Oh God, did we laugh. She's lying in that hospital bed and we started to laugh, right? So Chuck is laughing. He said, 'Did you really say that?' She said, 'Yeah, but I wouldn't tell you that now.' "

Steel's lucidity fluctuated; she was cognizant of who was with her but often confused. When a guest pointed out a snail on the plants in the hospital room, Steel reached out and tried to eat it, as if it were escargots. She almost died one night but miraculously survived. "And she said she definitely saw her body there. She didn't see the white light, but she was detached, floating above her body," recalls Fisher. "So she could kind of talk about it." Yet often she couldn't find the words, so she would gesture with her hands, attempting to convey what she was trying to say.

"Three weeks before she died, Lynda [Obst] and I went up to the house on a Sunday morning. In order to take her out, you had to detach her from all the stuff. And so she was downstairs and she was sitting in the wheelchair and it was sunny. And she was very responsive. She said, 'Chuck,' and he went over and bent down and he kissed her. It was really tender. He turned to me at one point and he said, 'It is times like this that I think it is really going to work.' I'm sure he probably tried to escape it and deny it, but he was there majorly. Majorly. And all she wanted was to see Chuck," recalls Howard Rosenman.

By the beginning of December 1997, Steel was coughing up blood. Her head, which was swollen like a pumpkin, had to be held up or else she would drown in her own blood. Even her friends no longer recognized her. As the cancer progressed, her nervous system shut down, and she slowly became almost entirely paralyzed. Yet she was conscious. Afterward she was given an emergency tracheotomy, and for almost two weeks Roven barred almost everyone from seeing her. "When she became so sick, it was too painful to be around her for Rebecca," adds Fisher.

Indeed, several days after the tracheotomy, Roven began to believe that his wife was only holding on for them. Another MRI had determined that the treatment in Texas hadn't done any good. He told Rebecca that Steel wasn't going to get better, and she sobbed with shock. She kept saying, "Mommy can't die. She's Dawn Steel." On Thursday the eighteenth, Roven told Steel there was no hope. He told her that if she wanted to go, it was okay. She asked to be taken off the steroids, and to see Rebecca. He called all her close friends—mostly her girlfriends, and Howard Rosenman, and told them to come to the hospital. Roven's mother, Blanca, came to ask for forgiveness.

When Rebecca walked through the door, her mother used what energy she had left to smile. Rebecca lay on Steel's hospital bed, kissing her and telling her it was all right to go. Steel was awake, but she couldn't talk. No one knew if she was actually hearing what was said to her.

"Dawn's eyes were alive, and they were roaming around really fast. And they were stuck inside somebody else's body. Like her soul was there, trying to get out," recalls Amy Pascal. "I held her. I told her everything I needed to say. I want to believe she heard it all. I think it was more for me than her at that point."

"I felt like there was still some pain there, you know, like maybe she wasn't ready to go," says Melinda Jason, who sneaked into the room later that night to see her.

The next night Roven and Rebecca went to dinner at Il Fornio with Amy Pascal and her husband, Bernie Weintraub. In the middle of the meal, Roven's cell phone rang. He picked it up and turned white. Steel had died. It had been twenty-one months since she was diagnosed with cancer.

She was buried three days later at Mount Sinai. "Larry, her brother, gave the greatest speech. He was very self-conscious. He said, 'Dawn is looking at me and saying, "What are you doing there, schmuck? How could you follow Sherry Lansing?" ' " recalls Howard Rosenman. "He told stories of Dawn. You know, when she was ten years old, he was sitting at the table, and he was annoying her, and she took her fork and she stuck it in his ass." For the women who memorialized Steel, it was as if a mother figure had died, a human hurricane who had left both destruction and awe in her wake. "It really wasn't until that day that it hit me about how much she changed my life," recalls Pascal, who sobbed through the service.

As is the Jewish custom, each mourner took a turn throwing shovelfuls of earth on the casket. No one wanted to leave. And so they stayed, and stayed. Until they reached the top, completely burying Dawn Steel.

"I'm the king of the world!" shouted the director James Cameron as he accepted the Academy Award for Best Director for the film *Titanic*, the highest grossing film of all time, his waterlogged tale of star-crossed, class-divided, superphotogenic lovers on the great disaster ship. Against long odds Cameron had brought forth Hollywood's first billion-dollar epic, but his tinny evocation of Leonardo DiCaprio's joyous line from the film fell like hubristic hail on the tuxedo-clad crowd of industry leaders and movie stars. Ebullience was becoming to the young and disenfranchised, but not the rich and dictatorial. At least Cameron had made an attempt to maintain a modicum of dignity. When he won his Golden Globe two months earlier, he had crowed, "Does this prove once and for all that size does matter?"

In his gloating, Cameron wrapped himself in machismo, in a kind of auteurist self-congratulation that had gone out of fashion in the buttoned-down echt-corporate Hollywood of the late nineties. With stupendous force of will and belligerent bravado, he had succeeded in wrestling two studios to the mat as the *Titanic* budget soared 100 percent past its initial estimate to become, at over $200 million, the most expensive movie in history.

Yet what he had made was the biggest women's picture of all time.

For many in Hollywood, *Titanic* proved once and for all that women went to the pictures and women could drive megahits. Sixty percent of its audience was female; 72 percent of the repeat business was female, 64 percent of whom were under twenty-five. The press filled with account after account of teenage girls who dressed up like Jack and Rose for *Titanic* parties, of professional women who convened in movie theaters over and over for the express purpose of huddling in the dark for a long, cathartic cry.

Cameron certainly had done his homework. His Rose is less a strait-laced English aristocrat than a daughter of Madonna, a beautiful, full-

Sherry Lansing (center) with John Wayne in the film RIO LOBO, 1970.

bodied Valkyrie in a pink party gown who smashes the chains imprisoning Jack with one wobbly slash of her fire ax, who learns to spit with impunity, and enjoys sex with whomever she pleases. While two decades earlier George Lucas had followed beat by beat the classic male hero myth laid out in Joseph Campbell's *The Hero with a Thousand Faces*, Cameron opted for a different sort of primal text: Mary Pipher's *Reviving Ophelia*, which focuses on the identity traumas facing late-twentieth-century teenage girls. Cameron, who'd created such fierce, maternal warriors as Linda Hamilton's gun-toting mama bear in his *Terminator* series, set about ingeniously crafting a narrative that would appeal to the prepubescent female. His heroine Rose didn't simply want to be rescued by her handsome prince, Jack. No, Jack was the avenue by which she became more fully herself. His unconditional love emboldened her to live out her fantasies. He freed her self-expression; he made possible the woman she wanted to be, and then gave up his life for her. The girl no longer had to die at the end of the picture: the guy did.

When Sherry Lansing first read the script for *Titanic*, she was "crying at the end," she says. "I remember saying, 'This is one of the strongest feminist pieces I've ever read in my life. She was the first feminist.' " It wasn't surprising that the simple strokes of *Titanic* appealed to Lansing. It features an iconic female protagonist dealing with one of the issues that had consumed Lansing's life: the terror that a woman would marry for security rather than love. Yet it was strange to hear Lansing tag Rose with the word *feminist*, as if with this avowal she again was washing away the antifeminist aroma that had clung to her professional life since *Fatal Attraction* and back to the earliest days of her career, when she would publicly profess to see no signs of discrimination in the movie business, to the intense chagrin of so many of her peers. Lansing saw herself in Rose, her version of feminism incarnate: sexy, man-loving, fun-filled, self-castigating rather than angry, and determined to walk her own path despite the fact that she really didn't want to hurt anyone's feelings.

Lansing had advocated that Paramount buy the domestic rights to the movie from Fox but cap their investment at $65 million, because she was convinced the budget would soar way past Fox's proposed $106 million price tag. With his blunt forcefulness, Jonathan Dolgen implemented the suggestion and later earned kudos for the best business decision of the year as he forced Fox to absorb the overruns. Lansing got along well with Cameron, who seemed to have a preference for strong women. Even so, she had questioned the casting of Leonardo DiCaprio as the romantic lead, and unsuccessfully tried to talk the director out of using a song over the end credits because it was corny. (The song turned out to be Celine Dion's hit.) On a wiser note, she recognized that Cameron needed more time, and led the charge to move the movie's release date from summer to Christmas—a battle that turned increasingly acrimonious with Fox.

Lansing professed not to mind that the glory for *Titanic* had traveled elsewhere. For her, Oscar night had a bittersweet note. She couldn't help thinking of Dawn Steel, whose face flashed before her in an Academy tribute to the Hollywood figures who had died in the preceding year. Steel's death had brought her close to many of Hollywood's other female players for the first time in her life. Steel's death was real, and final; a movie was only a movie.

As she sat in the Shrine Auditorium dressed in an off-the-shoulder gown, Lansing was the most powerful businesswoman ever to grace the motion picture business, with a long string of commercial and critical successes to her name. Even Paramount's initially derided cost-sharing practices had proliferated throughout the rest of Hollywood. Every year at Paramount turned into a profitable one. Success had made her more forthright, or at least made her forthrightness more apparent, despite her finishing-school manners. As the millennium neared, few doubted that Lansing was tough, very tough. Yet she was studiously careful not to wallow in self-importance; she didn't want to succumb to the arrogant God complexes that beset so many in Hollywood. That kind of vanity was unbecoming, particularly in a woman. Sherry was Margot's daughter, and Margot had ingrained in her all the worry and cautious restraint of a pogrom Jew. Now Lansing just cites Dolgen, her boss and friend: "Jonathan uses this expression, 'You don't do a victory lap, because the next day you're going to be stupid again.' "

Still, she basked in the attention of being part of the biggest movie of all time. When Cameron won his Golden Globe, it was Lansing who'd been the first to jump up and throw her arms around him, the way only a woman could. It was a move that put her on TV and irked her fellow studio executives at Fox, the ones who had almost lost their jobs over this production.

There is a reason why Lansing has lasted almost thirty years in the rough waters of the film business. Many of her original peers have faded away—brave, outrageous women like Julia Phillips and Sue Mengers, Marcia Nasatir, Roz Heller, and Dawn Steel. Yet Lansing endures and prospers, treading through the male enclaves of Hollywood as the girliest of girls, doling out warmth and good cheer, trying never to publicly bad-mouth others as she moves with tactical cunning, a master psychologist cum salesman. She does her homework, and often the work of everyone around her. She is comfortable with herself, her sexuality, and the mechanics of power. Long ago she banished bitterness and shame as useless emotions, unnecessary female baggage. She knew how to cater to male egos, yet still take what she needed to advance her agenda.

Unlike much of Hollywood in the eighties and nineties, Lansing recognized the economic power of women moviegoers and knew how to reach them. Her movies aren't politically correct, or even sophisticated, but visceral pulse-pounders designed to generate maximum controversy. Again and again she recycles little bits of her psyche for mass consumption—her obsession with moral quandaries, with untamed sexuality, with women's anger and indomitability. Her heroines are constantly testing the nature of their own power.

Most notably, she was, and is, ruthless in doing whatever it takes to make a hit.

Many of Sherry's peers—the ones who still toil in the business—have tempered their ambitions. Polly Platt found it difficult to orient her life without a male Sun God as an anchor. After a miserable experience on *Evening Star,* Polly Platt ran Carsey-Werner's nascent (and sleepy) film division, where, ironically enough, she worked in the same building as Cybill Shepherd, and the name of the show *Cybill* was emblazoned on almost every door. She devoted herself to screenwriting, churning out an adaptation of Jane Hamilton's *A Map of the World* and Kay Jamison's memoir of manic depression, *An Unquiet Mind.* In 1999, she quit drinking. She talks about directing *Real Feelings,* which is about "the early careers of actors like Jack Nicholson and writers like Bob Towne and the Roger Corman days, some of which I lived through."

Paula Weinstein seems less obsessed with changing the world. In 1998, she became business partners with the director Barry Levinson and, in 1999, produced the first unqualified hit of her entire producing career, *Analyze This*, an old-fashioned mafia spoof. She was thrilled and relieved to finally produce some real money for Warner Bros. Politics has begun to fatigue her, and she essentially withdrew from her prime political platform, the Hollywood Women's Political Committee, because she hated how institutionalized it had become and she "did not want to be a handmaiden to the Democratic party." In 1998, the HWPC folded anyway, in a ritualized hari-kari protest against the corrupting impact of money on the political process.

While Jodie Foster continues to earn $15 million to star in such splashy studio fare as *Anna and the King*, her own much-hyped Poly-Gram deal fell far short of its initial agenda of producing a slate of pictures. She executive-produced only one effort in which she did not star or direct, the cable movie *The Baby Dance*, and in 1999 she reestablished her shingle at Lansing's Paramount as a standard variety production company that traded explicitly on her stardom—it included a provision that she act in at least one Paramount project.

She is still dogged by the long shadow of John Hinckley. She recently spoke to *60 Minutes* about him, saying nothing she hadn't said before, only to find this small part of the interview trumpeted in every promotion for the show. "It was all over everything. I just thought, I'm such an idiot. This fascination that people have with celebrity pain is gross," she says angrily. "It's grotesque. It makes me feel like I'm being used, which of course I am, and I should be used to it, but I like to have some good feeling about humanity instead of being a misanthrope." She is increasingly hounded by the tabloid press, especially after the birth of her son, Charlie, in 1998, when she refused to publicly identify the father or even the means of conception. To escape scrutiny, she temporarily moved out of her home when the baby was born.

Foster remains obsessed with the issue of the female artist, and questions of morality. She speaks enthusiastically about her upcoming directorial effort, *Flora Plum* (*All About Eve* set in a circus), and her plans to do a biopic of the alternately revered and reviled Leni Riefenstahl, the director who masterminded *Triumph of the Will*, one of the most potent pieces of Nazi propaganda, although she knows, "I'm going to catch shit on that one." The one thing she sounds tired of is acting—or at least acting for other directors. "I want to make sure that I work with people I look up to and can learn something from, and feel a challenge from, instead of feeling that I'm the only one holding up the fort, and then I've still got to be rolling my eyes. I'll probably make a lot less movies, a lot less."

Of course, all lives have cycles. In the 1990s, Elaine May resurfaced the way true talent can. She joined up again with her old partner Mike Nichols and wrote *The Birdcage* and *Primary Colors* (and was nominated for an Oscar for the latter).

Most important, another generation has grown up in the wake of Lansing, Steel, Mengers, and Platt, a group of women who have bene-fited greatly from the battles they waged. In the seven years since I started the reporting for this book, the gospel of the female executive class proclaimed that the war on the male enclaves of Hollywood had been won, and why did the people—namely the media—have to con-tinue to harp on such meaningless distinctions as gender?

"You work your whole career to be at the table with the men, why at that point would you want to excuse yourself to go into the parlor with the women?" asks Stacey Snider, the recently anointed chairman of Universal Pictures. "I want to be part of the same conversation when it comes to my business that the guys are having. I've worked too hard, I've accomplished enough and I've given up some things, to earn that. It just seems the oddest time, to then be marginalized by stories about the girls, and the women." Indeed, Snider has even declined to be con-sidered for a Crystal Award.

The thirty-eight-year-old University of Pennsylvania graduate is part of a new breed of women—bright college graduates like Lisa Hen-son, Amy Pascal, and Nina Jacobsen—who dot the upper echelons of the studio world. Indeed, since Lansing's coronation and successful run at Paramount, every studio, save Warner Bros., has named a woman production president, or copresident. A generation younger, these women don't seem larger than life, their virtues and vices magnified by the scrutiny under which they live. They have grown up with allies, fe-male and male. They are less angry, more corporate, more confident that Hollywood is their birthright. As each was promoted, the town didn't circulate with rumors of whom they had slept with to get the job. Unlike Dawn Steel, they don't ape male theatrics or prove their man-hood with temper tantrums. By the year 2000, loud testosterone was going out of fashion. Sobriety and fiscal responsibility were the buzz-words. Both Snider and Amy Pascal, who was concurrently named chairman of Columbia Pictures, are famed for their story sense. Snider is the mother of two little girls who eat lunch with her every week in the Universal commissary or in her office. "It's great because it really takes the edge off if I'm beginning to feel anxious about missing them," says Snider.

The D-girls have won; indeed, they proclaim running a studio a task distinctly suited to their skills. The job once inhabited by such imperious moguls as Harry Cohn is now touted as "a job that really suits the female temperament," says Pascal, who is one of Hollywood's most aggressive promoters of female talent. "Because it's a job about compromise. It's a job about being in the background of things. It's about no fingerprints. It's a job that's about having other people stand out front. It's a traditional women's role. That's why it fits so well."

In the same breath Pascal points out that "there are no women owners. There is no female Michael Eisner or Ted Turner. There's no woman power broker, buying companies, selling companies." As soon as women arrive in the house, the ceiling gets raised again.

There is also no female James Cameron, a pop-culture mythmaker able to magnetize the resources of two major studios. While the few commercially successful women directors prosper, women continue to have difficulties breaking into the studio world, particularly as the cost of films skyrockets. They've had a harder time even seizing the boy-genius mantle that has descended upon such up-and-comers as Paul Thomas Anderson or David O. Russell, or the standard-bearer Quentin Tarantino. Still, the independent world has nurtured a new generation of female directors, women like Kimberly Peirce, Tamara Jenkins, Lisa Cholodenko, Patricia Rozema, and Nicole Holofcener. The 2000 Sundance Festival, the premier independent showcase, boasted more than twenty films by female directors, almost a third of its roster. At the big five film schools—UCLA, NYU, USC, Columbia, and the AFI—women constitute 36 percent of the incoming students. Actress-directors such as Diane Keaton and Anjelica Huston proliferate.

It's unclear whether these women will be able to translate their smaller successes into larger, sustained careers, where their work will be seen outside New York and L.A. If they get a second chance and if their films make money. While political revolutions are usually led by those with the least to lose, Hollywood revolutions are usually led by those who have won the most. Money has been Hollywood's biggest equalizer, the irrefutable measure of worth, and those who continue to make it—Sherry Lansing, Nora Ephron—prosper. While people mocked

Dawn Steel's inability to tell the difference between a good picture and a profitable one, she accurately gauged the defining ethic of the town. As Polly Platt quipped, "Barbra Streisand would have won the Oscar if *Yentl* made more money."

As the millennium dawned, money seemed an increasingly gender-less entity. Girl-empowerment stories appeared on every studio slate: the *Scream* series, *Shakespeare in Love, Notting Hill, Ever After, The Thomas Crown Affair, Runaway Bride, Double Jeopardy.* When Jodie Foster won the Academy Award for Best Actress for *The Accused,* four out of her five fellow nominees had played victims. Ten years later, when Gwyneth Paltrow won the Academy Award for Best Actress for *Shakespeare in Love,* four out of five of the nominees strode across the screen as iconoclasts or adventurers. Meryl Streep played the only victim. In 1999 Julia Roberts became the first female star to break into the $20 million club, the exclusive, unofficial price ceiling for male actors. Stacey Snider, who nurtured four other Roberts films, made that deal happen.

Even male-oriented films like *The Matrix* or the teenage gross-out comedy *American Pie* have added spirited female characters so as not to leave the women's audience at the door. At an average of $50 to $75 million a pop, movies cost too much to have their appeal depend solely on one gender. "Nobody wants to make movies that appeal primarily to young men," explains Pascal, noting the sea change. "If you can't get girls to go to the movies too, and other audiences, you're dead." Pascal staked her year 2000 fortunes—and her career—on the successful, postfeminist remake of the ultimate seventies jiggle show, *Charlie's Angels.* Its producer is the twenty-five-year-old Drew Barrymore.

It's perhaps fitting that the true measure of success is the ease with which it is taken for granted. To the women pioneers who paved the way for Pascal and Barrymore, nothing came for free. The price they paid for female ambition was high. It included marriages, children, decimated egos, pulverized self-esteem. They were unwanted guests in the business of American dreaming—their simple desire for presence seen as an affront, their personalities distorted by the pressures of being different, by unquenched yearning, by having to maneuver without power, constantly watching and waiting, assessing the enemy. Who knew there was anything cataclysmic going on when the sixteen-year-old Sherry Lansing used her forefinger to write out her life's goals in the sand? Who knew there was anything revolutionary about the words *I want to work?*

NOTES

Most of this book is derived from personal interviews I conducted from 1992 to 2000. I also drew heavily from books and various newspaper and magazine accounts. When possible, I asked the sources to speak on the record, but, this being Hollywood, some preferred anonymity.

INTRODUCTION

xi   "My mother could": Chuck Roven, author interview (hereafter cited as "Roven interview").

xii "Women as studio": Elaine Goldsmith, author interview (hereafter cited as "Goldsmith interview").

xiii "Women really don't": Lindsay Doran, author interview (hereafter cited as "Doran interview").

xiii "denial": Peter Biskind, "One on One: Nora Ephron," *Premiere* special: *Women in Hollywood,* 1996.

xiv "One of the great": Sherry Lansing, author interview (hereafter cited as "Lansing interview").

xv   "Nobody knows anything": William Goldman, *Adventures in the Screen Trade* (New York: Warner Books, 1983), 39.

xvi "The operator on": Roven interview.

CHAPTER 1. ROUGH BEGINNINGS

4   "She's the velvet glove": Wayne Rogers, author interview (hereafter cited as "Rogers interview").

4   "five-minute standing": Lansing interview.
5   "to talk to anyone": Judy Lansing Kovler, author interview (hereafter cited as "Kovler interview").
6   "apple of his": Lansing interview.
6   "Why is Sherry": Ibid.
6   "wasn't coming home": Ibid.
7   "a 'baby doll' ": Ibid.
7   "I remember seeing": Ibid.
8   "If you sing": Ibid.
8   "very cold, very demanding": Ibid.
10   "Everywhere we went": Polly Platt, author interview (hereafter cited as "Platt interview").
11   "I understand Jim": Ibid.
12   "I was stoned": Ibid.
12   "amazingly tough and": James L. Brooks, author interview (hereafter cited as "Brooks interview").
12   "That's just like": Antonia Bogdanovich, author interview.
12   "If I were young": Platt interview.
13   "It's in Texas": Ibid.
14   "I wouldn't say they": Larry McMurtry, author interview (hereafter cited as "McMurtry interview").
14   "I don't like for people": Platt interview.
14   "There's a mood": Brooks interview.
14   "She fills a huge void": Penney Finkelman-Cox, author interview.
14   "When you watch": Brooks interview.
15   "You know, I'm a woman": Platt interview.
15   "Because we didn't have a car": Ibid.
15   "Puritanical, original sin": Jack Platt, author interview (hereafter cited as "J. Platt interview").
15   "I think my mother": Platt interview.
16   "I was the older": J. Platt interview.
16   "And my father": Platt interview.
16   "I believe that my mother": Ibid.
16   "The one thing": Ibid.
17   "She was the first": J. Platt interview.
17   "He was a lost soul": Ibid.
17   "She didn't think he'd want": Ibid.
17   "I keep going, 'Fuck' ": Paula Weinstein, author interview (hereafter cited as "P. Weinstein interview").
17   "I would have": Ibid.
18   "they'd never have to": Maureen Orth, "Hollywood's New Power Elite: The Baby Moguls," New West, 19 June 1978.
18   "I grew up being told": Ibid.
19   "a Marxist and": Lisa Weinstein, author interview (hereafter cited as "L. Weinstein interview").

19   "If [our] program": Ronald Brownstein, *The Power and the Glitter: The Hollywood-Washington Connection* (New York: Vintage, 1992), 108.

19   "I was the youngest": P. Weinstein interview.

20   "I never knew any other way": Ibid.

21   "He was impossible": Ibid.

22   "You stole my gun": Platt interview.

22   "You should have watched": Ibid.

23   "a young man": Ibid.

23   "There was a lot of unhappiness": Ibid.

24   "You couldn't tell who": Robert Benton, author interview.

24   "I used to say": Platt interview.

25   "We're eating and I'm": Ibid.

25   "She used to ride": Michael Brownstein, author interview.

25   "We went to": Ibid.

26   "not to impart": Lansing interview.

26   "She talked about": Johnny Grant, interview with Sean Miner.

27   "a secretive rogue": David Thomson, *A Biographical Dictionary of Film* (New York: Knopf, 1994), 323.

27   "I wore makeup": James Bacon, "Hawks' Discovery Now a Leading Lady," *Los Angeles Herald-Examiner,* 15 April 1970.

27   "She has been able": Kovler interview.

28   "He was eighty": Lansing interview.

28   "Your body tells": Ibid.

28   "I was miserable": Ibid.

28   "You could have been": Ibid.

28   "Quitting acting was": Ibid.

29   "I was ashamed": Ibid.

29   "nobody would like me": Ibid.

29   "It's the best": Ibid.

CHAPTER 2. UNMARRIED WOMEN

31   "he could bring": Platt interview.

31   "I always thought": Ibid.

32   "Buy it at": Ibid.

32   "He came to me": Ibid.

32   "Yes, you do": Ibid.

33   "It's just a dirty": Ibid.

33   "What's the matter": Ibid.

33   "Of course, you're": Ibid.

34   "has a decency": Pauline Kael, *5001 Nights at the Movies* (New York: Holt, Rinehart and Winston, 1982), 317.

34   "You might have": Jeff Bridges, author interview (hereafter cited as "Bridges interview").

34   "She had as much": Ben Johnson, author interview.

34   "Peter and Polly": Bridges interview.

34   "I think sometimes she": Peter Bogdanovich, author interview.

34   "Oh, people are": Platt interview.

35   "It's like a bad": Ibid.

35   "I feel old": Ibid.

35   "I'll kill us": Ibid.

35   "It's either Cybill": Ibid.

36   " 'You wouldn't be' ": Ibid.

36   "That's my movie": Ibid.

36   "I love you": Ibid.

36   "I saw how they": Ibid.

36   "I realized I would": Ibid.

37   "He said he": Ibid.

37   "There was just": Ibid.

37   "covered with a": Ibid.

38   "I think Orson Welles": Ibid.

38   "It's such a bad": Ibid.

38   "Orson got so mad": Ibid.

38   "I didn't want them": Ibid.

39   "Sue called me": John Calley, author interview (hereafter cited as "Calley interview").

39   "It was a crazy": Ibid.

40   "ghastly": Calley interview.

40   "I think she": Platt interview.

40   "We embraced and": Ibid.

40   "There were stars": Ibid.

41   "Are you giving": Randall Riese, *Her Name Is Barbra* (New York: St. Martin's Press [paperback], 1994), 358.

41   "We're in a": Ibid.

41   "I remember we": Sue Mengers, author interview (hereafter cited as "Mengers interview").

42   "Imagine, you could be Polly": Platt interview.

42   "It's really an anesthetic": Ibid.

42   "my Cybill Shepherd": Ibid.

42   "pretty angry": Frank Marshall, author interview (hereafter cited as "F. Marshall interview").

43   "You can't be": Bud Yorkin, author interview.

43   "It's embarrassing that a person": Platt interview.

43   "I want to thank": Ibid.

43   "It never occurred": Ibid.

44   "I don't want to be humiliated": Ibid.

44   "On *Paper Moon*": Laszlo Kovacs, author interview.

44   "it never occurred": Platt interview.

44   "He was like": Peggy Sarno, author interview.

44   "I thought it would be only": Platt interview.

45   "She's very tough": F. Marshall interview.

45   "He liked me": Peter Biskind, *Easy Riders, Raging Bulls* (New York: Simon & Schuster, 1998), 213.

45   "People began to": Platt interview.

CHAPTER 3. SUE MENGERS IS HATCHED

47   "The reason women": Mengers interview.

48   "When I met Sue": Joan Hyler, author interview (hereafter cited as "Hyler interview").

48   "I was a little pisher": Sue Mengers, interview with Mike Wallace, *60 Minutes*, 1975.

49   "He didn't leave a note": Mengers interview.

49   "It all had": Marie Brenner, "Is Sue Mengers Too Pushy for Hollywood?" *New York*, 17 March 1975.

49   "I looked around": Paul Rosenfield, "Sue Mengers: The Agent Who Roared," *Los Angeles Times*, 6 December 1987.

49   "receptionist, theatrical agency": Ibid.

49   "the Octopus": Frank Rose, *The Agency: William Morris and the Hidden History of Show Business* (New York: HarperBusiness, 1995), 88.

50   "pastrami at the desk": Brenner, "Sue Mengers," *New York*, 17 March 1975.

50   "total aggression": Mengers interview.

50   "When I was": Ibid.

50   "Of course, the": Brenner, "Sue Mengers," *New York*, 17 March 1975.

51   "It was all the": Ibid.

51   "Sue appeared, spotted": Ibid.

51   "Personally, I think he": Mengers interview.

51   "I never thought": Ibid.

51   "Now I had my credentials": Ibid.

52   "interested in stars": Ibid.

52   "There must be something": Ibid.

52   "Well, now here I'm": Ibid.

53   "I was *charming*": Ibid.

53   "I remember her": Rosenfield, "Sue Mengers: The Agent Who Roared," *Los Angeles Times*, 6 December 1987.

54   "How could I": Mengers interview.

54   "didn't want Paul": Ibid.

55   "Tony said, 'Sue' ": Charles Winecoff, *Split Image: The Life of Anthony Perkins* (New York: Dutton, 1996), 266.

55   "It was because": Mengers interview.

55   "So, they didn't know what": Ibid.

56   "Who represents you": Brenner, "Sue Mengers," *New York*, 17 March 1975.

56   "Even Dr. Frankenstein": Louise Farr, "And Now from Hollywood: The Sweetening of Sue Mengers," *Ms.*, June 1975.

56   "Thank you, Uncle": Ibid.

56   "I'm not a little": Ibid.

56   "a grown-up woman": Ibid.
57   "You swore he": Boaty Boatwright, author interview.
57   "Agents are the": Confidential source.
57   "I thought being an": Mengers interview.
57   "Her manager arranged": Ibid.
58   "Elliott would say": Ibid.
58   "We were two single": Ibid.
58   "She didn't agree": Ibid.
59   "Don't worry, honey": Ibid.
59   "the hardest part": Ibid.
59   "Freddie is my": Ibid.
60   "It was very": Ibid.
60   "Our house became": Rosenfield, "Sue Mengers: The Agent Who Roared," *Los Angeles Times*, 6 December 1987.
60   "I never thought": Mengers interview.
61   "never thought any": Ibid.
62   "When Ryan O'Neal": Ibid.
63   "[Barbra and I] had to confront": Ibid.
63   "More than anyone else": Rosenfield, "Sue Mengers: The Agent Who Roared," *Los Angeles Times*, 6 December 1987.

CHAPTER 4. WOMEN CREATE

65   "Women have been": Judy Klemesrud, "At the Movies," *New York Times*, 13 October 1974.
66   "Famous actresses, writers": Susan Smith, "The AFI's Workshops for Women," *Los Angeles Times*, 13 September 1979.
66   "They're discriminated against": Farr, "And Now from Hollywood," *Ms.*, June 1975.
67   "People think I": James Power, "Dialogue on Film: Joan Tewkesbury," *American Film*, March 1979.
67   "There is nothing": *Time*, 20 March 1972.
67   "I don't know if": Ibid.
67   "At this moment Elaine": Andrew Tobias, "For Elaine May, A New Leaf—But Not a New Leaf," *New West*, 6 December 1976.
68   "You have your": Robert Rice, "A Titled Insight," *New Yorker*, 15 April 1961.
68   "She is a short": Ibid.
69   "I feel awful": Ibid.
69   "Look, sweetheart, you're": Ibid.
69   "It's a good thing": Ibid.
69   "The secret we share": Helen Markel, "Mike Nichols & Elaine May," *Redbook*, February 1961.
69   "I kept learning": Thomas Thompson, "Whatever Happened to Elaine May?" *Life*, 28 July 1967.
69   "whose chief occupation": Ibid.
69   "I feel in opposition": Rice, "A Titled Insight," *New Yorker*, 15 April 1961.

70   "May I sit down": Thompson, "Whatever Happened," *Life,* 28 July 1967.

70   "once you have money": Markel, "Mike Nichols," *Redbook,* February 1961.

70   "I told Mike": Thompson, "Whatever Happened," *Life,* 28 July 1967.

71   "I was onstage": Barbara Gelb, "Mike Nichols: The Special Risks and Rewards of the Director's Art," *New York Times Magazine,* 27 May 1984.

71   "They said it can't": Calley interview.

72   "Why don't you": Andrew Tobias, "For Elaine May," *New West,* 6 December 1976.

72   "I arranged a place": Thompson, "Whatever Happened," *Life,* 28 July 1967.

72   "Elaine is going": Ibid.

72   "Elaine didn't know": Ibid.

73   "We all go down": Ibid.

73   "I think Elaine": Ibid.

73   "When I started": Michael Rivlin, "Is Elaine May Too Tough for Hollywood?," *Millimeter,* 3 October 1975.

73   "She doesn't understand": Anthea Sylbert, author interview (hereafter cited as "A. Sylbert interview").

74   "We were in a pitch": Hillard Elkins, author interview (hereafter cited as "Elkins interview").

74   "When the camera": Howard Koch, author interview (hereafter cited as "Koch interview").

75   "She couldn't make": Ibid.

75   "Elaine does [all those takes]": A. Sylbert interview.

75   "She operates very emotionally": Richard Sylbert, author interview (hereafter cited as "R. Sylbert interview").

75   "They kept saying": Dick Lemon, "How to Succeed in Interviewing Elaine May (Try, Really Try)," *New York Times,* 4 January 1970.

76   "We went to court": Koch interview.

76   "Elaine was upset": Elkins interview.

76   "I went way over": Rivlin, "Is Elaine May," *Millimeter,* 3 October 1975.

77   "I kept saying": A. Sylbert interview.

78   "Once we cast": Edgar Scherick, author interview.

78   "I suspect part": A. Sylbert interview.

78   "She had a wonderful": R. Sylbert interview.

78   "She was always": John Gruen, "More Than Elaine May's Daughter," *New York Times,* 7 January 1973.

79   "Nice tits today": Biskind, *Easy Riders, Raging Bulls,* 145.

79   "No one was keeping": A. Sylbert interview.

79   "Cut": Paul Sylbert, author interview (hereafter cited as "P. Sylbert interview").

79   "You don't say": Ibid.

79   "I know": Ibid.

79   "Yes . . . but they": Ibid.

79   "Cut": Ibid.

79   "There's a big": Ibid.

80   "In all honesty": Sheldon Kahn, author interview.

81   "If you put any": Tobias, "For Elaine May," *New West,* 6 December 1976.

81   "I learned to judge": Todd McCarthy, author interview (hereafter cited as "McCarthy interview").

82   "She is a brilliant": Tobias, "For Elaine May," *New West*, 6 December 1976.

82   "Things will go right": Ibid.

83   "I was sued": David Blum, "The Road to *Ishtar*," *New York*, 16 March 1987.

83   "It was sort of": Ibid.

83   "I really do believe": McCarthy interview.

CHAPTER 5. A DIFFERENT KIND OF CHILD

86   "funny malice and": Pauline Kael, "Woman on the Road," *New Yorker*, 13 January 1975.

86   "She was already": Toby Rafelson, author interview.

87   "Jodie was never": Linda R. Miller, "Victor of Circumstances," *American Film*, October 1988.

87   "I was that vicarious": Jodie Foster, author interview (hereafter cited as "Foster interview").

87   "She wanted me": Ibid.

88   "savings and selling": Ibid.

88   "Let's just imagine": Hilary de Vries, "Command Performance," *Los Angeles Times Magazine*, 11 December 1994.

88   "Alexander the Great": Buddy Foster, *Foster Child* (New York: Dutton, 1997), 56.

88   "I was always on a skateboard": Foster interview.

89   "She could read": Brandy Foster, author interview (hereafter cited as "B. Foster interview").

89   "From the very": Foster, *Foster Child*, 61–62.

89   "when you allow yourself": B. Foster interview.

89   "My mother's very opinionated": Foster interview.

90   "The only way my": Foster interview with Holly Millea.

90   "There was a lot of hollering": B. Foster interview.

90   "It was like a partnership": Clara Lisa Kabbaz, author interview.

91   "Jodie strives to": Ibid.

91   "I used to have": Holly Millea, "The Woman Who Fell to Earth," *Premiere*, July 1997.

91   "When I was a little kid": Foster interview.

92   "They'd look at your": Ibid.

92   "I insisted that we get": B. Foster interview.

92   "She had never": Ibid.

92   "saucy": Henry Thompson, "Napoleon and Samantha," *New York Times*, 20 July 1972.

CHAPTER 6. THE ARSENAL OF SEDUCTION

93   "There were fights": P. Weinstein interview.

95   "She was scared": Ibid.

96   "It was such a big thing": Ibid.

96   "All these radical": Ibid.

97   "Mike thought that": Ibid.

97   "liars and hypocrites": Bill Davidson, *Jane Fonda: An Intimate Biography* (New York: Dutton, 1990), 190.

97   "graylisted": Christopher Andersen, *Citizen Jane* (New York: Henry Holt, 1990), 262.

97   "They were scared": P. Weinstein interview.

98   "Jane was my": Ibid.

99   "I want to produce": Ibid.

99   "I can't say we were friends": Ibid.

100   "people didn't talk": Ibid.

101   "Although it received terrific": Don Devlin, author interview (hereafter cited as "Devlin interview").

101   "Why are you": Lansing interview.

101   "would keep all her hours": Ray Wagner, author interview (hereafter cited as "Wagner interview").

101   "You can't speak": Lansing interview.

102   "People always kind": Wagner interview.

102   "She wasn't threatening": Ibid.

102   "I actually thought": Lansing interview.

102   "Jay Sandor was": Leonard Stern, author interview (hereafter cited as "L. Stern interview").

103   "Katie came home": Gloria Stern, author interview (hereafter cited as "G. Stern interview").

103   "living in a": Ibid.

103   "There were no women": L. Stern interview.

103   "It was open": Ibid.

104   "She brings out": Ibid.

104   "She can disarm": Ibid.

104   "Sherry's got a": G. Stern interview.

104   "Several of the": Lansing interview.

104   "There's an atmosphere": Martin Scorsese, *Scorsese on Scorsese*, ed. David Thompson and Ian Christie (London: Faber & Faber, 1989), 59–60.

105   "takes the idea": Gregg Kilday, "Scorsese: Virtuoso of Urban Angst," *Los Angeles Times*, 14 March 1976.

105   "It had just the": Paul Schrader, *Schrader on Schrader*, ed. Kevin Jackson (London: Faber & Faber, 1990), 120.

106   "And she knew": B. Foster interview.

106   "I don't remember having": Foster interview.

106   "were all doing blow": Julia Phillips, *You'll Never Eat Lunch in This Town Again* (New York: Random House, 1991), 212.

107   "I also remember Robert": Foster interview.

107   "It was like": Ibid.

107   "I remember getting": Ibid.

108   "He was nervous": B. Foster interview.

108   "She didn't exhibit": Michael Phillips, author interview.

108 "a raw, tabloid": Pauline Kael, *When the Lights Go Down* (New York: Holt, Rinehart and Winston, 1979), 132.

108 "diving elatedly into": Robert F. Moss, "The Brutalists: Making Movies Mean and Ugly," *Saturday Review*, October 1980.

108 "If Jodie Foster wins": Scorsese, *Scorsese on Scorsese*, 61.

108 "I broke out": Foster interview.

109 "This is going to really": Lansing interview.

110 "very self-centered": Confidential source.

110 "Sherry slept her": Ibid.

110 "We had created": Daniel Melnick, author interview (hereafter cited as "Melnick interview").

111 "What took you": Erika Mark, "Model Turned Mogul," *San Antonio Light*, 25 May 1980.

111 "She was an": Susan Merzbach, author interview (hereafter cited as "Merzbach interview").

111 "He just kind": Ibid.

111 "Melnick was one": Confidential source.

111 "we were part of MGM": Merzbach interview.

112 "She was very focused": Dick Shepard, author interview.

112 "We're not taking": Lansing interview.

112 "It was like": Biskind, *Easy Riders, Raging Bulls*, 245.

112 "If someone is": L. Stern interview.

112 "Melnick could have": Merzbach interview.

112 "I don't take": Lansing interview.

113 "She never had a bad word": Myra Silverman, author interview.

113 "She kept people": G. Stern interview.

113 "I remember looking": David E. Goodman, author interview.

CHAPTER 7. THE POWER OF BARBRA STREISAND

115 "That's *all* you can get": Marie Brenner, "Collision on Rainbow Road," *New Times*, 24 January 1975.

115 "Directing is a thing": Ibid.

116 "Do you know": Barbra Streisand, author interview (hereafter cited as "Streisand interview").

116 "I got the part": Ibid.

116 "The night before": Ibid.

116 "I loved Willy": Ibid.

117 "would collaborate with me": Joe Morgenstern, "Streisand's Rite of Passage," *Los Angeles Herald-Examiner*, 13 November 1983.

117 "The world is waiting": Brenner, "Collision," *New Times*, 24 January 1975.

117 "James Taylor and": John Gregory Dunne, "Gone Hollywood," *Esquire*, September 1976.

118 "I wanted Barbra": Calley interview.

118 "He didn't know": Streisand interview.

118 "You've got a great ass": Nancy Griffin and Kim Masters, *Hit & Run: How Jon Peters and Peter Guber Took Sony for a Ride in Hollywood* (New York: Simon & Schuster, 1996), 29.

118 "new, sensual Barbra": Jerry Parker, "Producer Peters: 'I'm Fighting For What I Believe In,' " *Los Angeles Times,* 7 November 1978.

119 "He just made her believe": Polly Platt interview with Nancy Griffin.

119 "I do believe": Platt interview.

119 "She'd done *Funny Lady*": Brenner, "Collision," *New Times,* 24 January 1975.

119 "Freddie Fields muscled": Calley interview.

120 "I wasn't crazy": Dunne, "Gone Hollywood," *Esquire,* September 1976.

120 "so passive": James Spada, *Streisand: Her Life* (New York: Crown, 1995), 347.

121 "I wanted Frank Pierson": Streisand interview.

121 "I couldn't just": Frank Pierson, "My Battles with Barbra and Jon," *New York,* 15 November 1976.

121 "I'm for women's lib": Riese, *Her Name Is Barbra* (New York: St. Martin's Press [paperback]), 418.

121 "You're the only one": Griffin and Masters, *Hit & Run,* 41.

122 "hadn't read the descriptions": Pierson, "My Battles," *New York,* 15 November 1976.

122 "Your turn—the Jewish": Ibid.

122 "I don't feel you": Ibid.

122 "She meant it": Platt interview.

123 "Two women can't": Ibid.

123 "Thank you! Thank": Pierson, "My Battles," *New York,* 15 November 1976.

123 "I'm neutral": Lawrence Grobel, *Playboy* interview: "Barbra Streisand," *Playboy,* October 1977.

123 "Barbra sings to": Pierson, "My Battles," *New York,* 15 November 1976.

123 "You have to be": Ibid.

124 "He was incapable": Platt interview.

124 "Frank was in": Confidential source.

124 "was out to lunch": Spada, *Streisand: Her Life,* 357.

125 "For God's sake": Pierson, "My Battles," *New York,* 15 November 1976.

125 "Their relationship was": Griffin and Masters, *Hit & Run,* 44.

126 "Jon Peters was like": Mengers interview.

126 "When Jon Peters": Ibid.

126 "We fought day": Ibid.

126 "If I had it": Ibid.

127 "broke through the": Ibid.

127 "It didn't work": Ibid.

128 "I think the first": Ibid.

128 "It is a job": Ibid.

129 "When you see Barbra": Spada, *Streisand: Her Life,* 383.

129 "We were standing": Ibid., 403–404.

130 "I remember it": Mengers interview.

131 "It was flattering": Streisand interview.

131 "She behaved very": Mengers interview.

131 "I said, 'How' ": Streisand interview.

131 "Barbra, you have": Griffin and Masters, *Hit & Run*, 103.

132 "My agent David": Streisand interview.

132 "anybody could be": Mengers interview.

132 "When you live": Ibid.

CHAPTER 8. PRETTY BABIES

133 "I was so afraid": Platt interview.

133 "drunk as a": Ibid.

135 "I wouldn't even": Ibid.

135 "Whether you're a": Ibid.

135 "Mainly what fascinated": Leticia Kent, "Malle: 'Pretty Baby' Could Be the Apprenticeship of Corruption," *New York Times*, 16 April 1978.

136 "Louis and I": Platt interview.

136 "Well, Nicholson": Ibid.

136 "I went running": Ibid.

137 "I don't know how": Ibid.

137 "It was kind of a nightmarish": Susan Sarandon, author interview.

137 "the mother was relegated": Platt interview.

138 "There was a": Joan Goodman, "Pretty Baby," *New York*, 26 September 1977.

138 "in Teri's own": Ibid.

138 "the biggest boost": Ivor Davis, "Baby Brooke Takes Her Stuff to Masses," *Los Angeles Times*, 13 January 1979.

138 "this may be": Penelope Gilliatt, "His Finest Yet," *New Yorker*, 10 April 1978.

138 "In leaving out": Molly Haskell, "When a House Is a Home," *New York*, 17 April 1978.

139 "in ways you": Platt interview.

139 "technician": Foster interview.

139 "She didn't quite understand": B. Foster interview.

139 "There's Tallulah walking": Foster interview.

140 "I made out with him": Jodie Foster interview with Holly Millea.

140 "I remember when I": Nicolas Gessner, author interview.

141 "It was the straw": Peer J. Oppenheimer, "Jodie Foster," *Family Weekly*, 16 April 1978.

141 "I hate to sound": Edwin Miller, "Here Comes Jodie Foster," *Seventeen*, January 1977.

141 "An Oscar is": *Los Angeles Herald-Examiner*, 17 March 1977.

142 "It seems to be": Philippa Kennedy, *Jodie Foster: A Life Onscreen* (New York: Birch Lane Press, 1995), 45.

142 "It felt pretty bad": Foster interview.

142 "I have to give her": Ibid.

142 "He had every right": Ibid.

143 "She and her mother": Andy Warhol, *The Andy Warhol Diaries* (New York: Warner Books, 1989), 10 April 1980.

143 "It's a horrible memory": Jodie Foster interview with Holly Millea.

144   "of a guy": Kandice Stroh, author interview (hereafter cited as "Stroh interview").

144   "I look at myself": Foster interview.

144   "It was a very male": Stroh interview.

145   "These kids are": Roger Ebert, "Jodie Foster Grows Up to Join the *Foxes*," *Us*, 4 March 1980.

145   "Just treat her": Thomas Baum, author interview (hereafter cited as "Baum interview").

145   "Before the read-through": Ibid.

146   "Some of it": Ibid.

146   "I just had": Foster interview.

146   "Someday I would": Ibid.

146   "People used to": Baum interview.

146   "Everyone wanted to": Holly Millea, "The Woman Who Fell to Earth," *Premiere*, July 1997.

147   "I actually was": Baum interview.

147   "He showed up": Jonathan Taplin, author interview.

147   "I don't overreact": Foster interview.

CHAPTER 9. D-GIRLS ON THE RISE

149   "Was it my fault": Lansing interview.

150   "Every possible chauvinistic": Michael Douglas, author interview (hereafter cited as "Douglas interview").

150   "She doesn't talk": Ibid.

151   "It was mostly guys": Dick Shepard, author interview.

151   "He was like, 'You're' ": Lansing interview.

151   "He was a very misunderstood": Ibid.

151   "The rumor about him": William Friedkin, author interview (hereafter cited as "Friedkin interview").

151   "When I was a kid": Lansing interview.

152   "The film falsely": George Will, "The China Syndrome," *Newsweek*, 15 March 1979.

152   "Incredible reactions": Budd Schulberg, *New York Times*, 27 April 1980.

153   "You're a writer": Ibid.

153   "She had always been": Lansing interview.

153   "She was the person": Stanley Jaffe, author interview (hereafter cited as "Jaffe interview").

153   "If you're that": Stephen Faber and Marc Green, *Hollywood Dynasties* (New York: Delilah, 1984), 280.

153   "I don't know who brought": Lansing interview.

154   "It really was instant": Jaffe interview.

154   "A few weeks": Meryl Streep, author interview (hereafter cited as "Streep interview").

155   "She would encourage": Ibid.

155   "They admitted they": Ibid.

156   "I won't be able": Confidential source.

156 "We fought to the point": Brad Darrach, "Enchanting, Colorless, Glacial, Fearless, Sneaky, Seductive, Manipulative, Magical Meryl," *Life*, December 1987.

156 "I think Bob": Streep interview.

156 "I remember the": Ibid.

157 "I didn't think of it": Ibid.

158 "tempestuous relationship": Rogers interview.

158 "If it hadn't been Melnick": Ibid.

158 "He really gave me": Lansing interview.

159 "Did you hear": Ibid.

159 "Is that your favorite": Ibid.

159 "It became clear": Jaffe interview.

160 "There was hellish": P. Weinstein interview.

160 "Sherry was never": Ibid.

160 "I felt like": Ibid.

160 "I made a passionate": Ibid.

161 "I kept thinking": Ibid.

161 "I had no notion": Ibid.

161 "There were times when": Ibid.

162 "everybody [including Sue Mengers]": Ibid.

163 "When I first": Ibid.

163 "It's fun, in": Ibid.

164 "I felt [Sue]": Lynda Obst, author interview (hereafter cited as "Obst interview").

164 "A love relationship": P. Weinstein interview.

165 "Mark was hired": Ibid.

166 "I was fired": Andersen, *Citizen Jane*, 299.

166 "They are often treated": Ibid.

167 "Basically [Jane] wanted": Patricia Resnick, author interview (hereafter cited as "Resnick interview").

168 "It was wonderful": P. Weinstein interview.

168 "Jane and Bruce": Resnick interview.

168 "The only trouble": P. Weinstein interview.

CHAPTER 10. THE FILM SCHOOL IMPERATIVE

171 "How could you": Joan Tewkesbury, author interview (hereafter cited as "Tewkesbury interview").

171 "I looked at her": Ibid.

171 "I thought it was": Ibid.

172 "The fact that the door": Ibid.

174 "It cast a chilling pall": Victoria Hochberg, author interview.

174 "I just got": Amy Heckerling, author interview (hereafter cited as "Heckerling interview").

175 "I'd always been": Ibid.

175 "She's got eight": Ibid.

176 "I was real excited": Ibid.

176   "I saw the AFI": Art Linson, author interview.
177   "Sean brought Chinese": Heckerling interview.
177   "He told me": Ibid.
177   "I was still": Ibid.
177   "My idiot husband": Heckerling interview with Eliza Bergman Krause.
178   "One day he": Ibid.
178   "Years later when": Heckerling interview.
178   " 'You can't be a director' ": Martha Coolidge, author interview (hereafter cited as "Coolidge interview").
179   "We talked about lots": Ibid.
179   "It was an": Ibid.
180   "a spiritual religion": Ibid.
180   "everybody advised me": Ibid.
180   "The reason was": Ibid.
181   "And the guy had": Ibid.
181   "And I sat there in shock": Ibid.
182   "women-libbed to": Ibid.
182   "I want you": Ibid.
184   "I was more advanced": Gillian Armstrong, author interview (hereafter cited as "Armstrong interview").
184   "she never liked": Ibid.
185   "There was terrible bitching": Ibid.
185   "I had a": Ibid.
186   "So any person": Ibid.
186   "They all thought": Ibid.
186   "climbing mountains or": Ibid.

CHAPTER 11. THE ASSUMPTION OF POWER

187   "I always was as": Lansing interview.
189   " 'What, are you' ": Ibid.
189   "Alan said, 'That's' ": Ibid.
189   "I had talked to her": Frank Price, author interview (hereafter cited as "Price interview").
189   "She was really": Ibid.
190   "I was a model": Lansing interview.
190   "I hope you can sell": Ibid.
190   "It really caught": Alan Hirschfield, author interview (hereafter cited as "Hirschfield interview").
190   "There were specious": Platt interview.
191   "Sherry got the job": Obst interview.
191   "Female executives suck": David McClintick, *Indecent Exposure: A True Story of Hollywood and Wall Street* (New York: Morrow, 1982), 520.
191   "She came to me once": Hirschfield interview.
192   "She turned down": Confidential source.
192   "When I went in to quit": Ibid.

192   "I just felt": Lansing interview.
193   "Norman would just": Melnick interview.
193   "She really was kind": Robert Cort, author interview (hereafter cited as "Cort interview").
194   "Jerry Lansing": Alex Ben Block, *Outfoxed: Marvin Davis, Barry Diller, Rupert Murdoch, Joan Rivers, and the Inside Story of America's Fourth Television Network* (New York: St. Martin's Press, 1990), 29.
194   "dollface": Lansing interview.
194   "This is not": Ibid.
194   "You can get": Block, *Outfoxed,* 39.
195   "Dollface, why don't": Ibid.
195   "He was not": Merzbach interview.
195   "I remember sitting": Lansing interview.
196   "She had reticence": Hirschfield interview.
196   "She frankly did": Ibid.
196   "You could just feel": Melnick interview.
196   "We showed it": Jaffe interview.
197   "The kids were": Block, *Outfoxed,* 50.
197   "The audience were all forty": Jaffe interview.
197   "She's like a politician": David Niven, Jr., author interview (hereafter cited as "Niven interview").
197   "I was one": Ibid.
197   "The work becomes": Rogers interview.
198   "Jean Adcock did": G. Stern interview.
198   "I had been programmed": Lansing interview.
199   "I don't think": Rogers interview.
199   "I'm sure being a mother": Lansing interview.
199   "It was like a nightmare": Ibid.
199   "I was in a room": Jaffe interview.
199   "She kept going": Ibid.
200   "She only likes domestic": Greg Kilday, "Sherry Lansing: Kiss Her Goodbye," *Los Angeles Herald-Examiner,* 21 December 1982.
200   "I remember going": Ibid.
200   "which I really, really loved": Lansing interview.
200   "indefinite extension": Block, *Outfoxed,* 55.
200   "none of us knew": Aljean Harmetz, "How a Hollywood Rumor Was Born, Flourished and Died," *New York Times,* 12 December 1982.
201   "You think you're": Lansing interview.
202   "Ned's and my": Confidential source.
202   "I was then going out": Niven interview.
203   "I don't think": Lansing interview.

CHAPTER 12. WAR GAMES

205   " 'Do you want it' ": P. Weinstein interview.
206   "People told each": A. Sylbert interview.

207 "Rothman was quite": P. Weinstein interview.
207 "We were in, I thought": Ibid.
207 "It was insidious": A. Sylbert interview.
207 "What bothered me": P. Weinstein interview.
208 "Fields came in": L. Weinstein interview.
208 "[Marty and I]": Ibid.
208 "She had a personal": Freddie Fields, author interview.
209 "I don't think he": A. Sylbert interview.
209 "The day before": L. Weinstein interview.
209 "Because I tend": Ibid.
210 "You have got the same": P. Weinstein interview.
210 "Paula and I": L. Weinstein interview.
210 "Marty had been": Ibid.
211 "I think the people at": P. Weinstein interview.
211 "They never went": Ibid.
212 "It was an unbelievable": Ibid.
212 "some prejudicial behavior": Ibid.
212 "You can't win": Ibid.
212 "So that was": Ibid.

CHAPTER 13. BROKEN BONDS

213 "Where's Peter Bogdanovich": Platt interview.
213 "We were very happy": Ibid.
215 "I was out": Ibid.
215 "He won't see anyone": Ibid.
215 "Why don't you": Ibid.
215 "As you know, your": Ibid.
216 "It was almost as": Ibid.
216 "It's Dorothy's birthday": Ibid.
216 "I don't know why": Ibid.
216 "It was almost as if Tony": Ibid.
217 "I finally became very angry": Ibid.
217 "I was deeply offended": Ibid.
218 "and when he": Ibid.
218 "I definitely was": Ibid.
218 "She was my": Garry Marshall, author interview (hereafter cited as "G. Marshall interview").
219 "And years later": Platt interview.
219 "I didn't blame her": Ibid.
220 "After tonight": "U.S. Agents Find Hinckley Shift to Violent Emotions," *New York Times*, 5 April 1981.
220 "Jodie Foster love": Stuart Taylor, Jr., "Hinckley's Father Tells the Court, 'I'm the Cause of John's Tragedy,' " *New York Times*, 13 May 1982.
220 "They're laughing at": John Hinckley, Jr./Jodie Foster, "Conversation," *Time*, 12 October 1981.

220   "Jody [sic], I would": "Text of Letter Found in Suspect's Room at Hotel," *New York Times*, 3 April 1981.

220   "It was really important": Foster interview.

221   "I felt very": "Actress Shocked After Learning Fan Held in Reagan Shooting," *Toronto Globe and Mail*, 2 April 1981.

222   "too beautiful to kill": Sam Kiley, "Fatale Attraction," *New York Times*, 12 May 1991.

222   "Why did Israel": Louis Chunovic, *Jodie: A Biography* (Chicago: NTC/Contemporary Publishing, 1995), 72.

222   "Jodie, I'll kill you": Laura Kiernan, "Hinckley, Jury Watch 'Taxi Driver' Film," *Washington Post*, 29 May 1982.

222   "I felt like a pariah": Linda R. Miller, "Jodie Foster: One Terrific Survivor," *Cosmopolitan*, February 1989.

222   "She was very flip": Harry Ufland, author interview.

223   "My body jerked": Jodie Foster, "Why Me?" *Esquire*, December 1982.

223   "It was a shattering": Foster interview.

223   "He just wanted": Ibid.

224   "Let's just say": Ibid.

224   "At the time": Natasha Richardson, author interview (hereafter cited as "Richardson interview").

224   "Jodie had a streak": Rob Lowe, author interview (hereafter cited as "Lowe interview").

225   "I sat down with Tony": Jodie Foster interview with Holly Millea.

226   "If the Hollywood": Lowe interview.

226   "an ironic thumbing": Ibid.

226   "That picture had": Foster interview.

CHAPTER 14. THE DAWN OF A NEW AGE

227   "I was a desperate": Dawn Steel, author interview (hereafter cited as "Steel interview").

229   "Dawn took the": Jeffrey Katzenberg, author interview (hereafter cited as "Katzenberg interview").

229   "She was severely": Marilyn Vance, author interview (hereafter cited as "Vance interview").

229   "Dawn thought she": Platt interview.

230   "And he said to me": Steel interview.

230   "There was no incident": John Taylor, "Bright as Day, Strong as Steel," *New York*, 29 May 1989.

230   "While I was": Steel interview.

231   "Dawn was a complete": Amy Pascal, author interview (hereafter cited as "Pascal interview").

231   "I always had a theory": Steel interview.

231   "Look what you did": Dawn Steel, *They Can Kill You . . . but They Can't Eat You: Lessons from the Front* (New York: Pocket Books, 1993), 11.

231   "King of the Giants": Ibid.

232   "I was always comfortable": Steel interview.

232   "the best calculator": Steel, *They Can Kill You*, 29.

232   "Every single one": Steel interview.

232   "I wanted great": Steel, *They Can Kill You*, 32.

233   "was the biggest": Ibid., 34.

233   "a dream come true": Ibid., 45.

233   "perfect for me": Ibid., 52.

234   "We all thought it was hysterical": Craig Baumgarten, author interview (hereafter cited as "Baumgarten interview").

234   "She had a ponytail": Hyler interview.

235   "I just kept saying": Baumgarten interview.

235   "She was actually a tad shy": Laurence Mark, author interview (hereafter cited as "Mark interview").

236   "She definitely made herself": David Kirkpatrick, author interview (hereafter cited as "Kirkpatrick interview").

237   "There was no support": Ibid.

237   "The zeitgeist of the second floor": Steel interview with Peter Biskind.

237   "I'm looking for commando": Steel, *They Can Kill You*, 142.

237   "It was overwhelming": Steel interview.

237   "I remember one of my": David Madden, author interview (hereafter cited as "Madden interview").

238   "But the whole thing": Ibid.

238   "I used to": Joel Silver, author interview (hereafter cited as "Silver interview").

238   "I remember trying": Steel interview.

239   "I needed people's approval": Ibid.

239   "Look at the rack": Confidential source.

239   "She would out-boy": Mark interview.

239   "my favorite truck": Dean Pitchford, author interview (hereafter cited as "Pitchford interview").

239   "I do have at times": Steel interview.

239   "She really loved being": Craig Zadan, author interview (hereafter cited as "Zadan interview").

239   "To some extent": Mark interview.

240   "I think that she had more fun": Katzenberg interview.

240   "She drank with": Howard Rosenman, author interview (hereafter cited as "Rosenman interview").

240   " 'You can't have relationships' ": Baumgarten interview.

240   "She wanted to": Katherine Reback, author interview (hereafter cited as "Reback interview").

241   "She used those relationships": Silver interview.

241   "She was in life": Melinda Jason, author interview (hereafter cited as "Jason interview").

241   "I remember one": Silver interview.

241   "One night we": Reback interview.

242   "The moment he ran": Steel, *They Can Kill You*, 79.

242   "Who are you": Ibid., 129.

242   "*Flashdance* for me": Steel interview.

243   "I think what is signature": Obst interview.

243   "*Flashdance* is a": Steel, *They Can Kill You*, 147.

243   "They had that kind of": Baumgarten interview.

243   "Could it get": Steel, *They Can Kill You*, 140.

243   "I said that if you don't": Dawn Steel, interview with Peter Biskind.

244   "we were very competitive": Obst interview.

244   "There was not enough": Steel interview.

245   "Here's what the movie": Steel, *They Can Kill You*, 151.

245   "everybody had a different": Jerry Bruckheimer, author interview (hereafter cited as "Bruckheimer interview").

245   "Dawn made it": Jennifer Beals, author interview.

246   "didn't seem to want": Reback interview.

246   "girl's dialogue": Ibid.

247   "When you start": Steel interview.

247   "So Don and": Bruckheimer interview.

247   "People were making": Silver interview.

247   "Dawn looked at": Bruckheimer interview.

247   "Everybody is so": Ibid.

248   "It was a disaster": Steel interview.

248   "Calm down and": Steel, *They Can Kill You*, 167.

248   "For this picture": Pauline Kael, *New Yorker*, 27 June 1983.

249   "She said, 'No' ": Zadan interview.

249   "he was 'fuckable' ": Ibid.

249   "to prove to them at Paramount": Ibid.

249   "I hope you": Ibid.

250   "She was the only": Ibid.

250   "Herbert, you old": Steel, *They Can Kill You*, 170.

250   "All we had": Pitchford interview.

250   "Baby, do you": Steel, *They Can Kill You*, 171.

251   "Want to have": Ibid., 175.

251   "She was like a little kid": Vance interview.

251   "Marty was all": Rosenman interview.

252   "She was in her office": Confidential source.

252   "you people": Steel, *They Can Kill You*, 179.

252   "from a green": Mary Pat Kelly, *Martin Scorsese, A Journey* (New York: Thunder's Mouth Press, 1991), 174.

253   "like praying": Ibid.

253   "God invented syphilis": Confidential source.

253   "I was the executive": Kirkpatrick interview.

253   "She never had any": Katzenberg interview.

253   "She knew it was": Baumgarten interview.

254   "She felt terrible": Vance interview.

254   "He could not forgive": Baumgarten interview.

CHAPTER 15. WOMEN DIRECT

255   "I think there's": Streisand interview.
255   "The same problem": Ibid.
257   "It appealed to": Ibid.
257   "Rusty, my assistant": Ibid.
257   "It scared me": Ibid.
258   "I was getting": Ibid.
258   "This is why": Ibid.
259   "I didn't put": Ibid.
259   "Telephone conversations with": Steven Bach, *Final Cut: Dreams and Disasters in the Making of* Heaven's Gate (New York: Morrow, 1985), 395.
259   "We'd have members": Rusty Lemorande, author interview (hereafter cited as "Lemorande interview").
260   "in matters Jewish": Chaim Potok, "Barbra and Chaim Potok," *Esquire*, October 1982.
260   "At times it": Ibid.
260   "I couldn't believe": Spada, *Streisand: Her Life*, 401.
262   "in love with": Bach, *Final Cut*, 393.
262   "I didn't know": Ibid.
262   "That's why you": Ibid.
262   "He said he'd": Spada, *Streisand: Her Life*, 409.
262   "They said she": Streisand interview.
262   "eat shit": Potok, "Barbra and Chaim Potok," *Esquire*, October 1982.
262   "I had to give up": Ibid.
263   "I was so dismayed": Streisand interview.
263   "No one is going": Ibid.
263   "I touch my": Ibid.
263   "I didn't pay": Ibid.
264   "If Barbra was": Lemorande interview.
264   "Cocksucker! Motherfucker! Shit!": Confidential source.
264   "Take it down": Lemorande interview.
264   "She can go": Ibid.
264   "I was worried": Jeannette Kupferman, "Streisand's New Direction," London *Sunday Times*, 4 March 1984.
264   "Jeez, I look": Ibid.
264   "Hers was not": Ibid.
265   "She wants all the attention": Confidential source.
265   "I had to": Streisand interview.
265   "My vision was": Ibid.
265   "I prayed and": Ibid.
265   "I'm going to die": Riese, *Her Name Is Barbra*, 465.
266   "all the candy": Spada, *Streisand: Her Life*, 417.
266   "the whole movie": Pauline Kael, "The Perfectionist," *New Yorker*, 28 November 1983.

266   "resembled a vanity": Janet Maslin, "Screen: 'Yentl,' A Drama with Barbra Streisand," *New York Times,* 29 January 1984.

266   "I must say": Isaac Bashevis Singer, "I. B. Singer Talks to I. B. Singer About the Movie 'Yentl,' " *New York Times,* 29 January 1984.

267   "I don't necessarily": Streisand interview.

267   "I didn't direct": Ibid.

267   "I was looking": Ibid.

268   "Before I met Gillian": Diane Keaton, remarks at the Women in Film Crystal Awards, 1995.

268   "an enticing image": Armstrong interview.

269   "Exploring that sort": Ibid.

269   "There must be another Mel": Ibid.

269   "We're giving this purple": Peter Bart, *Fade Out: The Calamitous Final Days of MGM* (New York: Morrow, 1990), 147.

270   "I actually had no sexism": Armstrong interview.

270   "Everyone kept forgetting": Ibid.

270   "It was an absolute": Ibid.

270   "They could not cope": Ibid.

271   "The grips were moving": Ibid.

271   "Thank God you're the": Bart, *Fade Out,* 155.

271   "I think they were all harder": Armstrong interview.

272   "this little black": Diane Keaton, remarks, Crystal Awards, 1995.

272   "She's getting great": Bart, *Fade Out,* 157.

272   "I checked the first": Armstrong interview.

CHAPTER 16. OWNING YOUR VOICE

273   "Not only did I": Nora Ephron, author interview (hereafter cited as "Ephron interview").

273   "I had this very clear": Ibid.

275   "Everything had gone": Ibid.

275   "Don't eat leftovers": Ibid.

275   "Never marry a": Suzanna Andrews, "The Ephrons Take a Story, Add Sibling Revelry," *New York Times,* 16 February 1992.

275   "She was so strangely": Ephron interview.

276   "When I was little": Peter Biskind, "The World According to Nora," *Premiere,* March 1992.

276   "I always envied": Ephron interview.

276   "I was completely different": Ibid.

277   "cold water on them": Nora Ephron, "A Few Words About Breasts," *Nora Ephron Collected* (New York: Avon, 1991), 13.

277   "They were very competitive": Ephron interview.

277   "This adorable person": Ibid.

278   "Take notes, Nora": Henry Ephron, *We Thought We Could Do Anything* (New York: Norton, 1977), 210.

278 "One day her stomach": Nora Ephron, *Heartburn* (New York: Knopf, 1983), 25–26.

279 "When I went into": Ephron interview.

279 "women pulled between": N. Ephron, *Nora Ephron Collected*, 22.

279 "sisterhood is difficult": Nora Ephron, *Crazy Salad: Some Things About Women* (New York: Knopf, 1975), 21.

279 "I certainly remember": Ephron interview.

280 "Did you see": Leslie Bennetts, "Nora's Arc," *Vanity Fair*, February 1992.

280 "How to keep": Ibid.

280 "Ten New York": Ibid.

281 "Everything is copy": H. Ephron, *We Thought We Could Do Anything*, 210.

281 "The man is capable": N. Ephron, *Heartburn*, 13.

281 "I think in some": Bennetts, "Nora's Arc," *Vanity Fair*, February 1992.

281 "I don't mind if people": Ephron interview.

282 "everybody wrote a": Ibid.

282 "which is of course": Ibid.

282 "a really nifty": Goldman, *Adventures in the Screen Trade*, 240.

282 "It was terrible": Ephron interview.

282 "The truth was": Ibid.

282 "I needed money": Ibid.

283 "I *had* to do the screenwriting": Ibid.

284 "The original impulse": Ibid.

284 "You're always looking": Ibid.

285 "Mike [Nichols] identified": Ibid.

285 "I was infuriated": Platt interview.

286 "parents who love": Ibid.

286 "I wouldn't say": McMurtry interview.

286 "He wanted to put": Platt interview.

286 "He thought he could shoot": Ibid.

286 "she came to lunch": Mark interview.

286 "With Jim I": Platt interview.

287 "Something in her does": Michael Leeson, author interview.

287 "Andy Hardy country": Brooks interview.

287 "I understood production": Platt interview.

288 "One of the things": Ibid.

288 "There was a time": Brooks interview.

288 "I said to him": Platt interview.

288 "Do you always": Shirley MacLaine, *My Lucky Stars* (New York: Bantam, 1995), 138.

289 "That's why I": Ibid., 138.

289 "weird and warped": Ibid., 148.

289 "I kept having": Platt interview.

289 "Jim was like": Ibid.

289 "I would come home": Ibid.

290 "I remember people": Brooks interview.

291 "I certainly don't think": Platt interview.

291 "Women were so racked": Ibid.

291 "Everybody said, 'You're' ": Ibid.

292 "Jim and Michael": Ibid.

292 "I didn't think": Ibid.

293 "He looked at me": Ibid.

294 "The film wavers": Pauline Kael, *New Yorker,* 7 January 1985.

295 "I quite literally": Platt interview.

295 "I felt like I was": Ibid.

296 "We'd meet in": Paul Verhoeven, author interview.

296 "It's his punishment": Platt interview.

CHAPTER 17. GO-GO YEARS AT PARAMOUNT

299 "Boy, am I": Steel, *They Can Kill You,* 203.

299 "She said, 'They're' ": Silver interview.

299 "Martin Davis in": Ned Tanen, author interview (hereafter cited as "Tanen interview").

299 "Congratulations. It's yours": Ibid.

300 "It's a white": Steel, *They Can Kill You,* 201.

300 "She'd say, 'I hate' ": Rosenman interview.

300 "You had about two": Madden interview.

300 "To her, a lot": Doran interview.

301 "She always thought": James Wiatt, author interview (hereafter cited as "Wiatt interview").

301 "She had a really": Doran interview.

301 "Look, I'm not going": Steel interview.

302 "I did seem to feel": Doran interview.

302 "I don't think she": Confidential source.

302 "She and I often": David Geffen, author interview (hereafter cited as "Geffen interview").

302 "She would not": Marcelle Clements, author interview.

303 "She had no": Madden interview.

303 "God knows, the": Tanen interview.

303 "She yelled at": Gerri Barton, author interview.

303 "She was at least": Madden interview.

304 "The first time I": Ephron interview.

304 "Okay, you're really": Ibid.

304 "And we sat": Obst interview.

304 "Within a year I": Ibid.

305 "We fought like": Vance interview.

305 "She tried really": Doran interview.

305 "I always compared myself": Ibid.

306 "David Caruso had": Ibid.

306 "Dawn left Paramount": Ibid.

307 "I was a workaholic": Steel interview.

307   "It's just so funny": Vance interview.

307   "It's about fucking": Steel, *They Can Kill You*, 196.

308   "Would you have called": Ibid., 198.

308   "power shower": Steel, *They Can Kill You*, 215.

308   "She told me": Platt interview.

309   "Oh, you can't imagine": Jason interview.

309   "It was much": Doran interview.

CHAPTER 18. PSYCHES ON-SCREEN

311   "It was just horrible": Lansing interview.

311   "Her mother was": G. Stern interview.

312   "When she was dying": Lansing interview.

312   "We served as a married": Jaffe interview.

313   "I would never take": Lansing interview.

313   "I said, 'Sherry' ": Jaffe interview.

313   "That's just his way": Lansing interview.

314   "She kind of brought": Tanen interview.

314   "You need to": Confidential source.

314   "The perception was": Jaffe interview.

315   "one of the great": Douglas interview.

315   "The short film": James Dearden, author interview (hereafter cited as "Dearden interview").

316   "I kept coming": Lansing interview.

316   "For a very long": Jaffe interview.

316   "For years I've heard": Lansing interview.

317   "The wife reaches": Ibid.

317   "I think when": Dearden interview.

317   "The blame, if": Ibid.

317   "[Lansing's] imprint must": Ibid.

318   "Stanley is very": Ibid.

319   "I think once": Madden interview.

319   "And, yes, we": Steel interview.

319   "Dark Woman and": Susan Faludi, *Backlash: The Undeclared War Against American Women* (New York: Crown, 1991), 120.

319   "a piece of shit": Lansing interview.

320   "I had an ongoing": Adrian Lyne, author interview (hereafter cited as "Lyne interview").

320   "The movie when we": Lansing interview.

320   "We would argue": Lyne interview.

321   "She separated us": Jaffe interview.

321   "She doesn't have a sense": Lyne interview.

321   "Anne Archer would": Ibid.

321   "I couldn't get anybody": Tanen interview.

321   "I called a really good": Lansing interview.

322 "Of the production people": Tanen interview.

322 "It became patently": Jaffe interview.

322 "It was tough": Lyne interview.

322 "I remember Stanley": Ibid.

323 "Michael had a very": Tanen interview.

323 "Yet when Dawn": Madden interview.

323 "responsibility of the": Douglas interview.

323 "Fuck it, I'll": Confidential source.

323 "I said, 'Danny, I'm' ": Lansing interview.

324 "During the film's": "The Dark Side of Love," *People*, 26 October 1987.

324 "In this film": Richard Corliss, "Killer," *Time*, 16 November 1987.

325 "When I started out": Lansing interview.

325 "One guy is": Ibid.

325 "If you want to know": Faludi, *Backlash*, 121.

326 "The other day, I saw": Ibid.

326 "She looks like a person": Tanen interview.

326 "It was really *Fatal*": Lansing interview.

327 "self-referential commercial": Pauline Kael, *New Yorker*, 16 June 1986.

328 "Faludi takes all": Steel interview.

328 "protest march": Steel, *They Can Kill You*, 177.

328 "That was the movie": Steel interview.

328 "I said, 'These people' ": Ibid.

329 "What I wanted to do": Lansing interview.

329 "Sherry talked about": Merzbach interview.

329 "I became totally": Lansing interview.

330 "walked away from": Jonathan Kaplan, author interview (hereafter cited as "Kaplan interview").

330 "This is horseshit": Madden interview.

331 "She was very tough": Kaplan interview.

331 "were okay, but": Foster interview.

331 "She is what he would": Kennedy, *Jodie Foster: A Life Onscreen*, 128.

332 "I get knocked": Dan Yakir, "Jodie Foster," *Interview*, August 1987.

332 "At the time": Tony Bill, author interview.

332 "I couldn't see": Millea, "The Woman Who Fell to Earth," *Premiere*, July 1997.

332 "See, *The Accused*": Foster interview.

332 "A lot of actresses": Kaplan interview.

332 "Jonathan begged and": Foster interview.

333 "The envelope please": Lansing interview.

333 "Foster wasn't 'rapeable' ": Kaplan interview.

333 "They said, 'She's' ": Foster interview.

333 "I don't think Stanley": Madden interview.

333 " 'Well,' she says": Foster interview.

334 "Sherry doesn't like": Kaplan interview.

334 "She reminds me": Foster interview.

334 "She's, 'Well, we're' ": Ibid.

334 "Let Stanley handle": Confidential source.

334 " 'Stop it. What' ": Kennedy, *Jodie Foster: A Life Onscreen*, 138.

334 "Jodie, Dawn, and": Kaplan interview.
334 "a real unconscious": Foster interview.
335 "She got really quiet": Kaplan interview.
335 "I felt, at times": Foster interview.
336 "That was the last": B. Foster interview.
336 "This is how I recovered": Foster interview.
337 "the single lowest": Lansing interview.
337 "They didn't crumble": Kaplan interview.
337 "to the lowest common": Barry London, author interview.
337 "If anyone thinks": Faludi, *Backlash*, 138.
338 "Someone said to": Ingrid Sischy, "Jodie Foster," *Interview*, October 1991.
338 "taught me that all": Jodie Foster, Academy Award speech, 1989, transcript.
338 "For me work was": P. Weinstein interview.
340 "Mark fell into": Griffin and Masters, *Hit & Run*, 123.
341 "There was that sort": A. Sylbert interview.
342 "After the first event": Ibid.
342 "allowed its members": Brownstein, *The Power and the Glitter*, 305.
342 "We are committed": Ibid., 306.
343 "We are not": Ibid.
343 "I did nothing": P. Weinstein interview.
343 "I remember getting": Ibid.

CHAPTER 19. A LEGEND RETURNS

345 "It was like the courtship": Mengers interview.
346 "foot soldiers marching": Rose, *The Agency*, 450.
346 "*tummler*": Toni Howard, author interview (hereafter cited as "Howard interview").
346 "Boys' Towns!": Confidential source.
347 "I wanted more": Mengers interview.
347 "Wouldn't it be nice": Confidential source.
348 "Now they'll really": Ibid.
348 "And I said": JJ Harris, author interview.
348 "And Kevin knew": Ibid.

CHAPTER 20. CULTURAL ICONS

351 "I know all": Penny Marshall, author interview (hereafter cited as "P. Marshall interview").
352 "Don't give up your childhood": Peggy Orenstein, "Making It in the Majors," *New York Times*, 24 May 1992.
352 "Don't be ashamed": Ibid.
353 "This is Penny's life": Brooks interview.
353 "I identified with her": P. Marshall interview.
353 "the bad seed": Ibid.

357   "This was a": Joe Morgenstern, "Penny from Heaven," *Playboy*, January 1991.

357   "We went from": P. Marshall interview.

357   "witlessness": Richard Schickel, "Viewpoints: The Second Season," *Time*, 9 February 1976.

357   "chosen not to": Ibid.

357   "We were blue-collar": P. Marshall interview.

358   "Cindy felt she": Garry Marshall, *Wake Me When It's Funny* (New York: New-market Press, 1995), 159.

358   "crap": Bob Woodward, *Wired: The Short Life and Fast Times of John Belushi* (New York: Simon & Schuster, 1984), 104.

358   "didn't go well": P. Marshall interview.

359   "If Penny could wring": Louis Armstrong, "It's Thumbs Up—Sort of—as Penny Marshall Copes with Life Without Meathead," *People*, 28 April 1980.

359   "If a bomb": Carrie Fisher, author interview (hereafter cited as "C. Fisher interview").

359   "I wanted to rest": P. Marshall interview.

360   "She always loved": Brooks interview.

360   "It was great": P. Marshall interview.

360   "I think I have": Patrick Goldstein, "Penny Marshall Makes 'Big' Impact," *Los Angeles Times*, 8 June 1988.

360   "She's a brilliant woman": Morgenstern, "Penny," *Playboy*, January 1991.

360   "little adventures that I": P. Marshall interview.

361   "She used to cut": Morgenstern, "Penny," *Playboy*, January 1991.

361   "He'd see me": P. Marshall interview.

364   "I go over there": Silver interview.

364   "I think Whoopi": P. Marshall interview.

364   "She didn't want": Silver interview.

364   "I'd try to": P. Marshall interview.

365   "Penny was and": Silver interview.

365   "Then he'd draw": P. Marshall interview.

365   "I was on": Brooks interview.

365   "There are things in it": Morgenstern, "Penny," *Playboy*, January 1991.

365   "But I think": P. Marshall interview.

366   "revealed she really": P. Sylbert interview.

366   "The story of *Ishtar*": Ibid.

366   "Give me a": Heckerling interview.

367   "You win the": Randa Haines, author interview.

367   "This is your": P. Marshall interview.

367   "I thought, Well": Ibid.

369   "She was up": Brooks interview.

370   "Barry was hard": P. Marshall interview.

370   "People don't get": Barry Sonnenfeld, author interview.

370   "I went into": P. Marshall interview.

370   "Penny Marshall has turned into": David Ansen, "Man-Child in the Corporate Land," *Newsweek*, 6 June 1988.

370   "Yeah, that sucks": P. Marshall interview.

371   "I was in a rehab": C. Fisher interview.

371 "I felt in it": Ibid.
371 " 'Maybe I shouldn't have given' ": Ibid.
372 "I did this thing for": Ibid.
373 "Cora had adapted": Carrie Fisher, *Delusions of Grandma* (New York: Simon & Schuster, 1994), 221.
373 "Lucille Ball used": Joan Juliet Buck, "Carrie Retakes Hollywood," *Vanity Fair,* August 1990.
373 "I worshiped my mother": C. Fisher interview.
374 "I decided so early": Ibid.
374 "As soon as I was": Ibid.
375 "I started writing": Ibid.
375 "I liked being": Ibid.
376 "So then I was Princess": Ibid.
376 "I was there for *Star Wars*": Ibid.
377 "I didn't like the diagnosis": Ibid.
378 "I wrote a lot of it": Ibid.
378 "He needed someone": Ibid.
379 "It's difficult to maintain": Ibid.
379 "I was brought": Ibid.
380 "Nora told me": Biskind, "The World According to Nora," *Premiere,* March 1992.
381 "sex ruins everything": Nora Ephron, *When Harry Met Sally . . .* (New York: Knopf, 1997), viii.
381 "He always wants": Ibid., 93.
381 "In the beginning": Ephron interview.
381 "The director is": Ibid.
382 "It was as much fun": Ibid.
382 "Everybody, one after": Ibid.
382 "Richard Dreyfuss turned": Ibid.
383 "I'll have what": N. Ephron, *When Harry Met Sally . . .* , xv.
383 "How did I": Confidential source.
383 "I felt like I": Meg Ryan, author interview.
383 "It was a big shock": Lizzie Francke, *Script Girls* (London: British Film Institute, 1994), 110.

CHAPTER 21. STEEL IN THE FURNACE

385 "green pea soup": Confidential source.
385 "I'm in the": Steel, *They Can Kill You,* 206.
385 "Ned never wanted": Madden interview.
386 "He thought she was being": Doran interview.
386 "I get in one": Confidential source.
386 "Dawn would simply": Madden interview.
387 "Ned's jealous of": Steel, *They Can Kill You,* 224.
387 "One day I called Dawn": Ephron interview.
387 "I used to race": Tanen interview.
387 "There is no way": Ephron interview.

387   "Dawn was not particularly": Roven interview.

387   "He just tortured her": Silver interview.

387   "She called John": Tanen interview.

388   "I had one of the woman's": Ibid.

388   "I was beginning": Steel, *They Can Kill You*, 222.

388   "I'm going to put": Roven interview.

388   "In terms of the whore-madonna": Confidential source.

388   "She was her own worst": Roven interview.

389   "It was an": Steel, *They Can Kill You*, 223.

389   "She actually called": Lucy Fisher, author interview (hereafter cited as "L. Fisher interview").

389   "My husband was convinced": Steel interview.

389   "I had heard about": Ibid.

390   "When I came out": Ibid.

390   "You must be": Steel, *They Can Kill You*, 235.

390   "I've never thought of myself": Steel interview.

390   "She would call up": L. Fisher interview.

391   "I've been discussing": Steel, *They Can Kill You*, 245.

391   "I didn't say to her": Roven interview.

392   "Ray and I, because": Melnick interview.

392   "I thought she would be": Victor Kaufman, author interview (hereafter cited as "Kaufman interview").

392   "Victor Kaufman was someone": Steel interview.

392   "She was thrilled": Baumgarten interview.

392   "The first time I looked": Steel interview.

393   "I remember thinking": Ibid.

393   "They gave away": Confidential source.

393   "It was so moving": Steel interview.

394   "She was completely electrifying": Pascal interview.

395   "These rumors seemed": Steel interview.

395   "She called one": C. Fisher interview.

396   "There was a": Hyler interview.

396   "You haven't finished": Steel interview.

396   "I never saw her so": Pascal interview.

396   "There was this guy": Steel interview.

396   "If there was something": Roven interview.

397   "It was pretty easy": Mark Gill, author interview (hereafter cited as "Gill interview").

397   "I had her": Ibid.

397   "This is the": Dawn Steel, remarks at the Women in Film Crystal Awards, 1989.

398   "My first question": Steel interview.

398   "I think she was so": Kaufman interview.

398   "I think she felt": Geffen interview.

399   "What about Bob": Griffin and Masters, *Hit & Run*, 225.

399   "Dawn, I want": Steel interview.

400   "Who the fuck": Griffin and Masters, *Hit & Run*, 255.

CHAPTER 22. THE DEMISE OF SUE; THE RISE OF THE SUE-ETTES

403   "from another world": Risa Shapiro, author interview (hereafter cited as "Shapiro interview").

403   "She acts like": Ibid.

403   "Sue asked, 'Haven't you' ": Goldsmith interview.

404   "She was harder": Howard interview.

404   "get close to the wives": Confidential source.

404   "breeding cows": Ibid.

404   "I used to walk": Hyler interview.

404   "She believed women": Bobbi Thompson, author interview.

404   "Go to CAA": Confidential source.

405   "It was a nightmare": Mengers interview.

405   "Let me tell": Rose, *The Agency*, 435.

405   "The good news": Confidential source.

405   "She's channeling Freddie": Confidential source.

405   "The one quality": Mengers interview.

406   "She was close to": Hyler interview.

407   "We thought if": Shapiro interview.

407   "We were talking": Goldsmith interview.

407   "There are no finite": Ibid.

408   "Toni definitely did": Shapiro interview.

408   "Now, they can really call": John Richardson, "California Suite," *Premiere*, May 1991.

CHAPTER 23. LEADING-LADY BLUES

409   "I'm barely able": Elaine Dutka, "Meryl Streep Attacks Hollywood Gender Gap at SAG Conference," *Los Angeles Times*, 3 August 1990.

409   "If the trend": Richard Corliss, "Women on the Verge of a Nervous Breakdown," *Time*, 18 February 1991.

411   "In her willingness": Molly Haskell, "Meryl Streep: Hiding in the Spotlight," *Ms.*, December 1988.

412   "I loved the problem": Streep interview.

413   "*Death Becomes Her*": Ibid.

413   "I went out there": Ibid.

414   "I hate being": Ibid.

CHAPTER 24. INDECENT PROPOSAL

415   "I wondered if": Lansing interview.

417   " 'I'll be forty-eight' ": Ibid.

417   "I'd thought you'd": Ibid.

418   "I'm going to hopefully": Ibid.

418   "There is nobody": Friedkin interview.

418   "which she took": Ibid.

418   "I was very surprised": Richard Zanuck, author interview (hereafter cited "Zanuck interview").

419   "She has a need": Friedkin interview.

419   "The first sex": Biskind, *Easy Riders, Raging Bulls*, 204.

419   "I think I was sort": Friedkin interview.

420   "Billy leaned in": Tita Cahn, author interview.

420   "Sherry said, 'Look' ": Friedkin interview.

421   "Billy is what I need": Lansing interview.

421   "I didn't want": Ibid.

422   "She genuinely loves": Friedkin interview.

423   "[Stanley] wanted Billy": Lansing interview.

424   "Truly, she took the job": Friedkin interview.

424   "There's no script": Lansing interview.

424   "You didn't expect": Ibid.

CHAPTER 25. A GIANT LEAP

425   "I'd like to see you": Callie Khouri, author interview (hereafter cited as "Khouri interview").

425   "You don't know who": Ibid.

427   "there was something": Ibid.

427   "I wasn't one of": Ibid.

427   "I loved production": Ibid.

427   "To me being a writer": Ibid.

428   "This idea just": Ibid.

429   "I knew I could convince": Ibid.

430   "It was weird to go": Ibid.

430   "They gave me": Sigourney Weaver, author interview.

431   "I have a lot of friendships": Khouri interview.

432   "A paean to transformative": Richard Schickel, "Gender Bender," *Time*, 24 June 1991.

432   "It justifies armed": Ibid.

432   "Call *Thelma & Louise*": Sheila Benson, "True or False: *Thelma & Louise*: Just Good Ol' Boys," *Los Angeles Times*, 31 May 1991.

432   "Its heroines are": Janet Maslin, "Lay Off *Thelma & Louise*," *New York Times*, 16 June 1991.

432   "It's exhilarating, that": Mary Cantwell, "What Were the Women Asking For," *New York Times*, 13 June 1991.

432   "After that initial": Khouri interview.

433   "I heard a conservative": Ibid.

433   "Jodie's film is": Richard Corliss, "A Screen Gem Turns Director," *Time*, 14 October 1991.

434   "to save the women": Foster interview.

435   "The way he tortures": Fred Schruers, "A Kind of Redemption," *Premiere*, March 1991.

435   "Jodie Foster, TIME'S": Michelangelo Signorile, "Gossip Watch," *OutWeek,* 20 February 1991.

435   "Absolutely queer. Oscar": Larry Gross, *Contested Closets: The Politics and Ethics of Outing* (Minneapolis: University of Minnesota Press, 1993), 219.

436   "The problem is, I": Foster interview.

436   "L.A. is a scuzzy": Ibid.

436   "I'm not somebody": Ibid.

437   "She's meticulous and calculating": Confidential source.

437   "bad, horrible crimes": Millea, "The Woman Who Fell to Earth," *Premiere,* July 1997.

437   "I'm somebody who in": Foster interview.

437   "outsiders trying to figure": Ibid.

437   "It showed the progression": B. Foster interview.

438   "Why do you want": Foster interview.

438   "I said, 'Well, you' ": Ibid.

439   "nightmare of being": Scott Frank, author interview (hereafter cited as "Frank interview").

439   "I was angry": Scott Rudin, author interview (hereafter cited as "Rudin interview").

440   "You're awash in": Frank interview.

440   "When I'm treated": Hilary de Vries, "She's Always Been Out There," *Los Angeles Times,* 6 October 1991.

440   " 'Just pretend really' ": Jon Van Meter, "Jodie Foster: Child of the Movies," *New York Times,* 6 January 1991.

440   "First-time directors": Gerri Hershey, "Jodie Foster," *Rolling Stone,* 21 March 1991.

440   "I'm not a pain": Ibid.

441   "We need a single": Schruers, "A Kind of Redemption," *Premiere,* March 1991.

441   "She never threw me": Rudin interview.

441   "bow to mothers like her own": Thomson, *Biographical Dictionary of Film,* 261.

441   "When I saw": B. Foster interview.

441   "I said, 'But wait' ": Foster interview.

442   "The people in the industry": Ibid.

442   "I didn't really": Ephron interview.

443   "Lynda [Obst, a mutual]": Ibid.

443   "We sort of got rid": Ibid.

444   "Jon Peters told": Ibid.

445   "Nora said to": Biskind, "The World According to Nora," *Premiere,* March 1992.

445   "One of the things I": Ibid.

446   "I waited until": Ephron interview.

CHAPTER 26. A QUEEN'S PREROGATIVE

449   "We were in": John Goldwyn, author interview (hereafter cited as "Goldwyn interview").

450   "It was Sherry": Mace Neufeld, author interview (hereafter cited as "Neufeld interview").

450   "irreversible hostility": Kirkpatrick lawsuit, 15 November 1993.

450   "it wasn't working out": Kirkpatrick interview.

451   "Fuck 'em!": Rod Lurie, "How Jaffe and Lansing Sucked Blood Out of a One-time Creative Blockbuster," *Los Angeles*, July 1993.

451   "She was standing": Confidential source.

452   "The preview process": Lansing interview.

453   "We would go around": Ibid.

453   "I find her very frank": Zanuck interview.

453   "It wasn't that as soon": Phillip Noyce, author interview.

453   "Sherry is very, very": Ibid.

454   "Sherry was right": Ibid.

455   "It's a masterpiece": Ibid.

455   "I think they pay": Neufeld interview.

455   "I don't use research": Lansing interview.

456   "I think Paramount": Rudin interview.

456   "I said to myself": Wendy Finerman, author interview.

457   "It's Norman": Richard Corliss, "The World According to Gump," *Time*, 1 August 1994.

457   "Let me say": Winston Groom, *Forrest Gump* (New York: Doubleday, 1986), 1.

458   "a blinking green": Lansing interview.

458   "I wouldn't have": Kristen O'Neill, "Gumption," *Premiere*, April 1995.

458   "board": Ibid.

459   "psycho": Confidential source.

459   "Look, Bob, Stanley's": Ibid.

460   "When they [the]": Ibid.

460   "It felt like": O'Neill, "Gumption," *Premiere*, April 1995.

CHAPTER 27. I'LL DO ANYTHING

461   "I said, 'I'll be back' ": P. Weinstein interview.

463   "He wanted me to go": Ibid.

463   "Part of the motivation": Ibid.

464   "baby derby": Ibid.

464   "I could never look": Ibid.

465   "Everybody would have": Ibid.

465   "I'm told from those": Ibid.

466   "Friday was the memorial": Ibid.

466   "A lot of my closest": Ibid.

467   "strong woman's disease": Ibid.

467   "The day I started": Ibid.

468   "I came to understand": Ibid.

469   "He lost respect": Platt interview.

470   "And I felt that it was": Ibid.

470   "he dismissed it": Ibid.

471   "He said, 'All I' ": Ibid.

471   "I do within": Ibid.

471 "serving somebody. I was": Ibid.

471 "It was upsetting": Brooks interview.

472 "I needed to": Platt interview.

472 "I just know that I approved": Brooks interview.

472 "I realized that": Platt interview.

CHAPTER 28. THE WORLD NEEDS A REWRITE

473 "which trashed [the]": Lansing interview.

475 "I can't tell you": Frank Biondi, author interview (hereafter cited as "Biondi interview").

475 "I think they were under": Lansing interview.

476 "You were right": Confidential source.

476 "She went into Sherry": Ibid.

477 "Okay, okay": Lansing interview.

477 "It's not okay": Ibid.

477 "I don't know": Confidential source.

477 "Shall we let her": Biondi interview.

477 "I started to": Claudia Eller, "A Tribute to a Demeaning Reflection," *Los Angeles Times*, 16 March 1995.

477 "Sherry has an ideal": Friedkin interview.

478 "It is very hard to get": Biondi interview.

478 "She has a desire": Rudin interview.

478 "I don't think Sherry's aware": Wiatt interview.

479 "I think there is a side": Rudin interview.

479 "It's normal for me": Goldwyn interview.

480 "It means a": Ibid.

480 "I don't think [my staff's]": Lansing interview.

481 "For Dolgen, every crisis": Friedkin interview.

481 "Jonathan's the only person": Lansing interview.

482 "Can't you even pretend": Ibid.

482 "It never ceases to amaze": Ibid.

482 "I have seen her be": Rudin interview.

483 "What I found was there": Kathleen Kennedy, author interview (hereafter cited as "Kennedy interview").

484 "I'm confused": Karen Rosenfelt, author interview.

484 "We'll go over the film": Goldwyn interview.

485 "You were right": Lansing interview.

485 "total bullshit": Kennedy interview.

485 "What does he have on": Confidential source.

486 "shameless": Ibid.

486 "Here's what I": Lansing interview.

486 "I did as much": Jaffe interview.

487 "everyone thought *Blue Chips*": Baumgarten interview.

487 "Sherry has never": Friedkin interview.

487 "No one was nuts": Biondi interview.

488   "crucified": Baumgarten interview.
488   "She did the very best": Confidential source.
488   "The head of the studio": Lansing interview.
488   "We made a lot": Friedkin interview.
488   "It just eats her": Wiatt interview.
489   "When the picture didn't work": Biondi interview.
489   "[following] his own": Lansing interview.

CHAPTER 29. THE BUTTERFLY CHASERS

491   "I was totally freaked": Khouri interview.
491   "Who would want": P. Weinstein interview.
493   "There's a very sweet": Ibid.
493   "We had one meeting": Resnick interview.
493   "Barbra thought Goldie's": Ibid.
494   "We talked a lot": Khouri interview.
494   "I kept not": Ibid.
495   "I had to finish": Ibid.
495   "It would have been": Ibid.
496   "The part was written": Ibid.
497   "It went to men": Ibid.
497   "I had total freedom": Ibid.
497   "It was an oddly painful": Ibid.
497   "The bottom line": Confidential source.
498   "That night Julia": Ibid.
498   "I have an 'I'm right' ": Khouri interview.
498   "She was not totally without": Ibid.
499   "I kept saying, As soon": Ibid.
500   "Ultimately I felt": Ibid.
500   "They just didn't want": Ibid.
500   "It makes no": Foster interview.
501   "defendedness": Ibid.
502   "I really thought": Ibid.
502   "I have a": Richardson interview.
503   "The play is": Foster interview.
503   "I believe women": Jodie Foster, remarks, Walker Art Center, 1991.
504   "Ten or fifteen": Foster interview.
504   "probably in terms": Ibid.
505   "I didn't care about the money": Ibid.
505   "I mean, *Nell*": Ibid.
506   "[People came] up to me and": Ibid.
506   "If we do something": Rudin interview.
506   "I'm sure that Sherry": Foster interview.
508   "emphasizes feelings over": Janet Maslin, "How Do You Reroute a Comet? Carefully," *New York Times*, 8 May 1998.

508 "being portrayed as": Kristine McKenna, "Not So Little Women," *Los Angeles Times*, 27 December 1994.

508 "I don't think we have": Ephron interview.

509 "When you're making a comedy": Ibid.

510 "I think that Ray Stark": Ibid.

510 "We sat with him": Ibid.

511 "Today, the older female": Ed Minz, author interview.

512 "It was a primal": Lansing interview.

513 "It is hard to think": Rudin interview.

513 "She was really interested": Ibid.

513 "every female in the DGA": Confidential source.

514 "They said it was": Rudin interview.

514 "Bette said, 'I signed' ": Hugh Wilson, author interview (hereafter cited as "Wilson interview").

515 "Does the name": Judy Bachrach, "Goldie's Big Splash," *Vanity Fair*, January 1997.

515 "She went ahead and let": Wilson interview.

515 "I thought she": Ibid.

516 "It's one of": Phil McCombs, "Men Take Revenge on 'First Wives'," *Washington Post*, 11 October 1996.

517 "Maybe this is": Claudia Puig, "Make Way for 40-plus 'Club,' " *Los Angeles Times*, 26 September 1996.

517 "I have always been": Jane Campion, author interview (hereafter cited as "Campion interview").

517 "Ada actually uses": Jane Campion, *The Piano* (New York: Hyperion, 1993), 138–139.

518 "People would say to me": Campion interview.

518 "It's scary how box-office-driven": Ibid.

CHAPTER 30. FADE TO BLACK

519 "It turned out": Steel interview.

519 "Mom and Dad": Steel, *They Can Kill You*, 285.

519 "Dawn kept caving": Roven interview.

519 "This is all about": Ibid.

521 "Jeffrey would have": Ibid.

521 "I don't think": Katzenberg interview.

521 "[Katzenberg] was giving over": Confidential source.

521 "She was in a fight": Ibid.

521 "She believed": Reback interview.

522 "She remembered it was": Baumgarten interview.

522 "She didn't have": Clements interview.

523 "I think that Dawn": Rosenman interview.

523 "I remember at one": Ephron interview.

523 "She said, 'Fuck' ": Roven interview.

523   "I always believed": Jon Turteltaub, author interview.

524   "In my opinion, the": Ibid.

524   "She kept saying": Ibid.

524   "Something like three": Lansing interview.

525   "the first woman": Diane Wayne, author interview.

525   "We were not": Lansing interview.

525   "She used to wear": Ibid.

525   "I was standing": Peter Biskind, "Good Night Dark Prince," *Premiere*, April 1996.

526   "I think that she saw": Roven interview.

527   "I need to go": Ibid.

527   "Most women would": L. Fisher interview.

527   "She said, 'I'm tired' ": Jason interview.

527   "These ex-hippies were": Ibid.

528   "It was some desire": Reback interview.

528   "We had some meeting": Pascal interview.

528   "The doctors told": Roven interview.

529   "I think that she felt": Ibid.

529   "She called my husband": Jason interview.

529   "I remember walking": Reback interview.

529   "I knew what the statistics": Lansing interview.

529   "She would have a drill": L. Fisher interview.

530   "She really didn't let": Roven interview.

530   "There was none of that": Ephron interview.

530   "Okay, that's done. It's over": Doran interview.

530   "Even in her dialogue": Roven interview.

531   "We were all lying": Reback interview.

531   "I had seen her": Lansing interview.

532   "It hadn't been done": L. Fisher interview.

532   "At the end": Lansing interview.

532   "I would tell her": L. Fisher interview.

532   "We had this visit": Reback interview.

533   "And she said": L. Fisher interview.

533   "Three weeks before": Rosenman interview.

533   "When she became so": L. Fisher interview.

533   "Mommy can't die": Roven interview.

534   "Dawn's eyes were": Pascal interview.

534   "I felt like there": Jason interview.

534   "Larry, her brother": Rosenman interview.

534   "It really wasn't": Pascal interview.

EPILOGUE: *TITANIC'S WAKE*

535   "Does this prove": Kurt Andersen, "Sore Winner," *New Yorker*, 16 March 1998.

537   "crying at the": Lansing interview.

538   "Jonathan uses this expression": Ibid.
539   "the early careers of": Platt interview.
540   "did not want to be a handmaiden": P. Weinstein interview.
540   "It was all over everything": Foster interview.
541   "You work your whole career": Stacey Snider, author interview.
542   "It's great because": Ibid.
542   "a job that really suits": Pascal interview.
542   "there are no women owners": Ibid.
543   "Barbra Streisand would": Christine Spines, "Behind Bars," *Premiere* special: *Women in Hollywood 2000,* January 2000.
543   "Nobody wants to make": Pascal interview.

ACKNOWLEDGMENTS

I'd like to thank Susan Lyne, the former editor of *Premiere*, who sent me on this journey, and Chris Connelly, who helped me marshal the initial interviews. My agent, Amanda Urban, and my editor, Ann Godoff, both believed in this book before I did, and waited years to see the final outcome.

I've had much support from my colleagues at *Premiere*, the staff at Random House, and the various researchers who worked on this project. They include: Jim Meigs, Kathy Heintzelman, Howard Karren, Corie Brown, Eliza Bergman Krause, Anne Thompson, Kindra Peach, Kate Niedzwiecki, Benjamin Dreyer, Amelia Zalcman, Lisa Thackaberry, Jacob Foreman, Kerrie Mitchell, Jay Fernandez, Jason Clark, and Sean Miner. Nancy Griffin, Holly Millea, and Peter Biskind offered friendship and wise advice about the arcane intricacies of Hollywood and its players. Deena Metzger helped me develop my writing voice. Kira Meers and Jodie Burke read early versions of the manuscript, and Jane Mendelsohn explained the vagaries of the publishing process.

Lisa Chase, Alice Naude, and Hanna Weg made excellent and invaluable editing suggestions, and indulged me with long conversations into the middle of the night about women and power. I also appreciate the lifelong encouragement of my parents, Morton and Sheppie Abramowitz. Mostly, I must thank my husband, Joshua Goldin, for his unfailing and tireless editorial advice, his patience, his love, and his uncommon insight into the human character.

I must also thank the women of Hollywood, many of whom sat for hours of interviews, and placed their faith in me to tell this story fairly and accurately.

INDEX

ABOUT THE TYPE

This book was set in Photina, a typeface designed by José Mendoza in 1971. It is a very elegant design with high legibility, and its close character fit has made it a popular choice for use in quality magazines and art gallery publications.